Recreation

IN AMERICAN LIFE

Recreation
IN AMERICAN LIFE

REYNOLD E.
CARLSON

THEODORE R.
DEPPE

JANET R.
MAC LEAN

INDIANA UNIVERSITY

Wadsworth Publishing Company, Inc.
Belmont, California

FOURTH PRINTING: JULY 1967

L. C. CAT. CARD NO.: 63-8481

PRINTED IN THE UNITED STATES OF AMERICA

Foreword

The inbuilt logic of our heavily industrialized society makes inevitable the widening distribution of three elements, the possession of which has always been the condition of civilized living. These liberating factors are *first*, increasing quantities of disposable time defined as hours unsold in the market place; *second*, increasing quantities of disposable energy defined as vital powers unspent in the process of earning a living and unwasted by ill health; and *third*, increasing quantities of disposable income defined as financial capability over and above the minimum needs of existence.

In our urban age, theoretical science and an intricate technology combine to produce conditions that alter man's habitual expectations in relationship to time. More and more circumstances enable him to enjoy unhurried and pleasurable living in response to his spontaneous and educated enthusiasms. To use the encompassing opportunity of leisure for inner development and satisfaction, man needs to understand the era in which he lives. He requires an equipment of performance skills and a guidance system of values.

At the moment when its service is most needed, *Recreation in American Life* provides this orientation. It is comprehensive in perspective, imaginative in outlook, and down-to-earth in its practicality. Incorporating the seasoned experience of eminent scholars at work with the superlative resources of a great university and daily in intimate contact with people, processes, and performance, the book explores a field of professional concern to which its authors have dedicated their careers. The presentation is characterized by clarity of disciplinary concepts; the interrelation of public purpose to private enjoyment; the description of the social structure and the values that sustain it; an awareness of the variety of human needs, interests, and physical conditions; a concern for professional skills in participant roles essential to continuing personal growth; a recognition of the obligation of leaders and the method of their training; and the requirements of citizen effort in the forging of public policy.

Reynold Carlson, Theodore Deppe, and Janet MacLean are my personal and professional friends of many years. They have produced a classic work. The reading of these pages provides its own testimony to their competence, integrity, and perception.

Paul Douglass
District of Columbia Bar

Contents

Preface

This book endeavors to present, in a broad, comprehensive manner, recreation in American life: its philosophy, historical background, leadership, organization, and program. *Recreation in American Life* is designed to serve both as a textbook in courses dealing with community recreation and as a reference book for practitioners in the field. It offers the general reader an overview of recreation in the United States today.

An ever increasing opportunity as well as a challenge currently exists in making satisfying and constructive uses of our new leisure. The need for professional leadership in the many public and private organizations that serve recreation needs has far exceeded the number of persons qualified for these careers; therefore, the professional education of potential leaders who can meet this need has become a major concern. We hope that this book will contribute to the educational preparation of those planning to enter this field of service.

Recreation in American Life is based on the premise that recreation has become a community responsibility worthy of every citizen's attention. Because this new attitude toward recreation is an outgrowth of contemporary modes of life, we have tried to provide an accurate description of current recreation problems, practices, and principles. While emphasizing the practical aspects of recreation in the lives of the American people today, we have attempted to provide sufficient theoretical and historical background to allow the reader to gauge the magnitude of recreation as a social phenomenon. The professional recreation leader must be familiar with all aspects of recreation as they apply to contemporary life; he also must possess the ability to foresee the place of recreation in the lives of future generations. We have tried to provide a book that will present an introduction to all those community organizations that share a responsibility for recreation: their challenges, their problems, their organizational structure, and their interrelationships.

We wish to acknowledge our debt to the many authors whose works have served as guideposts in the training of recreation leaders. We also recognize our debt to the professional leaders in communities throughout the United States from whom has come a steady stream of practical information and ideas. The national professional and service organizations with which we have been associated for many years have given us both inspiration and guidance. Their publications, conferences, and workshops have kept us alert and have widened our acquaintance with professional leaders.

We are proud to have had in our classes many young men and women who now occupy positions of influence and responsibility in recreation throughout the United States and in many foreign countries. A teacher must also be a learner; and to these students we are indebted for fresh enthusiasms and continuing awareness of changing needs. We are most appreciative also of the fine cooperation received from those who willingly supplied pictures, organizational charts, and facility plans.

To Ruth Carlson, who gave up many hours of her own leisure to analyze materials, to discuss ideas, to proofread, and to retype copy, the authors are sincerely grateful. Her excellent suggestions, her critical reviewing, and her endless patience with necessary details were a major contribution in the development of the manuscript.

Finally, to our faculty associates we wish to express thanks for their encouragement, guidance, assistance, and long patience.

REYNOLD E. CARLSON

THEODORE R. DEPPE

JANET R. MAC LEAN

1

THE PLACE OF RECREATION IN AMERICAN LIFE

1

What Is Recreation?

Change is an eternal phenomenon in human affairs, but in America the twentieth century has brought technological changes at such an accelerated pace that the lives of all have been revolutionized. New industrial machinery, incredibly fast transportation, television, miracle drugs, and atomic energy are but a few of the new and tremendous influences that have quickened the tempo of our lives and conditioned the variety and extent of our experiences. We, ourselves in the midst of change, remain essentially unchanged. We have the same elemental urges and desires our ancestors felt centuries ago; but today's scientific advances have given us one great gift that, above all others, could make possible the satisfaction of these basic urges and desires. That gift is leisure.

Throughout history, people have sought leisure. Once it was the prerogative of only the upper classes or of primitive tribes who dwelt where nature was bountiful. Today, in America, leisure reaches all classes in ever increasing amounts. Modern technology has provided, for the many, leisure that ancient slavery made available for the few. Never before have the people of any nation had at their disposal so much leisure and such varied outlets for its use.

In leisure may lie the final test of our civilization. The nature of our society is determined less by our accelerated work accomplishments than by the quality of our leisure. This leisure provides the means either for improving the quality of living or for destroying our civilization, and science has given us the tools to perform either task. Though our economic and indus-

3

trial progress is dependent upon work, our cultural, moral, and spiritual development is dependent, in large measure, upon the uses of leisure. Leisure itself is a two-edged sword; it carries no guarantee for Utopian happiness. It may bring opportunity for enjoyment of art, music, and science; for development of health, strength, and satisfaction; or for acquisition of inner resources that lead to contentment. Conversely, it may bring idleness, boredom, overindulgence, deterioration, or corruption. History has shown us that the world progresses or regresses not so much through what is done in our work hours but through what is done *or not done* in our leisure hours. Wise use of the gift of leisure is the challenge of our time.

Traditionally, our productive work life has been the major concern of society; our free time has been a matter of individual interest. In a democratic society, the use of leisure will always remain the prerogative of the individual; however, the great increase in the availability of leisure for large numbers of people places upon society some obligations and responsibilities for making adequate provisions for its use. Skills, interests, and attitudes developed through leisure are significant not only to the individual but to the society whose quality of culture and citizenship he helps to develop. Society is, therefore, concerned with recreation, which occurs during leisure.

The Nature of Recreation

What is recreation? What is play? Do the two terms differ? How does each differ from work? Are leisure and recreation synonymous? Recreation is such a highly personal experience that it nearly defies concrete definition. If we were to ask lay and professional persons to explain the term "recreation" we would be apt to get a variety of responses, each within a personal philosophy or conditioned by the connotations evoked by past experiences. Although there seems to be some agreement as to the nature and the function of recreation, succinct description is not readily forthcoming because definitions of recreation vary. Following are some examples of definitions of terms, which will indicate the variety of concepts:

Leisure

Leisure: "For purposes of social analysis the concept is usually narrowed —and widened—to mean simply freedom from activities centering around the making of a livelihood." [1] Craven

"Leisure: The state of having time at one's own disposal; time which one can spend as one pleases; free or unoccupied time." [2] Oxford English Dictionary

[1] Ida Craven, "Leisure," in *The Encyclopedia of Social Sciences* (New York: The Macmillan Company, 1933), V, 402.
[2] Oxford English Dictionary.

"Leisure is best defined as unhurried, pleasurable living among man's spontaneous and educated enthusiasms. In its enjoyment, the quickened spirit yields at once a feeling of vividness and of peace." [3] Paul F. Douglass

"Leisure is commonly thought of as the surplus time remaining after the formal duties and necessities of life have been attended to. It is the free time, enabling a person to do as he chooses." [4] Neumeyer and Neumeyer

"Leisure is popularly defined as the time we are free from the more obvious and formal duties which a paid job or other obligatory occupation imposes upon us." [5] Lundberg

Play

"Play is the means whereby the child, in fantasy, comes to know reality." [6] Slavson

"Play is a voluntary activity or occupation executed within certain fixed limits of time and place, according to rules freely accepted but absolutely binding, having its aim in itself and accompanied by a feeling of tension, joy, and the consciousness that it is different from ordinary life." [7] Huizinga

"Play is the purest, most spiritual activity of man. . . . It holds the sources of all that is good. It gives, therefore, joy, freedom, contentment, inner and outer rest, peace with the world." [8] Froebel

"That which is neither utility nor truth nor likeness, nor yet, in its effects, is harmful, can best be judged by the criterion of charm that is in it and the pleasure it affords. Such pleasure, entailing as it docs no appreciable good or ill, is play." [9] Plato

Recreation

"Recreation is looked upon as activity voluntarily engaged in during leisure and motivated by the personal satisfactions which result from it." [10] *The Recreation Program*, Athletic Institute

[3] Paul F. Douglass, in an address given at Milwaukee, Wisconsin, April 18, 1958. Reprinted by permission.

[4] Martin H. Neumeyer and Esther S. Neumeyer, *Leisure and Recreation*, 1st ed. (New York: A. S. Barnes & Company, 1936), p. 1.

[5] George A. Lundberg, Mirra Komarovsky, Mary Alice McInerny, *Leisure, A Suburban Study* (New York: Columbia University Press, 1934), p. 2. Reprinted by permission.

[6] S. R. Slavson, *Recreation and the Total Personality* (New York: Association Press, 1948), p. 3.

[7] John Huizinga, *Homo Ludens* (London: Routledge & Kegan Paul, Ltd., 1949), p. 7.

[8] Friedrich Froebel, *Education of Man* (New York: Appleton and Company, 1887), p. 55.

[9] Plato's *Laws*, ii, 667 E.

[10] Athletic Institute, *The Recreation Program* (Chicago: The Athletic Institute, 1953), p. 1. Reprinted by permission.

"Recreation is not a matter of motions but rather of emotions. It is a personal response, a psychological reaction, an attitude, an approach, a way of life." [11] Romney

"Recreation is the natural expression during leisure of human interests seeking satisfaction." [12] Fitzgerald

"The word recreation has come, however, without our willing it, to be the rallying word of those who work for a creative, cooperative expression of personality through sport, athletics, play, art forms—through recreation." [13] Braucher

"Recreation . . . may be considered any activity which is not consciously performed for the sake of any reward beyond itself, which is usually engaged in during leisure, which offers man an outlet for his physical, mental, or creative powers, and in which he engages because of inner desire and not because of outer compulsion." [14] Butler

"Recreation may be thought of as activity voluntarily engaged in during leisure and primarily motivated by the satisfaction or pleasure derived therefrom." [15] Brightbill and Meyer

Recreation is "any activity pursued during leisure, either individual or collective, that is free and pleasureful, having its own immediate appeal, not impelled by a delayed reward beyond itself or by any immediate necessity." [16] *Dictionary of Sociology*

A personal philosophy

It is evident from the definitions above that concepts and philosophies vary. Although there is some trend in sociology to try to equate leisure and recreation, they are not synonymous. Though recreation takes place in leisure, it does not and should not absorb all leisure hours. Man may also use his leisure beneficially for worship, education, or service, or may misuse it in idleness, overindulgence, or crime.

Leisure may be defined as the unobligated hours available after caring for employment or the activities mandatory for self-maintenance.

"Play" and "recreation" are terms that are often used interchangeably by

[11] Ott Romney, *Off the Job Living* (New York: A. S. Barnes & Company, 1945), p. 14.

[12] Gerald B. Fitzgerald, *Community Organization for Recreation* (New York: A. S. Barnes & Company, 1948), p. 32.

[13] Howard Braucher, *A Treasury of Living* (New York: National Recreation Association, 1950), p. 23.

[14] George D. Butler, *Introduction to Community Recreation*, 3rd ed. (New York: McGraw-Hill Book Company, 1959), p. 10. Reprinted by permission.

[15] Charles K. Brightbill and Harold D. Meyer, *Recreation: Text and Readings* (Englewood Cliffs, N. J.: Prentice-Hall, Inc., 1953), p. 50. Reprinted by permission.

[16] *Dictionary of Sociology* (New York: Philosophical Library, 1944), p. 251.

laymen and professionals alike. Common distinctions made between the two terms may describe play as spontaneous, physical activity for children and recreation as re-creative, organized, relaxing activity for adults. There are thin lines of differentiation, but the authors of this book accept recreation as the broad term that includes play.

Recreation is any enjoyable leisure experience in which the participant voluntarily engages and from which he receives immediate satisfactions.

Such a definition is broad enough to include many experiences. No specific activity, then, may be· designated as recreation. What is recreation for one individual may be drudgery for another. Recreation is person-centered; the attitude of the individual toward the activity is all-important. Recreation may include reading a book or planting a flowerbed, watching a puppet show or listening to a symphony concert, creating an oil painting or baby sitting with the grandchildren, camping with the family or playing football, collecting buttons or going to a dance, playing solitaire or greeting friends at a party. The potential of recreation for creative, satisfying, enriched living in increased leisure is limitless. Inspirational guidance to help individuals meet that potential in an ever more complex society is the challenge of the recreation leader in our century.

Community recreation denotes those recreation activities that society provides through various social institutions such as the municipal recreation department, the school, the home, and the church.

Although within the confines of the definition of recreation, an individual's personal choice of recreation could engage him in unwholesome activities, community recreation programs tend to provide recreation embodying only positive values.

Characteristics of recreation

There is difficulty in gaining common agreement in a definitive statement of the essence of recreation; however, most professionals agree upon certain basic characteristics that the term implies.

It is activity as opposed to idleness. The activity may involve quiet discussion or contemplation, participation in the most rigorous contact sport, or any degree along the continuum between the two extremes. In other words, the activity may be mental, physical, emotional, or a combination of these three.

Recreation occurs in leisure. The time for recreation is the unobligated hours, when one is free to do as he chooses.

The choice of activity is voluntary. The individual participates in recreation voluntarily, not through compulsion. He is free to choose those activities that interest and reward him; he acts not because of outside pressures but of his own free will. This freedom of choice offers at once a challenge and an obligation. It assumes that there is a wide offering of activities from which the individual may choose; it further assumes that he has had some guidance in developing the emotional mechanism that will allow him to make the choices that allow growth, not deterioration, in his leisure hours.

Recreation provides enjoyment. The participant finds enjoyment in his recreation; if this quality is lacking, he does not voluntarily return to the activity. The absorption, the involvement that allows the participant to lose himself in the fun of the moment, provides a balance for the obligations of the working hours.

Satisfactions are immediate and inherent in the activity. Recreation is its own paymaster; the rewards lie in the doing of the activity. No ulterior purpose is allowed to dominate, although long-range or postponed satisfactions may provide "dividend" rewards. For example, the avid collector who enjoys gathering and organizing stamps may find additional pleasures as he displays them later at a hobby show.

Recreation, at its best, is re-creative. The word "recreation" is sometimes used to include both activities that are beneficial and those that are dangerous, undesirable, or questionable. In its best sense, however, the word implies a renewal of spirit and body. The efforts of public and private agencies to promote recreation are justified by the assumption that it has this re-creative value and makes a positive contribution to the physical, mental, and moral welfare of the participants.

It provides a change of pace. Recreation usually involves a change of pace, which refreshes the individual and allows him to maintain physical, mental, and emotional equilibrium. It may also involve the same activity with a change of focus from work to pleasure. A swimming coach may play the piano for recreation, or he may possibly go swimming with friends. In the first instance, he has changed his pace; in the second, he has changed focus although participating in the same activity.

Recreation is broad in concept. Because recreation depends upon the attitudes of individuals toward activity, it encompasses a multitude of choices. The types of recreation are as numerous as human interests and desires. They include offerings in arts and crafts; drama; dance; literary, mental, and linguistic activities; music; outdoor recreation; sports and games; social recreation; hobbies; and special events. They involve all ages from the preschool child to the retired aged and all capacities from the paraplegic or retarded to the vibrantly healthy. They range from rigorous sport activities to quiet study; from watching an activity to creating it; from solitary enjoyment to group activity; from spontaneous participation to

Fig. 1   *Recreation—Many Things to Many People*

highly organized affairs; and from outlets requiring no leadership to those requiring highly skilled professional leadership.

Recreation should be wholesome, constructive, and socially acceptable. Since the adjectives listed conjure up a variety of connotations dependent upon qualitative opinions of individuals and the society in which they live, this characteristic has long been the source of controversy. What is wholesome to one person may be considered degenerating to another; local mores often dictate what is socially acceptable. Dancing may be quite popular as wholesome recreation in one community and banned as sinful in another locale. Although admitting that personal choices of activities may not always seem to qualify as recreation within the confines of this characteristic, the recreation profession would agree that programs by recreation agencies should meet this requirement. Hopefully, any worthwhile recreation activity will carry with it a personal challenge, social approval within the society in which it is offered, and a chance for the growth of the inner resources of the participants involved.

Misconceptions and Changing Attitudes

Changing times demand changing attitudes, and the lag often causes erroneous concepts. As is true with any new term, certain misconceptions have already formed with regard to recreation.

Recreation as a refresher after work

An editorial in *Life* magazine indicated one popular misconception in that it described recreation as "any kind of mental or physical change from work that enables you to work better, such as a stenographer's coffee break, a professor's detective story, or a factory worker's weekend in the woods." [17] Such a concept furthers the philosophy of the work-recreation cycle, which fosters the idea of the sanctity of work and sees the purpose of recreation as a reward for work or a tool for re-preparation for work. Although it may often be true that recreation provides renewal of spirit and energy to enable an individual to return to his job, those who do not work are in even greater need of finding the satisfactions of life in their enlarged leisure hours. Certainly, for many, work provides the great satisfactions and purposes of life; but in a world in which work hours are constantly decreasing and leisure time is increasing, the values of recreation that are totally unrelated to work are burgeoning. To consider leisure merely as a means of increasing work output is to deny individuals the opportunity for full lives in our century.

[17] From an editorial in *Life* magazine (December 28, 1959), p. 62. Copr. 1959 Time Inc. Reprinted by permission.

Recreation as sinful or evil

The Puritan, who held the concept that work and piety were synonymous, denounced any form of play as evil. Whatever was pleasurable had to be sinful. In years gone by, in which the production of necessities was the all-engrossing concern of society, the idea of the sanctity of work was understandable. In today's economy, which demands discretionary time for the masses if production rates are not to outstrip the ability to consume, recreation as a road to the "good life" must be interpreted as both respectable and necessary.

Recreation as a time filler

To justify recreation as a mere escape from boredom, a murmur of activity to fill empty hours, is to demean seriously its possible values. It would be a sad commentary on the cultural growth of American society if all that could be expected of recreation were the aimless consumption of periods of time.

Recreation as a panacea for social ills

Recreation is sometimes thought of as being of value chiefly because it may help solve such social problems as juvenile delinquency. There has been much discussion, with a lack of conclusive evidence, regarding the relationship between antisocial behavior and the lack of recreation opportunities. Delinquency is a complicated problem, one in which home, church, school, and all community agencies must cooperate. Recreation leaders are responsible for providing well-rounded wholesome experiences through which both children and adults may develop and remain emotionally and morally stable; these programs are aimed only indirectly at the reduction of delinquency.

Increasing a community's recreation program may not decrease antisocial behavior; but when programs and trained leadership are directed specifically toward problems in this field, significant reductions may be made. By offering a constructive use of leisure, recreation leaders can help individuals to avoid the unwholesome environment and undesirable activities that may lead to crime and delinquency.

Much of what is termed juvenile delinquency is based on misdirected urges for adventure and recognition, which should be satisfied through wholesome recreation activities. The pleasurable and thrilling sharpening of the senses that comes from pitting one's skill and intelligence against an adversary seems to be at the bottom of at least some forms of delinquency. Similar excitation can be found in healthful recreation pursuits such as skiing, diving, sailing, camping, mountain climbing, and certain organized sports. Institutions concerned with delinquency can well look to recreation for ways in which to satisfy, harmlessly, the urges that, when uncontrolled, lead to destructive behavior. If the traditional recreation programs are not sufficiently attractive to suffice as counter-attractions to delinquency, new ways must be found to hold the interest of the delinquent and the potential delinquent.

Although there is little question that wholesome recreation can help to prevent antisocial behavior, recreation is not a cure-all for unacceptable behavior. The values of recreation are in the enrichment of life for the majority; deterring the minority from delinquent acts is an important but secondary contribution. Fortunately, many misconceptions of recreation are no longer held by thoughtful people. Recreation as a *creative force* in the life of the individual and in the betterment of society is recognized as having ever increasing importance.

Recreation and Its Relationship to Other Areas

The objectives, purposes, and values of recreation are not dissimilar to those of other related areas. Recreation interrelates with work, social welfare, education, religion, and health, yet belongs exclusively to none of these. Although most of these are concerned with helping the individual and society to attain the highest possible potential, they differ in emphasis, method, and organization for achieving that goal. The following discussion relates some similarities and differences.

Recreation and work

Although work for some may be pleasurable and may contain some of the characteristics of recreation, activity is not recreation when its motive is money-making, prestige, or anything other than satisfaction in the activity itself. The Lindemans and Edisons who vowed that they experienced only pleasure in their work are in the minority. Work and recreation differ in five important respects although, hopefully, there are some enjoyable moments in any work day: (1) Work is compulsory, whereas recreation is voluntary. (2) Compensation in work is most frequently in the form of money or status, whereas satisfaction inherent in the activity itself is the reward for recreation. (3) The reward in work usually comes at the end of the week, the month, or the season; immediate enjoyment is the reward of those engaged in recreation. (4) Inability to perform at expected capacity in work means serious consequences and possible loss of job; recreation, except for the professional, does not mean loss of sustenance if the participant does not perform at top level. (5) An individual must adapt himself to the requirements of his life work; if he is unable to make such changes, the job goes to someone else. In recreation, the individual can alter the choice of activity to suit his mental, physical, or emotional capacities or urges of the moment.

Recreation and education

Recreation is a form of education if the latter is defined as including "any process shaping the potentialities of the maturing organism." [18] The goals of recreation and education are not poles apart, since both are working toward enrichment of life for individuals. Learning is more rapid and lasting if it is pleasurable and satisfying in itself, and the finest educational experiences take on a recreational nature. This is not to suggest that all education should be recreation. Learning with a purpose beyond immediate satisfaction is necessary in education, and we all must learn to do things that we might not enjoy doing.

Recreation and adult education

The profession of adult education most closely resembles recreation in goals, organization, and method. There is often no line of demarcation indicating when the adult education sewing class or the community center public-speaking club ceases to be adult education and becomes recreation, or vice versa. Generally speaking, if the activity is used for vocational progress, it is considered adult education. If it relates to skills and appreciations for use in leisure, it is recreation for adults.

The adult educator uses the recreation spirit to accomplish his task for the greatest satisfaction of his participants. The recreator adds a bonus of learning and personal growth to the enjoyment of the recreation activity. The qualified leader, be he in adult education, recreation, or any other profession that deals with human welfare, combines appreciations and satisfactions with learning.

Recreation and group work

Although many agencies engaged in group work are engaged in recreation, group work and recreation are not synonymous. Group work is a way of working with people to achieve desired goals. The method used may be participation in recreation activity. For example, a group worker in a neighborhood settlement may try to bring about changes in personality and behavior among members of a boys' group through sports and games that, to the boys, are forms of recreation. Recreation is a tool for the social worker. Group work is a method for the recreation leader.

Recreation and physical education

Although recreation and physical education are closely allied, they are complementary, not identical. Recreation and physical education have often been associated in the popular mind because many physical recrea-

[18] *Columbia Encyclopedia*, 2nd ed. (New York: Columbia University Press, 1950), p. 592.

tion activities are identical with those used in school-oriented physical education programs. The purposes of physical education are physical fitness and the development of attitudes, interests, and skills which will maintain that fitness. The purpose of recreation is enjoyment, though better physical fitness may be a by-product of wise choices in physical activities. Such physical activities comprise only one aspect of recreation. A well-rounded recreation program includes many kinds of experiences, and recreation should no more be identified with physical education than with education in the arts or sciences.

The Significance of Recreation in Modern Life

Recreation is as old as the human race; only in recent years, however, has its importance been appreciated. Today it stands, along with education, work, and religion, as a necessary part of a well-balanced life. All recreation is based on the satisfaction of certain urges or desires. Among these are the desires for security, for social contact, for recognition, for new experiences, for giving service, for belonging, for enjoying the beautiful, for learning, and for creating. For many people, satisfaction of these urges and desires exists in one or more of the wide variety of recreation activities.

The need of recreation for people of all ages

People of all ages need recreation. For the infant or young child, play is the natural expression of his very being. Play begins a few weeks after birth; through it the child learns to use his body and to communicate with others. A child that does not play is sick, and a child who is denied the right to play does not develop normally. Play is, for the very young, one of the most important aspects of living, the means whereby they grow in their own physical, mental, and emotional patterns and in their relationships with others.

Through play, the older child extends his acquaintance with the world outside his family. He takes part in games, expresses himself through music and art, explores his natural environment, and satisfies his curiosity. He establishes with children and adults relationships that will serve him in his maturity. He develops many patterns of recreation interests that may last throughout his life.

As a young person approaches maturity, recreation assumes new importance. Through it he gains experience in social living. His recreation serves a part in finding and evaluating a spouse. As important by-products of his recreation, he may learn respect for society and may develop self-sufficiency, independence, and ability to work with others.

It is not only children and youth who need recreation. The young adults, the middle-aged, and older people all find in it not only personal gratification but also a means for improving their communities and serving others.

Recreation and the needs of society

Several conditions arising out of modern social life affect the need for recreation. Changes in society have altered attitudes and formed a new philosophy of the importance of leisure expenditure. Following are some factors that have influenced the growth of recreation needs:

Increased leisure. The twelve-hour day and the six-day week of a few generations ago have given way to the seven- or eight-hour day, the five-day week, and paid vacations of from two to six weeks. The housewife and the young child also have less work, for the many labor-saving devices in the home have decreased the drudgery of household chores. Leisure time has especially increased among older people; a longer life span, early retirement with social security and pensions combine to give them time to use as they wish. Such increased leisure has demanded a change in the philosophy which dictated that work, of itself, was sufficient for existence. Although work still provides many satisfactions, growing leisure demands education for a capacity to use it wisely.

Changing home life. Work and play in early America centered in and around the home. There were many responsibilities for all members of the family; and when home chores were done, the children played around home. Although the home is still the basic institution in society, many modern conditions have weakened its influence. No longer does the economic success of the family depend upon the teamwork of each child and adult. There is more time for recreation, yet there are fewer opportunities for obtaining it around the home and thus a greater necessity for seeking it elsewhere.

Recreation can either weaken or strengthen family ties. Parents busy with activities away from home are often only too glad to let the children go their separate ways and are grateful to organizations that will fill the children's leisure hours. However, recreation can and should serve to strengthen a family and keep it together; it is possible through leisure-time pursuits to maintain family solidarity and unity of purpose. Through recreation children may learn the lessons in responsibility and consideration for other members of the family once learned through home chores.

Population factors affecting recreation. The growth of population has resulted in a great change in the way people must live. From a nation of less than four million in 1790 we have grown to over 185 million. In 1960 in the continental United States there was a density of 50.4 persons per square mile as compared with only 4.5 in 1790. Whereas in the early days of our country almost every child might fish, hunt, and roam the woods freely, today such opportunities are restricted. It is now necessary for society, through governmental or other means, to set aside lands for recreation; yet, with each passing year, intensifying population pressures make such lands more difficult to reserve.

Although the population center in the United States has moved each year further to the west, most of the people of America still live in the Northeast, the Great Lakes states, the Far West, and the South Central sections of the country. If present trends continue, the bulk of our population will cluster increasingly in metropolitan sections. A change in recreation habits must necessarily follow. Recreation requiring space must give way to other forms of recreation, or else society must provide the space needed.

Our population is tending toward greater homogeneity. Despite the great population increase from 1940 to 1960, the number of foreign-born has decreased. Immigration has been sharply reduced in recent years, and most of the immigrants who came to our land in the great tides of the 1800's have died, leaving descendants who have been absorbed into the American pattern of living. Cultural uniformity throughout the country has been accelerated through schools, newspapers, magazines, movies, radio, and television. Demands for recreation throughout the nation are likewise becoming more similar, subject, of course, to variations due to climate and geographical factors.

Industrialization and mechanization—automation. A century ago our nation devoted itself essentially to handicraft manufacturing methods; today we are highly mechanized and industrialized. Each of us has acquired, in terms of horsepower, the equivalent of many slaves. Electricity, steam, and the internal-combustion engine were great transforming influences; even these seem dwarfed with the development of atomic power. Needing our muscles less for work, we have more energy left for leisure.

Not all the steps toward industrialism have necessarily resulted in good. Most workers are now employees rather than owners. One of our greatest satisfactions in life should come from our work, but mechanized industry provides little opportunity for millions of workers to obtain satisfactions comparable to those of the independent farmer or the owner of a small business. A man on the assembly line may not feel the joy of creative effort; indeed, he may not even see his finished product. Tensions caused by high-speed production may increase his need for recreation; yet he may work in a congested city, in which he cannot find the kind of relaxation he needs. Specialization on the job makes more necessary an integrated experience in recreation. Automation not only has stimulated the need for recreation but has conditioned our use of leisure with automobiles, automatic golf carts, and television sets.

Increased income and mobility. Recent years have brought higher incomes and higher purchasing power for most of the people of America. Automobiles, electric lights, radios, television sets, telephones, and summer vacations are not restricted to the wealthy but are extended to a great majority. Better health, increased vitality, and greater opportunities for education have all accompanied the rise in income. When income rises above that needed for subsistence, there is more money to spend for recreation. Commercial recreation has grown in quantity and variety, and people have been able and willing to pay for it.

Good roads, automobiles, and rapid public transportation, accompanied by high income, have made the American people mobile and have placed within reach many recreation areas formerly of difficult access. A mobile population has also left many aged alone in their communities as their children have ventured to new abodes.

Urbanization. At the time of the Declaration of Independence, only about 2.5 percent of the American people lived in cities of over 2,500 people. The census of 1960 showed over two thirds of the population living in such cities.

As a result of the mechanization of agriculture, farms are larger, and fewer people are needed to produce the food, fibers, and lumber of America. The movement from country to city and the resultant change in living and working habits have had significant impacts on recreation. Commercial recreation has grown up in urban areas to meet the needs of city dwellers, and community recreation has had its greatest growth in cities. Co-existing with today's urban trend, and somewhat counterbalancing it, is the movement toward the suburbs, where families may have homes of their own with lawns and gardens and where the recreation pattern may differ considerably from that of the city dwellers.

Education. The present century has brought more formal education for greater numbers of people; those who are well educated usually demand higher standards of living, including more opportunities for recreation. One of the objectives of education is the development of leisure interests, skills, and attitudes. Many school courses, such as those in science, art, music, reading, physical education, and geography, have recreation values and stimulate interests that students may wish to pursue in their leisure. Such leisure pursuits may well continue throughout their lifetimes.

The Values of Recreation

Recreation is an end in itself, and as such it needs no justification beyond satisfying the participants. However, from the point of view of the agencies that provide recreation, certain values that make worthwhile the money and effort society invests in them are to be expected to accrue both to society and to the individual. With the increase in leisure opportunities, the more lasting satisfactions possible from leisure are a source of life enrichment.

Personal values

Physical well-being. The value derived from recreation depends obviously upon the type of recreation. The most evident value of many forms of recreation is their contribution to physical well-being. In addition to providing a satisfying outlet for excess energy, physical recreation may improve body tone, increase strength, develop coordination, and perfect manipulative abilities. In this age of sedentary jobs, it is ever more necessary that recreation help in the maintenance of physical fitness. Mrs. Calvin Coolidge once remarked, "I like to get tired; it feels so good to rest." Anyone who has come in from the ski run or the sailing regatta will know full well the exhilaration of healthful physical fatigue about which Mrs. Coolidge spoke. Sometimes, at any age, it is only recreation that offers the stimulus for physical activity, rigorous or mild. Dr. Marjorie Phillips, noted physical educator, sounded a warning in these words:

There are two factors of particular importance that make attention to the problems of fitness mandatory. Both of these factors are related to the conditions under which we are living today. The first of these is the imminent threat of total war that is constantly with us and which requires that we maintain a fitness level which can be rapidly raised to meet the emergency demands of a total war. The second is the ever-decreasing physical exertions imposed as our technological advances remove more and more of the physical tasks formerly performed as routines of the average day. We must be aware of the possible progressive deleterious effects of such a way of life. If we persist in blinding ourselves to these conditions and fail to take a realistic and determined approach to alleviating them, it is possible we may be courting immediate and eventual disaster.[19]

Recreation's contribution to physical fitness, then, may be involved not only with living healthfully but with living at all.

Mental and emotional health. Recreation makes a significant contribution to mental and emotional health, in that it provides a balance and a release. It offers outlets for frustrations and can effect a catharsis of harmful emotions. It contributes significantly to satisfaction of basic needs upon which psychological integrity as well as physical health depends. Petty worries and unnecessary concerns may be forgotten in the pursuit of an engrossing form of recreation. Through art, music, social activities, games, sports, and other activities, we may find opportunities for self-expression otherwise denied. Chapter 18 expands this topic.

Intellectual development. Mental development may be stimulated by many forms of recreation, for, as has been pointed out, recreation may be

[19] Marjorie P. Phillips, from an address delivered at American Association for Health, Physical Education, and Recreation conference, Kansas City, April 1958.

educational in nature. Recreation situations offer numerous opportunities for "learning by doing"—whether it be learning social relationships or learning to paint. Through direct experience learning is stimulated, hastened, and retained. The greatest lessons are not always confined to the classroom.

Ability to organize and carry responsibility. The ability to organize, to develop, and to carry out programs of action is often learned through recreation. We may learn to lead effectively and follow intelligently.

Character development. Recreation may help develop character traits such as initiative, self-reliance, restraint, courage, perseverance, ingenuity, honesty, love of fair play, and consideration for others. It is not accidental that all so-called character-building organizations use recreation as a major tool for the attainment of their objectives. One of the happiest attributes of wholesome recreation activities is the opportunity they offer to meet personality needs that will contribute to fruitful, well-adjusted living. In a relaxed environment in which the penalties for mistakes are not too costly, learning the joys of having taken responsibility and the unpleasantness accompanying shirked duty provides important lessons, which the individual can later apply throughout his daily life.

Social adjustment. Since recreation frequently involves groups, large and small, it may be one of the most rewarding situations for the development of certain social relations. It is one of the easiest routes to friendship. Through recreation there may develop respect and understanding for others and a recognition of one's own place in the social structure. Personal faults may be overcome through recreation. The retiring child may overcome fear of others through play, while the overaggressive child may be "toned down."

Aesthetic and spiritual values. The sense of well-being that comes with the development of inner resources that allow the individual to use his leisure creatively provides one of the highest values of recreation. With loss of pride in achievement in many labor situations and the steady decrease of the need for the craftsman, the search for the beautiful, the cultural, and the aesthetic belongs to the valuable leisure hours.

Values to society

Values derived by the individual may be said to be derived also by society, since happy and well-adjusted individuals make up a happy and well-adjusted society. There are, however, certain additional benefits from recreation that apply particularly to society.

Community attractiveness. People are attracted to places where there is an obvious concern for a better way of life and where parks are adequate and well cared for and a variety of desirable recreation opportunities is available. These are the communities in which parents prefer to rear their children and into which industries wish to move.

Civic spirit. Recreation can weld community spirit; it can develop an interest in civic projects, a pride in the progress of the community, a "know-how" in working together. Individuals may learn to be better citizens in a democracy—to adjust their demands to those of the group, to participate in group decisions, to work and play harmoniously together, and to win or lose with good grace.

Education for democracy. One of the best avenues for education in democratic citizenship is provided through recreation. When people organize themselves into groups and make decisions on a democratic basis, they strengthen the democratic way of life. Through recreation they may realize that race, creed, and economic status are secondary to qualities of character.

Safety. One of society's chief concerns is for the safety of its members. Recreation can contribute to safety. Well-planned and well-supervised play areas can do much to reduce street accidents, particularly in areas congested with heavy automobile traffic. Also, through recreation, such skills as swimming and life-saving, which contribute directly to safety, are learned. A relaxed person, free from tension, is a safer person, less prone to accidents.

Economy. Recreation has become a major direct as well as indirect force in American society. The recreation industry has a definite place in our modern economy. Chapter 3 deals more fully with the influence of recreation as a new frontier.

Limitations of recreation

In spite of its many possible values, recreation is not a cure-all for community ills; it is but one of many factors that may contribute to a healthy society. Good results depend upon a good program under good leadership. Recreation itself may provide situations in which to practice either desirable or undesirable behavior. Negative outcomes may result from participation in recreation activities: instead of honesty and good sportsmanship, for example, dishonesty and selfishness. When desirable behavior is practiced, however, good character traits may be developed and strengthened.

How can those responsible for recreation make sure that the recreation experience will have desirable effects upon its participants? The quality of recreation is determined by several factors, the most important of which is its leadership. Other influential factors are the wholesomeness of physical surroundings, the vitality of the program itself, the cooperation of individual citizens and organized groups, and the opportunities given for democratic decisions.

Although we cannot guarantee that character traits developed in recreation activities will always transfer to the home, the business world, or elsewhere, it is reasonable to assume that exercising desirable character traits in one situation will make it easier to exercise these traits in another situation.

The Case for Recreation

Recreation is a part of a whole. We would not wish to suggest otherwise. No claims are here made for recreation as the only answer for social ills, fullness of life, emotional balance, physical well-being, or an improved society. Recreation is not a panacea; it is not a substitute for work, economic security, or emotional stability. It is difficult to deny the value of wholesome recreation as a deterrent to personal and social difficulties, yet it is wholly recognizable that some leisure is devoted to recreation that degrades and degenerates. The abuses of leisure in an age of plenty are an ever present challenge to those who would recognize the potential heights that could be reached in more wholesome outlets.

Responsibility for the provision of leisure activities has been assumed by various commercial, educational, religious, and social organizations—public, private, and voluntary. It is generally agreed that, because of the potential benefits to society, it is society's duty to see that wholesome recreation opportunities are available and in some cases to protect the individual and society from undesirable enticements. That individuals and private agencies may indulge in activities for personal recreation or commercial benefit that fall short of the standards of acceptable practice is not denied; this book is concerned with the challenges faced, opportunities offered, and responsibilities accepted by agencies within a community who relate themselves to wholesome, constructive, creative recreation. It is their story, the story of community recreation, that is told in the following pages.

SUGGESTED REFERENCES

Braucher, Howard, *A Treasury of Living*. New York: National Recreation Association, 1950.

Brightbill, Charles K., *Man and Leisure: A Philosophy of Recreation*. Englewood Cliffs, N.J.: Prentice-Hall, Inc., 1961.

Huizinga, John, *Homo Ludens*. London: Routledge & Kegan Paul, Ltd., 1949.

Larrabee, Eric and Rolf Meyersohn, eds. *Mass Leisure*. Chicago: The Free Press, 1958.

Lee, Joseph, *Play in Education*. New York: The Macmillan Company, 1916.

Mulac, Margaret E., *Leisure: Time for Living and Retirement*. New York: Harper & Row, Inc., 1961.

Nash, Jay B., *Philosophy of Recreation and Leisure*. St. Louis: The C. V. Mosby Company, 1953.

Neumeyer, Martin H. and Esther S. Neumeyer, *Leisure and Recreation*, Third edition. New York: The Ronald Press Company, 1958.

Sapora, Allen V. and Elmer D. Mitchell, *The Theory of Play and Recreation*, Third edition. New York: The Ronald Press Company, 1961.

Slavson, S. R., *Recreation and the Total Personality*. New York: Association Press, 1948.

*"For there are three forms of life,
of which the first is the practical, the second, the contemplative,
and the third, the life of enjoyment."*

PLUTARCH

2

Recreation—
Past and Present

Although we do not know exactly how long human beings have existed on earth, the time may be measured in at least hundreds of thousands of years. Anthropologists have found little difference in man's mental and physical capacity over the years, and we may assume that the needs, urges, and longings of primitive man, although less complex than those of modern man, were in many ways similar to our own. Wherever or whenever man has existed, he has found some time for recreation. Even prehistoric man, when his needs for food and shelter were met, turned to some form of play to absorb his leisure hours. Ways of expressing recreation needs often vary, but the needs remain the same. Cultural, social, and economic changes have always influenced the breadth and scope of recreation and of course will continue to have a profound effect upon man's quest for a full life.

The Beginnings

Early life posed a struggle for mere physical existence, yet examples of ancient man's search for a more enjoyable life through forms of recreation are evident. Egyptian reliefs give evidence of an interest in hunting, spearing, wrestling, and fencing. Kite flying provided a dual pleasure for the artistic talent and the physical energy of the Chinese and other Asiatic peoples, 4,000 years before the Christian era. Expression in movement of sorrow or delight, or the interpretation of an occupation formed the dance patterns, which were highly developed in early societies. Clay modeling and basket weaving for pleasure or practical purposes have existed since primitive races took clay from the riverbeds and reeds from the marshes. Contests of speed and endurance gave evidence of the early Persians' use of recreation to train their warriors, and the Japanese board game of "Go" existed 2,200 years before the birth of Christ. The types of recreation and interest in those types are not new. Singing, dancing, arts and crafts, sports and games, social activities, story telling, drama, music, and nature activities have given recreation satisfaction throughout the ages, affecting and being affected by the life of the times.

In primitive cultures, the lines between work and play were not sharply drawn; and, as conditions fluctuated, various activities changed from labor to pleasurable leisure pursuits. It is interesting to observe that many present-day recreation activities, in which both children and adults engage, resemble those that had utilitarian or survival value somewhere in the history of the human race. Outstanding are the food-gathering activities such as fishing, hunting, gardening, and herb collecting. Few, indeed, are the recreation outlets today that did not have utilitarian origins: skiing, boating, walking, swimming, horseback riding, combative activities, and arts and crafts such as pottery, weaving, and leather work. To what extent the development of these interests today is due to our cultural environment and to what extent their development is due to basic physical and psychological needs is a problem better left to the psychologists. As permanent communities were established, time for work and time for recreation became more clearly delineated, and leisure classes emerged.

The Classical Age

From warlike Sparta to cultural Athens to the deteriorating Roman Empire, the importance of recreation pursuits was recognized, but the objectives varied. In the Golden Age of Pericles, in the fifth century B.C., the Athenian democracy was dedicated to the idea that to live was not enough; to live well was the goal. "A sound mind in a sound body" was the harmonious balance expected from leisure. The cost of this leisure was high, however; as wise a man as Aristotle condoned the enslavement of a large part of the population to allow leisure for a few. Attention to games in early Greek civilization constituted part of the education for the leisure class. The Athenian ideal integrated art, literature, philosophy, music, and sport into a unified concept. The concept of leisure as an opportunity for cultural development is evident in the Greek word for leisure, "schole," from which our English word "school" was derived.

The Spartan civilization and its Roman counterpart viewed play also as a means of education, but as education for the primary purpose of physically and emotionally conditioning the people toward the exigencies of war. Such a philosophy necessitated a heavy emphasis on physical feats of daring, accuracy, and endurance as recreation pursuits. Thus, both the military and the art attitude toward play existed intermittently during the classical age.

Recreation activities

The Athenian child had rattles, marbles, hoops, dolls, and kites, and engaged in tug of war, hopscotch, and other games similar to those found in any modern kindergarten. At seven, he entered the gymnasium, where he studied music, gymnastics, oratory, drama, poetry, and politics. His Spartan counterpart was drilled in contests of speed and endurance and exposed to a scouting education comparable to the modern scouting program for Explorers.

The early Olympic games, the most celebrated of the Greek festivals, included foot races, wrestling, boxing, chariot racing, and oratory—with the garland of wild olives as the coveted prize. Other Greek festivals included symposia and contests in singing, riddle solving, and drinking. Sixth century B.C. Panathenaic games included recitations, chariot racing, musical contests, and rowing. The Roman *Ludi*, or public games, provided spectator sports for scores of Roman citizenry, who gathered to view the *Ludus Troiae* (a sham fight on horseback), chariot racing, gymnastic contests, gladiatorial combats, or military reviews. Both Greeks and Romans engaged in cockfighting, games of gambling with knucklebones, and board games of all kinds.

Facilities

The large stadiums and gymnasiums housed athletic activities, whereas open air amphitheaters afforded areas for music, dance, and dramatic festivals. Friends of Plato bought a suburban recreation grove named Academus, where Plato founded an intellectual academy dedicated to "the means of living a life of philosophic leisure." There, cultural pursuits were directed for over 900 years. The Academy fostered intellectual and aesthetic interests, whereas the Forum, or public square, provided an opportunity for public discussion. The public baths offered a setting for diversion, relaxation, or business transaction, as the need arose.

The Middle Ages

"The Middle Ages" is a modern term coined to distinguish the 1,000 years after the fall of the Roman Empire, when Europe was held together primarily by the unifying influence of the church. Many references have been made to the influence of excesses of leisure upon the downfall of Roman civilization; the new age, permeated by religion, turned its back on many of the play activities that had been a part of the social and cultural life of the classical period. Medieval civilization was characterized by class distinctions and a categorized "belonging," which influenced choices of leisure activity. In a feudalistic system, people banded together for protection, and several social and economic divisions emerged: the lord and nobleman, who protected the land; the serf or peasant, who tilled the land; the guildsman, who worked at a craft; and the clergyman, who administrated both education and religion.

The "good life" was the ascetic life of abstinence; worldly pleasures were not goals for this existence. Life was a preparation for rewards beyond. The domination of church and manor exerted influence until such time as the introduction of gunpowder freed the serf from his dependence for protection on the noble knight, and the invention of the movable-type printing press relieved the clergy of sole control over education.

Amounts of leisure and the media for its expenditure varied, as would be expected, with social status. The lords and noblemen, between battles, had ample leisure; the serfs had little time for revelry after the fields were tilled, the animals cared for, and the grain pounded. The strong religious attitude of the church dominated choices of recreation activity, with a noticeable abstinence from the physical games and contests or arena spectator activities of classical times. Such authority had intermittent influences down through the Puritan period in American life.

That there existed during the Middle Ages a native vigor ready to burst the bonds of oppression is obvious, human nature being what it is; but the massive power of the church, sustained by ignorance and superstition of the people, hung like a conscience over any who openly sought to make pleasanter the life that was "only a prelude to an infinitely worse or infinitely better future."

Recreation activities

Outlets for recreation were varied, dependent primarily upon class distinctions, and were frequently related to the occupation at hand. The nobleman, when not actively engaged in warfare for protection of home and country, played at mock battles in the jousts and tournaments of the lists. His lady found her pleasure in embroidering his jacket or in being a spectator for such events. The male child spent the first 21 years of his life in training for his role of Protector. His play activities consisted of riding, hawking, lancing, singing, reading, and jousting, to perfect his ability as a chivalrous knight in the manor or on the battlefield. His female counterpart learned music, embroidery, and other crafts. Indoor sports of the nobleman included feasting, drinking, gambling, board games, and entertainment by the popular jester or the traveling bard of the day.

The poverty-stricken peasant also indulged in those activities that related to his daily tasks. Communal dances portrayed his harvesting labors or mocked the life of his manor lords. Quarter-staff tilting was a favorite pastime for those who watched the flocks. Fairs, pageants, and racing; bowling, cockfighting, and archery contests—all kept the serf in the out-of-doors to which his work related.

The craftsmen or guildsmen shared recreation as they shared their work, owing allegiance neither to the lords nor the serfs. Fairs in which their work was displayed were popular. Singing work songs to glorify or to stimulate progress on their craft formed a bond in leisure and in work hours. Possibly one of the most significant contributions of the guildsmen to literature and entertainment of the day was the development of the guild carts, which moved through the streets to play mystery and miracle dramas on street corners.

The church, too, added to cultural outlets involved with art, literature, and drama, though it did not condone the athletic contests and spectator sports of the day. If the literary accounts of the age can be accepted, many of the clergy strayed far from the church teaching in their own leisure hours, which might be spent as often in drinking bouts as in moments of contemplation.

Facilities

The lists, in which jousts and tournaments kept the noblemen playing at warfare, were descendants of the Roman arena and forerunners of the modern football stadium. In the lists, spectators thrilled to dual contests or mass combat, and the judges were no less barbarous than their Roman counterparts as they decreed whether or not tips should be removed from lances for a fight to the death.

The guild wagons, built by craftsmen when the church moved the drama from the altar and the churchyard, formed our first traveling theaters. These wagons allowed persons standing on neighborhood street corners to witness the Corpus Christi plays or more banal offerings. Other recreation activities required only the space of the out-of-doors, which was readily available to serf or nobleman.

The Renaissance

"The Renaissance" is a term used to designate a well-known but indefinite space of time between the Middle Ages and the modern world. The spirit of the age was questing and inquiring. The spread of popular education and the relief from the oppression of church authority brought about a revival of learning, a renewed interest in classical arts and activities, and a new philosophy of the meaning of life. In direct contrast to the former period, life during the Renaissance was lived, as Huizinga [1] indi-

[1] John Huizinga, *Homo Ludens* (London: Routledge & Kegan Paul Ltd., 1949). Reprinted by permission.

cates, as a "game of artistic perfection." The rules of the game were many and varied. The old identification with caste diminished, and new social, economic, and cultural strata were formed. The aristocracy and the bourgeoisie alike play-acted their leisure.

Recreation activities

The formal court balls and parties of the aristocracy were mimicked in lesser style by the rising middle class. Fairs, exhibitions, banquets, operas, and theater were prevalent and popular; falconry, cockfighting, and swordfighting were as frequent, if less sanctioned, sports. Hunting and gardening occupied leisure of adults, while children's games showed less emphasis on knightly combat.

Insecurity and instability characterized the age, but the relinquishing of static codes of living brought with it an inquiring spirit, which investigated the worth of pleasure and enjoyment as it explored other theories. Play activities were finally looked upon as essential to the physical health of individuals and later took their place as aids to liberal education itself.

Facilities

Theaters, courtly ballrooms, arenas for fencing or other contests, and formal parks and gardens were outstanding in the Renaissance era. Open areas for festivals and fairs were also prevalent. Game preserves offered hunting paradises for the aristocrats and the adventure of poaching for the poor. Beer gardens and, later, coffeehouses served as social recreation haunts or highly literary discussion centers for many classes.

Colonial America (1492–1775)

While Europe floundered in its search for a balance of security and meaning for life, the exacting demands of existence in a new country left little time for pleasure-seeking for colonial Americans. The need to survive put a high premium on labor for all. Sustaining life in the wilderness was serious business, but it had its gratifications. A man was his own employer; his resourcefulness and skill rewarded him, at least a good part of the time, with success. Making a living required long hours, but it offered satisfactions in social, creative, and physical achievements that are today often associated with recreation.

Because survival depended upon hard work, the early settlers in both Virginia and New England enforced rules against idleness. With the rigid zeal of their Puritan inheritance, New England laws prohibited all forms of amusement or misuse of time long after economic necessity for such abstinence had vanished. Thus, the earliest forms of recreation legislation were prohibitive rather than permissive. Governor Endicott of the Massachusetts Bay colony decreed that "no person shall spend his time unprofit-ably," whereas the Virginia Assembly, early in the seventeenth century, issued the edict that persons found idle could be bound over for work. To be idle was to be evil, a concept so deeply instilled by such paragons of virtue as Increase Mather and his son Cotton that its message has haunted the nation far into the present. The result of such a philosophy was not to eliminate recreation but to surround it with a sense of guilt. The average housewife of today who hurriedly makes excuses for playing with her young-ster in the yard before finishing her housework is suffering from the same Puritan guilt complex concerning the evil of recreation.

The eighteenth century brought economic prosperity, an increase in the population of coastal cities, and a widening of the western frontiers. Leisure had expanded for all parts of the country, but the slavery of the South gave the plantation owners the reputation for the most pleasure-loving society America had ever known. The New York and Philadelphia areas were taking on urban atmospheres, and the new frontiers of America were as unrestrained in their recreation as in other aspects of their adventurous existence.

Recreation activities

The hardy pioneers, as human beings, needed release from their arduous labor, and their behavior often did not mirror their laws. Communal work projects were an excuse for merrymaking. The rewards of wrestling, danc-ing, and games after the tasks were completed were motivation for the work of barn-raising, husking bees, and similar activities. Hunting and fishing were sanctioned; theaters were prohibited. As late as 1750, attempts to put on a play in Boston created a major riot.

Pleasure on a severe winter night confined itself to the social recreation enjoyed after the wedding or interment of friends or relatives. Many turned in desperation to taverns and liquor for want of more wholesome recrea-tion opportunities. Growing interest in card playing, dancing, bear baiting, and gambling produced more prohibitive laws and accompanying punish-ments. Only folk music and singing seemed to escape legal wrath. The wealthy of the South engaged in a renewal of English games and sports, enjoyed riding to the hounds, horse racing, and cockfighting. The Dutch settlers in New York indulged in bowling, ice skating, and ice carnivals, although all the colonists played shuffleboard, participated in shooting matches, foot races, and marching reviews.

As increasing migration brought large numbers of non-Puritans to New England, rebellion against restraints began to mount. By the end of the eighteenth century, dancing classes in New York, the social gaieties of the Boston aristocracy, or the foxhunts and theatricals of Virginia were being viewed with less jaundiced eyes by a population that had become more economically prosperous and more prone to accept the inevitability of some recreation pursuits. Even Boston was beginning to release the ban on theater, which New York and the South had enjoyed regularly during the last half of the eighteenth century.

Significant events

1565. The Spanish established a plaza in St. Augustine. The plaza might be considered the first park land in the continental United States.

1634. The establishment of Boston Commons represented the first city park in the English colonies. Set aside originally for communal pastureland, it soon became a social meeting-place.

1640. The Massachusetts Bay colony passed an ordinance opening bodies of fresh water over ten acres in size to the public for "fishing and fowling." Such sport was a means of survival as well as recreation.

1686. Mention was made of the game of football as early as 1686. The sport was then played with bare feet.

1716. The Theater of Williamsburg, Virginia, founded in 1716, is believed to be the earliest theater in America, although credit for the first permanent theater in America goes to the John Street Theater in New York, built in 1767. By 1760, Boston's Faneuil Hall was accommodating regular musical concerts and some theatrical productions, which were promoted in the guise of public lectures.

Recreation in a New Nation

At the close of the Revolutionary War, the trans-Appalachian country was still largely unsettled. Among the first moves toward westward expansion were the ordinances of 1785 and 1787, which provided for the development of the Northwest. As a matter of policy, government lands were sold or transferred to private hands as quickly as possible. With the Louisiana Purchase in 1803, the accession of the Floridas in 1819 and Texas in 1845, and the Mexican cessions (Guadalupe-Hidalgo Treaty of 1848 and the Gadsden Purchase of 1853), the present boundaries of the United States, except for Alaska and Hawaii, were substantially established.

The westward movement dominated the thinking of the American people of this period. In spite of the growth of cities along the eastern seaboard and the development of city culture, most of the people in America still lived on farms or in small communities. Recreation consisted principally of the simple pleasures of rural life—country dancing, social gatherings, mutual work projects, local fairs, hunting, and fishing. Recreation in frontier towns took on a rowdy character. The unrestricted, un-inhibited frontiersman indulged in wolf drives, brutal ring hunts, shooting matches, logrolling, dancing, tomahawk throwing, gambling, and heavy drinking. Interspersed with these were occasional religious revivals, camp meetings, or charivaris, which helped to fill recreational and emotional needs of the frontier folk.

In the slowly expanding cities on the eastern coast, people began to show a new dimension in their recreation choices. Gradually they threw off the Victorian cloak of inhibition and replaced the rural pleasures with com-mercial amusements and spectator activities, which have been an integral part of our twentieth-century leisure pattern. The shift from active to pas-sive diversions and the emphasis on minstrel shows, circuses, amusement parks, and other forms of commercial recreation, brought recreation voids that were not filled until late in the century with the beginnings of the recreation movement.

Cultural awakening

A vogue for self-improvement, affecting all classes, set in during the 1830's and 1840's. In 1826, the National Museum paved the way for cul-tural interests. Public lectures were popular and drew large crowds. Despite the disapproval of religious leaders, the theater was growing. Farce and variety shows, circuses, and exhibitions mingled with stagings of the legiti-mate theater. Lyceum courses and chautauquas provided music and drama as well as lectures. The singing classes and dancing assemblies gave way to musical concerts and grand balls. Popular entertainment in lectures, music, or drama proved to be "big business."

Early park planning

The great majority of the American people had access to land either because they were owners or because access to private land was considered, in many places, a right. Only in the large cities did a need for society to provide land for parks or gardens become evident. In New England, the traditional open spaces for communal pastures, such as the Boston Com-mon, were prevalent. In Georgia and in Pennsylvania, city planning re-ceived attention when General James Oglethorpe laid out a design for Savannah's Public Gardens and William Penn delineated five open squares in the Philadelphia plan.

Although such limited spaces had been provided in many cities, it re-mained for New York City to design and develop the first city park, which was to set the example for future park expansion elsewhere. Land for Cen-tral Park was acquired in 1853, when Mayor Kingsland and the Common Council set aside 850 acres. Development of the area was left to Frederick Law Olmsted, the first superintendent of the park, and Calvert Vaux, who helped in the design. The designers, who envisioned a future in which New York's populace would be cramped for space, attempted to supply New Yorkers with the joys of the country in the midst of the city. Central Park is still noted for those scenic and recreational objectives and has stood as an important pattern for similar city park developments.

Although Hot Springs National Park, in Arkansas, had been reserved for the public in 1832 because of the medicinal qualities of its water, it was not recognized as a national park until early in the twentieth century. The federal government's acquisition of Yellowstone Park in 1872, with the intention to preserve it for the enjoyment of future generations, marked the real beginnings of the national park movement.

School and recreation

Several other developments influencing recreation were taking place during the nineteenth century. This was the period of the rise of universal public education. The new republic staked its life on the conviction that an educated populace could be entrusted with government. Although universal education in its beginning was centered chiefly in teaching the "three R's" and informing the citizenry, its scope broadened through the years. Education widened the horizons of individuals and increased their wants. The use of leisure and the development of new skills began to interest more and more people.

As early as 1821, the Salem Latin School opened an outdoor gymnasium with crude equipment and no supervision. In the ten years that followed, outdoor gymnasiums were constructed in many of the eastern colleges (Harvard, Yale, Williams, Amherst, Brown), which introduced physical training in the curriculum and organized many athletic and sporting clubs. Subsequent developments were not forthcoming until health consciousness after the Civil War again focused attention on the school's role in physical health. It was not until nearer the end of the century, in 1888, that school buildings were opened for recreation purposes in New York and in Boston, and school areas were used to any great extent as playgrounds. Later experiments in Oakland, Los Angeles, and Boston emphasized the value of play by dividing school time, with half the hours spent in lessons and half in play.

Rise of voluntary agencies

The nineteenth century saw the development of certain voluntary agencies, which have now taken a share of responsibility for the provision of wholesome recreation opportunities and education for leisure use. In 1851, the Young Men's Christian Association was introduced from England, and the national YMCA was formed in 1866. By 1860, the first Boys' Club had been established in Hartford to attempt to counteract the ills of the city. The first Young Women's Christian Association was established in Boston in 1866, although the national YWCA was not founded until early in the twentieth century.

Golden age of the naturalists

These years may be thought of as the golden age of the great naturalists. There were new species to be discovered and described as the land was explored and settled. Expeditions moving into the West contributed greatly to scientific knowledge and laid the cornerstone for the outdoor-recreation movement of today. Educators, too, were beginning to see the values in outdoor education and recreation. In 1861, Frederick William Gunn of the Connecticut Gunnery School for Boys took his entire student body on a two-week camping trip for what is generally considered the first camping experience of its kind. Some twenty years later, Ernest Balch started the first private camp, and the YMCA initiated a camping program in its organization.

By 1867, concern for misuse of natural resources brought about the organization of commissions in Wisconsin and in Michigan to study conservation practices. Similar commissions followed in states on the eastern coast. By 1871, the Bureau of Fisheries had been set up in the Department of Commerce, and some fourteen years later, the Biological Survey became a part of the Department of Agriculture. In 1875, the establishment of the American Forestry Association helped unify the movement to save the forests. The end of the century saw the setting aside of the first federal forest reserve in the West. In a country that had been blessed with natural resources, there appeared to be growing a realization of their worth and the need to take steps to preserve them for future generations.

Beginnings of organized sports

During the early years of the nineteenth century, sports were in their infancy, although the interest of schools in physical activities had awakened some realization of need for such activities during after-school hours. Early participation in gymnastic games, tennis, foot races, and other rural pleasures had given way to spectator amusements, and the country's leaders began to lament the lost values. The social elite also further spurred the revival of active sports by making them fashionable in the post-Civil War period, when America was beginning to worry about the physical fitness of its populace. "A basic need for outdoor exercise to conserve national health and the sponsorship of social leaders thus served in large measure to break down the barriers that had formerly stood in the way of the development of organized sports." [2]

[2] *America Learns To Play* by Foster Rhea Dulles: Copyright, 1940, by D. Appleton-Century Co., Inc. Reprinted by permission of the publishers Appleton-Century-Crofts, an affiliate of Meredith Press.

The beginnings of modern baseball are sometimes traced to the 1839 diamond in Cooperstown, New York, or to the business and professional men's Knickerbocker Club, whose members played together in the Elysian Fields of Hoboken, New Jersey, in 1842. Baseball slowly spread until the public gave its stamp of approval by actually paying admission to watch the ball games. In 1869, when the Cincinnati Red Stockings were hired for a country-wide tour, professional baseball was born. Although the colleges took little active leadership in the growth of other sport activities, they introduced and developed football. The first intercollegiate game was played between Princeton and Rutgers in 1869. The sport aroused spectator interest from the start. The real need for an indoor activity to replace the fair-weather enthusiasm for football and baseball prompted James A. Naismith, a YMCA leader, to develop basketball in 1891. The new sport was to attain undreamed-of popularity.

Skating, bicycling, tennis, and croquet grew in favor; but it remained for organized baseball and football, then basketball, to stimulate the expansion that made attention to sports a significant development of the age. In 1885, new emphasis was placed on physical activities with the formation of the American Association for the Advancement of Physical Education, now the American Association for Health, Physical Education, and Recreation.

Initial playground efforts

Although significant impetus toward the development of the playground movement in America did not become apparent until the establishment of the Boston sandgardens in 1885, several isolated incidents prove that others in the new country were aware of a need to provide space and opportunity for play. As early as 1868, there is record of an outdoor playground for children in connection with the vacation school of the old First Church of Boston. Rainwater denied the importance of the event to future playground development in the following statement:

There is no evidence that it was related to subsequent developments in that city or elsewhere. It was, at most, but a sporadic expression of the consciousness of a need that did not gain lasting recognition until fully 20 years later.[3]

In 1872, Brookline, Massachusetts, became the first city in the United States to set aside public lands for playgrounds, when two tracts of land were bought for such purposes. The Brookline action failed to be significant to the playground movement, since the provision of apparatus or

---

[3] Clarence E. Rainwater, *The Play Movement in the United States* (Chicago: The University of Chicago Press, 1922), p. 15. Copyright (1922) by the University of Chicago. Reprinted by permission.

leadership never materialized. The next acquisition of space for play did not come until Boston purchased land for playgrounds, in 1894.

End of a century

With meager developments in facilities, breadth of program, and expansion of a recreation philosophy, the new nation embarked upon a period that signified adverse conditions in recreation, a period that very nearly revived the colonial period's intolerance toward any activity that did not produce fruitful labor. Growth of urban areas (with accompanying social problems), increasing leisure, flourishing commercial recreation ventures of questionable reputation, and gross exploitation of the nation's natural resources characterized the later years of the nineteenth century, at the same time giving birth to today's emphasis on educating the public regarding the importance of provisions for wholesome recreation.

Development of Organized Recreation

Any great social movement grows out of a pressing social need. The events of the last years of the nineteenth century brought realization of the growing need for recreation. Meager beginnings had already appeared before the turn of the century.

Boston sandgardens

Most historians of the recreation movement give credit to the sandgardens of Boston as the true beginnings of the recreation movement, from which stemmed other developments in gradual but linked progression. Dr. Marie Zakresewska, while summering in Berlin, noticed that youngsters were playing with heaps of sand in the public parks. At her instigation, the Massachusetts Emergency and Hygiene Association started a similar experiment in Boston in 1885. Whereas the Berlin project had been supervised by the police, the Boston sandpiles were supervised by interested volunteers until 1887, when women were paid for such duty. Similar activities extended to other Boston areas, and the idea was taken up by other cities including Philadelphia, Milwaukee, Pittsburgh, Denver, Minneapolis, New York, Chicago, Providence, and Baltimore. Butler reviews the stages that marked the evolution of the Boston experiment:

1. Started as a private project, it was later taken over and operated as a public responsibility.
2. Financed in the beginning through private philanthropy, support from public funds secured later.
3. The playgrounds originally on private property but were gradually transferred to public areas.
4. The playgrounds were at first under volunteer leaders, but soon matrons

were employed, and subsequently kindergarten teachers and other trained workers were used as play leaders.

5. The first centers were merely sandpiles for little children, but apparatus and areas for older boys were later provided.[4]

Settlement houses and the model playgrounds

Voluntary agencies played a part in the onward movement of recreation as the Neighborhood Guild in New York City introduced the settlement-house movement in 1886. Three years later, Jane Addams and Ellen Gates Starr established Hull House as a settlement house to serve Chicago's needs. Miss Addams later succeeded in securing enough land around Hull House to start the first model playground in 1892. Similar play areas were provided within the next six years at the Northwestern University and the University of Chicago settlement houses. The pattern of apparatus play, sport activities for older youth, and low organized games under supervision comprised a blueprint for like efforts in other large cities. Early objectives of the settlement houses to meet the needs of the poor were soon broadened to include education, health, and recreation as well as welfare.

[4] George D. Butler, *Introduction to Community Recreation*, 3rd ed. (New York: McGraw-Hill Book Company, 1959), p. 73. Reprinted by permission.

Fig. 2   *Jane Addams and the Original Hull House*

The small-parks system

Although Washington Park had been opened in Chicago as early as 1876, it was little used for recreation purposes for another ten to fifteen years. In 1888, New York passed a law that appropriated one million dollars a year for acquisition of land for parks and playgrounds. In 1889, the Boston Park Department converted ten acres along the Charles River into an outdoor gymnasium known as the Charlesbank Outdoor Gym. Here men, boys, and, later, women could wade, bathe, row, or use apparatus under supervision. Similar neighborhood parks with scenic and functional intention were created in New York and Louisville. Such dual purpose joined the park and playground concepts.

Chicago's South Park playground system, initiated in the early years of the twentieth century, made a tremendous impact on the growth of the recreation movement. With their carefully planned fieldhouses and their spacious outdoor areas, the playgrounds represented the first acceptance of public responsibility for indoor and outdoor recreation facilities, for varied interest programs, for recreation outlets for all ages, for year-round activities, and for leadership as well as facilities. The success of the small-parks system in meeting neighborhood needs was an inspiration to all those who came in contact with it. The long-range thinking of the fieldhouse planners in providing structures adaptable to a variety of types of programing has stood the test of time. The organization of the New England Association of Park Superintendents, now the American Institute of Park Executives, in 1898, gave further evidence of the growing concern for responsible leadership in the movement.

The recreation movement

Isolated individual developments in recreation were made throughout the nineteenth century. It remained for the pressures of a changing industrialized society to force individual leaders, municipalities, and private and public agencies to unify those efforts. Neumeyer and Neumeyer describe these social movements as follows:

Analyzed from the point of view of development, social movements normally involve a number of more or less distinct aspects or phases, even though they overlap and tend to merge into each other. (1) Movements grow out of unsatisfactory and disorganized social situations causing social unrest and concerns. (2) The situation must be defined by competent observers as constituting a social problem and requiring adjustment . . . (3) There must be a conscious effort to meet the situation . . . A movement involves a type of social change that is produced by deliberate action designed to improve a given condition. (4) To become a movement, a conscious effort or event must be followed by others connected by a cause-and-effect relation and extended in time and space . . . (5) The setting up of objectives and standards is evidence of maturation of a movement . . . (6) The final phase is the gradual realization of the objectives as disclosed through the stages of its development, transitions in its policies and activities, and trends in its organization.[5]

The movement starts, then, with a felt need. Let us explore those events, conditions, and feelings that created an expressed need for better recreation opportunities and resulted in an organization of the movement.

The need for unification of effort. Many of the conditions that gave rise to the modern recreation movement had their origins in the last half of the nineteenth century. The birth of the Playground Association of America, in 1906, is most often named as the true beginning of the organized movement. Why did it occur? What happened before 1906 to alert people to the need? What happened after 1906 to continue emphasis on recreation? Following are some of the conditions that stimulated the unification of the recreation movement:

1. DEPLETION OF NATURAL RESOURCES. At the close of the Civil War, the westward trend continued. The nation went about the business of filling the continent, freely using its natural resources. In the eastern states, practically all land had been turned over to private interests, although in the West there still remained vast areas of public domain that were to be held as a reserve. Characteristic of this period was the thoughtless exploitation of natural resources. Forests, grassland, wildlife, and water resources were laid waste with a prodigal hand; there was always more land to the west. Too soon the cost of this careless policy was made apparent; today America is still paying the cost of its early extravagance.

2. EFFECTS OF THE INDUSTRIAL REVOLUTION. The Industrial Revolution, which changed the American population from an agrarian to an industrial society, mushroomed in the late years of the nineteenth century. The rise of industry and the development of machine power brought drastic changes in the life of the people. As the machine replaced manpower, work hours were decreased, and *new leisure* became a right of all. The specialization of the assembly line and improved transportation made manufactured goods accessible to most people, and handcraft began to disappear as a means of livelihood. With the mechanized, mass-production approach to industry, the worker was *deprived of the pride in achievement* he had realized in his earlier craft. A distinct need for outlets that would exercise his creative energies and provide a sense of achievement and accomplishment became pressing for the industrial worker, who worked monotonous hours in tedious repetition of a small task. Curtis, in 1917, described the situation thus:

[5] Martin H. Neumeyer and Esther S. Neumeyer, *Leisure and Recreation*, 3rd ed. (New York: The Ronald Press Company, 1958), pp. 62–63. Reprinted by permission.

Recreation is necessary for an individual very much in proportion as the work he is engaged in fails to yield him the normal satisfaction which should everywhere attend it. Perhaps the greatest tragedy of modern times and a capitalistic organization of society is that we have so minutely specialized our industries that the person does not make the whole of anything, but repeats endlessly a single operation, with the result that the finished work is never wholly his own. . . . Whether it is possible that our great factory system should be so organized that the individual should, at his machine, find joy in the work he does, is a problem which we have scarcely tried to solve, inasmuch as we have sought to produce shoes and fabrics rather than human happiness. And we have not realized that out of these conditions of work has grown so much of our industrial unrest, strikes, and other social evils.[6]

3. URBANIZATION. With the increase in industry came a decided shift to urban living, with accompanying problems in choice of, opportunity for, and space for recreation activity. Whereas in 1850 only 85 cities boasted populations over 8,000, by the end of the century almost 600 cities were over 8,000 and 28 cities had populations exceeding 100,000. Factories encroached on residential sections, and slum areas grew. The rural resident had had ample space for recreation. With overcrowded conditions in the urban areas, the streets became the playgrounds. The spacious backyard of the country homes was gone. It remained for organization of effort to set aside space in which recreation opportunities could be offered.

4. RISE IN CRIME AND DELINQUENCY. The tremendous increase in the incidence of crime and delinquency in the latter years of the nineteenth century prompted such men as Jacob Riis in New York City to stimulate anti-slum campaigns to afford healthier living conditions, which he hoped would counteract the formation of delinquent gangs.

5. INCREASE IN POPULATION. The steady growth in population demanded better organization for work, for living conditions, and for play. The Industrial Revolution, with its accompanying rural-to-urban population shift, had found the municipalities unprepared for servicing the needs for the influx of humanity. A few people gathered in a given community can communicate their interests and needs and find solutions. When the numbers are doubled within the same space, more organization is mandatory if needs are to be met in recreation as well as in other services.

6. RISE IN INCIDENCE OF MENTAL ILLNESS. It is not surprising that the social-hygiene and mental-hygiene movements in the United States evolved at approximately the same time and for some of the same reasons as did the recreation movement. The increase in numbers of patients who needed psychiatric care gave ample proof of the existence of new tensions in the changing world. Recognition of the worth of recreation to relieve tension

[6] Henry S. Curtis, *The Play Movement and Its Significance* (New York: The Macmillan Company, 1917), p. 91.

and serve basic psychological needs was late in coming but has blossomed into one of the strongest causes for recreation programing.

7. UNWHOLESOME COMMERCIAL RECREATION. The broad expanse of unwholesome commercial recreation opportunities fostered the need for their replacement by more truly recreative activities. The dime novels, pool halls, billiard rooms, dime museums with freak attractions, spicy nickelodeons (the forerunner of today's cinema), shooting galleries, and saloons were easily accessible to all. Vaudeville attractions, which combined melodrama and burlesque, gave the legitimate theater heavy competition. Even the theaters sold plenty of liquor on the premises, and the saturated audiences proclaimed their pleasure or dissatisfaction with applause or cabbages as the actors plied their talents. Horse racing, professional baseball, and prizefighting were popular, with heavy concentration on the gambling aspects of such spectator sports. Dulles points to the low status of commercial fare:

> In 1898, the police of Gotham listed ninety-nine amusement resorts, including saloons with music and entertainment, on the Bowery alone. They classed only fourteen of them as respectable.[7]

The movie has been cheap and popular from the beginning. The peepshow kinetoscope, invented by Thomas Edison in 1889, progressed to the five-cent bawdy theater of the nickelodeon, and finally the first motion picture to tell a story (*The Great Train Robbery*) in 1903.

8. INCREASING MOBILITY OF THE POPULATION. Although boat and train excursions had been available, the electric trolley and the motor car at the end of the century forecast the greater mobility of the average citizen and created a demand for wholesome recreation areas to which he could travel on his weekends and holidays. The motor vehicle was soon to afford another means of spectator amusement; the first motor-vehicle race was run in Chicago in 1895. Two of six gasoline-driven cars finished a 52-mile course, and the sport of auto racing was born.

9. NEED FOR UNIFICATION OF INDIVIDUAL EFFORTS IN RECREATION. The early, scattered attempts of city after city to provide space, leadership, facilities, or methods of control for recreation finally alerted those involved with such problems to the need for channels through which each could profit by the experiences of others. The early Boston sandgardens; the model playgrounds of Chicago and New York; the provision of summer playgrounds in Philadelphia; the small-park systems in New York and Chicago; the initiation of Public Athletic Leagues by Luther Gulick in New York; the provision of a Board of Playground Commissioners as the first separate department of municipal recreation in Los Angeles in 1904; the use of school buildings as community centers in New York City, Rochester, and Pittsburgh, and early community recreation efforts in Oakland, Cali-

---

[7] Dulles, *America Learns To Play*, p. 221.

fornia, in Baltimore, in Washington, and in other cities all pointed to the urgency for some means of interrelating individual efforts and concerns and communicating information gained from experiences in different places. A plan for such interrelation was formulated when a few dedicated and visionary individuals, competent observers, who "defined the situation as constituting a social problem requiring readjustment," met in Washington, D.C., in 1906, to plan what was to become the first true attempt at organization of the American recreation movement.

The Playground Association of America

The need for a social movement had been felt, as is indicated by the increasing problems brought about by the nine points previously mentioned. The situation had been observed. The work of the Washington group in 1906, which culminated in the organization of the Playground Association of America, marked the "conscious effort to meet the situation." The organization of the Playground Association of America—named, in 1911, the Playground and Recreation Association of America, and presently called the National Recreation Association—is perhaps the most significant event in the history of the recreation movement. With President Theodore Roosevelt as honorary president, Dr. Luther Gulick as president, and Dr. Henry S. Curtis as secretary and acting treasurer, the members of the Association settled themselves to the following purposes expressed in their constitution:

> To collect and distribute knowledge of and promote interest in playgrounds and athletic fields throughout the country, to seek to further the establishments of playgrounds and athletic fields in all communities and directed play in connection with schools.[8]

That their original purpose has broadened considerably in scope is attested to by the many and varied services of the present National Recreation Association, which touches recreation services and problems wherever and whenever they are discovered. As it has grown and developed, this organization has tended to be concerned more directly with municipal recreation efforts, although it has made valuable contributions to many other agencies that deal with recreation. Settlement houses, parks, forests, youth agencies, camping, and related movements were developing independently and concurrently. Such fragmentation has become one of the foremost problems to plague the recreation movement.

In June 1906, the Association undertook the publication of the *Playground* magazine, now *Recreation* magazine, in an effort to help disseminate information. The following year, the first national meeting of recreation workers was held in Chicago to exchange ideas and information. This event

[8] Butler, *Introduction to Community Recreation*, p. 77.

marked the beginning of the annual conference, which today is called the National Recreation Congress. Records show that 336 cities had organized programs by 1910. Joseph Lee, commonly known as the "father of the American playground," had been chosen president of the Association; a normal course in play had been published; Lebert Weir had been named the first field representative, and Howard Braucher had taken his place as the first paid secretary for the Association.

Fig. 3   *Pioneers in Organized Recreation*

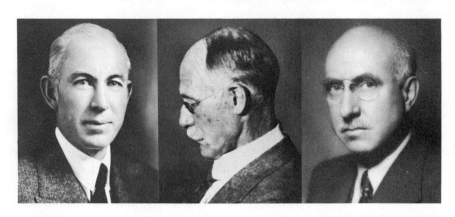

Lebert Weir   *Joseph Lee*   *Howard Braucher*

Since the formal organization of the movement, progress had been made in development of park and playground facilities, in efforts to improve the training of recreation leaders, in the contribution of youth-serving agencies, in school-oriented recreation, in acceptance by municipal and federal government as well as by private agencies of the responsibility for recreation opportunities, and in a concern for standards of facilities and leadership. Developments in the movement have continued, with a yearly meeting for evaluation of the present needs and concerns.

The second decade, twentieth century

In the second decade of the twentieth century, the disappearance of nineteenth-century attitudes toward leisure brought general agreement that recreation programs were necessary for all. Responsibility for provision for those needs was divided.

In 1910, the Boy Scouts of America was incorporated. The earlier youth agencies, Sons of Daniel Boone and Ernest Thompson Seton's Woodcraft Indians, were absorbed into the new organization. The same year saw the start of the Campfire Girls through the efforts of Dr. and Mrs. Luther Gulick. The year 1912 brought the introduction of the Girl Guides, later to become the Girl Scouts of America. Each organization played a part in the recreation education of youth.

The increase in public responsibility. The federal government assumed its role in recreation in several ways during this decade. In 1912, the Children's Bureau surveyed recreation opportunities for youngsters; the Smith-Lever Act of Congress, in 1914, called for demonstration and instruction in agriculture and home economics for those not attending college and made possible many recreation opportunities for rural residents. In 1916, the Sixty-Third Congress of the United States formed the Bureau of National Parks, which grew into the present National Park Service.

Schools also were exploring better means of providing recreation programs and facilities. The 1911 approval by the National Education Association of the use of school buildings for recreation services increased the numbers of schools who followed the Gary, Indiana, plan of schools designed as social centers. A Russell Sage Foundation survey, in 1914, found 50 schools giving courses for play leaders. The same year saw the inclusion of intramural-sports programs in many schools, whereas the next two years saw the initiation of experimental play schools at the University of California and the University of Wisconsin. Laws were passed in many of the states mandating physical-training classes and areas for recreation in school systems. Possibly the most significant contribution of education professionals during the decade was the inclusion of the "worthy use of leisure" as an important objective for education in the National Education Association's Seven Cardinal Principles of 1918, along with such goals as "command of the fundamental processes," "health," and "worthy home membership."

The 1913 Yearbook of the *Playground* magazine indicated that municipalities were continuing to build the playground systems peculiar to our country. The May 1915 issue listed 83 cities in 28 different states that reported full-time recreation workers. Surveys by the Playground and Recreation Association and Russell Sage Foundation reported a need for increased opportunities in music, drama, and the arts.[9] Social centers, settlement houses, and community centers had increased in such numbers as to stimulate the need for the formation of a National Community Center Association in 1916. Given impetus by both public and private agencies, the camping movement that had started in the previous century made great strides in an attempt to allow Americans to get back to the wonders of the soil.

Before 1900, only a small percentage of the American people had vacations, and pleasure travel was extremely limited. The middle of this period

[9] "A Brief History of the Playground Movement in America," *Playground,* IX, No. 2 (1915), 41–42.

(1910–1920) found over two million automobiles, which diminished the isolation of the country, changed the recreation habits of the populace, and literally altered the face of the United States as highways crisscrossed the land. The tourist and vacation industry got its start, the end of which is not in sight.

The effects of World War I. Before the entrance of the United States into World War I, there had been a heavy emphasis on decentralized neighborhood-center activities. The physical and psychological strains on individuals and communities were great as war camps flooded nearby communities with homesick soldiers, and military statistics shocked the nation by declaring one third of the draftees physically unfit for active duty. The Playground and Recreation Association, at the request of the War Department, mobilized recreation resources into the War Camp Community Service, which initiated recreation programs in over 600 communities near military centers and another fifty in strategic industrial centers. Although the organization was dissolved shortly after the fighting had stopped, the value of recreation to the community had been clearly demonstrated.

The pre-depression years

The decade after World War I, a period of prosperity, brought a marked increase in appreciation of the importance of recreation. An upsurge of interest in recreation facilities, both private and public, was demonstrated by the prevalence of new parks, community houses, swimming pools, dance halls, beaches, golf courses, picnic areas, skating rinks, and bowling alleys. In 1921, the National Conference of State Parks was organized to further the state park movement. Activity fads swept the country, bringing popularity for such current favorites as crossword puzzles, miniature golf, the Charleston, dance marathons, comic strips, board games, or skating marathons. Commercial recreation mushroomed for a population with increased purchasing power.

Henry Ford, with the assembly-line production of cars, gave easier transportation to the masses, and the tourist industry flourished. As early as 1922, the motion pictures established a self-censorship to improve their services to the public and eliminate adverse criticism. With the advent of the "talkies" by the end of the decade, the movie theaters gained tremendous popularity for all ages, with weekly attendance figures estimated at 110,000,000 in 1929.[10] Radio hams became engrossed in their new hobby, and the listening audience found effortless recreation at home with their wireless sets.

With the new appreciation of the assets that wholesome recreation could bring came a greater adult participation. Spectator sports increased in

[10] Dulles, *America Learns To Play*, p. 301.

popularity, and women began to join in sport activities without fear of reproof. New interest in every phase of programing brought publications on sports, art, drama, and music to aid in development of program areas. Use of leisure became a concern for research, and President Hoover's Research Committee on Social Trends, in 1929, gave special consideration to recreation. Earlier interest in the development of outdoor recreation had prompted the National Conference of Outdoor Recreation, called by President Coolidge in 1924. The awareness of the need for special training for recreation leaders occasioned the start of the one-year graduate course, in 1926, by the National Recreation Association. Known as the National Recreation School, it carried the principal responsibility for educating recreation executives until 1935, when institutions of higher learning were alerted to the need for special curriculums for recreation professionals. By 1927, 32 states had passed laws for use of school buildings as community centers; and by the end of the decade, half of the states had passed enabling legislation to provide for extended recreation opportunities at the municipal level.

The depression years

One result of the depression of the 1930's was an increased emphasis on recreation. The modified work week, shortened in order to spread available work among more people, gave more leisure. Commercial recreation programs closed for lack of business, since people no longer had the admission price for bowling, dancing, theater, and spectator events. A heavier demand was placed on facilities and programs of voluntary and municipal agencies, who were unable to handle the increased needs. The resulting increased demand for recreation and decreased supply of opportunities available caused federal agencies to try to take up the slack, giving the recreation movement more impetus than it had ever had before. Alerted to the seriousness of the situation, the administration furnished two different kinds of aid. First, through efforts to give jobs to those without work, it started construction projects that involved building new or extending existing recreation areas and facilities. Second, it provided finances for employing recreation leaders to initiate and supervise programs.

The blue eagle of the New Deal brought the "parade of the alphabet"; The Federal Emergency Relief Administration, The National Youth Administration, The Works Progress Administration, and the Civilian Conservation Corps all served to further the cause of recreation in a period of enforced leisure, at the same time aiding in the rehabilitation of the country. The FERA, the WPA, and the CCC gave people jobs and were responsible for the construction and improvement of centers, parks, picnic areas, roads, trails, and similar facilities. The WPA and the NYA hired recreation leaders and held institutes for training volunteers and recreation workers.

Dulles describes the scope of the construction program and its impact on municipal recreation offerings:

By the close of 1937 some $500,000,000 had been allotted for building 3,700 recreational buildings, 881 new parks, 1,500 athletic fields, 440 swimming pools, 3,500 tennis courts, 123 golf courses, and 28 miles of ski trails. Twelve hundred cities had in all seventeen thousand acres of parks reserved for sports activities, and they were annually spending $40,000,000 on their upkeep. Bathing beaches and swimming pools, with an estimated annual attendance of some 200,000,000, were the most popular of their facilities, but there were also 8,800 softball diamonds and 3,600 baseball diamonds at which the player attendance was estimated at 31,000,000; 2,400 ice skating rinks with an attendance of 13,-000,000; 11,000 tennis courts with an attendance of 11,000,000; and public golf courses used by a total of 8,000,000. Here was the truly democratic approach to this phase of recreation. These millions of urban workers—men, women, and children—were finally enjoying the organized sports that had been introduced by the fashionable world half a century and more earlier. Democracy was making good its right to play the games formerly limited to the small class that had the wealth and leisure to escape the city.[11]

Federal funds that were poured into state park and forest systems caused a great spurt in state outdoor-recreation developments. Forty-six Recreation Demonstration Areas were initiated under the National Park Service in 1936 and were later turned over to federal and state agencies. Recognition of the function of the state in providing areas and facilities to protect and improve game resources brought an increase in the ever popular outdoor sports of hunting and fishing. Skiing soon was added to the outdoor-recreation choices as private agencies capitalized on the lure of the snowy hills.

The Federal Arts Project of the WPA stimulated interest in music, painting, theater, writing, and historical research. The Federal Theater Project became an active force in the theatrical world. At a time when the audiences in commercial theaters were dwindling because of forced economies, some 500,000 amateurs were acting on stages in community theaters. Thousands more were introduced to the joys of participating in choruses and orchestras or listening to public concerts. Max Kaplan makes the following observation:

For the first time in American life, music was made an integral part of the recreation philosophy. Until then, leaders had been for the most part specialists in games and sports, drama and arts and crafts; and these were the activities associated in the public's mind with recreation. Music now became a community possession.[12]

[11] Dulles, pp. 348–349.
[12] Max Kaplan, *Music in Recreation* (Champaign, Ill.: Stipes Publishing Co., 1955), p. 4. Reprinted by permission.

The fads of the twenties subsided and gave way to less costly pastimes such as contract bridge, backyard gardening, inexpensive hobbies, Chinese checkers, and bingo. The Big Apple and the Lambeth Walk had replaced the Charleston for the dance enthusiasts. Americans were still spending five percent of their total income on travel and vacationing.

Fitzgerald lists the major contributions of the WPA and other federal aids in the new leisure of the depression as follows:

1. Increased participation by laymen in the recreation affairs of the community.
2. Closer cooperation between public and voluntary agencies.
3. The principle of recreation as a community responsibility was greatly advanced.
4. Recreation was brought to communities which previously had not experienced organized programs under leadership.[13]

Other spurs to the recreation movement came in publications designed to help in the training of recreation leaders in certain program areas.

The effects of the depression colored the recreation picture during the 1930's; but other significant events—which also had an impact, directly or indirectly, on the forward push of the recreation profession—must be mentioned. The White House Conference, called by President Hoover in 1930, firmly established through its Children's Charter the rights that the American child could expect as his deserved heritage. They include:

For every child from birth through adolescence, promotion of health, including health instruction and a health program, wholesome physical and mental recreation, with teachers and leaders adequately trained.

For every child a community which recognizes and plans for his needs, protects him against physical dangers, moral hazards, and disease; provides him with safe and wholesome places for play and recreation; and makes provision for his cultural and social needs.[14]

In 1933, the American Library Association included recreation in its three-point program. The American Physical Education Association adopted as one of its principles the "promotion of play and recreation as aspects of fine living." The International Recreation Department of the UAW-CIO, organized in 1937, emphasized the acceptance of employee recreation as part of the labor union's concern.

Perhaps most significant in the development of the profession was the recognition on the part of colleges and universities that recreation is a pro-

[13] Charles E. Doell and Gerald B. Fitzgerald, A *Brief History of Parks and Recreation in the United States* (Chicago: The Athletic Institute, 1954), p. 74. Reprinted by permission.

[14] *Children's Charter* from *White House Conference on Children and Youth,* 1930.

fession that demands a special education. The first College Conference on Training Recreation Leaders, sponsored by the University of Minnesota and the Recreation Division of the WPA, was held in 1937.

During the same year, at the request of Howard Braucher (then Executive Secretary of the National Recreation Association), a small group of recreation leaders assembled to discuss the need for a national organization for full-time professionals in recreation. The following October, the Society of Recreation Workers of America, now the American Recreation Society, was formed in Atlantic City. It attracted over 500 charter members its first year.

Recreation and World War II

World War II had started in Europe in 1939. Two years later, with the attack on Pearl Harbor, America went to war. Duplicating and extending the concern that it had felt for its servicemen in World War I, the government renewed emphasis on recreation and its values both on the fighting and on the home fronts, increasing interest in recreation and at the same time recognizing and interpreting its values. Statistics of numbers of draftees judged unfit for service spurred interest in means of promoting better mental as well as physical health. The USO, American Red Cross, Army Special Services Division, the Welfare and Recreation Section of the Bureau of Naval Personnel, and the Recreation Service of the Marine Corps promoted programs on the battlefront, in the rest centers, in the hospitals, and in the camps. Their main concerns were with relieving tensions of war, bolstering morale, and decreasing the psychological impact of the separation from home and sometimes country.

The United Service Organizations incorporated in 1941. They consisted of six agencies (Jewish Welfare Board, Salvation Army, Catholic Community Services, YMCA, YWCA, and the National Travelers' Aid), whose purpose was to serve the leisure needs of the armed services in community settings and to provide recreation for industrial workers engaged in the war effort. USO community centers enlisted thousands of volunteers to man their drop-in centers, in which a lonesome or bored serviceman might find food, dancing, a good book, or simply some friendly conversation. Hollywood stars promoted USO tours throughout the war, so that in the European theater or in the Aleutian Islands the "boys" might be treated to a performance by such personalities as Joe E. Brown, Bob Hope, Carole Landis, Jack Benny, or Martha Raye. Heavy demands were placed upon the profession when the armed services alone needed some 12,500 recreation directors. That the profession was not ready with adequately educated leaders was made all too obvious when servicemen's stories filtered back, telling of overemphasis on sports, lack of imagination in programing, dearth of cultural opportunities, and other deficiencies. That there were some excellent experiences is also obvious in the 1951 report of the President's

Committee on Religion and Welfare in Armed Services, a study of special services, which credited recreation with "shaping character, promoting national understanding and support of Armed Forces, and increasing efficiency of job performance."

American Red Cross services were carried to every part of the globe occupied by United States troops.

The number of overseas Red Cross service clubs, rest homes and recreation centres grew to 350 during 1943. . . . Important as were the activities for the able-bodied, far more vital was the service to the sick and wounded servicemen in military hospitals at home or overseas.[15]

On the home front, the American Junior Red Cross filled a desire on the part of teenagers to help with the war effort. Some 17 million members produced articles for army recreation rooms.

The Federal Security Agency (now the Department of Health, Education, and Welfare), initiated in 1939 to "promote social and economic security, educational opportunity, and the health of the citizens of the Nation," operated through its Community War Services program. It employed consultants for recreation programing and helped set up 250 to 300 new community programs. The Federal Works Agency made funds available for construction and operation of child-care centers and recreation centers. Through funds provided by the Lanham Act, the FWA took over some of the recreation functions of the defunct WPA.

Youth-serving agencies were busy on the home front. Boy Scouts, Girl Scouts, and Camp Fire Girls spent many leisure hours in collecting scrap metal and paper, selling war bonds and stamps, or making supplies for USO centers, while their 4 H neighbors were being trained in child care, gardening, and farm-aid projects. The personnel from the National Recreation Association went to war as active directors or consultants in battlefront or home-front recreation ventures. Increased war tensions and the restlessness and uncertainty of the times created a soaring rate of delinquency among children and youth, which stimulated the Conference of the Children's Bureau, in 1943, to concentrate on prevention of this social ill.

Lack of gasoline for travel necessitated a return to neighborhood activities. Teen centers, neighborhood adult programs, victory gardens, and increased industrial recreation opportunities all flourished. As the American soldiers traveled to distant lands, recreation ideas and customs were exchanged. The years of the war brought increased recognition of the contribution of recreation, a revelation of the need for more and better-prepared professional leaders, and a concern for the preventive and therapeutic possibilities in recreation activities.

[15] "American Red Cross," *Book of the Year*, 1944 (Chicago: Encyclopaedia Britannica, Inc., 1944), p. 596. Reprinted by permission.

Other significant progress occurred during the war years. The year 1941 saw industry taking a responsibility in recreation as it organized the National Industrial Recreation Association. In spite of forced economies in travel, attendance figures in the national forests increased. In 1945, the first bill to suggest the need for an agency concerned solely with initiation and coordination of recreation at the federal level was introduced in Congress. The Federal Interagency Committee was formed in 1946 to coordinate the efforts of those organizations in the several departments of federal government that relate to recreation. On the community level, the consolidation of the Los Angeles administration into a Park and Recreation Department was the start of a series of community actions following the Los Angeles lead. At the state level, three states (North Carolina, Vermont, and California) had established state commissions of recreation. The 1948 Jackson's Mills Conference and the 1950 Pere Marquette Conference evidenced the concern for better preparation of professionals at both undergraduate and graduate levels.

The war years had initiated and instigated many community programs. They had created an environment in which progress in development of programs could be made with people who had seen the need for such efforts. More tangible evidence of the dying away of nineteenth-century attitudes came with the introduction of living war memorials. In place of the monuments in the square or the towering obelisks offered in memory of the dead of previous wars, swimming pools, civic centers, parks, picnic areas, and playgrounds are today's evidence of the respect communities have paid to the heroes of World War II.

Mid-century to present

At mid-century, the National Recreation Policies Committee formulated a "Mid-Century Declaration of Recreation Policy." Its statement lists the following apparent needs, which "should be the concern of thoughtful citizens, educators, and statesmen."

1. A restatement of the nature and function of recreation, especially in the modern industrial era and consonant with the principles of democracy as a way of life. Literature bearing upon the subject of recreation is of a past age. The implications of the new leisure and of correlative changes in the mode of living should challenge the best minds in the nation and bring forth a basic philosophy upon which to plan.
2. Continued conservation of the natural resources of the nation, which may be utilized as one of their highest purposes for qualitative recreation for all the people. . . .
3. Formulation of a national policy concerning leisure and recreation. There is a need for a national agency that may guide the formulation of such a policy, enlist the leadership of the nation, alert the people to the purposes

and functions of recreation, and engage in social planning toward the beneficial use of leisure. . . .

4. Establishment of similar agencies and policies in each of the states of the union for the same purposes.

5. Creation of local governmental agencies in urban and rural areas to organize the local public resources in lands and structures and the cultural traditions and leadership for a better recreational life.

6. Education for recreation of all children through the public and private schools and educational opportunities in recreation for the adult public as well.

7. Encouragement of voluntary community recreation agencies in every community to utilize recreation activities effectively for an integrated and happy community life and for the development of good citizenship, all in accordance with the best American traditions.

8. Awakening of the commercial recreational entertainment and amusement enterprises to elevate the common taste and to provide recreation and entertainment that will not debauch the public but will contribute to good citizenship.

9. Enlistment of the churches of all faiths and denominations in a continuing crusade to infuse the recreational life of the American people with spiritual quality.

10. Suppressing and prohibiting by law and effective enforcement of recreational practices that degrade and debauch the people.

11. Implementing plans for redevelopment of slums and blighted and congested areas in cities so that the home and the immediate environment of the home may permit the safe play of children and the wholesome development of family and neighborhood recreation.

12. Cultivating a greater sense of family responsibility for the planning of recreation for all members of the family and for the improvement of family relationships.

13. Upgrading the qualifications of professionally employed personnel in community, governmental and commercial entertainment and amusement enterprises, and dignifying generally the calling of recreational leadership.

14. Enlisting, inspiring and training an adequate force of professional recreation leaders inbred with social zeal, technically prepared and dedicated to the advancement of humanity through recreation.

15. Instituting programs of recreation for mentally and physically handicapped persons and especially integrating these persons in the recreational activities and associations of normal citizens.

16. Safeguarding the ethics of recreational activities that are part of the American tradition, and by educational means improving the quality of expression of the people in their recreation so that through leisure they might achieve goodness and beauty in living.

17. Recognizing the values of recreation in building and sustaining national morale especially in times of national emergency and preserving the democratic recreational tradition and opportunity as essential to our national security.[16]

The beginning decade of the second half of the twentieth century found many in the recreation profession and in related fields who were consciously striving to meet some of the specified needs. The following developments have been instrumental in maintaining a national emphasis on recreation.

1. *Changing leisure pursuits.* Leisure has continued to increase for many sectors of the population, particularly those who have reached compulsory retirement age. Americans are finding themselves with more discretionary time, more discretionary income, and, in addition, the kinds of occupations that leave them enough energy to feel the need for further mental and physical diversion. Comparisons of expenditures in the five-year period from 1955 to 1960 indicate that one twelfth of total income was spent on recreation activities; increases in amounts spent for books, foreign travel, theater, opera, sports participation, and sports equipment were far greater for the five-year period than the increases recorded for radio, television, magazines, movies, and spectator sports.[17] Such indications of renewed interest in active participation in sports and in cultural activities are gratifying to recreation leaders.

2. *Upsurge in outdoor interests.* Boating, camping, and travel to national and state parks were gaining more and more enthusiasts. "Mission 66," a long-range program by the National Park Service to further extend the offerings of the national park system by 1966, was well under way, whereas in 1960 the state park attendance statistics totaled 259 million. The 1956 Congressional request that the Forest Service survey recreation use and needs provided impetus for "Operation Outdoors," a program of repair and rehabilitation of national forests. The year 1958 saw in Washington the first national conference to explore needs and concerns of outdoor education. The same year marked the creation, by an act of Congress, of the Outdoor Recreation Resources Review Commission, whose three-year survey of national needs prompted the establishment of the Bureau of Outdoor Recreation in the Department of the Interior in April 1962.

3. *Concern for fitness.* The decade of the fifties saw new concerns for and emphasis on mental and physical fitness. With the unveiling of the results of the Kraus-Weber tests,[18] which tended to prove American youths

---

[16] A *Mid-Century Declaration of Recreation Policy* (National Recreation Policies Committee, October 1950), mimeographed materials, pp. 4–6.

[17] "Leisure Spending," *Recreation*, LIV, No. 8 (1961), 429.

[18] Six tests for muscular strength and flexibility.

physically inferior to their European counterparts, national interest was centered on finding ways to correct this condition. Zealous attacks were made on television as a deterrent to physical recreation, on physical-education professionals for lack of success in programing, and on modern conveniences of all kinds for making life too easy to generate physical fitness. In 1956, Shane McCarthy was sworn in as Executive Director of President Eisenhower's Council on Youth Fitness. Programs to improve fitness were developed in most states, and National Conferences on Youth Fitness were held. With the change in administration in 1961, popular "Bud" Wilkinson of the University of Oklahoma was appointed Special Consultant on Youth Fitness to the President.

President John F. Kennedy re-emphasized the challenge of fitness for the nation in his article "The Soft American":

For the physical vigor of our citizens is one of America's most precious resources. If we waste and neglect this resource, if we allow it to dwindle and grow soft then we will destroy much of our ability to meet the great and vital challenges which confront people. We will be unable to realize our full potential as a nation.

Throughout our history we have been challenged to armed conflict by nations who sought to destroy our independence or threatened our freedom. The young men of America have risen to those occasions, giving themselves freely to the rigors and hardships of warfare. But the stamina and strength which the defense of liberty requires are not the product of a few weeks' basic training or a month's conditioning. These only come from bodies which have been conditioned for a lifetime of participation in sports and interest in physical activity. Our struggles against aggressors throughout our history have been won on the playgrounds and corner lots and fields of America.

Thus in a very real and immediate sense, our growing softness, our increasing lack of physical fitness, is a menace to our security.[19]

In addition to numerous state and national conferences on physical fitness, other evidences of the new concern for mental fitness and the role of recreation in mental health included the Washington Conference on Recreation for the Mentally Ill, sponsored by the American Association of Health, Physical Education, and Recreation, in 1957; the hiring of National Recreation Association personnel to handle special services for recreation for the ill and handicapped; the conference to explore curriculum needs in therapeutic recreation in 1961; and the provision of a Leisure Time Committee in the American Psychiatric Association.

4. *White House conferences.* Two major White House conferences discussed the needs and interests peculiar to two different age groups. In

[19] John F. Kennedy, "The Soft American," *Sports Illustrated*, XIII, No. 26 (1960), 16. Reprinted by permission.

each conference, recreation was a primary concern, and leaders in the recreation profession were called upon to participate.

WHITE HOUSE CONFERENCE ON CHILDREN AND YOUTH. The first such conference to give attention to the needs of this particular section of the nation's population was held in 1909 at the request of President Theodore Roosevelt. The 1960 conference marked the golden anniversary of the occasion and chose as its theme, "For each child an opportunity for a creative life in freedom and dignity." Some 7,000 persons representing all phases of youth work gathered in Washington "to study the problems, programs, and potentials of local and statewide organizations which seek to assist youth and children to discover, develop, and adopt moral and spiritual values as guides for life, and to relate these values to their responsibilities and to the challenges of our changing world." Youth itself was heavily represented in the delegates, and each participant was provided with extensive background materials for perusal before the conference in order to foster enlightened group ideation during the Washington meetings. Recommendations that pertained to recreation needs evolved from many of the sessions as groups discussed health, religion, education, and related topics. The recommendations that were formulated by the section on leisure embodied 42 statements on federal, state, and local action; youth participation; community programs; program objectives and philosophy; sports and physical activity; leisure-time reading; arts; and research and public education. Post-conference activities, stimulated by the Washington meetings, included organization of state youth councils, geographical-area discussion sessions, and local action to initiate youth programs or extend present program offerings.

WHITE HOUSE CONFERENCE ON AGING. The first national conference on aging took place in 1950 and was initiated by the Federal Security Administrator in the Truman administration to explore the growing problems of the aging. Two other conferences (the Conference of State Commissions on Aging in 1952 and the Federal-State Conference on Aging in 1956) preceded the first White House Conference on Aging held in Washington on January 9–12, 1961. The conference itself was preceded by a two-year period of study in the individual states. These studies were made possible by federal grants up to a maximum of $15,000 for each state. Perhaps more significant than the conference itself was this two-year period of preparation, which brought forth specific recommendations from each state for study and action by the conference delegates. Some 3,000 delegates dealt with twenty topics. As in the White House Conference on Children and Youth, many work groups discussed recreation as it related to their specific topic: education, rehabilitation, family life, community organization, and others. The section on Free Time Activities, which stood alone as one of ten major groupings, acted upon state recommendations that pertained to recreation, voluntary services, and citizenship participation. A policy statement was formulated, and specific recommendations were made pertaining to program, facilities, financing, organization, leadership, research, preparation for retirement, and public information.

Again, as in the previous White House conference, national publicity alerted local and state action for post-conference discussions and implementation of the recommendations. Further comments on the organization and implications of the conference will be discussed in Chapter 18.

5. *Increased emphasis on performing arts.* The 1958 act of Congress that made possible the National Cultural Center for the Performing Arts, to be located on a ten-acre site on the Potomac River in Washington, D.C., is evidence of the increased national impetus given to the performing arts as leisure outlets. The general concept of the center is stated in the bylaws:

> The National Cultural Center is destined to stand as a monument to America's cultural maturity and to her realization that the conquest of material things cannot stand the test of time until they find fruition in the realm of the mind and soul. The peoples of fifty sovereign states, sharing a love for the political freedoms of self-government, see in the creation of a cultural center a concrete expression of their common attachment to the arts.[20]

The advisory committee for the center, appointed by President Eisenhower, included Joseph Prendergast, Executive-Secretary for the National Recreation Association, who represented recreation interests. The national center, designed for the "participation, education, and recreation" of all the people, will be an important stimulus in the development of more cultural opportunities in leisure.

Many fine examples of cultural opportunities at the local level are found in such cities as Winston-Salem, North Carolina; Fort Wayne, Indiana; Milwaukee, Wisconsin; Boston, Massachusetts; and Los Angeles, California. The growth of arts councils for promotion and coordination of the arts programs such as those in Waterloo, Iowa, and Richmond, Virginia, evidence the awareness of recreation professionals of increased interest in the performing arts. The opening, in 1962, of the Lincoln Center in New York further demonstrates the increased attention being given to cultural interests.

6. *Progress in professional education.* Several professional conferences concerned with the better preparation of recreation personnel or with problems in education for leisure followed the Jackson's Mill and Pere Marquette conferences previously mentioned. Other evidences of professional progress include the development of a Code of Ethics for the profession by the American Recreation Society, the increased emphasis on

[20] Quoted in Joseph Prendergast, "The National Cultural Center," *Recreation,* LIII, No. 7 (1960), 306.

research, the NRA Southern Regional Study of "Recreation as a Profession" in 1952–1954, and the increased numbers of institutions of higher learning that offer curriculums for preparation of recreation professionals.

7. *Evidence of increased cooperation in the profession.* The establishing of the Federation of National Professional Organizations for Recreation, in 1954, was a significant attempt to coordinate the efforts of the many organizations having recreation as their professional responsibility. Problems of coordination will be dealt with in future pages, but the Federation, slow in starting, presently shows potential of becoming a firm voice for cooperative effort for the profession. Representative of other cooperative efforts is the joint sponsorship of the annual National Recreation Congress by the NRA and the ARS. Joint sponsorship began in 1957.

Increased cooperation and coordination of effort with schools, welfare divisions, youth-serving agencies, business and industry, and commercial recreation ventures are paying dividends, as such organizations accept a share of the responsibility for education for and expenditure of the ever increasing leisure.

8. *Other significant events.* The founding of the International Recreation Association, in 1956, brought the services of Tom Rivers as Director General to handle the purely international aspects of the world recreation movement. The same year saw the start of the first International Cooperative Community Recreation Exchange, in which America and foreign countries traded ideas through exchange of personnel.

The first National Workshop in Recreation for Leaders in Religious Organizations, sponsored by the Indiana University Department of Recreation in 1952, marked an effort at clarification of recreation philosophy for all denominations. Significant also was the September 1957 issue of the *Annals* of the American Academy of Political and Social Science, which was devoted entirely to "Recreation in the Age of Automation."

The 1960 National Social Welfare Manpower Study, initiated by the Personnel Committee of the National Social Welfare Assembly and conducted by the Bureau of Labor Statistics of the U.S. Department of Labor, presented current salaries, working conditions, and educational background of some 10,448 recreation workers. The Fourth Annual Convention of the Golden Age and Senior Citizens was held in New Orleans in 1960, and formally became a national organization. Further evidence of federal concern for the aged sector of the population came with the naming of Dr. Donald P. Kent to the special staff on aging in the Department of Health, Education, and Welfare, as Special Assistant for Aging.

The 1961 Curriculum Conference on Therapeutic Recreation made more emphatic the recreation needs of the ill and handicapped, already indicated by the establishment of a Hospital Recreation Section in the American Recreation Society, a Recreation Therapy Section in the American

Association for Health, Physical Education, and Recreation, the Consulting Service on Recreation for the Ill and Handicapped in the National Recreation Association, and the National Association of Recreation Therapists.

9. *Signs of the times.* The decades of the second half of the twentieth century are not without their fads and recreation fancies. Zeal rises and falls for such outlets as hula hooping, stock-car racing, miniature golf, trampoline-jumping centers, drag-strip racing, and go-cart racing by youths. The drive-in theaters have prospered as have the ornate amusement parks. New dances are popularized via television dance shows and last until new gyrations capture the imagination of the dance enthusiasts. The guitar and ukulele of the twenties have regained some popularity, and the smart set no longer considers folk singing "way out." The space age has introduced intriguing toys from space helmets to launchable missiles to atomic submarines. Card playing, golf, riding, and boating are no longer considered strictly for the country-club social bracket, and bowling has become quite respectable for all. The commercial bowling alley, golf courses, and billiard rooms are attempting to play a dual role in recreation service by offering table games, nursery-school service, and pleasant surroundings for their clientele. There is some evidence that those who deal in commercial recreation are recognizing their need for trained professional leadership and are probing for cooperation in this area.

Transitions in the Recreation Movement

Since its inception as an organized movement in 1906, recreation has come a long way. Significant gains have been realized; problems still remain. Following are some transitions obvious in the development of present concepts.

Change in attitudes toward recreation

Martha Wolfenstein describes "the emergence of fun morality" in the American culture: "Here fun, from having been suspect if not taboo, has tended to become obligatory. Instead of feeling guilty for having too much fun, one is inclined to feel ashamed if one does not have enough." [21] However facetiously such a statement is made, in it shines the element of truth. From the Puritan ethic that any recreation is sinful, the work of the devil, America transferred to the philosophy that recreation is admissible but only after one has earned the right to such relaxation in the work-play cycle. With considerable increases in leisure for all people, and the additional factor of sedentary or monotonous occupations, comes the revelation

[21] Martha Wolfenstein, "The Emergence of Fun Morality," in *Mass Leisure*, ed. Eric Larrabee and Rolf Meyersohn (Chicago: The Free Press, 1958), p. 86.

that leisure must provide some of the satisfactions of basic human needs not met elsewhere. With such a concept comes a broader philosophy in terms of both the objectives for and scope of the recreation program.

Extension of recreation programs

With a different attitude toward recreation came tremendous changes in the concept of a recreation program. From opportunities principally for youngsters, the program concept expanded to include offerings for all ages, both sexes, and all degrees of mental or physical capacity. From just outdoor programs on open areas in the summer weeks developed year-round programs, both indoor and outdoor. From open lots without equipment came creative facilities and equipment according to specific standards for number and excellence. From offerings to take care of the needs of urban industrial families came the realization that the rural population and finally the "megalopolis" must be administered to also. From emphasis on physical activity and games and sports as program content, the offerings have broadened to include creative, aesthetic, and cultural activities.

New concepts of leadership

From the complete absence of leadership, through the volunteer matron who watched youngsters play, through the play leader who passed out equipment and prevented accidents and fights whenever possible, the profession has progressed to the recognized need for creative, professionally trained leaders in all phases of programing. Even the armed services, industry, hospitals, and the commercial recreation forces—who, for many years, felt that recreation services could be handled by individuals from their own ranks—have turned to professionals in recreation for better results. Standards for leadership have been explored; research has been done relative to quality of, need for, and results of good leadership. No longer does the star athlete or the good-natured girl who "likes kids" qualify without training for leadership in a profession that demands creative maneuverings with all types of people and program ideas.

Change in responsibility for recreation

The first recreation opportunities were sponsored by philanthropic individuals or agencies. The broadening need for recreation demanded that recreation become a function of government. Public responsibility for recreation matters is growing at local, state, and federal levels.

Development of coordination of effort

Because recreation has been recognized as a universal need, many professions and organizations have felt impelled to become involved with provisions for recreation opportunities. The problem of responsibility for and coordination of recreation opportunities still looms large, but the joint efforts of national professional organizations and public and private agencies have made measurable progress. Councils at local levels, commissions at state levels, and inter-agency committees at national levels are increasing in numbers. Consolidation of parks and recreation departments has often strengthened programs in coordination of effort.

Growth of evaluation and research

Possibly one of the most significant developments in the growth of the recreation movement is the increased attention given to exploration of information that will augment the knowledge of leisure needs, the best way to meet them, and recreation's contribution to the participant. From a condition of basing programs on a casual survey of opinion or the recreation director's guess, communities have come to realize the value of critical evaluation of present recreation outlets and of exploration of those factors that will influence and guide future planning.

The Challenge of the Future

The recreation movement has made significant progress; however, it must continue to move as the face of the nation and of the world changes. Problems of land encroachment, loss of natural resources, lack of long-range planning in housing developments or in expansion of municipalities, duplication of effort by public and private agencies, increased mobility of the population, early retirement from the work force, and unmet recruitment needs of the profession are still with us. National magazines and newspapers have taken up the cause of recreation to focus the public eye on leisure needs as never before. Projections in terms of the expanded leisure of the future bring an ever present challenge to America to educate now for the recreation literacy of future generations. We have passed many milestones, but, in the road ahead, the American public must assume further responsibilities if the recreation needs of the emancipated citizen are to be met.

SUGGESTED REFERENCES

Curtis, Henry S., *The Play Movement and Its Significance*. New York: The Macmillan Company, 1917.

Doell, Charles E. and Gerald B. Fitzgerald, *A Brief History of Parks and Recreation in the United States*. Chicago: The Athletic Institute, 1954.

Dulles, Foster Rhea, *America Learns To Play*. New York: D. Appleton-Century Company, Inc., 1940.

Rainwater, Clarence E., *The Play Movement in the United States*. Chicago: The University of Chicago Press, 1922.

Steiner, Jesse F., *Americans at Play*. New York: McGraw-Hill Book Company, 1933.

"Prosperity is only an instrument to be used, not a deity to be worshipped."

CALVIN COOLIDGE

3

Impact of Recreation on the Economy

How the American "spends" his leisure and how he spends his money during his leisure are matters of great moment to the economy of the United States. Recreation pursuits in the twentieth century have become the basis of a large proportion of economic endeavor. Numerous industries, businesses, and services, with employees numbering into the millions, depend upon recreation in whole or in part for their existence. Expenditures during leisure affect community growth, land values, and governmental income.

The rising popularity of certain forms of recreation affects the stock market. When an old industry such as boat manufacturing grows, in a few years, from sales of a few million dollars annually to close to three billion dollars, the stock in boat companies soars. New recreation products, such as transistor radios, that are based on modern technology often receive immediate and enthusiastic adoption.

Direct effects on the economy are more easily understood than are the indirect relationships. The farmer, the miner, and the processor of raw materials are all affected by the use of their products in the buildings, supplies, and equipment used in recreation.

Productivity, Income, and Leisure

When high productivity, income beyond that required for necessities of life, and unprecedented leisure coincide in a nation, as they have in the United States today, the repercussions extend into the far sectors of the economy. Developments that occur under this combination of circumstances affect retailers, wholesalers, manufacturers, workers, and others who at first glance may seem remote from any connection with the economics of recreation. State, local, and national governments are also influenced by the economic activity resulting from recreation pursuits.

Increased productivity

The increased productivity of workers has been made possible through imaginative management, mechanization, and automation. George Soule wrote: "According to the most reliable statistical estimates, the real net national product in the United States grew about thirteenfold between the decade 1869–78 and the decade 1944–53." [1] The average worker in 1950 produced more than five times as much per hour as the average worker of 1850, and during the same period, the labor force increased so that the total number of man-hours worked multiplied approximately fivefold.[2] The real value of the total output thus increased about 25 times, while the population was increasing from 23 million to 151 million, or about 6.5 times.

The percentage of the population in the labor force has grown during the last century, largely because of the increase in the percentage of women in the labor market. Since 1950, however, there has been a drop in the percentage of the population in the labor force because of the large number of children under working age and the increasing numbers in the age bracket above 65 years. It is anticipated that in future years the older age group will constitute a larger and larger leisure class, the goods and services for which must be supplied by the working force.

Since fewer working hours are needed to produce articles and services that are essential to survival, a larger part of the working day is being devoted to producing goods and services that contribute to comfort and pleasure. Some of these goods and services are embellishments of necessities; for example, we have gourmet foods, luxurious homes, and fashionable clothing—things that are far more elaborate than we require for survival. We have professional services in education, law, medicine, dentistry, and social welfare that a less productive society could not afford. Finally, many

---

[1] George Soule, "The Economics of Leisure," in *Recreation in the Age of Automation* (Philadelphia: American Academy of Political and Social Science, 1957), The Annals of the Academy, Vol. 313, p. 17. Reprinted by permission.

[2] George Soule, "The Economics of Leisure," p. 17.

working hours are devoted to producing goods and services consumed in recreation pursuits. It is with the relationship of this aspect of man's work to his use of leisure that the following pages are particularly concerned.

Increased income

Personal income has been climbing to ever greater heights, surpassing $427 billion in the year 1961. Money available to the average person beyond that required for the essentials of living has correspondingly increased. This "discretionary income," which an individual may spend as he pleases, has risen nearly sixty percent in the past decade. According to The Chase Manhattan Bank of New York City,

In 1960, people received $123 billion over and above the income required for essential food, clothing, shelter, medical care, and fixed commitments. Thus, nearly one third of all after-tax consumer income—an average of $682 per person —was available for the consumer to spend as he wished.

Consumers are spending one third of this discretionary income—or twelve per cent of their total income—on leisure activities. So the market for goods and services connected with recreation has doubled in the past ten years.[3]

Studies indicate that the percentage of total income expended for leisure is not constant as income increases. The middle income group spends relatively less than either the higher or the lower income groups. The explanation of the high percentage in the lower income group may lie in the following considerations: (1) the lower income group includes many children and retired people, both of whom may spend more than they earn; (2) the lower income group may spend a smaller percentage of money on education and housing than the middle income group; and (3) the total spent for recreation by the lower income group may be no higher than that of the middle income group, although the percentage of the total income is higher.

The largest single item in the leisure budget is travel.[4]

Increased leisure

In the class-structured civilization of the past, leisure was enjoyed by the few at the expense of the many, who, with long hours and hard work, maintained leisure for a privileged class. In the early days of the United States, long hours of work were a necessity. Today, in the United States, fewer hours suffice to obtain basic goods and services. Leisure is the privilege of all groups in society, along with improved housing, food, and other

[3] "Leisure Activities," from *Business in Brief*, No. 39 (July–August 1961), p. 6. By permission of The Chase Manhattan Bank.

[4] "Leisure Activities," p. 6.

Fig. 4 *Disposable Consumer Income (in Billions)—1960 and Projected, 1976 and 2000. Source:* Outdoor Recreation for America (*Washington, D.C.: Outdoor Recreation Resources Review Commission, 1962*)

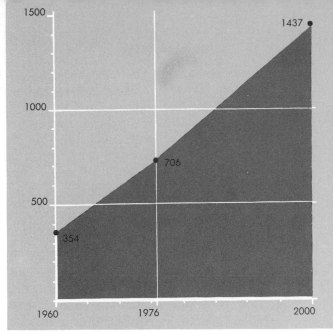

Fig. 5 *Average Scheduled Work Week for Nonagricultural Workers by Industry— 1960 and Projected, 1967 and 2000. Source:* Outdoor Recreation for America (*Washington, D.C.: Outdoor Recreation Resources Review Commission, 1962*)

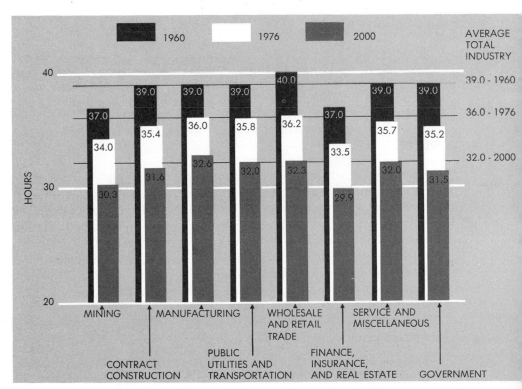

material comforts. The standard work week has been reduced from about 70 hours in 1870 to about 40 hours today. The Chase Manhattan Bank pointed out that employees will take 50 million vacation weeks over the summer months and another 32 million weeks during the rest of the year, in addition to some 467 million holidays. It was further pointed out that, even during ordinary weeks, one fourth of the average person's time is open to choices of activity and that families have more free time together because modern conveniences have reduced household chores. Figures 4 and 5 provide an indication of the levels that income and leisure are expected to reach by the year 2000.

Balance between productivity, income, and leisure

Productivity, income, and leisure are in a delicate and intricate balance. If workers should increase their working hours, they could presumably produce more and obtain more income. With reduced leisure, however, they would not enjoy the fruits of their labor. They would have no time for those recreation pursuits that today use up a large part of their income. There would be fewer purchasers for boats, books, television sets, and cars; and fewer patrons of vacation resorts, movies, concerts, and sporting events. The industries and businesses dependent upon recreation would accordingly suffer; unemployment would mount; and the economy would be thrown out of balance. Marion Harper wrote in *Business Horizons:*

Just as our present work week creates discretionary income, leisure, too, is directly responsible for discretionary spending. It takes a prosperous country to support a market for second cars, boats, fishing tackle and paperback books. That is to say, people must work long enough hours to produce wealth for this market. On the other hand, ample leisure time is needed to make use of these products. The right balancing of work and leisure, therefore, is necessary to a thriving economy.[5]

Each worker balances his life in terms of income and leisure. For the individual, time is a salable commodity. The amount of time he is willing to work for a given income indicates the value he places upon leisure. The worker who has a short work week may take a second job during weekends, thereby choosing increased income in preference to leisure. Executives and professional men who work long hours, even though they can usually afford leisure, probably do so in part for increased income, although they may be motivated also by a sense of responsibility toward their work and enjoyment of the work itself.

Like the value of material objects, the value of leisure depends in part upon the quantity available. The less leisure an individual possesses, the

[5] Marion Harper, Jr., "The New Conflict of Time and Money," *Business Horizons*, III, No. 4 (Winter 1960), 28–29. Reprinted by permission.

more he usually prizes it. This attitude is recognized in the time-and-a-half pay commonly given for overtime work.

Recreation and Economic Health

Recreation affects the economic well-being of individuals, businesses, industries, and government. It creates employment in many diverse fields. It can make a community a place in which individuals, businesses, and industries wish to settle and can have a tremendous effect on property values. Government income and expenditures are affected by recreation patterns through taxes received and programs provided. Hardly an aspect of the economy escapes the effect of the use of leisure.

Recreation creates employment

If recreation expenditure equals 12 percent of our income, a tremendous working force is involved in supplying recreation goods or services. Some of the workers are engaged directly with recreation. Many more are engaged indirectly.

Employment directly related to recreation. Increasingly, workers of many kinds are employed in recreation programs. Many thousands of people depend for a livelihood on work in parks, recreation departments, voluntary youth-serving agencies, camps, settlement houses, industrial recreation programs, religious organizations, private recreation centers, commercial recreation enterprises, hospitals, and institutions. Some of these workers are employed in the maintenance and management of recreation properties. Many others, including professional recreation workers, are engaged in direct leadership. Still other workers, among whom are some of the highest-paid individuals in our country, are professional entertainers.

Employment indirectly related to recreation. Many workers who are not directly employed in recreation programs are indirectly related to recreation through manufacturing, wholesale and retail businesses, building trades, services dependent upon recreational travel, and numerous other activities. Some concept of the numbers of people involved can be obtained by considering a few of the types of specialty shops serving recreation interests. They include stores specializing in sporting goods, toys, hobby supplies, photography, art, bicycles and motorcycles, garden equipment, rocks, riding accessories, music, pets, and many others. Thousands of people are employed in the many industries serving recreation needs, such as those manufacturing travel trailers, playground supplies, boats, photographic equipment, toys, television sets, radios, record players, home workshop equipment, sporting goods, and camping equipment.

A glance at recent catalogs of large mail-order houses reveals many pages devoted to recreation supplies and equipment. One such observation showed 23 pages describing television sets and record players; 12 describing guns; 10, photographic supplies; 11, sports equipment; 11, toys; 6, musical instruments; 6, bicycles; 3, telescopes and binoculars; 2, boats; 2½, fishing accessories; 5, camping and picnic equipment; and 3, pets. Many additional pages were given over to equipment used in do-it-yourself projects, such as garden tools, paints, workshop tools, and sewing supplies. Space was also allotted to saddles, archery equipment, gem-polishing tools, scooters, motorcycles, automobile accessories, books, clothes for various sports, and special hobby supplies.

These and other recreation-related products involve millions of workers. As an example of the extent of employment resulting from recreation, let us examine just one of its aspects: the use of the automobile. Probably one third to one half of the driving of the family car is recreation. The car is used not only for the pleasure of driving itself but also as the means of getting to places of recreation. It is often the only means of access to areas for picnicking, hunting, fishing, camping, swimming, or vacationing. Studies show that 80 percent of all vacation travel is by car. Pleasure driving ranks high as a form of family recreation. Wylie found that 86 percent of the families reported in his study of family recreation engaged in pleasure riding.[6] Although some cars are reserved exclusively for business, most family cars combine recreation use, business travel, and family convenience. Even where public transportation is available and cheaper, the family car is often preferred because it is more pleasant, in spite of traffic congestion, parking costs, and other difficulties. Ownership of an automobile, its model, and its cost are often regarded as a status symbol. The many economic interrelations of the recreational use of the automobile include:

AUTOMOBILE MANUFACTURING. The value of automobiles manufactured yearly approximates $10 billion. Around $4 billion to $5 billion of this amount might be charged to varied recreational uses. Huge as it is, this figure only begins to tell the story of the economic impact of recreational use of the automobile.

RELATED INDUSTRIES. The automobile industry in turn affects a staggering number of industries supplying the raw materials, such as iron, copper, aluminum, textiles, plastics, paint, and rubber. In the distribution of automobiles, not only are thousands of retailers concerned but also transport companies, advertising companies, and the mass media financed through advertising.

MAINTENANCE AND OPERATION RELATIONSHIPS. If we assume that the average family car travels 8,000 miles a year at a cost of about eight cents a mile, we have a figure of $640 a year, of which we might again assume that

[6] James A. Wylie, "Survey of 504 Families to Determine the Relationship Between Certain Factors and the Nature of the Family Recreation Program," *Research Quarterly*, XXIV (1953), 234.

around $300 can be charged to recreational use. Since there are about 70 million cars in the United States, it can be seen readily that the recreational use of automobiles has a tremendous impact on a variety of businesses—garages, body shops, car laundries, gasoline stations—and the huge industries, the oil companies and parts manufacturers, supplying them. Insurance companies thrive on liability and collision insurance; and government itself depends in large measure on taxes and license fees.

HIGHWAY DEVELOPMENTS. The construction and maintenance of highways and the operation of tourist accommodations along the highways are dependent upon the automobile.

ASSOCIATED RECREATION PURSUITS. Some forms of recreation businesses, such as the drive-in theaters and restaurants, could not exist without the automobile. Other forms are heavily dependent upon it. Businesses concerned with sightseeing, entertainment, photography, publication of travel books, advertising, maps, camping equipment, and the like, would suffer without the automobile. Many parks, picnic areas, beaches, campgrounds, and trailer parks could never have existed.

The employment of thousands of workers in many diverse industries depends on the recreation use of the automobile. Space here does not permit the citing of other examples of the far-reaching effects of recreation. Leisure interests have economic significance far beyond surface manifestations; the list of industries depending in some degree on recreation is endless.

Recreation as an attraction to residents and industries

The recreation opportunities—public, private, voluntary, and commercial —in a community affect, to a great degree, the ability of the community to attract and retain residents and industries. Families who have a choice select communities that offer a variety of leisure pursuits, in which the children will grow up in a wholesome atmosphere, and in which the whole family can find engrossing things to do. The movement to the suburbs during the past thirty years has taken place at least in part because of the belief that recreation and cultural opportunities are greater there than in the city. There can be no doubt that land values are higher in communities that have desirable living conditions.

Industries select sites for plants for many reasons, including the labor market, sources of raw materials, and transportation. The concern for the welfare of their employees leads industries to place the religious, educational, and recreational atmosphere of a community on their list of considerations in selecting a location. Industries are more apt to prosper in communities in which their workers are happy.

Recreation and property values

In many situations land values change drastically because of recreation developments. Although in not all cases is there clear evidence of cause and effect, the leadership, program, type of planning, and placement of the facilities can affect property values.

Municipal parks and playgrounds. Large, well-maintained municipal parks, with attractive landscaping or natural scenic beauty, seem to increase the value of property adjacent to them. The most striking evidence is the price of property adjacent to Central Park in New York City, Lake Shore Drive in Chicago, Fairmount Park in Philadelphia, and Golden Gate Park in San Francisco. In some cases the highest-priced residential property of a city is adjacent to such parks.

A heavily used playground or playfield may decrease the value of adjacent property, particularly if fields are night-lighted. If such areas are carefully planned, however, with plantings to muffle noise, protect privacy, and increase aesthetic qualities, adjacent property may rise in price. Property not immediately adjacent but a few blocks away is apparently improved in value by the proximity of play facilities. In a very poor neighborhood, the establishment of a playground or a community center of attractive design is very apt to increase adjacent property values.

Non-urban recreation developments. Many lands that have little value for any other purpose may attain economic significance because of their use for recreation. Desert areas such as Palm Springs, California, were practically worthless until they were developed as resorts; their recreation use created fantastic land values. Marsh lands may have more value as wildlife habitats, nesting sites for waterfowl, and hunting and fishing grounds than as agricultural lands. This lesson was painfully demonstrated by the unwise drainage of many marsh lands. The Horicon Marsh of Wisconsin, once drained, has been reflooded and now serves as a large waterfowl breeding area. In many parts of the West, poor ranch lands have been sold for cottage sites, hunting preserves, or resorts. These lands have brought better prices and realized much greater income from recreation use than from ranching. Eroded and almost worthless lands have been salvaged for recreation use by tree planting and lake construction. Such developments have given the lands a high value. Because of the demand for water activities and for shoreline homes, lands adjacent to newly developed reservoirs have sometimes multiplied fifteen to twenty times in value over a period of a few years. Much property on both the Atlantic and Pacific and along the Great Lakes is extremely expensive.

Private land and buildings for recreation. The demand for hunting and fishing grounds has produced a secondary income for some private landowners who grant the privilege to use their land in exchange for fees. The economic value of other private non-urban lands used for recreation— camps, lakes, resorts, and the like—is considerable. There is no way of accurately estimating the value of city lands and buildings devoted to recreation, although the figure runs into the billions. A specific piece of property may, because of its location, bring a much better price as a site for a recreation establishment than for any other purpose. The nature of the particular business and its relationship to the neighborhood combine to increase or decrease property values adjacent to it. A bowling alley might enhance the value of one section of a community but depress property values in another.

Recreation and government finance

Expenditures. Though governmental expenditures on recreation are far less impressive than commercial expenditures, they add up to a considerable sum. Today approximately $500 million is expended for community parks and recreation. Eighty million dollars was expended by the National Park Service in 1960, and state parks in the same year expended $87 million. These figures do not include the numerous expenses of various other bureaus of the government related to recreation.

Income. At the same time, governments derive income from recreation. Taxes on property, business, and manufacturing are of course applicable to recreation properties, businesses, and manufacturing. Licensing fees and taxes are often levied on luxury goods and pleasure activities. Licensing fees and taxes on amusements are two special methods by which governments obtain income from amusement industries. In some places, taxes on legalized gambling form a large part of the income.

Reduction of cost of delinquency and crime. The economic impact of recreation on government can be viewed also in the light of its effect on delinquency and crime. The costs of police protection, court procedures, incarceration, probation, and parole are high. In many communities recreation is regarded as a means of reducing these costs, since it is believed helpful in redirecting potentially criminal behavior into socially desirable channels. The benefits to the community in making it a safer and pleasanter place to live through recreation far exceed the benefits of financial savings resulting from a reduction of the costs of antisocial behavior.

Recreation Expenditures

Although we are concerned in this chapter with the expenditures for recreation, we do not wish to imply that we equate recreation satisfaction with dollars and cents. When we purchase material objects, we expect quality to be related to the price. This principle does not necessarily hold true in recreation. Some of the greatest joys of life are free. Unlimited expenditures for recreation do not insure unlimited satisfaction. Although we may assume that a ten-dollar seat at the opera has more value than the three-dollar seat, there may be free music experiences fully as satisfying as either. A five-thousand-mile vacation trip may be more frustrating and less satisfying than a vacation at home. A sunset may be more satisfying than an expensive excursion, or a home-made boat a source of more pleasure than a yacht. A child often shows preference for a simple toy rather than an expensive purchase. We must none the less recognize that those who spend money on recreation expect to get satisfaction from their expenditures and that an increase in expenditures is accompanied by an expectation of increased satisfaction.

Difficulties in determining recreation expenditures

Difficulties in assessing the significance and extent of recreation expenditures lie in terminology and in absence of compiled information. We may measure the number of visitors to a national park and determine their average daily expenditure, but these figures are only a small part of the cost to the park visitors; they do not include expenditures for gas, lodging, or meals en route to the park nor money spent on camp equipment and clothing to use while in the park. We also encounter problems in trying to determine which activities may be considered recreation and which should be considered in some other light. A particular trip may be made for pleasure, for education, or for business; or all three purposes may be involved. Further, it is impossible to draw lines between recreation and educational experiences, such as attending a museum, freely sought for their intrinsic satisfaction. We are also hindered by the problem as to whether we include questionable activities, such as gambling and drinking, which involve vast sums of money and, however undesirable from society's point of view, are nevertheless participated in for what the participant considers recreation.

Another difficulty in analyzing expenditures for recreation lies in the rapidity of change. New industries serving recreation needs arise daily. Some, such as boat manufacturing, assume mounting importance year by year. Others, such as miniature golf, may rise, wane, and die, only to be resurrected again. Still others, like the hula-hoop, enjoy a brief period of glory and disappear. Then, too, we are continually faced with fluctuations in definitions of necessities and pleasures. The automobile is considered a necessity for most families, though certainly much of its use is recreational. Something a poor family would regard as a luxury might be considered a necessity in a rich man's home.

The variance in estimate of the total expenditures for recreation reflects the problems listed above. Some estimates range as high as 50 billion dollars per year. A Department of Commerce estimate for 1961 was only 20.6 billion, but these figures did not include the travel and vacation business nor the cost of all the public and voluntary agency programs. While reading the following pages, the reader should bear in mind the limitations to accurate analysis of the expenditures for leisure pursuits and the difficulty of determining which activities are solely recreation.

Travel and vacation business

The people of the United States are on the move. By car, plane, train, bus, and boat, they are traveling greater distances and to more places than ever before—to Europe, Canada, Mexico, and around the world; to state and national forests and parks; to distant cities, historical sites, or simply to any section of the country they have not seen before. They go to learn, to fish, to hunt, to camp, to swim, to sail, to relax, or just to see. Many of them seem to be filled with restlessness, as though they had to be constantly on the move in order to make the most of their vacation time. It is a standard joke that one must come home to recover from one's vacation.

Extent of leisure travel. Before 1900 only a small percentage of the American people had either the time or the means for pleasure travel. The wealthy developed fashionable resorts, such as those at Bar Harbor, Newport, and Saratoga Springs, or developed summer homes and elaborate camps. People in moderate circumstances who could get away for vacations patronized boarding houses or rented small cottages. Without automobiles, people could not travel far; a vacation resort had to be near railroad or water transportation. The great majority of people stayed at home through the summer months. It remained for the automobile, higher incomes, and paid vacations to put the American people on the road.

Approximately two thirds of all vacationists use motel accommodations. Camping and trailer-court camping provide for about 5 percent of vacationists en route to their destinations; and there seems to be a rapid increase in trailer and tent camping, particularly in forests and parks. Fishing camps, dude ranches, and vacation resorts of all types serve the traveling public. The dramatic growth in numbers of travelers is evidenced in the increase in visitors recorded in national and state areas from the end of World War II to 1956:

Area	Average Annual Percent of Increase
National Park System	8%
National Forests	10%
State Parks	10%
Federal Wildlife Refuges	12%
T. V. A. Reservoirs	15%
Municipal and County Parks	4%
Corps of Engineers Reservoirs	28% [7]

[7] Marion Clawson, *Statistics on Outdoor Recreation* (Washington, D.C.: Resources for the Future, April 1958), p. 7.

It should be noted that during this period, when travel to outdoor areas was increasing from 4 percent to 28 percent annually, our population was growing at the rate of only 1.9 percent per year. The tremendous increase in the use of water areas, such as those under the jurisdiction of the Corps of Engineers, may be attributed in part to the many new areas established and in part to the boating boom of the post-war years.

Travel expenditures. Domestic and foreign travel expenditures by United States citizens were estimated in 1961 at from $13 to $20 billion, making the travel business one of the largest businesses in the country. Included in the lower figure are the costs of transportation, vacation homes, lodging, and meals, whereas the higher figure adds the cost of vacation clothing, sports equipment, and entertainment. Although much of the travel is for business reasons, it is estimated that about two thirds of domestic travel and four fifths of foreign travel is for nonbusiness or recreation reasons.

In Florida, the vacation business brings more money than the next two industries, agriculture and manufacturing, combined. In California alone, the travel and vacation business is estimated at a billion dollars annually. In many states the income from tourists is the second or third largest source of the total income of the state.

Reasons for increase in vacation traveling. The same factors that are responsible for the rise in general recreation expenditures—chiefly high income and increased leisure—have caused the great travel and vacation boom. Spurring the growth even further are the expanded networks of highways, the 70 million automobiles, and the jet planes, which annihilate distance. The higher average level of education adds another factor, since more education tends to stimulate the desire to travel.

TIME AVAILABLE FOR TRAVEL. Much of the increase in leisure has come in the form of longer vacation periods, with the three-week vacation rapidly supplanting the two-week vacation common in the 1940's. Thus there is time for extended trips. It is estimated that 85 percent of the workers now have paid vacations, with higher income groups having longer vacations than lower income groups.

Although most vacations are taken in the summer, the number taken at other times of the year is increasing. In the winter, vacationists go south to enjoy the warm weather or north to participate in winter sports. Many formerly seasonal resorts now operate on a year-round basis.

Longer weekends and extra days around the holidays make short trips possible at many times of the year.

INCOME. Although low income groups probably spend more vacation time in visiting friends and in activities near home than in extensive travel, they, too, have increased their ventures away from home. The popularity of family camping and trailering may be due in part to the fact that they reduce living costs on trips almost to the stay-at-home level. At the same time, family camping is one of the pursuits in which higher income groups engage. The travel-trailer and camper-coach boom is augmented by the numbers of retired persons traveling to find agreeable weather or to see the country.

Foreign travel, once largely restricted to the wealthy, is now within the means of teachers, industrial and professional workers, and operators of small businesses. The traveling of these groups has resulted in some decrease in per capita expenditures and a great increase in the total number of travelers.

Home-related recreation expenditures

Expenditures for home-related recreation vary depending upon economic status, section of the country, and degree of urbanization. Apartment-house dwellers in the city will be different in their pattern of recreation expenditure from the suburban or small-town residents. Modern urban living has decreased the sense of family solidarity that formerly came through family participation in the operation of a farm or small business. Members of today's families seldom work together, and family solidarity must develop during leisure rather than during work hours.

Homes as recreation facilities. With more time and more money, interest in family recreation has soared. New single-dwelling homes for middle and upper income groups reflect this interest. The family room, with its television, hi-fi, lounge chairs, and game equipment, is part of many homes. A recreation room, with a snack bar, space for dancing and cards, a ping-pong table, or a billiard table, is common. The backyard often contains play apparatus for children, a sandbox, or even a swimming pool. The number of swimming pools in 1961 was estimated as 310,700, a rise of 450 percent in a five-year period. Over a third of these pools were in California. Patios have been designed for outdoor eating, entertaining, and relaxing. The homes of many higher income families have become well-equipped recreation centers.

Do-it-yourself. The "do-it-yourself" movement has become big business, with estimates of expenditures running as high as 12 billion dollars a year. Although do-it-yourself activities are motivated in part by the desire to avoid the high cost of home services, they are also in many instances forms of recreation. Painting, home repairs, and tinkering in the home workshop, in which projects range from furniture making to figurine carving, are, to a certain extent, recreation.

Hobbies. About 30 million Americans garden, spending at least 2 billion dollars a year on this hobby. Specialized interests require investment in rare and expensive plants or seeds and even in home greenhouses. In one community of approximately 30,000 people, a survey indicated that 52 percent had gardens or yards that they cared for as recreation pursuits.

Special activities such as gem polishing, photography, ceramics, or copper enameling are illustrative of home-centered recreation pursuits. Photography involves an expenditure of more than 700 million dollars per year. Collecting hobbies, such as collections of stamps and coins, are usually home-oriented.

The home is often a center for musical activity. Millions of dollars are spent on musical instruments found in the home, such as pianos, violins, guitars, banjos, and recorders. Television sets, radios, record players, and records involve large expenditures for the home.

To this list of home-centered expenditures should be added art supplies, books, magazines, hobby equipment, pets, equipment for home sports, and toys. The toy industry has expanded materially, and its wide variety of offerings include expensive articles such as working bulldozers and moving dolls.

Economic aspects of outdoor recreation

Those activities that depend upon the natural environment we call "outdoor recreation." A large part of the travel and vacation business, already discussed, could be included under this heading. Some of the largest areas of expenditure are in outdoor recreation. Boating, hunting, and fishing alone involve over $5 billion a year.

Boating. An expenditure of $2.4 billion was reported for the purchase and maintenance of boats and accessories for the year 1959. This figure had trebled since 1950, and there is no end in sight. Sailboats, canoes, dinghies, rowboats, and all types of inboard and outboard motorboats have shared. in this growth. The new water areas, marinas, launching areas, water craft, motors, and boat trailers, combined with the efforts to decrease water pollution, make it evident that there will be continued rapid growth in boating. Once associated with the wealthy, boating is now an activity of the many. Of the more than 8 million boats in operation in the United States, most are owned by the skilled, semi-skilled, and white-collar labor force. With certain groups, the boat seems to have replaced the automobile as a status symbol.

During the last several years, two rather new activities related to boating have sprung into prominence: water skiing and scuba diving. Their emergence has resulted in a demand for new types of equipment.

The growth of water activities has made necessary stringent regulations in regard to restricting water areas for certain activities, establishing safety procedures, and licensing of both boats and operators.

Camping. There have always been a few families, fishermen, and hunters who have camped for enjoyment, for convenience, or for economic reasons. Following World War II, however, family camping burgeoned. Many families learned for the first time the pleasures of traveling at low cost and living close to nature independently. It was estimated that over 16 million people engaged in camping in 1961.

Sale of camping equipment has boomed. One of the larger suppliers had a 400-percent increase in business in ten years. Travel-trailer and camper-coach businesses have experienced phenomenal growth. Public camp-grounds have been unable to provide for the influx; Michigan in 1960 turned down an estimated 60,000 campers because of lack of space. In the same year the state parks of the United States showed an increase of 18 percent in tent and trailer camping. Private campgrounds are beginning to be developed to meet the growing need.

Organized camping for children has had a continuous growth during the twentieth century. Millions of dollars are invested in campgrounds and facilities, as well as in the provision of food, maintenance, and leadership. Even in camps operated on a nonprofit basis, weekly fees are seldom below $20 a week; and in private camps, fees may run as high as $100. With more than 5½ million children in organized camps each summer, camp opera-tion is a considerable segment of American business.

Hunting and fishing. Dangling a hook on a line has always been a popu-lar activity; but, like other aspects of outdoor recreation, it is even more popular today. Fishing is no longer a simple matter of a hook, line, and worm. Modern fishing costs money. Equipment is designed as much to attract the fisherman as the fish. A glance in a sporting goods store window reveals an elaborate and expensive array of rods, reels, lines, artificial lures, landing nets, waders, and special fishing clothes.

Comprehensive studies of the economics of fishing and hunting were made under the auspices of the Fish and Wildlife Service in 1955 and 1960. During this five-year period the amount spent in fishing rose from about $1.9 billion to $2.7 billion a year, with the mean expenditure per person rising from $91.98 to $106.26. The amount spent on hunting rose from $1 billion to $1.2 billion, though the mean expenditure per person dropped slightly, from $79.49 to $79.34. According to the 1960 study, about 15 million fishing licenses and 12 million hunting licenses were issued in 1960, but this figure did not include all fishermen and hunters, since many servicemen, veterans, aged or disabled persons, children, and others were exempted from license requirements and since licenses for salt-water fishing were required in only two states. It was estimated that nearly two out of five persons twelve years of age and over fished or hunted at some time during 1960.[8]

In addition to individual expenditures, we must recognize the expendi-

[8] *1960 National Survey of Fishing and Hunting* (Washington, D.C.: Fish and Wildlife Service, 1961), pp. iii, 4, 5, 59, and 66.

tures of governmental agencies in their efforts to maintain public fishing and hunting areas. Fish hatcheries and the planting of fishing waters are costly items of government. It is more difficult to provide for hunting than for fishing. Stocking programs are less successful, and the habitats for game are decreasing with the growth of population and the pressures on land for other purposes.

Costs, both personal and governmental, related to fishing and hunting, include: operation of private hunting and fishing preserves; manufacture, distribution, and sale of guns, ammunition, fishing tackle, boats, motors, special clothing, and equipment; boat rental and bait business; travel to and from fishing and hunting areas; housing, food, and entertainment; licenses and fees; provision and management of public areas; enforcement of fish and game laws; propagation and planting of fish and game.

Other outdoor recreation expenditures. No estimate is available on the amount of business created by horseback riding, mountain climbing, bird watching, rock collecting, hiking, outdoor photography, and other outdoor-related activities; but the total must make up a considerable segment of the economy. That these outdoor interests are growing and may be expected to grow is indicated by Clawson's prediction that, by the year 2000, if trends of the late 1950's and early 1960's continue, there will be 40 times the demand for use of our "resource-based" vacation lands.[9]

Economic aspects of sports

Expenditures on sports present a varying picture. Some sports have grown tremendously in recent years. Others have barely kept pace with the growth of population.

Participation sports. An encouraging sign, in view of the widespread picture of the American as "soft," is the growth of active participation in sports. The schools' emphasis on physical education and the impetus given to fitness programs by the President's Council on Youth Fitness have made Americans more conscious of the value of wholesome exercise. The investment in facilities, uniforms, equipment, and leadership for the conduct of sports is an impressive one. Although many sports programs are offered by schools, public recreation agencies, and other nonprofit groups, commercial establishments have a tremendous investment in many active sports.

Bowling, dependent almost entirely upon commercial facilities, has shown phenomenal growth. The new bowling alley has become a family-serving institution. According to Lloyd R. Ludwig, president of the American International Bowling Corporation, the number of participants grew from 12.5 million in 1946 to 33 million in 1961.

[9] Marion Clawson, "The Crisis in Outdoor Recreation," reprinted from *American Forests* (March–April 1959), p. 11. Used by permission.

The development of artificially refrigerated ice-skating rinks has proven a boon to skaters, emancipating them from dependence upon unpredictable weather and extending the season appreciably. Before St. Louis opened Steinberg Memorial Skating Rink in 1957, the city had been averaging only 4 to 7 outdoor skating days each season. The rink is now open about five months a year. The economic importance of ice skating is probably slight compared to that of skiing, inasmuch as many rinks are operated by municipalities on a nonprofit basis, and skaters do not usually travel extensively to indulge in this pastime.

It is estimated that there are more than 3 million skiers in the United States. Participants in this increasingly popular sport spend tremendous sums of money on ski equipment, suitable clothing, travel, ski lodges, ski lifts, and the services of instructors. New developments in parks and forests now provide for winter sports, and many private ski areas offer accommodations and instruction. Huge resort developments, such as that of Sun Valley, Idaho, owe their existence chiefly to the popularity of skiing.

Although figures vary greatly as to the extent of participation in various sports, the following rough estimates, gleaned from many sources, are somewhat indicative of the relative popularity of the various types: bowling, 31 million participants; swimming, 33 million; baseball and softball, 16 million; basketball, 11 million; golf, 8 million; badminton, 7 million; ice skating, 6 million; horseback riding, 5 million; roller skating, 4 million; tennis, 7 million; volley ball, 4 million; skiing, 3 million; and archery, 5 million.

Spectator sports. Spectator sports have been "big business" for many years. Although most of them have not grown in the past few years to the same extent as other forms of recreation, they still attract big crowds and require big money. Spectator sports drew the following attendance in 1950 and 1960:

	Attendance (in millions)	
	1950	1960
Major league baseball	17.7	20.3
Professional football	2.0	3.2
Collegiate football	19.0	20.4
Horseracing	29.3	46.9
Greyhound racing	6.1	7.9

Although at first glance it may look as if horseracing far overshadows baseball as America's No. 1 spectator sport, one should consider the fact that the baseball figures here given do not include minor leagues, amateur leagues, junior baseball leagues, and sandlot games, all of which claim their quota of devotees. The growth in attendance at horseracing events may be due to its greater acceptance as a respectable sport.

Amusement and entertainment

Though we may take hope at figures that indicate a wholesome growth of participation activities, there is another side to the picture. The amusement and entertainment industries, including television, radio, movies, amusement parks, and night clubs, also share in claiming a large part of the nation's increased money and leisure. The child glued to television for hours a day, despite the active recreation programs offered in most communities, is a not uncommon source of worry for those concerned with the welfare of youth.

Radio, television, and record players. It is hard to realize that those giants of the entertainment world, radio and television, were unknown in the early years of the century. Radio first became a factor in the recreational life of the people of the United States in the 1920's. The novelty of hearing music at will and tuning in on such shows as "Amos 'n Andy" soon made radio addicts of millions of people.

Television's great development followed World War II. Television broadcast revenues increased about ten times between 1950 and 1959, as compared with a mild increase of about one fourth in radio. By 1954 television broadcast revenues outstripped those of radio, and today are about double those of radio, as the following figures show:

Broadcast Revenues

	1950	1959
Radio	$443 million	$555 million
Television	$105 million	$1,163 million

None the less, more families own radios than television sets. An astonishing number of people own record players. The oldest of the three forms of entertainment, the phonograph went into temporary eclipse with the advent of radio, only to be revived with the vast new improvements that set off the hi-fi boom. The numbers of families owning these forms of entertainment in 1960 were:

	Families Owning, 1960	*Estimated Value*
Radio	50.3 million	$ .31 billion
Television (black and white)	46.2 million	$1.24 billion
Record players	36.5 million	$ .66 billion

Assuming a total of about 53 million homes in 1960, there were radios in about 94 percent of them.

Motion pictures. Motion pictures antedated radio by twenty years as a form of popular entertainment. The silent film held sway until 1927, when Al Jolson appeared in *The Jazz Singer*, ushering in the era of talking pictures and new prosperity for the motion-picture industry. The advent of television cut sharply into the attendance at motion-picture theatres, and there were many who predicted the early death of the industry. The motion pictures fought back with improved techniques, color, panoramic screens, drive-in theatres, heavy advertising, and stories often designed to attract through sheer sensationalism and capacity to shock. The industry has become somewhat stabilized but has not shared in the growth that other forms of recreation have experienced. Although the national income originating in motion-picture services has risen, it has not yet reached the high point of $930 million reached in 1945, before television became a competitor.

Other sources of amusement. Many other forms of mass entertainment, such as amusement parks, dance halls, night clubs, and the variety theatres, could be added to this list. All these forms of recreation are important not only in relation to expenditures and employment but also in their influence upon our culture. Never in history have such powerful devices existed to affect the thinking of adults and children as well.

Economic aspects of cultural activities

The term "cultural interests" has often been applied to reading, music, dramatics, and art. Some critics of modern society have deplored the growth in passive entertainment and spectator sports. There is reason to believe, however, that the cultural fields have had a far greater growth.

Music and drama. We have already noted the large numbers of households that own record players. It has been estimated that 30 million Americans are classical-music adherents and that $100 million per year is spent on classical records out of a total of $400 million spent on records of all types. There are twelve hundred symphony orchestras in the United States, and $500 million spent a year on musical instruments. The American Music Conference estimates that there were 32 million amateur musicians in 1961 as compared with 19 million in 1950. At least $300 million a year is spent on admissions to theatres, operas, and concerts. The remarkable growth of little theatres, children's theatres, and summer-stock playhouses is evidence of the interest in dramatics.

Ticket sales for the theatre and opera rose 115 percent since 1946. Theatre receipts in 1960 were more than one third above admissions to all spectator sports.

Books, newspapers, and periodicals. Although a very large percentage of reading should be classed as educational rather than recreational, reading is a favorite recreation of many millions of people despite the competition of television. The growth of the paperback book has made available to the masses at low cost the finest of fiction, science, biography, and history as well as the most sensational popular works. Magazines of general interest as well as those covering every conceivable specialty or hobby field, from Arabian horses to gemology, flood the newsstands. The newspapers are not mere carriers of news as they were long years ago; the Sunday papers especially would look lean without their comics, stories, book reviews, news of the entertainment world, travel sections, and articles dealing with such specialized fields as gardening, crafts, decorating, sewing, and woodwork.

Spending for books has risen phenomenally. Statistics comparing the year 1947 with 1958 indicate that in that eleven-year period there was a spectacular rise in the sale of books. Both the numbers sold and the revenues received approximately doubled. In 1947, 487 million books were sold and $435 million received. By 1958 these figures had jumped to 903 million books and $931 million.

The growth in newspapers and periodicals was less spectacular. Although the newspaper receipts nearly doubled in this period, rising from $1.8 billion to $3.5 billion largely because of increased advertising, circulation showed a more modest gain, from 119.6 million aggregate per issue to 136.8 million. Periodicals meanwhile registered a gain of from 384 million circulation and $1 billion receipts in 1947 to 392 million circulation and $1.6 billion receipts in 1958.

Art and museums. More interest in art is evident. Amateur art supplies now involve an expenditure of more than $30 million a year. More families are purchasing art objects for their homes.

There are over 2,500 museums of all types in the United States, and the numbers of visitors have steadily increased, thereby evidencing their enthusiasm for art, folklore, history, and science.

The number interested in art—as measured by museum attendance—is over 40 million. Visitors to the Metropolitan Museum of Art in New York City on a single Sunday would twice fill the Madison Square Garden sports arena.[10]

Planning Ahead

Unless international tensions increase, throwing our economy into heavier production of war materials, standards of living should continue to rise year by year. The amounts of leisure and income both should increase. What Americans do with this time and money will not only react upon the economy but will shape our very civilization. Discretionary time, the Utopian dream of past generations, has been coupled with discretionary money. Education for development of an emotional mechanism that will allow us to make wise expenditures of both is the responsibility of

[10] "Leisure Activities," from *Business in Brief*, No. 39 (July–August 1961), p. 7. By permission of The Chase Manhattan Bank.

our century. Therein lies a challenge that cannot be ignored: to plan so that the use of leisure will contribute to the happiness and well-being of the country as well as to its economic stability.

SUGGESTED REFERENCES

"A $40 Billion Bill Just for Fun," *Life*, XLVII, No. 6 (December 28, 1959), 69–74.

Dewhurst, J. Frederic and Associates, *America's Needs and Resources: A New Survey*. New York: Twentieth Century Fund, 1955.

The Editors of Fortune, "$30 Billion for Fun," in *Mass Leisure*, ed. Eric Larrabee and Rolf Meyersohn. Chicago: The Free Press, 1959, pp. 161–172.

Harper, Marion, Jr., "The New Conflict of Time and Money," *Business Horizons*, III, No. 4 (Winter 1960).

Kaplan, Max, *Leisure in America: A Social Inquiry*. New York: John Wiley & Sons, Inc., 1960.

"Leisure Spending," *Recreation*, LIV, No. 8 (October 1961), 428–429.

"On the Go and at Play," *Newsweek*, LIV, No. 24 (December 14, 1959), 53.

Soule, George, "The Economics of Leisure," in *Recreation in the Age of Automation*. Philadelphia: American Academy of Political and Social Science, 1957. The Annals of the Academy, Vol. 313, pp. 16–24.

U.S. Bureau of the Census, *Statistical Abstract of the United States*. Washington, D.C.: Department of Commerce. Published annually.

2

SERVING THE
LOCAL COMMUNITY

"The happiness of society is the end of government."
JOHN ADAMS

4

Responsibility of Local Government for Recreation

Modern urban living, with all its complexities, has brought with it a growing organism—municipal government—to meet the urban citizen's needs. Over two thirds of the people in this country now reside in metropolitan areas, living together in extremely complicated relationships. In an urban-oriented society, people are often subjected to a deterioration of social controls, with the result that crime, poverty, stresses of integration, and a multitude of other problems acquire new dimensions.

People being crowded together can multiply the dangers inherent in the maze of human relationships. But although people are living in ever closer proximity, it is strange to find a gradual breakdown of the neighborhood, which yesterday was the hub of social life in the city. Cooley stresses that "the intimacy of the neighborhood has been broken up by the growth of an intricate mesh of wider contacts which leaves us strangers to the people who live in the same house." [1] Burdened with these many problems, it is

[1] G. H. Cooley, *Social Organization* (New York: Charles Scribner's Sons, 1909), pp. 24–25.

no wonder that city dwellers turn to the city government as the instrument to aid them in seeking the "good life" within the city.

Municipal Functions

History and development

Life in the small borough in colonial times did not create the problems or demand the services that are evident in cities today. Prior to the nineteenth century, there were few cities of any size, and what cities existed performed few governmental functions. Public education, a function of New England colonial towns, was one of the earliest services performed by municipalities in the United States. In 1810, New York City, a city of approximately 100,000 people, spent only one dollar per capita for all municipal services.[2] It was not until the 1840's that police administration appeared as a municipal function. Fire protection, first regarded as a private concern, later appeared as a public service in the form of volunteer companies and finally became exclusively a municipal service during this same period. Public works administration started during the middle of the nineteenth century and developed rapidly in the second half of the century.

The greatest expansion of municipal functions came in the first half of the twentieth century. As the family gradually changed from independence to interdependence, increased demands were placed on local governments to provide additional services. It was under these conditions that health, parks and recreation, and similar items were added to the growing list of city services. The setting aside of open space and public parks preceded the development of organized recreation. The full history and development of recreation is found in Chapter 2.

Recreation—a function of government

Evolution of recreation as a municipal function came about under much the same circumstances as did the other services that the modern city provides. Starting first on a private basis, recreation gradually became a municipal function when local governments were confronted with demands for organized services, first in the establishing of parks and later in recreation. As the ever increasing list of municipal services more and more affected the taxpayers' pocketbooks, the need to justify these services became more imperative. Many people questioned the need for spending tax funds for an activity that they felt was a responsibility of the individual. Strong arguments for recreation as a municipal service quickly came forth.

There are many authorities of government who feel that the functions

[2] H. G. James, *Municipal Functions* (New York: D. Appleton and Company, 1917), pp. 18–19.

of a local government should be justified only on the basis of felt need and expressed demand for a particular activity that individuals themselves cannot provide. According to James, the various functions performed by municipal governments "find their justification only in the fact that they contribute to the welfare of society and the individual in it. In fact, all government finds its *raison d'être* in that fact alone." [3] Certainly, recreation's contributions to the safety, health, morals, and welfare of the individual and society alone merit community support along with such functions as education, public works, and police protection.

Legally, it can be shown that, by the enactment of state legislation authorizing cities to provide funds for recreation programs and by the judicial interpretation that follows such enactment, precedence has established recreation as a rightful function of government. It is obviously true that recreation should be considered primarily an individual responsibility, but the provision of some areas and facilities and the conducting of an organized program for all to enjoy are certainly not within the realm of an individual's means.

There are some things that can best be done by government; other things are better accomplished by voluntary agencies or commercial groups. Experience tells us that the over-all community recreation program should be a cooperative effort with all agencies, both public and private, having important roles. The major contributions—unique in the total community effort—that local governments provide to recreation can be summarized as follows:

1. *Government is best suited to acquire, develop, and maintain lands for the total community.* The municipal government is the only agency that has the resources and ability to acquire, develop, and maintain the necessary areas and facilities to meet the needs of the total community. Statutory provisions given local governments make it possible for the municipality to acquire land to be set aside for parks and playgrounds through subdivision control; to acquire needed land or waterways by powers of eminent domain; and, by means of careful long-range planning through the efforts of city planning bodies, to coordinate park and recreation resources as a part of the total community's master plan. Cities also have the financial ability, through taxation, special assessments, and bonding powers, to secure adequate funds to carry out these responsibilities.

2. *Municipal recreation is all-inclusive and views the total community effort rather than a limited segment of it.* Many of the community agencies in the recreation field are segmented with regard to their program and services. Religious agencies generally are concerned with providing opportunities to their own memberships. Youth agencies serve limited age

[3] James, *Municipal Functions*, p. 150.

ranges and, in some cases, limit participation according to sex (Boy Scouts, Girl Scouts, Boys' Clubs). Settlement houses are normally devoted to the lower income groups, and industry gears its program to its employees and their families. The municipal recreation agency is the only agency that is concerned with all areas of the city, all ages, and the total realm of services.

3. *Municipal recreation provides a large proportion of the urban population their major opportunity for a variety of wholesome recreation.* Through a well-rounded municipal recreation program, citizens of all income classes are provided with opportunities of a wholesome nature. To the poor, it might provide their only opportunity for wholesome leisure activities.

4. *Municipal recreation provides for equitable distribution of costs.* Just as public schools and other local governmental services are supported mainly by public taxes, it is appropriate that recreation be likewise financed. This principle of finance is based on the theory of assessing costs according to the ability to pay. By consolidating the total city's program under one agency, it is possible to provide programs at the lowest possible cost.[4]

Organization of the Recreation Department

When a community has identified and clarified its need for establishing a municipal recreation program, it is faced with the decision of determining whether an existing agency, such as the public schools or the park department, should conduct the program or whether it should establish a new administrative authority. Since recreation's scope is broad and its resources are varied, it is important not only to determine carefully the best administrative authority but also to consider the many interrelated arrangements that are essential, if the best use of tax funds is to be made and the best possible services and program are to be offered.

Several principles are important in guiding city authorities or the organizing committee in properly initiating the department. It is first recommended that all functions be placed under *one agency*. In some cities, municipal recreation is provided by two or more governmental agencies. This organizational pattern often results in overlapping and duplication of functions, competition for functions and responsibilities, and increased costs to the taxpayer. Second, a *separate budget* should be allocated for recreation. Where this practice is not followed, it is possible to siphon off money for purposes other than the recreation program. Finally, it is important that *widespread community support* be created and *lay partici-*

[4] For additional reasons justifying municipal recreation, see George D. Butler, *Introduction to Community Recreation*, 3rd ed. (New York: McGraw-Hill Book Company, 1959), pp. 59–63.

pation be initiated in the form of opportunities to serve on boards, committees, or in other volunteer capacities.

It is generally agreed that there is no one authority that is best suited to administer the recreation program. Practices reveal that recreation is usually administered by: (1) a separate recreation authority, (2) the park department, (3) the school administration, and (4), in more recent years, a combined department of parks and recreation. To a lesser degree, other forms of managing recreation are utilized. Conditions in each community differ, and it is important to weigh the several factors that might possibly affect the ability of the previously mentioned authorities to administer the program successfully.

Factors determining the type of administrative authority

City officials must carefully study the following factors that play an influential role in determining the best administrative authority for their community:

1. *Enabling legislation.* Since a municipality can perform only those functions authorized by the state government, it is important first to examine the existing state statutes to determine how such legislation will affect the local government in setting up a department. For example, in Wisconsin, state statutes make it desirable for local school systems to administer recreation programs. The 1955 Park and Recreation Law, passed in Indiana, provides definite advantages for a city in that state to set up a recreation program as a consolidated department of parks and recreation. In Illinois, the park department provides the best opportunity for a recreation program to be organized; and, in North Carolina, the advantages lie in a separate recreation authority.

2. *Ability to obtain funds.* It is also important to determine under what agency the most adequate funds can be provided. In some cases, legal requirements might influence the method or limitations of raising funds for yearly budgets or capital outlays. In other cases, personal bias might affect the possibility of financing a program. The attitude of the school board or superintendent of schools, for example, might influence the amount of money they would be willing to set aside for recreation purposes. The factors concerning finance are varied and many. They must be analyzed closely.

3. *Influence of political pressure.* The extent to which "politics" might be a detrimental influence on the management of various organizational setups merits careful study. Recreation should not become a "political football." The operation of the department should be void of outside political pressures in the matters of hiring personnel, purchasing equipment, or providing services. The 1955 Park and Recreation Law in Indiana

creates a nonpartisan board and provides that this board should hire the executive on the basis of qualifications and experience rather than for political reasons. Experience has proved that no administrative authority is immune to political pressures. Local conditions will determine the degree of susceptibility to such influences.

4. *Availability of areas and facilities.* The agency that either has the control of adequate areas and facilities or has the ability to enlist cooperative arrangements with other agencies should receive particular consideration. No one organization controls all the areas and facilities necessary to operate a comprehensive community program. The agency, therefore, that can develop policies, coordinate plans, and enlist cooperation with other community organizations might well be the logical authority to direct the community recreation program.

5. *Organization with most widespread community support.* An organizing committee should be interested in determining the public's attitude toward the various types of organizations. The agency that is held in the highest esteem, that has a reputation of providing quality service, and is looked upon with favor by other community and governmental agencies should be strongly considered as the proper agency to operate the municipal recreation program. In addition, consideration should be given to the organization and its leaders that would be the most successful in cooperatively working with other community organizations in providing a well-rounded program for the entire community.

6. *Quality of leadership.* Perhaps the key to the success of any organizational structure is the leadership that guides its fortunes. Since municipal recreation is often only one of the many organizations serving the recreation needs of a community and since the success of the total community program is based primarily on the highest level of cooperative relationships, the organization that already has such leadership or the agency that will hire this leadership should be given strong consideration when choosing the proper authority.

Types of administrative patterns

The practice of administering recreation as a separate function has gained the most widespread support of community officials throughout the country. Equally strong arguments, however, can be found for the other types of managing authorities. Examples of departments providing well-rounded programs and services under the guidance of qualified leadership can be found in each of the various types of organizations. Briefly treated, the main types of organizational patterns are as follows:

Administration of recreation as a separate function. Recreation professionals look with favor on organizing recreation under a separate commission, board, or department. Past studies have revealed that this approach is the one most commonly in practice today. The organization of recreation as a *separate department*, comparable to other city functions and directly under the mayor or city manager, has received widespread support from students of government. Advocates of this procedure claim that more prompt and efficient management of the department results, and closer integration and coordination with other municipal departments occur. Lay participation can be provided by establishing an advisory committee, which can act as a consultant and interpretive body to the department. The cities of Livingston, New Jersey, and Austin, Texas, provide examples of recreation programs established under separate departments in the city's over-all organizational system.

The majority of recreation professionals, however, advocate the establishment of recreation under a *recreation board* or *commission*. Under this system, a board (bipartisan is recommended), usually appointed by the mayor and approved by the council, guides the fortunes of the recreation program. Arguments for a board are many, but they chiefly center around the following: a board affords opportunities for more citizen involvement, it insures continuity of policy and program, it provides better opportunity for obtaining and reflecting public opinion, it offers guidance to administrators concerning community interest and problems, and it facilitates broad cooperative relationships in planning and coordinating programs with schools and other community agencies concerned with recreation. Long Beach, California; Cincinnati, Ohio; and Decatur, Illinois, are but a few examples of cities that utilize boards as the administrative authority for their programs.

Those who advocate a separate recreation agency, whether organized as a separate department or as a board or commission, justify their choice by citing the following advantages:

1. Recreation is considered the primary function; under schools and parks, recreation is usually relegated to a role secondary to education and maintenance of park areas and facilities.
2. Separate funds are earmarked for recreation, whereas in other administrative setups the budgets are often consolidated with the school's physical-education funds or the park funds.
3. Chances for a more stable and adequate financial support for recreation are enhanced. Schools and park departments are already faced with the difficult problem of financing their basic programs without adding recreation to their present budgets. If cuts are made, they will naturally cut recreation before they will cut their basic programs.
4. Chances for the employment of full-time recreation leadership to administer the program are greater under the separate recreation agency.

5. Recreation is of sufficient importance to merit the establishment of a separate agency to devote its full energies and capabilities solely to recreation.

The chief arguments advanced against having a separate recreation authority are generalized as follows:

1. The park department and public schools are already well established in most communities. Both are concerned with recreation and, therefore, should logically assume the responsibility; to set up another department would simply add to the complexity of local government.
2. A separate recreation department might possibly duplicate or be in competition with existing recreation programs provided by the park and school authorities.
3. A separate department would be confronted with the problem of having little or, in some cases, no property. Some of the best facilities for recreation are under the administration of parks and schools.
4. It would be more economical to integrate recreation into one of the existing agencies.

Park administration of recreation. In a large number of cities, the recreation departments have been outgrowths of already existing park departments. Since the park movement was a forerunner of organized recreation and became well established in most communities before the concept of municipal recreation was recognized, it is natural that recreation in its early developments joined forces with park departments. In the past, one of the main arguments against having park departments administer recreation programs was that park administrators were concerned mainly with administration of areas and equipment, and more involved with maintaining beautiful lawns or shrubs than with stimulating use of the recreation areas. Present-day park directors are more recreation-minded and realize that public parks have basically one chief function: the leisure enjoyment of people. The gradual changing of philosophy of park leaders has been instrumental in bringing park and recreation professionals much closer together. The results have been a more cooperative relationship and efficient administration of community recreation. Minneapolis, Dallas, Chicago, and Skokie, Illinois, all operate their recreation programs under park administration.

School administration of recreation. Milwaukee, Wisconsin, presents concrete evidence that recreation can be effectively administered under school authorities. Because school administrators are becoming increasingly more aware of recreation and realize that the school has definite responsibilities in this area, they are looking with favor toward fostering recreation programs under their administration. In most cities, the public school board and administrators command a high degree of respect from parents and the public in general, and it is felt that the public would look with favor upon the school's direction of the recreation program. Schools also have buildings, playgrounds, and other facilities that play a key role in affording recreation programs for the community.

Combined department of parks and recreation. The consolidation of parks and recreation into one department, each receiving appropriate recognition, has received considerable attention in recent years. Under this type of organization, recreation tends not to be subordinated to maintenance of park areas and facilities; and certainly better integration of maintenance and program results. By combining the park and recreation functions into one department, authorities hope that overlapping costs may be eliminated and that the combined functions may be organized into a unified effort. Under joint partnership, each function has an opportunity to gain real understanding and appreciation of its respective role. The cities of Los Angeles, Detroit, St. Paul, and Richmond, Virginia, have successfully combined parks and recreation into one department.

District organization. A comparatively recent trend in recreation administration has been the establishment of county, district, or metropolitan park and recreation departments. Departments of this type have been initiated to provide recreation services to the central city as well as to the surrounding suburbs. Many of these authorities administer recreation as a separate function; others establish recreation as a part of a district or regional park department, while still others treat park and recreation as a combined or joint function. Organization of recreation on a county or district basis has been instrumental in solving many of the problems resulting from big city growth and development and also has helped to serve the total recreation needs of all citizens in the large metropolitan area.

Organization means people

Organizations are made up of people, not things. The human element must be placed in front in attempting to consider any organizational setup. Each individual in the organization must be assigned specific tasks, broad outlines of interrelationships must be established, and definite lines of authority must be created. All personnel, from the executive to the playground leader, must understand the unifying purpose of the organization. The question often raised is whether proper organization or quality of employees takes precedence. It should be recognized that even the best organizational structure will break down with uninspired, uninformed, dissatisfied workers. Conversely, not even the best leaders, caught in the web of confusion resulting from poor organization, will achieve the goals of the department.

Community leaders should study thoroughly the various organizational patterns to determine the one that best fits their community. The factors that will influence their selection should be examined. To the pattern eventually chosen should be added qualified personnel that have the ability to initiate, organize, delegate, and coordinate. Final success will be based chiefly upon the attitudes, enthusiasms, and loyalties of these workers. As Aristotle wrote:

The form of government is best in which every man, whoever he is, can act best and live happily.

The test of ideal government is not its particular organization but the result of that organization in promoting the welfare and happiness not of any one class but of all classes.

Legal Authority for Recreation

Recreation as a function of local government must receive legal authority from the state before a program can be organized and conducted. The city itself is a creature of state government. Its very existence, its type of government, and the kind and scope of its powers are derived from the state constitution and statutes. As a political subdivision of the state government, the city is forced to look to this higher authority for legal authorization to deal with its problems. Recreation as a recognized governmental function must fit into this legal framework..

Organized recreation in its early history did not require specific legislation from the state. Existing school and park legislation was broadly interpreted to include recreation under school and park legal powers. In early years, cities based their authority on existing general-welfare and police powers. As needs for recreation began to grow and more money was requested, local officials looked for more specific legal powers that would authorize their communities to operate recreation programs. Efforts were made to broaden the existing park and school legislation to include recreation services. This approach did not prove to be entirely satisfactory, since many of the park and school authorities did not take advantage of the newly created powers. Recreation leaders stressed the need for specific recreation enabling laws.

In 1859, Indiana became the first state to pass school legislation permitting community use of school facilities. The intent of this early school legislation was merely to permit school facilities to be used by community groups and not to authorize schools to conduct recreation programs. Several states have since broadened their school laws to permit school authorities to appropriate funds and conduct organized programs. The first state to pass a general recreation enabling act for municipalities was

New Jersey, in 1915. Today, 46 states have such acts, with only Arizona, Nevada, Alaska, and Hawaii deficient in this respect.

State enabling laws for recreation

In each state, a myriad of laws can be found pertaining to recreation and parks. Some laws are direct in their influence, whereas others indirectly affect city government. Laws can be found that are general in scope or that pertain to a single community or to a specified class of cities. Laws in the field of health, welfare, parks, conservation, and education, to relate only a few, provide certain limitations or controls on local recreation administration. For example, in Indiana, some 58 laws related to parks and recreation were to be found on the books in the early 1950's. It is no wonder that this state was interested in establishing, in one act, broad enabling legislation to allow all communities in the state to establish municipal recreation programs. Such an act was passed in 1955. With such a complexity of laws, city and community leaders are perplexed as to what laws affect their city in setting up a community recreation program. Recreation authorities are in almost unanimous agreement that the passage of good state recreation enabling acts will do much to further the development of municipal recreation in this country.

A desirable enabling act grants a considerable amount of home rule for recreation. Such an act enables communities in the state to establish and conduct recreation programs under any type of administrative authority (park board, school board, separate recreation board) that the community feels would be most effective for its local situation. Legislation of this type is permissive in nature. In essence, it means that the local community has the prerogative of establishing or not establishing a local recreation program.

Many states have initiated laws that have authorized county, district, or metropolitan park and recreation districts. Recreation agencies of this type are found principally in large urban areas. Under such conditions, recreation services can be provided not only to the major city itself, but to the many suburbs surrounding it. The Huron-Clinton Metropolitan Authority, Detroit, Michigan; the Jefferson County Recreation Commission, Kentucky; and the Hayward Area Recreation and Park District in California are examples of such metropolitan districts. It is important to recognize that state enabling laws must conform to the existing constitution and general laws of the state.

The provisions of state enabling acts vary, with no state having what might be termed an ideal or perfect law. Since cities and politics differ and not all their features are considered desirable or pertinent for each situation, the existing laws are generally a matter of compromise. Although most states have some type of state enabling legislation for recreation, effort should be made to amend the present legislation to provide more desirable features, wherever possible. Some of the provisions normally found in state enabling acts are:

1. Method of establishing the managing authority and board
2. Powers of the administrative authority and executive
3. Fiscal procedures to be followed, including how money can be obtained, accounted for, and spent
4. Cooperative agreements among existing governmental agencies
5. Qualification and selection of personnel

Local recreation legislation

Once a city desires to establish a municipal recreation program, it must study the powers granted to the local community through state enabling legislation or included under home-rule provisions. Since most state legislation is permissive, it is up to the local government to establish the local recreation authority, which is based upon the specific powers authorized by the state. In the case of a city under home rule, the local charter may need to be amended to provide recreation services. Where a state enabling act is provided, the city must pass an ordinance to initiate the program.

Financing Municipal Recreation

The willingness of a community to provide sufficient funds for recreation indicates, in part, to what degree recreation has been accepted by the public as a governmental responsibility. Money is needed to provide adequate recreation opportunities for all citizens; this concept must be generally accepted by the public and their elected or appointed officials before adequate funds will be provided. The increased number of recreation programs and the increased expenditures for parks and recreation indicate that more and more communities are accepting recreation as a governmental function. Problems still exist; for instance, many individuals have the attitude that recreation is a personal concern and that people should pay for their own enjoyment. There are still people in cities who question why public funds should be expended for recreation.

Since recreation is a comparatively new community service, it is understandable that the average citizen has a questioning attitude toward it. Butler, in writing for the International City Manager's Association, describes this attitude:

He has never been personally confronted with the problem of providing his own fire protection or streets, and has assumed that they would be furnished at public expense. He takes them largely for granted and expects that he will pay for them through taxes. But not so with recreation which is a personal, individual matter in which each person feels he has a direct and immediate interest. He has been accustomed to choose his own recreation and to pay for it, to join with others in meeting common recreation expenses, and to weigh the benefits and the costs. He has not considered it as something which the city should provide for him.[5]

Certainly most individuals expect to pay for much of their recreation; however, government funds should be provided for services deemed essential for the over-all good of the community. Convincing the community that recreation is a basic community need is imperative before adequate funds can be secured. Justifications for recreation as a municipal function are found in the early pages of this chapter.

Once a community has accepted recreation as a governmental function, sufficient and dependable financial support must be supplied if the city is to provide appropriate facilities, services, and programs. The budget that is passed indicates the course of action that is felt necessary to provide an adequate program. This money determines the magnitude, the scope, and the quality of the services that can be offered. No department can function at its best without adequate financial support. Funds are needed to acquire areas and facilities, to employ qualified leaders, to purchase supplies and equipment, and to maintain the parks, community centers, and other facilities that are essential for a well-rounded program.

How much should a community spend?

It must be recognized that parks and recreation are only two of many municipal functions, and the amount that should be set aside for these two purposes from the total tax dollar is difficult to ascertain. Because competition among municipal departments plays an important part in budgetary procedure, councils and boards are confronted with the problem of determining functions and allocating sufficient funds to perform each function properly.

Recreation's share of the tax dollar and the proper allocation of money for parks and recreation are problems that have not been solved. In 1952, the Athletic Institute staged a National Recreation Workshop in which the participants reconfirmed the generally accepted standard by stating, "$6.00 per capita is needed in most communities that undertake to provide a comprehensive recreation program." [6] This amount does not include the money provided for recreation by semi-public, private, commercial, or other governmental agencies. It must be remembered that the value of the dollar has changed appreciably since such standards were set.

Most authorities consider that the $6.00-per-capita figure should include

[5] *Municipal Recreation Administration* (Chicago: International City Managers' Association, 1945), p. 399. Reprinted by permission.

[6] *Recreation for Community Living* (Chicago: The Athletic Institute, 1952), p. 147. Reprinted by permission.

the annual operating budgets for both parks and recreation. Capital expenditures for acquisition or development of new areas and facilities are excluded from this figure. The money spent for programs and for maintenance of areas and facilities should be in balance. One half of this amount, or $3.00 per capita, should be allocated to parks for the maintenance and operation of parks, zoos, and other areas and facilities under their direction. The remaining $3.00 would be spent for recreation programs and services.

As in all standards, the standard presented for park and recreation costs should be used only as a guide in estimating what should be spent for these two functions in a given community. Extreme caution should be used in applying these standards, since communities differ as to their recreation needs, economic standards, existing nongovernmental agencies providing recreation programs and facilities, cost-of-living indices, and other factors that should be considered when authorities concern themselves with how much to spend. It is possible that some communities might spend less than the suggested $6.00 per capita and still provide an adequate program, whereas other cities spending more than this amount could be short-changing their citizens with regard to recreation opportunities. The fact that many cities are spending much more than the amount suggested bears witness that the standard suggested is an attainable one.

Caution should be exercised in comparing community expenditures for recreation. In many instances, recreation expenditures are incorporated in park budgets and are not readily separated from the maintenance budgets. Also, there are varying policies of cooperative fiscal arrangements in using school facilities and personnel. In some cities, school areas are accessible to the recreation departments for athletic leagues and community center activities at no cost; in other cities, a charge is made for the use of school facilities. In communities in which the school administration is the official recreation authority, many of the costs for operating recreation programs are borne by the school budget. Where the park and recreation departments are administered as separate functions, it is sometimes impossible to determine the actual costs for the recreation program. In some instances, the park department maintains all of the areas and facilities for the recreation department, with the cost charged to the park budget. In other instances, the park department provides the same services for the recreation department but will charge the cost to the recreation budget. The previous examples illustrate only a few of the situations that make it difficult to determine what is actually being spent by cities for their recreation programs.

Methods of financing recreation

Funds for financing municipal recreation can be divided into two categories: those for the current operation of the department and those for capital development. Sources of these funds are varied; discussion of them will be categorized according to their main purpose.

Sources of current operating funds. The following are considered to be the principal sources of current operating funds.

1. APPROPRIATIONS FROM THE GENERAL FUND. One of the most widely used methods of securing money for recreation is the submitting of a budget to the appropriating body, normally the Common Council. Upon approval by the necessary reviewing boards, the money is drawn from the city's General Fund.

The General Fund is created and maintained to finance the over-all functions of a municipal government. The recreation department endeavors to obtain its fair share of the city's tax funds along with the police, fire, public works, and other departments. Where recreation is under the school administration, the recreation director presents his budget to the school administrators, and the money approved is considered a part of the over-all school budget. The amount of money received each year depends to a large extent upon the ability of the recreation board and administrator to win approval of their program from the council or school board, who must determine the budgets of several departments in relation to the anticipated revenue. With an efficient, civic-minded council, the recreation department is likely to receive its just share of the city's tax dollar. It is possible that the recreation department might also be subject to an economy-minded body that might drastically reduce the budget request, thereby cutting the planned recreation program.

2. SPECIAL RECREATION TAX. A special tax levy for recreation is authorized in a number of states, with the money derived from this source being set aside in a Special Revenue Fund. A fund of this nature is usually created through statutory provisions to provide definite revenues for such functions as parks, recreation, and schools. One of the advantages of this method is that the money cannot be spent for any other government service except the purpose for which it was created.

In some states, the local park and/or recreation authorities have been granted complete fiscal independence, since the boards have the right to levy taxes and spend the money without receiving approval from the mayors or city councils. In other states, special levies for park and recreation purposes are subject to city council approval. It is possible in special revenue funds to receive additional appropriations to supplement the money received from the special park and recreation tax.

The special tax is usually expressed in terms of a certain number of mills on each dollar of assessed valuation or so many cents per hundred dollars of assessed valuation of a community. The tax is determined as follows: the total cost of the recreation program for the coming year is calculated; then the anticipated revenues from all other sources, excluding the property tax, are deducted. The balance of the anticipated expenditures must come from the property tax. This remainder is then divided by the assessed valuation of the community, resulting in the recreation tax levy. For example:

Recreation budget request	$100,000
Anticipated revenue from fees and charges	40,000
Balance to be raised from property tax	$ 60,000

Tax rate = $60,000 ÷ $30,000,000 (net assessed valuation) = $.20 per $100 assessed valuation

3. FEES AND CHARGES. Municipal recreation is partially supported by fees charged for certain services or use of facilities. It is important to realize, however, that public recreation can no more be self-supporting than can public education. It is generally agreed that where certain facilities or services have a high initial cost and have limitations as to the number of people they accommodate, fees should be charged. Golf courses and swimming pools are two of the most common examples of facilities for which fees are normally charged. Traditionally, playgrounds, parks, and community centers that serve large numbers of people in the community are free to the public. Most cities open their recreation activities to children at no cost. Practices vary as to fees and charges, and a community that is determining its policies should remember first that the recreation program is for all people in the community and that a stringent policy of fees and charges might exclude a large number who most need the benefits of the program.

Sources of funds for capital outlay. The following are considered to be the principal sources of funds for capital outlay.

1. BOND ISSUES. Borrowing for capital acquisitions and improvements by the issuance of bonds has been considered essential if large and costly projects, such as swimming pools, camps, community buildings, or golf courses, are to be provided by municipalities. The expense of such undertakings would be prohibitive if imposed upon a community at any one time. It should be mentioned that bonds are a supplement to taxation and should not be considered actual revenue, since they create a liability that must be paid from future taxes.

2. SPECIAL ASSESSMENTS. Special assessments are used most commonly to finance permanent improvements, which are paid for in whole or in part by the property owners in the area specially benefited. This method is not used widely, nor is it highly recommended by community officials. The desirable feature is that it places the cost of services on those who benefit and are willing to pay. However, the low economic areas of the community, which most often need such facilities and improvements, generally are neglected if this becomes a common method of financing.

3. DONATIONS AND GIFTS. One of the main sources of funds for capital outlays for many of the semi-public agencies is gifts from philanthropic organizations and civic-minded individuals. Municipal park and recreation departments, possibly to a lesser degree, have also been presented valuable gifts from individuals. In their long-range plans, recreation authorities should be ever alert to this source of assistance.

Areas and Facilities

One of the major concerns of the modern city is the provision of properly developed recreation areas to meet the leisure needs of its citizens. This situation existed even in the early American city, wherein the expressed concerns of the people for the "disappearing land" and crowded, congested living, loss of privacy, and fear of having no place for children to play alerted city fathers to the need for setting aside areas (Boston Commons) and breathing spaces (Central Park) for present and future enjoyment. The tremendous growth of the American city has enlarged this problem so that today it is a most complicated and costly one. City after city and neighborhood after neighborhood lack the necessary playgrounds, parks, playfields, and other facilities to meet present needs, let alone future needs. It is indeed unfortunate that we are falling behind in our responsibility to provide these areas and facilities. Without adequate space, we cannot meet the wholesome leisure requirements of our people.

The provision of land properly spaced and creatively developed according to the needs of the city is essential if a well-balanced community recreation program is to be achieved. Experience tells us that the municipal government is best suited to provide appropriate areas and facilities for the whole community. The following are some of the main responsibilities of a city relative to this function.

Responsibilities of municipal park and recreation agencies for areas and facilities

There are several functions that every city, regardless of its size, must perform, if adequate recreation areas and facilities are to be provided. The park and recreation authority must:

1. *Acquire, develop, and maintain sufficient land for the total community needs.* Statutory provisions given local park and recreation authorities make it possible for the city to require land to be set aside (subdivision control), acquire the land where it is deemed essential (powers of eminent domain), coordinate present as well as future planning for recreation areas as it relates to the total community needs (city planning), and finance the acquisition, development, and maintenance of such areas in the most economical way (bonding and taxing powers).

In spite of the powers available to cities and the far-sighted examples of our forefathers in acquiring space for recreation, communities are failing to meet present as well as future needs. Economist Marion Clawson suggests, concerning scarcity of land for recreation, that we are approaching a "grade A crisis unprecedented in both size and character." He reminds us, "Recreational use of all kinds of public lands has more than trebled since the end of the war, and is still rising. Despite strenuous efforts, new recreation facilities are not being added nearly so fast." [7] Because of our bulging cities, massive highway developments, and exploding suburbs, land is fast disappearing, and what is left is astronomical in price. It is up to us to keep a step or two ahead of suburb developers; we must, therefore, look beyond our present city boundaries and buy or reserve sufficient land, in desirable locations, for future development.

According to Conrad Wirth, Director of the National Park Service, "the inadequacy of our parks today cannot be blamed on our not knowing the value of parks, but rather on a reluctance of many people to forego the possible commercial value of the land." [8] Once land is set aside or utilized for other purposes, it is almost impossible to reclaim it for public recreation purposes. Civic-minded leaders must take the lead in interpreting this crisis to our communities and must arouse a willingness in our taxpayers to pay the cost of land acquisition. Unless people are willing to pay the cost, park and recreation authorities are powerless in meeting the demands for recreation areas and facilities.

It is important that the land acquired be so located throughout the city that it meets the needs and interests of the neighborhood and community. It is not enough merely to set aside adequate acreage; it is important also that the land be developed and maintained in usable units so that a wide variety of activities can be fostered. Otherwise, the area might prove to be a liability rather than an asset.

2. *Provide an organized program or supervisory control.* An organized program or supervisory control must be initiated according to the area's purpose and the community needs and interests. In some areas, such as parks, golf courses, zoos, and swimming pools, the main functions of the administrative authority are to establish appropriate policies and exercise supervisory control, so that the best use of the area might be facilitated. On the other hand, in a camp, community center, or playground, the municipal authority has a responsibility for providing an organized recreation program, so that the maximum use of the facility may be achieved, the objectives of the program fulfilled, and the best interests of the individuals

[7] Marion Clawson, "The Crisis in Outdoor Recreation," reprinted from *American Forests* (March–April 1959), pp. 2–3. Used by permission.

[8] Conrad Wirth, Foreword in *The Crisis in Open Land* (Wheeling, West Va.: American Institute of Park Executives, 1959), p. 3.

met. A school building without planned educational experiences would be meaningless; a camp or playground without a well-organized program like-wise would be a waste of community efforts in providing such facilities. The provision of qualified leaders, more than areas, facilities, or equipment, will determine whether a well-organized recreation program will result. Sometimes a city spends money to acquire and develop beautiful recreation areas and facilities but fails to reap the harvest because another ingredient, good leadership, is missing.

3. *Coordinate use of existing facilities.* Cooperative relationships should be established between municipal recreation authorities and private, re-ligious, industrial, and youth-serving agencies. These community organiza-tions should be encouraged to utilize the areas, facilities, and services offered by the city. Recreation authorities should stimulate interest and give technical assistance to leaders of community groups who wish to use public property. Since cooperation is a two-way street, it might be necessary or economical for municipal recreation departments to use areas and facili-ties owned and operated by schools, industry, youth-serving and other community agencies. Such cooperative relationships will assure the fullest possible use of existing community resources and might decrease duplica-tion of physical developments. Public recreation agencies and the public schools should work closely in securing the most efficient use of their properties. Cooperation of all groups—public and private—will yield maxi-mum returns to the taxpayer's or the philanthropist's dollar. If coopera-tion exists, additional facilities will be built only when facilities of all existing organizations are being used to capacity.

4. *Develop immediate and long-range plans.* Comprehensive planning is essential to assure a varied and well-integrated system of park and recrea-tion facilities. Proper balance, harmony, and order can be assured only if plans of the many public and private recreation agencies in a community are coordinated. Since the programs of all agencies are in some ways related and interdependent, recreation planning cannot be made in a vacuum but must be done in relation to all.

5. *Guard against encroachment.* Not only are cities failing to acquire space fast enough for recreation purposes, but many are finding it difficult to hold what they already have. Schools, hospitals, libraries, highways, and factories are being built on land once acquired and in some cases developed for recreation uses. According to George Butler, park and recreation land represents the line of least resistance and involves less work and expense than the acquiring of other lands for a project.[9] Reports from all sections

[9] George D. Butler, "The Land Grab for Building Purposes," *Recreation*, L, No. 6 (June 1957), 204–206.

of the country reveal that the encroachment problem is widespread. In Murfreesboro, Tennessee, the city's only park was traded for a new industry; in Louisville, Kentucky, a new superhighway devoured one complete park and pieces of two others. The last ten years have provided many similar illustrations. On the other side of the ledger, we can take pride that some cities have had the foresight and willpower to resist such attempts. Recently, widespread interest was focused on the Cook County Forest Preserve's successful battle with the University of Illinois, which sought to develop a Chicago campus on one of the Forest Preserve's choice sites.

Park and recreation lands once lost can never be replaced. It is imperative that cities resist encroachment attempt with vigor and force. The American Institute of Park Executives, in a Statement of Principles on Land for Parks and Recreation, adopted a resolution, part of which stated:

Once lands have been secured for a system of parks and recreational facilities the land should be firmly held against the pressures that it should be used for other public purposes such as schools and other public buildings, parking lots and highways. This does not mean that parks are inviolate, or that the properties held for park and recreation purposes may never be encroached upon in outline, but it is a determined warning that such properties cannot be entered upon with impunity or without full compensation in sufficient amount to reestablish the damaged property in an equally efficacious location.[10]

Basic considerations in planning

Some of the basic principles that must be considered by the recreation authority are:

1. *Integrate.* Recreation should be a part of the city's master plan. A large number of cities today have established planning commissions or boards to develop master plans for the total development of the cities. Where such planning agencies exist, recreation authorities should work closely with the planning authorities in integrating the recreation plan with the master plan. Such things as the acquisition of new school sites, the development of streets and highways, housing developments, and industrial growth and development must be taken into consideration in planning future park and recreation space and facility requirements.

2. *Study.* Area and facility planning should take into consideration the people it is to serve. The recreation agency must study carefully such factors as the needs and interests of the individuals in each neighborhood, their nationality traits and customs, and the population indices, and fit the plans accordingly. Since people, neighborhoods, and cities differ, it is reasonable to assume that a stereotyped playground, playfield, or park will receive mixed responses in different neighborhoods and communities.

[10] *The Crisis in Open Land* (Wheeling, West Va.: The American Institute of Park Executives, 1959), p. 26.

Robert Crawford, Commissioner of Recreation for the City of Philadelphia, made a tremendous impact upon the development and redevelopment of park and recreation areas in that city. The amazing "Philadelphia
story" might be attributed to his careful adapting of a plan to each individual neighborhood and presenting the plan, in person, to a "town hall"
meeting of the people of that neighborhood, where the plan was discussed
and considered.

3. *Cooperate.* School-city cooperative planning should be encouraged.
Notable progress has been achieved in cooperative planning between school
and recreation administrators in the past decade. The location of playgrounds at elementary school sites and playfields at secondary school areas
has proved to be one of the most economical and effective ways of providing adequate recreation opportunities in the average community. The
use of these areas for recreation purposes has been effective only when the
needs of both the school and the recreation leaders are jointly considered
and when school facilities are planned with the concept of joint use in
mind.

The park-school plan, in which the park and the school authorities
acquire and develop adjacent areas as a single functional unit for mutual
benefits has received increasing recognition throughout the country. Minneapolis, Detroit, and Oakland are among the cities that have demonstrated successful accomplishment of the park-school plan. Schools may
serve as indoor recreation centers and may be used by community groups,
especially if they are properly designed for this joint use. Cooperative planning between these two governmental agencies seems imperative, if the taxpayer is to receive maximum benefits from his tax dollar.

4. *Coordinate.* Plans should be coordinated with voluntary agencies.
Voluntary and semi-public agencies, such as the YMCA, Boys' Clubs, or
settlement houses, conduct programs that are similar or interrelated in
many respects to recreation programs conducted by school and municipal
agencies. Also, the programs sponsored by these agencies often require use
of municipal park and recreation facilities and services. Organizations of
this nature need recreation buildings, gymnasiums, and camps that are also
needed by municipal recreation agencies. For these reasons, it is important
that these agencies and the public authorities cooperatively plan program
and facility developments so that duplication and maladjustments, or, in
some areas, deficiencies, will not occur.

5. *Interrelate.* Relationships between county, district, regional, state,
and national agencies should be considered. It is not enough to limit our
thinking and our planning merely to the many facets of recreation in our
modern communities. Our new "jet age," with higher family incomes and
improved modes of transportation and communication, has placed our

national parks, ski resorts, and seashores within reach of the mass of the American people. Our state parks are bursting at the seams. Under such circumstances, it is reasonable to assume that recreation authorities must broaden their planning to include these additional recreation outlets. Having state and regional parks within easy reach of our urban population for swimming, picnicking, fishing, hiking, or skiing influences local recreation offerings and opportunities.

The growth of large metropolitan areas with limitless boundaries creates a new dimension in community planning. This "urban sprawl," as William H. Whyte aptly describes it, is filling in our countryside "at a rate of some 3,000 acres a day." Whyte wrote:

With characteristic optimism, most Americans still assume that there will be plenty of green space on the other side of the fence. But this time there won't be. It is not merely that the countryside is ever receding; in the great expansion of the metropolitan areas the subdivisions of one city are beginning to meet up with the subdivisions of another. Flying from Los Angeles to San Bernardino—an unnerving lesson in man's infinite capacity to mess up his environment—the traveler can see a legion of bulldozers gnawing into the last remaining tract of green between the two cities, and from San Bernardino another legion of bulldozers gnawing westward. High over New Jersey, midway between New York and Philadelphia, the air traveler has a fleeting illusion of green space, but most of it has already been bought up, and outlying supermarkets and drive-in theatres are omens of what is to come.[11]

Similar illustrations can be found in most of our other large metropolitan areas. Urban sprawl is causing a squandering of land with no pattern for growth. Park and recreation areas are not being set aside in sufficient amounts to satisfy the leisure needs of people caught in this mesh of urban living. The establishment of county, district, and regional park and recreation departments has been one means of meeting the recreation opportunities in large metropolitan areas. Recreation administrators must broaden their planning to encompass these gigantic problems caused by twentieth-century progress.

Current standards for space and facility development

How much land and what types of developments are needed to provide a comprehensive system of recreation areas and facilities? These questions confront local officials concerned with providing organized park and recreation programs. Over a period of years, various national professional and service organizations, planners, and recreation leaders have developed standards to serve as guideposts for communities in establishing recreation areas and facilities. Attempts have been made periodically to revise these

[11] William H. Whyte, "Urban Sprawl" in *The Exploding Metropolis* by the editors of *Fortune* (New York: Doubleday & Company, Inc., 1958), p. 133.

standards to meet the needs of our changing society. At present, there seems to be no common agreement on facility standards. It is recognized that further studies must be directed toward the goal of "updating" our standards; until new and better standards are formulated, some of the most generally accepted ones must suffice. One of the most generally accepted standards is that a city should secure at least one acre of park and recreation space for each 100 people in the community. Of this land, from 30 to 50 percent should be developed for active recreation use.

Space alone is not enough. Each recreation area must be creatively designed and developed to meet its intended purpose and properly managed and maintained to ensure the fullest use of the facility.

Types of recreation areas and facilities

Some of the main types of recreation areas, with their intended purpose and appropriate facilities and features, are listed on the following pages.

Fig. 6 *Creative Play Equipment—Oakland, California (Courtesy Oakland Park Department. Photo by Harold Winder)*

1. *Tot-lot or play lot.* The smallest of all recreation areas, the "tot-lot," is an area for pre-school children. Such an area is sometimes developed as a separate functional unit, but more often it is an integral part of a neighborhood playground. The tot-lot should be enclosed by a hedge or fence and normally is equipped with some of the following facilities: sandbox, chair swings, low climbing devices, benches for mothers, a grassy area, and additional play equipment designed particularly for small children. An open shelter and a drinking fountain would add a great deal to its effective use.

2. *Neighborhood playground.* Operated on a neighborhood basis, the playground should provide space for all age groups, particularly children from five to fifteen years of age. The size of a playground should normally vary from 4 to 10 acres, depending upon the density of population of the neighborhood. In many communities, the grounds of elementary schools, which are generally located on a neighborhood basis, are utilized as part of the city's supervised playground program because of their location and facilities. Site and location do not, however, insure that an elementary school will fulfill the needs of a neighborhood unless the school and grounds are designed to be used for both school and recreation purposes. Some desirable features that should be included as a part of a neighborhood playground are a tot-lot, sports and games area, area for low organized games, apparatus area, multiple-use paved area, shaded area for crafts and quiet activities, and a shelter house. Where school grounds are used for the neighborhood playground, the school should serve as the shelter house and should be designed for this purpose.

3. *The park-school.* This comparatively new concept combines a school and playground or playfield with a park to form a single functional unit. Under this plan, the city officials would acquire sufficient land, generally 15 acres or more, to be planned and developed to serve not only the educational needs of the neighborhood or community but also the recreation and community needs. This concept involves joint use of school facilities by recreation and community groups as well as use of the additional park areas and facilities by school officials. With this type of thinking, both the school and the park or recreation agency supplement each other for mutual enrichment.

4. *Playfield.* The playfield usually serves several neighborhoods and all age groups. From 10 to 30 acres are needed. The playfield is sometimes developed in conjunction with a junior or senior high school. Although designed to serve all age groups, this area is mainly concerned with the leisure needs of older youth and adults. A neighborhood playground can be developed as one part of a playfield. Other features often found in this

Fig. 7   A *Park-School Plan*

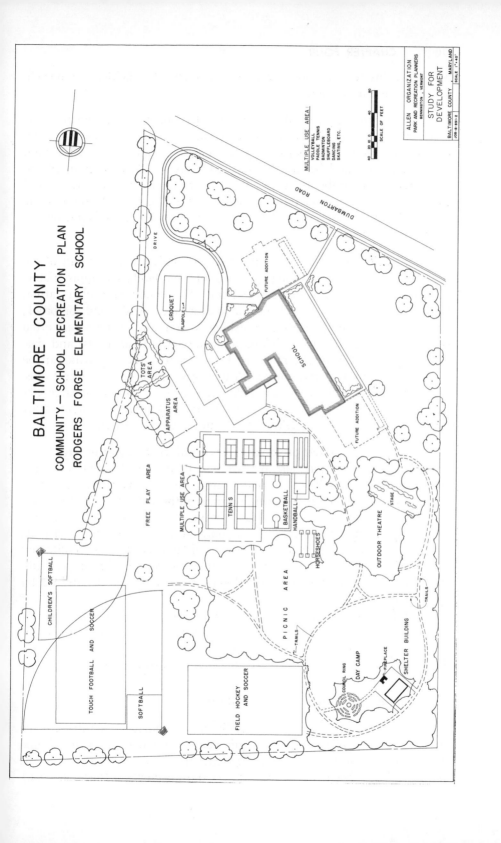

BALTIMORE COUNTY

COMMUNITY – SCHOOL RECREATION PLAN
RODGERS FORGE ELEMENTARY SCHOOL

MULTIPLE USE AREA:
VOLLEYBALL
PADDLE TENNIS
BADMINTON
SHUFFLEBOARD
DANCING
SKATING, ETC.

SCALE OF FEET

ALLEN ORGANIZATION
PARK AND RECREATION PLANNERS
BENNINGTON , VERMONT

STUDY FOR
DEVELOPMENT
BALTIMORE COUNTY , MARYLAND
JOB-B-691-2 | SCALE 1"=40'

DUMBARTON ROAD

DRIVE

CROQUET
FLAGPOLE

FUTURE ADDITION

FUTURE ADDITION

SCHOOL

TOTS' AREA

APPARATUS AREA

FREE PLAY AREA

MULTIPLE USE AREA

TENNIS

BASKETBALL

HANDBALL

HORSESHOES

OUTDOOR THEATRE

STAGE

PICNIC AREA

TRAILS

TRAILS

COUNCIL RING

DAY CAMP

FIREPLACE

SHELTER BUILDING

FIELD HOCKEY AND SOCCER

SOFTBALL

TOUCH FOOTBALL AND SOCCER

CHILDREN'S SOFTBALL

type of area are tennis courts, a swimming pool, baseball fields, a band shell, and a community center.

5. *Neighborhood park.* Neighborhoods often benefit from small scenic areas, attractively landscaped, which provide breathing spaces for quiet, passive recreation. Neighborhood parks sometimes are developed around formal plantings and beautiful gardens. Others are devoted primarily to grass, trees, and shrubs. Benches are often provided for people to sit and enjoy a moment of relaxation or the beauty of the park. Seldom is the neighborhood park developed for active recreation activities found on the playground or playfield.

6. *Large city park.* The large city park is generally found in a part of the city that offers interesting topography and sufficient land to be appropriately developed so that all city dwellers can enjoy the scenery and other natural features. Some city parks are built around a lake, small pond, or brook, which offers swimming, boating, or fishing. Woods and meadows are often developed into picnic areas, hiking and horseback-riding trails, and day-camp sites. In cities in the northern United States, the city park can be utilized as a winter sports center with toboggan slides, ski jumps and runs, ice-skating rinks, and sled slides. Additional facilities found in large city parks might include golf courses, swimming pools, tennis courts, nature museums, zoos, marinas, shelter houses, and outdoor theaters.

7. *Reservations—forest preserves.* Areas of this type consist of large tracts of land, 500 acres or more, left in a largely natural state. They are normally found on the boundaries of or outside large cities. Reservations are usually operated by city, county, district, or state authorities. Scenic drives are often maintained so that the natural beauty of the preserve can be enjoyed. Hiking and riding trails are the only means of access to other parts of the area. Some reservations have parcels of land set aside as wildlife and waterfowl sanctuaries. Developments of the preserve include camps, trails, picnic areas, trailside museums, developments for water sports, and winter sport facilities.

The mountain parks outside Denver and Boulder, Colorado; the Watchung Reservation in northern New Jersey; the East Bay Regional Park District, Alameda County, California; and the Cook County Forest Preserve in Chicago are examples of this type of outdoor-recreation area.

A Creative Approach for the Future

With impetus from Europe, especially the Scandinavian countries, many types of creative play areas and equipment have emerged in the United States. One of the most encouraging trends in parks and recreation in the past decade has been the resourcefulness and imagination that many park and recreation directors have illustrated in the development of areas and equipment that challenge the imagination of children of all ages. This movement to a more creative approach to park and recreation planning is in its infancy. Most schools and park and recreation departments are still designing areas and installing equipment along the same traditional lines that can be traced back to our early playground and parks. One of the greatest challenges facing today's recreation leaders is to revitalize the thinking of community planners.

Fig. 8   *School at the Zoo—San Diego, California (Courtesy San Diego Zoo. Photo by R. Van Nostrand)*

As our society radically changes, and automation takes many of the satisfactions and creative outlets from our daily tasks, unique and stimulating opportunities for leisure activities are of paramount importance. If cities are to meet successfully the challenges of today, planners must continue to experiment with new and exciting approaches to our tot-lots, playgrounds, playfields, and parks. The transition that has taken place in Philadelphia, Oakland, and Colorado Springs is worthy of high commendation. Park and recreation planners elsewhere are successfully experimenting with a creative type of areas and facilities that is functional, yet adds color, attractiveness, and adventure. In most instances, it has been the larger cities that have taken the lead. These cities have paved the way; others must follow.

SUGGESTED REFERENCES

Baker, Benjamin, *Urban Government*. New York: D. Van Nostrand Company, 1957.

Butler, George D., *Introduction to Community Recreation*, Third edition. New York: McGraw-Hill Book Company, 1959.

——————————, *Recreation Areas: Their Design and Equipment*, Revised edition. New York: A. S. Barnes & Company, 1958.

The Exploding Metropolis. New York: Doubleday & Company, Inc., 1958.

Gabrielsen, M. A. and Caswell M. Miles, eds., *Sports and Recreation Facilities for School and Community*. Englewood Cliffs, N.J.: Prentice-Hall, Inc., 1958.

Hjelte, George, *The Administration of Public Recreation*. New York: The Macmillan Company, 1940.

Meyer, Harold D. and Charles K. Brightbill, *Recreation Administration*. Englewood Cliffs, N.J.: Prentice-Hall, Inc., 1956.

Municipal Finance Administration. Chicago: International City Managers' Association, 1955.

Planning Facilities for Health, Physical Education, and Recreation. Chicago: The Athletic Institute, 1956.

Williams, Wayne, *Recreation Places*. New York: Reinhold Publishing Corporation, 1958.

5

The School's Role in Recreation

Human needs can be classified into two categories: those necessary for survival and those necessary for enrichment of life. Public schools not only serve as educational media for survival needs, but they also act as resources for life enrichment—as constructive influences upon society and avenues for community betterment. No other organization has a more vital role. In the past several decades, vast changes in community life have had a marked effect on the school and on other community agencies. Schools, along with the home, church, and other social institutions, must keep abreast of social and economic changes. In turn, these institutions have a great influence in determining the culture, customs, habits, and mores of a community.

At no time in civilization has the complexity of an age so challenged social and human values. Transitions in all phases of daily living have resulted in additional responsibilities for the school. Along with the ever changing society has come a multitude of new problems, including those brought about by increased leisure. Schools have been faced with the problems of preparing people for the new dimensions in living that leisure brings, for a future in which their leisure hours may outstrip their work hours in number and importance.

113

Traditionally, we have placed upon the schools the responsibility for teaching the basic fundamentals of education, the three R's. Present elementary school curriculums still emphasize these fundamentals as essential for every child. It is in the elementary grades that the child is expected to master the tools basic to further education. Added to these obligations, in the modern concept of "education for life" are many other tasks that pave the road to more complete living.

In recent years, demands have been placed upon the public school to provide a much broader range of experiences. Educators have felt that the child should develop desirable attitudes, make social adjustments, and grow in personality. This concept has resulted in an enlarged curriculum. Educators differ in their preference for the traditional intellectual approach as opposed to the progressive "preparation for life" approach. Within the confines of the latter philosophy, education for increasingly abundant leisure must assume vital importance. Bobbitt forecast such implications for the school as early as 1918:

> It is probable that in the newer schools of the oncoming humanistic age, education for leisure occupations will be recognized as one of the most serious educational tasks—if not the largest and most vital of all.[1]

If youth are to be prepared to handle the physical, social, and emotional as well as the intellectual problems of today's world, the broadening of curriculum that has evolved during the last half century is justified. Life is a series of changes. Education must continue to keep abreast of present needs and foresee future responsibilities, if society is to be composed of useful, resourceful, adjusted individuals.

In 1918, educators accepted "worthy use of leisure time" as one of the Cardinal Principles of Education. As education changed to meet the new developments in society, educators redefined their goals. The Educational Policies Commission of the National Education Association, in 1938, published a new set of aims for education in American democracy. The new objectives of education were concerned with self-realization, human relationship, economic efficiency, and civic responsibility. These objectives stress the importance of the individual and his relationships with people and society. They also include the concern for education for leisure as it affects one's ability to find self-realization. All educative forces in the community have a role to play in achieving the end product—a well-educated individual, capable of coping with his environment and achieving satisfaction from it.

In 1960, school authorities in California published a document that spelled out the role of the school in the total recreation program of the community. The following beliefs were recorded:

[1] Franklin Bobbitt, *The Curriculum* (Boston: Houghton Mifflin Company, 1918), p. 212.

We Believe

1. That recreation is a basic human need because creative use of leisure is vital to the conservation and strengthening of human resources and personality.
2. That recreation contributes significantly to the cultural advancement and to the well-being of the individual, the community, the state, and the nation.
3. That recreation requires the mobilization of all community resources to meet the present and the future needs of our citizens.
4. That school recreation is an integral part of education, and the school places emphasis on the avocational values of all school subjects, as well as providing recreational opportunities.[2]

Such a statement places recreation and education together to work interdependently toward similar goals.

The School's Recreation Responsibilities

In terms of facilities, leadership, and knowledge, schools have the potential to educate students properly for the worthy use of leisure, to conduct varied recreation programs, and to aid other recreation agencies in the interpretation and the conduct of their programs. The contributions that the schools can make toward recreation are noteworthy. Their efforts are needed, if communities are to meet the recreation needs of all citizens.

Education for the arts of leisure

Since recreation is voluntary and people may choose the type of leisure pursuits in which they will participate, education to develop the ability to make wise leisure choices is essential. The school joins with the home, church, and other agencies in this all-important role. There are several ingredients in the process of education for leisure. All of these ingredients must be considered if the child or adult is to receive the necessary background for leisure pursuits. Education for the arts of leisure must include the following:

1. *Aiding the development of a wholesome philosophy of leisure.* If we are to educate for leisure, then we must first interpret the importance of leisure and its possible contribution to a full life. The school must plan now for the leisure literacy of the future so that negative attitudes will not deny the value of extra hours. Attitudes and habits are best developed in the young, before their learned prejudices and inhibitions interfere.

2. *Teaching skills and knowledges.* A person who has been taught how to swim, paint, or play an instrument is prone to engage in these activities

[2] *The Roles of Public Education in Recreation* (Burlingame, Calif.: The California Association for Health, Physical Education and Recreation, 1960), p. 2. Reprinted by permission.

after lessons cease. It is generally agreed that proficiency adds to enjoyment and satisfaction in recreation activities. A broad program of education will develop skills and knowledges of a physical, intellectual, and social nature. Most of the courses offered in elementary and secondary school curriculums may contribute to education for the arts of leisure. The "three R's," history, science, and the arts form the broad foundation considered necessary for a basic education. These basic knowledges may also form the foundation for leisure experiences such as reading, scientific experiments, and discussion clubs. Courses or co-curricular activities in music, dramatics, physical education, home economics, and manual arts have definite leisure connotations. Emphasis should be placed on teaching activities with carry-over values as well as those with immediate values. For example, in physical education, such activities as basketball, football, baseball, and track should not complete the offerings. The development of skills in tennis, golf, archery, bowling, swimming, badminton, and sailing will prove valuable long after the participant's body has lost the ability to withstand the rigors of contact sports or his setting denies the numbers needed for a team.

There is no conflict between teaching the fundamental processes or attaining the highest intellectual achievement and teaching the arts of leisure. The latter may contribute to intellectual achievement. Some of our best learning takes place in relaxed leisure hours when we turn to books, nature lore, scientific experiment, or discussions because we choose to do so. Inspiration to use in leisure the basic skills and knowledges that must be learned anyway is often the teacher's greatest contribution.

3. *Developing desirable attitudes, interests, habits, and aspirations.* The creating of desirable interests and attitudes toward school courses and activities is as important as, if not more important than, the teaching of skills. If, during the impressionable school years, children are provided with satisfying, enriching experiences that provide positive values, they will be more disposed to choose these activities voluntarily. If, for instance, a teacher approaches her task of teaching literature in a dull, uninspiring manner, little, if any, carry-over value will be achieved. If she teaches literature in an interesting, enthusiastic manner, children may voluntarily continue to read for leisure enjoyment.

Social conditioning often denies us pleasures that we otherwise would find worthwhile. Attitudes are caught from, not taught by, parents, teachers, and associates. The idolized coach who attends the science fair and the dramatic production is teaching his boys a lesson as important as techniques of ball handling.

4. *Developing desirable personality traits.* The school is a laboratory for the development of personality traits. A considerable portion of a child's time is spent in school. The varied social contacts and experiences provided therein are powerful influences in shaping a child's personality. Ac-

cording to the Neumeyers, the development of a wholesome personality is mainly concerned with "the creation and integration of various personality traits that respond favorably to the best in the environment." [3] The school provides the environment in which children learn how to get along with others and join together to work on common projects. A boy or girl who has not developed friends in school or has not adjusted to the many opportunities that are provided will find himself lonesome and unhappy. Also, the child that does not have the emotional make-up or temperament to adjust to a social group, a club, or a team likewise becomes disturbed and needs guidance and help.

Personality traits are generally developed best through recreation experiences provided either in class learning situations or in the co-curricular activities. Frequently, play outlets in which the child is engrossed are excellent indicators of areas of concern or need in personality growth. The children that do make the proper adjustments to school activities are the persons who will develop desirable personality traits that are necessary in getting along with people.

If success in life is measured not only in terms of material possessions but in how an individual adjusts to everyday living, then education has a noteworthy function to develop desirable personality traits as an integral part of education for the arts of leisure.

5. *Guidance in the proper use of leisure.* Because of the many facets of leisure pursuits, both youths and adults are faced with choosing among the numerous activities offered. Whether a person will select activities with positive values or activities resulting in destructive or negative influences will largely be determined by whether desirable skills, attitudes, tastes, and personality traits have been created. Teachers and counselors have an additional responsibility—that of counseling and guidance, not only for mature tastes and wise choices but in attention to numbers of choices. Involvement in too many co-curricular activities, even though each separate choice is wholesome, is a cause for concern of parents and teachers.

Teachers also have a responsibility for suggesting programs that merit consideration for leisure. This might take the form of suggesting to children that they should watch a certain television show, explore the effects of erosion in a neighborhood area, or attend a musical concert. Attention might be called to a magazine article or a book that is worth reading.

Education for the worthy use of leisure does not necessarily mean adding additional courses to the already crowded curriculum. Present offerings can be taught with an enthusiasm that will inspire a desire for leisure use of the skills and knowledges of any subject.

[3] Martin H. Neumeyer and Esther S. Neumeyer, *Leisure and Recreation*, 3rd ed. (New York: The Ronald Press Company, 1958), p. 71. Reprinted by permission.

Provisions for co-curricular activities

Extracurricular activities, more recently termed "co-curricular" by many educators, are becoming more and more a part of the regular curricular program. The fences that once separated these activities from the formal classroom experiences have gradually disappeared because of the recognition of the educative values inherent in such offerings. In the past, extracurricular activities were tolerated and considered a frill by teachers and public alike. Today we find that activities such as clubs, orchestras, plays, debates, and other co-curricular activities are being accepted as a part of the regular school program and often are conducted on school time rather than relegated exclusively to after-school hours.

Almost all subject fields reap benefits from their corresponding clubs and activities because of the motivation they offer to the regular classroom program. In an informal setting, classroom knowledges and skills may be further utilized, interests stimulated, and hobbies initiated. In order that co-curricular activities may merit curricular status, school administrators must see that these activities are worthwhile educational experiences. Teachers must be oriented to the values and importance of these activities and be encouraged to provide creative leadership so that the aims of this portion of the curriculum will be realized.

Co-curricular activities are varied in their scope and contribute to the physical, mental, and spiritual growth of youth. Some of the activities that might be included are: musical activities (bands, orchestras, choral groups, and operettas), class plays, science clubs and fairs, conservation and nature clubs, intramural programs, dances, reading clubs, athletic programs for boys and girls, 4-H Clubs, Hi-Ys, Y-Teens, student government activities, journalistic activities, and convocations.

Offering of leadership and facilities for free time of students

With the trend toward school consolidation, it has become necessary for many schools to provide children with bus transportation. Most children find it necessary to spend the noon hours in school cafeterias or nearby lunch rooms. During this period of free time, many school administrators find it feasible to offer recreation programs under competent leadership. Gymnasiums and multi-purpose rooms are opened for dancing and physical activities; movies are presented, and lounge and reading rooms are provided as a part of a well-rounded noon-hour program for youth.

Recess time offers another period when organized or supervised play is desirable. Teachers must provide the necessary supervision of playgrounds when the children flood onto them. Playground equipment should be provided, and organized activities should be initiated to provide stimulating experiences during this period. During rainy days, organized indoor games and other activities should be provided in the gymnasium or classroom.

During vacations and after school hours, schools are often opened as community centers, with a wide variety of recreation activities offered. School playgrounds, under the direction of qualified leaders, provide excellent outlets for worthwhile outdoor recreation experiences. Playgrounds are operated after school, during weekends, and during summer vacations by school authorities in many cities.

Planning, developing, and providing school facilities for community use

Public schools no longer have the mandate to serve only children of certain ages. As a social agency, the school is obligated to serve the whole community. In most cities, schools possess valuable areas and facilities, strategically located, that can be utilized for recreation as well as for education. The extended use of the school plant beyond school hours and school needs provides for maximum use of expensive facilities and supplements the existing park and recreation facilities in the community. In order that effective use of these facilities can be made by both school and community groups, with a minimum of money and problems, cooperative planning and development of school areas and facilities must be undertaken. The use of school facilities by citizen groups or community agencies does not necessitate building expensive "palaces" or elaborate additional facilities. It does mean that schools must be properly designed, zoned, and adapted, and that sufficient area must be acquired so that the school plant can be utilized to its maximum. With this type of action, duplicate facilities need not be developed in the same neighborhood at additional expense to the community.

Planning school buildings for community use. School-city cooperation in planning is a must. To facilitate cooperative planning, mutually accepted policies should be established. Policies should cover the purchase of land, planning and designing the building and playground area, and the joint use of the school plant. Many cities have benefited from school-city joint planning. Richmond, Virginia, is one example where the schools and recreation department have practiced a cooperative approach to school and recreation development. For all new school buildings, the recreation department requested that the following be provided:

1. Outside entrances to wash rooms, cafeteria, auditorium, gymnasium, library, shops or any other special facilities. Also an arrangement whereby inside doors can be locked securely when outside entrances are in use and access through building is not desired. Separate buildings for auditorium and gymnasium are desired.

2. "Cut offs" (fire door or folding gates) so that cafeteria, gymnasium, auditorium, and six class rooms (more or less as needed), preferably on first floor, can be heated and used separately.

3. Folding gates or suitable arrangements that will prevent access to the entire building when only a portion is needed.

4. Movable tables and chairs in cafeteria and class rooms which are used for community purposes.

5. Storage space for recreation supplies, games and equipment—in the form of extra closets in class room or a separate storage room, conveniently located.

6. Softwood floors on auditorium stages; dressing rooms and storage space arranged in a practical manner for drama presentations.

7. Arts and crafts with running water, work tables, good lighting, and storage closets or cabinets.

8. Entrance lounge and check room.

9. Office space for the staff of large centers.[4]

The extent to which public schools begin to incorporate the ideas, already in practice in Richmond and other cities, will determine whether schools can effectively serve as indoor recreation centers.

Indoor centers. The indoor-center movement has proved to be popular in many communities. Schools are used afternoons (after school), evenings, and Saturdays for varied purposes. The municipal recreation department operates several types of indoor centers, which include:

ELEMENTARY CENTERS. Normally open several afternoons each week and on Saturday mornings and held in elementary school buildings, these centers offer a wide variety of activities geared to the needs of elementary children. Good leaders provide the stimulant to the program.

JUNIOR OR SENIOR HIGH CENTERS. School buildings are often opened evenings (Friday and Saturdays) and on Saturdays for junior- and senior-high youth. If several rooms are available, such as the shop, gymnasium, lounge, multi-purpose room, cafeteria, and classrooms, the municipal recreation department can offer a varied recreation program.

ADULT CENTERS. When school buildings are used for adult recreation activities only, they are called adult centers. High-school buildings offer the most appropriate facilities for adult use; however, some cities use their junior high and elementary schools for the adult-center program. Gymnasiums, shops, classrooms, or auditoriums provide places for class instruction, club meetings, or municipal league play. Adult centers are most often scheduled on weekday evenings. The role of the school for adult education or recreation is discussed later in this chapter.

ATHLETIC CENTERS. School gymnasiums are used extensively for athletic instruction and league play. Often the only facility of a school building that is used by the municipal recreation department or other recreation agencies is the gymnasium. An athletic center limits the use of the school to the gymnasium and for sports only.

[4] George D. Butler, "School-City Cooperation," *Recreation*, XLVI-A, No. 2 (1953), 101–102.

SOCIAL DANCE CENTERS. The opening of school buildings for square dance and social dance groups is frequent. Under these circumstances, the only parts of the building used would be the gymnasium, multi-purpose room, or cafeteria. The types of indoor-center programs vary from city to city. Some cities use their school buildings only for athletic leagues; others conduct dances for their youth. Where the need is evident, schools should be used to supplement the recreation program of the neighborhood.

The indoor-center program involves the municipal recreation department's use of school buildings. The use of school plants by civic and community groups is practiced almost everywhere. Boy Scouts, Girl Scouts, YMCAs, YWCAs, and other youth-serving agencies often use schools for their programs. Churches and industries use school facilities for recreation programs for their constituents. The over-all use of schools by the community makes a valuable contribution to the total community recreation program.

Hints for successful operation. The use of schools for indoor recreation centers is not without its problems. In far too many cities, public schools, especially the older ones, are not designed for community use. This often means that the community-used facilities are not zoned off from the rest of the school; most schools report that storage space is at a premium or nonexistent. School personnel frown upon outsiders using "their" classrooms and gymnasiums. If recreation administrations are to plan and operate indoor-center programs successfully, the following suggestions merit consideration.

1. INTERPRET PROGRAMS TO PERSONS INVOLVED. Recreation officials need to interpret to all school personnel recreation in general, as well as the particular indoor-center program. The manner in which each schoolroom will be used should be discussed. In turn, recreation leaders who are a part of the indoor-center program should understand school people and their problems. They must understand the over-all use of the school building, of which the recreation use is only a part. Efforts should be made to establish good working relations with all school personnel. Dual use of facilities demands good human relations. Careful interpretation of, orientation to, and consideration of the objectives of both the school and the recreation agency decrease sources of difficulty.

2. ESTABLISH DEFINITE POLICIES. Establishment of a clear agreement on policies is basic. The policies should be formulated in writing and distributed to both school and recreation personnel concerned with the operation.

3. ADAPT SCHOOL BUILDINGS FOR COMMUNITY USE. Since a large majority of school buildings are not designed for community use, recreation administrators will find it necessary to adapt existing school plants. Gates may be strategically installed in order to zone the building. Portable cabinets for

storage and portable bulletin boards for public-relations purposes can be developed. Portable wardrobes can be placed in the halls.

4. PROVIDE GOOD LEADERSHIP. Leadership is important to any community center or recreation program. In using another agency's building, leaders play an even more crucial role. Many departments operate on the premise that no schoolroom shall be open to the recreation program unless a leader, paid or volunteer, is present in the room or gymnasium. Employment of school personnel as a part of the indoor-center staff is considered essential by some administrators.

5. MAKE APPROPRIATE USE OF EACH FACILITY. The misuse of various school facilities has been one of the main problems of dual use. Each room should be carefully studied to determine whether the room should be used as a part of the indoor-center program and, if so, for what purposes. Craft activities in regular classrooms may create as great a hazard as a basketball game in the library.

6. LEAVE THE SCHOOL IN AS GOOD, IF NOT BETTER, CONDITION THAN YOU FOUND IT. This will pay dividends.

Conducting the community recreation program

In some instances, the public schools have proved to be the logical agency to organize and conduct the recreation program for the entire community. This situation is particularly true in smaller communities that cannot afford to operate a separate recreation agency. Under such circumstances, civic leaders normally look to the school to conduct the program. In many smaller cities, schools administer a part-time or summer recreation program utilizing school facilities and leadership.

Outstanding examples can be given of school authorities administering full time community recreation programs in large cities. Milwaukee, Wisconsin, is perhaps the best example. Milwaukee's program is administered by a superintendent who has the title Assistant Superintendent of Schools in Charge of Municipal Recreation and Adult Education. A complete recreation staff takes over the school plant at the end of the school day, and all resources are available for the recreation program.

Schools can be successful in this function if school authorities fully accept recreation as a significant aspect of community life and have a broad concept of recreation. They also must realize that teachers or physical educators do not necessarily have the requisite training or philosophy to assume the direction of such a program. With the provision of qualified leaders, adequate financing, and full executive support, public schools can be of real service to the community in conducting the recreation program.

Helping initiate or cooperating with community recreation programs

Public schools have an important function in integrating their leadership, physical resources, and program with the various agencies in the community providing recreation services. It has already been mentioned that schools can make available their valuable areas and facilities to the total community. School authorities can and should take the initiative in establishing a municipal recreation program if the need exists. School personnel are one of the key sources of community leadership. Teachers and principals should be represented on recreation boards or commissions, advisory committees, planning commissions, and community-wide civic organizations. Also, teachers offer tremendous resources of skills and leadership that can be of valuable service to the community recreation programs in either a paid or volunteer capacity.

In far too many cities, competition for a child's time and interests exists between the school and other leisure agencies. It is important that the various leisure offerings be correlated so that the community and the child can receive maximum benefits from the total community resources.

Outdoor Education

The outdoor-education movement and especially one of its components, school camping, are in their infancy. More and more school leaders are recognizing the values of outdoor education and how direct experiences in the out-of-doors can achieve the accepted objectives of education. Simply stated, outdoor education includes those guided experiences in the out-of-doors that utilize the natural resources in the area. It is generally recognized that some things in the curriculum can best be learned in an outdoor setting. Teachers find it effective to take their children around the block to study the trees indigenous to the area, to a local or state park for a nature jaunt, or on a field trip to observe and study plants, animals, or water resources.

School camping is that phase of outdoor education that involves living in the out-of-doors. Schools generally lease existing camps found in state parks or those operated by private agencies. Boys and girls, most often from the fifth or sixth grades, spend a week at camp during the fall or spring semesters. A part of the everyday living in camp brings to life activities related to science, geography, animals, weather, botany, conservation, plants and wild flowers, and other subjects found in the school curriculums.

Recreation for Adults

The public school should utilize its resources not only for the education of youth but also for the vocational and avocational needs of the adults in the community. Because a person's urge for personal growth never ceases, the school has a challenge to meet the wide needs and desires of the adult population. No definite lines can be drawn between adult education and adult recreation. People who seek to develop knowledges and proficiency so that they can equip themselves for a job, or better equip themselves for their present occupations, attend adult classes primarily for vocational reasons and not for enjoyment. On the other hand, there are large numbers of adults who seek cultural and recreational activities. They are the people who, according to Lies,[5]

have deep longings for creative expression, for extending their mental horizons, wanting to get equipped to understand more of the world about them including the world of affairs; they want more culture; they wish to pursue hobbies.

Schools and recreation agencies can offer a wide variety of opportunities to meet the needs of adults. Some of the adult activities conducted by the Department of Municipal Recreation and Adult Education of Milwaukee are illustrated by the program offerings of one of the department's social centers—the Wilbur Wright Center.

Arts and Crafts
  Art Crafts
  Metalcraft and Jewelry
  Painting and Sketching
  Rosemaking
  Woodworking

Home and Household
  Cake Decorating I
  Cake Decorating II
  Knitting
  Millinery I
  Millinery II
  Party Foods and Favors
  Sewing and Tailoring I
  Sewing and Tailoring II
  Skillet Skills—Men
  Lawns and Gardens

Family Living
  Just for You
    Boys and Fathers
    Girls and Mothers

Recreation and Health
  Bridge I
  Bridge II
  Bridge III
  Sheepshead
  Ballroom Dance I
  Latin American Dance I
  Latin American Dance II
  Round Dance
  Square Dance
  Chorus (Mixed)
  Ladies' Fun and Figure Gym
  Men's Indoor Sports and Gym
  Modern Dance Exercise
  Camera Art
  Film Skills
  Golf

General
  Business English
  Civil Defense
  Driver Education
  Effective Speech
  First Aid
  French for Travel
  Investment Planning
  Spanish for Travel

[5] Eugene T. Lies, *The New Leisure Challenges the Schools* (Washington, D.C.: National Education Association, 1933), p. 195.

Recreation Role of Colleges and Universities

Institutions of higher learning have varied responsibilities related to the field of recreation. Their role is concerned primarily with meeting the leisure needs of students, preparing leaders for the profession, conducting research, and providing consultant service, publications, and other assistance to communities within the state.

Campus recreation

The college or university must take the place of the home and community in providing leisure activities for its students. College unions offer varied recreation opportunities, which include theaters, snack bar facilities, club rooms, bowling alleys, game rooms, lounge and reading facilities, and many others, the number depending upon the size of the union and the university. Sororities, fraternities, and housing units normally have social or recreation committees, who plan for the needs of their residents. Ample opportunities are offered on most campuses in the form of convocations, operas, plays, concerts, symphonies, lectures, and other cultural activities for the students. Athletic contests and intramurals are conducted to satisfy the active physical needs or spectator interests. A student must learn to balance his recreational pursuits with relation to his academic program.

Preparation of professional leaders

Professionally trained leaders provide the lifeline of any profession. The demand for trained persons in recreation has risen sharply in recent years, and colleges and universities have initiated curriculums in recreation to meet the challenge. It is not necessary or feasible that all institutions of higher learning engage in this enterprise. There should be colleges in each section of the country that establish curriculums based upon acceptable standards that will assure the development of well-rounded professional personnel. Schools that do establish recreation curriculums should possess adequate facilities, qualified instructional personnel, a varied course selection, and adequate community resources. Chapter 15 provides a more detailed discussion of professional training.

If elementary and secondary teachers are to educate for the worthy use of leisure, it is important that our teacher-training institutions incorporate into their curriculums courses in recreation philosophy. Legislation for such strengthening of curriculums is already in existence in some state certification requirements.

Research in recreation

There is a great void in the recreation profession in terms of quality research. Because recreation is new and broad in scope, much of the progress of this movement has been based on research in related disciplines such as sociology, government, education, and physical education. It is only by increased research of the highest quality that the recreation profession can move forward and develop on a sound foundation. Institutions of higher learning are in an advantageous position because of their professionally trained staff and resources to engage in research that would add sound fundamental knowledge to the recreation profession.

Community service

Most state universities offer valuable service to communities within their state. It is through extension classes and correspondence courses that individuals on the job can further their education in the field. Conferences, institutes, workshops, and special leadership training courses are conducted by many of the universities. Such offerings are designed to aid in the training of professional and volunteer leaders. Colleges also provide valuable services to recreation and its leaders in communities through the preparation of printed materials, through film libraries, and through consultant services. It has been said that a state university extends its influence and assistance to all communities within the borders of the state. Colleges and universities with this philosophy can provide valuable services to the field of recreation by the many activities mentioned.

Education and the Challenge

The little red school house, with its meager facilities and limited curriculum, has vanished. Education has grown with the changing times.

Fig. 9   *Great Lakes Park Training Institute, Pokagon State Park, Indiana*

Although other social agencies have also evidenced dynamic growth, education for enlightened and enriched living will inevitably be anchored in the school program. That education for leisure must absorb an increasing portion of the school years is mandatory, if educational institutions are to meet their objective of "preparation for complete living." The fact that educating for leisure is not solely the responsibility of the school is undeniable. The church, the home, the recreation agency must accept their obligations. Education for the arts of leisure is, in essence, "everybody's business." Unfortunately, what is everybody's business often become nobody's business. The school is in an excellent position to condition future attitudes toward leisure, to stimulate action, and to cooperate with those community agencies that are concerned with leisure opportunities.

America is fast becoming a nation of individuals who are spending the greater portion of their lives not in work, but in leisure choices. Recreation and education must move cooperatively so that those choices will not degrade and dissipate but instead will enrich and enlarge the potential for the ultimate in living for present and future societies.

SUGGESTED REFERENCES

Conduct of School Community Centers. New York: National Recreation Association, 1946.

Education for Leisure. Washington, D.C.: American Association for Health, Physical Education and Recreation, 1957.

Leisure and the Schools. Washington, D.C.: American Association for Health, Physical Education and Recreation, 1961.

Lies, Eugene T., *The New Leisure Challenges the Schools.* New York: National Recreation Association, 1933.

Olson, Edward G., ed., *School and Community.* Englewood Cliffs, N.J.: Prentice-Hall, Inc., 1954.

Outdoor Education Through Park-School Programs. Wheeling, West Va.: American Institute of Park Executives, n.d.

Plunke, Harold H., *Community Uses of Public School Facilities.* New York: King's Crown Press, 1951.

Recreation for Community Living. Chicago: The Athletic Institute, 1952.

The Roles of Public Education in Recreation. Burlingame, Calif.: The California Association for Health, Physical Education and Recreation, 1960.

"The manner in which the hours of freedom are spent determines, no less than labor or war, the moral worth of a nation."

MAETERLINCK

6

National Voluntary Youth-Membership Organizations

Today numerous nongovernmental organizations sponsor leisure activities for children and youth. The rise, growth, and development of most of these agencies have occurred during the past century, particularly since the year 1910. In many communities, these voluntary agencies were the first groups to establish recreation programs for young people; and tax support was not given such programs until their worth was well proven. Today, in most communities, the tax-supported agency and the voluntary agency work side by side, each fulfilling its particular function in providing for the leisure hours of youth.

Nature of Organizations Serving Youth

In this chapter no effort can be made to discuss or even list more than just a few of the overwhelming number of organizations that offer recrea-

Fig. 10 *Voluntary Agencies Serving the Varied Interests of Youth*

tion for youth in the United States. Religious, political, social, civic, fraternal, labor, conservation, and veterans' societies and clubs sometimes sponsor, finance, and direct programs for young people. Organizations that pursue special fields, such as art, music, dramatics, nature, and sports, further their interests through work with young people. The three major faiths—Catholic, Protestant, and Jewish—are active in recreation as well as religious programs for young people. There are other organizations that concentrate upon services to special groups, such as neglected, underprivileged, handicapped, or delinquent children and older youth.

Some of the organizations that offer recreation as a means of achieving their purposes would describe themselves as "group-work" or "character-building" organizations or as health, education, or welfare agencies. Their primary purposes in many cases are developing personality, instilling certain beliefs and ideals, or retaining loyalties to the sponsoring group. There are two important types of youth-serving organizations: first, those that include youth in their membership; and second, adult groups that give assistance to youth programs by providing financial help, seeking special legislation, sponsoring community planning, or by some other means. This chapter is devoted to the major national voluntary youth-membership organizations. Other youth-serving organizations are considered in various other chapters in this book.

The large, nationally constituted, youth-membership organizations are in great measure a twentieth-century development. These groups have evolved in response to adults' recognition of their responsibilities to youth in a changing society and to the youths' needs for adventure, companionship, social participation, and self-expression.

All of the major youth-membership organizations are open to young people regardless of race or religion. The fees vary, but most of them are extremely low so that, in most cases, cost need not prevent membership. Although the objectives are educational, the methods are recreational. The "play way" of learning is employed. The youth organizations base their programs on the assumption that children's personal and social development can be promoted through their participation in activities, voluntarily chosen, taking place in peer groups under adult leaders.

In certain foreign countries national youth programs are established, encouraged, financed, and dominated by government. In the United States, however, youth services have developed on a voluntary basis, giving young people the opportunity to select from a number of organizations those to which they wish to belong. Financial support has come, not from taxes, but from contributions. Leadership has likewise been, to a large extent, voluntary; organizations have depended upon this leadership for their very existence. As a result, these organizations are close to the pulse and thinking of the communities in which they exist. They are "voluntary" in a fourfold sense—in origin, in membership, in finance, and in leadership.

Common Objectives

The Educational Policies Committee of the National Education Association has stated, as desirable outcomes for a growing child, the following: self-realization, desirable human relationships, economic efficiency, and civic responsibility. Each of the major youth-membership organizations is concerned with these goals, though they are variously expressed and emphasized. Here are some of the special objectives that these organizations have in common.

Personality development. Personality may be thought of as the sum of one's social, physical, and mental attributes. It consists of physical features, intelligence, emotional make-up, social drives, character, philosophy of life, social expression, and the concept of one's self.

Character development. Character is one of the aspects of personality. Good character is indicated by honesty, courage, perseverance, self-reliance, self-control, self-restraint, ambition, enthusiasm, good sportsmanship, unselfishness, kindness, and similar qualities. Poor character is revealed by lack of dependability, dishonesty, selfishness, and lack of concern for others.

Social integration. A well-integrated person will make and keep friends, adjust to others, work within groups, function democratically, and respect the rights of others, particularly those different from himself.

Development of new skills and interests. The youth-serving groups introduce young people to a variety of interests, including those that are vocational in nature, those that give service to others, and those that enrich cultural life.

Constructive use of leisure. Through guidance, education, and participation, high standards for the use of leisure are encouraged. An effort is made to instill leisure attitudes and teach skills with a carry-over value to adult life.

Physical health, growth, and development. Good health habits and healthful activities have a place in the program. Cleanliness, adequate rest, and adequate diets as well as participation in wholesome activities, indoors and out, are stressed.

Spiritual growth. Though the major youth-membership organizations are nondenominational, all are rooted in certain spiritual concepts. Many local units are sponsored by religious organizations.

Development of Youth-Membership Organizations

Even among ancient primitive societies, various types of organizations for boys and girls were to be found. These ranged from temporary informal groups to highly organized ones with religious and educational functions. The origin of American youth organizations is, however, a comparatively recent phenomenon. Of the seven largest youth-membership organizations, four were established after 1909. The remaining three trace their origins to the nineteenth century.

Origin and development

During the last part of the nineteenth century, industrialization brought with it serious city slum conditions, child labor, long hours of work, and high rates of crime and delinquency. The establishment of the Young Men's Christian Association, the Young Women's Christian Association, and the first Boys' Clubs can be attributed to attempts to alleviate the unwholesome conditions of crowded city living.

Four additional important national youth organizations came into existence in the United States from 1910 to 1914: the Boy Scouts, the Girl Scouts, Camp Fire Girls, and the 4-H Clubs. It is significant that no major youth-membership organization has been established since 1914 but that the existing organizations have altered their programs to keep pace with the changing interests and needs of youth.

The organizations today

The voluntary youth-membership organizations form an accepted part of the pattern of American life today. Children in almost every part of America have the opportunity to belong, and the percentage of children participating increases year by year. In many homes, membership in one of these organizations is considered an essential part of growing up, like going to church or school. The participation of adult volunteers, either in administration or in direct leadership, continues to expand. The numbers of professional leaders have grown rapidly, and means of financing these agencies is becoming more stable and more firmly entrenched as part of community fund drives.

It is impossible to state what percentage of young people are members. Membership figures are misleading, since "membership" may range from a brief and casual contact to intensive, long-term participation. Moreover, many young people belong to two or more national organizations as well as to locally organized groups. For example, a study of adolescent Boys' Club members showed that six out of ten belonged to other organizations, including local clubs, church groups, and national activity clubs.[1] Interpretation of membership figures is further complicated by the frequent inclusion of both child and adult members. Communities differ greatly in the extent of membership in the various organizations. In the crowded sections of

[1] *Needs and Interests of Adolescent Boys' Club Members* (New York: Boys' Clubs of America, 1960), p. 88.

certain large cities, membership in certain organizations may be relatively small, whereas in the suburbs of the same cities the membership may be considerably above 50 percent of the children of eligible age. Such differences may be attributed in part to the way children from various backgrounds respond to the offering of the youth agencies.

The agencies considered in the pages that follow are: Boy Scouts of America, Boys' Clubs, Camp Fire Girls, 4-H Clubs, Girl Scouts, Girls Clubs, Young Men's Christian Association, and Young Women's Christian Association. These eight were selected for discussion from the great numbers of youth organizations because of their large membership, rounded programs, influence, and widespread acceptance as a part of community life in the United States. They are open to young people regardless of race and religion and, with the exception of 4-H Clubs, are financed primarily from voluntary gifts. Youth-membership organizations that are restricted in membership or in fields of interest and organizations that sponsor youth programs but do not include young people in their membership are considered elsewhere in this book.

Boy Scouts of America

The Boy Scouts of America, the nation's largest organization for boys, extends to every portion of the country. There are over five million members in the United States, about one fourth of whom are adults serving in leadership capacities. Of the boy members, about 1.9 million are Cubs; 1.6 million, Boy Scouts; and 270,000, Explorers. Total membership from the inception of the organization to the end of 1960 has numbered 33 million persons.

A half century of Scouting

The origins of Scouting are both English and American. Preceding the Boy Scouts in the United States was an organization known as the Woodcraft Indians, founded in 1902 by Ernest Thompson Seton. This was the first boys' organization to emphasize woodcraft and camping skills. When the Boy Scouts were established in the United States, Seton cooperated in the movement, and the Woodcraft Indians were disbanded.

The Boy Scouts themselves were first organized in England in 1908 by Sir Robert Baden-Powell (later Lord Baden-Powell). His experiences in the Boer War had shown him the great deficiencies of the English soldiers in outdoor knowledge and skills. After the war, he was determined to help boys secure what he considered to be essential training in the out-of-doors. Thus Scouting was born. When William D. Boyce, a publisher from Chicago, visited England in 1909, he learned of the Boy Scouts from Baden-Powell and was deeply impressed. He enthusiastically brought the idea back to America, and in 1910 the Boy Scouts of America was founded. It was granted a federal charter by Congress in 1916.

The new movement grew rapidly. In 1914, there were about 112,000 Scouts. The one million mark was passed in 1935, the two million mark in 1946, and the five million mark in 1959. The movement has spread throughout the world. There is today an international structure composed of about 60 countries, with headquarters in Canada. Representatives from each nation form the council.

Structure of Scouting

The national council is the governing body of the Boy Scouts. It is composed of honorary members, members at large, and local council representatives. Its work is carried out through officers, an executive board, committees, and a professional staff at the national headquarters in New Brunswick, New Jersey. Twelve geographical regions, professionally staffed, help the national council carry out its functions. At the local level, Scouting is under the jurisdiction of a citizens' council which works through voluntary committees and employed personnel. It operates under charter from the national council.

Scouting is open to boys of all religions and races. Though nondenominational, it encourages its members to observe religious lives, and about half of its approximately 130,000 units are sponsored by religious institutions. Another one third are sponsored by civic groups and about one fifth by schools and parent-teachers' associations. Sponsoring groups frequently provide meeting places. The program is designed as a "game," in which the boys participate because they find fun and excitement. The game has the serious purpose of developing character, health, mental alertness, manual skills, self-reliance, and the ability to work with others.

Cubs, Scouts, and Explorers. There are three main divisions of Scouting: Cub Scouting, Boy Scouting, and Exploring.

CUB SCOUTING. Launched in 1930, Cub Scouting passed Boy Scouting in membership by 1955 and now claims 200,000 more members than the Boy Scouts (excluding Explorers). A boy can become a Cub Scout at eight years of age. The program is home-centered, and many of the projects are such that the whole family can enjoy them together. Mothers and fathers help the boys learn and pass simple "achievements" (twelve for each rank), through which they progress from "Bobcats" to "Wolf Cub" Scouts, to "Bears" and then to "Lions." "Arrow points" are awarded for additional work in 23 elective fields, including science, dramatics, construction, social activities, music, photography, animals, conservation, cooking, and sports. The work in the elective fields is adapted to different age levels. At age ten-and-a-half, a boy can begin the Webelos program. Meeting requirements for the Webelos badge prepares a boy for Scouting.

A "Den" is a small neighborhood group of Cub Scouts who normally play together and who meet weekly with one of the mothers (a "Den Mother") and a Boy Scout (a "Den Chief"). A Cub Scout is elected "Denner" to help the Den Chief, and a "Den Dad" is also chosen. Several Dens come together with parents for a monthly "Pack" meeting led by a "Cubmaster."

BOY SCOUTING. At eleven, a boy may join a Scout Troop, which is composed of smaller units called "Patrols." A boy progresses from Tenderfoot to Second Class to First Class. He can work for merit badges in over one hundred subjects. The games, stunts, outings, and special projects, though engaged in for pleasure, all have underlying educational values. The importance of teamwork, democratic procedures, and the development of leadership are stressed.

EXPLORING. For fourteen to seventeen year olds, Exploring offers an advanced program in outdoor adventure, service, social activities, personal fitness, citizenship, and vocational explorations. Members enroll in Explorer Posts, Air Explorer squadrons, and Sea Explorer ships. Attention is given to special-interest groups. A revised Exploring program was embarked upon in 1958 after an extensive study of adolescent boys made by the Institute of Social Research of the University of Michigan and by the Research Service of the National Council at the request of the Boy Scouts.

Success of Scouting

The reasons for Scouting's success are numerous.

1. It is based largely on outdoor adventure, which captures the imagination of the growing boy—particularly in a society that is becoming more and more urbanized.

2. The careful outlining of the program has contributed markedly to the growth of Scouting by making it possible for relatively untrained volunteers to succeed as leaders. The handbooks and detailed manuals of procedure are easy to follow. The system of step-by-step progression enables a leader to work with his boys without having had a great deal of experience himself. Therefore, Scouting spreads on the basis of volunteer initiative without a large financial investment.

3. The award system is intended to give each boy goals to strive for and a definite sense of accomplishment. His badges are tangible evidence of his achievements.

4. The program offers variety. The opportunities in Scouting are so numerous that there is something to challenge almost every boy, whatever his interests and abilities.

5. Finally, the leaders of Scouting have not been content with their program, even though it was successful from the start. It has been frequently tested, studied, and up-dated to meet the changing needs and interests of youth and to hold the maximum number of boys. Scouting

today is a powerful influence in the thinking and acting of millions of men and boys, an achievement which reflects the ability, flexibility, and confidence of its leaders.

Boys' Clubs of America

City-dwelling boys, aged 8 to 20, from low-income families, inadequate homes, and poor neighborhoods are the special concern of the Boys' Clubs. The large-city clubs are located in the districts of greatest need, such as those in which population is most dense or the incidence of juvenile delinquency highest. The small-community Boys' Clubs reach boys from all classes of society, inasmuch as many small communities lack other forms of recreation for boys.

Background of Boys' Clubs

Boys' Clubs were established in New England in the 1860's by groups of people who recognized a need for a nonsectarian organization providing after-school and evening activities and leadership for less privileged boys. The first club was opened in 1860 in Hartford, Connecticut. The early clubs were established chiefly in big cities, and even today 99 percent of the members are urban residents. In order to provide services to existing clubs and to help communities start new clubs, a national organization, the Boys' Clubs of America, was founded in 1906. It was chartered by Congress in 1956. There are today about 600 Boys' Clubs with over 600,000 boy members.

An open door for boys

The purpose of the Boys' Clubs of America is "to promote the social, educational, vocational, health, and character development of boys." The program by which attempts are made to achieve this purpose is not a national pre-arranged one, such as the Boy Scouts employ. Although program ideas are offered through the national office, each club sets up its own program in the way it deems most serviceable to its members.

A building is necessary to a Boys' Club program, since an important policy of a Boys' Club is to be open every weekday during hours when boys have leisure so that no boy needs to seek activity and companionship in the street. In some large communities a central building and smaller neighborhood branch clubs are maintained. Boys' Clubs usually contain gamerooms, libraries, gymnasiums, locker rooms, shower baths, shops, classrooms, and group rooms. Swimming pools, playgrounds, athletic fields, kitchens, craft rooms, quiet rooms for studying and reading, and auditoriums are considered desirable.

Since the maintenance of health is an important part of Boys' Club work, medical and dental examinations are often provided. Pre-vocational training and guidance are stressed. Reading, opportunity for study, dramatics, music, Boy Scouts, group clubs, and other interests may also be included. Day, overnight, and resident camps are conducted. Counseling with boys on their individual problems and needs is considered a valuable service of the Boys' Clubs.

The National Council, made up of representatives of each autonomous member club, is the policy-making body of the Boys' Club of America. The National Council elects officers and members of the Board of Directors, who are responsible for the operation of the organization. Seven regional offices have field staffs to promote new clubs and assist existing ones. The Boys' Clubs, with their "open-door" policy and low membership fees, fill a definite niche in the youth services of the cities. A Boys' Club is open when boys have free time and are looking for something to do. The club thereby serves to a certain extent as a substitute home for boys whose home lives are unhappy, unwholesome, or in other ways unsatisfying.

Camp Fire Girls

Around the fires of a camp in Maine in the early years of the twentieth century evolved many of the ideas that became the program of the Camp Fire Girls, founded in 1910. Dr. and Mrs. Luther Halsey Gulick, the founders, had tested their theories with their own children at home, in schools, and at their summer camp. The organization was incorporated in 1912. Today there are over a half million members in about 400 units throughout the country. The movement has spread to Great Britain, France, Germany, China, Spain, Holland, Mexico, and South America.

Nature and purpose

The purposes of the Camp Fire Girls, as stated in the Articles of Incorporation as amended in 1955, are:

To make available to all girls for daily living an educational-recreational program which shall include activities designed to encourage the development of spiritual and ethical values; love of home and family; pride in woman's traditional qualities—tenderness, affection, and skill in human relationships; love of country and the practice of responsible citizenship; the capacity for fun and friendship; the formation of healthful habits; initiative, self-reliance and satisfaction in work; interests and hobbies to be enjoyed alone and with others; the appreciation of nature and skill in outdoor living; the ability to see beauty, romance, and adventure in the common things of life.

Based on the philosophy that a girl's experiences as she matures affect her entire life, Camp Fire Girls provides opportunities for enjoyable and worthy leisure activities through which girls may develop into alert and responsible women. Emphasis is laid on self-realization and appreciation of aesthetic values. Members are drawn from girls from seven years of age through high school and from every race, religion, and economic background.

Camp Fire Girls presents a practical training in citizenship. Girls are encouraged to take an active interest in the affairs of their community, to respect the rights of others, to obey the laws of the land, and to give service to their country. Services to local charitable institutions are common parts of Camp Fire Girls' activities. Girls are stimulated to make international friendships through writing "pen-friend" letters to foreign lands, assisting in drives conducted by international relief agencies, and the like. In addition to the basic program, special themes are chosen nationally to receive special emphasis. For example, the Golden Jubilee theme, "She Cares. . . . Do You?," was a two-and-one-half year project devoted to conservation, during which 2 million trees were planted, areas beautified, wildlife improvements made, erosion-control measures taken, workshops held, displays made, and publicity distributed.

Camp Fire Girls have camped since their origin—a time when camping for girls was a novel thing. Camping is not only a summer activity but a year-round one. Both resident and day camps are maintained. While learning about swimming, dramatics, cookouts, handcrafts, and nature lore, a camper learns to take care of herself and to work for the good of the whole camp community.

Four age groupings

Until 1962, the Camp Fire Girls' program was divided into three groups: Bluebirds, Camp Fire Girls, and Horizon Clubs. As a result of study and research, the program was revised as follows:

Blue Birds. The youngest girls, aged 7 and 8 years (second or third grades in school), comprise Blue Birds. The program, organized in 1913, consists largely of creative play activities suitable to the younger children and planned to help them adjust to their environment, both physical and social. For most girls who join, Blue Birds is the first opportunity to be a part of a voluntary group. Simple handcrafts and trips to help them know their community are included among their activities. Blue Birds meet weekly in homes, schools, churches, or other places made available by sponsors. Not more than 20 girls, with their leader and assistant leader, comprise the Blue Bird group.

Camp Fire Girls. Camp Fire Girls are in the fourth, fifth, and sixth grades or are aged 9, 10, and 11 years. The program is based on the Seven Crafts: home, outdoors, creative arts, frontiers (of science), business, sports and games, and citizenship. The law of the Camp Fire Girls, which is a distillation of its objectives, is similar in some respects to the Boy Scout and Girl Scout laws.

The program abounds with symbolism, idealism, and beauty. American Indian lore, which was imaginatively used in the Gulick camp, is woven into the program. The girls choose Indian names and make extensive use of Indian symbols. Members progress through the ranks of Trail Seeker, Wood Gatherer, Fire Maker, and Torch Bearer by working for "honors" in the seven crafts and meeting other requirements. Honor beads, a different color for each craft, are worn on the blue ceremonial jackets or Indian gowns. The Book of the Campfire Girls lists over a thousand suggestions in the Seven Crafts, so that there is leeway for individual interests, particularly in the advanced stages of the program.

Groups are led by adult "guardians" and meet weekly in groups of not more than 20 girls. Each group must have a sponsoring committee of 3 to 5 adults. The crossed logs and flame of the insigne symbolize the hearth of the home and the campfire of the outdoors. The watchword, "Wohelo," is composed of the first two letters of "work," "health," and "love."

Junior Hi Camp Fire Girls. This is a new division, established in 1962 for girls in the seventh and eighth grades. Girls in this program can achieve the rank of Group Torch Bearer and begin work on Individual Torch Bearers. They engage in activities related to the home, the arts, science, service, sports and games, outdoors, and having "fun."

Horizon Clubs. Organized in 1941 and open to girls from the ninth grade through high school, this program stresses personality development, social skills, vocational exploration, community service, and activities in which boys may also share. The members plan their own programs. Community services include such activities as working as hospital aides and doing office work for the United Fund. Dances, parties, charm courses, and camping trips are frequently included in Horizon Club activities.

Under the new program, there are no prerequisites for rank. A girl entering the program at any stage engages in activities suitable for her age even though she has not worked on ranks that younger members engage upon.

National Council

The National Council, which is the policy-making body, has under it a National Board of Directors with 10 administrative regions. The national body is financed from dues and income from publications and royalties.

Camp Fire's contribution

The development of the individual girl is the primary objective of all age groups. Through Camp Fire Girls, girls may make new friends, cultivate skills, and become both self-reliant and cooperative. The organization accentuates the importance of the distinctly feminine role, in which the woman is seen "as a strong, healthy, intelligent human being, the chief preserver of beauty, compassionate, dedicated to the preservation and enrichment of life." [2]

4-H Clubs

Though subsidized by government funds, 4-H is included here among the voluntary youth-membership organizations because, in its membership and in most of its leadership, it is truly a voluntary organization. 4-H Clubs are active in more than 3,000 counties and have about 2.5 million members. There are nearly 100,000 4-H Clubs in every state and about 400,000 volunteer leaders, trained by county agents.

A rural movement

The 4-H Clubs grew out of rural America, but their origin cannot be traced to any single group. Around 1900, in several localities, rural young people began forming groups to engage in activities to improve agriculture. Various agricultural leaders believed that one of the best ways to promote the use of scientific methods on farms and in homes was to work with youth.

Between 1901 and 1905, leaders of these groups began to meet to talk over their common aims and set up general patterns for organization and activity. Later they adopted the 4-H name and emblem. In 1914, Congress passed the Smith-Lever Act, which provided for cooperative extension work in agriculture and home economics, including what was then known as "boys' and girls' club work." The law set up a system of federal funds to be matched by the states and counties to provide financial support for the program. The 4-H programs are financed today, therefore, on a three-way basis: county, state, and federal. The local organization usually stems from the office of the county agricultural agent, and state guidance comes from the state land-grant college extension services. The Federal Extension Service of the United States Department of Agriculture gives national leadership. Two nongovernmental agencies, the National 4-H Service Committee and the National 4-H Club Foundation, assist the movement. Although no place or date can be designated as the start of the national 4-H Club movement, various states honor their own beginnings and their pioneers. The 4-H Club idea, with adaptations to meet the needs of other parts of the world, has spread to more than 50 countries. Through the International Farm Youth Exchange, young Americans may go to other countries and young people of other countries come to the United States to live and work for several months with farm families. In 1961, about 220 young people from 42 countries participated in the IFYE program.

[2] *Gift to the Nation* (New York: Camp Fire Girls, Inc., n.d.), Brochure. Reprinted by permission.

Place of volunteers in 4-H

The leadership is almost entirely volunteer. Older club members may assist as junior leaders. Leaders are trained and assisted by the county agents of the Cooperative Extension Service, who have available to them the resources of the state land-grant colleges and the United States Department of Agriculture. Leaders advise members, attend meetings, visit homes to see how projects are getting along, and accompany members to club events outside the community. County, district, and state council groups in many areas help plan and conduct the club work.

A program for farm, home, and community

The members of 4-H, who come chiefly from farms and suburbs, carry on a wide variety of projects in farming, homemaking, and community service. Among these projects are raising livestock, trees, and poultry; gardening; conserving soil; sewing; cooking; making things for the home; and working for community betterment. Any boy or girl between 10 and 21 years of age may join by agreeing to follow 4-H ideals and standards. "Learn by Doing" is the club slogan, and "To Make the Best Better" is the motto. Character development and good citizenship are long-range goals.

The club colors are green and white. The national emblem is a four-leaf clover, with a letter "H" on each leaf. The term "4-H" refers to "head," "heart," "hands," and "health."

4-H members usually run their own clubs, electing their officers, conducting their meetings, and selecting their projects. Each club drafts its own program to suit its own members and the localities in which they live. Active participation in community affairs is encouraged. Requirements for the completion of 4-H projects are flexible. The programs may include team demonstrations; judging demonstrations; special 4-H Club days; work in music appreciation and dramatics; tours and hikes; 4-H camps; special club ceremonies; and exhibits at local, county, and state fairs. Camping has increased in the 4-H program in recent years. There are special recreation leadership projects through which many club members receive recreation training.

4-H has brought enjoyable leisure activity to rural young people whose time and transportation difficulties often inhibit their membership in other groups. It has broadened the cultural horizons of its members and has been instrumental in building esteem for farm life, appreciation of the responsibilities of citizenship, and ambition for education.

Girl Scouts of the United States of America

With about three and a half million members in the United States, the Girl Scouts is by far the largest girls' youth-membership organization today. The Girl Scouts are dedicated to the "purpose of inspiring girls with the highest ideals of character, conduct, patriotism, and service that they may become happy, resourceful citizens." [3]

Origin and growth of Girl Scouting

Girl Scouting followed closely upon the heels of Boy Scouting. The Boy Scout idea had been received with such success in England that the enthusiasm spread to the girls, who demanded an organization of their own. In 1909, Miss Agnes Baden-Powell, sister of the founder of Boy Scouts, became the first president of a companion movement for girls, known as the Girl Guides. Just as Boy Scouting was brought to America by an American who had become acquainted with the movement in England, so was Girl Guiding. Juliette Gordon Low, a friend of the Baden-Powells, had led Girl Guide groups in Scotland and England. In 1912, on one of her visits to her native city of Savannah, Georgia, she organized the first Girl Guide group in the United States. In 1913, the name was changed to Girl Scouts. The organization was given a Congressional charter in 1950.

Though somewhat slower than its brother movement in getting under way, the Girl Scouts had increased membership to 5,000 by the end of 1915. By the 1930's, the Girl Scouts' membership had outstripped that of any other organization for girls. It more than doubled in the decade between 1950 and 1960, with the greatest rate of growth taking place in the Brownie program.

Girl Scouting has spread all over the world. National groups are joined in the World Association of Girl Guides and Girl Scouts, which promotes the movement throughout the world and encourages international friendship. The organization functions through a National Council, which elects a National Board. There are 12 regional branches of the national organization to carry on its work.

What is a Girl Scout?

If one were to draw a picture of the ideal Girl Scout based on the laws, slogan, and motto, one would find a girl with an outgoing personality, eager and able to assume responsibility and excelling in such virtues as loyalty, honesty, courtesy, and gentleness. The slogan, "Be Prepared," and the motto, "Do a Good Turn Daily," are identical with the slogan and motto of the Boy Scouts. The laws, like the Boy Scout Law, stress honor, loyalty, courtesy, obedience, and similar virtues.

A program adapted to each age

Girl Scouting includes girls from 7 years of age through high school, with a program adapted to the needs and interests of each age. Until September 1963, the following age groupings are to prevail:

[3] From Constitution of Girl Scouts of the U.S.A. Used by permission.

Brownie Scouts. In their brown beanies and light brown dresses, the Brownies, aged 7 through 9, are encouraged to emulate the good-natured goblins for whom they are named by helping unobtrusively around the house. Brownies meet weekly with their leaders, usually at the homes, schools, or churches. The program stresses being useful to other people, particularly family members. Games, parties, crafts, trips, and camping are all part of a Brownie's experience.

Intermediate Girl Scouts. Intermediate Scouts, for girls from ten to fourteen, are organized into troops, usually of eight to twenty-four girls, which meet weekly. Some troops are divided into small groups of six to eight members each, called patrols, with an elected leader called a patrol leader. The patrol leaders and other officers, with the adult leader, act as a Court of Honor (executive committee) to make plans for the troop. Suggestions are sent to the Court of Honor by the patrols through their leaders, so that each girl may have a voice in planning.

An Intermediate Scout joins as a "Tenderfoot" and advances through meeting certain requirements to Second Class and First Class. Additional work earns her the Curved Bar, the highest Intermediate rank, which serves as a link between Intermediate and Senior Scouting. The program activities are grouped under four headings: the home, the arts, citizenship, and the out-of-doors. Badges may be earned in eleven program fields: agriculture, arts and crafts, community life, health and safety, homemaking, international friendship, literature and dramatics, music and dancing, nature, out-of-doors, and sports and games. Badge work varies in difficulty and age interest. Some badges are designed for younger Girl Scouts, others for older. "Co-ed" activities have a part in the older Intermediate program.

Senior Girl Scouts. Senior Scouts are in high school or between fourteen and eighteen years of age. They have their own troops, distinctive uniforms, and programs. Instead of a rank-and-badges program, Senior Scouts choose a special interest on which they concentrate and name their troops accordingly. Thus we have Mariners, Wings, Trail Blazers, Explorers, and International Friendship troops. Service to others and vocational exploration are part of all troop programs but are highlighted by the Aide programs: Child Care, Hospital, Museum, Ranger, Occupational Therapy, Office, Library, Program, Public Relations, Laboratory. Boys are sometimes included in the social activities.

An updated program

It is a difficult process for a large national organization to make basic changes either in structure or program. The Girl Scouts nevertheless have kept alert to the changing needs of girls and have met these needs through frequent reexamination and revision of both their structure and their program. As a result of independently conducted research in the late 1950's [4] the entire Girl Scout program was reviewed and analyzed. Major changes based on this review were approved at the National Council meeting in St. Louis in 1960. To bring the revised program to girls, the total adult personnel is to be trained. Four new handbooks, incorporating these changes and delineating four age groups, are scheduled to be ready in September 1963.

The four new age groupings are to be as follows:

> *Brownie Girl Scouts*, aged 7 and 8 years;
> *Junior Girl Scouts*, aged 9, 10, and 11 years;
> *Cadette Girl Scouts*, aged 12, 13, and 14 years;
> *Senior Girl Scouts*, aged 15, 16, and 17 years.

There is to be no change in the fundamental elements of the Girl Scout program. The entire structure is to be streamlined, however. A major objective is to make the Girl Scout program of informal education a more effective complement to the present-day school curriculum.

Another major change now being effected in Girl Scouting is the merging of many councils and lone troops into larger councils in order that the entire country may be served more effectively. In 1960 the total number of Girl Scout councils was 1,014; 437 less than in 1950.[5]

Girls Clubs of America

A Girls Club, designed for girls from 6 years of age through their teens, is intended to supplement today's homes with training in the fundamental requisites of homemaking and motherhood during the years when little girls are impressionable enough to absorb these skills as they play. Like the Boys' Clubs, its greatest service is to children from low-income families and crowded neighborhoods.

Purpose

The main purpose of the Girls Clubs is "the encouraging of daily, out-of-school programs for girls in heavily populated areas." They are "dedicated to the belief that every girl from the age of 6 through the teens should enjoy the advantages of a wholesome recreation program devoted especially to the promotion of health, emotional security, cultural values, and community understanding." [6] The attainment of a complete, well-balanced personality is a goal sought for each girl member.

[4] Survey Research Center, Institute for Social Research, University of Michigan, *Adolescent Girls* (New York: Girl Scouts of the U.S.A., n.d.).

[5] *1960 Annual Report* (New York: Girl Scouts of the U.S.A., 1961), p. 31.

[6] *Why Girls Clubs?* (New York: Girls Clubs of America, Inc.), Brochure.

National organization

The oldest Girls Club dates from 1864. The Girls Clubs of the United States and Canada, representing about 100 clubs, are federated into the Girls Clubs of America, which was founded in 1945 in Springfield, Massachusetts. A national headquarters was established in 1947. Each local club retains its autonomy. To maintain the national office, each club pays one and one half percent of its total operating budget to the national organization. The Girls Clubs of America seeks to strengthen the Girls Club movement through assisting member clubs and citizen groups interested in forming Girls Clubs. Field services are given in organizing new clubs, surveying needs, giving advice on buildings and standards of operation, and suggesting programs. Workshops, institutes, and forums are conducted.

To be admitted to membership in the Girls Clubs of America, a Girls Club must have a written statement that its purpose is to promote character development; to train girls for citizenship, homemaking, and motherhood; and to maintain high standards of Girls Club work through program, leadership, and sponsorship. Another important requirement is that the Girls Club program must be operated for a minimum of five half-days per week during nine full months of the year.

Unique program for girls

Like the Boys' Clubs, the Girls Clubs maintain central club buildings which provide daily programs of varied activities. This structure makes the organization different from any other service for little girls. The program includes homecraft, handcraft, music, dramatics, art, games, reading, sports, dancing, health, good grooming, charm, co-recreation, parties, community service, camping, and outdoor summer programs. Competition is not stressed. Special attention is given to younger girls, aged 6 to 12.

Each Girls Club follows a basic pattern yet retains its own individual qualities dependent upon the needs and interests of the girls it serves. Each club has a great deal of leeway in determining its own policies and programs. There are no barriers of creed or race in the membership requirements. Dues are purposely kept low.

Young Men's Christian Association

Oldest of the existing large voluntary organizations of youth, the YMCA was begun in London in 1844 by twelve young drygoods clerks headed by 22-year-old George Williams, a farm boy who, on coming to London to work, was appalled by the moral conditions of the city. At this time, the Industrial Revolution had caused serious upheavals. Clerks worked from fourteen to seventeen hours a day. No constructive recreation was provided for them, and their few idle hours were spent largely in drinking, gambling, and immoral living. The YMCA was a reaction by youth itself against the inadequacy of life offered them in the city.

Over a century of growth

The movement spread rapidly across Europe. It reached the United States in 1851, when Thomas V. Sullivan, a retired sea captain, gathered together in Boston the group that became the first American YMCA. In seven years, YMCAs dotted the country from coast to coast. The national organization was formed in 1866. The first YMCAs were primarily religious discussion groups. The program of physical education, with gymnasiums and later swimming pools, began in the 1860's. The first formally organized Boys' Department was set up in Salem, Massachusetts, in 1869.

A worldwide fellowship

The Young Men's Christian Association we regard as being, in its essential genius, a world-wide fellowship united by a common loyalty to Jesus Christ for the purpose of developing Christian personality and building a Christian society.

This statement, as revised in 1957 from a statement adopted in 1931 by the International Convention and by the National Council of YMCAs of the United States, today is the official purpose of the YMCA. Boys, girls, men, and women of every age, race, and creed are welcome in the YMCA. There are in the United States today about 2.6 million members in over 1,800 associations. About one fifth of the members are girls or women.

The "Y" building

In the larger cities, the YMCA typically operates a building or buildings wherein a variety of facilities is to be found. Many are equipped with inexpensive hotel accommodations, restaurants, gymnasiums, swimming pools, lecture halls, craft shops, and meeting rooms. However, a large part of the YMCA program is carried on in neighborhoods without central buildings, with meetings held in schools, houses, or other places.

Clubs

Most of its work with youth is carried on through its clubs, among which are the following:

Y-Indian Guides. Primarily for 6-, 7-, and 8-year-old boys and their fathers, this program is unusual in that boys cannot participate without their fathers or vice versa. There are no rigid tests to pass and there is no severe grading system. The groups are called "tribes." The program is very flexible and may include handicraft, trips, storytelling, team games, discussions, swimming, hikes, camping, picnics, or nature lore. Tribes meet in the homes of members twice monthly. The purpose of the program is to foster the companionship of father and son.

Gra-Y and Tri-Gra-Y. Boys from about nine through twelve years of age make up the Gra-Y Clubs. Each club must have at least eight boys with an approved adult leader and a sponsoring committee. Clubs meet weekly, elect officers, and conduct simple rituals. The first Gra-Y Club was organized in 1924 in Morris Cove, Connecticut. There are now thousands of clubs, organized in neighborhood groups, in school, through the church, or through a YMCA building. The Tri-Gra-Y Clubs are the counterparts for girls.

Junior Hi-Y, Junior Tri-Hi-Y, Hi-Y, and Tri-Hi-Y. The Junior Hi-Y is intended for boys of the seventh, eighth, and ninth grades; the Junior Tri-Hi-Y, for girls of the same age; the Hi-Y, for boys in the upper three grades of high school; and the Tri-Hi-Y, for girls of the same age. Each club must have a sponsoring committee, a written constitution, and an approved advisor. All members share in planning, conducting, and evaluating the meetings. Worship is usual at each meeting. The programs deal with personal and social problems, such as vocational guidance and boy-girl relations; promotion of good will and understanding among those of different nationalities, races, and creeds; and social recreation. Variety of methods in program presentation is encouraged. The first high-school YMCA club that has operated continuously since its inception was formed in Chapman, Kansas, in 1885. Such clubs spread rapidly, although the name "Hi-Y" was not used until 1911. Meanwhile, high-school girls' clubs sponsored by the YMCA began to grow. The Tri-Hi-Y was admitted into the National Hi-Y Fellowship in 1946.

The YMCA carries on an extensive program with young adults. Among the adult club groups it sponsors are Phalanx, Y's Men's International, YMCA Spouse and Sparkle Club, Gradale Sororities, and Young Men's Industrial Club.

Classes at the "Y"

Since its early years, the YMCA has conducted classes of an informal nature, mostly for students from about 18 to 24 years of age. Subjects covered may include social and recreation skills, arts and crafts, music, drama, reading, writing, speaking, marriage, home, family, psychology, business, religion, and public affairs. Informal education is carried on through forums, special-interest groups, social affairs, programs with religious emphasis, counseling and guidance, and sports. In many states, model state legislatures are sponsored to teach boys and girls the meaning of citizenship.

Specialized "Y" services

In addition to the programs described, the YMCA carries on many specialized services. There are numerous college associations, dating from 1858, when college YMCAs were established at the University of Michigan and the University of Virginia. An intercollegiate association was formed in 1877.

The welfare of members of the armed forces was a concern of the YMCA as long ago as the Civil War. During every war since that time it has been active in social service. In World War II it worked as a member organization of the United Service Organizations (USO) to provide recreation and carry on welfare projects.

A special division for railroad employees was established in Cleveland, Ohio, in 1872. Railroad YMCAs later became an important part of YMCA work. Associations for Negroes began in 1853; for Indians, 1879.

Two colleges have been established primarily for the training of YMCA workers. These are Springfield College, in Springfield, Massachusetts, and George Williams College, in Chicago.

National and international affiliations

Each local YMCA is a self-governing unit affiliated with other YMCAs throughout the country through the National Council. Local associations, through their representatives, control the area councils, and through these groups the National Council. Actions of the National or area councils are binding upon local associations in the sense that, having participated in formulating the actions, they are under moral compulsion to cooperate.

Area councils serve as coordinating agencies, decide on program emphasis, formulate policies, provide direct services to local associations, conduct inter-association activities, and organize new YMCAs or branches. The National Council deals with other national institutions, including government agencies, assembles facts, formulates policies, establishes standards, publishes program resources, fosters national program organizations, provides specialized services, maintains personnel services, and affiliates with the YMCAs of other nations.

The YMCA is at work throughout the world. The World's Alliance of YMCAs, founded in 1855, is a federation of national YMCA movements. Its elected executive body, called the World's Committee, has headquarters in Geneva, Switzerland.

The "Y" as a pioneer

To the YMCA goes a great deal of credit for inventing or pioneering in a number of programs that have become highly successful and have been adopted by other agencies, public and private. Among its pioneer efforts are:

> the development of health and fitness programs;
> introduction of the game of basketball;
> learn-to-swim campaigns;

camping for boys; and

night-school education.

The Boy Scouts and the Camp Fire Girls were aided in the early days of their organization by YMCA leaders.

The YMCA thus offers an outstanding example of the unique contributions that a voluntary organization can render in experimental programs. Through such an organization, new approaches may be tried, which tax-paying organizations may later adopt.

Young Women's Christian Association

The emblem of the Blue Triangle, familiar in large cities from coast to coast, marks a "home away from home" for many young women and a recreation center for many more. Any girl over 12 years of age, regardless of race, creed, or national origin, may become a member of the YWCA. Most members are between 15 and 35 years of age. About 3 million women and girls avail themselves of the services of the 1,600 YWCAs of the United States; and over 50,000 boys and men are associate members.

Purpose

The purpose of the YWCA has been stated as follows:

To build a fellowship of women and girls devoted to the task of realizing in our common life those ideals of personal and social living to which we are committed by our faith as Christians.

In this endeavor we seek to understand Jesus, to share his love for all people, and to grow in the knowledge and love of God.

Emphasis is on Christian living. The association helps girls and women to acquire habits, knowledge, and skills to meet their basic needs and to aid in their emotional and spiritual adjustment.

A Product of the Industrial Revolution

Like the YMCA, which it parallels in many respects, the YWCA emerged during the Industrial Revolution out of the needs of young workers coming to the cities. In 1855 Mrs. Arthur Kinnaird brought together a group whose object was to provide homes for young women in London. About the same time, a prayer union was founded by Emma Robart. The movements spread rapidly and were merged in 1877.

Similar migrations of women workers to the cities were occurring in the United States, and the movement found an early footing in industrial centers. The earliest association in the United States was the Ladies' Christian Union in New York, founded in 1858; and in 1866, in Boston, the first organization bearing the name of the Young Women's Christian Association was formed. In 1906, the present national organization was created by the union of two national groups, one of which had grown up in the Middle West and the other in the East.

A World's YWCA was formed in 1894. Its headquarters is today in Geneva, Switzerland. Its membership encompasses about fifty countries. The executive body of the national organization is the National Board, chosen to carry out policies adopted at the national conventions. It directs four community divisions and nine regions.

Flexible program

Through its program, the YWCA attempts to advance the spiritual, moral, intellectual, physical, and social welfare of girls and women. The program is not rigidly fixed. The YWCA has taken the position that the program must be built on the basis of the needs of individual groups and individual girls. The use of awards as a means of stimulating interest is avoided. Although the top leadership is professional, most YWCAs depend upon volunteer leadership. There are three major types of work in the YWCA.

1. *Community associations.* In large cities, YWCAs commonly maintain buildings with dormitories, restaurants, classrooms, lecture rooms, gymnasiums, and social rooms. The buildings are of course less pretentious in small towns, and, in many small communities, the YWCAs function with no buildings. Various cultural, social, and recreation projects are carried on by community associations. Among them are forums for discussing problems, personal and vocational guidance, religious observances, community services, festivals, parties, and dances. Frequently, employment bureaus are maintained. Classes are offered in homemaking, health, typing, shorthand, English, psychology, and Bible study. Recreation is offered through music, arts and crafts, dramatics, swimming, archery, badminton, volleyball, and bowling. Camping and outdoor activities are important in the program. Clubs are organized for business and professional women and for factory workers.

2. *Student associations.* There are about 475 student associations in universities and colleges. These associations offer counsel to girls and opportunities for worship, fellowship, and community service. Like the YMCA, the YWCA established itself in colleges early in its history, the first association for college girls being organized at Normal University in Illinois in 1873.

3. *Y-Teens.* Work with younger girls began in Oakland, California, where in 1881 the Little Girls' Christian Association was originated. Many other girls' clubs soon appeared. They were united under the name of "Girl Reserves" in 1918 and changed their name to "Y-Teens" in 1946. There

are about 350,000 members between 12 and 18 years of age. The program is one of service, worship, and play.

YWCA as a social force

The YWCA can look back upon years of effort and achievement in many welfare fields. Although primarily concerned with the welfare of girls and women, it exerts its influence in wider spheres, as the following examples of its activities show.

1. Health education for women has been a part of YWCA work since the 1870's.
2. Low-cost vacation camps, day camps, and child-care centers are maintained.
3. Classes in various subjects are offered to enrich the intellectual, physical, and cultural lives of its members.
4. The principle of full equality for all races and nationalities is stressed. Work with Negroes, Indians, and the foreign-born is extensive.
5. Standards for the improvement of working conditions for women have been promulgated.
6. World cooperation through international organizations, especially the United Nations, is vigorously supported.

The activities of the YWCA stem from its basic intention of making its Christian beliefs achieve reality. In seeking this goal, it has made happier, richer, and more purposeful the leisure lives of girls and women around the world.

How the Youth Agencies Function

Broadly conceived, a "program" includes everything that happens in a group, including casual and unscheduled activities as well as the planned events more commonly designated as "program." It is through the program that the agencies attempt to meet their objectives. Carrying out a program for a particular group is influenced by several factors. Among them are the needs of the participants—physical, mental, emotional, social; the skills of the leaders; finances; facilities, areas, and equipment available; and the time available.

Because membership is voluntary, the programs must consider the desires of young people, such as to have new experiences, adventure, and self-expression; to be emotionally secure and free from danger (in counterbalance to the desire for adventure); to give and receive love and affection; to participate as a member of a group; to experience beauty; to engage in physical activity; to be important to others; and to serve others.

Three ways of conducting programs

There are three major ways in which programs are carried out—through small-group activities, through large-group activities, and through individual activities. However conducted, the activity is less important than the individual who participates in it, and a particular program may be good or bad depending upon what it does to the participant.

Small-group activities. The most common method of carrying out the program in youth-membership organizations is in small groups or clubs under adult leadership. In these informal groups, planning is democratic, and all members are urged to express their opinions. Learning takes place through doing and, by means of games, assumes the mantle of play. All the members of a small group may carry on the same activity at the same time, or the small group may be subdivided into interest or hobby groups, so that the members can carry on various activities simultaneously.

Large-group activities. Large-group or "mass" activities are carried on to a lesser extent by most of the youth organizations. Those organizations that maintain buildings may perhaps carry on large-group activities in the gymnasiums, swimming pools, and auditoriums while carrying on small-group activities in the clubrooms and craft shops. The program may be in large part determined by the facilities. Organizations that have no buildings usually operate in small groups, limiting their large-group activities to special events, such as city-wide parades and banquets or national events such as jamborees and conventions.

Individual activities. Much of the badge work in Scouting, the honor work in Camp Fire Girls, and the project work in 4-H Clubs is carried on by members working individually outside of club meetings. The highest awards usually require spending considerable time and effort on individual pursuits. Guidance on an individual basis is a feature of all the major youth-membership organizations, although some stress this aspect of their programs more than others.

Nation-wide programs

Programs of the major youth organizations are either established definitely on a national basis or set up according to the interests of individual local groups. The Boy Scouts, Camp Fire Girls, and Girl Scouts are outstanding examples of organizations with nation-wide, uniform programs, whereas the YMCA and YWCA are set up primarily in accord with local interests.

Similarities in program. The programs of the Boy Scouts, Camp Fire Girls, and Girl Scouts result from studies of the interests and needs of young people of various ages, and experimentation through the years with various program activities. Handbooks for members and leaders give detailed guidance through the various steps. In these three organizations, the programs are clearly defined into age groups, each with its own uniform as well as its own program, adapted to its particular age level. The programs for the youngest children are home-centered, whereas programs for the intermediates are more achievement-centered, with greater variety and adventure. The senior programs provide opportunities for community service, vocational explorations, social experiences, and specialized interests.

Many parallels may be pointed out in the program fields of the three organizations. All are strongly outdoor-oriented. Camping is an integral part of their programs and is carried on more or less throughout the year as well as in the summer. Resident camps, troop camps, and travel camps are all encouraged. The Girl Scouts are credited with being the first to establish day camps, having introduced this form of camping in 1922. They have promoted day camps extensively, finding them successful in introducing camping to younger girls who are not yet ready to leave home for established camps.

Use of awards. Systems of progression by means of meeting definite requirements characterize all three agencies. For example, a Boy Scout rises in rank or receives awards when he passes certain tests of knowledge or skill. Differences in the interests and capabilities of individual members are met by the inclusion of a great variety of fields in which to win awards.

There has been some criticism of the award system. True, in the hands of an inexperienced or incautious leader, the awards may become goals in themselves and the learnings mere side issues. Correctly used, the awards may become spurs to greater achievement and may arouse interest in worthy fields of endeavor. Moreover, since the programs are subject to the constant test of use and are revised from time to time, there is reason to believe that they are well suited to the needs and interests of the children they serve. There can be little doubt that many a lifelong career was born in the enthusiasms aroused in the award program.

Locally determined programs

In the Boys' Clubs, Girls Clubs, YMCA, and YWCA, no such definite programs as those described above exist. There is little use of achievement awards. Though, in general, the programs may be similar from one city to another, the precise program of local units depends upon the interest and needs of the particular groups served, the facilities and leadership available, and the financial resources. Since all three of these organizations maintain buildings wherever possible, much of the program revolves around use of the facilities contained therein. These organizations do not necessarily compete with the organizations using prescribed programs. On occasions, they may supplement one another. For example, a Boys' Club may sometimes organize a Boy Scout troop within its membership and the troop may hold its meetings in the Boys' Club building. Whether their programs are set up nationally or determined locally, all of these organizations have resource materials and staff guidance available from their national and regional headquarters.

Leadership and administration

The organizations with the most carefully outlined programs can most successfully use volunteer leaders. The wide extent of the Boy Scouts, Girl Scouts, and Camp Fire Girls can be attributed in large measure to their ability to use volunteers, particularly parents of the members. In these organizations, the professional workers have very little contact with the children; and the volunteers are the direct leaders of the groups. The organizations conduct training courses for the volunteers, which, combined with the manuals or handbooks with their clear descriptions of the preplanned programs, make it possible for the volunteer leaders to proceed easily and confidently with but little additional help. Even the training courses for volunteer leaders are sometimes given by other volunteers, so that the services of the professional workers can be chiefly supervisory and administrative. Under such a system, a large number of children can be served with a small paid professional staff. The dependence upon volunteers is expressed in a sentence in the Preamble to the Girl Scout Constitution, which reads, "We hold that ultimate responsibility for the Girl Scout movement rests with volunteers." [7]

In agencies such as the YMCA and YWCA, in which programs are determined on a local basis and may vary considerably from community to community, there is a much greater need for professional leaders in direct relationship with the children. In these organizations, the professional workers themselves often lead the groups. Volunteers are used to a considerable extent as assistants, particularly in areas demanding specialized skills. Volunteers play a major role as members of boards of directors of all the youth-membership agencies.

Each of the major youth organizations is administered by a national lay council and has a national headquarters with a professional staff to give advice and consultation, prepare literature, represent the organization nationally, and give other help. To facilitate administration there are also state offices or regional offices, which cover several states. Local units are administered by local lay councils or, as in the case of 4-H, advised by local committees.

Facilities

Boy Scouts, Girl Scouts, and Camp Fire Girls own very few facilities. They meet chiefly in churches, schools, and homes, in which rooms are

[7] 1960 *Annual Report* (New York: Girl Scouts of the U.S.A., 1961), p. iv.

sometimes reserved for their exclusive use. It is common, however, for them to own their own camps. The Boys' Clubs, Girls Clubs, YMCA, and YWCA, on the other hand, are dependent upon buildings by the very nature of their programs, although the YMCA and YWCA have extended into programs that do not require buildings. These agencies usually maintain centers that are open daily, so that many of the activities are conducted on a drop-in basis rather than a pre-scheduled one. These organizations, likewise, often own their own camps.

Financing

With the exception of 4-H clubs, which receive some support from tax sources, all the major youth-membership organizations depend primarily upon local contributions and membership fees for their existence. Membership fees are usually kept at a minimum so that cost is not a serious bar to membership.

Annual finance drives, frequently as part of United Fund or Community Chest drives, are the usual sources of local contributions. The YMCA and YWCA, which maintain buildings, have additional sources of revenue from the operation of restaurants, hotel services, and swimming pools. Local units often supplement their funds through special money-raising projects, such as cookie sales, calendar sales, and magazine subscription drives. Fees are charged for special services like camping, but frequently such charges cover only part of the cost. National headquarters are financed in some of the agencies primarily by fees from individual members. In other agencies, the member clubs pay for the support of the national headquarters. Gifts, bequests, royalties, and the sale of literature and equipment are further sources of national income.

Special Advantages and Problems of the Voluntary Youth-Membership Organizations

With the great expansion of programs for youth, both tax-supported and voluntary, it is well to examine the nature of the services rendered by the voluntary organizations as distinct from those of public agencies.

Advantages

There are some advantages resulting from the means of financing voluntary agencies.

Freedom to experiment. Because of their relative independence from governmental control and from tax support, the voluntary agencies have a high degree of freedom. They are able to offer a diversity of approach, to experiment, and to act as proving grounds for new ideas. The voluntary organizations may on occasion act with dispatch and boldness in matters in which the public agencies may hesitate because of political repercussions. Many programs that have subsequently been adopted by tax-supported recreation or educational agencies originated with the voluntary agencies.

Opportunity to specialize. By the very nature of their support, tax-supported programs have an obligation to serve all groups. The voluntary agencies may focus their attention on segments of society and offer individualized programs to certain groups, their only limitation being the extent to which they may obtain financial support. Thus, the voluntary organizations may maintain close relationships with religious groups, as public agencies may not.

Appeal to altruism. Although tax-supported programs may sometimes receive voluntary contributions, they do not serve as effectively as the voluntary organizations as channels for the altruistic efforts of individuals and groups, upon which voluntary agencies depend for sponsorship, leadership, and finance.

Disadvantages

There are special problems encountered by the voluntary organizations from which the public agencies are relatively free.

Uncertain financial support. Financing is often uncertain. The organizations, particularly those with widespread membership, must constantly maintain good public relations and prove themselves worthy in the public eye in order to receive financial support. If they depend upon general public backing, they must answer to the public in much the same way tax-supported agencies must. Their income may fluctuate markedly from year to year, particularly if they are dependent upon a few large contributors. By comparison, the cost of a public program is distributed among all the taxpayers rather than a limited number of contributors, a factor that contributes to stable financing.

Expenditure of time and energy in money-raising. Much of the time and effort of the voluntary agencies may be dissipated in money-raising, although United Funds and Community Chests have considerably lessened this responsibility. Although tax-supported agencies, like the voluntary ones, must maintain good public relations if they wish to have their budgets approved, they usually expend less effort in raising funds.

Uncertainty of volunteer leadership. Another major problem encountered by voluntary organizations is the securing of volunteer leadership, upon which most of them depend heavily. Although volunteer leadership may often be of a very high quality, it is often difficult to secure, train, and hold. Continuity in the program is disrupted because of a high turnover in volunteer leadership.

Lack of land and facilities. A further problem of the voluntary groups lies in their need for land and facilities. Some of the agencies own very little themselves but depend upon the use of public lands and facilities. Their requirements, by necessity, are placed second to those of the public agencies themselves. For example, a voluntary group that wishes to operate a day camp in a public park may find that public use of the park makes such a program impossible.

Overlapping of services. The sheer numbers of voluntary organizations create another problem. When many different organizations function within one community, there may be overlapping of services and competition for members and funds. In many communities there is a serious attempt to coordinate efforts through such organizations as councils of social agencies. A successful program of service to youth demands cooperation not only among voluntary agencies but also between voluntary and public agencies. Duplication of programs and competition are wasteful and undesirable. Each organization has its own valuable service to render.

Trends

The half century since the founding of most of the youth organizations has witnessed more changes than has any other period in history. It is an impressive fact that these organizations have been able to adapt themselves to these changing conditions and continue to flourish, grow, and meet the needs of the young people they serve. The programs themselves have undergone revisions based upon research in the needs and interests of youth. As a result of four studies made in the late 1950's,[8] for example, the Boy Scouts, the Boys' Clubs, the Camp Fire Girls, and the Girl Scouts reexamined their programs, making alterations where advisable and retaining features that were still of evident worth.

When first established, the organizations laid emphasis on the provision of wholesome experiences and opportunities for self-development. Later, the programs became highly organized. The leaders, although concerned with activities that had "character-building" values, tended to try to fit the child into the program. This stress on the program has today shifted to a concern for the development of individual personality.

One of the greatest challenges to the organizations has been that of sim-

[8] (a) *Needs and Interests of Adolescent Boys' Club Members,* Boys' Clubs of America; (b) Survey Research Center, Institute for Social Research, University of Michigan, *A Study of Adolescent Boys, 1955* (New Brunswick, N.J.: Boy Scouts of America, 1956); (c) Survey Research Center, Institute for Social Research, University of Michigan, *Adolescent Girls* (New York: Girl Scouts of the U.S.A., n.d.); (d) *Leadership-Program Studies,* conducted by Audience Research, Gallup Enterprises, New Jersey, for Camp Fire Girls, 1957 and 1958.

ply providing enough leadership to serve the growing population. All of the major agencies grew phenomenally in size during the 1950's; and the provision of trained leadership was an enormous task. Accompanying it was the task of extending membership to hard-to-reach groups. The enlargement of Girl Scout Councils and experiments in California to bring Girl Scouting to daughters of migratory workers are examples of this trend. The problems of interracial and intercultural relationships have been eased somewhat by the work of the youth organizations. International festivals, visits to homes of those of other races, international camping, and friendships between those of different ethnic and national backgrounds have been encouraged.

With the increase in juvenile delinquency, some of the youth organizations, particularly the Boys' Clubs and the settlement houses, have attempted with increased vigor to reach the juvenile delinquent and the potential delinquent. Special workers have been assigned to these groups. Other groups to receive attention have been the handicapped and the institutionalized. With vast new fields of employment opening up for youth, the youth organizations have placed increased emphasis upon vocational guidance with older youth. Health and physical fitness have been granted more attention, as the organizations have cooperated with the program of the President's Council on Youth Fitness.

The camping programs of the youth organizations have grown, with more camping during seasons other than summer. Day camps, resident camps, and other forms of camping have shared this growth.

The participation of the whole family in the program of the youth organization has received increasing attention. Cub Scouting, the phase of Scouting that has grown most rapidly, involves the whole family, with parents as active leaders. The Y-Indian Guides, for small boys and their fathers, is another example of parent participation. The other organizations also include parents in various ways. It is worth noting that the greatest growth in membership in recent years has taken place in the groups under ten years of age—the groups that most frequently include parents.

A voluntary organization cannot remain static. Unless it is sensitive to the needs and interests of its members and quick to find means of gratifying them, it cannot continue to find the support necessary to its existence. The youth-membership organizations that are firmly entrenched in the lives of children today have achieved this position by keeping themselves flexible and alert in a complex society of shifting values. Their task is exceedingly difficult and important.

SUGGESTED REFERENCES

Chambers, M. M., *Youth-Serving Organizations: National Non-Governmental Associations*. Washington, D.C.: American Council on Education, 1948.

Neumeyer, Martin H. and Esther S. Neumeyer, *Leisure and Recreation*, Third edition. New York: The Ronald Press Company, 1958.

Sapora, Allen V. and Elmer D. Mitchell, *The Theory of Play and Recreation*, Third edition. New York: The Ronald Press Company, 1961.

Handbooks and other literature published by the following youth-membership organizations:

Boy Scouts of America, Rt. 1, New Brunswick, N.J.

Boys' Clubs of America, 771 First Avenue, New York 17, N.Y.

Camp Fire Girls, Inc., 65 Worth Street, New York 13, N.Y.

4-H Clubs, Federal Extension Service, U.S. Department of Agriculture, Washington 25, D.C.

Girl Scouts of the United States of America, 830 Third Avenue, New York 22, N.Y.

Girls Clubs of America, 22 E. 38th Street, New York 16, N.Y.

Young Men's Christian Association, 291 Broadway, New York 7, N.Y.

Young Women's Christian Association, 600 Lexington Avenue, New York 22, N.Y.

"Towers and ships are nothingness
Void of our fellow men to inhabit them."
SOPHOCLES

7

Community Centers and Playgrounds

A city's playgrounds and community centers serve as the backbone and lifeblood of the typical recreation department's offerings. These are the facilities that are found in most communities and neighborhoods. When well-organized, comprehensive programs and qualified leadership are added, these facilities begin to meet the expectations of the city fathers and public, who planned, constructed, and financed their development for satisfaction of the neighborhoods' basic year-round recreation needs.

In some instances, community centers and playgrounds are developed on separate sites. In other settings community centers are an integral part of playfields or park developments. A current practice is to have the elementary school and playground serve as the neighborhood's indoor and outdoor recreation center. Regardless of the approach, the programs of these two recreation outlets should be geared to the needs and interests of all persons residing in the neighborhood.

Community Centers

In cities of all sizes, the need for establishing indoor recreation centers that will facilitate year-round programs is of ever increasing importance. Community centers sponsored by municipal recreation departments are one of the common approaches to the problem. In some instances, YMCAs,

YWCAs, Boys' Clubs, Girls Clubs, and neighborhood settlement houses serve the indoor recreation needs of a neighborhood. It must be recognized, however, that these organizations are limited in scope (boys only, girls only, the underprivileged only, and members only) and are usually not in a position to serve the over-all needs of the neighborhood. It is important that duplication of indoor facilities be avoided and that municipal recreation departments open school buildings or establish separate building-centered programs only when the need is evident. Because the many semi-public or private agencies, mentioned previously, have been discussed at length in other chapters, only community centers operated by municipalities will be discussed here. The use of school buildings as indoor recreation centers is discussed in Chapter 5.

Why community centers?

City life has changed drastically in the last century. Much has been written about the social and physical deterioration of modern cities. Danford points out some of the following characteristics of city life that "threaten the foundations of our democratic society."

1. Breakdown in neighborhood solidarity.
2. Narrowing of the basis of unity among men and a decrease in their points of contact.
3. Friendliness replaced by a formalized impersonality of relationships. People are physically near but socially distant. Increase in social isolation.
4. Increasing vocational specialization resulting in a decreasing concern for a common life and a common destiny.
5. Disruption of a common social life as achieved through the ice cream socials, spelling bees, and harvest festivals of the village and rural areas.
6. Weakening of the sense of civic responsibility and the spirit of cooperation for the common good.
7. Increasing anonymity of the individual resulting in a lack of accountability.
8. Weakening of the moral and ethical senses.
9. Increasing bureaucratism and its corollary, absence of direct action.
10. Decreasing opportunities for participation in vigorous activities thus resulting in biological deterioration.[1]

These social implications are a real challenge to all civic, social, educational, religious, and recreation agencies in the community. It is under the influence of this environment that habits, personality traits, attitudes, and leisure pursuits are fostered. The solutions must be approached in this very setting. The church, school, and home must do their part. Youth-serving agencies have an important role to play. The community center can also

[1] Howard G. Danford, *Recreation in the American Community* (New York: Harper & Row, Inc., 1953), pp. 210–211. Reprinted by permission.

serve as a social instrument for community betterment. Its responsibilities are many.

Community centers serve as the common meeting place for all age groups. They should be designed and developed to offer a wide variety of wholesome civic and recreation opportunities. Centers normally provide facilities such as playgrounds, pools, shops, gymnasiums, and game rooms, which are not found in the ordinary home. Their leaders offer planned programs, personal and group guidance, and equal opportunities for all participants. Centers provide a place where people of all ages, religions, races, and social and economic status may participate in activities of mutual interest. Recreation programs range from the informal to the organized, from the simple activity to the more complex; they must include physical, mental, cultural, and social activities.

Community centers must do more than merely provide a meeting place or activities; they must contribute positive values and satisfy creative outlets for all persons involved in the program. To do anything less is to fall short of the goal.

Community-center buildings

Buildings vary from renovated garages or former USO centers to beautifully designed recreation buildings; from small four- to five-room buildings to spacious plants that include swimming pools, auditoriums, and gymnasiums. The type of physical plant depends on the finance available, size of the city, existing agencies and programs, school facilities available, and needs and interests of the people in the neighborhood or community.

Building facilities. It is recommended that each neighborhood have some type of indoor recreation facility, whether it be a school building or a separate recreation building. Facility standards indicate that a community center should be located within one half mile to one mile of every home, the distance depending on the density of population of the area. When civic leaders are considering a new building or the renovation of an old building, it is essential that the building be adaptable to the recreation functions for which it will be used. Facilities must also adhere to the principle of multiple use; rooms should be adaptable to many different uses. Above all, the center should be a symbol of community pride. It should be attractive, appropriately landscaped, tastefully decorated, and well lighted. The community center will be an important factor in meeting community needs only if it is carefully planned, properly maintained, and wisely administered.

Rooms and facilities found in community-center buildings are listed below; not all are found in the average building.

1. Gymnasium—locker room and showers
2. Auditorium—assembly hall

3. Game rooms—ping pong, billiards, table games
4. Club and meeting rooms
5. Arts and crafts shops
6. Kitchen or snack bar
7. Swimming pool
8. Library—reading room
9. Lounge
10. Offices
11. Service rooms—storage, rest rooms, et cetera

Justifying a separate building. A question often raised is: "How can a community justify a separate recreation building when school facilities are available?" This question does not have an either-or answer. Where school buildings are planned, designed, or adapted for community use and school authorities approve the principle of total community use, it would seem unwise and uneconomical to duplicate school facilities. However, it is generally recognized that one or more separate recreation buildings are needed in most cities to supplement school resources. Some of the arguments used to justify this statement are listed on the following pages.

Fig. 11   *Community Center—Clayton, Missouri*

1. A separate recreation building can be used all hours of the day; schools are available only after school hours. Even then, facilities are reserved for school groups engaged in co-curricular activities.
2. The joint use of any facility raises problems. Custodians, teachers, and principals who have not been convinced of the need for groups to use "their" buildings may cause conflicts.
3. Many schools, especially the older ones, are not designed for community use.

Even though the authors believe that many of these difficulties can be solved by a cooperative school-city relationship, a separate building can be justified in most communities.

Organization

Most community centers, operated as functions of municipal park and recreation departments, are administered by a community-center director and staff. In larger cities, the director is generally a full-time professional person. In smaller communities, the superintendent of recreation might also serve as the director of the center. The community-center staff is responsible to the superintendent of recreation and to the recreation board or commission.

Hours of operation. Centers are generally open mornings, afternoons, and evenings, six days a week. Some operate on Sunday afternoons and evenings. During school hours, the program is geared to adults and senior citizens. In some cases, the building is used for a nursery-school program. On weekday afternoons following school and on Saturdays, school children have priority in using the facilities. Policies differ as to the use of centers on school nights. Some directors limit the facilities to older children and adults on school nights. In other instances, children are allowed limited use of the center.

Advisory councils. The success of many centers has been attributed to a community-center advisory council. The council applies the democratic principle of working with, rather than for, the participants. Advisory councils vary in size and composition. They generally are made up of representatives of community or neighborhood leaders and supporters (PTA, schools, churches, labor, and others) and clubs or participant groups using the center. Advisory councils provide aid in planning and coordinating the program and in interpreting the center operation to the community.

Leadership

The key to a center's success is its leadership. The many positive values that come from a community center's program are based wholly upon the number and quality of leaders available. Without good leaders, a center would be wise not to open its doors, for its purposes and values cannot be achieved and it may provide a breeding ground for antisocial behavior. Leadership has many functions, which include:

1. establishing goals that are acceptable to the group
2. offering varied opportunities so that participants may develop new skills, knowledge, and appreciations
3. giving individual or group guidance so that goals may be achieved and individual differences can be met
4. influencing individuals and groups to act in a socially acceptable manner
5. offering opportunities for participant leadership

Good leaders inspire the confidence and respect of the participants as they work together toward mutually satisfying goals.

Program

Activities offered by centers vary, depending on the facilities, leadership, and expressed needs of individuals. In discussing the many activities sponsored by community centers, it should be recognized that activities in themselves are not important; it is what happens to the person that counts. The various types of activities can be classified according to the method in which they are organized and administered. Few centers will sponsor all activities presented; the following suggests a comprehensive picture of activities that might be conducted.

Informal activities. Every center should provide facilities in which children and adults may engage in informal, unorganized activities of their own choosing. Under these circumstances, persons may drop in to the center to play table tennis, read a magazine, watch television, shoot baskets, swim, or develop a film. These persons do not have to be members of a team or club, be enrolled in a class, or play in a tournament to take part in center activities.

Organized activities conducted by the center staff. Organized activities can generally be classified under four major categories: clubs, classes, leagues and tournaments, and special events. These activities make up the core of the center's program.

1. CLUBS. Most centers are instrumental in establishing one or more clubs that serve various age groups or interests. The following are some of the more common types of clubs.

a. Youth clubs: Teenage clubs or youth centers received a tremendous boost during World War II. Some youth centers were established in their own exclusive buildings, although many were incorporated as a part of community-center programs.

Youth clubs are responsible for planning activities for high-school youth, from 14 to 18 years of age, through youth-center councils. These councils are responsible for planning and operating the program under the guidance of adult leadership. Youth centers, organized as a part of community-center programs, generally take over the building one or two nights (Friday and Saturday, for example) a week for their planned activities. Programs include such activities as dancing, picnics, talent shows, costume parties, sport events, hay rides, bowling leagues, and community-service projects.

b.   Young-adult clubs: Young adults, ages 18 to 35, are often one of the most neglected groups. Some centers sponsor young-adult clubs as a part of the total program. They are organized in much the same manner as youth centers, with elected officers and committees functioning to plan and operate the program. Also, the programs of young-adult clubs, like those of youth centers, vary greatly to meet the needs and interests of the age group.

c.   Senior-citizen clubs: A comparatively recent trend in community-center programs has been the establishment of golden age or senior-citizen clubs for those sixty years of age and older. Some cities provide separate buildings for programs for the aged; in other places, community-center programs are expanded to include this age group. When community centers are used, facilities are set aside one or two nights a week, or during the morning or afternoon periods of operation. The enthusiastic response of the aged population to programs of this type has been encouraging.

A partial list of activities for the aged includes: arts and crafts, hobbies, literary discussion, social events, square dancing, movies, trips, choral groups, and day camping programs. There is no stereotyped program that can be applied to senior-citizen programs. Programs vary according to the desires of the oldsters and the recreation leaders' skillful handling of the group.

d.   Special activity clubs: People having special interests often join together and form clubs to further their hobbies and share ideas. Community centers have the responsibility of providing the needed facilities and leadership. Clubs of this type include: photography, square dancing, coin collecting, dramatics, music, hiking, and book-review clubs.

2.   CLASSES. Instructional classes, as well as the clubs mentioned previously, are considered to be the heart of community-center programs. An almost unlimited variety of classes can be offered. In arts and crafts alone, numerous classes are conducted. A few examples include: ceramics, lapidary, sketching, jewelry making, leathercraft, enameling, and woodworking classes. Classes can be offered in other program areas. Examples of some of the more typical class offerings include: ballet, charm school, modern dance, physical fitness, cooking, golf, badminton, tumbling, swimming, square dancing, bridge, make-up, photography, and furniture refinishing.

3.   LEAGUES AND TOURNAMENTS. Leagues and tournaments provide an excellent means of stimulating interest and conducting competition in various sports and games activities. They can be conducted on weekly, monthly,

or seasonal bases. Examples include basketball, volleyball, handball, bridge, cribbage, table tennis, billiards, and chess.

4. SPECIAL EVENTS. Special events provide the "frosting on the cake" to the basic program offerings. Each of the clubs may conduct special events as highlights for their club activities. Special events may be promoted for all persons in the neighborhood or community. Hobby shows, Christmas parties, flower shows, carnivals, fashion shows, square-dance festivals, or billiard exhibitions are but a few of the common "specials" promoted by community centers.

The types of programs previously mentioned incorporate the offerings sponsored and promoted as a part of the community-center planned program. It is the responsibility of the director of the community center to work cooperatively with all clubs and center personnel to develop a master plan of activities. The space or facilities and the leadership needed to operate the program will be established in the plan. If after this plan has been made, rooms and other facilities are available for community use, requests can be accepted.

Organized activities carried on by outside groups. Centers must establish policies to determine what types of community or civic groups may use the center and for what purposes. If room is available, community groups should be allowed to use the center. Many of these organizations need a meeting place and, in some cases, special facilities to conduct their programs. League of Women Voters, Council of Social Agencies, women's clubs, Boy Scouts, and Girl Scouts are but a few examples of those groups whom the center might serve.

Community centers equipped with adequate facilities and manned by qualified leaders can serve as social instruments for good to communities or neighborhoods if the needs and interests of the participants are considered and met. They form the greatest potential for consistent, continuous program effort in the easily accessible confines of neighborhood areas.

Playgrounds

Playgrounds are universally accepted as the center of recreation life for neighborhoods, a must for every community, and the very foundation of the municipal recreation department's program and services. Playgrounds started as a big-city movement. They resulted from the social and industrial conditions concomitant with the Industrial Revolution, growth of cities, and social degeneration of society. The Boston Sandgardens, initiated in 1885, was the first playground. The sandgardens and like areas that followed laid major emphasis on social, health, and safety objectives. They were usually first developed in slum areas to keep youngsters out of mischief, off the streets, and outdoors in the healthful sunshine.

From a total of ten cities with established playgrounds prior to 1900, the playground movement has grown rapidly. Today, playgrounds are found in all sections of the country, in small as well as in large cities, and in neighborhoods of all types. One important ingredient has been added to the early playground movement—qualified leadership. Creatively planned, professionally staffed playgrounds have become the firm basis on which and from which other community recreation programs may develop.

Fig. 12   *This . . .   . . . or this?*

Why playgrounds?

Playgrounds have been accepted by the public and city officials as one of the major features of municipal recreation programs. Over the years, justification of playgrounds as preventive measures for juvenile delinquency has gradually given way to an emphasis on the many positive values of supervised playgrounds. Neighborhood playgrounds, along with community centers, are the focal points for neighborhood recreation. Qualified leaders help make a playground not only more than just a play or recreation area, but a laboratory for good citizenship and a place where children and adults can engage in a variety of wholesome, constructive activities.

Leaders have the responsibility for planning activities and teaching new skills and interests to all age groups. They must assure all children equal opportunities to participate. They provide the environments in which the bullies or gangs cannot take over, and the shy, unaggressive child may find his place in the daily program offerings. Supervised playgrounds contribute to the health, safety, and character development of participants. Cities have spent considerable sums of money in developing and maintaining attractive neighborhood recreation areas. The placing of good leadership on these areas has stimulated increased attendance and maximum use of the investment.

Physical features of playgrounds

Playgrounds are the chief recreation areas of neighborhoods. They may be parts of playfields or developed as separate functional units. Large numbers of cities use elementary schools for their summer playground programs because they are usually located on a neighborhood basis and often have adequate playground space.

Playgrounds serve primarily children from 5 to 15 years of age. The current trend is for playgrounds to serve all age groups; therefore, if playgrounds are to meet the needs of all ages, they should be carefully planned and developed. The size of playgrounds varies from 4 to 10 acres, depending upon the population of the neighborhood. It is generally agreed that playgrounds should be located within easy walking distance (one fourth to one half mile) from every home. The features and development of playgrounds are dependent upon the needs of the neighborhood.

Well-designed playgrounds have the following features: tot-lots, apparatus areas, multiple-use areas, open spaces for informal play, areas for field games, areas for crafts and quiet games, and shelter houses. Furthermore, playgrounds should be properly lighted, appropriately landscaped, and creatively developed. The trend toward creative design in equipment and facility development merits consideration. The physical features of playgrounds influence, in no small measure, the scope of opportunities and the effectiveness of the supervised playground program.

Organization

There are several types of playground operations, including fall, spring, and summer playground programs. In larger cities, year-round programs are operated. The fall and spring programs normally last only a few weeks; they are held during after-school hours and, in limited cases when lights are provided, during the evenings. Summer is the time when most cities sponsor supervised programs. During the vacation period, playgrounds are operated from 8 to 14 weeks. Because this is the most universally accepted period of operation, the remaining discussion of supervised playgrounds will be concentrated on the summer program.

Program planning. In organizing summer playground programs, recreation administrators and staffs must devote considerable time, effort, and planning to the following management concerns, if the objectives of the program are to be successfully achieved.

1. selecting playground locations
2. determining length of season and the days and hours of operation
3. staffing the program with qualified leaders
4. determining the type and scope of programs
5. establishing policies and cooperative relationships
6. maintaining areas and facilities
7. purchasing supplies, materials, and equipment
8. providing over-all supervision of leaders and program

Playground councils. Playground councils are often called booster or parents' clubs. Administrators have found playground councils to be of value in enlisting interest or support, providing leadership or funds, sponsoring various events, and promoting the playground program in the city. Decatur, Illinois, has received wide recognition for its adult recreation clubs. The aid and support given to the recreation department, and especially the neighborhood playgrounds, have been phenomenal. According to Russell Foval, Superintendent of Recreation, one of the major contributions to the department came from donated money. To mention only a few, some of the playground facilities and equipment purchased by the clubs are: floodlights, playground equipment, fences, bleachers, storage buildings, scorebooks, public-address systems, spray pools, and bicycle racks.[2]

Leadership

Leaders are the engineers that make the playground program move. There can be no substitute for good leadership. The degree of success that

[2] Russell J. Foval, "Adult Recreation Clubs," *Recreation*, XLVI, No. 10 (March 1953), 579.

playground programs achieve can be correlated with the quality of leaders that make up the staff. The size and composition of the playground staff are dependent upon the size of the community and the number of playgrounds. The use of adult and junior volunteer leaders is highly recommended.

Personnel standards have not been developed concerning the number of leaders needed on each individual playground. On some of the smaller playgrounds, one leader is often found. Danford believes this is unwise and gives the following reasons:

1. If the leader is a woman the older boys will be neglected and, in many cases, either will not attend the playground or, if they do, may be constant disciplinary problems.
2. If the leader is a man he is very likely to neglect the younger children and girls, because his interests and abilities lie in the area of recreation for older boys.
3. One person cannot provide the individual attention the children ought to have if the program is to yield the values which it should.
4. Accidents are very likely to increase. Studies have shown that accidents increase as the degree of supervision decreases.
5. Many phases of a well-rounded program cannot be developed because of the lack of adequate leadership. Field trips cannot be made unless the playground is closed for the duration of the trip. Where two or more leaders are available one can be away on trips, or hikes, or interplayground athletic contests, while the other remains on the grounds.[3]

Most cities follow the practice of two leaders per playground, usually a male and a female. In larger cities, especially on the larger playgrounds, additional leaders are added. Robert Ruhe, Superintendent of Parks and Recreation, Skokie, Illinois, experimented on a higher leader-participant ratio. By adding additional leaders to one of his playgrounds, he found that significant improvements in program, interest, and attendance resulted. His findings merit careful study by the recreation administrators in the profession.[4]

Program

If playground programs are to serve higher purposes than just keeping kids busy, off the streets, and out of mischief, recreation administrators should carefully and intelligently plan their goals and how they can accomplish them. In the development of the program, the basic principles (see Chapter 16) that affect program planning in any recreation setting should be carefully studied.

[3] Danford, *Recreation in the American Community*, pp. 131–132.
[4] *Effect of Increased Leadership and Its Relation to Interest and Participation* (Skokie, Ill.: Skokie Park District, 1961). Reprinted by permission.

Factors influencing planning. Any approach to planning must take into account the following factors:

1. the playground—its facilities, distance between playgrounds, and the neighborhood environment.
2. the leaders—their age, experience, skills, and interests, and the number of leaders on each playground.
3. the people served—the numbers of people on each playground, predominant age groups, and their needs, interests, and abilities.
4. the length of operation—the number of weeks, days per week, and hours per day.

The master plan. No standardized program that is suitable to every neighborhood can be developed. Programs must be adapted to the needs and conditions of each neighborhood; however, a definite, but flexible, master plan is necessary. Pre-planning is as essential to playground programs as building plans are to the construction of homes. The master plan is important in that it sets program standards and provides direction. Since leaders differ in attitudes and abilities, the master plan helps to provide generally uniform programs for all playgrounds. It sets minimum standards that will tend to make the weakest leaders hustle; it is administratively sound because it makes the most efficient use of personnel and equipment. Finally, a master plan can be justified on the premise that playground leaders need and want help and direction.

A master plan is more than setting playground hours, providing equipment, giving leaders program ideas, and setting up the routine activities. It might be viewed as the "core curriculum" for the supervised playground. A master plan determines the scope, content, and approach to arts and crafts, sports and games, and other program areas on the playground. It establishes the schedules and relationships of supervisors and specialists with the program and leaders. The scheduling of the day-camp program, interplayground competition, weekly tournaments, and city-wide special events is often incorporated in a master plan. Finally, this kind of planning strives for an integrated program of events rather than an unrelated list of activities.

The daily and weekly schedule. With the master plan as a framework for development, playground leaders must build their daily and weekly schedules for their particular playground. It is here that the individual differences in neighborhoods and people are taken into account. Playground leaders are usually asked to submit their own weekly plan to the superintendent prior to the start of a week of playground operation.

Playground activities. As neighborhoods and people vary in their needs and interests, so must the playground program. The program must be planned to include a wide variety of activities coming from all program areas. The scope and type of activities are almost unlimited. A creative, imaginative leader will stimulate activities in crafts, music, dramatics, sports and games, nature and outings, dance, and social recreation. A good playground program will have balance in the types of activities presented but not necessarily equal treatment of each of the program areas. For a more thorough treatment of recreation activities, see Chapter 17.

Activities can be conducted as informal, self-directed activities, classes, clubs, teams, contests, tournaments, interplayground competition, trips and excursions, and special events. Playgrounds that incorporate a wide variety of activities, that are manned by qualified leaders, and that are directed by creative planners and administrators can serve as the recreation center for the neighborhood. Together with community-center programs, they provide year-round recreation activities for all age groups.

SUGGESTED REFERENCES

Butler, George D., *Introduction to Community Recreation*, Third edition. New York: McGraw-Hill Book Company, 1959.

Butler, George D., *Playgrounds: Their Administration and Operation*, Third edition. New York: The Ronald Press Company, 1960.

Colborn, Fern M., *Buildings of Tomorrow, Guide for Planning Settlements and Community Buildings*. New York: Whiteside, Inc., and William Morrow & Company, Inc., 1955.

Danford, Howard G., *Recreation in the American Community*. New York: Harper & Row, Inc., 1953.

Ledermann, Alfred and Alfred Trachsel, *Creative Playgrounds and Recreation Centers*. New York: Frederick A. Praeger, Inc., 1959.

Making Teen Centers Succeed. Albany, N.Y.: New York State Youth Commission, 1953.

Musselman, Virginia, *The Playground Leader—His Place in the Program*. New York: National Recreation Association, 1952.

Summer Programs on California Playgrounds, A Guide. Sacramento, Calif.: California Recreation Commission, 1953.

Williams, Wayne, *Recreation Places*. New York: Reinhold Publishing Corporation, 1958.

"Afoot and lighthearted, I take to the open road."
WALT WHITMAN

8

Camping and Outdoor Education

Man is still a child of nature. For certain periods of time he may wall himself up in a cubbyhole, breathe smoky air (or air that has been heated or cooled, filtered, humidified or de-humidified, and re-circulated), walk on a straight cement path in a canyon of steel and concrete, and work and play by artificial light. But sooner or later he breaks loose from his casing and seeks the land—to bask in the sun, to plunge his hands into rich black soil, to cast his line after an elusive trout, or to test his skill against a mountain's height. He seeks for his children the outdoor opportunities that they, too, are often denied in everyday urban living. From this seeking, modern camping was born.

"Camping" means simple living in the out-of-doors. The term usually implies that the camper assumes some responsibility for his own food and shelter and engages in activities related to his surroundings. Whether camping involves large groups or a few individuals, its one and only distinctive aspect is its close contact with the natural environment.

Organized Camping

The term "organized camping" has come to be applied to a program, usually for young people, that includes leadership, educational objectives, living in a group outdoors, and a more-or-less planned program related to the out-of-doors. At its best, organized camping is the blending of education and recreation in the natural environs of the woods, open fields, rugged mountains, or water's edge. To the child it must spell fun and adventure; to the parent it must imply a safe and satisfying vacation; to the camp director it means the opportunity to make significant contributions to the child's physical, intellectual, and emotional growth. All three viewpoints are carefully integrated in the program of the superior camps.

Types of organized camps

There are many kinds of camps and many ways of categorizing them. In terms of basic organization, the following types of organized camps are recognized.

Resident or established camps. A resident or established camp is an organized camp in which children live for a period of time that usually ranges from five days to eight weeks. This type of camp has a permanent base, usually with permanent buildings and other developments.

Small group or troop camps. A group or troop camp is an organized camp consisting of a pre-existing group, such as a scout troop, which goes to camp as a unit, usually under the direction of the leaders who regularly work with the group. Camping is done with a bare minimum of facilities; groups bring their own equipment and plan their own programs.

Travel camps. Organized groups traveling by car, bus, covered wagon, boat, bicycle, or canoe constitute travel camps. These camps generally have no permanent bases. Campers carry their own equipment and use public or privately owned lands for overnight or longer stays.

Day camps. The day camp is a camp in which campers participate during the day but sleep at home at night. Because many kinds of programs are labeled "day camps," it is desirable to set up certain criteria if the term is to be used. The following are suggested:

1. LOCATION. The program takes place in an outdoor setting suitable for camp programs. A natural area with varied topography is preferable. The day camp must be located within a reasonable distance of the campers' homes so that a disproportionate amount of time will not be consumed in travel.

2. SMALL-GROUP STRUCTURE. The day camp provides opportunities for small-group activities under leadership, either in interest groups or in counselor groups.

3. DURATION. A day camp lasts at least six hours per day, for five or more days, and includes at least one meal daily. The camp may operate three, four, or five days a week. Less frequent operation tends to destroy continuity of experience.

4. PROGRAM. At least part of the program is outdoor-related. It includes campcrafts, nature and conservation, outdoor-related games, music, campfires, arts and crafts, and other activities similar to those of the resident camp.

5. LEADERSHIP. Leaders are eighteen years of age or older, and there is at least one leader for each ten campers eight years of age and over and for each eight campers under that age. Good leadership is as essential in the day camp as in the resident camp.

Origins of organized camping

So far as we know, organized camping had its origins in the United States. There are no precedents in other countries for such outdoor-living programs under leadership. It may well be that the romance of the westward movement and the American tradition of outdoor living manifest in the lives of the Indian, explorer, trader, trapper, overland immigrant, cowboy, and lumberman played their part in capturing the imaginations of young Americans and in developing the great appeal of organized camping.

It is difficult to trace the backgrounds of a movement that began as a mode of life, even if we restrict ourselves to a country with a comparatively brief history. "Camping" as an organized movement with educational objectives could not have originated in America until man had abandoned camping as a way of life. It was not until the wilderness yielded to cultivated fields, towns, and cities, and until the hunter, trapper, Indian, and explorer were supplanted by settled residents in permanent houses, that there was a reason for a return to the out-of-doors through group camping.

Informal camping by small groups of youth with leaders preceded the establishment of planned camps with educational objectives. The following, described by Mitchell and Crawford, are considered among the first organized camps:

1861—A school camp (Gunnery Camp, founded by Frederick W. Gunn)
1876—A private health camp (North Mountain School of Physical Culture, founded by Dr. Joseph T. Rothrock)
1880—A church camp (founded by Reverend George W. Hinckley)
1885—A YMCA camp (Camp Bald Head, founded by Sumner F. Dudley)[1]

It should be noticed that the above group includes a school camp, a private camp, a church camp, and an agency camp. These four are still the major types of camps operating today. Camp Chocorua, founded by Ernest Balch in 1880, is often considered the first private camp with educational objectives similar to many modern camps.

[1] A. Viola Mitchell and Ida B. Crawford, *Camp Counseling*, 3rd ed. (Philadelphia: W. B. Saunders Company, 1961), pp. 19–21.

Organized camping today

The camping movement expanded slowly before 1900, but its growth rapidly accelerated in the years following. It is estimated today that each summer more than five million children attend resident camps. There are at least 13,000 organized camps in the United States, about 7,500 of which are resident camps; the rest are day camps, troop camps, and others. Studies indicate that the rate of increase in the number of children attending camps has been greater than the rate of increase in the number of children in the general population. Camp growth has been particularly marked in day camps, camps for handicapped children, camps operated by religious organizations, and school-operated outdoor education programs in camp settings. Agency and private camps have also shown a healthy gain. Organized camping has now spread to all parts of the world. It has developed into a major education-recreation movement, and its place as a part of the accepted pattern of youth services seems secure.

American Camping Association

As organized camping developed, it was natural for camp operators to come together to discuss their common problems. In 1910 the Camp Directors' Association of America was organized, followed in 1916 by the National Association of Directors of Girls' Camps and in 1921 by the Mid-West Camp Directors' Association. These three organizations joined together in 1924 to become the Camp Directors' Association, which in 1935 adopted the name of the American Camping Association. The membership and purposes of the Association were broadened, and a period of growth ensued.

Today the American Camping Association is the primary voice of organized camping in the United States and represents all types of camps in its membership.

Services of the American Camping Association include improving camp standards and programs, acquainting the public with the values of camping and the importance of good camping practices, reviewing studies and encouraging research, keeping abreast of legislation affecting camping, giving consultant services, developing leadership training courses, placing counselors and campers, and conducting conventions and workshops.

Camping's powerful influence

There are certain characteristics of the organized camp that make it extremely significant in influencing behavior patterns of children, teaching skills, and developing new interests.

1. The out-of-doors makes a very strong appeal to children, who are normally responsive to the natural setting.

2. Living in a small group with others of similar age and interests in an informal and friendly relationship with a counselor for 24 hours a day has a profound effect on a child.

3. The camp program is one of *doing*. It consists of first-hand experiences.

4. In the child's mind the total experience is surrounded with an aura of fun and adventure.

This combination makes the camp a powerful educational setting and places on the camp the responsibility of seeing that its influence is constructive and that the outcomes of camping are socially desirable.

Objectives of camping

The following objectives of camping, as stated by Dimock, are widely accepted.

1. The development of a sense of at-homeness in the natural world and of the arts of outdoor living.

2. Education for safe and healthful living.

3. Education for a constructive use of leisure.

4. Contribution to personality development.

5. Education for democratic group and community living.

6. The development of spiritual meanings and values.[2]

It will be immediately recognized that these objectives, except for the one concerned with the out-of-doors, are held in common with youth-serving groups and in part with public schools.

Camp programs must be planned with these objectives in mind. A camp is not merely a place in which to keep children entertained; it is a place where children may achieve, assume responsibility, learn to live with others, and find satisfaction in the manifold associations of the world of nature.

How camps differ in sponsorship

Many agencies conduct organized camping programs. Considered in terms of sponsorship, camps fall into four major categories.

1. *Camps conducted by voluntary agencies.* This category constitutes the largest number of camps. It includes the camps of Boy Scouts, Girl Scouts, Camp Fire Girls, YMCAs, YWCAs, Boys' Clubs, 4-H Clubs, Salvation Army, settlement houses, agencies for handicapped children, and various adult service agencies. Generally, agency camps are short-termed, of one or two weeks' duration. They are reasonable in price, since part of the cost is usually borne by the sponsoring agency. Camps of this type are integral parts of the programs of the major youth-serving agencies.

[2] Hedley S. Dimock, *Administration of the Modern Camp* (New York: Association Press, 1952), pp. 33–36.

2. *Private camps.* Private camps are operated by individuals or groups and are financed by fees that provide the total cost of operation and an income for the operators. There are about 3,000 such camps in the United States. Camp periods are usually longer than in the agency camps, four to eight weeks being common.

3. *Camps operated by religious organizations.* The three major faith groups in the United States—Catholic, Protestant, and Jewish—all carry on extensive camping programs. Camping sponsored by religious organizations has been one of the most rapidly growing forms of camping since 1950. These are generally short-term camps, usually not over one week in duration, and are moderate in price. The sponsors commonly assume part of the expense, and in most cases counselors are not paid. These camps normally include religious instruction or observances to a greater extent than do other types of camps.

4. *Camps operated by tax-supported agencies.* Schools, park and recreation departments, and, less frequently, other public agencies assume responsibility for camp operations. The school outdoor-education program will be discussed later. Most of the camps conducted by public park and recreation departments in the United States are day camps, but there are a number of resident camps operated by these agencies also, particularly in the West.

How camps differ in program emphasis

In terms of program emphasis, there are three types of camps.

1. *Varied-program camps.* Most camps appeal to the normal child and offer varied programs covering a wide range of activities. These camps frequently include handicapped children, or children with other problems, in their camp population, but their programs are geared neither to special interests nor to special problems. The great majority of organized children's camp programs fall into this category.

2. *Special-interest camps.* There are camps that specialize in particular fields, such as music, arts and crafts, woodcraft, natural science, dramatics, athletics, riding, folk dancing, language, and even work projects. Such camps usually carry on some general program activities in addition to their specialties in order to give variety. Some of the camps of religious organizations might be included as special-interest camps.

Special-interest camps appeal to older boys or girls. Interests tend to become specialized as children grow, and older boys and girls often wish to pursue program areas to a greater depth in order to develop more skill and competence than they can develop in the general camp program.

3. *Special-purpose camps.* One of the most interesting developments in recent years is special-purpose camps organized to serve children with

unusual problems or needs. The programs of these camps, though varied, are adapted to the special requirements of the campers they serve.

Health camps and camps for handicapped children have existed for many years, but their numbers and types have multiplied since World War II. There are camps today for diabetic, orthopedically handicapped, blind, cerebral palsied, and mentally retarded children, as well as those with other kinds of disabilities. These camps are intended to give handicapped children experiences often denied them because of their physical ailments. Such camps are not planned primarily as means of treatment, although therapy may be a part of their concern. Living with other children in the camp and participating in varied programs under good leadership are themselves good forms of therapy. A few of the camps have staff members especially trained to carry on the particular types of program. If a handicap is not so severe as to keep a child from adjusting to life in a camp with normal children, it is usually preferable to place him in such a camp rather than in a special-purpose camp.

Another type of special-purpose camp serves children with emotional and behavior problems. Some camps are for children whose emotional problems make their adjustment to school difficult; other camps are for offenders against the law. Where good leadership is available and programs are carefully developed, the camps may contribute effectively to the rehabilitation of these young people.

Children are not the only ones to benefit from special-purpose camps. Camps for the aged, particularly day camps, have recently come into being as attention has been focused upon the needs of this portion of our population.

Camp program

The camp program consists of everything that happens to the camper, including both the organized activities and those that are casual and unplanned. It is the program which attracts a child to a camp, and it is through the program that the purposes of the camp are attained. The camp organization, facilities, equipment, and supplies are merely means of making the program possible. Leadership acts through the program, whether through scheduled activities or informal relationships with the campers.

Factors determining program. We have pointed out that a camp may have a general program, a special field of interest, or a program adapted to campers with special needs. Even camps with general programs differ a great deal in their program emphases. Some of the factors that determine the program in a particular setting are:

1. Philosophy of the organization or individual conducting the camp.
2. Location of the site—topography, climate.
3. Leadership—interests, skills, and concept of education.

4. Clientele—background, age, physical characteristics, and interests of the campers.
5. Facilities and equipment available.
6. Length of camp period.
7. Expectations of campers' parents.

Ideally the leadership, location, facilities, equipment, and even the length of the camp should be determined by the program, but in practical application the program must operate within the limitations of these factors.

Unique program possibilities of camping. Increasing numbers of camps are evaluating their programs in terms of camping objectives and are coming to realize that camps can best contribute to the welfare of youth by utilizing their unique opportunities. The camp situation, in which children live together outdoors and use the natural environment, offers indigenous program possibilities not available in other situations. By concentrating on these possibilities, rather than repeating activities that can be done as effectively or even more effectively in the school, playground, club, or community center, camps can fulfill their most significant function.

How the program is carried out. The agency or individual conducting the camp usually determines how the program is organized, but the actual day-to-day planning in most camps involves the total camp staff and the campers themselves. The staff must be prepared with program ideas, but the campers can participate in the planning and should have opportunities to make choices within the limits of program possibilities. There are four groupings in which the program may take place.

1. First is the small group of campers that live together. In some camps, most of the program revolves around this basic unit; whereas in other camps, unit activities are at a minimum.
2. Second is the interest group, such as a group concerned with arts and crafts, swimming, sailing, or innumerable other activities. Many camps make it possible for campers to select, from a variety of interests, the ones in which they wish to participate. Campers who are in the same living unit may be in completely separate interest groups. Advocates of this type of organization feel that it offers both the advantage of free choice and the opportunity to develop high levels of proficiency in particular skills.
3. Third is the entire camp, with activities in which all campers participate together. These activities may include campfire programs, camp meals, and special celebrations.
4. Last is the individual camper himself. Campers should have some free time. The day should not be so completely scheduled that there is no opportunity for campers to read, relax, and do some of the personal things they wish to do.

Most camps provide program opportunities in all of the above categories. The length of the camp period and the age of the campers help determine the emphasis given to a particular means of grouping.

Flexible scheduling. In recent years, camps have turned away from scheduled class periods to more flexible scheduling, with long blocks of time available for various types of programs. Certain aspects of camp living must, however, be scheduled on a definite time basis. Time must be clearly allotted for sleep, rest, meals, and camp chores. Campers from 9 to 11 years of age require about 10½ hours of sleep each night, whereas campers from 15 to 17 years of age need about 9 hours. In addition, camps provide a daily rest period, usually just after lunch. Apart from this basic scheduling, considerable freedom may be allowed. A camp group may take a morning for a hike, for example, instead of scheduling an hour for crafts, an hour for dramatics, and a half hour for swimming instruction.

Balanced activities. Efforts are made in good camp programing to keep a balance in terms of strenuous and quiet activities and in terms of individual and mass programs. Good programing also affords diversity in order to appeal to the individual interests of the campers.

Some camps are criticized because their programs are too active and too stimulating. Programs must be inviting and challenging, but over-stimulation produces a camper who is tired and irritable, who does not rest well, and whose human relationships deteriorate.

Camps must allow time for the care of personal equipment and camp living quarters, for letter writing, and for the fellowship of the camp counselor and the cabin or tent unit. In many camps, these aspects of camp life are a major part of the program.

Program areas. The following list indicates program possibilities that are especially suited to the camp environment.

AQUATICS—swimming, diving, and life saving; canoeing, rowing, and sailing; water skiing, games, and pageants.

CAMPCRAFT AND WOODCRAFT—camp tool craft, shelter construction, selection and care of duffel, fire care and fire building, camp cooking, use of conservation measures and nature knowledge in outdoor living, health and safety, lashing, knotcraft, and use of the axe.

ARTS AND CRAFTS—using the arts to interpret the out-of-doors; using native materials in arts and crafts; making casts and prints of natural objects; constructing tools and equipment needed out-of-doors; constructing tools and equipment for the nature and conservation programs; preparation of natural materials for preservation and display; and preparation of costumes, settings, and decorations for dramatic and social events.

NATURE AND CONSERVATION—field trips, excursions, and explorations; developing nature trails and displays; making collections; maintaining gardens, aquariums, and terrariums; erecting weather stations and making observations; making star observations; campfire talks related to natural science; work on conservation projects such as erosion control; and making natural-science surveys.

INDIAN LORE—Indian dancing, construction of drums and costumes, Indian ceremonials and crafts, and Indian-story nights.

SPORTS AND GAMES—hiking and mountain climbing, trailing games, wide-area games, Indian and pioneer sports and games, orienteering, team sports requiring minimum equipment, horseback riding, archery, target shooting, and fishing.

DRAMATICS—informal campfire dramatics, short plays and original skits, dramatized story telling and readings, pageants, circuses, and stunt nights.

MUSIC—informal group singing, solo and group performances in singing or instrumental music, rhythm bands, listening to good recordings, and song writing.

SOCIAL ACTIVITIES AND DANCING—social and folk dancing, games of all types, intercamp parties, and special events.

The camp site and its facilities

Site. A good camp program is dependent in large part on a site with varied natural resources and suitable facilities. In resident camps and troop camps, there should be at least one acre per camper, and most of this acreage should be in a natural condition. Day camps may often operate on smaller sites, but the land should be adequate to give some sense of isolation and to provide different kinds of program opportunities. Water resources for swimming and boating are generally considered desirable for the day camp and essential for the resident camp.

Facilities. Camp facilities range from the rugged to the luxurious. All types of camps must provide for access, parking, safe water, sanitary handling of all food, adequate refrigeration, and sanitary disposal of wastes. Facilities must be maintained in a safe and healthful condition. State boards of health generally assume responsibility for inspection and supervision of camps to insure safe and sanitary operations.

Group camps or troop camps, to which campers bring their own equipment, provide little beyond the basic requirements. Many of them maintain trading posts where campers may purchase supplies, shelters for meetings on rainy days, and sites where groups may cook and erect tents. Day-camp facilities can be even simpler, since overnight shelters and trading posts are not required. Some day camps, in which children do not do their own cooking, maintain dining halls and kitchens; but in most day camps children bring their own lunches or cook outdoors.

Resident camps require the most elaborate facilities. They generally have dining halls, well-equipped kitchens with electricity and refrigeration, tents or cabins, central lodges, infirmaries, campfire circles or council rings, central wash-houses, laundries, docks, and beaches. To these, some camps add stables, craft shops, museums, chapels, game courts and diamonds, garages, and recreation halls.

Most modern camps are arranged on a "decentralized" basis: that is, instead of being in a formal, close arrangement, living quarters are grouped into units or small camps at a moderate distance from one another. Such seclusion makes possible the conducting of programs in small groups without prohibiting programs on a total-camp basis.

The camp staff

More than two hundred thousand leaders are required to man the camps of the United States. Most of these leaders are teachers or college students employed only in the summer.

The counselor. The general counselor, because of his close relationship with the camper, is the basic program person in most camps. Because of the close personal relationship between campers and counselors, the counselor needs to be a person of the highest quality. There should be at least one adult counselor for every eight children 8 years of age and older; one for every six children under 8 years of age.

Much has been written on the qualifications of the good counselor. These qualities fall into three groups:

1. PERSONAL QUALIFICATIONS. The counselor should be at least 19 years old; should have interest in and sympathy with the problems of youth; and should have an exemplary character, good physical health, stamina, and emotional maturity. He should enjoy outdoor living, be able to work with others, and be dedicated to the purposes of the camp.

2. QUALIFICATIONS OF KNOWLEDGE AND UNDERSTANDING. The counselor should have an insight into child and group psychology, understanding of health and safety in camping, and knowledge of the out-of-doors. The counselor with a good background of education and experience and with varied interests is much to be desired. At least two years of college or the equivalent is recommended.

3. QUALIFICATIONS OF SKILL. The counselor needs skill in democratic leadership, individual guidance, and leadership of several types of program activities.

The director. The director should have many of the same qualifications as the counselor but should be at least 25 years of age, should have a college degree or the equivalent, and should have had some successful experience in administration and in camp leadership. The director may be a full-time professional camp worker, particularly if he is the owner of the camp. Because there are not many year-round programs in camping, except in the field of school outdoor education, such full-time professional workers are few in number. The director-owner of a summer camp may, however, find year-round work in promoting his camp, maintaining his facilities, and arranging off-season use of the camp by his own clientele or other groups.

Other staff members. Staff members who specialize in particular aspects of the program, such as swimming, horseback riding, or crafts, should have essentially the same qualifications as the general counselors and, in addition, training and skill in their specialties. Qualified staffs are also required for business, health, food service, and maintenance aspects of camp operation. The basic organization of personnel in a resident camp is indicated in Fig. 13.

Fig. 13   *Administrative Structure of a Resident Camp*

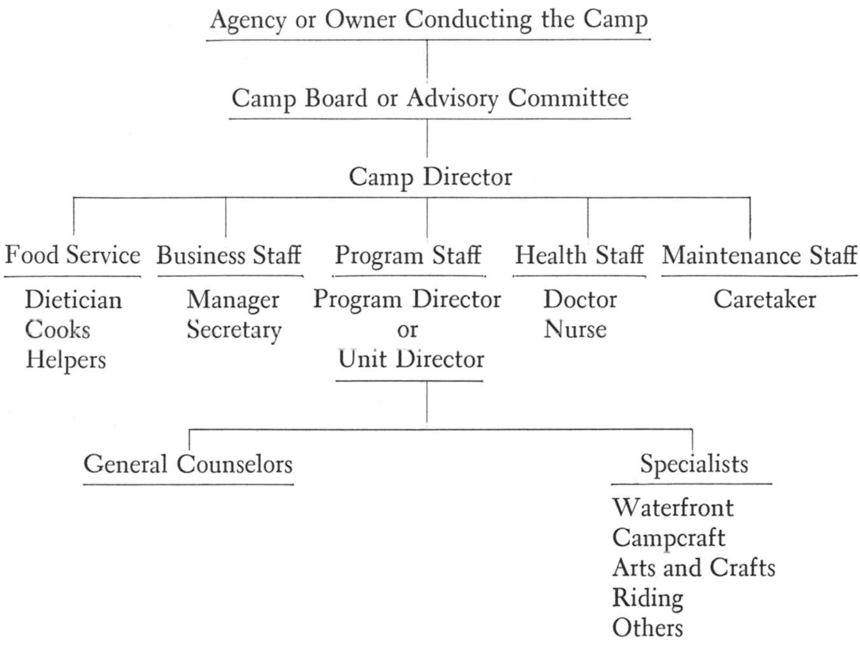

Agency or Owner Conducting the Camp

Camp Board or Advisory Committee

Camp Director

Food Service	Business Staff	Program Staff	Health Staff	Maintenance Staff
Dietician	Manager	Program Director	Doctor	Caretaker
Cooks	Secretary	or	Nurse	
Helpers		Unit Director		

General Counselors

Specialists

Waterfront
Campcraft
Arts and Crafts
Riding
Others

Outdoor Education in the Camp Setting

Closely related to organized camping but with different purposes is the school-sponsored outdoor education program in the camp setting. For many years schools have used the out-of-doors as a resource for learning. School classes have taken field trips and engaged in outdoor projects in forestry, agriculture, wildlife, and other fields of science. School gardens, farms, and forests have served educational purposes.

How outdoor education grew

Although the Gunnery School, a private school, is credited with conducting the first organized camp in the United States, this was an isolated event. The taking of numbers of school groups to resident camps for educational purposes is rather new. Dr. Lloyd B. Sharp, founder and head of the Outdoor Education Association, pioneered in advocating school outdoor education programs and assisted numerous communities in their experimental efforts with school camps. In 1940 he established National Camp, a leadership training camp in New Jersey. The W. K. Kellogg Foundation advanced the outdoor education movement in 1940 by initiating, in cooperation with educational leaders of Michigan, a pattern for outdoor education that has been adopted generally by school systems throughout the country. San Diego's extensive system, by which camp experiences are provided for school children, was embarked upon in 1946. Since then, outdoor education programs have been adopted extensively in California, Michigan, and elsewhere. There were at least six hundred school systems in the United States in 1960 that conducted at least a one-week program in a camp setting. Outstanding and well established are the programs of Battle Creek, Michigan; Cleveland Heights, Ohio; Tyler, Texas; San Diego, California; and Long Beach, California.

Why outdoor education is accepted as a school responsibility

A statement by Dr. Sharp, which has become a byword for advocates of this form of education, succinctly expresses the basic philosophy underlying the inclusion of outdoor education in the school curricula.

That which can best be learned inside the classroom should be learned there.
That which can best be learned in the out-of-doors through direct experience, dealing with native materials and life situations, should there be learned.[3]

There are a number of reasons why outdoor education has developed in schools in recent years.

1. *Nature of modern life.* Urbanization has divorced most youth from the soil, and city children have little knowledge of the age-old problems of growing food and little understanding of man's dependence on nature.

2. *New understandings of the learning process.* Some things can best be learned through direct observation and experience. The outdoors offers many opportunities to learn in this manner. Life cycles and the behavior

[3] Julian Smith, ed., *Outdoor Education for American Youth* (Washington, D.C.: American Association for Health, Physical Education, and Recreation, 1957), introductory page.

and interrelationships of living things are made more understandable through contact with the natural environment. In addition, where interest is high, learning takes place more rapidly and is retained longer than under other circumstances. Outdoor education can take advantage of this principle and, by capturing the moment, teach when the interest is most keen.

3. *Enrichment of the school curricula.* Many subjects taught in the classroom may be supplemented and enriched through outdoor experiences. Actual experience lends reality and dimension to textbooks on science, history, geography, and health. Incentives to verbal expression, both written and oral, may come from the outdoor experience.

4. *Need for work experiences.* The camp setting offers work experiences often lacking in a child's home or school environment. Taking care of himself, keeping his quarters clean, helping with camp chores, and engaging in projects to improve or conserve the campsite help a child to assume responsibility and attain self-reliance.

5. *Need for education in human relationships.* Successful experiences in outdoor education improve the relationships of teachers to children and children to one another. In some instances, the improvement of mutual understanding and the building of class morale are of greater value than the other educational benefits of the school camp. The school outdoor education program has much in common with the organized summer camp. The chief difference between the two lies in the integration of the school camping program with the school curriculums.

Usual pattern

The most common pattern for the school camp is the one-week resident camp program conducted during school time. The fifth, sixth, or seventh grades participate more frequently than the other grades. The departmentalization of school subjects at the upper grade levels and in high school makes it difficult to organize the program in these grades.

Usually the classroom teacher accompanies the children. Other teachers, principals, supervisors, and student teachers add to the staff. In some of the larger school camp programs, special teachers are employed to give their full time to the outdoor education programs. Pre-camp planning customarily takes place in the classroom and involves a study of the science, history, and geography of the campsite. Menus may be planned ahead of time in the classroom, and decisions may be made regarding educational and personal equipment to take along. The projects to be undertaken and the experiences to be enjoyed may also come into the planning sessions.

Typical experiences in outdoor education

In camp itself the schedule may be roughly similar to that of the resident camp, with personal chores, camp duties, rest period, evening programs, and campfires. The heart of the program consists of educational outdoor experiences. Some of the typical experiences are:

Science and conservation—constructing and operating a weather station; making field trips to study geology, forestry, farming, water life, land wildlife, soil, and plants; making collections and preparing exhibits; working on conservation projects such as tree planting and trail construction; learning about proper fire building and forest fire control.

Social studies—gathering information on local pioneer and Indian history; visiting local farms and industries; studying changes in rural living; learning to use topographic maps and compasses.

Health, physical fitness, and safety—observing good practices in eating, resting, exercising, and keeping clean in camp; learning about meal planning and food preparation; observing safe practices in swimming and exploring; recognizing and avoiding poisonous plants and reptiles.

Arts and crafts—interpreting the out-of-doors through art forms; using native materials in crafts.

Language arts—enlarging vocabularies with words associated with the camp experience; keeping camp diaries; writing letters; presenting oral reports and dramatic productions; writing poems and stories based upon camp experiences.

Manual skills—learning outdoor-living skills such as camp crafts, use of tools, outdoor cooking.

Other possibilities include learning songs, games, boating, and fishing, depending upon the school and the locality. The program emphasized in a particular camp may relate to the subject matter taught in particular grades and may be employed to give vitality to the classroom subjects.

Leadership in the school camp

The lack of teachers prepared to carry on programs in outdoor education has been a principal deterrent to the development of these programs. Two types of attacks on this problem are illustrated by leadership training at Northern Illinois University and at the New Jersey State School of Conservation. At Northern Illinois University, every student preparing to be an elementary teacher spends two and one half days as a sophomore, three days as a junior, and a week as a senior in the Lorado Taft Field Campus. New Jersey requires a week's participation in its State School of Conservation for all students seeking elementary school credentials. In some school systems, the employment of fifth- and sixth-grade teachers is contingent upon their ability and willingness to carry on outdoor education programs with their classes.

Family Camping

The second half of the twentieth century has witnessed an explosive growth in informal camping, in which families or groups of friends take their own equipment to sites of their own choice and set up their own camps. Our public parks and forests have been besieged with millions of families who seek such places each summer. Most families take tents. Others sleep in cars, station wagons, or under the stars. The small travel-trailer has added a new dimension to camping, and on some of the western campgrounds from one third to one half of the occupants use these trailers. The number of people going by canoe, horseback, or foot into wilderness areas has also grown and has accentuated the need for maintaining our last vestiges of wilderness.

Land for family camping

The demand for family campsites has resulted in increased attention to the provision of campgrounds. Two approaches are:

Commercial family camps. Commercially operated camping facilities are being developed rapidly in many parts of the United States. These camps are of two types: those designed primarily for travelers, in which one night is the ordinary length of stay; and those designed for vacationers. In the latter, the site must be large, attractive, and inviting for extended stays. There must be fishing, riding, hiking, swimming, or other interesting things to do. Commercial developments must of necessity make charges sufficient to make the ventures profitable. The public has evidenced its willingness to pay reasonable fees and, by so doing, has encouraged expansion of these camps.

Public campgrounds. Public lands still bear the major burden of accommodating family campers. The national and state forests and parks, which are the major land resources for outdoor recreation, are providing more campsites. The public has been requesting more and more comfortable facilities; and, where these are provided, charges are often made to cover the costs. It is to be hoped, however, that small, simple campgrounds will continue to be available, free or at low cost, so as not to deter great numbers who wish to camp.

Organized family camping

Organized camping for families has also continued to grow. Such programs are conducted by churches, YMCAs, settlement houses, industries, labor organizations, and municipal recreation departments. They provide places where families can spend a week or more, each family living by itself but usually eating in a common dining hall. A more or less organized

Fig. 14   *Family Camping in a National Park (Courtesy United States Department of the Interior. National Park Service Photo)*

program is commonly provided, with some activities for families, some for children only, and some for parents only. The camps relieve mothers from cooking and extensive housekeeping and provide relaxing outdoor experiences.

Present-Day Developments in Camping and Outdoor Education

As organized camping, school outdoor education programs, and family camping have increased in recent years, several developments are discernible. Organized camping has assumed an important place in the recreation-education experiences of youth. Standards for leadership and camp practices have risen, largely through the efforts of the American Camping Association, state boards of health, and the major youth-serving organizations. Decentralized facilities and flexible programs geared to the natural environment are commonly accepted, and many opportunities are offered for campers to participate in program planning. Camps for those with special interests or needs, such as camps for the handicapped or day camps for the aged, are increasing. Literature dealing with camping is abundant. Public agencies are providing more areas and facilities for camping agencies. If sufficient natural lands can be preserved to meet the needs of a growing population, the future of camping is bright.

SUGGESTED REFERENCES

Benson, Reuel A. and Jacob A. Goldberg, *The Camp Counselor*. New York: McGraw-Hill Book Company, 1951.

Burns, Gerald, *Program of the Modern Camp*. Englewood Cliffs, N.J.: Prentice-Hall, Inc., 1954.

Dimock, Hedley S., *Administration of the Modern Camp*. New York: Association Press, 1952.

Freeberg, William H. and Loren E. Taylor, *Philosophy of Outdoor Education*. Minneapolis, Minn.: Burgess Publishing Company, 1961.

Hammett, Catherine T. and Virginia Musselman, *The Camp Program Book*. New York: Association Press, 1954.

Irwin, Frank L., *The Theory of Camping*. New York: A. S. Barnes & Company, 1954.

Mitchell, A. Viola and Ida B. Crawford, *Camp Counseling*, Third edition. Philadelphia: W. B. Saunders Company, 1961.

"It is far more important that a man should play something himself, even if he plays it badly, than that he should go to see someone else play it well."

THEODORE ROOSEVELT

9

Recreation
Is Where You Find It

Major contributions to the recreation needs of any community are offered by the local government, the schools, and the voluntary youth organizations. Chapters 4, 5, and 6 outlined their roles. Chapter 9 is concerned with other agencies that also have key responsibilities in providing recreation services in the local community. Recreation activities can take place in many settings, which include such areas as the church, the home, the playground, the factory, the settlement house, or the museum. For some of these settings, such as playgrounds, community centers, and zoos, recreation is the chief concern; for others, recreation plays a secondary but important role. The contributions that the latter settings make to the recreation movement is the subject of the following pages.

Family Recreation

In present days of expanded leisure, the home, the oldest of our social institutions, must be alert to the challenge for education, for leisure, and for wholesome, creative use of that leisure. Families can be fun. Let us begin with that premise. Families should be fun, and—stronger still—families must be fun, if they are to continue to uphold their proper responsibility in the present social order.

The influence of home and family is a basic foundation from which community environment is shaped. Any culture is dependent primarily upon three factors: human nature, physical surroundings, and social heritage. The first, human nature, remains fairly constant the world over. Inventions, technological advancements, and scientific discoveries have tended to minimize the effect of our physical environs. Our social inheritance, however, continues to move the nation through successive waves of readjustment. All too frequently, in the realm of social changes that affect family use of leisure, readjustment has not kept pace.

Early interdependence of families

The family was the basic unit of even the ancient primitive cultures. It was the organization for procreation and education of children, bound together through social and economic necessities. In the last two hundred years, nearly every new force in our civilization has been instrumental in weakening those original ties. Years ago, the individual's ability to survive was enmeshed with interdependence within families or tribes. It was literally impossible to stay alive without contributing to or accepting from the daily life of other members of the family.

The early American pioneers banded together for protection from their enemies. In a rural setting, life was a cooperative family affair. While father and grandfather farmed, mother and grandmother baked and cleaned, sister helped with the younger children, and brother kept the animals or brought in the firewood. Economic necessity put all family members on the same team, rubbing elbows, pushing shoulder to shoulder, with a keen sense of unity and belonging. When the work was done, the leisure hours were spent in singing, backyard games, quilting bees, Bible reading, or parlor games with the same closely knit circle. There were few distractions from this pattern. When such distractions did come, they arose in broadening of the same work-and-play activities to include other relatives or close neighbors.

There were few alternatives. Grandfather could not have his clothes tailored at the nearest shop, nor could he drop in at the local restaurant for a chicken dinner or find his entertainment needs at the nearest theater. Grandmother relied on grandfather for the ingredients for the family meal, and the children's recreation was of their own improvisation. The scope of such possible improvisations was, of course, widened by the fact that most families contained at least five youngsters, from whom the ideas would be forthcoming.

The back lot was the original playground; the home was the original community center; the parents were and, in the opinion of the authors, still should remain the first play leaders. Education, whether for work, leisure, or worship, was provided for the family, by the family, and with the family.

Changing times and concepts

Today's mass productionized, social welfarized, institutionalized world has all but eliminated the early *raison d'être* for the family group. As the population moved from a simple rural to a highly complex urban setting, the responsibility for training children for adult roles in such an environment became too specialized for individual parents successfully to fulfill their obligations. Other factors also decreased family interdependency and cohesiveness. In a world in which nurseries are available for child care, lucrative positions are accessible for the emancipated wife and mother, and shelter and food satisfactions are prevalent outside the home for the male members of the family, the concept of family teamwork, mandatory for existence in the past, has all but vanished.

Twentieth-century life has contrived to pull the family away from the home to work, to learn, to play, and even to worship. In many homes, there are few meals at which all family members are present. The salvation of the family as a social unit may yet lie in its concentrated effort to get acquainted with its members through recreation pursuits. The pioneer father learned to know his son as the boy followed his lead in the barn or in the fields or explored the joys of whittling or playing the jew's harp. The pioneer girl and her mother or grandmother gained mutual respect and understanding as the youngster was introduced to the joys of cooking, the intricacies of quilting, or the vibrant notes of the harpsichord. Today's job rarely allows the father to take his son to work; frequently, the other members of the family have little concept of the demands of the breadwinner's position. Today's housewife, emancipated through modern conveniences, has little need for the child's help in her daily chores.

The Industrial Revolution has opened up new blocks of leisure not only for those who work but for those who are too young or too old to join the work force. Economic affluence has increased the opportunities for varied use of such leisure; social changes have influenced what can be done with impunity in such free hours, and many organizations—private, commercial, public, and voluntary—are involved with educating for and ordering our leisure. However, it is our sincere belief that training for the wise use of leisure is first the responsibility of the family and home.

In the present day, when article after article is written about delinquency and crime among juveniles, broken homes of adults, and the lonely desperation of the isolated aged, parents may shake their heads and place the blame on television, comic books, movies, or the current political tensions. In reality, some of the blame must rightfully be directed at the home. Parents may help stem the tide of discontent and delinquency in the ever increasing leisure by giving time and space for recreation in the family environment. In a study indicating where high-school students seek "good times," 95 percent of the boys and 83 percent of the girls found their fun outside their homes.[1] The pendulum of common sense is hopefully swinging back from the parent who discharged his responsibility by buying the most expensive bicycle or the newest car model for his son to the father who spends time wisely opening for his children new vistas for adventurous hobbies, which will outlast the sturdiest of wheeled vehicles.

The new philosophy of child rearing helps to stimulate such a mutual enjoyment. Early precautions had new parents regimented to a schedule that allowed neither the stimulation of baby's gurglings nor the bliss of the rocking chair. Their main responsibility was educating the child systematically for the day when he would leave the home. The modern mother and father are encouraged to enjoy their youngsters at any age. Emphasis is put upon a balanced inter-relatedness within the home, in which life is lived not just as preparation for tomorrow but as healthful, meaningful experience of today.

The importance of family recreation cannot be ignored when research shows that, for the most part, our recreation choices and our development of leisure appreciations, skills, and interests occur before the teen years. In a study of current hobby interests of persons in New York City, Nash[2] found that 70 percent of those interests had started in the home and 70 percent of all hobbies had been initiated before the age of 12. Such statistics place on the home a heavy responsibility for early training in education for leisure.

Leisure can strengthen or weaken the family ties. In the words of Howard Braucher:

> The home and the family are the foundations of life in America. Nothing good outside the home can fully compensate for lack of abundant living in the home.
> The family that plays together and prays together stays together. That family really lives. That family has memories. There is no substitute for family recreation and family living. Upon such family life is America built.[3]

Wisely, community recreation leaders work to help fathers and mothers acquire skills and wisdom in regard to home recreation.

Approach to family recreation

Abundant living, for Howard Braucher, means the inclusion of family good times. Ideas for family fun crosscut all of the program areas. Families

[1] George A. Lundberg, Mirra Komarovsky, and Mary Alice McInerny, "The Amounts and Uses of Leisure," in *Mass Leisure*, ed. Eric Larrabee and Rolf Meyersohn (Chicago: The Free Press, 1958), p. 187.

[2] Jay B. Nash, *Philosophy of Recreation and Leisure* (St. Louis: The C. V. Mosby Company, 1953), p. 15.

[3] Howard Braucher, "The Home and Recreation," *Recreation*, XLIII, No. 2 (May 1949), 49.

or parts of families can find enjoyment together in active or spectator participation in music, drama, sports and games, and others.

As the conscientious parent takes over in his role of play leader, he needs a word of caution. Family recreation does not necessarily imply that the *entire* family must participate in *each* activity. There should be a planned balance of activity and participation in the family recreation program so that family recreation, like any other form of recreation, becomes an involvement because of attractive choice, rather than because of a sense of family obligation or responsibility.

All too frequently, overanxious parents feel that family fun consists of just playing with Junior, doing whatever he wants to do at that moment. Too often, Father, when he joins his teenage son and his buddies around the basketball backboard, insists upon an unpopular "togetherness" to prove he is an interested pal. There should be times and places when just the youngsters have fun together, when the whole family assembles to enjoy the backyard Four-Square or a picnic, and when the teenagers can have full use of an area without the heckling of "small-fry" brothers or sisters. Last, and most important, there should be a time when parents or adults have fun together without feeling guilty because they are not catering to small Susie's latest whim. In short, the interests of family unity are best served when there are times for doing things together and times for doing things individually or in groups of individuals. Wise families will not deprive any member of the household the joy of solitary reading or the pleasure of helping plan the anticipated vacation.

Settings for family fun

Houses today are being built with an eye to space for recreation activity for the whole family. Literally any room in the house can be used for recreation: from the bathroom (where miniature boats sail in the bathtub), to the hobby workshop in the basement, to the kitchen in which Mother introduces Daughter to the fun of baking, to the patio where Father dons the chef cap, or to the bedroom in which convalescent Grandmother tends to her window gardens. Space is important; the rest is provided by the ingenuity of the people involved—their ability to balance utilitarian and recreation experiences.

Architects are prone to include a family room in the plans of new homes. The tendency in "suburbia" is to seek a larger backyard for outdoor-indoor family living. Furniture or room subdividers often provide intentional climbing devices for youngsters to stimulate fun activities in their own rooms. There is a recent trend in home planning to return to the dining room, for several years omitted from post-depression years' blueprints. Sitting together at the family table sometimes is the only stimulus needed for conversation or game fun on those occasions when the entire family is home for dinner at the same time. The once-popular kitchen snack bar only heightened the feeling that mealtime was a necessity, to be dispensed with as quickly as possible.

New community emphasis on family recreation

Churches, municipal programs, youth-serving agencies, clubs, schools, and even commercial ventures are awakening to the realization that each has a responsibility for a greater emphasis on the need to reunite the family in recreation. For years, the efforts of organizations dealing with leisure pursuits segregated age and sex groups in the families, calling Father to his club, Mother to her sewing circle, Son to the basketball league, Sister to the craft class, and the youngsters to the neighboring tot-lot.

In the last ten years, there has been a decided increase in efforts to include programing that will entice whole families or parts of families to the same place at the same time. Community centers are sponsoring family dances; playgrounds are having family fun nights; churches are finding success with family dinners; PTAs are encouraging family potluck and carnival nights, and the service clubs are doubling the number of ladies' nights, so that wives may be a part of their husbands' club affiliation. Evidences of this new and healthful emphasis may be found in the following examples:

1. Backyard play kits and picnic kits furnished to families by municipal recreation departments on a sign-out basis.

2. Television shows, sponsored by recreation programs, which provide ideas for fun at home.

3. The several "fun-en-route" game pamphlets for travel fun furnished by insurance companies, oil companies, or recreation departments.

4. Attempts on the part of such organizations as the YMCA to make their offerings family affairs. The Krannert Memorial YMCA in Indianapolis, Indiana, incorporated indoor and outdoor activities for the entire family in its new facility opened in 1959.

5. Offering of leadership training classes to help parents with ideas and techniques in recreation activities.

6. Newspaper columns that explore new ideas for family recreation.

7. Increased attempts by agencies to encourage participation by the family in activities such as swimming and boating through substantial decreases in costs for family membership.

8. Increased emphasis on family community centers such as the Jewish Family Centers in Louisville, Kentucky, and Cincinnati, Ohio.

9. Contests for home decorations, which activate hours of work, fun, and pride for families.

10. "How to" bulletins such as those published by the Decatur, Illinois, Recreation Department, which stimulate building of games and areas for backyard play.

11. At state level, William E. Schupp [4] notes a decided increase in efforts of state parks to provide facilities that will entice family participation.

Such evidences are heartening, but the American family still has a long way to go. In a study of family recreation, James Wylie, of Boston University, found that, although a significant percentage of families felt that they achieved stronger family unity through recreation, a high percentage of families felt that their recreation program was unsatisfactory. An alarming 51 percent of the recreation took place outside the home.[5]

Moses Abramovitz, in a paper prepared for the Golden Anniversary of the White House Conference on Children and Youth, reinforces the increasingly important role of the family in recreation with the following statement:

The child is the father of the man. For better or for worse, the attitudes towards work, leisure, and consumption which will give tone to American civilization during the next generations are now being formed in our children. Their values and aspirations are emerging from the experience they now share with their parents and peers as we all learn to enjoy—to use or dissipate—our still new-won prosperity. Our own lives, private and public, will tell whether the affluence we now enjoy and the still more abounding productive powers which our children will control will be worthily used or most thoughtlessly squandered.[6]

Everything that professional recreation personnel can do to stimulate or educate the parent or child for more active, wholesome family recreation roles will be a boon for balanced and healthful living for the future community.

Recreation and Religious Organizations

The title for this section was carefully chosen, for it embraces more extensively the relationships between religion and recreation than does the more common term "church recreation." From the beginnings of time, religion and recreation have been closely associated, sometimes because of mutual benefits and interests and sometimes because of fierce antagonisms

[4] William E. Schupp, "Families Play in State Parks," *Recreation*, XLVIII, No. 5 (May 1955), 216.

[5] James A. Wylie, "Family Recreation, What Is Its Status?," *American Recreation Society Bulletin* (July 1953), p. 20.

[6] Moses Abramovitz, "Growing Up in an Affluent Society," in *The Nation's Children*, ed. Eli Ginzberg (New York: Columbia University Press, 1960), p. 179. Reprinted by permission.

and attempted restraints. The development of recreation throughout history has been alternately spurred and restricted by attitudes of religious organizations toward the spiritual value and meaning of man's recreative outlets. Extremes in attitudes of religious groups toward recreation have run from the philosophy of the Puritan, "the hours of play are the devil's workshop," to the inclusion of worship as a kind of supreme recreation, as noted in an excerpt from Kaplan's report of the 1956 Conference on Leisure. Several modes of leisure are presented in a classification that judges them in reference to freedom. In addition to mass entertainment, hobbies, and play, he adds:

Finally and the most preferable is recreation, which consists of three groups: artistic creation and appreciation, study and discourse, and prayer and worship. All these have intrinsic values of their own. In performing these acts, we are engaged "in the very reformation and recreation of ourselves." This is freedom par excellence. Worship is placed above the rest, for in addition to the element of freedom, worship "seeks the aid of the transcendent." [7]

These two widely diverse concepts have the span of centuries between them, yet elements of both philosophies can be found in religious organizations today.

Religion and recreation

Should recreation and religion be poles apart? Are they related? If so, how are they related? Does the church or the synagogue have any responsibility in recreation for its own members or for society as a whole? Here are some comments on such questions by leaders in religion or recreation. Dr. Walter Stone asks:

What is the relation of recreation to religion? Both are concerned with the things of the spirit. Both are concerned with the good life. Life is not good when social relations leave us unrefreshed. Life is not good when as we get closer together physically, we get farther apart spiritually. Leisure time provides the opportunity for refreshing social relations, and for community of interest, if we are smart enough to use it. There is a re-creational way of living at home, at church, at school, at work, in the community. [8]

The Most Reverend John Wright emphasizes the need for family responsibility in leisure use to strengthen spiritual ties, in the following excerpt from his contribution at the 1960 White House Conference on Children and Youth:

[7] Max Kaplan, *Leisure in America* (New York: John Wiley & Sons, Inc., 1960), p. 155. Reprinted by permission.

[8] *Proceedings, First National Workshop in Recreation for Leaders of Religious Organizations* (Bloomington, Indiana: Department of Recreation, Indiana University, 1952), p. 7.

The family should occupy a key place, too, in our planning for health and education, and for the solution of our problems of value.

Training in the use of leisure time would be a constructive contribution to family life. With a 30 hour week in prospect ten years hence, American men may eventually devote most of their time to activities of their own choice. They must be trained to use their leisure in a humane and divine way—to lead the good life in a family which will be part of the family of families, the American fatherland.

The current American attitude toward the family is akin to what happens when a man gets hit by a truck—no one dares to touch him for fear of hurting him more. Some pray; and all resolve not to get involved. But the family has no hospital to go to, and the main physician—God—has trouble getting his prescriptions filled.[9]

The need for involvement of religious organizations with community interest including recreation was delineated rather specifically by members of several faiths in a preliminary report [10] to the 1960 White House Conference on Children and Youth. They indicated that if the church or synagogue is to become a genuine force for good, it should emulate the churches and synagogues of colonial days, which were places of leadership and community activity as well as religious centers. E. O. Harbin, long-time leader of Methodist recreation activities, extends such thinking as part of his philosophy of recreation:

There are three reasons why the church must interest itself in community recreation: (1) The members of the church do not grow up in a vacuum. Children, young people, and adults have community contacts that are inescapable. The church must be intelligently concerned, therefore, about what goes on in the community. (2) Then, too, the church's interest in human welfare makes it imperative that it cooperate with other community agencies in providing adequate recreation opportunities of such quality and variety as to meet community needs. (3) The church often has space and equipment that should be made available for community recreation activities, if such space and equipment are not available elsewhere.[11]

The closeness of religion and recreation as fundamental human needs is recognized by Brightbill in these comments:

The chain which links the healthful recreational life with the wholesome spiritual life is most evident in their mutual attributes: love and respect for

[9] Most Reverend John Wright, "The Key Role of the Family," *Proceedings, 1960 White House Conference on Children and Youth* (Washington, D.C.: Government Printing Office, 1960), p. 99.

[10] Msgr. Raymond J. Gallagher, Rev. Dr. William J. Villaume, and H. Tannenbaum, "Religion in American Life," in *The Nation's Children*, ed. Eli Ginzberg (New York: Columbia University Press, 1960), p. 219.

[11] E. O. Harbin, "The Church and Recreation," *Journal of Educational Sociology* (January 1948). Reprinted by permission.

humanity, justice and fair play, truth, faith, hope, and joy, and the fortitude to stand for what we believe to be right. Each of these is what gives buoyancy, purposefulness, zest, and worthwhileness to life. It is this compatibility of the religious and recreational life—this dual dedication to abundant, fruitful, and joyous living for all people—as well as the mutually broad dimensions of these fields, which bind them together so strongly.[12]

A look at the past in religion-recreation associations

In America, as in other countries, the forces of religion and recreation have influenced and have been influenced by each other. The traditional early link came with the origins of such recreation activities as dance, music, and drama evolving from the ceremonials and religious festivals through which man worshiped and expressed his faith. Huizinga states that "the spirit of playful competition is, as a social impulse, older than culture itself and pervades all life like a veritable ferment. Ritual grew up in sacred play."[13]

Colonial New England Calvinism condemned amusement of any kind; strict Puritanism ruled against the theater and many other types of urban entertainment; the Virginia colony legislated against idleness, yet in both the North and the South, the church often provided the only facility except the tavern in which young or old could socialize. The end of the nineteenth century found a softening of the Puritan tradition as religious leaders came to a realization that changing social and economic conditions demanded a changing philosophy. Dulles [14] reports that the church, having lost its power to enforce arbitrary prohibitions, took a more realistic attitude. When it disapproved of commercial amusements, it tried to substitute wholesome activities that were of a social equivalent to those denied.

So it was that new, church-sponsored recreation activities arose in the form of games, bazaars, church suppers, lectures, concerts, sports activities, and study and discussion groups. Facilities such as libraries and gymnasiums were built. Not without some furor being stimulated in religious ranks, churches became highly involved in the business of recreation and have remained thus involved up to the present. With the evolution of the shorter work week and the gift of leisure for the masses, the church that still clung to the piety and sanctity of work could not reconcile such a concept with the reality of increase of leisure and diminishing need for all-con-

[12] Charles K. Brightbill, *Man and Leisure, A Philosophy of Recreation* (Englewood Cliffs, N.J.: Prentice-Hall, Inc., 1961), pp. 99–100. Reprinted by permission.

[13] John Huizinga, *Homo Ludens* (London: Routledge & Kegan Paul, Ltd., 1949), p. 173. Reprinted by permission.

[14] *America Learns To Play* by Foster Rhea Dulles: Copyright, 1940, by D. Appleton-Century Co., Inc. Reprinted by permission of the publishers Appleton-Century-Crofts, an affiliate of Meredith Press.

suming work ideals. The depression of the 1930's again emphasized the need for wholesome leisure use and the churches responded to try to fill the gap.

The first significant attempt to convene national leaders of all faiths to discuss their responsibilities and philosophies with regard to recreation came in 1951. Dr. Robert Tully, of the Department of Recreation at Indiana University, initiated a seminar for leaders of religious faiths, who planned the First National Workshop in Recreation for Religious Organizations, held at Spring Mill Park, Indiana, in 1952. Some 56 delegates and consultants attended the workshop for which the following acted as cooperating advisors: Monsignor Joseph E. Schieder, National Catholic Welfare Conference; Robert Morrison, National Jewish Welfare Board; and Dennis Savage, National Council of Churches. The workshop participants drafted a statement of basic concepts, which openly affirmed the responsibility of religious organizations for recreation pursuits.

Broadening patterns of recreation services

Specific and heartening advances in both philosophy and action have been made in Jewish, Protestant, and Catholic faiths. The Mormon Church has one of the most highly organized systems for provision of wholesome recreation for its members. Early in the arduous trek across the country, Brigham Young recognized the need for wholesome recreative outlets. One of his first acts in the new territory was to erect, in 1852, a social hall for recreation events. The Mutual Improvement Association, initiated for young women in 1869 and for young men in 1875, is charged with the responsibility of leadership in recreation, initiation of programs, guidance of activities, and maintenance of wholesome standards. Carefully prepared programs in sports, dance, music, public speaking, and drama are concluded with annual festivals. The MIA Bulletins are some of the most extensive publications available on church recreation programing.

The Jewish movement toward involvement in recreation activities traces its origin to a spontaneous youth movement that developed in the 1840's from the Jewish Literary Societies. The first Young Men's Hebrew Association was formed in Philadelphia in 1850, about the same time that the YMCA was initiated in America. New York City boasts a Jewish Community Center that has existed since 1874. The activities of the present Young Men's and Young Women's Hebrew Associations are coordinated by the National Jewish Welfare Board. There has been an active camping program since 1901. B'nai B'rith Hillel Foundation has existed since 1923 as a cultural influence in administering programs of religion, education, social activities, and sports. Jewish Community Centers have long been active, and increased opportunity for the aged has been seen in special Senior Citizen Centers in the last few years.

The Methodist recreation activities, pioneered by E. O. Harbin, in the

1920's, have been responsible for many recreation programing books as well as stimulation of social recreation outlets for youth fellowship groups. Recreation workshops and laboratories have been held by many of the Protestant faiths. The Church of the Brethren sponsored its first fellowship workshop in 1931 and has conducted numerous recreation leaders' laboratories on a regional basis. The publication *Social Recreation Primer* by Robert Tully (1944) marked the beginning of a hitherto undeveloped area in the Brethren church. *Recreation and the Local Church*,[15] in 1958, gave further evidence of its continued interest. The Southern Baptists hold annual conferences and program aid sessions and, in 1960, initiated a magazine, *Church Recreation*, to provide practical help in church-centered recreation.

Many churches and synagogues have built extensive indoor and outdoor facilities such as gymnasiums, community centers, camps, and auditoriums. Denominations have encouraged their membership to take advantage of such opportunities as Camp Ihduhapi, which has served as the scene of the Northland Recreation Leaders' Laboratory since the 1930's. Northern New Mexico is the site of Ghost Ranch, a gift of the Board of Christian Education of the United Presbyterian Church, in 1954. The American Baptist Assembly has a 1,100-acre outdoor area in Green Lake, Wisconsin.

The National Catholic Welfare Council organized a youth department in 1940 and operates Catholic Youth Organization camps. The young people's groups are active on local and national bases in service projects and fellowship programs. Most religious organizations have fellowship groups as a part of the church or as separate but closely related units. Most are trying to serve all age groups by limited or extensive social, physical, and cultural activities.

Recreation programs sponsored by religious organizations

Many churches have outlined their tasks with regard to recreation. For instance, the Mormon Church, as early as 1926, included in its goals and purposes of church recreation programs such objectives as: making the joys of recreation a vital part of the life of each member; developing better brotherly feeling through wholesome social contacts; promoting opportunities for leadership; bettering physical and mental health; maintaining an environment for the cultural and social refinement of youth; and developing the power of self-expression through such activities as drama, music, and debating.[16] Such a code for a varied recreation program would not be too deficient even by more recent standards.

Other denominations define their responsibilities as, first, to provide some

[15] Frances Clemens, Robert Tully, and Edward Crill, eds., *Recreation and the Local Church* (Elgin, Ill.: Brethren Publishing Company, 1958).

[16] *Recreation Organization and Leadership* (Salt Lake City, Utah: Mutual Improvement Association, 1926), p. 31.

recreation for their own membership to answer needs and build fellowship; and, second, to lend support to community recreation programs acceptable to their religious concepts.

The number and kinds of recreation programs found in various faiths and denominations vary with the philosophy of the religious organization, the leadership available, the community relationships and mores, and the facilities at hand. Following is a partial list of activities sponsored by one or more religious groups:

1. Camping and other outdoor activities, including church camping, family camping, camp conferences, and retreats in which Christian education is the main goal. Campers are introduced to recreation activities and are encouraged to pick up recreation skills wherever they are available.

2. Social recreation, including family nights, picnics, banquets, potluck suppers, game nights, bazaars, and dances.

3. Vacation Bible schools, which run the gamut of recreation activities with the educational program.

4. Arts, crafts, and hobby workshops.

5. Fellowship groups, youth clubs, Scout programs, and adult interest clubs.

6. Sports activities, including bowling, basketball leagues, and baseball.

7. Volunteer services.

8. Study and discussion groups.

Reverend Edward D. Head at the 1960 White House Conference for Children and Youth reiterated the need for assumption of responsibility for recreation activities by religious groups and his philosophy of organization in these words:

Over and above religious ceremonies, a healthy parish and synagogue will have developed a maze of other activities which will allow the youth to practice what has been preached to him.[17]

Signs of the times—changes in recreation within religious organizations

The new socialized movement within religious organizations has formed its pattern gradually but with mounting evidence of the acceptance by all faiths that the church and synagogue have a responsibility not only for the recreation of their own members but for the coordination of recreation effort within their communities. Following is a partial list of some devel-

[17] Rev. Edward D. Head, "Our Brothers' Keepers," *Proceedings, 1960 White House Conference on Children and Youth* (Washington, D.C.: Government Printing Office, 1960), p. 162.

opments that are evidence of better cooperation between community and religious organizations.

1. Courses in recreation are now being initiated and promoted for theological seminaries, so that religious leaders may better understand the meaning and the methods of recreation.

2. The Puritan prohibitions against amusement of any sort have given way to conscious effort to improve standards of entertainment and to replace unwholesome activity with wholesome opportunities for recreation. The Legion of Decency, which tried to improve film offerings during the 1930's, and the Catholic committee to investigate television programs in the 1960's are results of such concerns.

3. There is a vast increase in the numbers of recreation facilities erected and administered by religious organizations. Some of the facilities are separate activity buildings; others are areas of the church itself in the form of auditoriums, recreation rooms, bowling alleys, or gymnasiums. Williams comments thus on the role of the church in recreation facilities:

> In the search for existing facilities that seriously must be pursued before constructing new facilities, no single center comes under closer or more recurrent scrutiny than the neighborhood church. Traditionally, the planning and the use of church property have personified designing for the individual or special interest group. More and more, however, church planners are taking into account community needs as well as those of their parishioners. Church youth programs have come to depend upon so many other community facilities, both public and private, that there is a growing awareness of their responsibility to do their part in providing facilities for at least limited community use.[18]

4. The church conference camp has given way, in many instances, to a decentralized camp. Guidance to improve camp programs has been provided by the Committee on Camps and Conferences of the National Council of Churches. Annual training sessions are held. Family church camps are gaining in popularity. More religious organizations are trying to meet American Camping Association standards.

5. Several Protestant denominations, Catholic, and Jewish groups have hired national directors of recreation to initiate and integrate recreation programs.

6. Local churches and synagogues are hiring professionally trained recreation leaders to minister to the needs of their members of all ages.

[18] Wayne Williams, *Recreation Places* (New York: Reinhold Publishing Corporation, 1958), p. 69. Reprinted by permission.

7. Sections on the recreation needs and interests of religious organizations have been initiated in the American Recreation Society and in the American Association for Health, Physical Education, and Recreation.

8. There is an increasing awareness of the part that recreation and religion must together play in setting and maintaining better standards of recreation activity.

Current problems and criticisms

Programs with the best of intentions are often abused and misinterpreted by an uninformed or a prejudiced public. The following difficulties are still existent in many areas.

1. Some religious organizations are being accused of making their faith attractive to nonmembers through their social and recreation programs. Using recreation as a "vestibule" for proselyting is not to be condoned, according to some critics. Others feel that recreation is a responsibility and an obligation and if that phase of programing attracts those who would otherwise not have been enticed into the religious program, then this is an accomplishment of which to be proud, not ashamed.

2. Churches and synagogues sometimes limit the programs in terms of both the extent of their offerings and the people whom they serve. Dictums such as, "Those who have not attended church or Sunday school may not attend recreation programs for the week," and restriction of activities to "members only" have been the source of much criticism. Bans on particular activities such as dancing and card playing have also been prevalent.

3. The duplication by a religious organization of facilities or programs already being offered successfully by another agency in the community often causes dissension and lack of community support and cooperation.

4. Church recreation programs that attract participation of those members already too heavily scheduled in similar activities have been a source of concern.

5. Many feel that the religious organization has a large enough job if it deals exclusively with spiritual needs and that this major function may suffer if leadership energies are siphoned to recreation or other concerns.

6. Religious organizations do not have adequate facilities or leaders for extensive recreation offerings. Many leaders are untrained and inadequate. Some groups feel strongly that religious organizations should

get out of the active leadership role and, instead, support wholesome community recreation programs.

7. Religious organizations, because of historical background or religious emphases, may not feel that they can support certain program areas. They are often condemned for these restrictions.

Coordination of effort

There are many areas of possible coordination and cooperation as the religious organization takes its place with the school, the home, the private agency, or the public agency to minister to the recreation needs of the community. Many cities and towns throughout the nation have already experienced the assets of such joint cooperation. Interrelationships among the religious organizations or between the religious organizations and other community agencies may produce achievements such as the following.

1. Joint use of facilities by community groups can result in fuller program for all. The church may open its recreation areas to other groups such as the Scouts, discussion groups, schools, and drama clubs. The municipal facilities, in turn, may be reserved at special times for use by the religious organizations. Camps owned by the city may be leased by the churches, or church campsites may be made available to community groups.

2. Mutual benefits can be gained from institutes, conferences, and workshops, jointly sponsored by community agencies, using the qualified leaders from church or municipal programs.

3. A calendar or clearing house for activities may list church activities so that other agencies will try to avoid conflicts with religious events. Religious organizations can help promote participation in wholesome recreation offerings of other agencies.

4. Interchurch ministerial associations in some communities can sponsor recreation programs or facilities for different age groups.

5. The religious organization can aid appreciably in the total effort by building a recreation philosophy for its members and interpreting the goals of wholesome recreation, as well as giving leadership to recreation programs.

Recreation and religious goals are not dissimilar. Truly recreative activity carries spiritual values. It would be logical to expect that, in the future, communities will find more and better cooperation between the ministerial and the recreation professions.

Areas of cooperation, interpretation, promotion, provision of facilities, and actual leadership were reviewed in this section, in exploring the role of religious organizations in recreation. In the last analysis, however, the most important contribution that religion can make to recreation is to help society establish codes of conduct so necessary for modern-day living. If the church has met the challenge, the individual and the group of today will be prone to choose those recreation experiences that are truly beneficial.

Rural Recreation

Progress and development of the recreation movement in the United States have moved, for the most part, much more rapidly in industrial urban environments than in the hinterlands. Although the concept that rural populations are as much in need of recreation as their urban counterparts developed fairly early in the recreation movement, concrete solutions to the problems of supplying such needs have been slow in arriving. A survey of almost any state will reveal inadequacies in program offerings for those who do not live within the confines of the city. Close scrutiny of the daily schedules of those who live in rural areas will reveal many of the same deterrents to the pleasure of leisure use that existed for half a century or more after the inception of the Industrial Revolution.

Curtis, in 1914, voiced his fears for the loss of opportunity for full living in the country environs.

To one who has observed how the small stump patch of the pioneer has given place to the broad, smooth acres of the modern farm, how the log cabin or dugout has been replaced by the modern house, how the lumber wagon has been succeeded by the carriage and automobile, it appears that rural communities have made tremendous progress. The industrial development of America has been one of the wonders of the world; but it cannot always be taken for granted that a larger farm will mean a larger life, that more wealth will mean more leisure, or that a better house will also mean a better home. We may well inquire if almost the opposite effect has not taken place in each case. . . .

Rural life has become overserious and sordid. It must perceive that life and love and happiness, not wealth, are the objects of living. There must be injected into it the spirit of play. The isolation of the farm home must be broken by establishing some place where farm people will frequently meet together, and the colder and freer months must be more largely utilized for education, recreation, and the public good. The hours of work must be reduced, and the half holiday must be brought in. The country must discover again in its daily life the adventure and romance and beauty that have passed.[19]

Rural—defined

The clarity of distinction between the farm and the municipal populations of the early 1900's has been clouded today by a series of degrees of "becoming urban" in the character of daily living. There is no longer a strict dichotomy with the farm on one side and the highly industrialized city on the other. The concept of rural recreation must change to include

[19] Henry Curtis, *Play and Recreation for the Open Country* (New York: Ginn and Co., 1914), pp. xiii, xiv. Reprinted by permission.

not only the farmer but those who live in small villages and towns. They share with the farmer some of the same opportunities and the same difficulties for leisure outlets.

For the purpose of discussion, the rural population will be defined as those who live either in the open country or in towns and villages of not more than 2,500 population. Such arbitrary classifications are again influenced by the geographical location of the community and its proximity to metropolitan areas. The trend toward "suburbia" has had a tremendous impact on the rural-urban recreation concepts and their interrelationships.

Problems in organization for rural recreation

Some of the problems found in attempts to broaden the scope of recreation opportunities for people who live in rural areas have changed but little in the last half century. Additional problems have been added with the changing character of those who now seek residence outside the city limits. Factors that tend to increase the difficulty in implementing rural recreation programs include:

1. *The heterogeneous nature of rural residents.* No longer is the rural resident necessarily a farmer or a small-town resident in the early concept of these terms. Whereas, at the time of the Civil War, over 97 percent of the rural population was engaged in agriculture, estimates for the year 2000 anticipate a decrease to 7 or 8 percent who will be involved with the growing of food or fiber.

Many rural residents are employed in the metropolitan areas and commute long distances daily to their place of employment. Their habits, amounts of leisure, leisure interests, and needs may differ greatly from the person who farms his land daily or maintains his dairy herd. The youngster whose country home is a ranch house surrounded by the woods has some difficulty entering the 4-H activity that highly emphasizes livestock projects. Although the housewife may be energetically involved with cooking and sewing projects, her factory-employed husband may find little to interest him in preparation for the county fair, though both people are rural residents. It is becoming increasingly less accurate to classify leisure interests into those for rural and those for urban populations. As the term "rural" moves from the country to the small town, the problem may be lessened or intensified.

2. *Urbanization of rural culture.* Radio, television, the telephone, electricity, faster delivery service of newspapers and magazines, and improved highway systems have made more accessible to the rural population many of the recreation outlets of their city neighbors. Modern communication devices keep the rural resident informed of the available recreation opportunities, and better transportation places such opportunities within reach.

3. *Attitudes of rural populations.* Danford [20] indicates that the reluctance of people in rural areas to accept the need for organization of recreation opportunities has been a deterrent to rapid growth of rural recreation. The rural church, also, has been slow in relinquishing the Puritan idea of recreation as "devil's time" although, conversely, it has offered many social activities that could be termed recreational.

4. *Comparative isolation of rural residents.* As farmers have prospered and farms have enlarged, the isolation of farm life has been accentuated, even though better communication and transportation are available. The early contacts with neighbors, made necessary by group interdependence, have all but vanished. The farmer who sells to the co-op or to the city dispenser is no longer in intimate contact with his neighbor down the road who used to help him with harvesting, barn-raising, or planting. This same isolation not only deprives the rural resident of mandatory group contacts from which might spring recreation experiences, but it increases the burden of organization for programing. Within a few city blocks, personal contact will entice several individuals who may wish to be involved with any specific program area. Access to the same number in the rural areas necessitates long hours of travel. This problem is less bothersome in the small village, in which almost everyone "knows what's going on."

5. *Lack of facilities.* Although the rural church and the rural school have made some progress in attempting to provide recreation facilities, the rural areas and small towns are, for the most part, without adequate meeting places for outdoor or indoor recreation activities. An increase in the number of county parks has aided in the growth of use of picnic and camping facilities for individual families but has done little to foster facilities for organized programing for other recreation opportunities. A scattered population and few families to pay the costs are deterrents to long-range planning.

6. *Ill-defined responsibility for leadership.* Because the rural residents are frequently not a cohesive group, the placement of responsibility for developing recreation programs is somewhat vague. The acceptance by government of tax-supported programs has been slow in coming, partially because of economic factors and partially because of the reluctance of the rural residents to unite their voices to force governmental action. Professional and volunteer personnel from youth agencies, Agricultural Extension Services, churches, and schools have all made contributions, but definitive responsibility for leadership and organization has moved at a snail's pace in most areas.

7. *Lack of financial support.* Problems of facilities and leadership are directly related to the reluctance of the rural population to further tax

[20] Howard Danford, *Recreation in the American Community* (New York: Harper & Row, Inc., 1953), p. 50.

themselves for recreation opportunities. Many, whose mobility makes it possible for them to use nearby metropolitan facilities, see no need for organization toward recreation opportunity nearer home. Others are deterred either by their independent attitude of being able to care for their own or by the meagerness of their earnings, which demand expenditures of a more immediate nature.

8. *Nature of work.* Although government subsidies and mechanized equipment have opened up more hours of leisure for the farmer, the physical challenges of his work and the irregularity of his hours evolve difficulties in program scheduling that are almost absent in larger cities.

9. *Competition from commercial recreation ventures.* The bowling alley, the skating rink, the trampoline center, the dance hall, and the drive-in theater have, in many areas, moved to the country. The proximity of such outlets does not erase the need for other wholesome programing, which will involve nature and social emphases or participation in all the arts. Those who resist efforts to provide for a broader pattern of rural recreation opportunities often excuse their attitude by pointing to the variety of commercial recreation avenues as "plenty to do."

10. *Municipalities' increasing resistance to allowing county residents to use city facilities.* The municipal recreation boards in many sections of the country are being bombarded with constant criticism regarding rural residents' easy access to parks, swimming pools, golf courses, and other facilities to whose support they do not contribute. Such resistance may finally force the county governments into more definitive action, if residents of rural areas are to have a variety of recreation opportunities. Many counties have already solved the problem with county organization of outlying districts of city areas. Pooling of resources with an administrative board in control has made possible recreation facilities and leadership comparable to metropolitan districts. Other cities are demanding higher fees from county residents for use of such areas as golf courses, swimming pools, and parks.

Early efforts in building rural recreation

The early pioneers in America felt little need to organize themselves to build a variety of recreation opportunities. What few hours and physical energies were left after the arduous labors of the entire family were usually spent in work-related recreation activity. The neighborhood barn-raising was occasion for social festivities after the work was done; the clearing of land, the planting or harvesting of crops, or the quilting session, which brought families together, might end in feasting, steer roping, dancing, wrestling, woodcutting, logrolling, or milking contests.

Early schools in rural communities provided the fun of the spelling bee or the singing school, and the small churches opened their doors for box suppers, seasonal celebrations, or club work. The county fair, expanded and even more popular today, grew out of the farmers' early practice of taking livestock or farm produce to common meeting grounds for sale or trade.

These occasions naturally developed into gala days for the community because of the opportunity they afforded rural people from widely separated districts to meet for recreation and social contact, and because the finish of the harvest found the people in a festival mood.[21]

County school fairs originated in Campbell County, Virginia, in 1908, in an attempt, on the part of rural schools, to give youngsters a chance to display their work and play interests. Other efforts to organize play of children were found in the numerous corn-and-calf clubs that flourished in the first decade of the twentieth century, and the Playground and Recreation Association of America focused attention on the problems of rural recreation in its fifth annual meeting, in 1911.

The Patrons of Husbandry, more commonly known as the Grange, which originated in 1867, made strides toward providing social gatherings for both men and women as a part of their objective to provide a "more satisfactory rural life." In the second decade of the century, the schools in West Virginia led the way to acceptance of school responsibility for better recreation in rural areas when 1,000 rural teachers volunteered to organize their schools as social centers. Small inroads of success were being made as early as 1914 with the passage of laws that empowered counties to form county parks for better appreciation and enjoyment of natural surroundings. By the end of World War I, a number of Community Councils had been formed in rural areas to integrate existing agencies concerned with development of services for country districts.

Other organizations such as the Farmer's Union, Farm Women's Clubs, and Agricultural Extension agents also contributed to the early opportunities in recreation for rural youth or adults.

In 1919, following the first national conference on country life, held at Baltimore, the American Country Life Association was formed. It included among its concerns the recreation and social life of the rural population along with education, home making, and other related activities. It was a first attempt at national level to form a channel of organization and communication among all agencies dealing with problems in rural districts.

The changing scene in rural recreation

As has been indicated in previous pages, the characteristics of the area and of the people of rural districts have undergone many changes that affect

---

[21] *Encyclopaedia Britannica* (Chicago: Encyclopaedia Britannica, Inc., 1944), I, 387. Reprinted by permission.

the need for and success of rural recreation programs. Included in these changes are:

1. *The improved living conditions.* No longer is the typical rural resident without central heating, plumbing, electricity, or mechanized labor-saving devices. Such modern conveniences free all members of the family for leisure opportunities unknown in the arduous days of the pioneer, when it took all members of the family from sunup to sundown to eke an existence from the land.

2. *The influence of mass media.* With the advent of radio, television, and telephone, the country dweller may be alerted to or involved in many situations that his former isolation denied him.

3. *The trend toward consolidation of schools.* Although consolidation of schools upgrades educational opportunities for rural youngsters and may offer superior facilities for recreation, the long hours of riding the bus and the losses in community solidarity that existed as families gathered at the smaller schoolhouse make additional problems in servicing the recreation needs of the district.

4. *Greater mobility of the rural population.* The perils and trials of the horse-and-buggy era made travel for recreation purposes beyond the means of most rural families. Today's farm family, no longer left to their own recreation resources, find the urge to move toward city theaters, stadiums, and service-club meetings.

5. *The decreasing interdependence of rural families.* The farm family that ships its produce to market has lost many of the opportunities for social contact that brought its pioneer ancestors together for work and recreation. Specialization has decreed that the nurses will care for the sick, the preachers will conduct church services, the contractors will do the building, and the professional educators will teach the children. The "we'll all do it together" philosophy of community effort has all but vanished from the rural scene.

6. *Lack of common occupational interests.* As has been mentioned, those who have chosen to live in the rural environs are no longer necessarily tillers of the soil. They may commute to a variety of jobs and do no farming. The common work interest that was a basis for contacts in former years no longer exists. Such changes have frequently complicated the already prevalent problems that face those who wish to organize rural recreation programs. Again, such changes differ somewhat as the term rural moves in its connotation from the open country to the small village, in which contacts are more easily made but financial support is just as difficult.

Present opportunities in rural recreation

The past half century has seen a tremendous expansion of club activity in the rural districts. The county programs of YMCA and YWCA, the 4-H Clubs and Home Demonstration Clubs of the Agricultural Extension Service, the Farm Bureau, the Grange, the Farmers' Union, the Farm Women's Clubs, Boy Scouts and Girl Scouts all attempt to service some of the recreation needs of the residents in the countryside. Future Farmers of America and Future Homemakers of America carry on active programs of leadership training. The County Agent and Home Demonstration Agent foster training institutes, and the National 4-H Recreation and Rural Arts program is now functioning in every state in the union.

Educational systems and extension divisions are promoting better facilities and opportunities for learning recreation skills through use of itinerant special supervisors. Municipal recreation programs are helping by supplying professional recreation leadership for noon-hour or after-school leisure outlets. Rural churches are accepting greater responsibility for facilities and leadership in wholesome recreation. County parks are being constructed for fishing, hunting, picnicking, camping, and hiking opportunities. Libraries are becoming increasingly more aware of their responsibility for whetting the reading appetites of the rural youngsters and adults. Bookmobiles have proved successful and popular for summer and winter service.

Industries in small towns and villages are easing some of the financial burden by contributing money for facilities and leadership for better recreation opportunities in the community. The American Music Conference has stimulated interest in and emphasis on music in rural areas. Interesting and successful experiments in family camping have been initiated by E. H. (Duke) Regnier, extension recreationist for the University of Illinois.

Some of the early problems remain. Isolation, inaccessibility, lack of sufficient funds, and absence of community solidarity still prevail. Other aspects in terms of changing attitudes, greater mobility, greater literacy, and more leisure hours are brightening the picture. The rural recreation situation is a long way from Utopia, but significant progress is being made, if at a slower pace than in the more heavily populated, more prosperous urban areas.

Trends

What of the future? As the numbers of leisure hours have increased for rural residents, the demands for adequate and satisfying use of those hours have multiplied. Some communities have solved the problem by joining forces to hire professional leadership to train and supervise volunteers for their areas. Flourishing tax-supported programs have grown in such places as Jefferson County, Kentucky; Union County, New Jersey; Los Angeles County, California; and Cook County, Illinois. Although these communities are composed of a series of rural areas, in their organization they have enabled themselves to have extensive programs. In some rural areas, county conservation boards perform recreation functions.

As the trend toward suburbia increases, visionary planners and subdividers are including land for community playgrounds within each division. The swimming pool and surrounding play area are most frequently operated on a membership basis for those who live in the area. Many farmers have found new use for untilled soil by offering their lands as vacation spots for city dwellers. Caught in the government soil-bank restriction, some rural residents of Monroe County, Pennsylvania, now have 80 percent of their land in use for recreation. Others have opened their doors to cooperate with the American Youth Hostel for overnight guest houses. The establishment of hunting preserves, fishing lakes, and commercial park and picnic areas has sometimes brought income that has resulted in greatly increased land values.

University extension departments are extending recreation services through consultation, training of volunteers, and publications. The inclusion of recreation courses in the education of the elementary teacher who is to staff the rural school of the future may foster some changes in the philosophy of and opportunity for recreation within the school day. The new consolidated schools are being designed for community use as social centers and recreation areas after academic classes have closed for the day.

National organizations are including education in recreation skills in almost every agency that deals with rural residents. The recreation needs of rural people have never been drastically different from those of their urban neighbors. People's needs are primarily the same, wherever they reside, and the few characteristics that did somewhat distinguish the rural resident are fast dissolving as, in a vast race for land, the American city and country blend into an almost indistiguishable spectrum of rural-suburban-urban living.

Industrial Recreation

The vast industrial development in the United States since the nineteenth century has been accompanied by labor and management's increased awareness of their obligation to counteract some of the problems that have arisen from this expansion. Among the personnel services that were initiated to alleviate these problems, the industrial recreation program has gained high recognition for its contribution.

A look at the past

Recreation programs in industry are not entirely new. The earliest provision of recreation by industry has been attributed to the Peacedale Manufacturing Company of Peacedale, Rhode Island. It included library resources and singing classes in its program offerings as early as 1854. During the next 50 years, other industries such as the Pullman Company of Chicago, the Conant Thread Company of Massachusetts, Ludlow Manufacturing Associates, Johnson and Johnson, the Metropolitan Life Insurance Company, and the National Cash Register Company introduced recreation services, which ranged from athletic programs, picnics, and outings to buildings and golf courses constructed for employees' use.

In 1868, the YMCA became the first private agency to cooperate with industry in serving the needs of industrial workers. Its early affiliation with the Union Pacific railroad company was the beginning of a series of attempts on the part of the YMCA to enhance off-the-job hours for industrial workers. The movement culminated in the organization, in 1902, of the YMCA Industrial Department, whose purpose it was to share the responsibility of employee recreation. Facilities were established in lumber camps, mining towns, steel industry locations, and textile villages to provide better leisure opportunities.

The years prior to and during World War I augmented the need for recreation in industrial as well as in camp communities. In 1913, a survey [22] by the United States Bureau of Labor Statistics showed that over half of the 51 firms polled were offering some form of recreation for their employees. A more inclusive study [23] by the Bureau, in 1916, showed an increase in recreation facilities and services in some 431 companies in 31 states. By 1918, the first city-wide industrial recreation association had been established in San Francisco to coordinate industrial recreation offerings. Similar associations were soon formed in New Haven, Connecticut, and in Oakland, California.

The period following World War I found a slow but steady increase in the number of industries offering recreation programs and a vast broadening of the types of opportunities available. With the growing impact of labor forces, a need for better employee-employer relations was obvious. The recreation services were expanded as a means to that end. The depression years served to deplete resources in industrial recreation as they did in municipal recreation, but since the value of recreation to industry had been recognized, programs in most firms were not eliminated, even though they were curtailed.

In the late 1930's, a comprehensive study [24] of 639 firms in 38 states indicated not only a significant increase in the numbers and kinds of recreation programs but a singular lack of leadership trained for this particular

[22] Elizabeth Otey, *Employer's Welfare Work* (Washington, D.C.: Bureau of Labor Statistics, 1913).

[23] *Welfare Work for Employees in Industrial Establishments in the United States* (Washington, D.C.: Bureau of Labor Statistics, 1919).

[24] Leonard J. Diehl and Floyd R. Eastwood, *Industrial Recreation—Its Development and Present Status* (Master's thesis, Purdue University, 1940).

responsibility. Although the study seemed to show that numbers and variety of programs increased with the amount of leadership available, none of the leaders of the industrial recreation programs had been trained for their work, and only one third had been trained in such related fields as physical education or personnel management.

In 1938, Purdue University became the first university to set up requirements for a degree for professional industrial recreation workers. The program was under the direction of Floyd R. Eastwood, who had been instrumental in stimulating and performing much of the research in this special area. The Purdue campus at Lafayette, Indiana, is still the scene of annual conferences on the concerns of industrial recreation.

By 1941, many industrial recreation leaders felt the need to cooperate and coordinate industrial recreation on a national level. As a result, the Recreation Association for American Industry, later named the National Industrial Recreation Association, was incorporated as a nonprofit service organization with Dr. Eastwood as president.

The NIRA is still flourishing with increasing membership. Special sections in ARS, AAHPER, and NRA also concern themselves with industrial recreation.

World War II brought expansion of recreation programs in industry, and the years since World War II witnessed additional expansion. A study in the late 1940's indicated that 92 percent of the firms surveyed were providing some recreation services. The demand for an appreciation of recreation services continues to grow.

Beginning with the establishment, in 1937, of the international recreation department of the United Auto Workers, union-sponsored recreation spearheaded new emphasis on recreation in industry. At the present time, the union recreation budget in any large factory may well exceed the recreation funds for some small communities.

In establishing locations for industry, administering operations to their greatest potential, and furthering human and financial interests of both employer and employee, industry finds much to be gained from developing and expanding industrial recreation programs.

Structure and organization

There is no set pattern of organization that has proved infallible or most desirable in establishing a recreation program in industry. Eastwood,[25] after studying different types of organization, evolved a model of organization and administration principles for conducting industrial recreation programs. His model included such items as administrative independence, democratic representation, financial independence, and all-inclusive mem-

[25] G. Herbert Duggins and Floyd R. Eastwood, *Planning Industrial Relations,* Purdue University, 1941.

bership. The choice of structure and administration seems to depend somewhat on the size of the industry. The several methods of organization that are now existent include the following:

1. The management takes complete responsibility for facilities, leadership, and program.

2. Complete responsibility is taken by an independent employee association.

3. Facilities and areas are provided by the employer; the program is administered by the employees.

4. Facilities and areas are provided by the management, and the employer and employees take joint responsibility for the administration of the program. The recreation director may be paid by management, but he is guided by an employee advisory committee.

5. The company union organizes the program without help from management.

6. Industry provides a committee and funds to cooperate with an existing community recreation program that includes opportunities for industrial workers.

Management and labor agree that the program usually has better success if the employees have some financial as well as operational responsibility for recreation. The recreation director, who is employed by management, is most frequently responsible to the personnel director, though several other channels of authority are used. Those who favor an autonomous employee association feel that the association allows opportunity for acquisition of facilities, freedom from company authority in programing, and absolvement of management responsibility in accidents that occur in leisure pursuits.

Industrial recreation programs

The extensiveness and variety of industrial recreation programs depend on many of the same factors regarding program planning discussed in Chapter 16. The amount of money available, the amount and the quality of the leadership involved, the size of the factory, the needs and interests of the people, and the facilities all influence the amount and kind of program offerings. W. H. Edmund, Director of Recreation for the Goodyear Tire and Rubber Co., in an address at the Personnel Conference of the American Management Association described the foundation for the ideal industrial recreation program in these words:

We in personnel build carefully, soundly, and objectively. An employee activities program in any company or plant, regardless of size, should be planned and built somewhat on the same blue-print as a 3-sided park shelter-house. 1. It should be located in an attractive environment, and should be attractive from the exterior. 2. One side is open as a welcome to those interested or casually exploring. 3. It is sturdy by being built on a fundamentally sound plan to invite confidence and security. 4. It must be attractive enough on the inside to invite participation and cooperation. BUT—there is still that one open side so that we don't have a feeling of compulsion or "have to." [26]

The open side and idea of freedom from compulsion that Edmund expressed are important in all recreation programs, but they are doubly important in industrial settings, especially if the program is being run entirely by management. Morale wanes under conditions in which employees feel that their participation is necessary to maintain good relations with management.

Classification of activities. Anderson [27] states that most industrial recreation programs classify their activities into the following divisions: social activities, cultural activities, physical activities, and outing activities. Basic program-planning principles apply in each division. In most cases, surveys have found that a company will offer any activity in which there are at least ten people interested. Programs that are found most frequently or are seemingly most popular in industrial recreation programs include the following:

LUNCH-HOUR ACTIVITY. Gameroom activities such as ping pong, cards, and board games are popular during lunch hours.

SOCIAL RECREATION. Picnics, section parties, family outings, awards banquets, and dances are numerous.

LIBRARIES. Noon-hour and take-home reading is available.

SPORTS. League play in everything from bowling to softball involves both men and women in the plant.

HIKES AND EXCURSIONS. Travel is a popular concern. Some industries have planned economy trips to Europe for their employees. Others encourage tours to concerts, plays, or art centers.

HOBBY GROUPS. Club activities centered around photography to ceramics or bird watching are numerous.

Programs must be constantly evaluated in light of changing conditions.

Facilities. The location of the plant and the distribution of the employees within the community are important conditioning factors in the decisions to create special facilities for employee recreation. The philosophy of the administrative board also colors the decision. Some companies choose to

[26] Charles K. Brightbill and Harold D. Meyer, *Recreation: Text and Readings* (Englewood Cliffs, N.J.: Prentice-Hall, Inc., 1953), p. 243. Reprinted by permission.

[27] Jackson M. Anderson, *Industrial Recreation* (New York: McGraw-Hill Book Company, 1955), p. 66. Reprinted by permission.

use community facilities when available in order to economize or to seek closer relationships with the community. Others, because of the absence of adequate community facilities or the distance involved in access to community offerings, prefer to build and operate their own areas. Facilities range in scope from simple gamerooms and open areas for sport activities to golf courses, country clubs, camps, swimming pools, and parks developed and maintained either by management, by employee associations, or by cooperation of the two.

Leadership. Recent studies have shown a definite increase in the numbers of companies who employ full-time recreation professionals to direct their programs. The lack of trained leaders is still a very real problem. When a full-time director is not available, the responsibility for conducting a recreation program most frequently goes to a member of the personnel staff. Until the recreation profession can recruit and educate professionals in such numbers as are presently needed, industrial recreation leadership cannot hope to meet its highest potential in servicing the needs of either management or labor.

Finance. Methods of financing industrial recreation programs vary from company to company. The present inclination is to involve those who benefit from the program in some financial responsibility. Methods of financing include any one or a combination of the following: contributions from management, voluntary dues from the employees, receipts from vending machines, receipts from money-making projects, admission charges for entertainment, appropriations from the union, and fees and charges for activities.

Community cooperation. A new industry may be attracted to a community because of a satisfying recreation program. Once an industry has located in an area, there are still lines of cooperation that will be advantageous for both industry and community. In some small towns, industry finds that it is much more expedient to contribute to the existing recreation program than to establish a separate one. The employees are thus not segregated from the community in their leisure hours, and the community recreation program is strengthened by additional funds and leadership from industry. Other areas of cooperation include joint use of facilities by industrial and community groups; joint leadership training institutes for in-service training; cooperative ventures with the YMCA or YWCA in special programs for industrial workers; cooperation on pre-retirement or retirement programs; distribution of public-relations materials from municipal programs by industry or vice versa; cooperation with youth-serving agencies by providing meeting places in plant facilities; utilization of city parks on an annual basis for social outings for plant personnel; and use of plant personnel on recreation advisory boards.

Values and benefits from industrial recreation programs

Industrial recreation programs were born out of a pressing need to boost the morale of all personnel, both labor and management. Because of the bigness of industry, face-to-face contacts between employees and employer are few, and relationships become too impersonal. The recreation program helps attract better workers and bolsters morale by offering opportunities to meet colleagues or superiors in relaxed situations in which interpersonal relationships can develop. Specialization and automation have reduced work hours and have created monotonous jobs, which stifle creative outlets. Recreation programs offer challenging activity in leisure hours. Don Neer, Executive Secretary of the National Industrial Recreation Association, has listed the following benefits that American industry hopes to gain from employee recreation programs.

Physical Health: the increase in the number of deaths due to heart and circulatory diseases, the overweight problem, especially of executives, increased working days lost from common head colds, and general lack of physical fitness have prompted the establishment of extensive athletic programs in plants.

Mental Health: boredom from routine jobs, noise, tensions, conflicts, and increase in mental illness have led to the provision of activities that check fatigue and relieve tensions, such as the coffee break, noon-hour recreation programs, and recorded music.

Leadership Training: recreation activities provide a means for employee recognition; new leaders are discovered and developed who make a bigger contribution on the job.

Employee Stability: today's employee is choosy; he looks carefully at the company's benefits. Recreation activities are often an incentive for employment. Industrial recreation combats absenteeism and job turnover. It helps a firm to attract and hold good employees.

Community Relations: recreation is the backbone of good community relations which is typified in recreation activities for the family—Little League, Junior Achievement, Boy and Girl Scouting, picnics and day camps. Every company wants to be known as a good place to work.

Social Relationships: in recreation activities all are equal. There is no race, creed, color, management, or labor distinction, and this leads to a better understanding of one's fellow employees.

Work Atmosphere: recreation offers an atmosphere which is conducive to developing friendships. In this day of the migrant worker it is essential to help the new employee to adjust and feel at home, meet new people, get acquainted, and find a wife or husband.

Environment: company programs with good leadership protect the employee from adverse commercialized recreation areas and exorbitant entertainment expenditures.

Democracy: the employee program, governed by employees, gives workers a voice in company activities.

Morale: the company appears human—it shows that employers are interested in the employees, their welfare, leisure, and chance to enjoy life both on and off the job.[28]

Trends in industrial recreation programs

Industrial recreation programs, which originally started with meager offerings in athletic contests or leagues for men, have given way to broad and varied choices for company employees. Changes include the following.

1. There is a greater tendency for employees to help defray the cost of recreation programs through dues or voluntary contributions.

2. There is decidedly less emphasis on the paternalistic direction of recreation by management.

3. Labor unions have taken a strong lead in the development of industrial recreation programs.

4. More self-supporting activities are being included.

5. There is more emphasis on a broad scope of program; cultural and social activities are getting wider recognition.

6. More activities are being included for families.

7. There is a healthy concern for involving employees in pre-retirement activities that will have carry-over value in retirement.

8. There is a decided growth in the development of senior citizens' programs for retired employees.

9. A greater number of areas of cooperation between industry and community recreation agencies have been promoted.

In the words of Thomas J. Watson, Sr., Chairman of the Board of International Business Machines, as he presented trophies to IBM employees at the IBM Country Club, Endicott, N.Y., "People who play well together, work well together." This, in essence, is the *raison d'être* for industrial recreation.

Commercial Recreation

There exists in people today a willingness or even a desire to pay for their recreation. Many public and voluntary agencies have found that fees and charges, rather than reducing participation, have increased it. Certain segments in society will not participate in free programs but will spend considerable amounts of money for programs of similar or even of lower quality

[28] Don Neer, "Industry," in *Recreation in the Age of Automation* (Philadelphia: American Academy of Political and Social Science, 1957), The Annals of the Academy, Vol. 313, pp. 80–1. Reprinted by permission.

offered commercially. The feeling that paying for one's own recreation denotes a certain status probably accounts for this phenomenon.

In Chapter 3 the economic significance of leisure, including the extent of commercial recreation, was discussed. We are now concerned with the contribution of commercial recreation to the recreation needs of modern society. "Commercial recreation" may be defined as recreation that is established as private enterprise, for which the participant pays, and from which the purveyor makes a profit. This form of recreation is one of the most important and growing aspects of American culture today. Expenditures for commercial recreation far exceed expenditures for nonprofit programs, such as those offered by public and voluntary agencies.

Too often students of recreation and those concerned with the recreation programs of public and voluntary agencies have ignored the impact of commercial recreation. As William and Charlotte Astor commented, "Although leisure activity through private associations and commercial agencies constitutes one of the major segments of the recreation movement, the subject is generally given as little academic attention as a church organist gives to calypso music." [29]

Place of commercial recreation in the community program

Certain types of recreation responsibilities have come to be regarded as the responsibilities of public or voluntary agencies. Parks, playgrounds, playfields, and community centers under leadership are for the most part operated by public recreation agencies. The philosophy underlying public provision of these programs is that they are wholesome and constructive and that our social structure should make them available to all of the population on an equal basis. Programs concerned primarily with particular segments of society come under the responsibility of voluntary organizations.

Mass entertainment, such as movies, television, radio, and magazines, is largely in the hands of commercial interests. Activities subject to the fluctuations of popular fancy yet requiring expensive equipment, such as trampolines and miniature golf, are usually commercially operated.

There are many activities, such as organized camping, golf, swimming, and team sports, for which provision may be made by public, voluntary, or commercial agencies. An increasing number of forms of recreation that have hitherto been more or less the prerogative of nonprofit agencies are being offered commercially. For example, land and facilities for hunting, fishing, and camping have in the past been provided primarily by state and

[29] William Astor and Charlotte Astor, "Private Associations and Commercial Activities," in *Recreation in the Age of Automation* (Philadelphia: American Academy of Political and Social Science, 1957), The Annals of the Academy, Vol. 313, p. 92. Reprinted by permission.

federal governments. An increasing number of farmers, ranchers, and private forest owners are today opening their lands to the public for a fee. Artificial lakes, stocked with fish, are operated privately for profit in some places. Many large lumber companies, especially in the Pacific Northwest, now permit campers, hunters, fishermen, picnickers, and skiers to use their lands. Some of these companies, according to Brockman, provide picnic tables, fireplaces, sanitary facilities, piped water, shelters, children's playground equipment, boat ramps, bathhouses, and nature trails.[30] Although some of the companies make a charge, most do not; and these measures are taken primarily for good public relations.

Problems in commercial recreation

Commercial recreation runs the gamut from the best in music, art, and literature to amusements that cater to the lowest of appetites. There are those who look askance at commercial recreation because its primary purpose is profit, not the welfare of the people. It is true that many purveyors of commercial recreation put profit foremost, disregarding the effect of their activities on consumers and justifying their actions on the basis that they are merely meeting the demands of the public. This contention is true only in part; through advertising and glamorization, sellers can create demands where none existed previously.

Another charge against commercial recreation is that it encourages "spectatoritis." Many enterprises prosper on the theory that people want their recreation spoon-fed to them. Neumeyer and Neumeyer wrote: "Commercial amusements are designed to provide the largest amount of entertainment with a minimum of effort on the part of the spectators or participants." [31]

Among the forms of commercial recreation to receive heaviest attacks are those that reach the largest numbers of people: movies, television, and printed matter. There is considerable difference of opinion regarding the effect of violence portrayed in movies and on television and the preoccupation with sex in movies, magazines, and paperback books. A study made by Dr. Paul Witty indicated no serious ill effects from television and "little or no decrease in outdoor activities and hobbies." [32] Many people are none the less deeply concerned about the moral standards presented to impressionable children through these forms of entertainment.

[30] C. Frank Brockman, *Recreational Use of Wild Lands* (New York: McGraw-Hill Book Company, 1959), p. 38.

[31] Martin H. Neumeyer and Esther S. Neumeyer, *Leisure and Recreation*, 3rd ed. (New York: The Ronald Press Company, 1958), p. 316. Reprinted by permission.

[32] Max Kaplan, *Leisure in America*, p. 224.

Determination of standards. Perhaps it would be logical to assume that the mass media both shape and are shaped by our culture and that they can be influences for the best as well as for the shoddy. The same statement applies to other types of commercial operations. Many commercial operators are aware of their social influence and conscientiously attempt to contribute to the well-being of participants and to give full value for expenditures. That high standards are not incompatible with profit may be demonstrated by many examples. An outstanding enterprise is Disneyland, in Southern California, which has combined certain aspects of amusement parks, playgrounds, fairs, and museums into an imaginative compound that is not only a delight in itself but a challenge to park and recreation planners everywhere. Bowling alleys and pool halls have improved immeasurably in recent years so that they are no longer considered hangouts for persons of questionable character, but instead are wholesome, attractive centers for family fun.

Contributions to community recreation. The values of commercial recreation to the community may be enumerated as follows.

1. PROVISION OF RECREATION OPPORTUNITIES. It would be a crushing and unfair burden upon the taxpayer and the philanthropist to offer all recreation through public and quasi-public means. Types of recreation that are unduly expensive, that cater to only a limited clientele, or that may be only passing whims or fancies are better left to commercial enterprise.

2. EXPERIMENTATION. Public money is seldom obtainable for new and untried facilities or programs. Commercial recreation can pave the way, through experimentation, for acceptance of desirable forms of recreation into public programs.

3. SOURCE OF IDEAS FOR PUBLIC PROGRAMS. Commercial recreation can serve as a goad to prevent leadership of nonprofit agencies from becoming lethargic. Because a commercial operator must compete with others and must make a profit, he is under constant pressure to improve his efficiency and make his enterprise attractive. Many lively and imaginative ideas that originate from commercial recreation can be borrowed by public recreation authorities. Commercial recreation dares not be dull; other recreation should be equally alert to the needs, interests, and comforts of the public.

The control of commercial recreation

One of the most serious problems that communities face is that of the control of certain segments of the amusement industry, such as taverns, night clubs, burlesque shows, dance halls, gambling houses, and dealers in salacious literature. There are four main approaches to the control of commercial recreation.

1. *Legal control.* State laws and county and municipal ordinances are the legal basis for control. These differ from state to state and community to community. Gambling in various forms—from slot machines to pari-mutuel betting—is legal in some states. Forbidden in some states, it is a major form of income in others. Laws governing the sale of alcoholic beverages also differ. Some states grant "local option"—that is, the right to regulate the sale of liquor—to local governments; other states abide by state-wide laws. Enforcement of legal restrictions depends upon public support and the morale of the police force. Regulations are enforced by licensing and censorship.

LICENSING is one of the most common methods of control. It is usually accompanied by inspection. Licenses are revoked for failure to comply with regulations.

CENSORSHIP is another device used. It is difficult to apply and sometimes defeats its purpose. For example, the banning of certain books or the barring of certain scenes from movies often succeeds in publicizing them and making them more popular.

2. *Trade control.* Standards are sometimes set by an industry, which exerts pressure on individual operators to secure adherence.

3. *Public opinion.* In the last analysis, control lies in the hands of the public. Commercial ventures can operate only if they make a profit; profit depends upon public support. The attitudes of civic groups, parent-teacher associations, and religious organizations are extremely important in determining standards. Action groups from these community agencies may improve or eliminate undesirable commercial undertakings. Education in the schools, youth agencies, public recreation agencies, and particularly the home should be directed toward the development of interest in the constructive and wholesome use of leisure.

4. *Competition from desirable alternatives.* A positive approach to the problem is through provision of wholesome recreation activities as alternatives to the undesirable. Where beneficial recreation opportunities are presented in an attractive fashion, participation in the tawdry and unworthy can be expected to dwindle. Community recreation agencies of all types bear responsibility for providing wholesome outlets. Commercial recreation can successfully operate such enterprises. The clean, well-equipped bowling alley, designed for the family, may be not only better socially but also more profitable than one with a shady reputation.

In many communities youth centers are maintained on the assumption that young people will not be attracted to degrading activities if there are desirable places in which to spend their leisure. The establishment of service men's centers during the war years was predicated, at least in part, on the same assumption.

Principles

Some basic principles relative to commercial recreation may be briefly listed:

1. Where commercial recreation operators can supply good wholesome programs at a reasonable cost, they should be encouraged to do so. Well-conducted bowling alleys, swimming pools, skating rinks, organized camps, and other enterprises with high standards contribute to the community program and relieve the financial burden of taxpayers and voluntary givers.

2. Operators of acceptable commercial recreation ventures should be represented on any committees or boards concerned with planning for future recreation needs.

3. Worthy commercial recreation should receive the support and patronage of citizens interested in community improvement.

4. Communities should develop procedures to control or eliminate commercial recreation of questionable influence.

5. Elimination of the undesirable is not sufficient; it must be accompanied by substitution of the desirable.

Libraries

Gone are the days when a dull, musty repository for shabby books was considered an adequate library for a community. Today a library that is considered effective is inviting to the eye, cheerful, bright, and comfortably furnished. It carries on a public-relations program to keep the people informed of its new acquisitions and special activities, keeps its door open at hours most convenient for the public, and offers visitors pleasant surprises in its changing and timely displays.

Through the library, persons with interests in history, art, science, religion, philosophy, or music have access to the best of thinking. Hobbyists and do-it-yourselfers find the guidance necessary for pursuit of their interests. Whether the reader wants to plan a party, conduct a club for children, garden, care for pets, plan a vacation, or have a cookout, he will obtain information from the library.

The library is a gold mine of information on community recreation, with material on city planning, on means of organizing recreation programs, and on home recreation activities. Its supply of current magazines gives new information to public, private, and voluntary organizations.

The development of libraries

Libraries date back as far as the clay tablets of Babylonia in the twenty-first century B.C. Libraries in America are believed to have originated as early as 1653, in Boston. Today it is estimated that about one third of the children and one tenth of the adults make use of the 7,000 libraries and their 125 million books.[33]

Special library services

The library of today does far more than lend books. Among its numerous other services are: maintenance of libraries of records, photographs, manuscripts, pictures, clippings, and maps; story hours for children; reading clubs; book reviews; great books courses; discussion groups; lecture programs; meet-the-author programs; courses in gardening, arts and crafts, music, dramatics; and displays. Displays may consist of books and pamphlets dealing with subjects of seasonal interest, such as spring wild flowers or summer travel; exhibits of art, photographs, and manuscripts; what to see and do in the community; and many others. In some communities without museums, the libraries assume some of the functions of museums and display museum materials.

Since the library is one of the most important leisure resources of a community, its staff should be present in any program planning for the use of leisure in the community. Also there should be included the representatives of museums, nature centers, zoos, botanic gardens, and similar establishments that help to fill leisure needs. Discussion of these organizations follows.

Museums and Nature Centers

The old-fashioned museum was a place for miscellaneous displays, study, research, and the storage of collections. While still serving these functions, it is now an institution for popular education and enjoyment, attracting millions of visitors each year. The modern museum, well lighted, artistically planned, with highly selective displays, is a far cry from its predecessors. New techniques of display are employed to give continuity and significance to the exhibits. The museums are more concerned with large abstract concepts than with isolated and unrelated facts. There are unified themes that progress chronologically or in terms of complexity of thought from display to display. Exhibits include habitat groups, murals, models, restorations, diaramas, displays involving action, and self-testing devices. The museum has come to life.

Museums in America began in 1773, when the Library Society of Charlestown, South Carolina, began to collect materials in natural history.[34] Throughout the nineteenth century many museums were founded by in-

[33] *Recreation for Community Living, Guiding Principles* (Chicago: The Athletic Institute, 1952), pp. 24–5.
[34] *Recreation for Community Living,* p. 25.

dividuals and societies and financed chiefly by contributions, memberships, and endowments. Indiana, in 1914, was the first state to pass an enabling law for the use of tax money to support museums. Today museums, numbering in the thousands, are supported by local, state, and national governments and by universities as well as by private groups. Though differing widely in scope and interest, museums may be generally described as follows.

Large comprehensive museums

Museums such as the Smithsonian Institution in Washington, D.C., endeavor to include interests ranging from fine art and history through various branches of science. Such museums serve the public through numerous means, such as: sponsorship of expeditions; research; publications and audio-visual materials; field trips; lecture programs; courses of various types; special-interest clubs; traveling displays; leadership training courses for teachers and youth leaders; libraries; kits and starters for hobbyists; programs for junior leaders and junior teachers; conducted tours of the museum; radio and television programs; school services, such as visits to the schools, lectures to school groups, and the lending of movies and exhibits.

Special-interest museums

Many museums center on special interests, such as particular forms of art or science. There are museums of history, archeology, anthropology, astronomy (planetariums), oceanography, ethnology, applied science, and industry. Some of these museums are as large as some of the comprehensive museums and offer similar services but within the limits of their specialties. Particularly outstanding in originating special services were the American Museum of Natural History in New York and the Chicago Natural History Museum.

There are many unique museums that are major tourist attractions: the Henry Ford Museum; the Baseball Hall of Fame; the George Eastman House of Photography; the Corning Glass Center; and historic structures, such as homes of famous persons, forts, churches, and even whole communities.

Nature centers and children's museums

Children's departments are often part of the large museums, but there have also developed special children's museums. The Brooklyn Children's Museum and the Boston Children's Museum were among the first. In recent years a great many others have sprung up, some being referred to as junior museums and others, in which the emphasis is on natural history, as nature centers.

Children's museums, although they may contain extensive displays, are considered essentially activity centers. Children themselves may sometimes prepare the exhibits, which are changed often enough to encourage more participation in the preparations. The programs may consist of special-interest clubs, classes, field trips, demonstrations, lectures, viewing of movies and slides, and the like. Some children's museums are located in parks or other natural areas and make use of adjacent land for their programs. One of their most fruitful services is rendered to outdoor education groups from schools. School classes with teachers come on regular schedules to the centers to participate in days of demonstrations in the center and field trips in adjoining areas.

Trailside museums

The term "trailside museum" is applied to the small museum, usually located in a natural area, which is intended primarily to interpret the local features. Its displays explain the environs and encourage the visitor to venture outdoors and observe for himself the phenomena explained. Naturalist-guided field trips, lectures, demonstrations, and self-guiding nature trails are typical developments. National, state, and metropolitan parks contain many such museums. The national parks are tending to include the museums in developments to which they refer as "visitor centers," since they include information centers and meeting places.

Zoos and Wildlife Displays

Living animals are among the objects most intensely interesting to both children and adults. The tremendous numbers of visitors to zoological gardens attest to this interest. Like the better libraries and museums of today, zoos have undergone a facelifting and modernization. Instead of smelly aisles lined with close-packed cages, today's zoo is more apt to be a spacious park with animals living in areas resembling their native habitats, in which the means of confinement are cleverly concealed.

Exhibits are not limited to exotic animals. City zoos, recognizing that to city-bred children a domestic goat may be as rare a sight as a llama, sometimes maintain exhibits of domestic animals. Small communities that find it financially prohibitive to purchase expensive animals or maintain large zoos may concentrate on local wildlife. Local wildlife may also be displayed in nature centers and trailside museums.

Zoos are beginning to recognize their potentialities educationally and recreationally by providing livelier programs and better publications than in the past. Services include field trips and conducted tours; lectures; printed information on animal life; well-prepared labels; television shows; special children's programs, including clubs and classes; performances of trained mammals; and research. In the average zoo, there is still room for expansion of these services.

Though many people visit our national and state parks primarily to see

Fig. 15 *Sea Lion Exhibit (Courtesy San Diego Zoo. Photo by R. Van Nostrand)*

large animals, such as bears, the keeping of animals in captivity in these parks is extremely limited. Sometimes a paddock for deer, elk, or buffalo is maintained; and sometimes a few live specimens of small forms of life, such as snakes and turtles, are kept at nature centers. The trend in national parks is away from keeping any animal in captivity; instead, effort is made to protect animals so that the interested visitor may find them in their native habitats.

Botanic Gardens and Garden Centers

Particularly in large cities, extensive programs have developed around garden centers and botanic gardens. These are usually located in municipal parks, although they may be conducted on private grounds under private auspices. Garden clubs and horticultural organizations are usually strong supporters of these programs and in many cases may have some type of affiliation with them.

The botanic gardens or nature centers often contain libraries, herbariums, lecture halls, study rooms, and research facilities. Wild and horticultural plants from all over the world are displayed in greenhouses, along nature trails where plants are labeled, in formal gardens, and in children's gardens. Information centers, which serve as sources of information on lawn and flower care to community residents, are frequently operated. Other services include clubs and classes; lectures; seasonal flower shows; radio and television programs; research; children's gardens, clubs, classes, and field trips; and provision of horticultural materials, publications, and lecture services to schools.

By arousing an interest in plants and gardens and an awareness of their beauty, these centers contribute not only to the leisure life of a community but also to its attractiveness as a place to live.

Lodges, Clubs, and Fraternal Organizations

There exists in every community a large number of voluntary organizations, clubs, lodges, fraternities, and societies that are organized for the purpose of personal growth and social relationships of their members, as well as for over-all betterment of the community. Reasons for joining these organizations are extremely varied, but the desire for sociability, status, and sense of belonging ranks high. Recreation is not the primary function of most of these agencies, but their contribution to youth activities and community recreation programs is significant. Through these varied community organizations, a channel for altruistic service to the community and to youth is fostered. Max Kaplan, in his book *Leisure in America*, puts it this way:

As a member of a club or group with a goal, one's leisure takes on direction and the perceptions of constructive living. This is especially needed by persons who feel guilt at wasting time or doing nothing. A deep psychological, perhaps even a religious, sense of duty or ethics enters here.[35]

Most of the community organizations, to a greater or lesser degree, provide recreation activities as a part of their program for their own members. These may range from music, social events, and sports to rituals and games. The very gathering at meetings, although generally initiated for other purposes, serves an important leisure function.

Recreation agencies should be concerned with the relation of these organizations to the community recreation programs. The members of these groups generally constitute the more well-to-do, more civic-minded, and better-educated members of any community; as such, they collectively and individually have the desire, influence, and resources to strive for a better

[35] Kaplan, *Leisure in America*, p. 181.

community. The following are some of the general types of service projects that are rendered by these organizations:

1. *Serving as sponsors to recreation groups and programs.* This sponsorship often involves service on committees and provision of actual leadership and meeting places. In many cases, these organizations serve as cosponsors with the recreation agency in conducting a program.

2. *Working for the establishment of more adequate community recreation facilities and programs.* This work may take the nature of support and promotion of public park and recreation services or the initiation of a YMCA, Boys' Club, or other voluntary agency.

3. *Assisting in the financing of community recreation projects.* Community agencies have contributed millions of dollars toward financing recreation programs and facilities. Their efforts vary from the financing of an athletic team in an industrial basketball league or underwriting the expenses for a city-wide costume, wheel, and pet parade, to the spending of thousands of dollars for a new battery of tennis courts or a dining hall for a Girl Scout camp.

It is interesting to examine the services rendered by the various civic and fraternal groups and to notice that a large percent of such services have a recreation connotation. The types of services sponsored by these local agencies are often initiated and promoted from the national headquarters of their respective agencies. The Junior Chamber of Commerce and the Veterans of Foreign Wars, to mention only two, have recreation or youth activity consultants on their national staffs and publish materials that suggest ways that local chapters and posts can provide adequate recreation services and programs in their cities. The community agencies being considered here are great in numbers and are difficult to categorize. The following listing is intended to be indicative of types of organizations rather than an exhaustive list.

Men's service or luncheon clubs

Men's service or luncheon clubs are composed of business and professional men of the community. Examples of such organizations are Kiwanis, Rotary, Lions, Optimists, and Exchange. The purposes of these clubs are primarily good fellowship and community service. Most luncheon clubs have youth committees that serve as the motivating and supporting forces back of many of the youth programs of the community.

Types of recreation projects undertaken by service clubs include the financing of recreation, park, camp, or playground equipment or facilities, sponsoring of Scout troops, and often, as in the case of Optimist Clubs, the sponsoring of programs for boys. Also, service clubs sometimes pay the camp fees, youth-center fees, YMCA or YWCA memberships of underprivileged youth.

Fraternal organizations

Organizations such as the Elks, Eagles, Moose, Masons, and Knights of Columbus can be classified as charitable, fraternal organizations. Each organization is mainly concerned with promoting the welfare and enhancing the happiness of its members. Because of the latter purpose, these organizations conduct many types of recreation programs for their members. For example, in some cities, the Elks Club operates recreation facilities of the following types: bowling alleys, golf courses, billiard rooms, and card rooms. Bowling leagues, golf tournaments, bingo parties, dances, and picnics are sponsored for Elk Club members and their families. These fraternal organizations have given generously to many types of recreation programs in the community.

Veterans or patriotic organizations

Two of the most prominent veteran groups in this country are the American Legion and the Veterans of Foreign Wars. Both organizations have long been concerned with promoting wholesome recreation for youth. It is through these agencies that veterans can work in the interest of their community and for youth, who some day will take their rightful roles in the leadership of this nation.

For years, the American Legion has sponsored its well-known nationwide program of Legion Junior Baseball. The Veterans of Foreign Wars, through its Youth Activities Department, prepares for local post use a booklet that gives ideas for youth programs to the local post director. The VFW sponsors a marble tournament, a Teen-er Baseball program, and a Huckleberry Finn and Becky Thatcher Costume Contest, all on a national basis. A few of the suggested youth activities for the post level include: holiday parties and contests, athletic programs of all types, club activities, sponsoring of Boy and Girl Scout troops, and establishing youth canteens.

Local VFW posts are urged to assist city officials and other organizations in surveying community recreation needs and to finance or assist in improving the recreation facilities and programs found in the city.

Women's organizations

In almost every city in America, a fantastic number of women's organizations can be found. They serve much the same functions as the men's civic, service, and fraternal organizations, offering recreation to their members and aiding community efforts. Women's clubs are varied but generally are considered social, philanthropic, or service in nature. A sample of several women's organizations might include: the Junior League, Altrusa, General Federation of Women's Clubs, League of Women Voters, and Business and Professional Women's Clubs. These organizations are well known for their community service efforts.

Junior Leagues have been instrumental in stimulating cultural activities in many cities throughout the country. Arts Councils, embracing musical, dramatic, and fine arts activities, have been established in many cities, chiefly owing to the efforts of the Junior League. The establishment of the Arts Council of Winston-Salem, North Carolina, is but one example of the Junior League's influence in this area of community life. In Winston-Salem, Miss Virginia Lee Comer, consultant on arts for the Association of Junior Leagues of America, surveyed the city's cultural facilities and recommended possible courses of action. The Junior League of that city gave considerable money to help establish the Arts Council. Many other women's organizations play beneficial roles in aiding community recreation projects.

Other service organizations

There are other types of community organizations that do not necessarily fall under the previous categories. The Junior Chamber of Commerce, police organizations, and National Congress of Parents and Teachers should be mentioned because of their concern for youth. The Junior Chamber of Commerce, made up of the young and energetic business and professional men in the community, has aided many recreation programs. The police organizations have been active in sponsoring PAL Clubs in their effort to establish a closer relationship with boys.

The PTAs are primarily concerned with parent-teacher relationships and the welfare of the children in the local schools. These organizations have proved to be valuable to recreation agencies. PTAs generally sponsor Scout troops and provide equipment and financial help for school-related recreation programs. They also provide a channel for interpretation of recreation needs and services to the community.

The contributions of the many community organizations have been instrumental in broadening the recreation opportunities of their own membership as well as aiding other agencies who are responsible for providing recreation services.

Settlements and Neighborhood Centers

Settlements or neighborhood centers are generally considered social welfare agencies. Their prime responsibility is that of serving as social instruments for neighborhood betterment. Found most often in slums or low economic areas of larger cities, settlements are concerned with the health, welfare, education, and recreation needs of all persons living in these social environments.

Backgrounds

Like many other social movements, the settlement movement originated in England. The first settlement was Toynbee Hall, established in 1884 in east London. Samuel Barrett, its founder, described the settlement as a place in which individuals in a neighborhood could join together to discuss common problems, attempt to bring about improved conditions, and foster a better way of life for all people living in the area.

The original settlement in this country was the Neighborhood Guild, later named the University Settlement, founded in 1886 in the lower east side of New York City. Three years later, in 1889, the renowned Hull House in Chicago was started under the direction of Jane Addams. Other settlement houses followed until today there are over 850 settlements in this

Fig. 16   *Hull House Today*

country. In 1911, leaders in the settlement-house movement founded the National Federation of Settlements and Neighborhood Centers. Similar organizations also exist in Canada and in several European countries. This federation serves as the national agency for the settlement-house movement, serving the existing settlements as well as promoting new ones. The various national federations throughout the world established, in 1926, the International Federation of Settlements, with headquarters in the Netherlands.

Purposes

Settlements serve the constituency of the complete neighborhood, not just those who come to the settlement for advice, assistance, or planned activities. Social-work leaders operate on the premise that neighborhood environment greatly affects the development of individuals and families; thus, the settlement serves as the laboratory in which the people, guided by trained leaders, can bring about social reforms and better living for all persons residing in these poorer sections of large cities.

The objectives of neighborhood centers are generally acknowledged as broader in scope than those of most community recreation agencies. Settlements are concerned with all aspects of neighborhood and family living, with recreation being only one of their functions. The Arden House Conference included in its purposes the following: "To help promote cultural activities—an active participant culture: countering pressures toward passivity in American life, helping to develop ways of using our increasing leisure for creative activities." [36]

Organization

Settlements are governed by boards of directors composed of representatives from the contributing public, sponsoring agencies, and, in some cases, from the neighborhood served. The board is the legal entity and has complete control over the operation of the center. Neighborhood centers are often financed through United Funds or Community Chests. If the center is not incorporated as a part of the united community drive, money is received mainly through gifts from foundations, large industrial firms, or wealthy individuals. The staff is headed by a "head worker" who is responsible to the board. A majority of the staff are social group workers. Volunteer leaders are encouraged and considered important to the success of most centers.

Program

Programs of settlements differ greatly from community to community. There is no traditional pattern. In most cases, the entire family and the whole neighborhood are considered. The group-work approach is generally used in working with both youth and adults. The philosophy and methods are based upon the principle of individual development through group participation in various activities under trained leadership. Counseling on personal problems is an important service. Programs are not necessarily building-centered, since many of the activities and services take place in homes and in the neighborhood.

The program offered in the center depends upon its facilities. Recreation facilities might include many of the following: clubrooms, shops, game rooms, gymnasiums, nurseries, swimming pools, camps, ball fields, playgrounds, and libraries. Recreation programs are often similar to those of municipal recreation centers. Activities offered are: playground program, camps, hobby or interest clubs, athletics, arts and crafts, and cultural activities.

Neighborhood centers serve as recreation centers for sections of the community where they are located. It is recognized that these centers have all-encompassing roles to play—recreation is one of them. With the provision of a varied recreation program, the leisure needs of people in these low economic areas may be satisfied.

[36] *Social Work Yearbook* (New York: National Association of Social Workers, 1960), p. 527.

SUGGESTED REFERENCES

Anderson, Jackson M., *Industrial Recreation*. New York: McGraw-Hill Book Company, 1955.

Brightbill, Charles K. and Harold D. Meyer, *Recreation: Text and Readings*. Englewood Cliffs, N.J.: Prentice-Hall, Inc., 1953.

Clemens, Frances, Robert Tully, and Edward Crill. *Recreation and the Local Church*. Elgin, Ill.: Brethren Publishing Company, 1958.

Curtis, Henry S., *Play and Recreation for the Open Country*. New York: Ginn and Co., 1914.

Douglass, Paul F., et al., eds., *Recreation in the Age of Automation*. Philadelphia: The American Academy of Political and Social Science, 1957. The Annals of the Academy, Vol. 313.

Kaplan, Max, *Leisure in America*. New York: John Wiley & Sons, Inc., 1960.

Meyer, Harold D. and Charles K. Brightbill, *Community Recreation, A Guide to Its Organization*. Englewood Cliffs, N.J.: Prentice-Hall, Inc., 1956.

Neumeyer, Martin H. and Esther S. Neumeyer, *Leisure and Recreation*, Third edition. New York: The Ronald Press Company, 1958.

Pylant, Agnes Durant, *Church Recreation*. Nashville, Tenn.: Convention Press, 1959.

Recreation for Community Living, Guiding Principles. Chicago: The Athletic Institute, 1952.

Social Work Yearbook. New York: National Association of Social Workers. Published yearly.

10

Working Together
at the Local Level

Part 2, "Serving the Local Community," interrelates the many different leisure opportunities found on the local scene. Not all of these exist in every American city, but certainly a large number can be found in many progressive communities. Most leisure agencies have the same major goal, that of individual and community betterment. Although they have somewhat common objectives, agencies do differ as to the scope of their organizational efforts and the way they achieve their goals. For instance, such organizations as the Boy Scouts, Girl Scouts, and Boys' Clubs are concerned with specific age groups, whereas other agencies, such as municipal recreation departments, are interested in the total population. Organizations like the school, church, and industry consider recreation as a secondary function, whereas the foremost reason for the existence of public parks is the leisure interests of the public. Hospital recreation leaders are concerned mainly with those individuals confined to their respective institutions for treatment. Private clubs limit their offerings exclusively to their membership. On the other hand, some organizations open their doors to the entire community.

Regardless of each agency's individual approach, membership, or program, all are interested in the individual and how he can adjust to his social environment. Because community recreation encompasses many

239

varied relationships and experiences, many of the previously mentioned agencies offer recreation or related civic or social services. In most cities, there is a need to coordinate the efforts of these agencies, so that the best interests of the whole community are achieved. Butler presents the problem of coordination as follows:

The multiplicity of agencies undertaking some form of recreation activity or serving some recreation interest is largely the result of independent and unrelated attempts to meet specific recreation desires and needs rather than of concerted action to render recreation service according to a carefully devised cooperative plan of action. The rapidity and extent of the changes which have given recreation a place of prominence in American life . . . account in part for the relative lack of coordination among recreation agencies in the past.[1]

In far too many instances, interests of individual agencies are placed ahead of the over-all good of the neighborhood or community. Willingness to join hands in cooperative undertakings is often nonexistent. Competition for the leisure interests of youth and duplication or overlapping of programs, facilities, and services are frequent. The end result often is that, in in spite of the many different programs and facilities offered, recreation opportunities are inadequate in the majority of our communities. It is only through an integrated and cooperative approach that the best interests of the total community can be achieved and a well-rounded community recreation program can be maintained. Recreation comes the closest to people at the local level; it is here that "working together" must be practiced.

Community-Wide Relationships

Working together for a varied and comprehensive community recreation program involves public, private, semi-public, and commercial agencies. It requires the effort of the church, the home, the school, and other civic and social institutions sponsoring recreation activities. It is up to each agency to determine its special and unique function and how it can work with the other agencies in the community so that the total interests can be furthered. As each agency limits itself to its specific responsibility, it is essential that there be an understanding among organizations of how each contributes to the community effort.

It is generally agreed that public agencies must provide the basic facilities, services, and leadership that will enable them to offer recreation opportunities for the greatest number of people. On the other hand, private and semi-public agencies may limit their offerings to specific segments of the population. In many cases, their programs are directed to particular age groups.

[1] George D. Butler, *Introduction to Community Recreation*, 3rd ed. (New York: McGraw-Hill Book Company, 1959), p. 54. Reprinted by permission.

The manner in which the various agencies pool their resources will largely determine the degree to which the total community needs are met. Cooperation is a two-way process. Each agency has much to give as well as to gain. Not only does each organization benefit from this cooperative process, but also it contributes to more unified total community effort.

There are many ways in which communities work toward unified action. Whatever the methods used, they must be accompanied by a real desire on the part of the lay and professional leaders of each agency to gain a full knowledge and understanding of how other agencies operate and how their agency can best share its resources for the benefits of the community. Machinery must be provided as a framework for organized cooperative action. A community council has proved effective in many communities.

Community councils

If a community need is apparent or problems exist, a community council may be instituted to survey, plan, and instigate action to improve community life. Community councils are broad in purpose and function. Some of the community needs to which councils give attention are health, welfare, schools, government, economic improvement, and recreation. Recreation can be considered as only one of the areas of concern. Generally, committees or interest sections are established for each of the phases of community life, depending upon the needs of the particular community. The council, through its committees or sections, attempts to approach community problems by a survey of existing conditions, by study and discussion of various needs, and by recommendations as to ways of improving the existing conditions.

The council might be termed an "inter-agency" council at the local level. In order to be successful, the council should represent all community groups, such as governmental agencies, churches, youth-serving agencies, health organizations, women's groups, luncheon clubs, lodges, business organizations, recreation clubs, and interest groups. Recreation needs are approached through a "youth and recreation" or a "group-work and recreation" section. Both lay and professional leaders of representative recreation agencies should actively participate in the activities of this section if a coordinated recreation effort is to be achieved.

Various types of coordinating organizations have been established. Examples of such councils include: Councils of Social Agencies, Coordinating Councils, and, more recently, Health and Welfare Councils. No one type of council merits recommendation over another. The council, its type and its organization, is dependent upon local needs, conditions, and community organization.

Coordinating councils. Coordinating councils were first organized in California during World War I. In the early years, coordinating councils had as their main purpose the prevention of juvenile delinquency. As the movement expanded in numbers and to other states, the interests and functions also expanded to include all phases of community betterment. In 1938, Coordinating Councils, Inc. was formed to further the movement in California and other states. In small communities, coordinating councils are normally organized on a community basis, whereas in larger cities these councils are operated on a neighborhood basis. Recreation has proved to be one of their chief concerns.

Councils of social agencies. Councils of this nature were first established to serve as coordinating and planning instruments for the agencies in the federated financial drive in the community—the community chest. A need was evidenced to coordinate efforts, eliminate duplication, and fill gaps in services of these social agencies. Established first in Pittsburgh and Milwaukee in 1909, councils of social agencies have tended to locate in larger cities. Larger communities are more often financially able to employ professional personnel to guide and direct the operation.

Over a period of years, experience showed that all agencies in the community had to be involved, if effective cooperation was to be achieved. Membership of the council was expanded, therefore, to include public and private agencies, as well as agencies in the community chest. Also, membership was enlarged to include lay leaders as well as the professional workers representing the agencies involved. Because of this broadening of membership, many councils changed their names to *Community Welfare Councils* or *Health and Welfare Councils*. A Council of Social Agencies or Community Welfare Council may be organized as an integral part of the Community Chest or United Fund, or may operate as a separate organization. The latter is the most common method of organization. If the council is a part of the fund-raising organization, the agency programs, needs, and services can be appropriately weighed and correlated with the financial plan and drive. A council may serve as a review board for all new agencies seeking United Fund or Community Chest support. It may also analyze budget requests of both old and new agencies and conduct studies of their programs.

Relationships Among Local Governmental Agencies

In most cities, there is a need to develop closer relationships among the various public agencies providing education or recreation services to the community. These agencies include schools, park departments, recreation boards or commissions, libraries, museums, housing agencies, and others. It is most desirable that close working relationships and goodwill be maintained among such agencies as well as divisions of government, such as purchasing, planning, personnel, and finance. In most cities noteworthy examples can be observed of beneficial relationships between recreation and other departments of city government such as the police, fire, public works, welfare, and health departments. Cooperation from all segments of government must be maintained, if the best interests of the taxpayers are to be served and the widest possible recreation opportunities are to be provided. The following are some approaches to cooperative action among public agencies.

School-city relationship

Chapter 5 presents the various recreation functions of the school. The coordination of school resources with those of other community and recreation agencies should be considered one of the more important roles of the school. Cooperative planning of areas and facilities, joint use of facilities, coordination of program ventures, and provision of leadership are but a few ways in which schools can establish better cooperative relationships. The school and city administrations in Austin, Texas, to mention only one specific example, have developed a comprehensive list of policies to facilitate better school-city relationships. Detailed policies have been written for each of the following concerns: purchase of sites, planning new construction, use of buildings and grounds, and the program to be conducted. Muskegon (Michigan), Glenview (Illinois), Grand Rapids (Michigan), Minneapolis (Minnesota), and Denver (Colorado) are other cities that have been successful in establishing good city-school relationships. In many cities and states exist conditions that enhance the possibility for excellent school-city interaction. Favorable legislation, public opinion, and understanding school authorities provide climates for coordinated action. Cities have used various methods to secure cooperation; three specific approaches to the problem can be illustrated.

1. *School board representation on the recreation board.* Having a member of the school board serve on the recreation board has provided school authorities with a better understanding and appreciation of recreation services and has been beneficial in interpreting school philosophy and problems to recreation officials. Where this procedure is used, the school board member, serving on the recreation board, often takes the initiative on cooperative actions. He appropriately serves to establish liaison between the two boards.

2. *Joint employment of recreation executive.* In Hammond and in Bloomington, Indiana, the recreation executive is compensated from both the school and city budgets. Since he receives part of his salary from school funds, the recreation superintendent is considered a school employee; thus, he is a part of the school team. Certainly better school-city relationships are bound to be achieved under these conditions.

3. *Cooperative planning committees.* The establishment of joint planning committees has proved to be successful in coordinating the acquisition, planning, and utilization of school, park, and recreation areas and facilities. In Denver, Colorado, a committee of seven members has proved invaluable in coordinating school-city developments. The membership of the committee consists of: the president of the city-county PTA, a high-school principal, a member of the board of education, the chairman of the city council's recreation committee, the director of planning, the director of parks, and the director of health education, physical education, and recreation for the public schools.

Park-recreation cooperation

Where park and recreation departments are operated separately, cooperative action is essential if the fullest recreation opportunities are to be offered and the maximum use of park and recreation areas and facilities is to be achieved. In far too many cities, park authorities confine their interest mainly to the development and maintenance of areas and facilities, whereas recreation leaders are interested in recreation programing. Friction and lack of cooperation exist between the two departments. It is essential that the two departments work together in harmonious relationships. Joint agreements and policies should be made to serve the best interests of both departments. The modern trend of combining parks and recreation has been fostered mainly so that maximum services can be had at minimum cost.

City planning agencies

Official planning commissions, found in the majority of our cities, are concerned with all phases of the cities' growth and development. Recreation administrators should work closely with these official bodies so that adequate recreation space and facilities are acquired and developed in relation to the total growth of the cities.

Other Approaches to Joint Action

Community agencies have found it mutually advantageous to join hands in many other ways. The joint sponsorship of training institutes or workshops strengthens interagency solidarity and makes full use of the special talents available. In some instances, specialists are brought in from colleges or service organizations to conduct institutes on various phases of recreation. These institutes are generally open to volunteer and professional leaders representing the many agencies offering recreation programs. In other cases, specialists representing local community agencies may join forces to sponsor an institute. In either case, more than one agency benefits from this approach to in-service training.

Multiple use of a camp, school building, church basement, or swimming pool makes it possible for community agencies to conduct their programs at the most economical cost to the taxpayers. In one city, a Boy Scout resident camp was turned over to the Girl Scouts for a few weeks each summer so that both groups might offer camping opportunities. In another city, a large industry made its gymnasium available to the local recreation department for its municipal basketball league.

The development of master recreation calendars for communities is an effective tool for informing the public about the many recreation offerings. It may help agencies improve their scheduling. Community-wide studies under the direction of community councils have proved invaluable in many locales. Such undertakings demand cooperation from all agencies and groups sponsoring leisure activities. Some communities have established volunteer bureaus that maintain current listings of individuals who are willing to share their talents and energies with recreation agencies.

Advisory Councils

It is generally recognized that the strength of community recreation is developed and maintained by citizen interest. Public recreation agencies find that recreation advisory councils or committees are one means of exercising the principle of creative participation—that is, of working *with* rather than *for* individuals within the community.

Advisory councils are generally composed of citizens interested in community-wide public recreation programs. Councils are generally formed at the recommendation of recreation boards or commissions and have advisory rather than legal powers. In cases in which the recreation department is directly responsible to the mayor or city manager, an advisory council or committee is generally formed in lieu of an official recreation board or commission. If the council is formed as an adjunct to the official recreation authority, it should work directly with the board or commission. In order to be successful in its purpose and long-lived in operation, the council should be given specific functions. The value and effectiveness of the council will vary according to the degree of recognition and responsibility given to it by the legal authority.

Functions of advisory councils

The functions of an advisory council are dependent upon the purpose specified by the creating authority. Generally, advisory committees or councils are formed to:

1. *Conduct studies.* Often councils are charged with the responsibility of solving specific problems that confront the recreation department. Councils may utilize all available resources in seeking solutions to the problem.

Committees make their recommendations to the official recreation authority.

2. *Create good public relations.* Sometimes committees are asked to develop public understanding and support for specific projects or programs. They may also serve as a weathervane of public opinion. In this role, councils keep the board advised as to community needs, interests, and attitudes.

3. *Furnish technical advice.* Many recreation superintendents look to advisory committees for technical assistance on various problems related to medicine, law, architecture, and engineering. A smart executive is always alert to "pick the brains" of some of the community's best minds.

4. *Serve as liaison.* Many advisory councils are asked to serve as liaison between the recreation department and the community. They may meet with other community groups and recommend ways of providing cooperative services. In this capacity, advisory committees broaden the span of communication of the official recreation board.

Hazards to watch for

Citizens' advisory committees and councils have definite roles to play; however, in many instances they fail to fulfill the purposes for which they are created. Failures can often be attributed to one or more of the following:

1. Indiscriminate use of these committees
2. Poor selection of committee personnel
3. Failure of the board to define clearly the purposes and goals for the committee to achieve
4. Failure of recreation superintendents to work with advisory committee members
5. Establishment of an advisory committee without any real purpose or function

Principles Guiding Cooperative Action

To develop the fullest possible cooperation among community organizations in recreation, the following principles should be carefully considered.

1. It must be recognized that, in most communities, public, private, and commercial agencies have contributions to make in the field of recreation.
2. Each recreation agency must determine and continually evaluate its particular function in the total community program. It must operate

within this framework and not branch out to include functions adequately performed by other recreation agencies.

3. A sincere desire on the part of the leaders of each recreation agency to cooperate is essential before cooperative action can be achieved. This attitude is more important than the mechanical framework initiated for community cooperation.

4. In most communities, a community council should be established to coordinate systematically the resources of the community in a way that will facilitate more adequate community recreation offerings.

5. It must be recognized that cooperation is a two-way process and that each agency involved has much to give to as well as to gain from a cooperative approach to its problems.

6. The effectiveness of the total community recreation efforts is directly proportionate to the cooperative planning and coordinated action of the various agencies participating.

7. Any organizational structure developed for community planning must be based upon broad representation of community agencies and active participation of lay as well as professional leaders.

SUGGESTED REFERENCES

Community Planning for Social Welfare, A Policy Statement. New York: Community Chests and Councils of America, n.d.

Hillman, Arthur, *Community Organization and Planning.* New York: The Macmillan Company, 1950.

Local Planning Administration. Chicago: International City Managers' Association, 1948.

Meyer, Harold D. and Charles K. Brightbill, *Community Recreation, A Guide to Its Organization.* Englewood Cliffs, N.J.: Prentice-Hall, Inc., 1956.

Miracles Every Other Tuesday. New York: Community Chests and Councils of America, n.d.

Recreation for Community Living, Guiding Principles. Chicago: The Athletic Institute, 1952.

Teamwork in Our Town Through a Community Welfare Council. New York: Community Chests and Councils of America, 1954.

3

THE STATE, THE NATION, AND THE WORLD

*"Good government obtains
when those who are near are happy
and those who are far off are attracted."*
CONFUCIUS

11

The States' Responsibility

Recreation is generally thought of as the responsibility of local government and of locally operated voluntary and private organizations. The state, however, has an important and distinct place. In accordance with the United States Constitution, all powers not delegated to the nation reside in the states, and it is thus a state responsibility to authorize the establishment of local services. Moreover, state agencies render statewide services that are beyond the scope of the subdivisions of the state.

Recreational Functions of the States

Not all of the functions discussed in the pages that follow are performed in every state. A responsibility assumed by a state government in one state might be shouldered by local governments or private agencies in another. The recreation functions described, however, are characteristic of most states.

Enactment of permissive legislation

The legal authority for the operation of public programs, whether by schools, parks, or separate recreation agencies, is granted to the local communities by the states. Each state designates through its own enabling laws the means by which counties and municipalities may operate recreation programs. The legislation may indicate the administrative structure, the functions to be performed, the methods of financing, tax limitations, and

251

the like. Thus the states perform the essential service of providing a base upon which local communities may build.

Services to local units of government

In such fields as education, health, and welfare, the state renders direct services to communities through separate state offices and staffs. In only a few instances have the states given comparable services in the field of recreation; but where they have done so, local recreation programs have shown improvement both in numbers and in quality.

For many years the National Recreation Association, a nongovernmental service organization, has rendered invaluable advisory service to communities. With the growth in the numbers of community recreation programs, state governments are called upon to help meet the need. Many states have been slow to assume this responsibility. Legislators are often reluctant to create new agencies, yet existing agencies that might perform this function are sometimes unable or unwilling to do so. The proponents of separate recreation commissions or boards insist that recreation should receive recognition as a separate function of government and point to the improvements achieved where such commissions or boards exist.

Where special recreation agencies do not exist, recreation advisory services to local units of government are frequently rendered by departments of education, or agencies concerned with health, welfare, planning, parks, forests, and conservation. Colleges and universities and extension services of the colleges of agriculture may also give such services. Inter-agency committees have been organized in some states for this purpose.

State services to local communities include: studying recreation needs and programs and making recommendations for meeting needs through the expansion of present services or the establishment of new ones; providing information to local communities on methods of financing, administering, and conducting community programs; helping local communities enrich and improve recreation opportunities; acting as a means of exchange of information and ideas among local communities to effect improvements in programs and services; assisting in the recruitment and selection of personnel; conducting training courses and workshops for recreation leaders; and developing standards for the conduct of programs. Some states give financial assistance as well as advisory services for the development of local recreation programs.

Provision of areas and facilities

All of the states own land, with about three fourths of the state-owned land lying in the seventeen western states. States with large holdings usually have parks, forests, wildlife reserves, and income-producing lands, which they lease to private users for grazing, mining, and oil producing.

Other states have only small parks and lands on which state-owned buildings are placed.

States not only hold land specifically for recreation but in addition hold vast acreages that, although acquired primarily for economic purposes, are increasingly receiving recreation use. It may be said that the major service of states in recreation, apart from granting authority to local units to operate programs, is the provision of outdoor areas.

States hold title to about 80 million acres of land, about 50 million of which are grazing lands held for income purposes, primarily for schools.[1] State lands upon which outdoor recreation is a recognized use totaled 36.6 million acres in 1960, distributed approximately as follows: [2]

Type of Land	Millions of Acres	Number of Areas
State parks	5.1	1,758
State forest agencies	16.6	457
Fish and wildlife agencies	12.5	2,714
Water development agencies	1.2	295
Other agencies	1.3	341

State holdings are small compared to federal holdings. The states hold, roughly, less than one third as much parkland designated for outdoor recreation as the federal government holds; one tenth as much forest agency land; one eighth as much water development agency land; but one and one half times as much fish and wildlife agency land; and over eighty times as much land of other agencies, such as land offices, city administrations, schools, historical societies, special districts, and agencies not elsewhere classified.

Public demand has resulted in the development on state-owned land of many recreation facilities, such as roads, trails, picnic grounds, shelters, lodges, cabins, hotels, museums, swimming pools, beaches, bathhouses, and camp grounds. Emphasis is placed generally on the development of such facilities as will aid in the enjoyment of the outdoors.

Provision of programs under leadership on state-owned lands and in state-owned institutions

Although they were at first satisfied merely to reserve areas and provide facilities, state governments soon found that program services on these areas were also in demand. Personnel employed for safety or protection of prop-

---

[1] Land, 1958 Yearbook of Agriculture (Washington, D.C.: Department of Agriculture, 1958), p. 72.

[2] Based upon information from Progress Report (Washington, D.C.: Outdoor Recreation Resources Review Commission, January 1961), p. 20. Figures are rounded. Alaska and Hawaii are excluded.

Fig. 17   *Potawatomi Inn, Pokagon State Park, Indiana*

erty, such as lifeguards, wardens, and caretakers, were augmented by recreation specialists, lecturers, and guides. The state is engaged in direct recreation programs also in its state institutions: correctional, mental, medical, and charitable. Recreation has been proven to be a valuable tool in rehabilitation.

Propagation and distribution of plants and animals

In most states there exist programs to improve wildlife habitats and to propagate and distribute fish or game. State-maintained nurseries provide forest tree seedlings for distribution. The states attempt to improve conditions for plants and animals not only on public lands but also on private lands. The federal government cooperates with the state in projects affecting wildlife and forests.

Planning and research

Planning for recreation may be carried on by state agencies concerned with economic development, land acquisition and management, wildlife preservation, and others. These agencies must base their long-range planning on research, whether such research consists of analyzing the tourist business or the pheasant population of the state. In states in which recreation commissions or boards exist, much of the planning and research revolves about the development of community recreation.

Education and information

Education for the use of leisure is part of the concern of state departments of education. However, agencies concerned with natural resources offer various educational services, including: slides and films; radio and television programs; traveling exhibits; conservation workshops for adults and camps for children; lecture programs; and services to camps and schools.

Education for recreation leadership

Recreation programs have progressed slowly in many areas because of lack of adequate leadership. The number of state colleges and universities that include professional education for recreation in their curriculums is increasing. They offer not only formal courses of study but also experiences in practice leadership. Various other state agencies conduct conferences, conventions, workshops, and training institutes for teachers and leaders in recreation.

Promotion of the tourist business

So remunerative have businesses catering to travelers and vacationers become that some states make concerted efforts to attract tourists. State agencies engage in advertising; preparing and distributing booklets, maps, and folders; and maintaining information centers for the convenience of tourists. These services may be under the direction of planning departments, highway departments, departments of natural resources, or other divisions of state government. Private associations, such as state chambers of commerce, also participate in such promotion programs.

Services to special groups

There are certain special groups to which the states offer recreation services. Among them are state-maintained institutions such as hospitals, correctional institutions, and homes for the orphaned or the aged. Mental-health institutions particularly recognize the values of recreation and sponsor therapeutic recreation programs. Another service to a special group is that provided through state agricultural extension services. Rural residents, both adults and children, benefit from these programs. The state cooperates with the county agricultural agent and the home demonstration agents at the local level.

Establishment of standards and regulations

Regulations affecting recreation are of two types: those protecting the users and those protecting the resources. The state assumes the responsibility for regulating activities that might be harmful to the health, safety, and morals of its citizens. Certain types of commercial amusements, such as gambling, are regulated or prohibited, as are other activities in which there is potential danger to children or adults. Organized camps, fishing lodges, and resorts are regulated and inspected to safeguard the health and safety of their patrons. Swimming pools are required to maintain certain standards of cleanliness. State laws protecting natural resources include those controlling hunting and fishing, protecting land from fire and vandalism, preventing water pollution, and preserving plant life.

The variety of recreation functions performed by states is matched by the variety of agencies to which these functions are assigned. State governments differ not only in structure but also in the names designating agencies with similar functions. All of the agencies discussed in the following pages, therefore, may not operate in every state nor may the terminology used fit any particular state. In most of these agencies, the recreation functions are minor or at least secondary to their principal functions; in only a few is recreation the principal function.

For purposes of discussion, state agencies concerned with recreation are herein divided into five groups: (1) state recreation commissions or boards; (2) state departments concerned with natural resources—parks, forests, fish and game, and water resources; (3) agencies concerned with education— departments of public instruction, colleges and universities, museums, and libraries; (4) agencies concerned with health, welfare, and correction; and (5) other agencies—agricultural extension services, highway departments, commerce and planning agencies, and, finally, inter-agency committees, which attempt to coordinate the recreation efforts of all the other agencies. A description of each of these divisions of state government follows.

State Recreation Commissions or Boards

Many leaders in the field of recreation believe that only through recognition of recreation as a separate function of state government, along with health, welfare, and education, can recreation services contribute in the fullest extent to the well-being of the citizens of the state. In spite of this point of view, few states have established separate commissions or boards.

The state commissions and boards do not operate recreation programs themselves. Their functions are to advise local communities, sponsor training institutes, organize conferences, and make surveys. North Carolina, which established a State Recreation Commission in 1945, was the first state to have a separate recreation agency. Vermont was second in 1947, when its State Recreation Board was established. California followed, also in 1947, with a Recreation Commission; its functions were later transferred to the Department of Natural Resources.

Washington and Colorado created state park and recreation commissions. Some other states have recreation consultants, responsible either to an established agency or directly to the governor.

State Departments Concerned with Natural Resources

Many of the recreation services provided by the states are related to the management of natural resources. In spite of diverse terminology and varied administrative patterns in the different states, there are in most states agencies with four distinct responsibilities in regard to natural resources: management of state parks, management of state forests, management of fish and game, and management of water resources. In some states these four responsibilities are borne by four separate agencies; in others the functions are combined into one department of conservation or of natural resources.

The National Conservation Conference of Governors, called by President Theodore Roosevelt in 1908, was responsible for the appointment of state conservation agencies in 41 of the states. There are today in each of the 50 states one or more agencies concerned with conservation.

State parks

State parks vary tremendously in size and character. They range from large natural lands such as Adirondack State Park in New York, with over 2 million acres, to small parks of only a few acres. State park authorities may have jurisdiction not only over state parks (including arboretums, reservations, reservoirs, lakes) but also over state monuments, historic sites, recreation areas, parkways, and waysides. Thirty-five percent of all areas have fewer than 50 acres each.

State parks differ from local parks in that usually—not always—they are more remote from centers of population, are of wider significance, attract visitors from greater distances, contain greater acreage, retain more natural characteristics, and carry on programs more suited to the natural environment.

Administration. There are three main patterns of administration of parks in the various states: (1) administration within a department that also administers forests and wildlife; (2) administration within a department that also administers forests; and (3) administration by a separate department. Most of the states operate within one of these types of structure. The few remaining states administer their parks through a highway department, state historical society, state publicity and parks commission, department of public lands, and department of public works.

Purposes of state parks. State parks in their inception were set aside as historic shrines or places of outstanding natural beauty, somewhat intermediary between municipal parks and national parks. Some parks were intended to protect typical scenery so that future generations might know what the land was like before the coming of the white man. As time passed, there were included within the state park systems certain areas with a different emphasis, in which the land itself was subordinate to the recreational usage. These were places devoted for the most part to active recreation pursuits—swimming beaches, boating waters, campgrounds, winter sports areas, or, in some cases, playfields similar to those in city parks.

There is a difference of opinion among state park leaders as to the extent to which state parks should provide for active recreation. In many parks, swimming, horseback riding, camping, fishing, canoeing, boating, and hiking are accepted as appropriate activities, although the understanding and appreciation of natural and historic features are still regarded as the chief reason for state parks. In coming years, state park agencies may find it necessary to provide for more of the active recreation pursuits.

Provisions for visitors. Hotels, inns, vacation cabins, campgrounds, concession stands, picnic shelters, and amphitheaters are usually provided for the comfort and convenience of the visiting public. Swimming pools and beaches with lifeguards are commonly found. In some parks, personnel to conduct recreation activities are employed.

Because many park administrators are convinced that the fullest and wisest enjoyment of parks depends upon understanding them, interpretive services have been instituted in some places. Naturalists or historians conduct field trips, give lectures, arrange displays, conduct evening campfire programs with slides and films, and prepare publications. In many cases there are trailside museums, small zoos, nature trails, and trailside displays to inform the visitors. Historic parks often include buildings, burial grounds, or sites of important events around which the parks' interpretive programs center.

Background of state parks. The first state park in the United States was the Yosemite Grant, created in California in 1864 from land committed to the state by Congress. The concept of reserving superlative natural areas for public use was a new one. This grant, comprising a spectacular glacier-cut valley and the nearby Mariposa Grove of Big Trees, was a forerunner of our vast system of national and state parks. It was transferred to the national park system in 1890. The second state park, established by Michigan at Mackinac Island in 1885, was especially interesting because of its historic backgrounds, having served French, English, and Americans in the dramatic days of the fur trade. A small piece of property was set aside by the state of New York at Niagara Falls in 1885. The first parks were administered individually; state park systems were a much later development.

Following these beginnings, a number of other states moved to establish parks. The movement lagged, however, until the 1920's. In 1921, Stephen T. Mather, dynamic first director of the National Park Service, brought together in Des Moines, Iowa, a group of people interested in furthering the development of state parks. As a result of this meeting, the National Conference on State Parks, which has devoted itself ever since to state park improvement, was organized.

It remained for the depression years of the 1930's to bring to fruition the development of state parks. A number of states, particularly in the southern United States, trace their park program to these years. The National Park

Service was given the responsibility of working with the states to develop parks. From 1928 to 1941 the parks grew from 484 areas and 2.7 million acres of land to 1,335 areas and 4.2 million acres of land. Many camps, lodges, picnic areas, roads, trails, shelter houses, and the like, on state park land also had their inception as a part of the public works program of the depression years. Reduction of travel during World War II caused a decline in state park programs, maintenance, and attendance. Expansion came to a virtual standstill.

Expansion in state parks. After World War II, attendance increased sharply, from 92.5 million in 1946 to 259 million in 1960. Land acreage did not increase proportionately to attendance during this period. There were 4.6 million acres in 1946 as compared with 5.6 million in 1960. The numbers of areas increased somewhat more rapidly, from 1,531 in 1946 to 2,664 in 1960.[3]

The most startling increase in state park usage has come in camping. State parks in the South and parts of the East, which campers once used only slightly, have been overwhelmed with demands for campsites. Provisions for campers increased markedly in state parks between 1955 and 1960 alone, yet not as fast as the numbers of campers. During this period there was a 60 percent increase in the number of individual campsites, while the number of tent and trailer "camper days" increased from 7.6 million in 1955 to 16.2 million in 1960. The numbers of hotels, lodges, cabins, group camps, restaurants, and refreshment stands likewise increased, but at a much slower rate.[4] The following figures provide an indication of the increased public interest in state parks during the period from 1941 to 1960.

Growth in State Park Attendance, Areas, and Acreages [5]

	1941	1946	1955	1960
Total attendance	97.5 million	92.5 million	183.2 million	259.0 million
Camper days (organized camps)	.8 million	1.0 million	1.7 million	2.2 million
Camper days (tent and trailer camps)	1.6 million	1.1 million	7.6 million	16.2 million
Total number of areas	1,335	1,531	2,034	2,664
Total number of acres	4.3 million	4.6 million	5.1 million	5.6 million

[3] *State Park Statistics—1960* (Washington, D.C.: Department of the Interior, July 1961), p. 6.

[4] *State Parks—Areas, Acreages, and Accommodations, 1960* (Washington, D.C.: Department of the Interior, March 1961), p. 4.

[5] Based upon information in *State Park Statistics—1960*, p. 6. Figures are rounded.

The use of state parks has expanded about five times as fast as the population since World War II. Several states have made strenuous efforts to meet demands and to prepare for anticipated growth. In 1960, New York authorized a $75 million bond issue for the development of 25 thousand additional acres of state park and recreation land. California embarked in 1956 on an enormous program of acquisition and development, particularly of ocean shore properties. The program was financed by royalties from state-owned oil lands.

States differ greatly in the way in which they secure land and finance the development of state parks. Much land has been given to the states. In some cases, federal land has been secured. Increasingly, however, states are finding it necessary to buy their land.

Some state park systems have found an answer to the problem by charging fees to help meet expenses and finance improvements. Some authorities feel that, although fees should be kept at a minimum, at least 50 percent of the cost should be borne by the park users. The sources of funds commonly employed are gate fees, charges for automobile stickers that admit visitors to all parks in a given state, parking fees, admission charges for the use of special facilities such as swimming pools, and returns from concession operations.

State forests

State forests were originally reserved principally for the production of timber, although watershed protection was also important. In many cases cut-over lands and abandoned farms that no one else wanted were acquired. The reforestation of these lands through artificial or natural means not only increased timber resources but also protected watersheds and prevented further land deterioration.

Origin of state forests. Just as state parks preceded national parks, state forests preceded national forests. As early as 1867, when Wyoming appointed a forest inquiry commission, states showed interest in the preservation of trees. In 1885, six years before the national forest system began, New York created, in the Adirondacks, the first state forest preserve. California, Colorado, and Ohio established forestry departments that same year. During the next fifteen years, several other states followed suit.

Extent. State forests and related lands totaled 19.3 million acres in 1956, not including the forests in state park lands. Most of this acreage was commercial timber-producing land. Five of the states held three fourths of all state forestry acreage. They were Minnesota, Michigan, New York, Pennsylvania, and Washington.

Recreational use of state forests. Though less developed, state forests are much more extensive in area than state parks. State forests have always received a certain amount of recreational use and today most of the forest areas are open for recreation. A brief description of some of the recreational uses of state forests follows.

HUNTING AND FISHING. Unlike state parks, state forests are usually open to hunting, at least in certain areas. Fishing is likewise usually permitted, and provisions often are made for boat rental and private boat launching.

CAMPING AND PICNICKING. Day-use areas for picnickers and casual visitors are increasing in numbers. Camping areas for families and, in some cases, leases for resident youth camps, are available. Much of the growth of family camping in recent years has taken place on state forest lands.

SUMMER HOMES. Sites are leased for summer homes in some state forests.

OTHER ACTIVITIES. Hiking, sightseeing, horseback riding, sailing, swimming, canoeing, boating, and skiing are accommodated in state forests.

State fish and game agencies

More than 30 million Americans fished or hunted for recreation in 1960; these pursuits are major forms of recreation. Since 1940, sales of hunting and fishing licenses have increased by about 120 percent, while population has increased about 33 percent. The management of wildlife resources, the protection of fish and game, and, in some cases, the provision of public hunting and fishing grounds are major recreation responsibilities. For the most part, these are responsibilities of the states. Unlike other resources, wildlife does not belong to the private landholders but, rather, to the state. Wildlife that crosses state and international boundaries is the concern of the federal government, and, therefore, migratory birds are under the joint control of the state and the nation.

All states have some state machinery to handle the problems of wildlife. California and New Hampshire were the first to establish fish and game commissions (1878), but other states soon followed. In some states, the responsibility is divided among two or more agencies, although more commonly a department of fish and game is the single authority.

Provision and protection of habitats. All states are faced with difficult problems connected with the protection and management of wildlife habitats. Many of these problems arise out of the popularity of hunting and fishing. The numbers of hunters and fishermen are growing rapidly at the same time that industry, highways, homes, and agriculture are pre-empting the natural habitats of fish and game. The problem of retaining sufficient land and water areas and managing them in the interests of sportsmen has become difficult. Some states have embarked on programs of expanding public fishing and hunting areas. Sometimes these are state forest lands, but more frequently they are lands administered by state fish and game agencies. Occasionally, private land is under public lease to provide areas. Through stocking and planting of fish and game and through the management of the lands and waters to provide food and cover, the state endeavors to improve hunting and fishing in places open to the general public.

Cooperation with the federal government. The federal government co-operates in improving habitat through the provisions of several acts of Congress, notably the Pittman-Robertson Act of 1937 and the Dingell-Johnson Act of 1950. The former provides for a tax on firearms and ammunition, the proceeds of which are distributed to the states on the basis of the numbers of hunting licenses issued. The money is used for the improvement of habitats and the development of special wildlife areas. Some funds go to private landholders for the improvement of wildlife population by plantings in special, protected areas. The Dingell-Johnson Act provides for a tax on fishing tackle, and the funds made available therefrom are granted to the states for the improvement of fishing.

Opening of private lands to the public. One of the most difficult problems related to wildlife is that private lands have been increasingly closed to sportsmen, largely as a result of a few sportsmen's lack of consideration. Private land is, however, a major wildlife habitat in most parts of the country. Numerous steps have been taken by state fish and game authorities to open private lands to the public and to make them more productive of wildlife.

Competition with commercial interests. Commercial fishing and trapping are regulated in all states. The growing competition between commercial interests and the sportsmen often results in conflicts difficult to resolve. The state must give consideration to the man who makes a living from these activities while at the same time satisfying the demands of sportsmen.

Propagation and stocking. Most states maintain fish hatcheries and game farms. They provide seed stock when certain species have become depleted and in some cases plant fish in areas in which there is extremely heavy fishing. Financial support for these programs comes largely from hunting and fishing license fees.

Enforcement of game laws. All states endeavor to control wildlife through legal restrictions. Licenses for fishing and hunting are required, although specific provisions differ from state to state. Conservation officers are employed to enforce the licensing system and the laws governing seasons, bag limits, and the like. Enforcement varies considerably because of the differences among states in the adequacy of enforcement systems and in public acceptance of wildlife laws.

Education. Most state fish and game agencies conduct education programs. Conservation clubs are often organized, for both children and adults, school conservation programs are promoted, magazines and periodicals are published, voluntary agencies are assisted, news releases are prepared, motion pictures are distributed, and, in some cases, staff members are available for talks and consultation. Instruction may be given in such activities as casting, use of firearms, and archery.

Research. Protection and improvement of wildlife depend upon research. Research programs are usually carried on by state fish and game agencies in cooperation with educational institutions.

It is only through the most strenuous efforts of propagation, habitat improvement, legal control, and public education that wildlife can be assured for future generations. In the future, more emphasis must be placed upon the enjoyment of wildlife without destroying it. It is possible that hunting can be provided in years to come for only a small percentage of people and that hunting with field glasses and cameras will for most people replace hunting with guns.

State water resources agencies

Water resources are frequently administered by separate agencies in state governments, although the responsibility is often assigned to departments of health, geology, or natural resources. The development of water resources bears upon recreation in two ways:

1. Lakes, streams, and ocean shores are themselves recreation attractions.
2. Pure water for drinking, bathing, and other use is necessary for the development of resorts, camps, and lodges in recreation areas.

Agencies Concerned with Education

State departments of education or public instruction, colleges and universities, museums, and libraries, though concerned primarily with education, render significant services in recreation. Educational functions related to recreation are also performed by most of the other agencies discussed elsewhere in this chapter.

Departments of public instruction

In many states, departments of public instruction employ special recreation consultants or include recreation services to communities in the divisions of physical education and health. Recreation is promoted through consultation, financial aid for community programs, and training for recreation leaders. The use of school facilities for recreation is encouraged. These departments may stimulate the inclusion of recreation of various types in the school curriculums. Assistance is sometimes given in the development of school camping programs.

State colleges and universities

State colleges and universities generally provide opportunities for higher education for qualified students; offer professional and vocational training in such fields as medicine, law, education, business, and agriculture; conduct research; and render community services of various kinds through numerous departments. Services in recreation are today among the functions of many of these institutions.

Education for leadership in recreation. The education of professional leaders in recreation and park management is probably the most important service these institutions can offer to recreation. Courses offered may consist of only one or two subjects or may include a full range of subjects leading to advanced degrees.

Research. Research into the needs, administrative structure, and present status of organized recreation is continually under way. Studies are frequently published by both faculty and graduate students.

Field services. Some colleges and universities offer direct field-consultant services to communities in the state, either with the part-time services of the faculty or, as in the case of the University of Illinois, the employment of a field staff. In-service training courses, workshops, and conferences may be organized and efforts made to mobilize the recreation resources of the state.

Direct recreation services. Sports and cultural activities, such as musical and dramatic productions and lectures, are fostered by all institutions of higher learning. Many such events are open to the public as well as to the students and greatly enrich the recreation opportunities of the communities in which the schools are located. The various contributions of colleges and universities to recreation are discussed more fully in other sections of this book.

State museums and libraries

State museums and libraries may be thought of as primarily educational, but, at their best, these educational offerings become recreation.

State libraries are of special value to small-town and rural residents to whom city libraries are not easily accessible. State libraries give service to local communities and schools, encouraging reading and making available bookmobiles, films, records, art reproductions, and lecture services.

A state museum usually emphasizes the history, art, folklore, anthropology, geology, or biology of the state in which it is located. It may carry on field work and supply exhibits and audio-visual materials to schools and communities. Museums are frequently located in state parks and are under the jurisdiction of state park agencies. Others are maintained at state universities and historic sites.

Agencies Concerned with Health, Welfare, and Correction

Each state is concerned with welfare, health (physical and mental), and correction. These concerns may be administered separately or in different combinations. Many direct services are rendered; others are purely advisory. The numbers of special commissions, such as those assigned to problems of juvenile delinquency or the aging, have been increasing in recent years. These commissions may be appointed by state legislators, by governors, or both.

Health agencies

State health agencies, whose chief responsibilities lie in the protection and education of people on health matters, affect recreation by their insistence on standards of health and safety in the operation of camps, resorts, swimming pools, beaches, amusement parks, theaters, and other recreation facilities. Their concern for health leads them to the recognition of the importance of recreation in physical and mental fitness and the encouragement of improved physical-education programs in schools. Their field services in some states include the encouragement of good community recreation.

Where state health agencies operate hospitals, either general or mental, direct recreation services are given as part of the therapeutic treatment of patients. Hospital recreation programs are discussed in Chapter 17.

Welfare agencies

One of the major responsibilities of the state welfare agencies is that of providing financial assistance to the needy. Special grants to the blind, to dependent children, and to the aged are usually available, with county welfare departments as agents for the state and with the federal government cooperating in the cost. Child welfare, services for the handicapped, vocational rehabilitation, child placement, legal aid, and the like, are often the responsibility of state welfare agencies. Recreation is a concern particularly when homes or day-care centers are maintained. Legislation has been effected in some states to make recreation facilities and programs mandatory in the licensing of nursing homes and homes for the aged.

State youth commissions or councils

Youth commissions or councils, found in a number of states, are usually concerned with youth with problems. The growth in reported cases of juvenile delinquency has led many such commissions to encourage recreation. In New York, the Youth Commission has assisted local communities in the establishment and improvement of recreation programs, basing this service on the assumption that wholesome activities for youth deter anti-social behavior. Many other youth councils actively support various youth recreation programs for the same reason.

Elsewhere, youth councils give their major attention to studying delinquency and approaching its solution through work with those segments of youth with special difficulties. They make efforts to improve correctional facilities, court procedures, and services to children living in environments that might be considered contributing factors to delinquency. In some states, youth work is administered by public welfare agencies rather than by special commissions.

Commissions for the aged and aging

Problems of the growing numbers of people in the older age group are the province of many commissions of state government. These commissions encourage research, conduct educational programs, hold conferences, and cooperate with the federal government in the study of these problems. Employability, income, education, health, housing, and use of leisure are among the matters considered. Study and recommendations regarding recreation for the aged are particularly undertaken or promoted by these commissions, since recreation activities can determine whether the leisure with which most of the aged are endowed will be a burden or a blessing to them.

Correction agencies

Some states have separate boards dealing with penal institutions; in other states these functions are combined with public welfare activities. State education departments frequently supervise the schools of these institutions. Instruction is given in elementary and high-school subjects, and university extension or correspondence courses are available in a few institutions. Vocational training, especially industrial and agricultural, is stressed, and libraries are maintained. Recreation for institutions is discussed at further length in Chapter 17.

Other Agencies

There are several other agencies that serve recreation functions. Looming large in services to rural residents are the extension divisions of the state land-grant colleges. Highway departments contribute to the recreation of almost everyone who travels. Agencies concerned with commerce cater to the tourist recreation business, and planning agencies consider long-range recreation needs. State inter-agency committees, like oil on wheels, help the complex machinery of government to operate more efficiently within its existing framework.

Agricultural extension services

The state agricultural extension services are directed through the state land-grant colleges as provided by the Smith-Lever law of 1914. The programs are financed jointly by the state, the federal government, and the counties. In 1961, there were 19 states with full-time recreation specialists on their staffs and 18 states with staff members who devoted part time to recreation.[6] The Extension Service carries on work in three main fields: agriculture for farmers, home economics for rural women, and 4-H Club work for rural boys and girls. Volunteer leadership is used on the local level.

Recreation activities. The program is determined by each individual state. The most common forms of recreation activities are folk games, dancing, drama, choral groups, community singing, handicrafts, sports, camping, nature study, and family recreation. Camping is popular both as a 4-H activity and as an activity for rural women. Vacation camps for rural women have been sponsored by home demonstration agents since the early 1920's. Outings, picnics, and hikes are also sponsored.

Important parts of the state extension services are: recreation leadership training institutes and conferences, the planning of fairs and festivals, the maintenance of loan libraries, and the publication of recreation materials such as bulletins, game and song books, and program materials for the use of rural leaders. The extension personnel help small communities, counties, and rural-oriented organizations in analyzing their recreation needs and working out recreation programs.

Educational activities. Through its educational efforts, the Extension Service further promotes recreation. Its work in conservation, by which farmers are assisted in improving their soil, reforesting, building farm ponds, and making improvements for wildlife, increases the desirability of lands for recreation use. The nature programs of the clubs contribute to the enjoyment of outdoor areas.

The 4-H Clubs are considered in more detail in Chapter 6.

Highway departments

In a broad sense, one might consider the highways of the state a major recreation resource. They are not only means of travel to recreation areas but means by which travel itself can become recreation. It has been estimated that over half of the use of major highways is for recreation purposes.

The scenic location of highways is considered in their construction. Plantings hide construction scars and make the roadside attractive and can

[6] *Role of the Federal Government in the Field of Public Recreation,* No. 3, revised (Washington, D.C.: Federal Inter-Agency Committee on Recreation, 1961), p. 20.

transform highways into things of beauty. Parkways, roadside parks, and scenic turnouts add to the enjoyment. Roadside parks, frequently equipped with drinking water, picnic tables, and fireplaces, are a boon to the traveler, breaking the routine of a day at the wheel and giving needed relaxation.

Commerce agencies

State departments and bureaus dealing with commerce and economic development are designed to promote business, attract industries, and conduct economic studies. The tourist business is of such great economic benefit that many states make concerted efforts to entice vacationing visitors and to inform them regarding recreation opportunities through literature, the maintenance of information centers or tourist bureaus, and the like. Chambers of Commerce, which are nongovernmental, also perform these functions.

Planning agencies

An agency concerned with long-range planning is usually authorized to study the natural resources of the state, its potentialities for agriculture and industry, and its population trends. The agency is expected to make recommendations based on such studies. In many states, the recreation needs of the population are given consideration, and communities are helped to design recreation areas and plan their administration.

Coordination of state services

With a multiplicity of agencies in some way giving recreation services, there is a need in most states for some method of securing coordination and cooperation. In many states, inter-agency committees or advisory committees serve this purpose. The first such committee was established in 1946.

Some of the functions of these committees are: exchanging information, planning, conducting studies of recreation resources and needs, organizing and conducting conferences and workshops, sponsoring leadership-training institutes, providing information to the general public, encouraging communities to establish recreation programs, and rendering field service to local communities on request.

Membership in inter-agency organizations may consist exclusively of state agencies or may also include private agencies. State agencies concerned are usually state recreation commissions and agencies dealing with education, natural resources, and health. A successfully functioning committee can make the work of the agencies more effective by preventing overlapping of services and revealing areas where further services are needed.

Principles Regarding State Responsibility for Recreation

We have seen the many ways in which states are involved in recreation, including education for the use of leisure, provision of areas and facilities, setting up of legal controls, and education for leadership. Because of the great diversity of structures and the divergence in the degree of acceptance of state responsibility, it is questionable whether any recognized standards for state services exist. The following principles are probably more important than the organization structures themselves.

1. Each state should have well-constituted legislation to enable school districts, municipalities, and counties to finance and conduct community recreation programs.

2. Adequate state lands should be set aside for outdoor recreation.

3. Consultant service should be available to local communities.

4. State agencies should encourage education for the arts of leisure as part of the school program.

5. State institutions of higher learning should assume responsibility for the preparation of professional leaders.

6. Some state structure should exist to act as a clearing house, to plan on a statewide basis, and to bring together the various state agencies with responsibilities for recreation.

7. The state should assume the responsibility for the conservation of recreation resources, including wildlife, forests, and waters.

8. Agencies in the park, recreation, and conservation fields should maintain high professional status and continuity of program through employment and retainment of personnel on a nonpolitical merit basis.

9. A state agency should assume the responsibility of interpreting recreation to the general public.

SUGGESTED REFERENCES

Brockman, C. Frank, *Recreational Use of Wild Lands*. New York: McGraw-Hill Book Company, 1959.

Clawson, Marion, "The Crises in Outdoor Recreation," *American Forests*, March–April 1959.

Clawson, Marion, *Statistics on Outdoor Recreation*. Washington, D.C.: Resources for the Future, Inc., 1958.

Meyer, Harold D. and Charles K. Brightbill, *State Recreation—Organization and Administration*. New York: A. S. Barnes & Company, 1950.

National Park Service, Department of the Interior, *The Park and Recreation Problem of the United States*. Washington, D.C.: Government Printing Office, 1941.

National Park Service, *State Parks—Areas, Acreages, and Accommodations, 1960*. Washington, D.C.: Department of the Interior, 1961.

National Park Service, *State Park Statistics—1960*. Washington, D.C.: Department of the Interior, 1961.

"This will not be a good place for any of us to live until it is a good place for all of us to live."

THEODORE ROOSEVELT

12

Services of the Federal Government

The federal government, with the passage of time, has recognized more and more that recreation contributes to the "general welfare" and that federal activity in this field is, therefore, in accord with the purposes of the United States Constitution. At the present time more than thirty federal agencies are directly or indirectly involved in providing recreation or assisting other groups in making such a provision. These services extend from maintaining bird refuges and conducting campfire programs to planning roads in national parks.

Policies and Functions in Recreation

Because of the many agencies concerned with recreation, no unified federal policies have evolved. Each agency has determined its own policies and has altered them as time and circumstances have dictated.

Policy statement

An attempt to reach a common agreement was made by the Federal Inter-Agency Committee on Recreation in 1951, when its members developed a statement, *Recommended General Policy of the Federal Government Relative to Public Recreation*. The statement was reaffirmed in 1958. In this statement, the importance of recreation to the national welfare and the necessity for providing it through all levels of government and through both public and private agencies were recognized. The statement clarified the responsibilities of each level of government and expressed the opinion that the federal government should complement state and local governments without assuming responsibilities belonging to either of them. The statement continued:

Therefore, it shall be the policy of the Federal Government to promote and to facilitate the development of adequate and coordinated recreation facilities and services throughout the nation, and for this purpose the Federal Government shall:

(a) Recognize and appraise the recreation potentialities on all Federally-owned lands, water areas, and facilities; and, consistent with the fullest national interests, conserve and make provisions for adequate and appropriate facilities for the use of those resources for public recreation.

(b) Set aside or acquire lands needed for public park and recreation purposes, and administer and use them for such purposes, in accordance with the basic legislation covering their acquisition and use.

(c) Permit and encourage the States, their political subdivisions and others, to construct and operate recreation facilities and programs on Federal Government land when it is in the public interest to do so, taking into account the long-range recreation plans of the States.

(d) Work with the States and Territories on request, and with their political subdivisions with the consent of the States, in planning sound, long-range programs and services for State and local areas to the end that the total recreation provisions by all levels of government shall be cooperatively planned.

(e) Encourage National, State, and local leadership, both public and private, to develop recreation facilities and services adequate to meet the needs and desires of the people.

(f) Provide technical leadership and guidance in the planning and development of recreation facilities and services including the collection and dissemination of necessary and desirable data, pertinent to such planning and development through Federal agencies concerned with recreation.

(g) Develop and maintain in cooperation with State and local governmental agencies and private interests a national recreation plan which will serve as a guide to public and private agencies in integrating their activities into the over-all recreation needs of the country.[1]

Functions

Some of the major functions in recreation now being performed by the federal government are listed here. Many of the functions overlap. Others

[1] *Recommended General Policy of the Federal Government Relative to Public Recreation* (Washington, D.C.: Federal Inter-Agency Committee on Recreation, n.d.). Mimeographed.

are by-products of activities that are not recreational in themselves. For instance, the conservation efforts of the government are directed largely for economic reasons toward the soil, wildlife, forests, crops, and water; yet the recreation value of the resources conserved may be as great as or even greater than their economic value. The conservation education programs themselves have recreation value; they become recreational when, for example, they are part of an interpretive program in a national park or part of a hobby interest pursued by a 4-H member.

1. Management of land resources in the public interest, including the use of such land for recreation
2. Development of access and facilities to enable the general public to use and enjoy land and water areas
3. Construction of reservoirs with high recreation potential
4. Administration of recreation programs under leadership
5. Management of wildlife resources on public lands as well as the propagation of wildlife
6. Protection of wildlife resources and enforcement of certain legal restrictions on fish and game
7. Education in the wise use of natural resources as well as information about recreational possibilities
8. Research related to various subjects related to recreation, such as recreational land use, wildlife, and water resources
9. Cooperation with and services to state and local governmental units concerned with parks, recreation, wildlife, and other matters bearing on recreation
10. Operation of recreation programs in veterans' hospitals and other federal institutions
11. Operation of recreation programs for the armed services and other federal employees
12. Services to special groups, such as rural residents through the Agricultural Extension Service
13. Making of international agreements

Recreation and the Land-Administering Agencies

The interest of the federal government in recreation evolved chiefly from its position as custodian of public lands. From the early history of the United States, public lands were used for recreation, particularly hunting and fishing, though at first people participated in these activities more for food and fur than for pleasure. Recreation usage at that time was officially unrecognized or incidental to the management of land for other purposes.

The land we own

Of the nearly two billion acres of land once in the public domain, over a billion were disposed of through the years by sale; by homesteading; by grants to states, railroads, schools, institutions, and veterans; and the like. With its vast holdings, particularly in the West, the government seemed determined to dispose of its lands as quickly as possible so that they might

Fig. 18 *Naturalist Service— Cumberland Gap (Courtesy United States Department of the Interior. National Park Service Photo)*

be developed. However, over 718 million acres of the public domain or almost one third of the total average of our fifty states still remain in the hands of the federal government. Through other means, primarily purchase, the government has acquired another 50 million acres, bringing the total to over 768 million acres. Of these, about 200 million acres are definitely designated as recreation areas, including parks, monuments, historic sites, memorials, geologic areas, archeological areas, forests, recreation areas, public hunting and shooting grounds, water access areas, and fish hatcheries and wildlife areas in which the public is allowed to engage in recreation activities.[2]

Types of land-administering agencies

The agencies holding federal land may be divided into two groups: those administering natural lands and those that acquired lands for the purpose

[2] *Progress Report* (Washington, D.C.: Outdoor Recreation Resources Review Commission, January 1961), p. 19. These figures exclude Alaska and Hawaii.

of developing dams and reservoirs. The latter group of agencies frequently turn the administration of their lands over to state and local agencies or to one of the federal agencies in the former group. Agencies administering natural lands are National Park Service, Forest Service, Fish and Wildlife Service, Bureau of Land Management, Bureau of Indian Affairs. Water-resource-developing agencies are Corps of Engineers, Bureau of Reclamation, Tennessee Valley Authority.

National Park Service (Department of the Interior)

To a small group of men gathered around a historic campfire one night in 1870 the world owes a debt for a new idea in conservation and recreation —the setting aside of part of a nation's land for the enjoyment of generations to come. The men were members of the Washburn-Doane-Langford expedition, exploring the then little-known Yellowstone area. The loftiness of their ideal and the unselfishness of their purpose remain the core of national park philosophy even today. When, as a result of their efforts, the bill establishing Yellowstone National Park as a "public park or pleasuring ground for the benefit and enjoyment of the people" was passed, it was the first federal legislation recognizing parks and recreation as a federal responsibility. It was signed by President Grant on March 1, 1872.

The jurisdiction of the National Park Service extends to 189 areas comprising over 24 million acres of federally owned land. Included are 30 national parks and numerous monuments, historic sites, and cemeteries. The designation "national parks" is reserved for the superb treasures of the national park system. Most of them are large primeval areas with outstanding or unique features, such as Grand Canyon, Yosemite, and Yellowstone. A national park is established by an act of congress. "National monuments," unlike national parks, may be established on federal lands by presidential proclamation. Usually they protect some specific feature of archeological, historic, scientific, or scenic interest. They are considered of somewhat less national interest than the national parks. The size of the area has nothing to do with its designation as a "park" or a "monument."

By far the largest acreage in national parks lies west of the Mississippi River, partly because private holdings have made park acquisition difficult in the East and partly because the spectacular nature of certain western areas makes them especially worthy of national park status.

Although in its early history the National Park Service accepted only land essentially in a natural condition and refused national park status to inferior areas, there is today a changing point of view. Large natural tracts are now practically impossible to obtain, yet other areas have recreation potentialities. In the words of Ben Thompson, Chief of the Division of Recreation Resource Planning of the N.P.S., "such areas should be acquired at the earliest possible date, regardless of some undesirable complications—and this is particularly true of seashore and other shoreline areas—

so that the major public recreation potentiality of the area will not be lost." [3]

Growth of the national parks. As early as 1832, congress had shown a glimmer of interest in public ownership of lands valuable for their social use. At that time it established Hot Springs Reservation in Arkansas (which became a national park in 1921), not as a park but as a health resort, valued for the supposed medicinal qualities of the waters. In 1864, eight years before Yellowstone National Park was created, congress had granted Yosemite Valley and the Mariposa Grove of Big Trees to the State of California upon condition that they be held "for public use, resort, and recreation." [4] In 1905, these areas became part of Yosemite National Park, which had been established in 1890. Also in 1890, General Grant and Sequoia National Parks were created.

Until 1916, when the National Park Service was established in the Department of the Interior, responsibility for administering parks and monuments was divided among several agencies. Under the aggressive leadership of Stephen T. Mather, the first director, the National Park Service enlarged its system of parks. In 1933, all national parks and monuments, national military parks, national battlefield parks and sites, national memorials, the National Capital Parks, and certain national cemeteries were consolidated under the administration of the National Park Service. The scope of the National Park Service was enlarged further in 1936, when congress authorized the National Park Service to aid the states and their subdivisions in planning park and recreation areas. In this same year the National Park Service began its program of developing 46 Recreational Demonstration Areas, which demonstrated how worn-out lands could be built up into desirable recreation areas. Most of these areas were eventually transferred to state agencies.

During World War II, congress curtailed civilian appropriations drastically, and park maintenance and services declined. Attendance dropped to a third of its pre-war level.

Post-war developments. After the war, travel to the parks was resumed and mounted with terrifying rapidity year by year. The number of visits in 1943, when the war was still being waged, totaled less than 7 million; by 1946 it was nearly 22 million, and by 1955 it was over 50 million.

The National Park Service, limited in funds and unprepared for such an increase, faced the greatest crisis of its history. Its facilities were "inade-

---

[3] Ben H. Thompson, "Trends in Park Practice," *Selected Papers Presented at the 42nd National Recreation Congress, Washington, D.C. September 25–29, 1960* (New York: National Recreation Association, 1961), p. 112.

[4] *A Study of the Park and Recreation Problem of the United States* (Washington, D.C.: Department of the Interior, National Park Service, 1941), p. 107.

quate, obsolete, uneconomical of operation, maintained in usable condition only with great difficulty." [5] Therefore, in 1956, "Mission 66" was inaugurated. This was a ten-year plan to safeguard the national parks while at the same time providing facilities for an anticipated 80 million visitors by 1966, the fiftieth anniversary of the service. With $100 million authorized by congress, the National Park Service obtained or improved visitor centers, museums, campsites, utility systems, roads, trails, and parkways. It also greatly expanded its interpretive services.

The growth in the number of visitors continued uninterruptedly and promised to exceed the 80 million planned for by 1966. In 1960 over 72 million people visited the parks and other areas administered by the National Park Service.

Recreation policies and programs. Until 1962, when the Bureau of Outdoor Recreation was established, the National Park Service was the only federal agency concerned exclusively with recreation. The areas under its management are, however, reserved for a special kind of recreation—that which is related to the enjoyment of the resource itself in such a manner as to leave the rescurce unimpaired for future generations. This is a high purpose, and its attainment is beset with many difficulties. How many people can enjoy a spectacle without impairing its natural beauty? To what extent can roads, campgrounds, hotels, and lodges be built without ruining the very thing the people come to see? As Newton B. Drury wrote, "Many a great landscape carries in its beauty the seeds of its own destruction." [6]

Against pressures from many sources, the National Park Service, as guardian of the nation's natural treasures, restricts the form of recreation therein. Millions of visitors drive, fish, swim, boat, climb mountains, camp, picnic, ride horseback, hike, and engage in winter sports. These pursuits are secondary in the eyes of the National Park Service, however, to the main purpose of seeing, understanding, and appreciating the areas themselves. In attempting to preserve unspoiled the natural characteristics of each place, the National Park Service allows no hunting, no exploitation of timber or other natural resources, and no commercial fishing. Not even souvenirs such as rocks may be removed.

Attempts are made to provide essential accommodations, suiting all types of pocketbooks. These are so designed and so located as to detract as little as possible from the natural features. The management of the profit-making operations of the National Park Service areas is assigned to conces-

[5] *Annual Report of the Director, National Park Service, to the Secretary of the Interior, for the Fiscal Year Ended June 30, 1952.*

[6] Newton B. Drury, "State Park Philosophy," in *American Planning and Civic Annual* (Washington, D.C.: American Planning and Civic Association, 1957), p. 154.

sionaires. Hotels, lodges, restaurants, stores, and garages are all operated by private companies. Campgrounds, however, are operated by the National Park Service itself.

Facilities common to city park and recreation departments, such as golf courses, playground apparatus, baseball fields, and the like, are generally discouraged. Emphasis is given to recreation that will enhance appreciation of the parks. An interpretation program has long been a part of the National Park Service. Nature guiding was begun on a limited scale in Yosemite in 1918 and soon spread to other parks. About the same time, museums began to be developed. A plan for the educational work was made in 1924, recommending that each park feature its own individual phenomena rather than a general field—a policy that has governed the national parks ever since.

Interpretation in the individual parks is carried out by a staff of naturalists, historians, and archeologists. The program includes publications; visitor centers including museums or exhibits; guided trips such as auto caravans and hikes; nature trails; exhibits in place; displays; lectures; campfire programs; libraries; traveling exhibits; slides, photographs, television, and motion pictures; and research. The interpretation program is the means whereby the visitor is led to enjoy, understand, and appreciate the parks. The popularity of the program has increased even more rapidly than has attendance at the parks. In 1958, for example, the number of visitors using interpretive services increased over 1957 at a rate 69 percent greater than the rate of increase in total park visitation. The most significant advance was in the use of self-guiding devices.

Forest Service (Department of Agriculture)

About one acre out of each twelve in the United States, including some of the finest recreation lands, is administered by the Forest Service. The importance of the forests as a recreation resource can hardly be overestimated. Here one may find those types of recreation that require abundant space and offer escape from the bustle of metropolitan life. These forests contain rare wilderness—land where the only transportation is by horse, by canoe, or afoot; and the visitor must depend upon his own resources for food and shelter. A large part of the high western land, including spectacular mountains, clear lakes, thousands of miles of fishing streams, and a major part of the big game of America, is in Forest Service lands. In the forests are campsites developed both for families and for organized youth groups, lodges, ski resorts, hunting camps, and private cabins, all for the accommodation of visitors with less vigor than the wilderness seekers. Fishing, hunting, riding, picnicking, swimming, winter sports, camping, canoeing, boating, hiking, mountaineering, and other forms of recreation on these lands lured about 102 million visitors in 1961.

A *proud tradition*. The story of the national forests, like that of the national parks, contains colorful personalities, dramatic conflicts, and high idealism. Theirs is a proud tradition. Despite their wide recreational use today, our national forests were founded not for recreation but for economic reasons. A few timber reserves for naval purposes were established during the early nineteenth century. It was not, however, until after the Civil War that public opinion forced congress to halt the ruthless depredations of forest lands that resulted from the liberal policies by which public lands were obtained, laid bare, and abandoned.

In 1876 congress authorized the employment by the Department of Agriculture of a forestry agent. In 1881, a small Division of Forestry, purely educational, with no jurisdiction over forest land, was established in the Department. The despoiling of forest land none the less continued, and it was evident that stronger measures were needed.

The American Forestry Association, founded in 1875, helped to unify the movement to save the forests. Its efforts resulted in the passage by congress in 1891 of a bill authorizing the President to withdraw public lands as "forest reserves," which were areas closed to all use. Before his term expired, President Harrison set aside thirteen million acres. Since no policy had been established for the use of these first reserves, their withdrawal was severely opposed. In 1897 congress passed the Act for the Administration of Forest Reserves, which opened the reserves for use and became the basis for the operation of national forests to this day. Under the leadership of Gifford Pinchot, who in 1898 became Chief of the Division of Forestry (renamed Bureau of Forestry in 1901), the scope of the Division was greatly enlarged.

Until 1905, the Department of Interior administered the forest reserves, with the Division of Forestry of the Department of Agriculture giving technical advice. In that year the forest reserves were transferred to the Bureau of Forestry—renamed Forest Service—in the Department of Agriculture. During Theodore Roosevelt's administration more than 148 million acres became national forest lands. By 1910, approximately 400,000 people used the forests for recreation, though little was done for their convenience. Functions of the Forest Service were enlarged by the Weeks Law of 1911 and the Clarke-McNary Bill of 1924, amended in 1949, which authorized the purchase of land and provided for cooperation with states in fire protection and forest planting. Later laws further extended the holdings and functions of the Forest Service.

Meanwhile, recreational use of forests continued to grow. The idea emerged that forest recreation was both a service to the public and a means for winning converts to conservation. The public could, through its visits to the forests, be convinced of the value of protection, game preservation, and reforestation. Recreation thus became recognized as compatible with timber and watershed protection. During World War II, when the nation's forests were called upon to provide timber for many war uses, recreation was curtailed. The forests had few recreational visitors.

Like the national parks, the national forests witnessed a dramatic upsurge in the numbers of visitors during the post-war years and could offer only overcrowded facilities that had been constructed for the most part in the 1930's and had depreciated greatly. In order to bring its facilities in line with the demand, a five-year program, Part 1 of Operation Outdoors, was begun in 1957. Under this program campgrounds and picnic sites were rehabilitated and new ones developed at a cost of $85 million dollars. Part 2 of Operation Outdoors, presented in 1961, set forth objectives in the management of wildlife habitats which the Forest Service planned to achieve as rapidly as possible.

In 1960 the Multiple-Use Bill was enacted, giving statutory recognition to the principles of multiple use, which the Forest Service had practiced for many years. The objectives of multiple-use management include management for water, timber, grazing, wildlife, and recreation concurrently, though not all of these uses necessarily occur on the same land. Each resource must be managed according to its capabilities.

The Forest Service today. There are today about 186 million acres in national forests—about one acre for every person in the United States. The areas range from sea level to mountain peaks and are scattered throughout the country, with almost nine tenths of them lying in the West. Some of the land is commercially worthless yet has high recreation value. John Sieker, Director, Division of Recreation and Land Uses of the Forest Service, reports:

144,000 acres are developed for camping, picnicking, winter sports, organization camps, resorts, swimming and boating sites, and summer homes.

15,000,000 acres are managed as Wilderness, Wild, Primitive and Scenic areas. These lands also produce water, wildlife, and other uses consistent with wilderness.

2,625,000 acres are lakes, reservoirs and streams used for water storage, flood control, power, and recreation.

1,350,000 acres are water-front zones reserved to protect recreation values along the shores of lakes and streams.

2,800,000 acres are highways and roads and the zones along these reserved to protect roadside attractiveness.

120,000,000 acres are regularly used for hunting game animals, and game birds, and considerable waterfowl hunting takes place on national-forest lands.[7]

Except for restrictions because of fire danger, all of the forests are open to the public for recreation.

[7] John Sieker, in a speech at the National Conference on State Parks, reported in *Planning and Civic Comment* (December 1960), p. 30. Reprinted by permission.

The general public has frequently confused the National Park Service in the Department of the Interior, with the Forest Service. The National Park Service is dedicated to a single-use concept of the preservation and enjoyment of natural areas. Mining, grazing, lumbering, hunting, and other uses of the land that disturb the natural habitat are forbidden. The Forest Service, on the other hand, has continually held to what is known as the "multiple-use concept," as a result of which several uses may take place concurrently. Timber production, watershed protection, grazing, wildlife management, and recreation may all be found on national forest lands, though perhaps not all of them may be found on the same piece of land. Recreation uses may predominate in one place, timbering in another, or watershed protection in a third.

Recreation in the national forests. Recreation is the fastest-growing activity on national forest lands today. The national forests received 102 million visits for recreation during 1961, more than triple the number of visits in 1950. With the numbers of visitors constantly increasing, it is estimated that if present trends continue there will be 195 million visitors annually by 1969.[8]

Areas and facilities. Public recreation areas are found in all national forests. There are about 5,600 camp and picnic places, which can accommodate 430,000 persons at one time. Safe drinking water, sanitary latrines, fire grates, and tables are provided. In some camp areas a small charge is made for picnicking and camping; others are free. No cabins or tents are provided, and campers must bring their own equipment. A time limit, usually of two weeks, is placed on campers in the more populous areas. In recent years family camping has grown at a rate that can be called explosive. Much of this growth has focused on the national forests. Expansion of camping accommodations was part of the Operation Outdoors program. There are no developments in the camps in wilderness areas.

About 600 organization camps, including camps for Boy Scouts, YMCAs, YWCAs, municipalities, and churches, have been constructed by agencies on leased land in national forests. In addition, the Forest Service itself has constructed nearly 100 camp facilities, which are leased to youth groups that might not otherwise be able to conduct camps. Provision for camping, whether it be for a family in a developed campsite, for canoeists in the wilderness, or for children in an organized camp, is one of the major recreational services of the Forest Service. Nearly five hundred privately owned hotels, lodges, and cabin camps have been constructed, and about 19,000 private summer homes have been erected in places not needed for public use.

Access to national forests is made possible by means of its numerous

[8] *Conservation News*, November 1, 1961, p. 9.

waterways and 145,000 miles of roads and 118,000 miles of trails, including such famous trail systems as the Appalachian Trail from Maine to Georgia, the Cascade Crest in Oregon, and the John Muir and Sierra Trails in California.

There are about 81,000 miles of fishing streams on national forest land, over 2 million acres of fishing lakes, and extensive lands where game animals abound. Hunting and fishing on all national forests are subject to state game laws. The stocking of fish in streams and lakes and the management of wildlife assure a continuation of these forms of recreation. The growing interest in skiing has resulted in the development of about 100 winter sports areas in the national forests. Many of these areas have lifts and tows operated by commercial concessionaires. Some have toboggan slides.

Recreation leadership. The year 1960 witnessed the beginnings of the Visitor Information Service, a program somewhat similar to the interpretive services so well developed in the national parks. Guided walks, tours, demonstration areas, information centers, and campfire programs are included. Other possible recreation developments that have been proposed include a system of camps or huts for wilderness hikers and additional provisions for fishing, hunting, camping, and swimming.[9]

Wilderness. About 8 percent of the national forest land, or 14.5 million acres, are preserved as wilderness. The designation "wilderness" was first applied to national forest land when Gila Wilderness in New Mexico was set aside in 1924. Two years later, parts of the finest canoe country in America, the present Boundary Waters Canoe Area in Minnesota, were protected as wilderness. There are today 83 such areas, classified in four ways: wilderness areas (over 100,000 acres each) wild areas (identical, but smaller, yet with over 5,000 acres each), roadless areas, and primitive areas. These lands are preserved in as primitive a condition as is consistent with their protection. The character of the wilderness is preserved by prohibiting mechanized transportation; and the areas are penetrable only by foot, horseback, or canoe. No commercial timber cutting, hotels, stores, resorts, summer homes, organization camps, or hunting and fishing lodges are allowed. Grazing may be permitted in some cases. Hunting and fishing are allowed. Each year the American Forestry Association, the Wilderness Society, and other groups conduct trips through some of these areas. Thousands of Americans annually spend their vacations in these wildernesses.

Constant pressures are brought to bear for the opening of the wilderness

[9] John Sieker, in a speech at the National Conference on State Parks, reported in *Planning and Civic Comment* (December 1960), p. 29. Reprinted by permission.

by permitting roads, airplanes, motor boats, accommodations for the public or commercial use. Wilderness, however, is too fragile a thing to survive much use. Ours would be a poor nation, indeed, if it could not reserve some small part of primitive America in its natural and unspoiled condition for those who can and will make the effort to visit it. Even those who may never enter the wilderness may take satisfaction in knowing that it still exists and will exist for their children and their children's children.

Areas designated as wilderness exist also on lands under the jurisdiction of other federal agencies, such as the Fish and Wildlife Service and the National Park Service, which has been called "the reservoir of wilderness."

For all the people. From time to time there have been efforts to reduce the holdings of the Forest Service and turn its lands over to private individuals or to the states. In recent years, however, there has come a recognition of the importance to the national interest of public land carefully managed for its timber, water, and wildlife. These vast areas, open to the general public for recreation and inspiration, are the property of all the people for the use of all the people. Without them and the other state and federal lands, outdoor recreation would be denied to great numbers of Americans. In the face of population pressures, it is more important than ever that public reserves be held for public benefit.

Fish and Wildlife Service (Department of the Interior)

Many people consider fishing to be the favorite sport of Americans. Hunting also ranks high in popularity. It is estimated that about one sixth of the population fishes or hunts. These popular outdoor activities depend upon a continuing supply of fish and game. The involvement of the federal government in their preservation originated, however, with regard for their economic value rather than their recreation value.

Establishment of the Fish and Wildlife Service. Although abundant in our pioneer days, both fish and game suffered from the inroads of civilization. Widespread stream pollution and watershed destruction played havoc with the supply of fish, while indiscriminate shooting and the elimination of breeding grounds and habitats diminished the game supply. Some species were reduced to extinction or near-extinction.

It was in recognition of the federal responsibility for protecting and increasing the fish and wildlife supply that the Bureau of Fisheries was established, in 1871, in the Department of Commerce, and the Bureau of Biological Survey was established, in 1885, in the Department of Agriculture. In 1939, these two bureaus were transferred to the Department of the Interior and, in 1940, were consolidated to form the present Fish and Wildlife Service. In 1956, the Service was reorganized and two separate bureaus were set up: the Bureau of Commercial Fisheries and the Bureau of Sport Fisheries and Wildlife.

Several other agencies of the federal government are also concerned with fish and wildlife. In the national parks, all animals except fish are protected. The Soil Conservation Service, the Bureau of Land Management, and the Forest Service all take prominent part in the preservation of fish and game or the improvement of their habitats. International aspects of wildlife administration call upon the services of the Department of State.

Duties. The Service is concerned with birds, especially game birds; mammals, both land and marine; reptiles and amphibians; and commercial and sport fish. It exercises jurisdiction over birds migrating between the United States, Canada, and Mexico. It administers laws designed to increase and protect fish and wildlife resources; provides and maintains wildlife refuges; conducts research studies; furnishes advice and leadership in the control of destructive or injurious animals, birds, and fish; conducts educational work; enforces federal game laws; and cooperates with state fish and game agencies. Though wildlife is controlled in large measure by the individual states, the federal government has certain authority over birds migrating across state and national boundaries.

Fish propagation is another important responsibility of the Service. About 100 national fish hatcheries are maintained. They distribute millions of fingerlings annually through state cooperation to stock and restock fishing waters.

A program to acquire 4.5 million acres of wetlands to aid migratory waterfowl was authorized in 1961 with the passage of the Dingell Bill. As population increases and the competition for land and water becomes more intense, the maintenance of desirable habitats for fish and game becomes increasingly difficult. Very probably, stricter controls of fishing and hunting will become necessary. Forceful efforts are now needed to set aside land and waters for wildlife. The wetlands acquisition program of the federal government and the stepped-up pollution-control program are giant strides toward the protection of our fish and game.

The Fish and Wildlife Service administers about 290 national wildlife refuges and ranges, with an aggregate of over 28 million acres. Although most of the refuges are on lands controlled primarily by the Fish and Wildlife Service, 5 million are on lands controlled by the Bureau of Land Management and some are on lands controlled by other federal agencies. All forms of wildlife are protected in the refuges, but they are particularly significant in the protection of migratory waterfowl and game such as the bison, antelope, mountain sheep, and others that need special protection.

The refuges as recreation areas. In addition to assuring a continuing sport for fishermen and hunters, the refuges themselves are centers for outdoor recreation. Among them are lands that, like many lands of the Forest Service, are wilderness of outstanding quality. Okefenokee, in Georgia, is an example.

Fishing is permitted on most of the refuges. Hunting, camping, boating, picnicking, nature study, swimming, photographing, and sightseeing are allowed in certain areas. The facilities, somewhat limited, are provided by the Service, by local governmental or civic groups, or by commercial concessionaires. The use of these areas for recreation has increased rapidly. About 10 million people visit them annually. About one third are fishermen, and one twentieth are hunters. The great majority enjoy forms of recreation other than fishing and hunting.

Aid to states and local groups. There is liberal federal aid to the states in their fish and game programs through laws administered by the Fish and Wildlife Service. Funds for this program are secured in large part from the Migratory Bird Hunting Stamp Act of 1934, which requires hunters of migratory fowl to buy a stamp that is affixed to their state licenses; from the Pittman-Robertson Act of 1937, which makes available to the states funds from a federal excise tax on sporting arms and ammunition; and from the Dingell-Johnson Act of 1950, which makes available to the states monies raised from the excise tax on the sale of fishing tackle.

The Service cooperates with public and private agencies in the making of recommendations regarding water projects in connection with maintenance of marshes for waterfowl and wildlife food and cover plantings, fences to control grazing and poaching, dams and waterways to provide for fishes that leave the ocean to spawn in fresh waters, and the like.

Bureau of Land Management (Department of the Interior)

The Bureau of Land Management has jurisdiction over the public domain, which is that portion of federal lands not reserved by other agencies. The Bureau was formed in 1946 by combining the General Land Office and the Grazing Service. Its function is to manage land and resources of the public domain so as to obtain maximum use in the public interest with consideration of their conservation and development of productive capacity. Its custody extends to 477 million acres, nearly 300 million of which are in Alaska and most of the remainder of which are in the western states. Much of the land is open range; some, particularly in Alaska, is forested. The lands sustain game populations of considerable size.

Recreation on lands in the public domain. The recreational values of the public domain in Alaska, where about 99 percent of the land is still in the hands of the federal government, were recognized by congress, which appropriated funds to construct public campgrounds along the highways. With 125 million acres of forests in the public domain in Alaska, inherent recreational possibilities are as yet largely unexplored.

Determination of use. The Bureau has authority to classify lands for public recreation, and it attempts to put lands best suited for recreation to that use. It cooperates with state and local governments in arranging for recreation developments on its lands. Under this plan the Bureau does not itself construct facilities but leases or sells sites for the development of museums, restaurants, cabins, and the like, itself retaining and administering the surrounding recreation areas. To encourage public provision of recreation areas, the Bureau now makes land available to states and their political subdivisions at nominal cost. This new policy is expected to help relieve the critical need for public recreation lands.

Small tracts (five acres or less) may be leased or sold to individuals for private recreation purposes such as weekend residences or camping. Use of these lands has skyrocketed in recent years. Under multiple-use management, recreation takes its place along with grazing, wildlife management, forestry, and urban and mineral development.

Bureau of Indian Affairs (Department of the Interior)

The American Indian, subject for many romantic tales, is also an attraction recreationally. Tourist travel to Indian reservations rises largely from interest in the ceremonials, architecture, arts and crafts, and mode of life of the Indian. Visitors are also attracted by the scenic and historic sites and the opportunities for swimming and hiking. Hunters and fishermen use these lands with the permission of the Indian tribes, which sometimes require that special reservation licenses be secured.

The Indian tribes themselves are beginning to realize the value of developing tourist attractions. Most of the ceremonials are held during the summer and early fall, at times when visitors are most numerous. There are very few tourist accommodations on Indian lands, but plans are being made for picnic and campgrounds, hotels, motels, boating facilities, and the like. The new man-made lakes created on many of the reservations as a result of federal programs of river-basin development are expected to attract more people.

The Bureau of Indian Affairs, created in 1824, was primarily intended to give services in health, education, and land management. The lands under its jurisdiction in 1960 aggregated about 58 million acres. The Bureau of Indian Affairs maintains museums at several reservations. These display modern Indian arts and crafts as well as historical materials.

Corps of Engineers (Department of the Army)

The Corps of Engineers, organized in 1775, is authorized to improve and maintain rivers and other waterways in the interest of navigation and flood control. In so doing, it affects recreation by constructing reservoirs, protecting and improving beaches along the shores of the Great Lakes, and providing harbors and waterways used by recreation craft. The areas adjoining the water developments also become desirable recreationally.

Reservoir recreation. The many reservoirs create opportunities for boating, swimming, fishing, picnicking, and camping, although priority is given to flood control, navigation, consumptive water use, and power development. The Flood Control Act of 1944 authorized the establishment and maintenance of public park and recreation facilities in reservoir areas under the control of the Department of the Army and provided that the waters be open, without charge, for such uses as boating, swimming, bathing, and fishing, when such uses were not contrary to the public interest.

The Corps of Engineers collaborates with federal, state, and local authorities and other interested individuals during the initial study of a proposed project in order to explore fully its recreation possibilities. State and local units are particularly encouraged to develop public parks, since it is believed that the benefits are largely state and local ones. Over the past ten decades, states, local governments, and private enterprise have invested over ten times the amount the federal government has spent in developing recreation on Corps of Engineer lands. Preference in recreational use of reservoir areas is given in the following order:

1. Public day-use facilities such as observation points, picnic grounds, access roads, and trails
2. Public boat launching and docking facilities
3. Public campgrounds
4. Organized camps operated by governmental or other nonprofit organizations in the public interest

Private exploitation is not permitted. The Department of the Army licenses state and federal agencies to develop and manage fish and wildlife resources; grants commercial leases for dock and restaurant construction and furnishing of boats; leases lots to private groups and individuals where such uses will not conflict with public recreation needs; and provides needed roads, boat launching sites, parking areas, toilets, wells, picnic sites, and campgrounds. Facilities for handling visitors are provided by the Department of the Army in the vicinity of dams.

Recent increases. Attendance at the reservoir areas has mounted in recent years more rapidly than in any other type of area for which data are available, largely as a result of new additions to the system. About 6 million acres of land and water are now included. The 250 water areas are located in 40 states and vary considerably in size. They have about 23,000 miles of shoreline. In 1960 these reservoir areas attracted nearly 109 million visitors.

Bureau of Reclamation (Department of the Interior)

Although many state and federal agencies are concerned with the development of water sources, the Bureau of Reclamation, established in 1902, has as its special responsibility the water-resource development, primarily for irrigation and power, in the seventeen western states. During its existence it has constructed over 170 dams and reservoirs.

Planning for recreation. Recreation is recognized as one of the purposes of the Bureau. As early as 1936, when the Bureau entered into agreement with the National Park Service to develop recreation facilities and administer the area around Hoover Dam, recreation was one of its considerations. Since 1944, the Bureau has included recreation in its planning. However, only in recent years have funds of appreciable size been allotted for the construction of recreation facilities.

When studying reservoir projects, the Bureau considers recreation possibilities or the destruction of existing values that might result from a reservoir. In so doing, it cooperates with several other federal agencies, particularly the National Park Service, which investigates and appraises the recreation potentialities, prepares plans, and supervises facility construction. The Smithsonian Institution assists in archeological surveys and salvage operations, whereas the Fish and Wildlife Service makes recommendations relating to sport fishing and hunting.

Transferring of authority. It is Bureau of Reclamation policy to transfer reservoir areas wherever possible to other agencies for administration and development. Certain recreation areas of the Bureau of Reclamation at reservoir sites are, if they have national significance, administered by the National Park Service. The Forest Service develops and administers reservoir recreation areas located in national forests. Other recreation areas created by Bureau of Reclamation reservoirs are administered by state and local agencies. The national recreation areas under the jurisdiction of the National Park Service differ in administration from national parks in that emphasis is on active recreation such as swimming, boating, picnicking, camping, hiking, hunting, and fishing rather than on scenic or historic features. Facilities not normally found in national parks may be built.

The recreation use of Bureau of Reclamation lands has zoomed. In 1951, 6.5 million visitor-days were recorded. By 1959 this figure had increased to 22.7 million. To a large extent, this growth has resulted from the tremendous popularity of boating activities.

Tennessee Valley Authority

The Tennessee Valley Authority, created by an act of congress in 1933, affects recreation in connection with its primary purpose of development of the Tennessee River for navigation, flood control, and production of electric power. Its reservoirs have become extremely important as recreation resources in Alabama, Georgia, Kentucky, Mississippi, North Carolina, Tennessee, and Virginia. The lakes lie within a two-day drive of more than half the people of the United States.

At full pool level there are over 600,000 acres of water surface and more than 10,000 miles of shoreline, almost all of which are available for recreation. Recreation use totals about 40 million person-days a year. The TVA does not itself develop or operate any recreation services but encourages private groups or other public agencies to offer them. Its lands are made available for such recreation developments as public parks, group camps, fishing camps, boat docks, vacation resorts, summer residences, and bathing beaches. Lands may be transferred to other federal agencies, leased or deeded to state and local governmental units, or sold or leased to quasi-public groups (such as Boy Scouts) or to private individuals.

Fishing, with its accompaniment of boating, camping, and picnicking, is the outstanding activity on TVA lakes. Speedboat races, sailboat regattas, and other such events are held. Thirteen state parks and 62 county and municipal parks are located on the shorelines. About forty group camps are located on TVA property, and over six thousand summer cottages have been built along the shores. The lakes have revolutionized the economy and the leisure pattern of many of the communities near the reservoirs.

Changing concept of land use

Since the land-holding agencies have a primary responsibility toward the land itself, there is justification for the statement by the Outdoor Recreation Resources Review Commission: ". . . the orientation of Federal activities to date has been more to the resource than to the user. This is in contrast to local governments, which have been concerned with providing recreation opportunities for their residents." [10] That this attitude is undergoing a change, however, is indicated by the several ways, already discussed, in which these agencies are making increased provisions for use within the limits of the capability of the land.

Agencies with Advisory, Consultant, and Research Functions

Although the federal government today makes its greatest contribution to recreation in relation to resource use, it also offers other services to states and communities through several agencies. Most of the land-administering agencies previously described give consultant services and carry on extensive research. There are many other agencies that, although they do not administer lands used in recreation, give services related to recreation. These agencies form the subjects of the pages that follow.

[10] *Progress Report* (Washington, D.C.: Outdoor Recreation Resources Review Commission, January 1961), p. 68.

Extension Service (Department of Agriculture)

An outstanding example of cooperation among the counties, the states, and the federal government lies in the work of the Extension Service of the Department of Agriculture. This program of cooperative extension work between the land-grant agricultural colleges of the individual states and the United States Department of Agriculture began when congress, in 1914, enacted the Smith-Lever Act, which provided for the giving of instruction and practical demonstrations in agriculture and home economics to persons not attending or resident in the colleges.

Organized for the welfare and education of rural people, the Extension Service was inevitably concerned with recreation in carrying out its principal function. Although the federal government supplies about 45 percent of the funds, it is strictly advisory and gives assistance only upon request. The federal office serves through the land-grant colleges in the 50 states and Puerto Rico. Various publications emerge both from the federal and the state offices. Further discussion of the work of the Extension Service is contained in Chapters 6 and 11.

Soil Conservation Service (Department of Agriculture)

The Soil Conservation Service, established in 1935, carries out its activities principally by extending assistance to about 3,000 locally organized and managed soil conservation districts formed under state laws. By urging the conservation of soil and water on privately owned land, the Soil Conservation Service promotes the improvement of recreation resources.

Farmers are encouraged to build farm ponds, used for swimming, boating, and fishing. Waterfowl and game birds may also benefit from the pond areas. The improvement of wildlife areas is another concern of the Soil Conservation Service, and suggestions for plantings to attract wildlife are made. The Soil Conservation Service specialists, upon request, make land-use plans, whereby long-range planning for the use of land in terms of its best capabilities is developed. This service is available to camp operators as well as to farmers and can aid them in rehabilitating land, developing water resources, and restoring wildlife.

Office of Education (Department of Health, Education, and Welfare)

The U. S. Office of Education, established in 1867, promotes the improvement of school systems throughout the United States. It conducts studies, disseminates information, develops standards, and provides consultants in various educational areas.

Background. This was one of the first federal agencies interested in recreation. Even in its earliest report, in 1868, it recognized the significant role of recreation in the education of children. All aspects of the school program, including the teaching of the arts of leisure and the provision by schools of recreation opportunities both to students and to communities, are its concern. Its interests extend not only to recreation as an end in itself but to recreation as a method of teaching. The Office of Education renders its services to members of congress and to other federal agencies. It coordinates its efforts with those of other units within the Department of Health, Education, and Welfare through the Departmental Committee on Recreation. It also works with various national organizations, with state and local school systems, with colleges and universities, and with individuals.

Services. Some specific services include: sponsoring of workshops and conferences on school-community recreation; assembling and disseminating information relative to school-community recreation; giving consultative help on request; working to improve professional preparation for recreation leaders; advising state and local school systems in plans for buildings to include facilities for school-community recreation; and conducting studies and research on recreation problems and practices in relation to schools.

Children's Bureau (Department of Health, Education, and Welfare)

Created in 1912 to "investigate and report upon all matters pertaining to the welfare of children and child life among all classes of our people," the Children's Bureau includes among its responsibilities consideration of the recreation needs of children and youth. Recognizing the importance of recreation to the welfare of young people, it attempts to strengthen state and local recreation services of all types.

The Bureau works through state and national agencies and organizations concerned with youth. The encouragement of communities to provide for recreation for children, either through public or private agencies, is therefore a responsibility of the Bureau. It currently is concerned with juvenile delinquents, children of migratory workers, the physically and mentally handicapped, and children in foster homes and institutions. It is also concerned with recreation for the whole family. Its publications include suggestions for recreation programs, including games, social recreation, arts and crafts, music, drama, and nature activities.

The Children's Bureau carries major responsibility for the White House Conferences on Children and Youth. The 1960 Conference placed a great deal of emphasis on the role of recreation and the constructive use of free time. Extensive recommendations on recreation were incorporated in the conference's action plan for the future.

Public Health Service (Department of Health, Education, and Welfare)

Since sanitary conditions determine in large measure the usability of lands and waters for recreation, the work of the Public Health Service is important to recreation. The agency has frequently assisted in planning sanitary developments in parks, camps, and other recreation areas for federal, state, and local agencies. Its advice is sought in such matters as bathing sanitation, food handling, and disposal of refuse and sewage.

Water Pollution Control Program (Department of Health, Education, and Welfare)

Sewage and industrial pollution of rivers and streams is not only an important health problem but also a recreation problem. It can eliminate swimming, boating, water skiing, and fishing from the waters themselves and make picnicking and camping unpleasant or impossible along shore-lines. One of the recommendations of the National Conference on Water Pollution, called by the U. S. Surgeon General in December 1960, was that "public policy formally recognize the recreation value of our water resources as a full partner with domestic, industrial, and agricultural values in water quality management policies and programs."

The Federal Water Pollution Control Act of 1956 authorized the Public Health Service to engage in a broad program for water pollution control. Because of the severity of the problem, the act was amended and strengthened in 1961, providing increased grants to municipalities for construction for waste treatment and increasing federal enforcement authority over navigable waters. The water pollution control program was taken out of the hands of the Public Health Service and became the direct responsibility of the Secretary of Health, Education, and Welfare.

United States Travel Service (Department of Commerce)

The significance of travel was acknowledged by congress in 1961 with the establishment in the Commerce Department of a U. S. Travel Service authorized to operate branch offices in foreign countries to encourage residents of other countries to travel in the United States. With over $2 billion spent by Americans in foreign travel and only about $1 billion spent by foreigners in the U. S., an important aspect of the establishment of this service was its economic value.

Bureau of the Census (Department of Commerce)

The statistical information compiled by the Bureau of the Census that particularly affects recreation planning includes the size, nature, and distribution of population and projections into the future; land acreage, ownership, and recreation usage; recreation activities and expenditures; and other useful information. The studies are of assistance in understanding the present status of recreation and recreation resources but of even greater value in long-range planning.

Bureau of Public Roads (Department of Commerce)

The Bureau of Public Roads cooperates with state highway departments in developing access to recreation areas and with the National Park Service and Forest Service in constructing roads on lands under their control. Roads serve recreation purposes not only as means of travel to recreation areas but as sources of satisfaction themselves. In planning roads, the Bureau of Public Roads takes advantage of scenic features if possible and tries to eliminate construction scars, protect areas against erosion by plantings, and conserve landscape features. Roadside parks, parking areas, and turnouts for points of interest are included. In order to encourage retention of the natural beauty of the roadsides, the Bureau establishes standards for the control of billboard advertising along federally financed highways. States accepting these standards qualify for a bonus of one half of one percent of the federal share of the cost of the affected projects.

Housing and Home Finance Agency

As administrator of the war housing program, the Public Housing Administration of the Housing and Home Finance Agency during World War II stressed the providing of recreation activities in these projects. After the war, it concerned itself with low-rent housing and recreation facilities and services to meet the needs of residents of the developments. The recreation facilities constructed by the Public Housing Administration are frequently leased to public or voluntary agencies for program operation.

Under the Housing Act of 1961, the Urban Renewal Administration of the Housing and Home Finance Agency was authorized by congress to administer a $50 million appropriation to help states and communities acquire open spaces in urban communities. The proposed use of land financed in this manner must fit into a comprehensive plan to preserve open space. This appropriation is one step toward meeting the crying need for recreation areas in crowded population centers.

Federal Communications Commission

There are about 50 million homes in the United States that have one radio or more and almost as many that have television sets. Since these media act as major forms of entertainment for several hours a day in many homes, it is obvious that the Federal Communications Commission, which authorizes stations of all types, is closely concerned with recreation. Although the Federal Communications Commission does not censor radio and television programs, it makes periodic checkups to see that stations fulfill community needs and desires and meet their commitments in providing programs of a public-service nature.

Bureau of Outdoor Recreation (Department of the Interior)

Established in 1962, the Bureau of Outdoor Recreation resulted from the recommendations of the Outdoor Recreation Resources Review Commission, created by an act of congress in 1958. The report of this commission, of which Laurance S. Rockefeller was chairman, was presented in January 1962 and contained the most complete information and analysis available regarding outdoor recreation interests, needs, and resources.

The Outdoor Recreation Resources Review Commission's recommendations fell into five general categories:

A *national outdoor recreation policy:* The Commission recommended that the national policy should be "to preserve, develop, and make accessible to all American people such quantity and quality of outdoor recreation as will be necessary and desirable for individual enjoyment and to assure the physical, cultural, and spiritual benefits of outdoor recreation." It was further emphasized that the cooperative participation of all levels of government as well as private enterprise would be required.

Guidelines for management: The classification of outdoor recreation resources was urged so that planning for their use would be logical and effective. The proposed classification is given in Chapter 17.

Expansion, modification, and intensification of present programs: Among the recommendations were long-range planning; interstate cooperation; research; immediate acquisition of water, beach, and shoreline areas; provision for public access to shorelines in reservoir developments; open-space programs for metropolitan areas; congressional enactment of legislation to provide for the preservation of wilderness areas; protection of the natural character of certain rivers; zoning for recreation; defending recreation areas against encroachments; intensification of interpretive and educational programs; emphasis on outdoor recreation in federal multipurpose water developments and pollution control; flood-plain zoning; recognition of recreation values in highway construction and agricultural conservation programs; encouragement of public use of private lands for recreation; and increased financial aid to outdoor recreation through such channels as bonds, fees, gifts, and tax policies.

A *Bureau of Outdoor Recreation:* The Commission recommended the establishment of a Bureau of Outdoor Recreation in the Department of the Interior to have over-all responsibility for leadership of a nationwide effort by coordinating the various federal programs and assisting other levels of government to meet the demands for outdoor recreation. The Bureau would not manage any land.

A *grants-in-aid program:* The Commission recommended the establishment of a federal grants-in-aid program to stimulate and assist the states in meeting the demand for outdoor recreation. The grants-in-aid program would be supplemented by a program of loans to the states.[11]

Action upon these recommendations was prompt. On April 2, 1962, a new Bureau of Outdoor Recreation in the Department of the Interior, headed by Dr. Edward C. Crafts, was created. On April 27, the President established the Recreation Advisory Council, consisting of the Secretaries of the Interior; of Agriculture; of Defense; of Health, Education, and Welfare; and the Administrator of the Housing and Home Finance Agency. The new Bureau was to carry out planning functions already assigned to the Department of the Interior and administer a program of federal assistance to state agencies. Other duties included sponsoring and conducting research and surveys relative to recreation, developing a nation-wide recreation plan, and disseminating outdoor recreation information.

Functions formerly performed by the National Park Service but not related to the administration of the National Park Service areas were transferred to the Bureau of Outdoor Recreation.

Agencies Serving Special Purposes or Special Groups

There are several agencies of the federal government that serve special groups or special purposes. Among them are important and extensive services to military personnel and to veterans. Among them also are programs for the national capital itself and for employees of the federal government. There are also special committees set up to perform specific tasks not provided for otherwise in the government.

The armed forces

Recreation has become accepted as a valuable contribution to the well-being of men and women in the military forces. As stated by the Department of Defense:

It is the policy of the Department of Defense to promote and provide a well-rounded morale, welfare and recreational program to insure the physical and mental well-being of its personnel. Adequate free-time facilities should be provided, operated and maintained through financial support tendered by the Federal Government.[12]

Wartime programs. Although it is generally accepted today that the federal government has a responsibility to provide recreation for armed forces personnel and their families, recognition of this responsibility is

[11] *Outdoor Recreation for America* (Washington, D.C.: Outdoor Recreation Resources Review Commission, January 1962), pp. 6–10.

[12] *Department of Defense Directive* 1330.2 (Washington, D.C.: Department of Defense, January 1953), paragraph 2.

relatively recent. In World War I, the burden of providing recreation rested on the shoulders of voluntary agencies, including the Young Men's Christian Association, the Salvation Army, the Knights of Columbus, the Jewish Welfare Board, the American Library Association, the American Red Cross, and the War Camp Community Service.

It was not until World War II that the government itself accepted responsibility. All recreation on military bases was handled by the military. The war-time programs were organized hurriedly, and civilian recreation directors were commissioned to direct the military programs. The Navy and the Marines organized extensive programs of sports; and entertainment was stressed in all branches of the military. Off-base recreation for the armed forces was the concern of several agencies in World War II. Those providing recreation were:

UNITED SERVICE ORGANIZATIONS. Six national agencies—the Young Men's Christian Association, the Young Women's Christian Association, the Salvation Army, the National Travelers Aid Association, the National Catholic Community Service, and the Jewish Welfare Board—combined to foster and further religious, welfare, educational, and recreational needs of the men and women in the armed forces, calling the combined effort "The United Service Organizations." The USO served millions of men and women through its clubs, mobile units, and centers in the United States. The USO Camp Shows brought the cream of theatrical talent to entertain the troops overseas.

AMERICAN RED CROSS. The American Red Cross provided recreation in various places throughout the world on request of the armed forces and, in addition, conducted extensive hospital recreation programs.

PUBLIC RECREATION AGENCIES. In communities near military bases, extensive recreation programs were organized for the armed forces. Federal agencies were established to assist communities in the United States that were beset with problems accompanying an influx of military personnel and workers in war industries. The Division of Recreation, which was set up in the Office of Community War Services in the Federal Security Agency, gave advice to communities on organization, program, finance, and leadership. As a result of its work during the war, between 250 and 300 permanent community recreation programs were established and state recreation services were strengthened. Through the auspices of the Federal Works Agency, the federal government took the responsibility for providing recreation centers in communities affected by military posts or war industrial activity. Most of these buildings were later turned over to the communities for their use. The Federal Works Agency also administered the Lanham Act funds for recreation facilities and programs.

NATIONAL RECREATION ASSOCIATION. As a voluntary, nongovernmental agency contributing to the war recreation effort through its field work, conferences, and publications, the NRA promoted the organization of community programs in "defense recreation" for both soldiers and civilian war workers.

Today's program. With demobilization, the recreation programs were as a matter of course reduced, although they were kept in effect in the armies of occupation. Recreation was placed on firmer ground in the armed forces with the report of the President's Committee on Religion and Welfare in the Armed Forces in 1951, in which the contribution of recreation in shaping character, in increasing efficiency, and in promoting understanding and support of the armed forces was recognized.

It was found that peacetime needs differed from those of wartime. During the periods of warfare, those on active duty naturally sought relaxation during their free time. Recreation was brought to the soldiers of World War II by means of movies, big-name stars of the entertainment world, and other nondemanding forms of amusement. When the war ended, the men and women in uniform, freed from many of the physical and emotional tensions of war, discovered more value in active and creative participation. Today's program stresses both activity and creativity.

SPORTS. Today in the armed forces active and competitive sports are among the most popular forms of recreation, and the program stresses maximum participation through organized competition at the lowest organizational levels. Activities include conditioning exercises, mass games, football, baseball, softball, soccer, bowling, horseshoes, tennis, table tennis, billiards, handball, volleyball, badminton, archery, golf, boxing, weight-lifting, wrestling, track and field sports, swimming and water safety, cross-country sports, skiing, hockey, ice skating, croquet, shuffleboard, and judo. Organized intrabase and interbase competitions are held, and armed forces teams participate in world-wide competitions with teams from other services and from colleges, universities, and communities.

SERVICE CLUBS. A Service Club is "a facility on a military installation designed for use during off-duty time by enlisted personnel, their families, and friends." [13] Facilities commonly include a ballroom-lounge, music room, television room, and snack bar. Many service clubs have craft shops and outdoor recreation facilities. Emphasis of the program is on active participation by individuals and groups. The Service Club offers a self-directed program and a directed program under the supervision of professional recreation supervisors.

The self-directed program is made available through the provision of facilities and equipment for individual and group use, such as meeting rooms for hobby and special-interest groups, billiards and table tennis equipment, musical instruments, popular and classical record libraries, small games, reading and writing materials. Self-directed activities may extend to tennis, badminton,

[13] *Recreation in the Armed Forces* (Washington, D.C.: Armed Forces Section, American Recreation Society, n.d.), Brochure, p. 1.

archery, and other outdoor activities if facilities are provided in connection with the Service Club. The directed recreation program provides for participation in those activities which are organized and conducted by the Recreational Leader and staff. The standard directed program includes, but is not limited to, instruction in small crafts, dramatics, music and dancing classes, as well as scheduled activities, such as discussion groups, holiday observances, special parties, picnics, all-base events, tournaments, contests, exhibits, dances, and tours.[14]

ARTS AND CRAFTS. Craft shops, intended for the use of military personnel and their families, provide opportunities in ceramics, graphic arts, metal work, lapidary, wood work, leather work, plastics, model building, painting, photography, and other activities. The activities are organized into classes and clubs and are sparked with contests, exhibits, and demonstrations.

ENTERTAINMENT. Active participation is encouraged in drama and music through local production of dramatics and musicals. Contests are sponsored, and winners are sometimes organized into touring troupes. Vocal and instrumental groups are encouraged. Motion picture entertainment is offered at minimum fees at military installations.

LIBRARIES. Libraries are considered an integral part of the recreation program. The Library Service offers, in addition to recreational reading material, literature of a technical, reference, or general educational nature. The service includes discussion groups, audio-visual aids, and recordings.

LEADERSHIP. Professional leadership is offered in arts and crafts, dramatics, music, radio and television, social activities, sports, and general recreation.

More and more emphasis is being laid upon the employment of trained professional leadership to direct recreation activities in the armed forces. With most of today's young men and many young women spending at least part of their lives in the military service, the importance of recreation programs of sound value cannot be overestimated. The armed forces provide recreation in the following branches:

Army—Special Services Division, Adjutant General's Office, Department of the Army.

Air Force—Special Services Branch, Personnel Services Division, Directorate of Military Personnel, Deputy Chief of the Staff Personnel, Department of the Air Force.

Navy—Special Services Division, Office of Assistant Chief of Naval Personnel, Department of the Navy.

Marines—Special Services Branch, Personnel Department, United States Marine Corps.

Civilian assistance today. The USO and the American Red Cross continue to serve the armed forces. The National Recreation Association

[14] *Recreation in the Armed Forces*, p. 1.

has assisted communities near military bases in providing wholesome recreation for military personnel and their families. That the communities should bear this responsibility is recognized. However, when the base is large and the community is small, community resources are unduly burdened; and assistance from other sources, governmental or voluntary, becomes necessary. In such communities the USO, Red Cross, and special services of the military branches of government are particularly needed.

Veterans Administration

The Veterans Administration was created in 1930 to combine the functions of the Veterans Bureau, Pension Bureau, and National Home for Disabled Volunteer Soldiers. It administers laws relating to the benefits provided for former members of the military and naval forces. Its program has three aspects: medical care, insurance, and financial assistance for veterans. The Veterans Administration operates 172 hospitals with over 140,000 patients treated daily. The hospitals are of the following types: neuropsychiatric, general medical, surgical, tuberculosis, and domiciliary centers.

It is in connection with hospital operation that recreation becomes an important aspect of Veterans Administration responsibility. Under professional leadership, the recreation program is considered part of the medical treatment. It includes sports, dramatic entertainment, social recreation, motion pictures, and music. Although entertainment in the form of movies and stage productions is offered, stress is laid upon participation to the extent to which the patient is capable. Sports, social recreation, arts and crafts, and music offer opportunities for active involvement. Professional leaders act as recreation directors, assistant directors, and program specialists.

The objectives of the recreation programs are several: to facilitate patients' adjustment to hospital life, give doctors opportunities to observe patients' behavior, help patients adjust to their limitations, maintain the physical condition of patients while they are in the hospital, and develop interests in activities with carry-over value after patients are discharged from the hospitals.

Programs in the national capital

National capital parks. The parks and memorials of the District of Columbia and its vicinity are administered by the National Park Service. An estimated 45 million persons used the park facilities in 1960, with over 2.5 million attending special events and over 5 million visiting the national memorials.

District of Columbia Recreation Department. The recreation department of the District of Columbia is similar to such departments in other large cities except that it receives its funds from congress. Playgrounds and centers are maintained as part of a year-round recreation program.

Smithsonian Institution. The Smithsonian Institution is one of the world's largest historical, cultural, and scientific centers; its several branches include the National Museum, the National Gallery of Art, the National Collection of Fine Arts, the Freer Gallery of Art, the International Exchange Service, the Bureau of American Ethnology, the National Zoological Park, the Astrophysical Observatory, the National Air Museum, and Canal Zone Biological Area. A National Cultural Center was organized in 1958 as a bureau in the Smithsonian Institute. The board of trustees has the responsibility to construct in Washington D.C. a center for presenting music, opera, drama, dance, poetry, lectures, and related cultural activities from this and other countries, and for developing programs for all ages, for participation, education, and recreation. This recognition by the federal government of the cultural forms of recreation should do much to stimulate interest and create support for such programs throughout the country.

National Capital Planning Commission (Department of the Interior). This commission was created to plan and acquire parks, parkways, and playgrounds, to preserve the forest and natural scenery in and about the national capital, and to prepare a coordinated city and regional plan for the District of Columbia and its environs.

Recreation for federal employees

In addition to the recreation programs provided for military personnel and their families throughout the world, there are programs for employees in many of the civilian departments of government. These are comparable to programs that industries provide for their employees.

Special committees

Numerous special committees are set up from time to time to make particular studies or perform duties not carried on by established agencies of government.

The President's Council on Youth Fitness. Established in 1956, this council promoted activities to improve the physical, emotional, mental, social, and spiritual fitness of youth through community agencies of all kinds. The council was made up of the Secretaries of Interior; Defense; Agriculture; Commerce; Labor; and Health, Education, and Welfare; and the Administrator of the Housing and Home Finance Agency. The President's Citizens Advisory Committee on the Fitness of American Youth brought representatives of youth-serving groups of all types into the program. The change of administration in 1960 brought the program into the Department of Health, Education, and Welfare.

Interdepartmental Committee on Children and Youth. This committee assists federal agencies that have programs affecting children and youth. The Secretary of Health, Education, and Welfare, as chairman, has delegated his responsibility on this committee to the Children's Bureau. Others on the committee represent the Departments of Agriculture, Defense, Interior, Justice, and Labor. Also represented are the United States Courts, Housing and Home Finance Agency, Selective Service System, the United States Information Agency, and the Veterans Administration.

Federal Council on Aging. Established in 1956 in the Department of Health, Education, and Welfare, the Federal Council on Aging is intended to coordinate the activities of the federal government concerned with the aging and to make recommendations to the President and to appropriate governmental units. The Secretary of Health, Education, and Welfare is the chairman. Other permanent members are the Secretaries of Agriculture, Commerce, Labor, and the Treasury; and Administrators of the Housing and Home Finance Agency and the Veterans Administration. A special staff is maintained.

Coordination of Federal Activity in Recreation

As the program in recreation grew in the federal government, it brought with it problems of coordinating the work of the various federal agencies and minimizing overlapping and rivalry among them. A certain amount of informal cooperation took place, and inter-agency agreements were reached. Certain legislation permitted cooperation. For example, the Park, Parkway and Recreation Area Study Act of 1936 authorized the National Park Service, among other things, to cooperate with other federal agencies in the conduct of park and recreation studies.

Federal Inter-Agency Committee on Recreation

To help coordinate the recreation activities of federal agencies, the Federal Inter-Agency Committee on Recreation was organized in 1946. This committee was an unofficial bringing together of representatives from various agencies to discuss common problems and exchange points of view. The National Recreation Association led the way in setting up the Committee by financing the salary of its director. Present members of the committee are the Department of Agriculture (Forest Service, Federal Extension Service); the Department of the Army (Corps of Engineers); the Department of Health, Education, and Welfare (Office of Education, Public Health Service); the Department of the Interior (Bureau of Indian Affairs, Bureau of Land Management, Bureau of Reclamation, Fish and Wildlife Service, National Park Service); and the Housing and Home Finance Agency (Public Housing Administration).

In the words of a statement of the Federal Inter-Agency Committee:

The Committee serves as a clearing house for the exchange of information on policies, plans, methods, experiences, and procedures among the agencies; considers all current agency problems and projects presented to it and recommends basic principles which might well be followed in these and similar projects and problems; and endeavors to facilitate provision of information about the recreation activities of Federal agencies.

The Committee seeks to clarify the proper responsibilities of the Federal Government in the recreation field, to discover and insofar as possible to fill existing gaps in Federal recreation programs and services, with special attention and consideration of the needs of small communities in rural areas, minority groups, young people, and older adults.

The member agencies of the Committee cooperate in stimulating and assisting State agencies in the development of needed recreation facilities and services, in accordance with cooperative plans developed by the Committee so far as resources make this possible.[15]

The committee provides information to individuals and organizations, facilitates exchanges of information between the member agencies, cooperates with many organizations in the exchange of information, prepares reports, and publishes pamphlets.

Attempts to establish a federal recreation agency

During the depression years of the 1930's the federal government took part in the development of recreation facilities and programs on a community level. Many communities got their first taste of public recreation through Works Progress Administration projects. State recreation committees were established, and state services were encouraged. These federal services were discontinued as economic conditions improved, but those who witnessed the good that federal aid had accomplished began to visualize the day when a permanent federal recreation agency might be established to devote itself exclusively to the promotion of recreation on a state and community level.

In January 1937, the Technical Committee on Recreation of the State Departmental Committee to Coordinate Health and Welfare Activities recommended that the federal government coordinate its recreation services through the establishment of a permanent bureau of recreation. Its efforts never materialized.

During World War II, the federal government again stepped into community recreation. The Division of Recreation in the Office of Community War Services (Federal Security Agency) helped communities affected by wartime conditions to set up recreation programs. Many

[15] *The Role of the Federal Government in the Field of Public Recreation* (Washington, D.C.: Federal Inter-Agency Committee on Recreation, July 1961), unnumbered page of duplicated draft.

recreation centers used by the United Service Organizations were built with federal funds under the direction of the Federal Works Agency. These wartime agencies were dissolved after the war ended. Once more the value of a federal recreation agency was demonstrated.

After the close of the war, several bills were introduced over a period of years proposing the establishment of a permanent federal recreation agency. The first such bill was introduced in 1946. The American Recreation Society assumed the major responsibility for developing support for such legislation but did not succeed in having any of its proposed bills reported out of committee.

Many groups are continuing to press for the establishment of a federal recreation agency or for the enlargement of the Bureau of Outdoor Recreation to include all aspects of recreation. The Federation of National Professional Organizations for Recreation and its member organizations are giving study to the role and responsibilities of the federal government in the whole field of recreation in the hope that a clearer understanding of the responsibilities of all types of recreation agencies and organizations may be attained and a cooperative approach toward a solution of problems be made. Although complete agreement is an impossible dream, there should be a somewhat unified support if any new federal recreation service is to be rendered.

Unsolved Problems

Although the federal government has made bold steps in the interests of recreation, several unsolved problems remain. Many of them stem from the basic dilemma: how to provide recreation on limited land and water resources to meet the expanding demands of a growing public.

How, for example, can the use of natural lands increase without destroying the natural lands themselves? How can the uses of water for recreation increase while wastes from sewage and industry continue to pollute the streams, lakes, and bays? As government grows ever more complex, how can we avoid the rivalries among bureaus, which lead to overlapping, competition, and inefficiencies? Do we need still another bureau to devote itself exclusively to advisory services to states and local communities? If so, can its duties be so defined that it will not further complicate the already complicated functions of the federal government in recreation? In our fast-changing society, these problems will not wait. They must be faced and solved in order that the best interests of the people may be served.

SUGGESTED REFERENCES

Brightbill, Charles K. and Harold D. Meyer, *Recreation: Text and Readings.* Englewood Cliffs, N.J.: Prentice-Hall, Inc., 1953, pp. 154–167.

Brockman, C. Frank, *Recreational Use of Wild Lands.* New York: McGraw-Hill Book Company, 1959.

Clawson, Marion, *Statistics on Outdoor Recreation.* Washington, D.C.: Resources for the Future, Inc., 1958.

Meyer, Harold D. and Charles K. Brightbill, *Community Recreation, A Guide to Its Organization.* Englewood Cliffs, N.J.: Prentice-Hall, Inc., 1956.

National Park Service, *A Study of the Park and Recreation Problems of the United States.* Washington, D.C.: Department of the Interior, 1941.

Outdoor Recreation Resources Review Commission, *Outdoor Recreation for America.* Washington, D.C.: Government Printing Office, 1962.

Tilden, Freeman, *The National Parks.* New York: Alfred A. Knopf, Inc., 1954.

"We certainly can't create conditions of peace through recreation alone, but we can contribute considerably to establishing the value of human life and the decision of every person as to whether it is worth saving."

MARGARET MEAD

13

World Relationships Through Recreation

All nations and all races, whether progressive or retarded, rich or poor, have as part of their culture a wide variety of recreation pursuits. The underdeveloped countries of the world are today in a state of foment as their peoples strive for a share in the "good life" that their industrialized neighbors enjoy. They seek better food and shelter, medical care, easier working conditions, and some of the luxuries of living. Along with a more equal share of the world's material wealth they seek better educational opportunities so that their children may improve their position in life. They desire better opportunities for the use of the leisure that, if they lack now, they hope will be theirs in the future.

The search for some of the benefits of industrial civilizations does not always include a desire to emulate our American forms of leisure use. Each nation has its unique cultural background, and American imports do not necessarily improve upon the cultures of underdeveloped countries. Each country has contributions to make; with better transportation and communication removing the walls of distance, interchange of ideas on all cultural fronts is possible and necessary. In the words of Adlai E. Stevenson:

A hundred years ago, even fifty, perhaps even fifteen, to speak of world brotherhood was, I suspect, to adorn with rhetoric what was at most a remote idea. Today, brotherhood has become an insistent, demanding reality, thrust upon us whether we accept it or not by a science that has broken down the fences which had before separated the peoples of the world.[1]

Contributions from Other Lands

Many American forms of recreation originated in Western Europe. The first colonists brought with them their Old World songs, games, folk dances, drama, sports, hobbies, and the concept of public parks. The continued migration of people from Europe kept alive many of the folkways of the old country, even though the children forgot the language of their fathers.

Folk songs, folk dances, and folk games from England, Czechoslovakia, Sweden, Germany, and France still live in many parts of America, although in many cases regional modifications seem to have made them distinctly American. Music speaks to all peoples; and the opera and classical music of Europe are loved by American audiences as well as European. The influence of European schools of art has dominated much of our art. We see counterparts of the French formal gardens and parks in our own early city park developments. Denmark and Germany for many years supplied our parks with their landscape architects.

We are indebted to Europe for many games. Football had predecessors in ancient Greece and Rome and, in more recent times, England. Even baseball, as American as the Fourth of July, traces its ancestry to similar English games of the early nineteenth century. Many of our children's games have been played for thousands of years in Europe. Europe, in turn, owes a debt to other people. Some of its recreation activities had beginnings in Egypt, Asia Minor, India, and China. Origins of many forms of play are lost in antiquity. Even those of recent origin are often difficult to trace.

Our Contributions to the Rest of the World

Though most of the recreation interests of the United States originated in other parts of the world, a considerable number are native born. Some have found acceptance in widely scattered parts of the world.

Music and stories

Negro spirituals are generally regarded as one of America's contributions to music. They originated in the South among the slaves. Also of American origin is jazz, which began in the late nineteenth century among Negro musicians of New Orleans and reached full development in the 1920's and 1930's. Songs of the western cowboys are another distinctively American form of music.

[1] Adlai E. Stevenson, in *Recreation*, LIV, No. 2 (February 1961), 92.

The lore of the American Indian and the westward movement have inspired stories that have found their way around the world, particularly through the medium of the motion picture. Indian games and ceremonials have been accepted in many countries.

National parks

The national park, as far as is known, is a concept that originated in the United States. Governments throughout the world have followed our example in setting aside natural scenic, scientific, and historic areas for preservation or for public use. Much of the development resulted from the visits of foreign dignitaries to the national parks of the United States. Though a few parks in other parts of the world were reserved before the turn of the century, most of their developments have taken place since the 1920's.

First to follow in the footsteps of the United States was Canada, which in 1885 set aside a small portion of what is now Banff National Park. Canada today has national and provincial parks throughout the country, administered somewhat in the pattern of United States parks.

African countries have preserved some of the most magnificent national parks in the world, including world-famous Kruger National Park in the Union of South Africa and Victoria Falls in Rhodesia. The Sabie Game Reserve, forerunner of Kruger National Park, was established in 1898. Tanganyika, Uganda, Algeria, the Congo, and other African countries today maintain national parks. The movement to reserve natural areas has been slow in Asia except in Japan, where, in 1931, a national parks law was adopted. Today Japan's park system is highly developed. Its parks provide for boating, camping, hiking, fishing, and skiing. Burma, Indonesia, Lebanon, Malaya, and other Asian countries have made small starts.

National parks in Europe began when Sweden passed laws relative to their establishment in 1909. Belgium, Finland, Great Britain, Greece, Iceland, Italy, Poland, the Soviet Union, Spain, Switzerland, and Yugoslavia have since established parks—although, in land as heavily inhabited over the centuries as Europe, national parks are not the natural areas we find in the United States. France has no national parks but does have botanical and faunal reserves. Australia and New Zealand have set aside extensive areas. Mexico and the South American countries of Argentina, Brazil, Chili, Peru, and Venezuela have national parks.

The first international conference on national parks, held in Seattle, Washington, in 1962, under the sponsorship of the International Union for Conservation of Nature and Natural Resources, emphasized the theme that national parks are of international significance. The national park movement may well prove to be one of the greatest contributions America has made to recreation for the peoples of the world. In a growing world population, the preservation of natural lands is of prime importance.

Organized camping

The organized camp with planned programs and educational objectives originated in the United States. The romance of the American Indian and the drama of the westward movement with the frontiersman, settler, cowboy, and lumberman may account in part for the camp development in the United States and have probably helped its spread to other lands. Today the organized camp is found in many parts of the world. The camps in general have followed the American pattern, although in many countries they have incorporated their own outdoor living traditions. Camps are conducted by youth-serving agencies, religious organizations, and tax-supported schools. The private camp as we know it in the United States is rather rare in most parts of the world, although there are a number in Western Europe. Russia has seized upon the camping program as a method of carrying on a most effective youth indoctrination program.

Community playgrounds

Playgrounds of various types have been in existence for a long time, but the publicly financed, supervised playground, with a planned program, probably originated in the United States. Such playgrounds are not to be found in many parts of the world. In general the playgrounds of other countries have not attained the extent of leadership that is found in the United States, although there is a trend to obtain more and better-trained leaders. There are many playgrounds and playfields in England. Two national organizations, the National Playing Fields Association and the Central Council of Physical Recreation, have given attention to their development. In Amsterdam and Stockholm, the city-wide recreation programs are reminiscent of those of American cities, with playgrounds and playfields as basic children's facilities. France, Germany, and Italy also have many playground programs.

Each country develops its program along somewhat different lines, and each can learn from the others. The United States has many things to learn from developments in other countries. Some of the European play equipment is extremely creative. The so-called "junk" playgrounds, particularly in Denmark, appeal to the imaginative and creative urges of children. European playgrounds as a rule give special attention to muscle-building apparatus for young children, with an emphasis on a wide variety of climbing devices.

Sports and games

The American game of basketball, invented in 1891 by Dr. James A. Naismith at Springfield, Massachusetts, has spread throughout the world. The growth of popularity of American baseball has stimulated its development in other countries. Lacrosse, the national game of Canada, was inherited from the North American Indians.

The Exchange of Recreation Interests

The modern world's ease and speed of transportation and communication have made possible the dissemination of culture to a degree not previously possible. Events taking place around the world are reported almost immediately, and television makes possible their visual portrayal. Rapid air and surface transportation has revolutionized travel. Languages reflect internationalization; even the language of recreation is affected, as is evident in the international use of words such as *camping, baseball,* and *park.* In coming years, there should be better international understandings and, in recreation, better exchange of information and sharing with other nations.

Travel

Modern transportation and high income, particularly for the people of North America and Europe, have resulted in an international travel boom. Travel by Americans to Canada, Mexico, Europe, the Mediterranean, the West Indies, and Central America is especially popular, but Americans are also traveling in increased numbers to other parts of the world. Europeans have always traveled extensively in nearby countries. The number of Europeans visiting the United States is growing, though it is small compared to the number of Americans visiting Europe. Efforts are being made in the United States to induce greater numbers of tourists to visit this country.

Travel offers opportunities to observe and study the culture of other countries and to enjoy their recreation. If tourists study and plan before they travel, their trips can be more valuable. Making contacts in foreign countries with people of like interests, either vocationally or avocationally, enriches the pleasure of the trip and increases mutual understanding. In Denmark, the tourist organization assists Americans in making contact with people of like interests and developing acquaintance with them.

Mass communication media

The American movie has blanketed the world. Many times foreign people's impressions concerning American life result from motion pictures. Too often the true picture is distorted, and it is difficult to correct some of the misconceptions that develop. Whether the influence of American motion pictures is good or bad may be questioned, but they do provide entertainment to people the world over and tend to spread American tastes, songs, and ideas. The more recent popularity of films from other countries has helped to make the motion picture a many-channeled medium of exchange of cultural ideas. Radio, newspapers, magazines, and books cross national boundaries and help to break down national barriers. They also create worldwide audiences for sporting events, music, and drama.

International games and contests

Among the most enthusiastically received of international events are the Olympic Games, in which athletes from all over the world live and compete in a setting designed to improve international understanding and respect. The games date back to ancient Greece. According to tradition, games were held every four years in Olympia, beginning in 776 B.C. They reached their height in the fifth and fourth centuries B.C., when an Olympic victory was one of the greatest honors attainable. Later, professionalization subjected them to much criticism, and they were abolished in the fourth century A.D.

The modern games were begun in Athens in 1896, with but few countries represented. Except when interrupted by war, the games have been held in various parts of the world every four years since that date. The number of participating nations has grown, and along with it the number of contests and contestants. Track and field athletics have been supplemented by swimming, rowing, yachting, fencing, boxing, wrestling, winter sports, and numerous other events. The Pan-American Games, like the Olympic Games, stimulate international relationships.

There are a large number of other ways in which athletes meet across international boundaries. Touring teams move from country to country; and special tournaments, competitions, and demonstrations bring athletes of the various countries into contact with one another.

Recreation in Other Lands

The emphasis of this book is placed on recreation in the United States. It would not be feasible, therefore, to give detailed descriptions of developments in other lands. A few generalizations might give some indication of the character of recreation offerings throughout the world.

The Americas

The recreation developments of Canada are more nearly like those of the United States than are those of other parts of the world. Canadian parks—local, provincial, and national—resemble those of the United States. The youth-serving agencies, community centers, school recreation activities, camps, and playgrounds are comparable to those of the United States.

The Latin American countries carry on a variety of recreation services, largely under private auspices, although in some cases governments have developed programs. In recent years there has been a considerable development of sports areas and playgrounds. At least four Latin American countries—Argentina, Brazil, Ecuador, and Peru—have in recent years established national recreation associations similar to the National Recreation Association of the United States.

Asia

In June 1959, an Asian Recreation Congress was held in Yokohama, Japan, under the auspices of the National Recreation Association of Japan. Representatives from various Asian countries participated. This event is illustrative of the growing recreation interests in Asian countries. Japan itself has a strong national recreation association and an ever increasing interest. There are recreation and adult-education centers in Hong Kong and a new youth sports center in Singapore, along with recreation programs in parks and on school grounds.

In India there is a concerted effort to improve the well-being of the people, to raise the living standard, and to improve health conditions. This effort has been accompanied by an increase in community centers, sports opportunities, and outdoor play areas.

Western Europe

There are similarities and differences between the recreation developments of Western Europe and those of the United States. Europeans are extremely sports-minded, both as participants and as spectators. Provisions for spectator sports are abundant. Soccer and other events draw large crowds. Interscholastic competition as we know it in the United States is quite limited. A large number of private sports clubs exist, particularly in the northern European countries.

Municipal parks have been in existence in Europe for many years. Many of them trace their origins to gardens and hunting grounds owned by royalty. City planning, particularly in German cities, has been practiced for a long time. Cities such as Cologne, Germany, have developed comprehensive systems of small and large parks, well distributed throughout the cities. Continental parks tend to be formal, whereas the parks of England more generally retain the natural landscape. In recent years, recreation facilities such as play courts, swimming pools, and stadiums have been developed.

Playgrounds and playfields, though not as abundant as in the United States, are found in many European cities. Community centers of various types are sparsely distributed. Following World War II, a number of centers were developed in German cities through the efforts of Americans. Most of the centers of Europe function under private auspices.

Interest in music, the theatre, and arts is widespread. A large number of private associations provide opportunities for participation. Government subsidies for the opera, ballet, and symphony are common. In many European cities, theaters, opera houses, and museums are publicly owned and operated.

Outdoor recreation has many devotees. Hiking, mountain climbing, canoe-ing, and camping have a strong appeal, particularly in northern Europe. Walking trips are frequent. Youth hostels, much more numerous than in the United States, make possible low-cost travel for European youth. Mil-lions of Europeans camp as families or small groups. There are camping sites not only in natural areas but in the shadows of the large cities. For example, family campsites are available in the Bois de Boulogne, only a short distance from downtown Paris.

Gardening is an important pursuit for many Europeans, particularly the working classes, not only for its economic value but also for its leisure satis-factions. In the allotment garden system, large tracts of land, consisting sometimes of hundreds of acres of city-owned property, are divided into small plots, which are rented at low cost to city-dwelling families who do not have land of their own. Families plant and care for their gardens them-selves and often erect small huts where they may spend week-ends and vacations.

In many European countries, extensive recreation programs are carried on by industry or employee organizations. Outstanding is the Italian Ente Nazionale Assistenza Lavoratori (National Foundation for Assistance to Workers). There are more than 2.5 million members of the organization. Local clubs, usually with their own clubrooms and recreation facilities, are organized within a particular industry or business, such as a steel plant or

Fig. 19   *A Unique Youth Hostel—Stockholm, Sweden*

an insurance company. In Rome alone there are over 400 such clubs. Their activities include music, dramatics, arts, hobbies, camping, sports, and social events. Recreation is not the only function of these organizations, as they are active in health, education, and welfare programs; but the recreation activities are among the most important.

Many of the same voluntary youth-membership organizations that we find in the United States are to be found in Europe. Boy Scouts, Girl

Fig. 20   *A Modern Youth Center—Stuttgart, Germany*

Guides, YMCAs, and YWCAs are found in most countries, although the percentage of youth in membership is not nearly so high as in the United States. Religious and political youth organizations are common, and they carry on a variety of recreation activities. There is little joint solicitation of funds through any type of United Fund for these organizations. The precedent of supporting youth services through voluntary giving is not established in Europe. Public funds are often made available to youth organizations. Income from soccer betting pools is collected by the governments in some instances and distributed to youth organizations, sports groups, and youth hostels.

Few European universities provide specific education for professional leadership in youth and leisure areas. There are generally special schools for music, art, and physical education. The many leadership training centers provide short courses in the various skills and in leadership techniques. These are generally resident centers to which leaders come for periods of one to four weeks. Music, folk dancing, camping, and sports of all kinds are among the areas of training. Some of these centers are operated by private associations and some are publicly supported.

Russia

Russia has developed extensive recreation services. Parks and centers of rest and culture exist throughout the country, and there is today a boom in the building of parks for mass sports. Vacation centers for families have been established by the government, and vacations away from home are becoming possible for great numbers of Russian citizens.

Youth programs of Russia are highly organized. Children belong to the Pioneers, an organization offering numerous recreation activities but intended primarily as a means of political indoctrination. When the children reach their teens, they join the Komsomol, or party cell.

Channels for International Recreation

Almost from the beginning of the recreation movement, there was an exchange of information from country to country. In 1932, the first International Recreation Congress was held in Los Angeles. There were delegates representing 29 countries who participated in the Congress and shared experiences. The result was a heightened interest in the recreation of other lands. In 1937, *Europe at Play*, by Lebert H. Weir, was published. This book gave Americans their first comprehensive picture of the recreation developments of the countries of Europe.

Events leading to World War II and the war itself brought an end to many of these early efforts. Following the war, the vast numbers of service men who had crossed the seas brought back to the United States renewed interest in the recreation of other lands. The second International Recreation Congress was held in Philadelphia in 1956.

Since the war, there have developed several channels for the exchange of information and the promotion of recreation services. The purpose of these programs extends beyond mere exchange and promotion to the development of better international understanding through recreation. There are many who feel that international contacts through recreation are among the best means of developing friendships and appreciation of different cultures.

International voluntary organizations

The major youth-serving organizations are affiliated internationally. Outstanding examples are International Boy Scouts, World Association of Girl Guides and Girl Scouts, World Alliance of YMCAs, and World YWCA.

Young people from such organizations attend international conferences, camps, training courses, and workshops. There are exchanges of information and discussions that lead to better understandings and strengthen the respective organizations. The International Farm Youth Exchange enables farm youth to become acquainted with those of other lands.

The American Red Cross is affiliated with the International Red Cross, and the settlement houses of the United States are related to the International Federation of Settlements. Some of the service clubs and civic organizations have international affiliations. Rotary International, for example, has clubs in 116 countries. Leisure activities are promoted internationally by numerous specialized organizations. There are international organizations for all major sports—archery, basketball, boxing, bowling, canoeing, golf, tennis, skating, skiing, and yacht racing, to name only a few. Cultural organizations exist to promote drama, music, dancing, and art on an international level. Stamp and coin collectors, bridge enthusiasts, and chess players have international affiliations.

International Recreation Association. As a result of the meetings of the Second International Recreation Congress and the planning that had gone into them, the International Recreation Association was established on October 3, 1956. Lord Luke of Pavenham, delegate from England, was elected Chairman of the Board, and Thomas E. Rivers of the United States was appointed Director General. The officers and board of directors come from 34 countries. The central office is in New York City adjacent to the United Nations building.

In the first years of its existence, the IRA was given financial assistance by the National Recreation Association. Contributions and memberships are its source of funds today. The IRA provides a means of bringing to the United States many leaders from foreign countries to study American programs. It has sent representatives, mostly on a volunteer basis, into many countries of the world to give service, to study, and to observe. Its office is a clearing house of information on international aspects of recreation. It has promoted the establishment of strong national recreation agencies, which now exist in 28 countries. It has carried on an exchange-of-persons program.

Objectives of the association are to:

Serve as a central clearing house for the exchange of information and experience among recreation agencies of the world.

Aid countries to establish central recreation service agencies upon request.

Forward the development of a world recreation movement designed to enrich the human spirit through wholesome use of leisure.

Encourage the provision of land and facilities, training of leaders, development of varied programs, and public interpretation of the values of play for children, recreation for youth, and creative use of leisure for all ages.

Provide a medium through which the recreation authorities of the world may work in unity on one of the common problems of man.[2]

The International Cooperative Community Exchange Project is administered through the International Recreation Association under the sponsorship of the United States State Department. It brings to the United States young men and women who spend four months in visitation to communities and in study of problems of recreation. Begun in 1956, this program has given leaders from other countries a glimpse of American life and an opportunity to see programs in action. It has stimulated recreation developments in other countries.

International Recreation Service, National Recreation Association. The National Recreation Association maintains an International Recreation Service as one of its important functions. A staff member of the Association is assigned to this service, and a committee of outstanding recreation leaders of the United States serves as a national advisory committee. Some of its services include:

providing information to other countries on the community recreation services of the United States;
conducting meetings and workshops related to international recreation;
assisting exchange students and visiting leaders from other countries in securing the maximum benefit from visits to the United States;
working closely with the People-to-People Sports Committee in scheduling sports activities on an international basis; and
cooperating with the International Recreation Association, particularly in regard to helping exchange visitors.

International Youth Hostel Federation. Youth hostel associations in 33 countries, including the United States, belong to the International Youth Hostel Federation. The "hostel way" has become for many young people the most effective method of seeing a country and getting acquainted with its people. A youth hostel provides low-cost dormitory and cooking accommodations, primarily for members who do not use mechanized means of travel but walk, cycle, or canoe from place to place. The hostels are centers not only for overnight stays but for making friends, singing songs, exchanging experiences, and learning about the customs, history, and scenic attractions of a country.

The youth hostel movement originated in Germany in 1910, when Richard Schirrmann, a German school teacher, began taking his students on walking trips. The problem of finding shelter led to the establishment of simple lodgings. Schirrmann spent the rest of his life in the expansion of

[2] Thomas E. Rivers, "The Launching of the International Recreation Association," *Recreation* (January 1957). Reprint.

the hostel idea. The early hostels were used primarily by school children. They are still popular among school children, but older youth and young adults on vacation make up a large part of the membership.

Youth hosteling is a significant force for the development of international understanding, as youth from many countries mingle and exchange points of view. Hosteling has made possible foreign and domestic travel for thousands of young people who could not otherwise afford the experience. Through the coming years, its role should expand, both in its international aspects and in its domestic provisions for wholesome travel and outdoor enjoyment.

People-to-People program

In 1956, President Eisenhower invited some 50 leaders from diverse fields of American life and work to determine how international understanding might best be developed through person-to-person communication. Out of this meeting emerged the People-to-People program. Since its inception, the program has endeavored to stimulate contacts between individuals and organizations from various countries of the world. Thirty-six committees have been organized. The following two committees illustrate the functions performed:

The Youth Activities Committee is concerned with the interchange of information among youth groups and the encouragement of foreign travel among youth.

The Sports Committee is concerned with the exchange of information and the provision of opportunities for sports groups from other countries to meet in regular sporting events.

Other committees involve music, reading, education, industry, and other interests.

Intergovernmental cooperation

United Nations. It may well be that in coming years the United Nations will assume a larger role in the encouragement of recreation. Through their efforts to raise living standards throughout the world, many agencies of the United Nations inevitably touch upon leisure needs.

The United Nations Educational, Scientific, and Cultural Organization (UNESCO) has held a number of international meetings concerned with youth services and recreation. Its program fosters mutual appreciation of cultural values through international visits and exchange of ideas, literature, and art. The International Labor Organization (ILO), another specialized agency of the United Nations, has evinced interest in recreation and has held meetings with sessions devoted to recreation problems, particularly those related to working people. The United Nations Declaration of the Rights of the Child includes the statement, "The child shall have full opportunity for play and recreation"; and the Declaration of Human Rights affirms the need for opportunity for culture and for satisfying use of leisure time.[3]

The Organization of American States. Through its Fellowship Program, the Organization of American States contributes to the economic, social, scientific, and cultural development of member states. The OAS supported the First Inter-American Music Festival in Washington. The Pan American Union gives encouragement to art through its exhibitions.

Play speaks a universal language. All human beings respond to the opportunities for recreation, however much they differ in language and customs. The possibilities of international recreation exchange as a means of developing better understandings among the peoples of the world are barely beginning to be realized. Contacts and exchanges in recreation should, through coming years, contribute much toward a better world.

[3] "UN We Believe," *International Recreation Association Bulletin,* III, No. 4 (October 1960), 7.

SUGGESTED REFERENCES

Annual Report. International Recreation Service, National Recreation Association, 8 West Eighth Street, New York 11, N.Y.

IRA Bulletin. International Recreation Association, 345 East Forty-sixth Street, New York 17, N.Y.

4

THE RECREATION PROFESSION

"The final test of a leader is that he leaves behind him
in other men the conviction and the will to carry on."
WALTER LIPPMANN

14

Recreation Leadership

In recreation, as in many other fields of professional endeavor, one dominant factor emerges. Conditioned by, but more essential than, finance, areas, facilities, or program opportunities is the importance of one human being's impact upon another. The power of leadership is one of the great mysteries of human nature; without it, the best facility lies idle; without it, program offerings stagnate. Even in our accelerated age, human leadership is a most essential tool in work or in leisure. It is *the* factor on which all others depend. In a century in which each day brings some new device to absorb the work hours of some individual, there will always be room for inspired, creative leadership in the recreation profession.

The Need for Leadership

Joseph Prendergast, in his foreword to *Personnel Standards in Community Recreation Leadership*, states, "There is no substitute for qualified leadership, and any compromise in this matter is false economy." [1] A community that tries to refute such thinking in practice is doomed to disappointment and disaster. Charles Vettiner, himself an example of inspired leadership, expressed the importance of leadership in the following terms:

[1] *Personnel Standards in Community Recreation Leadership* (New York: National Recreation Association, 1957), foreword.

The best way to kill a program of recreation before it has a chance to live is to assign to playgrounds and recreation centers supervisors who are poorly trained or have no training at all.[2]

Charles Brightbill emphasized the need for quality leadership with his comment:

Because leisure will impose challenges heretofore unknown to free men, because its impact upon the democratic social fabric can be either a generating influence or a devastating force, and because recreative living requires human perceptions different from the traditional, the finest kind of leadership is needed.[3]

At both the White House Conference on Children and Youth (1960) and the White House Conference on the Aged (1961), both lay and professional leaders from every walk of life throughout the nation concurred in statements relative to the importance of professional leadership in meeting recreation needs for all ages.

A host of examples can be cited of communities, large and small, who, from frugality or ignorance, sought to erect beautiful facilities without adequate provision for leadership. The outcomes have been essentially the same, a meager use of the facility and a disappointing response to the recreation program. The addition of a dynamic, professional leader has increased the use of an area as much as 500 percent.

In its study *The Effect of Increased Leadership and Its Relation to Interest and Participation*, the Skokie (Illinois) Park District describes an experiment in which it increased the number of leaders on one of its playgrounds from two and one half to ten leaders. Conclusions from the study include the following:

1. From a standpoint of attendance, interest, and participation, the increased leadership program was extremely successful. This is established in attendance and participation records, parent attitudes, as well as the staff reports.
2. The two outstanding differences between 1959 and 1960 proved to be: (1) the high relationship between the number of registrants and the average weekly attendance and (2) the increased interest and participation on the part of those who attended in activities under leadership. This tends to substantiate that where sufficient leadership is available, children will be attracted by programs and activities under direction rather than merely attending to take advantage of physical facilities where no leadership is required.[4]

[2] Charles J. Vettiner, *A New Horizon of Recreation* (Louisville, Ky.: A New Horizon of Recreation, 1956), p. 116. Reprinted by permission.

[3] Charles K. Brightbill, *Man and Leisure, A Philosophy of Recreation* (Englewood Cliffs, N.J.: Prentice-Hall, Inc., 1961), p. 281. Reprinted by permission.

[4] *The Effect of Increased Leadership and Its Relation to Interest and Participation* (Skokie, Ill.: Skokie Park District, 1961), p. 4. Reprinted by permission.

Changing concepts of leadership

The twentieth century has seen a changing attitude toward the need for and importance of leadership in recreation situations for all ages. For many years, the literature was filled with protests over the trend toward direct leadership of child or adult recreation. Heard from many corners were such protestations as: "Why teach a child to play? No one ever taught me." "No one ever taught me to swim; I just fell into the old swimmin' hole and paddled." "Adults can take care of their own fun." The old attitude still prevails in statements similar to those of Robert Smith:

When I was a kid, the way we got to play baseball was this: school was out, we ran home and hooked a handful of cookies, hollered "I'm home, goin' out on the block" and met a friend who had an old first bascman's mitt and a ball, went down the block a little and hollered at the kid who had the bat.... We went to the vacant lot and played a game resembling major league baseball only in that it was played with a bat and bases. It was fun.[5]

The game probably was fun for those who could find a vacant playing area, who were aggressive enough to insist on being a part of the team effort, or who played by right of ownership of equipment.

But what about the ones left out? Do children want leadership? The old idea that leadership or direction will thwart freedom of play is fortunately giving way to the newer concept that a certain amount of direction and control is necessary and inevitable and that it is imperative that we get the right kind of control. The old sandlot ballgame was controlled and directed by those who emerged with status either by virtue of their physical stature, their mental ingenuity, or their ownership of the necessary equipment. The impulse to play is natural for children or adults. The form of play is not innate; the opportunity for recreation in a crowded America does not materialize magically when needed. Our American capacity to idle away the new hours of Utopian leisure is mute evidence of the fact that all ages, from the nursery-school cherub to retired senior citizen, need inspired leadership for best consumption of their leisure hours.

The one product that flows from our assembly lines faster than any other is leisure time. How we use this time may well be the supreme test of our civilization. Freedom of choice in wholesome recreation pursuits in leisure hours demands leadership to provide creative opportunities and to give guidance to forming the emotional mechanism with which to make satisfying choices. Boredom is a twentieth-century disease; to leave a bored people to themselves is to invite disaster for civilization.

The old, untrained play leader who passed out the equipment and stayed to see that the facility was not harmed or to break up the ensuing battles

[5] Robert Smith, "Let Your Kids Alone," *Life*, XLIV (January 1958), 103–104. Reprinted by permission.

is gradually being replaced by the personable recreation leader, trained in the mechanics of interrelationships of people as well as in the broad field of recreation pursuits. The new leader does not thwart those who are ready to engage in recreation without direction, but he creates an environment that may give them wider opportunities in self-directed activities. On the other hand, he is prepared to direct those activities and persons who need and desire guidance.

Inevitability of recreation leadership

That we will have leaders and leadership whenever people gather in recreation activities is inevitable. Leadership exists as the heart of success or failure in all areas in which human relationships are involved. No machine can replace man as inspiration.

Every group is composed of leaders and followers. Our problem, then, is not a question of leadership or the lack of it; it is, rather, a determination of the kind of leadership. The recreation leader is to the playground, the Scout troop, the community center, or the hospital what the parent is to the home, the teacher to the school, or the clergyman to the church. L. H. Weir, first field representative of the National Recreation Association, states: "It is plain common sense to order the use of leisure just as it is needful to order work and to order the general relationships of people to each other in modern society." [6] To accomplish such ordering as Weir describes demands trained, qualified leaders so that enrichment, not deterioration, may evolve.

The Nature of Leadership

What is a leader? Who qualifies in the name of leadership? Early concepts of leadership fall into two major patterns. The first and earliest idea of a leader conceived him as emerging at birth with the correct combination of genes that would make for skilled and inspired leadership. Leaders in earlier civilizations gained status merely by having been born into the ruling class of their era; their wisdom in matters of work or recreation was uncontested because of class distinctions. It was extremely difficult or impossible for those not so fortunately born to acquire the skills and knowledges needed for the leadership of the day.

Later concepts of the recreation leader described him as an affable person with good intentions, an example to be imitated by those who gathered around him. Careful scrutiny of the nature of leadership has since evolved a totally different connotation. The modern idea sees leadership not in a passive role but in dynamic, constantly changing growth, a working relationship for which dedicated persons can train. Today's leaders are made

[6] Lebert H. Weir, *Europe at Play* (New York: A. S. Barnes & Company, 1937), p. 1.

through a process of carefully educating those who have a real desire to take leadership roles. Leaders of twentieth-century America are no longer born; they are made.

Leadership in a democracy

A democratic society gives many opportunities for leadership in work and in recreation. In other nations and in other times, when a man was born into a leadership position he remained in that position, regardless of the situation. In a democratic way of life, situations often make the leaders for recreation activities, as they do for other involvements. On the ballfield, one person may assume the direction of the group. When the play-reading club meets, perhaps a different person assumes the role of leadership, though the two groups may be composed of the same adults or youngsters. Within the broad scope of recreation choices, a multitude of opportunities can arise for the emergence of leadership roles. The recreation leader will make the most of these opportunities to develop new leaders.

Definitions of leadership

Perusal of the literature of recreation and of other professions will uncover many and varied definitions of leadership. A brief review of the definitions seems pertinent at this point, for the description of a leader remains essentially the same whether he be a leader of recreation or any other phase of humanitarian endeavor.

Overstreet: "A leader is one person who counts as more than one." [7]
Tead: "Leadership is the activity of influencing people to cooperate toward some goal which they come to find desirable." [8]
Douglass: "A leader is the catalyst who provides opportunity for everybody to be at his best. The creative leader is the kind of human being who dreams, pioneers, invents, acts, and leads." [9]
Wolf: "Leadership is the Art, or Science, or Gift by which a man is enabled and privileged to direct the thoughts, plans, and actions of his fellow men by honorable and legitimate means, for noble and altruistic ends." [10]
Wilson and Ryland: "Leadership is a natural phenomenon in group life, a dynamic process which emerges in the interaction of individuals one with another." [11]

[7] Harry A. Overstreet and Bonaro W. Overstreet, *Leaders for Adult Education* (New York: American Association for Adult Education, 1941), p. 1.
[8] Ordway Tead, *The Art of Leadership* (New York: McGraw-Hill Book Company, 1935), p. 20. Reprinted by permission.
[9] Paul Douglass, unpublished speech, at National Recreation Congress, Long Beach, California (October 1957). Reprinted by permission.
[10] Frederick E. Wolf, *Leadership in the New Age* (Rutland, Vt.: Tuttle Publishing Co., 1937), introduction.
[11] Gertrude Wilson and Gladys Ryland, *Social Group Work Practice* (Boston: Houghton Mifflin Company, 1949), p. vii.

Funk and Wagnalls' dictionary: "A leader is one who guides and conducts."
Stone: "A leader is a person with a magnet in his heart and a compass in his
    head." [12]

Definitions of leaders vary from descriptions of those who are able to guide
and direct to those who pursue the process of development "through time,
experience, and tribulation." Inherent in all definitions is the importance
of the influence of one individual upon another.

Stone's definition of the kind of person who makes a good leader connotes many qualifications for leadership desirable in the recreation professional. Within the magnet and the compass can be found most of the
components for inspired guidance. The magnet has drawing power; if the
leader does not possess enough personal magnetism to attract others to
him, there will be no one to lead in recreation. The magnet also holds; the
leader must be skilled enough to wear well with people, to offer varied
opportunities, to perpetuate enthusiasm. It is no accident that the magnet
is located in the leader's heart, rather than in another part of his anatomy.
The issues of inspired leadership are always of the heart. Unfortunately,
at some time, we have all found those persons who could attract people as
a garbage truck attracts flies, but the magnetism was of no avail, since the
attractor had no sense of direction. The compass in the head conveys significantly the idea that the leader has enough skill, knowledge, and common
sense to delineate possible and desirable objectives toward which to guide
his group.

Qualities of leadership

Any definition of leadership inevitably breaks down into a survey of qualities found to be essential or desirable in the individuals who are to assume
leadership roles. Studies [13] have been made to identify those character traits
found consistently in recreation leaders. Many lists of personality traits of
leaders have been compiled. *With the full knowledge that combinations of
character traits do not necessarily determine leadership, except in a particular environment or in a special set of circumstances, and with the realization that leadership is not so much a matter of characteristics as it is of
working relationships, let us examine some personality traits that seem to
have loomed large in the making of successful recreation leaders.* Needless

[12] Walter L. Stone and Charles G. Stone, *Recreation Leadership* (New York:
William-Frederick Press, 1952), p. 19.
[13] (a) John K. Hempkill, *Situational Factors in Leadership* (Columbus,
Ohio: Ohio State University, 1949), p. 9; (b) W. W. Charters and Vaughn
W. Fry, *The Ohio Study of Recreation Leadership Training* (Columbus, Ohio:
Bureau of Educational Research, Ohio State University, 1942); (c) Ralph
Stogsdill, "Personal Factors Associated with Leadership," *Journal of Psychology*,
XXV (1948).

to say, the person who possesses these characteristics to a high degree would be the ideal. Possession of the traits to a moderate degree might be considered mandatory for the leader.

1. *Love of people.* Basic to leadership or any involvement dealing with human nature is a sincere interest in people, an acceptance of them as they are, and an acknowledgment, in practice and feeling, of the dignity and worth of each individual.

2. *Enthusiasm.* The recreation leader needs enthusiasm that at times must approach a missionary zeal. Ralph Waldo Emerson once said, "Every great and commanding movement in the annals of the world was the product of enthusiasm. Nothing great was ever accomplished without it." Enthusiasm is essential, but we hasten to add that the enthusiasm must be sincere, and it must be competent. The leader does not put on a false show. He genuinely believes what he sells, be it ceramics or the lure of the nursery rhyme. Sincerity is the basis upon which trust and confidence are built. Without it, there is no great leadership.

Competent enthusiasm implies a knowledge of things to do and the ability to define feasible goals. Sometimes the most important single thing a leader can do with a group is to guide them toward suitable objectives. Enthusiasm also implies vitality, a dynamic energy, which, in turn, suggests good physical and mental health. Lack of enthusiasm for his job, sometimes expressed by an individual, may be merely the outward manifestation of too little sleep, too much worry, or a malfunctioning liver. Enthusiasm stems from a peaceful inner zest, though the outward show of enthusiasm does not necessarily have to bubble and fume. With some groups, a quiet approach will be much more potent than a frenzy of zeal. The leader knows when to enthuse dramatically and forcefully and when to let quiet sincerity stimulate interest for productive action.

3. *Awareness.* A two-way hookup must exist between the leader and the group. Such a communication system implies that the leader is sensitive to the reactions of the group, can tell when interest is waning, can sense when to tighten and when to ease the reins. Awareness implies that he is an engineer in human relations. He knows what's in each boxcar, how much weight he must pull up the hills, and how often he must apply the brakes to prevent some overactive individual from running away with the group.

4. *Intellectual capacity.* A leader needs, in addition to awareness of the reactions of others, a mind that can grasp knowledges, skills, and understandings. This single quality is the only one that experimental research tells us cannot be learned. Idiots rarely become leaders of people, even of other idiots.

5. *Initiative, imagination, and vision.* Vital to the essence of leadership is the courage to start something new; fear stifles initiative. Vital, also, are

the imagination to conceive untried and intriguing activities that whet the recreation appetite and the vision to anticipate consequences. Osborne [14] puts tremendous emphasis on the leader's need for creative imagination as he discusses the coined word "Imagineering," which means that you "let your imagination soar and then engineer it down to earth." This kind of intelligent, creative vision is mandatory in a field in which people participate in activity, not through compulsion, but through attractive persuasion.

6. *Humility, self-confidence, self-significance.* To link these three traits may seem paradoxical, yet all are found in good leadership. All are needed and must be in balance. The true leader knows himself for the things he can do, for the importance that is his, and for the influence he possesses; yet he fully realizes that no man is infallible, and no man is indispensable to any organization. The great leader is humble. Donald Laird, noted authority in human relations, writes of Abraham Lincoln that it would have been impossible for Lincoln to have had a valet; the servant would have been, instead, Lincoln's companion. Such is the humility of a truly great leader.

7. *Sense of humor, sense of the dramatic, sense of timing.* The ability to laugh even when the joke is on you is essential, if one works with people. Seeing the funny side will often ease a tense moment and will make unity in a situation in which controversy is running high. Man is the only animal that can laugh; it is one of his happiest attributes, a privilege of nature to be used frequently.

Comparable in importance to this sense of humor is the sense of the dramatic. A good leader capitalizes upon emotional reactions. Look back on your life span. Where are the memorable moments? They came in the dramatic situations: the times when you caught your breath at the fiery sunset, at the "almost made" stolen base, at the first emergence of your print in the photography lab. Being sensitive to those teachable moments and capitalizing on them make inspired leadership.

The third sense, timing, can make success or failure in a leader. When to command, when to cajole, when to be silent, when to be direct, when to initiate a new idea, when to give credit—all are important. Time is a natural resource available to all. The leader learns to work with time. The leader makes a friend of time.

8. *Persistence, flexibility.* Again, the leader seems to embody a paradox. Enough persistency is necessary to prevent easy discouragement, but flexibility that allows one to know when to bend so that he will not break is just as important. Strangely enough, the ability to learn depends in part upon the ability to relinquish what has already been learned. Titus re-

[14] Alex F. Osborne, *Applied Imagination* (New York: Charles Scribner's Sons, 1953).

marks that "leadership cannot afford the luxury of being obsessed with an idea." [15] However well trained the leader is for today, tomorrow may bring new situations. The wise leader adopts and adapts, rearranges, modifies, or substitutes. Dr. Herbert True, of the Chicago Institute for Creative Leadership, points up such need for flexibility with the comment, "If you are thinking the same things today that you were yesterday, you are not progressing, you're just practicing."

9. *Fairness, consistency.* You can be extremely firm, if you are fair. The leader must be an objective, impartial observer. He must isolate and analyze his prejudices, which prevent him from being fair to his followers. Disciplinary measures and restrictions for young or old are much more readily accepted, if the leader is consistent. Children and adults need to know what to expect. Impartiality is essential. "A favorite has no friends." The playgrounds in Fort Wayne, Indiana, find most effective their brief slogan, "Be firm; be fair; be fun."

10. *Patience, optimism.* People are human. Patience with their frailties is mandatory for good human relations. A leader cannot expect the same quality of contribution from his followers that he himself can give. If such were the case, there would be no followers. An optimistic outlook helps in difficult times. Optimism does not convey a Pollyanna, unrealistic approach. The good leader knows the facts, plans within that knowledge, and hopes for good things to evolve. He expects the best, but if the results in followers or programs are less than the best, he is patient and tries again; or, better still, he tries a different method.

11. *Judgment, dependability, and responsibility.* Rarely does a person rise to heights of leadership without the ability to see the whole situation and to judge concerning its merits. Followers are attracted to those who will take major responsibilities and will make decisions, those on whom they can depend for vision and courage. Implied in the term "judgment" is the plain, old-fashioned kind of common sense. The leader must be extravert enough to know when he must take the spotlight and sensible enough to know when best results will come from a quiet, rear-guard instigation.

12. *Integrity.* Last, but by no means least, on the list of essential character traits in a leader is integrity, upon which all other traits are based. The leader who does not have basic personal honesty will be a menace to his generation, for he provides an example to his followers. If the pattern is faulty, the possibility of perfected products is remote. Integrity is doubly important for the recreation leader, since his followers come to him willingly and thus can be presumed to be in a more receptive attitude to learn by the leader's example.

[15] Charles H. Titus, *The Process of Leadership* (Dubuque, Iowa: William C. Brown Co., 1950), p. 57.

Abilities, knowledges, and skills needed

What kinds of things must a successful recreation leader know? There is no magic in leadership, no sleight-of-hand tricks. Leadership in recreation is based firmly on specific, trainable skills, concepts, and abilities that must be used in concrete situations. A leader must know himself, know his group, know what to do, and know when to stop.

1. *Knowledge of self and others.* Knowing ourselves implies that we know our abilities, our strengths, and our weaknesses, and that we allow for them. Knowing others involves an understanding of human behavior, an ability to read and interpret men. People may be misread as frequently as is the printed page. The recreation leader understands the importance of human relationships and the total community process.

2. *Knowledge of the organization and its purposes.* Basic to leadership are a sound philosophy of recreation and a cognizance of the aims of the profession and the organization to which loyalty is owed. An abiding faith in those aims is essential, if others are to be convinced that the goals are feasible and desirable. A recreation leader must know his reason for being, the "why" of his program, as well as the "how."

3. *Ability to plan and organize.* The leader learns to visualize, then organize toward objectives. Logical, organized planning is essential to effect a good recreation program. The leader learns to discriminate intelligently, to encourage the group toward attainable goals. His next step, the one most difficult for many leaders, is to assign tasks to move toward those objectives and then to allow the followers time and environment for accomplishing the desired ends. The final step in the process is to follow up the action of others to the successful conclusion of the effort. This step is all too frequently ignored.

4. *Ability to encourage initiative.* The intelligent, far-sighted leader trains other leaders. The real test for leadership is found in the ability to inspire action. Leadership, it is said, rises to its greatest height when it "sets men on fire." All fires are the same size at the start, but the energies and enthusiasms of people can be whipped into irrevocable action by a wise, inspirational leader.

5. *Ability to work democratically.* Building group morale, enlisting cooperation, sharing the task, learning to give credit where credit is due, all blend in the fostering of democratic working relationships within a group. There are no easy formulas for group morale, but the leader who creates an environment in which people may share plans, decisions, problems, success, and achievements with a sincere respect for the contribution of each

person is well on his way to cementing relationships that make a "group" of an assortment of individual personalities.

6. *Ability to observe and be sensitive.* The leader trains himself to be a keen observer, to be sensitive to the reactions of people. He knows how to stretch the members of his group; he is well aware that persons stretched to extended capacities never return to their original dimension. He is sensitive to the touchy spots; he handles situations so that the child or the adult does not lose face in his difficulty or grow unduly boastful in his successes.

7. *Ability to make decisions.* Leadership, at times, demands action. The leader accepts the responsibility for making decisions. When quick decisions must be made on the playground or at camp, he does not hesitate; he has the courage to take action. When the situation affords time for more leisurely decision-making, the wise leader takes time to weigh all aspects before plunging into motion. The executive may be involved with more numerous and consequential decisions, but the face-to-face program leader must learn that decisive choices are also necessary in his job.

8. *Ability to communicate.* The ability to communicate, so necessary to leadership, insures that the spirit as well as the intent of ideas is shared with the group. It has been said, "Man is an island; there is always a place to land, if we choose to row long enough." A pleasant approach and an infectious personality ease the road to communication, but certain knowledges and skills are needed also.

Voice tone is a conditioning factor in communication. Ninety percent of the friction in everyday life has been attributed to voice tone. Train your voice to inspire. A thin, complaining tone denotes tension or, perhaps, ill health; it seldom motivates action. A low, pleasing voice with clear enunciation commands more respect and is more apt to light the fires of enthusiasm. Monotones seldom arouse individuals; variety in inflection facilitates transfer of feelings and ideas. The leader uses simple, forceful language; he uses graphic illustrations in words or pictures whenever possible. Language is alive; proper use of it for communication purposes is mandatory.

9. *Ability to act, not react.* The leader does not allow other people to sway his action against his better judgment. A strong person does not allow himself to rebuff because he has been rebuffed. He does not wait for the other person to act, so that he can retaliate in kind. His action is positive, definite, and independent.

Research on characteristics associated with leadership

For many years, researchers in various disciplines have tried to decipher the mystery of exactly what composite of characteristics seems to have proved the most effective in successful leadership. Stogsdill,[16] in studying personal factors associated with leadership, concluded that the average man who occupies a position of leadership exceeds in intelligence, scholarship, dependability in exercising responsibility, activity and social participation, and socio-economic status. He also observed that the leader exceeds the average in sociability, initiative, persistence, self-confidence, alertness, co-operativeness, popularity, adaptability, and verbal facility.

Hempkill,[17] investigating situational factors in leadership, found that the leader must be a member of his group, have prestige, have knowledge of the existing field structure or nature of the situation, and have a vision of the long-time trends of his organization.

In recreation situations, the leader is many things to many people. The nature and scope of recreation leadership have such breadth that categorization becomes difficult. In his study of leadership, Tead states:

> For convenience, the qualities considered will be grouped under ten designations; the ten which together seem desirable are: physical and nervous energy, a sense of purpose and direction, enthusiasm, friendliness, and affection, integrity, technical mastery, decisiveness, intelligence, teaching skill, and faith.[18]

Freeman and Taylor conceive the "uncommon man" as "one who has excessive social adaptiveness, energy and drive, and better than average intellectual aptitudes, social proficiencies, emotional control, conscience, and integrity." [19]

In short, the leader is a person who can theorize, analyze, organize, improvise, deputize, synthesize, harmonize, supervise, summarize, and, if necessary, compromise. He has vision to create ideas, intelligence to investigate possibilities, logic to assemble a plan, ingenuity to make substitutions in his plan, common sense to delegate responsibility, personality to integrate group action, human understanding to observe what his group is accomplishing, executive ability to tie in loose ends, and the wisdom to be flexible, if the tension of the situation makes his plan undesirable.

Is there such a person in the recreation profession? Lindeman struck an optimistic note after careful observation:

> A modern professional worker, according to my criteria, becomes a skilled practitioner, a scientist, a philosopher, a sociologist, a cultural anthropologist, and a social psychologist. Have I set an impossible standard? Can these diverse qualities be anticipated in any single individual? My answer to that first question is an emphatic "no!" The standard is not too high. And I take courage in re-

---

[16] Ralph Stogsdill, "Personal Factors Associated with Leadership," *Journal of Psychology*, XXV (1948).

[17] Hempkill, *Situational Factors in Leadership*, p. 9.

[18] Tead, *The Art of Leadership*, p. 83.

[19] G. L. Freeman and E. K. Taylor, *How to Pick Leaders* (New York: Funk & Wagnalls Co., 1950), p. 7.

sponding with an emphatic "yes" to my second question, because I have seen this combination of qualities in some of our best recreation leaders. Standards cannot be set too high for a profession which has a task of such profound importance.[20]

Aims, Functions, and Values of Leadership

Whither recreation leadership? In a profession in which thousands of individuals are employed as leaders in various phases of programing, an inspection of over-all objectives is important. Objectives define the field of desire and delineate direction of effort. The general aim in all recreation activity is simple, direct, and so basically honest that many professionals feel compelled to expound, academize, or embellish the just goal.

Fig. 21 *Leadership in Crafts*

Aims of recreation leadership

For what is the executive, the craft supervisor, the play leader striving: one simple, but tremendously important goal—human happiness. It is as straightforward and simple as that. To try to justify, elaborate on, or explain such an end is useless; the recreation profession is the only profession that has man's enjoyment as its basic goal. The method for obtaining that happiness will take different routes, but if the goal has been attained for each person in the group, many other secondary objectives will have been

[20] Edward C. Lindeman, "Qualities of a Professional Recreation Worker," *Recreation*, XLIV, No. 10 (March 1951), 89.

reached also. If *all* have enjoyed themselves, some will have learned responsibility, human compassion, judgment, outlets for expression, and many other facets of skill or character growth. The recreation professional need make no excuse for his general purpose; the goal of enriched life in leisure is its own justification.

Functions of leadership

Why have leaders? What are the functions of leadership? Many lists of categories of leadership functions have been devised. Whether we are talking about executive leadership, playground supervision, or youth-serving agency personnel, it is important to remember that the functions of leadership are exercised always with relationship to people, rather than to materials or to activities. *Recreation leadership is people centered.* The craft instructor is more interested in the zest that Johnny displays in fashioning his clay elephant than in the formation of a perfect specimen. The hospital recreationist is as concerned with the enjoyment brought about by engaging in a checker game as he is with the therapeutic effect of the patient's ability to interrelate with another person through the checker board.

Secondly, it is important to remember that leadership functions in a complex, ever changing setting. The basic functions of leadership remain somewhat the same, however, and can be organized into five main categories: instruction, inspiration, organization, guidance, and evaluation.

1. *Instruction.* The leader represents the undertaking and gives information concerning the purpose of the activity. It is not exciting to be "on your way" without some concept of where you are going. The leader informs; he interprets; he develops skills; he teaches youngsters and adults media for recreation. The child who has not mastered the swing of the bat is not so enthralled with baseball as one who has. The adult who has never learned one note from another is less apt to thrill to the symphonic concert. By instruction and information, the leader makes possible increased enjoyment. He attempts purposely and purposefully to broaden recreation horizons.

2. *Inspiration.* The leader creates an environment for individual or group ideation. Titus includes as a function of leadership "the promotion and discipline of controlled imagination." [21] The leader whets the recreation appetite and stimulates a desire to try new offerings. He functions as an example in his own choice of recreation menu. He inveigles, stimulates, motivates, and inspires with a wide range of interesting choices made appealing for the novice and challenging for the experienced or the talented.

3. *Organization.* The leader insures the success of a program by creating the proper environment. In some cases, the proper environment will in-

[21] Titus, *The Processes of Leadership,* p. 57.

clude only the availability of essential equipment and materials; in other cases, the activities will demand more extensive initial measures before people, setting, and atmosphere for activity can be brought together. For example, the space set aside on the playground with swings and slides may be adequate organization for some physical recreation. On the other hand, to insure opportunities for all to participate in a drama festival or the league ballgames, it may be necessary for the leader to extend his energies far past the point of merely providing an area in which the festival or ball-game can occur. Organization implies and involves inauguration of programs, control of planning, and delegation of responsibility for execution of plans.

4. *Guidance.* In his role of guidance, the leader helps to identify and select feasible goals, which the group comes to find worthy of its attention. He helps the individual or the group make timely and wise decisions; he is a resource from whom factors conditioning decisions can be learned. He helps to administer the undertaking or draws leadership from the group. Once action is taking place, he supervises; he is aware of reactions; he confers and suggests; he feels the pulse of his group; he counsels individually.

5. *Evaluation.* The person who is leading others must objectively and effectively interpret and evaluate the paths that have been taken. He has a responsibility not only to study himself in his progress toward his goals but also to give those whom he leads an opportunity to analyze the efforts they have made, the decisions that have succeeded or failed, and the goals that have been reached or lost.

A recreation experience can be a learning experience just as can any other type of human activity. Growth in learning how better to achieve the goals enhances the enjoyment of the activity the next time that the individual or group may choose to participate. Evaluation also involves the selection and distribution of appropriate honors. Such honors do not necessarily mean tangible trophies or blue ribbons. Proper distribution of appropriate honors may, to the leader steeped in the values of human relations, sometimes confine itself merely to a casual, "That was a much better job," to the small child who is trying his hand at candle making. It may mean a coveted prize for the finest amateur oil painting at the community-center art show.

Values of leadership

The advantages of leadership over lack of leadership have been inferred and implied in many of the statements of qualifications and functions of leadership. Specifically, a qualified leader in a recreation situation should:

1. *Provide a safe setting in which play experiences can take place.* Provision of a safe environment is invariably involved with instruction, infor-

mation, and guidance. The youngster who learns to handle a bat safely learns also consideration for the safety of others.

2. *Equalize the opportunities for participation.* There is no true freedom in recreation situations unless all can participate within the structure of the activity. The leader, far from interfering with the participation, makes enlarged participation possible.

3. *Broaden recreation horizons.* The leader is not content with allowing recreation tastes of individuals to stagnate. He is ever watchful for the right time to initiate new interests.

4. *Teach skills or help develop appreciations.* A youngster or adult will go back to a recreation activity in which he can find some success. Knowing how to do something will increase recreation enjoyment.

5. *Get people of like interest together.* In a study of the aged in Bartholomew County, Indiana, it was found that men interested in horseshoe pitching, living within two blocks of each other, were not engaged in this activity for recreation. Each stated that he had no one with whom to play.

6. *Draw out leadership from the group.* The wise recreation leader involves his group in leadership. In adult situations, he may bow out of the leadership position completely when others in the group have been drawn into a position of authority and respect.

7. *Provide an environment for character growth and development.* Though character growth and development are not the primary aims and objectives of the provision of leadership in recreation, many desirable personality traits may be developed under careful guidance of a recreation leader. In a relaxed situation in which the consequences for error are not too serious, the child or adult does what he feels is the best thing to do under given circumstances and learns by his successful or unwise decisions. In a fair setting, he learns how to get along with others, a skill basic to our democratic way of life. Under wise guidance, he learns to accept others for what they can do; he has the opportunity to lead and to follow; he learns to create for himself a set of values, to learn his own capacities and limitations. He enjoys the rewards of having taken his responsibilities and suffers unpleasant repercussions when he shows his lack of dependability. Again, because the consequences are not too serious, he dares to try new things.

Hazards of Leadership

Leadership must be held as a sacred trust. It is not enough that we study the qualities of wise leadership and the values therein; we must constantly guard against the misuses of leadership by ourselves and others. The recreation leader, by the very nature of his work, comes into intimate contact with his followers. His pleasant personality, his attractive appearance, draw people to him; their acceptance of his offerings feeds his ego. What are some of the principal abuses of leadership to observe and deny?

Leading selfishly

The leader who unites his followers so that his personal goals may be accomplished has fallen into a hazard of leadership. The Little League coach who inspires and drills his team so that he may emerge the victorious mentor, who eases the frustrations of his own unsuccessful athletic experience by whipping his team into a frenzy of competition to boost his own morale is abusing his sacred trust of leadership. If the entire playground population must work all summer long toward a grandiose special event, which the leader may flourish at the end of the season as his personal triumph, then the leadership role has been violated.

Abusing the power of authority

The leader's position gives him some influence over others. If he uses that influence to increase his power at the expense of others, he has fallen into one of the pitfalls of leadership. If he uses his position to whip up blind emotional attachments, he increases his power and feeds his love of it but may lose sight of the greatest good for his group and their objectives. It is flattering to the leader at first to see the open looks of adoration on the faces of the youngsters as he walks into the Scout group or onto the playground. Some people grow with responsibility; others just swell. The sense of power is a heady elixir; the wise leader accepts authority with humility.

Inability to delegate responsibility and authority

Many good leaders fall into the erroneous idea that they alone can get the job done properly. Only they can lead the square dance; only they can plan special events. Such thinking is dangerous, for it at once destroys the involvement so important to group action and rapport, and it ties the hands of the leader with so many details that he has no time to function properly in his position of over-all leadership. The secure leader is willing to relinquish some of his power, to delegate authority as well as responsibility to one of his followers. Important, too, is the emphasis on delegating the authority to get a job done, once the responsibility for the job has been passed on to the subordinate.

Moving too far too fast

A successful leader has vision but does not force his plans too quickly. The poor leader often leaves his followers far behind, speechless, uninterested, and uninvolved.

Inability to understand and communicate

Lack of ability to understand and interpret the philosophy of the recreation profession in terms all can understand may undermine the most carefully planned program.

Types of Professional Recreation Leaders

The types of recreation leaders fall generally and logically into three categories. In community recreation are found the executive, the supervisor, and the face-to-face leader, all functioning on each of the several different levels. In each type are found, to a greater or lesser degree, the qualities indicated as necessary for leadership; each type functions at his own level within the broad categories of instruction, inspiration, organization, guidance, and evaluation. Each, however, has his special functions to which attention should be given.

Executive or administrator

The executive, whether he be a superintendent of recreation in a large city or an executive secretary of a youth organization, has several functions, which include:

1. *Planning.* It takes no more effort or energy to plan than it does to wish. Good long-range planning and definition of policies under which plans can be made grease the administrative wheels and allow the executive to fit each part of his program effort into a workable whole. Planning involves facilities and personnel, as well as programing. Freedom of choice in recreation offering is impossible without some planned order, consistency, and regularity.

2. *Organization and coordination.* The executive, seeing the whole plan, so orders and coordinates existing facilities, program, and personnel, or initiates new areas that maximum program offerings will be facilitated. He leads his personnel by organizing them. Accurate job descriptions keep clearly in mind the responsibilities of internal personnel, and proper coordination with other agencies eliminates duplication of effort.

3. *Control.* The executive must set a framework of control of his subordinates. A gathering of talented musicians may make a farce of a symphonic concert, if no leader directs them toward the desired results. Some measure of common control is necessary to protect the reputation of the organization within the eyes of the public it serves. Control can insure fair working conditions, opportunities, and status for employees.

4. *Reporting.* The recreation executive is responsible for reporting to his advisory board and to the public whom he serves, in intelligible, attractive media, the workings of his organization and its accomplishments.

5. *Finance, budgeting.* The financial plan and its efficient administration again lie usually within the functions of the recreation executive. Justification of and accounting for the expenditure of public or private monies loom large in the success or failure of a department.

6. *Evaluation.* Studies of existing conditions, interests, opinions, and attitudes, in order to improve services, bolster employee morale, evaluate existing program offerings, equalize job loads, or simply as a public-relations tool for letting the public know what the organization is doing, represent an important function of the executive.

7. *Personnel management.* Recruiting, orienting, guiding, supervising, and evaluating employees and keeping harmony within the organization are also functions of the recreation executive. Some staffs, such as those of the Chicago Park District, utilize house organs like the *Administrative News Bulletin*, to inform, to stimulate, or to distribute appropriate recognitions.

8. *Public relations.* The executive, in the last analysis, is responsible for the two-way street that brings about harmony of relationships between his organization and the public it serves. He must interpret his organization to his advisory board, employed staff, participants in his programs, and to the public at large. He must be ever alert to their attitudes, opinions, and ideas, so that the organization, measured by its quality of service, may be above reproach.

9. *Cooperation.* The executive should understand the role of his agency in relation to the total community needs and should seek to establish within his agency policies of cooperation whereby those needs may be met most effectively.

Supervisor

The supervisor in the recreation profession may be responsible for a particular program area, such as drama or arts and crafts, or he may serve as a deputy officer in a particular geographic area. As a supervisor for a special activity, he is responsible for the planning, promotion, development, and supervision of a special phase of the total community program. His specialty must interrelate with other program offerings and must be administered within the policies of the organization.

Supervision can be described as a process by which workers—volunteer or paid—who, as individuals, have a direct responsibility for carrying out some part of the agency's program plans, are *helped* by a designated staff member to learn according to their needs, to make the best use of their knowledges and skills, and to improve their abilities so that they do their jobs more effectively and with increasing satisfaction to themselves and to the agency.[22]

The general supervisor, therefore, has the following functions:

1. *To interpret the aims, objectives, and policies of the organization.* The executive must depend upon the supervisor to inform subordinates with regard to operating aims and policies.

2. *To act as liaison between staff and executive.* A two-way communication channel between personnel and administration is provided by the supervisor, who interprets the wishes of the administrator to the staff and the reactions or ideas of the employees to the executive.

3. *To aid in formulating and interpreting job descriptions.* The immediate supervisor clarifies the responsibilities of each of the personnel under his jurisdiction, so that they may know what is expected of them.

4. *To guide leaders to attain expected accomplishments.* As part of the administrative staff, the supervisor, through interpersonal relationships with those for whom he is responsible, insures that the objectives of the organization will be attained. Such guidance may involve teaching skills, encouraging initiative, or motivating action through individual conferences, inservice training, or observation of active leadershp.

5. *To assist in the management process.* The supervisor aids in the planning of program, budget, or facilities, after careful observation of the needs.

6. *To evaluate.* Measuring the efficiency or progress of those persons or programs with which he is directly involved is an important role in supervision.

7. *To build creative human relationships.* In the last analysis, the supervisor must make possible an environment in which creative human relationships can take place for the good of the total organization. A supervisor is, literally, a person with an abundance of vision, who sees the total plan of the administration and stimulates action to make that plan materialize.

Recreation program leader

The face-to-face leader dealing with the participating public on the playground, in the hospital, in the center, or at the camp is aided by the executive and the supervisor—their administration, organization, and supervision. In turn, he carries out policies and procedures within the framework of the organization and feeds back information through proper channels

[22] Margaret Williamson, *Supervision: Principles and Methods* (New York: Association Press, 1950), p. 7.

so that his executive may be informed of current successes, problems, or interests. He teaches skills, stimulates activities, guides action, observes results. Most of the functions of leadership discussed in previous pages relate directly to the program leader as he inspires, organizes, instructs, guides, and evaluates his group and their participation. In summary, effective leadership of the organization demands a working relationship, loyalties, and vision with a mutual respect and dependency among all the leaders at each level, if the success of any recreation venture is to be achieved.

The Volunteer Leader

Efficient and intelligent use of volunteers is essential to the recreation program. Before the evolution of the professional, all leadership in recreation, as in other kinds of social work, was accomplished by the zealous volunteer. When the nature and kinds of service became so diverse as to demand professional attention, the volunteer was given the position of an assistant, important though that assistantship is. Traditionally, the youth-serving agencies have depended largely on volunteers for face-to-face program leadership in their organizations, but such volunteers are carefully screened and trained by the professionals. There is no adequate substitute for trained leadership.

The trend in most community recreation situations has been for the professionally trained leader to accept the major burden for the smooth operation of his organization. Help, nevertheless, is always needed and welcome. In every community, there are persons, young and old, who seek, for their own recreation, a chance to serve others. Thus, the use of volunteers to aid in programing provides a double service: it expands the existing program possibilities, and it supplies an outlet for satisfaction for the volunteer himself.

Reasons for use of volunteers

The philosophies concerning the balance of advantage over disadvantage in the use of volunteers are varied. The following reasons are usually stated for using the volunteer leader:

1. The supply of professionally trained leaders has not yet caught up with the demand. The volunteers fill the gap.

2. Public recreation agencies have been unable for financial reasons to employ the number of recreation leaders needed to program adequately for today's expanded leisure. Economy demands the use of volunteers.

3. A special area such as oil painting, dramatic production, music instruction, and facility planning is sometimes handled by a volunteer whose talent is of such caliber that his fees would be beyond reach.

The highly skilled person may willingly donate a service that the organization could not afford on any reasonable wage scale.

4. Good public relations are fostered by properly oriented volunteers. They become liaisons between the organization and the public, interpret offerings, and act as sounding boards for public opinion and interest. The use of volunteers invites participation of the total community. The more persons involved with an organization and thoroughly informed about its functions, the more support is possible for program plans. An active volunteer has a personal stake in the success of the program.

5. The volunteer, as a differently trained individual, may bring a fresh enthusiasm and different point of view to the activities.

6. Work as a volunteer offers self-realization for the volunteer himself. It gives him the feeling of service, of being needed. Many aged people in the community have time, experience, and talent left unused by leaders too short-sighted to recognize their potential leadership wealth.

7. The use of the volunteer often augments interest in the adult recreation programs. Leaders in the community who are volunteering bring with them many followers who otherwise might not have embarked on any given program.

8. More manpower, in the person of a volunteer, expands program offerings in quantity and allows more children and adults to participate safely.

9. Volunteers provide a "we" feeling, a loyalty to the organization, which may permeate the community.

Problems in use of volunteers

Is the use of the volunteer without drawback? "Definitely not," say the professionals. Following is a list of difficulties often discussed when professionals gather at conference time:

1. The recreation leadership task is, to the volunteer, a secondary job. His full-time job at the school, office, industry, or home must, of necessity, come first with him. The executive cannot demand time, excellence of performance, or long-range commitments.

2. Lack of dependability is sometimes experienced within the ranks of the volunteer. An activity must be scheduled for a specific time. All too often, the volunteer has a more pressing obligation or more interesting outlet that keeps him from meeting his continuing responsibility.

3. The volunteer must be oriented and trained. Such training takes precious time from the schedule of the professional. Frequently, just

as the volunteer is thoroughly trained and oriented, he drops out of the program because of waning interest, a job transfer, or illness in the family.

4. Volunteers sometimes give difficulty because of vested interests in some particular area of the program. The person who offers service so that his daughter may star in the play, his son may make the ball-team, or his wife may be soloist in the glee club must be tactfully handled.

5. The volunteer who lacks knowledge of the entire community program effort will sometimes decrease good public relations, as the volunteer is often mistaken for the professional leader.

6. The complaint of the volunteer that he is actually doing more work than the paid leader may sometimes be a realistic observation, which causes unrest. The volunteers frequently feel that they should be hired after they have worked without pay for a period of time with the organization.

7. Professionals who have had poor experiences with volunteers often maintain that the biggest source of difficulty is getting rid of the undesirable volunteer. Proper selection practices could perhaps avoid the need for the dismissal, but it is difficult to refuse an offer of volunteer service. It requires the utmost tact to refuse, without giving offense, a person who is eager to serve your objectives.

Development of volunteer service

Volunteers can effectively enhance the recreation program, but the selection, training, and supervision must be as carefully planned with the volunteer as with the professional.

1. *Selection.* The first steps in the use of the volunteer are recruiting individuals, analyzing their qualities, and screening them for the tasks to which they will be assigned. The qualities sought in the volunteer are essentially those needed in the professional and include, as a minimum, integrity, a willingness to learn, dependability, emotional balance, and a realization of the objectives of the organization. Although specific abilities and skills are appreciated, the novice volunteer may also hold as important a role as that of the skilled and proficient volunteer. Many of the details of operation may be handled successfully by willing volunteers to free more highly skilled professionals for more demanding jobs.

2. *Sources of volunteers.* Recruiting of volunteers can be accomplished in a number of ways:

a. Interest surveys made in clubs, church groups, neighborhood centers, schools

b. Talks before civic groups, PTAs, and similar organizations with an invitation to participate in leadership

c. Guidance programs in high schools, which enable students to find outlet for exploration of career choices in various phases of programs

d. Investigation of the rosters of persons retiring from business, industry, and the professions

e. Perusal of newspaper articles to obtain the names of hobbyists

f. Careful observation of active participants skilled enough to be used in leadership positions

g. Establishment of a city-wide volunteer bureau to assist all agencies, public and private. Such bureaus may evolve from the work of councils of social agencies

The city of Evansville, Indiana, has designated the Civic Club as the official clearing house through which volunteers may be processed and assigned. The Village Recreation Commission in Bennington, Vermont, used high school students as volunteers in cooperation with the high school. The participating students received high-school extracurricular credit and grades for their volunteer services on the summer playgrounds.

Assignment of volunteers

Because of the broad scope of the recreation profession, the uses to which the director may put qualified people are as limitless as the capabilities of the people. Careful assignment of the volunteer to a specific task in which he has interest and capability is important. Here are some broad categories of participation in which volunteers have made contributions to community recreation programs.

1. *Advisory boards or councils.* Whether the organization is a tax-supported or a private agency, the use of a lay board is extremely helpful to its success. Civic-minded community leaders who evidence interest in leisure developments give valuable service either as members of a legal, policy-making recreation board or of an advisory liaison committee between the public and the organization.

2. *Special committees.* Frequently, qualified business and professional persons can be recruited to organize fund-raising ventures, aid in training institutes, initiate survey or status studies, or support legislation.

3. *Program participation.* Participation in programs by skilled persons may take the form of direct leadership, administration, or service incidental to the functioning of an activity. The drama enthusiast may qualify to direct the community play, but many volunteers with other talents are needed to help with costuming, staging, promotion, and lighting. The aged volunteer who can no longer play ball may be eager to keep score or time

for the playground or adult league. The professional planner may be willing to design new areas and facilities. Many a prominent citizen has learned the worth of the recreation program just by judging some special event. A mothers' club may act as an advisory board for a neighborhood or may take an active part by helping with the leadership on a tot lot or making the awards for a pet parade.

4. *Miscellaneous services.* Garden clubs may actively contribute to the recreation program by designating planting days for beautification of a center or playground. Registering children, preparing or distributing bulletins, writing news articles, making photographs, and assembling scrapbooks of activities may keep volunteers active and informed. Homebound individuals can be of tremendous help on telephone committees. Other opportunities for volunteers include such functions as transportation, repair of equipment, clerical work, recruitment, and story telling.

Principles for working with volunteers

In the discussion of the role of the volunteer, certain basic principles evolve as guidelines for acting.

1. It must be recognized that volunteer leaders can make important contributions, but that the volunteer only supplements the professional leader; he does not replace him.

2. In selecting volunteers, caution should be used. Get to know the volunteer, his personality, and his abilities before accepting his services. Careful screening is necessary. The quality of the volunteers is more important than the quantity.

3. The volunteer must be oriented to the procedures and the policies of the organization so that he may work within them. He must be given not only information, but inspiration—a sense of loyalty, of belonging.

4. The volunteer needs to see specific objectives. The jobs he is given to do must fit into a long-range pattern, but, at the same time, must involve short-term successes and aims.

5. For best mutual satisfaction, the talents of the volunteer must be matched against the needs of the job; the tasks to be accomplished must be definite and specific. The enthusiasm of many good volunteers can be killed by the lack of challenging, specific responsibilities to which they can apply their energies.

6. Proper attention to assignment, training, supervision, and guidance must be given, if the volunteer is to grow with his experience. Training institutes, staff meetings attended by volunteers, individual conferences, encouragement of attendance at professional conferences, all are rewarded by more and better service from the volunteer.

Manuals tailored to the needs of the volunteer have been found to add information and incentive. The Wilton (Connecticut) Teen Center Manual for volunteers includes items that cover operational policies, rules, regulations, and recording forms.

7. Volunteers should be included in the planning of assignments and program events.

8. The contributions made by volunteers must be properly evaluated and recognized for satisfactory relationships. Recognition may come in many ways. The Long Beach, California, department awards certificates of merit to volunteers. The Evansville Community Recreation Center in Evansville, Indiana, staged a "Danke Schön" party for its volunteers as a public "thank you" for services rendered. A playground system in the New England area issues a small ticket, which reads:

Dear St. Peter,

Please place another star in the crown of
_____ for his service to the _____
Department in _____.

Sincerely,

Superintendent of Recreation

Other departments have buttons similar to service-club buttons, proudly indicating years of volunteer service. Newspaper publicity or an expression of appreciation during staff or board meetings may suffice, but the volunteer must know along the way that his services are observed, evaluated, and appreciated.

9. Opportunities should be given for the volunteer to improve and advance to greater responsibilities.

10. A good volunteer should not be abused by overwork.

Basic Principles of Leadership

Certain underlying principles concerning recreation leadership can be summarized as follows.

1. With the exception of intelligence, qualifications for leadership may be developed, and skills and abilities may be trained.

2. Tools for recreation leadership are rooted in the basic philosophy of worth and value of recreation in a world of increasing leisure.

3. Recreation leadership is person centered, not activity or product centered.

4. The existence of leadership implies that the leader has some status and prestige within the group he leads.

5. Recreation leadership stems from the understanding of the needs and interests of the followers.

6. Methods of leadership will vary both with the personality and skill of the leader and with the situation in which he finds himself.

7. For greatest success in leadership, the best-qualified person is selected, oriented to his responsibilities, given opportunities to grow, supervised carefully, and evaluated fairly.

8. Professional leadership can and should be supplemented by carefully selected and trained volunteers.

Need for Creative Leadership

In the second half of the twentieth century, there is a critical need for inspired recreation leadership to stimulate and to motivate worthy and satisfying use of the expanded leisure of all age groups. An increasing supply of qualified recreation leaders must be trained to meet the demands for more and enriched programing.

No longer will the laissez-faire leader, who was little more than a caretaker, meet the ever widening popular recreation demands. Professionally trained men and women, educated in the understandings of people and their needs, skilled in a breadth of recreation outlets, must meet the challenge of the Utopia of leisure. In Chapter 15 opportunities for the recreation professional will be explored. The seeds of leadership do not grow "like Topsy."

Until it is fully appreciated that trained leadership is the key to the successful organization and operation of public programs of recreation, we will not move forward as rapidly in the field as we should. Training is as important in recreation as it is in medicine.[23]

Scientific miracles and technological advances have catapulted this century into ever increasing material affluence. A resulting increase in leisure requires creative leadership in the recreation profession, so that man may truly prosper in his off-the-job hours. Paul Douglass defines the creative process as the "inner illumination which lights an oath to productive action into hitherto unexplored territories."[24] Such fires must be cultivated in leadership for leisure.

The recreation profession must be constantly alert to seek out and recruit intelligent youth to be trained to meet the demand for opportunities for enriched living. The educational curriculums must be visionary enough to

[23] Vettiner, A New Horizon of Recreation, p. 111.
[24] Paul Douglass, unpublished speech on creative leaders, given at the Great Lakes Park Training Institute, Pokagon, Indiana, February 1957. Quoted by permission.

inspire in the new leaders the courage to evaluate the past and to move forward on untried paths. To the recreation leader goes a twofold challenge: guiding and educating the spontaneous enthusiasms of young and old. It is a matter not of life and death, but of life.

SUGGESTED REFERENCES

Bass, Bernard M., *Leadership, Psychology and Organizational Behavior*. New York: Harper & Row, Inc., 1960.

Bellows, Roger, *Creative Leadership*. Englewood Cliffs, N.J.: Prentice-Hall, Inc., 1959.

Browne, Clarence G., *The Study of Leadership*. Danville, Ill.: The Interstate Printers & Publishers, Inc., 1958.

Overstreet, Harry A. and Bonaro W. Overstreet, *Leaders for Adult Education*. New York: American Association for Adult Education, 1941.

Personnel Standards in Community Recreation Leadership. New York: National Recreation Association, 1957.

Ross, Murray G. and Charles E. Hendry, *New Understandings of Leadership*. New York: Association Press, 1957.

Stone, Walter L. and Charles G. Stone, *Recreation Leadership*. New York: William-Frederick Press, 1952.

Tead, Ordway, *The Art of Leadership*. New York: McGraw-Hill Book Company, 1935.

Titus, Charles Hickman, *The Processes of Leadership*. Dubuque, Iowa: William C. Brown Co., 1950.

Wilson, Gertrude and Gladys Ryland, *Social Group Work Practice*. Boston: Houghton Mifflin Company, 1949.

15

Recreation—A New
Profession

Recreation, like any other social movement, grew out of an expressed need. The recreation profession was a result of increased public pressures for recreation programs and services. The many agencies concerned with various facets of these services made unprecedented demands for qualified leadership. Thus, a new profession was born. Like many of those preceding it, such as medicine, education, and law, it experienced the normal growing pains.

The fact that recreation is attaining professional status can be attributed to several factors, chief among which is the general acceptance of recreation as a basic human need, as a community responsibility, and as a field of service to humanity. In recent years, the increased awareness of the need for specialized training for those who take the leadership roles in the areas of recreation has been another factor in creating professional status for recreation. Like other professions, recreation has been concerned with the components that characterize a profession.

Components of the Profession

It is generally agreed that the following ingredients are basic to the development of a profession: general acceptance of the field, specific body of knowledge, basic research, professional education, certification, person-

349

nel standards, recruitment, and professional organizations. The present status of recreation will be briefly considered to determine how well recreation is meeting its responsibilities as a profession.

General acceptance and growth

The contents of this textbook offer evidence of the tremendous growth of the field of recreation and its general acceptance as a vital community service. Opinions vary as to how recreation might best be provided and as to the boundaries of the total field. The need for promulgating and interpreting recreation programs is still present, but the vast amount of money spent on recreation, the increasing number of agencies offering programs and services, and the basic concern with the intelligent uses of leisure offer evidence of the general recognition that recreation is receiving across the nation.

Basic body of knowledge

A person interested in becoming a recreation professional must possess basic knowledges in several fields if he is to become the type of leader outlined in the preceding chapter. Professional leaders who are steeped in a philosophy of recreation, who understand people and the community, who know the techniques of leadership, and who have knowledge of the varied program areas and their organization and promotion are sorely needed. Leaders must know the "why" as well as the "how" of promoting and conducting recreation programs. The competencies needed by a recreation leader, supervisor, or director are many. Realizing that such competencies cannot be absorbed along with the preparation for physical education, group work, or any other area, colleges and universities have been alert to develop special curriculums to train future leaders for the field.

Students majoring in recreation, like any other college students, need basic knowledge in such subjects as sociology, government, science, philosophy, history, literature, language, and speech. To this background must be added professional courses and experience in education and recreation.

Recreation research

For many years, recreation as a new discipline relied upon government, education, physical education, and sociology as sources for basic truths concerning leisure and recreation. Recreation research was slow to "earn its wings," first because it was easy for a new profession to rely on closely related disciplines for answers to basic problems, and second because recreation education in institutions of higher learning was a comparatively new venture. The establishment of graduate education programs in recreation was responsible for increasing attention on research.

Many agencies, including service organizations, foundations, industry, government—local, state, and federal—and colleges and universities, have conducted research in recreation. Municipal recreation departments and youth-serving agencies have conducted studies in order to solve some of their common problems. It is apparent that the colleges offering graduate degrees in recreation are best equipped with skilled technicians, laboratories, and trained faculty to take the lead in recreation research. The results to date, on all fronts, have been far from what is needed if recreation is to maintain status as a profession. The gap between researcher and practitioner must be narrowed if studies are to become a meaningful adjunct to the profession.

Professional education

Although specialized training of recreation personnel has existed for some time, actual professional preparation of recreation leaders by colleges and universities is a comparatively new undertaking. It was the National Recreation Association that spearheaded the drive for well-trained, inspired professional leadership. For years, this organization has conducted workshops and institutes for recreation leaders in an effort to upgrade the profession and supply better-prepared leaders to meet the demands of communities throughout the country. The National Recreation School for Professional Graduate Training, established in 1926 and conducted yearly until 1935, must be recorded as "a first" in the formal training of leaders. Not only has the National Recreation Association been responsible for these and many other successful approaches to in-service and professional training, but the Association was instrumental in stimulating colleges and universities in developing recreation courses and, later, complete curriculums in recreation. A few institutions of higher learning initiated courses as a part of existing curriculums, chiefly physical education, in the early 1930's; however, the real surge in professional education has taken place since World War II. Today some 65 to 70 institutions are offering "recreation majors" to future leaders in this field. Several national conferences [1] on professional education for recreation have been instrumental in establishing the basic framework for colleges interested in establishing curriculums in recreation.

[1] National Conferences on Professional Preparation of Recreation Personnel:
    University of Minnesota, 1937
    University of North Carolina, 1939
    New York University, 1941 and 1948
    Washington, D.C., 1954, 1956, and 1962
National Conference on Undergraduate Professional Preparation in Health Education, Physical Education, and Recreation: Jackson's Mill, West Virginia, 1948
National Conference on Graduate Study in Health Education, Physical Education, and Recreation: Pere Marquette State Park, Illinois, 1950.

Undergraduate preparation. If recreation is to attain the status of other professions, a graduate in recreation must possess a broad liberal education, which will allow him to take a respected place in the community. The recreation graduate must also have the necessary competencies to fulfill his position as a direct leader or a supervisor. The undergraduate curriculum must be designed to meet these two important requisites.

The many national conferences on professional preparation of recreation personnel have formulated standards that institutions of higher learning can use in initiating undergraduate curriculums. Like most standards, they must be adapted to the administrative and academic framework of the colleges and universities. Most recreation and education leaders agree on one point—a recreation curriculum should be established only in schools that can offer the proper courses under a qualified faculty. Of what should an undergraduate curriculum in recreation consist? What competencies should a recreation graduate possess?

It is generally accepted that at least 50 percent of the course content should be concerned with a broad cultural education, 33 percent should be directed to specialized professional preparation, and the remaining 17 percent should be concerned with related areas. The courses and experiences of the recreation curriculum should be developed to meet the competencies needed in the three categories mentioned. It is recommended that an undergraduate recreation major should strive for proficiencies in the following areas.

HUMANITIES—SOCIAL SCIENCE: An understanding of the social sciences that contribute to an awareness of social and physical environments and their effect on man and society; an understanding of the role and structure of social institutions, political philosophies of government, and community organization.

NATURAL AND BIOLOGICAL SCIENCE: An understanding and appreciation of man and his environment.

COMMUNICATION: Knowledge of and skill in the use of the basic tools of effective written, oral, and graphic communication arts.

EDUCATION: An understanding of the learning process and how to expedite it; an understanding of the needs, desires, and capabilities of individuals at all age levels; an understanding of special needs of exceptional groups.

BUSINESS ADMINISTRATION: A knowledge of and skill in business procedures related to the operation of recreation programs.

PUBLIC ADMINISTRATION: An understanding of the framework of government.

PUBLIC RELATIONS: Ability to interpret the role of recreation in twentieth-century living to colleagues, to community groups, and to participants; ability to use the tools of public relations effectively.

HEALTH AND SAFETY: A knowledge of and skill in health and safety practices and procedures with regard to recreation programs.

GROUP PROCESSES: An understanding of the principle and skill in the use of group processes.

HISTORY, THEORY, AND PHILOSOPHY OF RECREATION: Knowledge and understanding of organization, history and development, structure, and purposes of community agencies related to recreation; understanding of philosophies of recreation and the development of a personal and professional philosophy of recreation; knowledge of the nature, history, and development of the recreation movement; knowledge of professional and service organizations that pertain to recreation.

PROGRAM AND INTRODUCTION TO ADMINISTRATION: Knowledge, understanding, and appreciation of the following program areas: arts and crafts, camping and outdoor education, dance, dramatics, mental and linguistic activities, music, service activities, social recreation, sports and games, and special events; introduction to the administration of community recreation programs.

DIRECTED FIELD EXPERIENCE: Ability to put recreation skills and knowledge into practice.

A college or university that endeavors to provide a curriculum for recreation students must possess the courses, faculty, facilities, and field-work opportunities if it is to do a creditable job. It is generally agreed that there should be one or more full-time qualified recreation faculty members teaching recreation courses, counseling students, and participating in the affairs of the department. Cooperative relationships should be developed with community agencies in recreation so that the best possible field experiences are available.

Specialization at the undergraduate level is not advisable if the chief objective, a broad liberal education, is to be attained. Some schools have developed courses giving an orientation to the special areas of recreation (hospital, park management, industrial) that demand competencies beyond those acquired through the basic curriculum. This practice is acceptable if the general education courses and the core recreation courses are still held constant. The addition of a few specialized courses tends to eliminate only some of the elective courses normally permitted in most curriculums.

Graduate preparation. The demand for highly qualified administrators, teachers, planners, and research specialists has made graduate study in recreation essential. Increasingly, communities are requiring a master's degree for the chief administrator. The doctoral program provides college teachers and other individuals with special competencies in research.

The objectives of a graduate program are as follows:

1. TO DEVELOP KNOWLEDGES AND TECHNIQUES IN ADMINISTRATION. An undergraduate curriculum can only touch the area of administration. It is

at the graduate level that the various phases of administration are covered. Emphasis is placed upon planning, management, promotion, organization, and maintenance of various recreation areas, facilities, and programs.

2. TO PROVIDE OPPORTUNITIES FOR RESEARCH. Courses in research and statistics are found in most graduate programs. Basic research tools and methods are put into practice in theses, independent research, and practical field investigations. The quality of recreation research in colleges leaves much to be desired. Schools providing programs of graduate education must become more alert in upgrading the quality of research conducted as a part of graduate study.

3. TO PROVIDE OPPORTUNITIES FOR SPECIALIZATION IN VARIOUS AREAS. Most people agree that specialization in such areas as therapeutic recreation, employee recreation, camping, outdoor recreation, and park administration should be reserved for graduate study. Courses should be designed to teach the competencies that recreation personnel need in each of these special areas. Schools providing a specialization should have a faculty member who is experienced in the specialization and should afford opportunities for field work or internship in the area of specialization.

4. TO OFFER GUIDANCE IN PERSONAL, ACADEMIC, AND PROFESSIONAL PROBLEMS. Guidance is even more important at the graduate level than at the undergraduate level because of the opportunity for a wider choice of courses and the problems of thesis writing and independent research. Even though a basic curriculum is required in most schools, graduate faculty members must work out a course of study that best fits the needs of the student.

5. TO GIVE STUDENTS OPPORTUNITIES TO OBSERVE, SURVEY, AND EVALUATE PROGRAMS. Students should be given opportunities to put into practice some of the experiences and theories developed in the field and as a part of graduate study.

6. TO ENCOURAGE CONTINUOUS PROFESSIONAL GROWTH. Students should become acquainted with and be encouraged to join one or more professional organizations in recreation. Many colleges have graduate societies that are affiliated with the American Recreation Society. It is through the activities of these societies that many students first have the opportunity to serve the profession.

Institutions of higher learning should have the proper resources and environment before graduate work in recreation fields is offered. The number and quality of the faculty, selection of graduate courses, and the libraries and laboratories available will determine the type of graduate education. Not all schools are equipped to nor should, offer graduate work.

Accreditation of colleges. The rapid growth of recreation curriculums has created questions about the caliber of these programs. In many cases, the recreation curriculums were attached to existing curriculums, such as physical education, sociology, or group work, by merely adding a professional recreation course or two. Far too often, the recreation faculty possessed inadequate experience and professional training. The need for strengthening recreation education programs became apparent, and the process of evaluating these programs according to standards has received increased attention among leaders.

Accreditation in most professions signifies that the institution is meeting existing standards in its training efforts. The process of accreditation requires the establishment of standards for professional education, the development of criteria or evaluative schedules to determine adherence to standards, the inspection of colleges by a recognized accrediting agency, and finally the enforcement of standards. Where does recreation stand with regard to accreditation?

As a result of the Jackson's Mill, Pere Marquette, and Washington conferences, standards for the professional preparation of recreation personnel were established. Following the first two conferences, a continuing committee, now called the National Committee for the Improvement of Professional Preparation in Health, Physical Education, and Recreation, was formed. The committee was made up of representatives from most of the professional and service organizations in recreation. Its main function was to develop schedules and evaluative criteria that could be used by an accrediting agency in evaluating recreation education programs. This phase of the accrediting process was completed in 1951. The final and most difficult steps, the visitation and inspection of an institution by an acceptable accrediting agency and the enforcement of standards, are yet to be completed. Differences of opinion exist as to the agency best equipped to serve as the accrediting group for recreation. A majority of the professions (law, medicine, education) have established accrediting agencies of their own. Some recreation leaders feel that the American Recreation Society should serve as the accrediting agency. Others feel that recreation should fall under one of the existing teacher-education accrediting agencies.

The National Committee for the Improvement of Professional Preparation in Health, Physical Education, and Recreation has worked closely with the accrediting agencies in education and feels that recreation should be a part of the National Council on Accreditation in Teacher Education. A solution must be worked out. Much still needs to be done in the years to come if accreditation of colleges offering recreation degrees is to become a forceful tool in improving recreation curriculums.

Placement. For the graduate in recreation, the opportunities in the field are varied and many. The need for qualified leaders by the various agencies in recreation far surpasses the number of trained persons available. The situation presents a real crisis for the profession but creates an ideal climate for those entering the field from colleges or universities and related fields. Positions can be found in the administrative, supervisory, or direct-leadership areas in most agencies. Positions requiring professional leadership are normally found at the administrative or supervisory levels, whereas the direct-leadership jobs (playground leader, camp counselor, life guards, or center leader) in most instances are considered part-time areas of employment. The following is a sample of some of the types of positions open to graduates in recreation.

MUNICIPAL RECREATION: Superintendent of recreation; assistant superintendent of recreation; superintendent of parks and recreation; recreation supervisor (general); recreation supervisor (special activity)—for example, supervisor of music, dramatics, nature and camping; recreation center director; camp director.

VOLUNTARY YOUTH AGENCIES: Director of Boys' Club; executive director —Boy Scouts; executive director—Girl Scouts; physical director—YMCA, YWCA; field representative; camp director.

COLLEGES AND UNIVERSITIES: Faculty in recreation departments; campus recreation consultants; program director—college unions.

HOSPITALS: Recreation director; recreation specialist; recreation leader; coordinator of activity therapy; volunteer services director.

CAMPING AND OUTDOOR EDUCATION: School camp director; agency camp director; private camp director.

ARMED FORCES: Service club director; program director; program specialist; Red Cross area director; youth activities director.

STATE AND FEDERAL: Naturalist; park planner.

RURAL: 4-H Club director; rural recreation specialist.

CHURCH: Christian education and recreation specialist.

INDUSTRIAL: Program director; program specialist; director of recreation for labor union.

Recruitment

A serious gap exists between the supply of and the demand for qualified leaders in recreation. It is alarming to find that the profession is not even keeping pace with current personnel needs, to say nothing of meeting the increased demands that are forecast for the future. Institutions of higher learning offering recreation curriculums report that they could accommodate many more students without adding additional facilities and faculty. Willard C. Sutherland, Director of the National Recreation Association's Personnel Service, states that the need for recruiting young people for the recreation field is urgent. Studies by the NRA indicate that approximately 2,000 new, trained leaders are at present needed by recreation agencies each year. Reports from colleges offering professional training programs in recreation reveal that approximately 600 students receive degrees each year. Many of these graduates are lost to the armed forces, to marriage, to further graduate study, and to professions offering more lucrative positions. Sutherland indicates that by 1970, nearly 30,000 vacancies can be expected because of turnover and newly created jobs. Sutherland estimates that, if recruiting efforts are not vastly improved, only about one sixth of these openings will be filled by trained persons. The supply of leaders must be multiplied if recreation agencies are to meet the demands for increased programs and services. The answer lies chiefly in a united, well-organized, comprehensive program of recruitment, with all professionals and professional organizations taking part.

There are many problems that face such recruitment effort. In a study of high-school students and their awareness of recreation as a profession, it is astonishing to note how few students actually are familiar with recreation and its potential as a career. One of the first steps in recruitment is telling the recreation story to these students and their counselors. Next, it must be recognized that recreation must compete with the older and more established professions for the best high-school youth. Competition is keen when industry, nursing, and other professions spend large sums of money each year in enticing students. Recreation as a career must be presented as a satisfying, socially accepted vocation with benefits that match many of the other areas of employment. Professionals in the field must constantly work for better salaries, freedom from political pressures, better working conditions, and other improvements in personnel standards. Recreation, like other professions, must seek and demand the best of our youth.

Through the efforts of the National Recreation Association and the many professional organizations serving the field, an awareness of the need for recruitment has been created. A comprehensive personnel study,[2] conducted by the National Recreation Association and the Southern Regional Education Board, was instrumental in alerting the profession to the deficiencies of qualified personnel in the South. Many approaches to the recruitment problem have been initiated by local, state, and national agencies. Recruitment committees have been established by most of the state and national professional organizations. Spearheading the drive has been the National Advisory Committee on Recruitment, Training, and Placement of Recreation Personnel of the National Recreation Association. A comprehensive but not necessarily unified campaign, which has resulted in some of the following projects, has been instituted.

1. Many local and state societies have established scholarships for students interested in recreation as a career.
2. Both state and national organizations have prepared and distributed recruiting pamphlets and brochures to high-school students and counselors.
3. Recruiting information on recreation has been supplied for the Annual Guidance Index of the Science Research Associates, Inc.

[2] *Recreation as a Profession in the Southern Region* (New York: National Recreation Association, 1955).

4. Local recreation personnel have been taking part in high-school career days.

5. The Athletic Institute has produced a film, *Careers in Recreation*, which has had wide distribution.

If the recruitment effort is to obtain maximum results, each professional must take an active part. Service and professional organizations at the national level must work out a comprehensive unified approach so that the full potential of the profession is obtained.

Certification and registration

To be accepted as a lawyer, doctor, dentist, nurse, or architect in most states, practitioners must be qualified by education and experience and duly certified by professional organizations before they are allowed to seek employment or set up practice. Most states require teachers to be licensed before they can teach. Unfortunately, mandatory certification is not yet possible in recreation because of the insufficient number of qualified professionals. The field has been open to people from related fields; in many instances, positions have been filled because of the applicant's political affiliation rather than his qualification for the job. The need for establishing a licensing or certification plan that will serve as a prerequisite to employment is urgent. Public officials, school authorities, and recreation boards that have the responsibility for employing recreation personnel must be convinced of the importance of hiring only certified personnel, if they are available. The door must be closed to people not qualified for full-time recreation positions, if the profession is to achieve status and if recreation is to gain widespread support and community acceptance.

State recreation societies have taken the lead in establishing voluntary registration plans administered by their state chapters. Several states have developed plans for certifying full-time recreation administrators, supervisors, and leaders. Other states are feeling their way slowly and have certified only recreation administrators. Certification plans have been universal in awarding certificates, without examination, to full-time recreation personnel employed in the field. In most instances they must make application to be certified during a "blanketing in" period and must be members of the state society. After this period, recreation personnel must meet the standards established by the plan with regard to education and experience.

No plan has yet been accepted to identify and certify qualified recreation personnel on a national basis. The Personnel Standards Committee of the American Recreation Society has been given the assignment of drafting a plan. Authorities seem to agree that certification and registration of recreation personnel are the responsibilities of the individual state chapters. It is important that state standards meet those established by the national committee. Perhaps the real value of establishing a national plan would be the creation of more uniformity among state plans, and the establishment of reciprocal agreements among states in accepting certified personnel moving from one state to another.

The process of establishing higher standards through the certification of professional workers is, at the most, in its beginning stage. Much needs to be done. The acceptance of present and future plans by lay and professional workers will determine the quality of leaders for the future, and will influence the status of the profession.

Personnel standards

Recreation administrators and the agencies they represent must constantly strive to improve the personnel practices that affect employees in their attempts to do effective work. An organization should have as a sound foundation personnel practices that will enable it to recruit successfully and hold highly qualified people. Written job descriptions and specifications should be used in employing personnel, and high standards regarding education and experience should be maintained. In the past, the inability to obtain qualified personnel was largely responsible for the lowering of selection standards and the employment of unqualified persons. Thus agency programs suffered, and the misconception that "anyone can be a recreation leader" was established in the minds of many people.

It is encouraging to note that salaries for professional recreation personnel have been steadily increasing and, in some instances, are now comparable to salaries for personnel in the fields of education and community services. Continuous efforts must be made to raise salaries of recreation personnel at all levels of service. Salaries of top administrative personnel vary depending upon the size of the city and the acceptance of recreation as a vital community service.

Recreation agencies are placing more emphasis upon better working conditions, opportunities for development and advancement, security and protection against undesirable political and public pressures, and sound retirement plans. Through the efforts of the National Advisory Committee on Recruitment, Training, and Placement of Recreation Personnel of the National Recreation Association, an up-to-date and revised report on personnel standards was developed and presented in a pamphlet entitled *Personnel Standards in Community Recreation Leadership*.[3] The work of this committee and the report published have done much to strengthen and improve professional leadership in recreation. The standards developed are realistic and attainable and can be used by communities concerned with the employment of qualified personnel.

[3] *Personnel Standards in Community Recreation Leadership* (New York: National Recreation Association, 1957).

Code of ethics

The establishment of a code of ethics by the constituents of an organization is the expression of their desire to adhere to sound practices and relationships that will develop status and integrity for the profession. The establishment and enforcement of a code are basic in providing better services to communities and are progressive steps that an organization must take before it can gain professional recognition.

Many of the professional organizations, both state and national, have adopted codes. In most cases, they have been established only after considerable study, frequent revisions, and final approval by the governing body and the society's membership. A majority of the codes adopted by these organizations are somewhat similar in content. Perhaps the purposes of these codes can best be described by a statement found in the American Recreation Society's code: "Canons express desirable relationships in duties, obligations, and conduct of members of the profession to one another and to the groups, agencies, authorities, and participants engaged in Recreation." Not only has a profession the responsibility to establish standards of professional "right or wrong behavior" but it must police or protect its members on violations of the standards set.

Until those who are in leadership positions find some means of effecting acceptance of stated standards by all recreation professionals and some means of enforcing adherence to the codes, these documents will fall short of their intended purpose.

Professional organizations

A professional organization serves as the mouthpiece and the backbone of professional endeavor. It is primarily concerned with giving service to its members, improving their programs and services, helping to achieve status and recognition, setting qualifications for entrance into the profession and standards of performance for the workers, recruiting new members, and aiding members with problems related to the movement that they endeavor to serve.

There are a large number of organizations that are directly or indirectly related to recreation. This number is due partly to the many different facets of community recreation and the varied types of agencies, private, semipublic, and public, that are involved with recreation pursuits. Some of the individuals working for schools, social welfare, and youth agencies feel that their work draws them closer to the education, group work, or other allied professional groups. Personnel in Scouting organizations, Boys' Clubs, YMCAs, and YWCAs look mainly to their national organizations for professional guidance and assistance. Likewise, those individuals employed in churches, camps, industry, hospitals, armed forces, and rural agencies find that their problems and situations are unique to their peculiar settings and have formed professional affiliations appropriate to their individual needs. Because of the many organizations, the recreation profession has become fragmented, as each organization competes for members and services. The new and even the older person in the profession is confronted with the problem of deciding what organization he should join and where his major emphasis and loyalty lie. Most professionals have found it beneficial to join several organizations. Some of the major professional and service agencies in recreation are briefly treated in the following pages.

American Recreation Society. The American Recreation Society was founded in 1938 as the Society of Recreation Workers of America. Its primary and only concern is that of serving the recreation movement. The Society is open to all full-time recreation workers and to students majoring in recreation.

The Society is governed by an administrative council composed of the elected officers and geographic representatives, the chairmen of standing committees, section chairmen, and the presidents or appointed representatives of state chapters, student societies, and other organizations affiliated with the Society. A small paid headquarters staff is headed by an executive director. Because of the lack of paid personnel, much of the work of the ARS is done by its members, through its elected officers and seventeen standing committees. These committees are concerned with the conduct of the routine affairs of the Society as well as with the stimulation of professional growth for its members in such areas as research, personnel standards, certification, code of ethics, professional training, and legislation.

Members of the Society have the opportunity to participate in the activities of ten different sections. They include: armed forces, hospital, industrial, parks, private agencies, public recreation, religious organizations, rural, recreation education, and state and federal agencies. Each section is vitally concerned with the up-grading of professional activities and standards pertinent to its particular area of interest.

For years, the American Recreation Society held its Annual Meeting in conjunction with the National Recreation Congress. Now the Congress has become a joint venture of the American Recreation Society and the National Recreation Association. The official publications of the Society are its *Recreation Annual* and the *Recreation Journal.*

The growth and development of the American Recreation Society has been slow since its inception. With the hiring of an executive director in 1957 and an increase in membership and dues, many feel that the ARS is beginning to fulfill its creators' fondest dreams and eventually will take its place as *the* professional organization in the field of recreation.

American Institute of Park Executives. The American Institute of Park Executives, organized in Boston in 1898, serves as a clearinghouse and a professional agency for the park and recreation movement. During the first half century of existence, the members of the AIPE were predominantly park executives. The major concerns of the Institute were those of horticulture, maintenance, park development, zoological gardens, and zoo operations. In recent years, the organization has broadened its objectives and functions to include recreation. The consolidation of parks and recreation in many communities and the recognition of the vital importance of recreation in the total park operation have influenced this change in emphasis. Although the organization is still composed primarily of park administrators, more recreation executives are becoming members of the AIPE, and the conferences and workshops sponsored by the Institute are concerned with many aspects of recreation as well as the more traditional park problems.

The Institute functions through its elected officers, a seven-member board of directors, and its many operating committees. The Institute is headed by an executive secretary and an able supporting staff. Many branch and affiliate associations, institutes, and organizations have become affiliated with the AIPE in its years of operation. The American Association of Zoological Parks and Aquariums is one of the Institute's earliest and largest affiliate groups. Zoological park executives and other executives having zoos under their jurisdiction can become members of this association.

The AIPE has been active in sponsoring training institutes for park and recreation workers. It has cooperated with other professional and service groups in conferences and workshops related to the improvement of park and recreation service. The official publication of the organization is the *Parks and Recreation* magazine, which includes sections on parks, recreation, zoos, and horticulture.

In 1952, the AIPE and Michigan State University launched a park education program for the purpose of preparing and disseminating literature for the park profession. Several workshops were held, with administrators, technicians, and resource people taking part. A series of bulletins resulted from this joint effort. As a service to its membership, the AIPE has instituted a Management Aids Series.

American Association for Health, Physical Education, and Recreation. The AAHPER is a professional organization for four major areas of interest: health, safety, physical education, and recreation. The Association's membership, some 25,000 strong, consists mainly of physical-education teachers, supervisors, and coaches. Recreation personnel active in the affairs of the Association come mainly from colleges and universities and from recreation departments that are operated as a function of the public schools. The AAHPER is a department of the National Education Association. The headquarters staff, located in Washington, includes an executive secretary and several professional associates, two of whom are primarily concerned with recreation and outdoor education.

Each of the areas of professional endeavor is headed by a vice president who serves as chairman of the division. Within the recreation division are six sections that function in the following areas: industrial, public recreation, recreation in religious organizations, recreation therapy, school recreation, and voluntary and youth-serving agencies.

The Association sponsors workshops and institutes and is a source of information on professional matters. It has done outstanding work in promoting outdoor education and conferences on professional preparation of recreation personnel.

American Camping Association. The American Camping Association is the national professional camping organization of the organized camping movement. Formed in 1910, it is dedicated to furthering "the interests and welfare of children and adults through camping as an educative and recreative experience." [4] Membership includes camp directors, members of camp staffs, and interested individuals from allied or related fields of education and recreation. It includes workers in all types of camps—organization, institutional, private, religious, and special purpose.

There are about 7,000 members. The Association maintains a national office with professional personnel at Bradford Woods, Martinsville, Indiana. For purposes of more efficient operation and servicing, the Association is divided into seven geographical regions. There are 43 sections, most of them organized on a state basis. The activities of the ACA are illustrated by the following: national and regional conventions; national and local workshops; leadership training for counselors; legislation related to camping; formulating standards of camp operation and working to secure adherence to these standards; publications; studies and research; program improvement; public relations; and area and facility research.

As organized camping assumes a larger place in recreation interests, the ACA exerts its influence towards the improvement of camping and the provision of increased opportunities for good camp experiences.

Other related agencies. Several other organizations play an important role to their respective constituents. They include: Association of College Unions, National Conference on State Parks, National Industrial Recreation Association, National Association of Recreation Therapists, and Society of State Directors for Health, Physical Education, and Recreation.

Service organizations

There are several organizations, national in scope, that offer service to the recreation profession. In many instances, service organizations co-sponsor workshops, institutes, or other projects of a professional nature with

[4] *What Is ACA?* (Martinsville, Ind.: American Camping Association, n.d.). Brochure.

Fig. 22   *National Head-quarters, American Camping Association, Bradford Woods, Indiana*

one or more of the professional organizations. A number of the projects performed by service organizations are professional in nature and in some cases duplicate or extend the efforts of the professional organizations.

The primary source of income for service organizations comes from donations from individuals and organizations. Control is placed in a private board of directors; this administration differs from that of the professional organization, in which democratically elected officers guide the affairs of the organization.

The National Recreation Association and the Athletic Institute are the two principal service organizations in the field of recreation. Their background, organization, and chief contributions to the profession are as follows.

National Recreation Association. The National Recreation Association, established in 1906 as the "Playground Association of America," is the major service organization for recreation. In the early years of the movement, the NRA was chiefly responsible for the promotion of the recreation profession. It is a nationwide, nonprofit organization financed by private contributions and individual and group memberships. Its membership is open to all persons interested in recreation; its services are available to individuals, communities, and organizations.

No other professional or service organization in recreation is as well equipped to give service to the profession. The headquarters staff, headed by an executive director, consists of a large number of able executives and specialists. The national field service is rendered through eight districts, with each district having one or more district representatives who provide service to communities in their district.

The NRA has established several national advisory committees that work in the following areas: recruitment, training, and placement of personnel; research; defense-related services; federal recreation; state recreation; programs and activities; administration; and publishing of recreation materials. These committees, made up of professionals from all parts of the nation, have been instrumental in stimulating research, developing standards, conducting institutes, publishing pamphlets and reports, and alerting the profession to basic deficiencies and problems. Some of the major services of the NRA are:

1. Sponsors the National Recreation Congress in conjunction with the American Recreation Society; sponsors district conferences.
2. Publishes *Recreation* magazine.
3. Operates a recreation book center with members receiving a discount on most books.
4. Publishes monthly affiliate newsletters.
5. Provides an extensive recreation personnel service.
6. Conducts leadership training institutes.
7. Operates an on-the-spot field service.
8. Gives aid and consultation to individuals and communities.
9. Keeps the profession posted as to the trends and scope of recreation.
10. Conducts community surveys and area and facility planning.
11. Operates an intern program in selected communities for graduates in recreation.
12. Provides scholarships for further education of outstanding students.

Athletic Institute. Founded in 1934 by a group of athletic goods manufacturers, the Athletic Institute had as its objective the stimulation of participation in sport activities throughout the nation. Today the Institute's functions have broadened considerably to include physical education, athletics, and recreation. Like the NRA, the Athletic Institute's sole purpose is one of service to the professional groups in these three areas. The Institute is supported financially by the manufacturers of athletic, sport, and recreation equipment. A board of directors, made up chiefly of executives from the various sporting goods firms, and an advisory committee consisting of leaders in the fields of athletics, physical education, and recreation, guide and direct the operations of the Institute.

The Institute has been active in three main fields of service: development of visual aids, financing various sports programs and projects, and organizing and financing workshops, which have produced publications for the three related fields. As the result of national workshops of professional leaders, the Institute has printed several publications, which include: *Essentials for Developing Community Recreation; A Guide for Planning Facilities for Athletics, Recreation, Physical and Health Education; Recre-*

ation for Community Living; The Recreation Program; and A *Brief History of Parks and Recreation in the United States.*

The Institute made an outstanding contribution to professional education for recreation when it financed and helped organize the two national conferences on undergraduate and graduate preparation in physical education, health education, and recreation at Jackson's Mill, West Virginia, and Pere Marquette State Park, Illinois.

The production of motion pictures and other visual materials has been another major service of the Institute. The films, *Playtown U.S.A.*, *Leaders for Leisure, $1,000 for Recreation*, and *Careers in Recreation*, have been widely distributed and have proved to be effective in creating understanding of the values of recreation and its leadership.

Coordination and Cooperation of National Organizations

There is a definite need for securing cooperation among the numerous national organizations concerned with recreation. In far too many cases, conflict, competition for membership, and overlapping of services have resulted in dividing the profession. Many have advocated consolidation of organizations so that recreation might speak professionally as one voice. According to Eppley,[5] an outstanding leader in both parks and recreation, such consolidation would be difficult to realize. He points out that "vested interests, different concepts of recreation philosophy, divergent policies in membership requirements, dues and scope of service, as well as historical roots and personal imperialisms, present difficult hurdles to be surmounted." The best approach toward establishing a strong national professional organization, Eppley concludes, is through a "long-range program accomplished through evolution and not revolution."

Federation of National Professional Organizations for Recreation

The establishment of the Federation of National Professional Organizations for Recreation in 1954 was an important step in establishing coordination among organizations. The Federation is made up of representatives of seven of the national professional organizations in recreation, with officials from the National Recreation Association and the Athletic Institute serving as consultants. The membership is as follows:

American Camping Association
American Recreation Society

[5] Garrett G. Eppley, "Professional Associations," in *Recreation in the Age of Automation* (Philadelphia: American Academy of Political and Social Science, 1957), The Annals of the Academy, Vol. 313, pp. 46–50. Reprinted by permission.

American Association for Health, Physical Education,
   and Recreation
American Institute of Park Executives
Association of College Unions
National Industrial Recreation Association
Society of State Directors of Health, Physical Education,
   and Recreation

The Federation constitutes a meeting ground for professional and service organizations in consulting on common problems, working together on projects important to all members, providing a clearing house for activities, and exchanging information.

The Worker's Responsibility to His Profession

The manner in which a profession grows and achieves status correlates strongly with the individual worker's personal growth and effectiveness on the job. A worker can gain much from a professional organization in the way of increased personnel benefits, higher salaries, and better working conditions. Joining together as "one voice" adds strength to the recreation cause.

The profession and "its voice" can gain in strength and can enjoy status only when each individual participates in the activities of his professional organization and strives to raise his personal competencies. A person can rightfully expect to receive benefits from his professional affiliations; in turn, the professional organization must have the support of its constituency. The professional worker should:

1. *Belong to his local, state, and national professional organizations.* With the several national professional organizations operating for the recreation professional, it is neither practical nor essential for workers to join all organizations. Most individuals find it possible to join one or two organizations.

2. *Be active in the work of professional organizations.* Being a member is not enough. Members should attend conferences, write articles for professional journals, serve on committees, and actively support the activities sponsored by the professional organizations.

3. *Keep up-to-date with current professional literature.* The development of a personal or departmental library is basic if workers are to keep abreast of the specialized body of knowledge needed by the professional worker. Since it is possible for the busy executive, supervisor, or leader to read only a small fraction of the material published, care must be exercised in selection of the most pertinent readings.

4. *Be alert in recruiting potential leaders for the profession.* The need for leaders has been treated extensively in this chapter. Each administrator, supervisor, and leader must assume this undertaking as his professional responsibility. No one else can do the job as effectively. The motto might be, "Each professional should recruit at least one individual."

5. *Advance himself educationally.* Some workers find it possible to take leaves of absence for the purpose of further graduate study. Others supplement their professional training by attending institutes, workshops, extension classes, or by registering for correspondence courses. Education is a continuing process, and the future of the profession is based upon how well each member develops personally in meeting the responsibilities of his job and profession.

Advantages and Problems Facing the Professional Worker

There are many advantages and problems that should be explained to a person who is considering recreation for his profession.

Advantages

Being a new profession has many advantages. A person entering the field will find that he is on the ground floor. In this situation, the opportunities for employment arc varied and many, and rapid advancement is possible for the competent, trained individual. Since the broad scope of recreation program includes contacts with all age groups and many different agencies and organizations, the new recreation professional will find himself an integral part of the total community. The worker's daily routine is seldom the same, and his assignments do not have the many restrictions found in a classroom or office job.

Opportunities to use ingenuity, to experiment with programs, and to initiate new ideas prevent a stereotyping of the recreation professional's responsibilities. Tremendous satisfactions are received from the enthusiastic responses of the boy or girl in the center, the handicapped child in the camp, or the elder participant in the senior-citizens' club. In cities in which the values of recreation have been sold to the community, salaries of recreation personnel are commensurate with those of workers in allied professions (education, social work, and others) that have similar responsibilities. Recreation is a field of service to mankind, and, as such, provides many intangible rewards in addition to the paycheck.

Problems

All professions have their problems; of course recreation is no exception. It has been said that recreation is confronting many of the same problems experienced by the older professions.

First and foremost of the problems is the lack of understanding on the part of the general public as to what recreation is and what it involves. The recreation worker must use every opportunity to interpret his field to the public. In some communities, salaries have tended to be lower for persons in recreation than for those in other fields. Since recreation interests are explored in leisure hours, the recreation leader must often work nights and holidays. In some instances, public and political pressures influence the management of the recreation department thus hampering efficient operation.

Since its early years of organization, recreation has come a long way. People who work in the recreation profession find it challenging, exciting, satisfying, and rewarding. Most of them are enthusiastic about their jobs. Such contagious enthusiasm has attracted persons from all walks of life into recreation; but, with the expansion of recreation offerings, the need for more personnel is still crucial.

Recreation professionals must continue to put diligent efforts into recruiting for and building their profession into one that will stand proudly on equal footing beside the more established ones, maintaining high standards of personnel and program, and developing a clear philosophy and objectives that will lead the profession to new heights in the future.

PROFESSIONAL AND SERVICE ORGANIZATIONS IN RECREATION

Professional organizations

American Recreation Society, Inc.
622 Bond Building
1404 New York Avenue N.W.
Washington 5, D.C.

American Camping Association
Bradford Woods
Martinsville, Indiana

American Association for Health, Physical Education,
  and Recreation
1201 16th Street N.W.
Washington 6, D.C.

American Institute of Park Executives
Oglebay Park
Wheeling, West Virginia

Association of College Unions
Willard Straight Hall
Cornell University
Ithaca, New York

National Conference on State Parks
901 Union Trust Building
Washington 5, D.C.

National Industrial Recreation Association
203 North Wabash Avenue
Chicago 1, Illinois

Society of State Directors of Health, Physical Education,
    and Recreation
c/o Division of Health and Physical Education
1330 West Michigan Street
Indianapolis, Indiana

Service organizations

Athletic Institute
209 South State Street
Chicago 4, Illinois

National Recreation Association
8 West Eighth Street
New York 11, New York

SUGGESTED REFERENCES

Brightbill, Charles K. and Harold D. Meyer, *Recreation: Text and Readings.* Englewood Cliffs, N.J.: Prentice-Hall, Inc., 1953.

Code of Ethics. Washington, D.C.: American Recreation Society. n.d.

Graduate Study in Health Education, Physical Education, and Recreation. Chicago: The Athletic Institute, 1950.

National Advisory Committee on Recruitment, Training, and Placement of Recreation Personnel, *Personnel Standards in Community Recreation Leadership*, Revised edition. New York: National Recreation Association, 1957.

National Conference on Undergraduate Professional Preparation in Physical Education, Health Education, and Recreation. Chicago: The Athletic Institute, 1948.

National Recreation Association and the Southern Regional Education Board, *Recreation as a Profession in the Southern Region.* New York: National Recreation Association, 1955.

Personnel Practices Committee, *Personnel Practices for Recreation Departments and Agencies.* Washington, D.C.: American Recreation Society, 1959.

Professional Preparation of Recreation Personnel. Washington, D.C.: American Association for Health, Physical Education, and Recreation, 1957.

5

THE RECREATION
PROGRAM

16

Program Planning

Planning is essential in almost any phase of human endeavor. The builder, as he constructs the new home or school, is guided by an architect's carefully considered blueprint. The housewife uses time-tested recipes in making a chocolate cake. The highway patrol defines a step-by-step plan to capture the fugitive. The school approaches the education of the young through a thoughtful curriculum progression. Whether the end result is in terms of people, events, or things, achievement in every avenue of endeavor is firmly grounded on intelligent, creative plans toward feasible goals.

Recreation programing is no exception to this concept. Unless the recreation professional scrutinizes and re-evaluates present offerings and seeks to rejuvenate his program to meet more creatively the ever increasing demands, he may find that the leisure population has drifted from his door. Intelligent, continuous planning is mandatory for efficient, successful, stimulating programs.

The community recreation program is composed of all recreation offerings, individual or group, formal or informal, organized or unorganized, made available to segments of or the total community population by individuals, agencies, or organizations. Planning such a program demands coordination of all concerned, if desired results are to be achieved. Desired results, in the last analysis, are achieved through satisfying the basic needs and desires of the participants and of the society of which they are a part. If three-year-olds are looking for action, story telling does not suffice; when teenagers are seeking social contacts, the center club program is too confining; traditional Bingo and checkers may fail to intrigue the spirited seventy-year-old. Unless changing needs are met, the program does not prosper, and all ages go elsewhere for their leisure activity.

What constitutes good programing? Is it availability of expanded areas, expensive equipment, and grandiose facilities? Is it adequate financing or quality leadership? Such elements are involved, of course; the quality program in any community, large or small, comes from a thoughtfully planned, systematically coordinated, and efficiently executed wide range of offerings under competent leadership with creatively developed facilities and adequate budget. The quality program offers a broad horizon of wholesome recreation choices.

Pitfalls in Planning

How do program plans evolve? How does the director strive to meet the needs? Danford [1] describes four unsound bases for guiding program efforts. Fallacies for each are delineated here.

1. *The traditional approach.* The program repeats itself each year. Because the program has been offered for twenty years does not necessarily make it infallible. Continuous evaluation must take place. Last year's ideas may be outmoded for this year's participants. Careful scrutiny will allow the program director to keep elements of merit and discard those that no longer appeal.

2. *Current practices.* Other communities of like size are observed and their programs are copied. Even if everyone is doing certain programs, they may not be right for you. Glean the good from other programs; then initiate your own.

3. *Expressed desires.* The participants are polled to see what they want. The fallacy here lies in the fact that individuals are conditioned by what they have already experienced. The creative program should offer new opportunities to expand recreation satisfactions.

4. *Best guess.* The director arrives at his decision for programing ideas by using his own best judgment. Without benefit of facts, his best guess may be wrong.

As Danford points out, the above bases for program planning are not without some merit, but they cannot, in isolation, hope to achieve the ultimate in effective program planning. A successful venture might well be worth repeating, if conditions under which it was successful still exist. It

[1] Howard G. Danford, *Recreation in the American Community* (Harper & Row, Inc., 1953), pp. 71–72. Reprinted by permission.

is true that what exists should be investigated for its strengths and weaknesses, whether it be in your program or in that of other communities. One of the real values of professional workshops and conferences is the interchange of ideas to alert professionals to what others are doing. It is reasonable, also, to expect that a checklist of recreation interests could be of value in attempts to satisfy recreation needs in the community. Inevitably, there are times when the director must use his own best judgment, but only after the facts have been investigated to weigh that judgment. All four processes may be employed in combination to improve program planning.

Guiding Principles for Program Planning

What then are some guiding principles for planning that have evolved from the experience of leaders through the years? Principles of program planning that community leaders might consider are here summarized.

1. *The recreation program should attempt to meet the individual and group needs and desires of the people.* The final test of success or failure in a program will lie in its ability to satisfy the people for whom the program was planned. If needs are not met, desires not fulfilled, the participants feel no inclination to return to the program.

Basic psychological needs are universal. Each individual seeks new experience, recognition, security, response, a feeling of belonging, or a search for aesthetic rewards. Individuals find satisfactions for these universal desires in a variety of ways. A game of chess may satisfy an old man's wish to relate to others, whereas the teenager may appease the same desire by attending a party or a dance. The adult may find aesthetic expression in the symphony concert, whereas the nursery tot creates through his finger painting. In a world in which it becomes increasingly difficult to find satisfactions in the work day, it is the responsibility of the recreation program to gratify expressed needs, stimulate new interests, and develop skills to explore those interests in alignment with the total objectives of the sponsoring agency.

2. *The program should be diversified.* All too often, recreation connotes only sports and games. The effective community program must include: sports and games; arts and crafts; dramatic activities; music; dance; literary, mental, and linguistic outlets; service to others; social recreation; camping and outdoor recreation; hobbies; and special events.

The program should be in careful balance to include opportunities for: active and passive recreation; physical, social, cultural, and creative activities; programs that allow individuals with varying degrees of skill to participate; programs that allow progress in proficiency within the activity; indoor and outdoor interests; activities for individual and for group participation; and interests that involve long-range as well as short-term participation.

3. *The program should provide equal opportunity for all, regardless of race, creed, social status, economic need, sex, age, interest, or mental or physical capacity.* Although it is often expedient to run programs on the basis of the "greatest good for the greatest number," wise program planning for community recreation will include activities for all ages, for both sexes, and for groups with special interest, varying ability, or economic, geographic, or social problems.

AGE. Program opportunities must not be limited to any one age grouping. Some programs should be provided especially for youngsters, teenagers, adults, or the aged; other programs should attract mixed age groups by crosscutting the interests of entire families or other social units. The young adults and adults are all too frequently ignored in favor of an accent on youth needs.

SEX. Opportunities should be offered in equal balance to meet the needs and interests of each sex. Other programs should seek to offer wholesome outlets for co-recreation at many ages.

SOCIO-ECONOMIC STATUS. Community recreation should not be apportioned according to one's ability to pay, nor should the recreation program be dedicated to the needs of only the lower social or economic strata. Recreation must service basic recreation outlets for rich and poor alike.

MENTAL AND PHYSICAL CAPACITY. Communities are increasing their awareness of their responsibility to provide programs for the atypical child or adult. The mentally retarded, the physically handicapped, and the homebound are getting a fairer share of consideration in the program, but there is need for greater concentration in these areas.

SPECIAL-INTEREST GROUPS. Although leadership and facilities are sometimes hard to find in the daily program for those who would like to indulge in sculpture, sailing, composing symphonies, or discussing philosophies, the skillful program planner will make every attempt to create outlets for those special interests through specialists, hobby groups, classes, or volunteer leaders.

RACE, CREED, OR ETHNIC GROUPS. It seems superfluous to mention that any program organized on democratic principles will avoid prejudices for or against racial or religious groups. Racial discrimination is one of the basic issues that recreation administrators, along with other community leaders, must face. Too often, program planning ignores particular needs of ethnic groups in special neighborhoods.

4. *Programs should be offered at a wide variety of times to meet the diverse living schedules of the population.* Timing is important to the success of any program. Activities must be available during the times when people are free to participate. Too frequently, the morning hours, the weekends,

and the winter months are overlooked, as program emphasis is geared too strongly to school children or working adults. Although there is a credible tendency to avoid interference with church services on Sunday, many agencies also close their doors on Saturday, a day when families might best avail themselves of community offerings.

The center that operates only in the afternoon and evening forgets the early-rising aged, who often do not care to travel at night. The playground that operates adult programs only in the evening ignores the many workers who labor on the night shift.

5. *Recreation programs for the community should be planned and coordinated to make best use of community facilities and personnel resources.* No one organization in the community is capable of satisfying all of the leisure needs and interests of the people. It is important that there be cooperative planning and coordination among individuals or agencies that offer recreation programs so that intelligent use can be made of existing facilities, leadership, and finance. For example, youth agencies frequently use churches, schools, and city recreation facilities for their programs. In-service training institutes should utilize capable leaders from all community agencies. Efficient cooperation will prevent needless duplication of programs or facilities or will fill voids in these areas. Involvement of participants and leaders in planning will also aid in successful programing.

6. *Quality leadership must be employed as the backbone of successful recreation offerings.* The capabilities of the leaders will make or break the programs. Optimum recreation outlets are possible only when qualified, professional leaders are employed and given authority parallel with their responsibilities.

7. *Adequate financial backing is necessary, if programs are to succeed.* Intelligent program planning gives the best possible variety of opportunity for the money available. Many activities must be free to the participants, in order that equal access for participation is possible. Other activities may be properly financed by fees and charges. Creative planning, careful coordination, and intelligent evaluation will produce the maximum in recreation benefits for the number of dollars expended.

8. *Best practices to insure the safety and health of the participants must be employed.* There is an ever increasing emphasis on the responsibility of the sponsoring organization for insuring adequately safe and healthful conditions for those who are participating in recreation. Albert Whitney comments on the relation between safety and recreation as follows:

Teach a boy to play football safely, or to sail a boat safely, or to use a gun safely; in each case, you are showing him how he can have a good adventure instead of a bad one. Instead of the bad adventure of breaking his collarbone he can have the good adventure of carrying the ball across the goal line; instead of the bad adventure of tipping his boat over . . . he can have the good adventure of sailing on to a thrilling finish; instead of ending his hunting adventure with a bullet through his leg, he can have the better adventure of the chase. . . .

From this point of view, the relation between safety and recreation is immediately clear. Safety rids us of the bad adventure and opens the way for the good adventure, but it remains for recreation actually to bring the good adventure. We must not put the children off the streets (for playing in the streets is better than no playing at all), unless we can furnish them with other, safe places in which to play. The two movements must go hand in hand. The safety movement needs the recreation movement in order to supply the better adventure. The recreation movement needs the safety movement in order to free life for the better adventure. They are both bound together as inseparable parts of the movement for a richer, better, more spiritual, more truly adventurous life.[2]

For safer program efforts constant research must be made on accidents and their causes. Leaders must be constantly alerted to the difficulties of unhealthful or unsanitary practices whether they be found in continuing physical activity in the face of participant fatigue, unsanitary facilities, debris on playground, or easy accessibility of acids in the craft center.

9. *Program planning should adhere to the best available standards as evolved by national leaders.* Many agencies and organizations have developed standards for facilities, leadership, or program. Conscientious program planners will utilize the standards put forth by such organizations as the American Camping Association, National Recreation Association, American Red Cross, or the Division of Girls' and Women's Sports of the AAHPER.

10. *Programs should be constantly re-evaluated in light of objectives and public acceptance.* Surveys to investigate and to promote recreation activities, continuous evaluation of existing programs, and planned observations of response to new offerings should guide program efforts. Constant awareness of changes in interest and needs will avoid wasting budget money on activities that have outlived their appeal.

Factors That Influence Program Planning

Intelligent planning for wholesome recreation suited to the needs and interests of individuals and groups in the community is based essentially upon six factors that condition the type, scope, and amount of program. These factors include: participants involved, settings available, number and capabilities of leaders, the budget approved, objectives of the sponsoring

[2] Albert Whitney, "The Relation Between Safety and Recreation" in *Family Recreation and Safety* (New York: New York University Center for Safety Education, 1961), p. 47. Reprinted by permission.

organization, and kind and extent of recreation programs offered by other community agencies.

People involved

Any program must be geared to the varying interests of the participants, encouraging them into further activity in areas with which they have had pleasant experiences and stimulating them into new ventures that will broaden their recreation horizons. Several factors concerning the participants condition the planning.

Age. Although all persons do not mature physically and mentally at the same rate, chronological age still remains as a conditioning factor in planning. Psychological, social, mental, or physical attributes that characterize different age spans are also considerations. Children, who are willingly enticed into many recreation activities, active and passive, for short periods of time, grow into teenagers, who must be involved with the planning, if the program is to function successfully. Once involved, they may maintain their interests for long periods. With the exception of heavy physical activity, age plays a lesser role in the choices of adults, as they range in interest from sports to Schubert.

The ages of the prospective participants in any area will color planning. The sophisticated teen program will inevitably go astray in a neighborhood of young families in which the majority of the youngsters have not yet reached a sixth birthday. By the same token, the response to the tot-lot program will be meager in a neighborhood that is predominantly aged.

Sex. Program planning must take into consideration whether the group will be all male, all female, or mixed. Social conditioning has done much to create definite differences in interest choices between the sexes. Even small youngsters are imbued with the idea that the dollhouse is for Susie and the trucks are for Jimmy, although the two join willingly in other play. It is sometimes extremely hard to entice boys into craft projects with which they are really intrigued or the girls into softball leagues, which they might heartily enjoy.

Although avoidance of sports requiring body contact as co-recreation activity is customary and laudable after girls and boys reach the age of ten or eleven, almost all of the other recreation offerings could be enjoyed equally by male or female, if social tastes were geared to their acceptance. To insist upon steering the boys toward heightened sports roles and the girls toward the so-called more cultural activities is to deny both sexes recreation outlets that could be extremely enjoyable. Plans cannot, however, ignore existing concepts. Horizons of interest are broadened gradually through education.

Mores and prejudices. No program should be planned without full knowledge of the customs, folkways, and prejudices of the community. Too many leaders have deprived themselves of goodwill and confidence by introducing programs that are in disrepute because of local mores. In some areas, for instance, dancing is considered sinful; in other areas a card party would be boycotted; in still others racial or national prejudices exist. Careful investigation of the community code is mandatory for good planning.

Interests and skills. The interests and capabilities of the participants will condition the program. It is not surprising that attendance is small at a social dance in a community in which few people know the rudiments of dance movements. A tennis club fails when few have learned to play the game. The planner must start with a program geared to the interests and skills of his participants, and then build new skills and stimulate new interests.

Socio-economic or educational status. The broadening of recreation horizons to include exciting vistas for all social, economic, and educational groups is a challenge for the director in any community. All too frequently, programs are directed toward the middle social or economic brackets, and the extremes in each category are ignored. The municipal authority may feel that the upper bracket can better use the facilities and offerings of private or commercial recreation ventures, but total community offerings should include opportunities for all groups. The types of program and the media for organization change as opportunities are offered to different social or economic brackets. In communities in which large numbers of foreign-born exist, different promotion is needed.

Needs. The needs of participants, expressed or unexpressed, affect choices in program. Some groups need social outlets, a chance to get acquainted; others need opportunities for physical activities. Some need outlets for creative desires; others need opportunities to be of service. A broad program creates offerings to satisfy basic physical and psychological yearnings in a variety of media.

Health. The physical and mental health of expected participants condition recreation offerings. The aged and arthritic are often absent because the activity is not readily accessible, either because of distance or because the building in which the program takes place has too many stairs and too few handrails.

Numbers. The size of the community and the numbers expected affect planning and promotion of activities. In large cities, decentralization of the program on a neighborhood basis is sometimes more efficient than an attempt to interest the whole population at any one time or in any one activity. Although the servicing of large numbers is important, leaders must be cautioned not to use the numbers involved as the only criterion for evaluating the success or failure of the program. Those outlets that attract only a few enthusiasts still have their place in the total program. Most new popular activities started with a handful of interested persons who spread their zeal to others.

Setting

The *time* of day, week, or year; the *facility* available; the *climate* and the *geographical location* all influence program planning. The timeliness of an activity is a most important factor. Knowing when to initiate a special event, what hours are most apt to attract the participants for whom the program is intended, how frequently to offer different programs, and how long activities may run without loss of enthusiasm are all factors that allow the planner to balance his schedule successfully.

The facilities and areas available also are key factors in planning. Accessibility of outdoor areas may accent nature lore, whereas the availability of a community theater may stimulate drama. Climate and geographical location must be considered so that the broadest possible programing can be offered within the limitations of humidity, temperature, or topographical features. Mountain climbing may be a popular pastime in Colorado, whereas swimming may be more feasible in a lake region. Humid summers are not conducive to enjoyment of heavy physical activity, whereas skiing programs would be quite in vogue for the Vermont winter season.

Types of leadership

The number of professional or volunteer leaders available is an important factor in planning. Activities cannot be initiated or executed successfully unless there are sufficient leaders capable of carrying on the activities. The organization that does not have a leader who engenders enthusiasm for drama finds a minimum of emphasis on dramatic activity. The secret of good planning is to employ professional staff members educated in a sound curriculum of recreation education, and steeped in a knowledge of the breadth and scope of recreation opportunities. Such leaders will capitalize on their own skills and seek out volunteers to expand program areas in which they feel less competent. Cooperation among the leaders of all organizations who offer recreation can considerably broaden the total program services in the community.

Finance available

How the program is financed, and by whom, will substantially affect the amount and kind of program possible. It is extremely unwise to base the continuance of a program on unit costs alone, but monies available may shorten the length of time programs are offered, eliminate entirely those activities in which unit costs cannot be justified, or make fees and charges mandatory.

Objectives of managing authority

Churches, schools, industries, youth-serving organizations, commercial ventures, or tax-supported agencies that govern portions of the total community recreation program operate under certain policies and move toward definite objectives. The policies, scope, program, and methods of organization of many youth agencies are dictated by the parent organization. The agency that is trying to serve youth is not primarily interested in stimulating activity among the adult population; the church that has strong feelings against the advisability of dance as a social program cannot be expected to further the dance interests of other members of the community. The commercial bowling alley will not have the same consuming interest in the art center that it has in promotion of bowling, yet some degree of cooperation between these diverse interests may be achieved. Only when all agencies and individuals concerned with wholesome recreation, whatever the activity or whatever the age, get together to coordinate their efforts will the total community achieve a maximum in recreation opportunities.

Other program offerings

Before activities are planned by an organization, the staff should look at other agencies in the community and try to avoid duplication of program, leadership, or facility. Each agency's effort should complement and be complemented by the programs offered by other agencies. Few organizations have budgets that they feel are adequate. Careful planning and coordination of energies could insure the fullest and most diverse program possible with the monies available in the total community.

Hazards To Be Avoided

Few professions have been plagued by as many misconceptions as has recreation. It must be confessed that many prevalent misconceptions stem from existing offerings that fall short of the ideal in effective program planning. Following are a few of the pitfalls that recreation directors must studiously avoid.

The welfare concept

An overemphasis on provision of programs in low economic areas at the expense of general geographic coverage gives the impression that only the poor need recreation. When such an impression exists, people in other economic brackets, who need recreation outlets just as badly, are deprived of opportunities. All people need creative and recreative outlets. Values in recreation are alike for the privileged or underprivileged. The program cannot be confined only to those who live "across the tracks."

Unequal opportunities for sexes

With the exception of space travel, probably nothing in the twentieth century has been so dramatic as the emancipation of women. Programs that do not include a gamut of recreation activities for girls of all ages are fostering the old misconception that organized sports leagues, outings, and club affiliations are for the male only. Lack of co-recreation opportunities may also send potential participants to other forms of recreation where meeting the opposite sex is a certainty.

Lack of variety in program offerings

Too much emphasis on sport activities to the exclusion of other program areas continues to support the idea that recreation consists primarily of sports and games. Physical activities are important in the total picture but must take their place as only one of many attractive and challenging recreation opportunities. Organized sports and league activity must not be allowed to dominate participation or public relations.

Overemphasis on children

The program that confines itself primarily to elementary children, with a few occasional special events for older groups, fosters in the public eye a continuation of the old image that the recreation program is designed merely to keep youngsters off the streets and out of trouble. The beginning program may start with children but must branch out to all age groups, if its obligation to the community is to be fulfilled.

Static program offerings

Many programs fail to continue to attract participants because of their inability to provide a progression of challenging activity. The child who learns to splash water colors on the easel may wish to continue to the exploration of techniques in oil painting. The oldster who learns to mold with clay may want to progress to the intricacies of ceramics. The adult who falteringly joins in square dancing at a special event may wish to pursue this pleasure to its more complicated forms. Imaginative program planning allows a progression of activities from the simple to those that take increasingly more talent, skill, or effort.

Activities for only the healthy

Failure to minister to the recreation needs of those who are mentally or physically incapacitated ignores many who most need recreation services. Cooperation with clinics, doctors, hospitals, schools, and private agencies to enlarge opportunities for the ill, the handicapped, and the retarded brings new challenges to the recreation professional.

Limited times of operation

Programs that open their doors only in the "out-of-school" hours, in the summertime or after school, are denying opportunities to the majority of the population. Such time limitations emphasize the old concept that recreation is "just for kids."

Too much organization

Some individuals resent constant ordering and organization of their activities. Programs must broaden those opportunities for individual or group use of facility or activity without direct leadership. Creating an environment in which groups may find wholesome recreation with their own leadership is a part of intelligent program planning. Too often, the recreation leader is visualized as a person who herds others into mass activity.

Lack of involvement in planning

Failure to involve participants, other agencies, activity leaders, and the community at large in the planning of the total program effort inevitably leads to dissatisfied workers; duplication of time, effort, energy, and facilities; confused participants, and a poor public image.

Lack of continuous evaluation

Directors who say they do not have time to make studies of what is happening in their recreation activities and how effectively their program is being executed are fostering the devastating misconception that recreation professionals are interested in just keeping people busy without knowing why or how. Careful surveys of the acceptance of program offerings, purposes and values, costs of activities, adequacy of areas, safety factors involved, areas of duplication of effort, and exploration of expanded program ideas are mandatory. If community leisure needs are to be successfully met, waste, misuse, and inefficiency must be avoided.

Planning in Action

Well-made plans usually bring satisfactory results; this concept is especially true in recreation. Just as the planner has an important role to play in the administration of a program, so the leader, who is responsible for putting the plans into action, has an equally important responsibility. The diversity of the recreation program and the many approaches to conducting programs make it imperative that the recreation leader have the proper training, resourcefulness, and management ability to accomplish his work.

Approaches to planning

Approaches vary as to the method of organizing and conducting activities. Agencies that have somewhat the same goals often differ as to how these goals are achieved. For instance, the Boy Scouts, Girl Scouts, and Campfire Girls have nationally prescribed programs that determine not only the program content but the methods that should be followed in carrying out the plans. Social welfare agencies are concerned with providing opportunities to their constituents through small-group activity. The social group workers seek to guide these groups in a way that will meet the needs of the individuals within the group or will help the group democratically bring about social change in the community.

The approach for carrying out the program sponsored by the park and recreation department varies according to the type of program and setting. In operating certain facilities, such as parks, tennis courts, picnic areas, beaches, and swimming pools, the department is concerned mainly with the establishment of policies, maintenance, and supervision. When a recreation department sponsors an organized camp, the amount and complexity of organization is much greater. Within each of these operations, varied methods might be used in fulfilling the objectives.

Programs can become too highly organized; when this happens, activities often become regimented and stereotyped. A program that is made up mostly of "drop-in" or unorganized activities also leaves much to be desired. Often, an overemphasis on special events tends to short-change the basic program. A balance between organized and unorganized activities should be sought.

Organizations should attempt to obtain balance in the different types of recreation activities offered. Such balance does not mean that equal portions of arts and crafts, sports and games, or other program areas should take place in every setting. Not all activities are of equal importance for given circumstances, nor do they require the same degree of supervision or the same type of organization.

Recreation activities differ as to the manner in which they are conducted as a part of the recreation program. Administrators, supervisors, and leaders should be aware of the various methods of conducting activities.

Methods of organization

Methods of organizing and conducting recreation can be generally classified as either informal or organized.

Informal activities. There are large numbers of people who desire to pursue their recreation interests on their own initiative, at their own speed, and with a minimum of interference. They wish only for a place to play, fish, hike, or read, where they may enjoy their leisure pursuit by themselves or with friends of their own choosing. Even in an organized camp program, time is needed for a child to seek relaxation or time to satisfy his inquisitive mind in exploring the wonders about him.

Informal or self-directed activities always will have an important place in recreation. They need little direct guidance and satisfy large numbers of the recreation public at a minimum of expense. An organization's responsibility with regard to informal activities may involve:

PROVISION OF ENVIRONMENT. Access to or availability of an attractive, safe, well-maintained facility in which recreation can take place may well be all that is needed for some pursuits.

SUPERVISION. In many cases, the drop-in activities, such as ping pong, jukebox dancing, and card playing in the community center need general supervision to assure wholesome participation and equal opporunity.

STIMULATION OF NEW EXPERIENCES. A leader has a challenge and responsibility, even in informal play, to whet the appetite of individuals for broader recreation horizons at home or in other settings.

PERSONAL GUIDANCE AND COUNSELING. Informal activities allow time and atmosphere for guidance and more personal attention to the problems of single individuals or small groups.

Organized activities. The main types of organized activities include clubs, classes, contests and tournaments, leagues, and special events.

CLUBS. Clubs are considered one of the basic elements of community recreation programs. They normally consist of persons who seek to associate with each other to promote some common interest or object. Club members elect their own officers, adopt a constitution, and establish qualifications for membership. There are basically two types of clubs: special-interest and general-interest.

Special-interest clubs are comprised of persons who are concerned with a particular interest such as stamp or coin collecting, model airplanes, square dancing, gardening, photography, or sailing. Age or sex is generally insignificant, since it is the interest that brings the group together that is all-important. A philatelic club normally is composed of as many persons who are beginning their stamp collections as those with substantial accumulations.

General-interest clubs are composed of persons who seek social interaction. The reason that keeps the members together is not so much the program sponsored as the chance to meet with others. Clubs of this nature may be established for most age levels. Teenage, young adult, or senior citizen clubs are examples of general-interest clubs commonly found in most communities.

Clubs can be established on a community-wide, nonsponsorship basis or may be sponsored by recreation departments, schools, settlement houses, or youth-serving agencies. When an agency sponsors a club, several different methods of organization can be used. They include:

a. complete sponsorship—agency organizes club, supplies leadership, and provides meeting place

b. provision of leadership and facilities—when enough interest is evident, the organization will provide facilities and direct guidance

c. provision of meeting place only

d. provision of leadership only

e. provision of stimulation of interest

CLASSES. Another method of conducting recreation in communities is the provision of instructional classes in various recreation pursuits. Agencies are almost unlimited as to the types of classes that can be offered. Their program should supplement the classes sponsored by the public schools in their regular school curriculums or in the adult education opportunities. When needs and interests are evident, classes should be planned, scheduled, and conducted. The success of this method of organization is based upon the quality of instructors available. Classes that are developed as a part of playground programs are generally more informal in nature than those that are given in indoor settings.

LEAGUES. Leagues are established to facilitate competition in various sports. They range from the informal intraplayground type to the highly organized and efficiently run city sport leagues. Most team sports, such as basketball, baseball, softball, volleyball, ice hockey, and soccer, are conducted on a league basis.

League play is organized on a round-robin method of competition, which provides for each team to play the other teams in the league. In double round-robin competition, games are scheduled on a "home and home" basis. The amount of organization needed in league play is largely determined by the formality desired and the number of teams taking part.

Municipal recreation departments usually guide and direct the operation of leagues in the city. In larger cities, a supervisor of sports and athletics has this responsibility. Some cities organize sport associations, which are invaluable in assisting departments in promoting leagues of various types. Associations are usually formed for the promotion of a particular sport and are composed of sport enthusiasts and team representatives. In some cases, there is a community-wide sport association that promotes all sports events. Sports leagues are prevalent for youths, adults, churches, and industries. In many communities, Little League, Babe Ruth, and American Legion baseball leagues are operated separately from the municipal program. Other cities find it beneficial for the recreation department to sponsor those leagues so that the various leagues can be better coordinated and kept in proper perspective.

CONTESTS AND TOURNAMENTS. Tournaments are series of contests that are conducted to determine winners in various activities. Most playgrounds and community centers sponsor tournaments as one of the main features of the weekly program.

Tournaments can be conducted on an informal or formal basis; they can be organized to determine a winner of a weekly event on the playground or can be used to stimulate continuous competition over a longer period of time. The type of tournament method used will be dependent upon the purposes for which the activity is conducted. Recreation leaders should be familiar with the different kinds of tournament methods and the specific advantages and disadvantages of each.

SPECIAL EVENTS. Since special events can range from a simple, spontaneous talent show around the campfire to a week-long, city-wide winter carnival, description of methods of organization that would be pertinent to all special events would be an endless task. Suffice it to say that the larger the spectacular, the more organization and coordination will be necessary. Types of special events in different settings and methods of organization are treated more fully in Chapter 17.

Virginia Musselman's Challenges to Program

Virginia Musselman, in a speech at the 42nd NRA Congress, listed the following weaknesses and inherent challenges to leaders in recreation programing.

First, many of the states and national agencies mentioned the unevenness of services—some lucky places, some lucky groups getting wonderful opportunities, and others getting little or nothing. . . . Challenge I, therefore, is the *Challenge of Distribution.*

A second weakness . . . is the failure to provide adequate programs for girls, for young married couples, for ethnic groups, particularly the Negro and the Spanish-speaking groups. . . . Challenge II, then, might be called the *Challenge of the Minorities,* whether it be the minority of sex, race, language, or interests.

A third weakness . . . was the failure to provide programs for the family as a unit. Recreation programs were accused of separating families. Challenge III, then, is the *Challenge of the Family.*

Many states and agencies pointed out what we all know—the need for recreation programs for the handicapped. . . . Challenge IV, then, is the *Challenge of the Unfortunates,* the hidden groups, with us, but all too often not *of* us.

Many states reported an overemphasis on a few sports, particularly baseball, football, and basketball, to the neglect of really good, long-term instruction in the individual sports. Challenge V, then, is Sports—not the few for the few, but the many for the many.

Closely allied with Challenge V, is the lack of physical activities that offer a personal challenge. . . . Where can boys and girls in their teens or early twenties, or any age for that matter, find anything to do these days that's adventurous, daring, and a little bit dangerous? Everyone has an instinctive need, at some period of his life, to pit himself against some force that is out of control; to find out what sort of person he is under stress; to fight natural forces. I am convinced that this unsatisfied need is behind the increasing popularity of skin diving, water-skiing, quarter midget racing, drag strips, motorcycling, motor boating, etc. None of our nice legitimate games, played with specific rules in specific limits, fill this primitive need. . . . Challenge VI—and a big one—is the *Challenge of Adventure.*

Interest in and a liking for, the great outdoors must be started early, when children's curiosity about the world around them is at its strongest. It is then that the beginnings of adventure can start, as the youngster learns how to be comfortable in and to enjoy the forests, waters, mountains, plains, and deserts. . . . Call it what you will, Challenge VII, is the *Challenge of the Wild,* and if we want to preserve our wilderness areas, we had better meet that challenge.

One of the most often stated criticisms . . . is the lack of, or inadequacy of, creative, cultural activities. Literally millions of children and youth have never seen a live play, listened to a live concert, seen a great painting or piece of sculpture, read or heard, or written poetry, seen an opera, played any form of musical instrument. Too few have had any creative outlet in painting, dancing, drama, or music. Too many receive their only art experience through the programs they passively watch on television. . . . Challenge VIII is the *Challenge of Community Culture.*

Lack of coordination between all community agencies, lack of joint planning, duplications of facilities, leadership, and programs, lack of policies for joint use of facilities were all cited as weaknesses throughout the nation. . . . Challenge IX might be called the *Challenge of Joining Hands*—the challenge of working for the good of the community, not just the good of a department or agency, whether public or private. It means change, mobility, flexibility. It means analysis, questioning, adaptability to community changes, and the keeping of a constant eye on ultimate values.

The severest indictment of recreation programs is the last. . . . Agencies have been concerned with methods rather than with social goals and social values. This then is our greatest challenge—the *Challenge of Lasting Values.* Virtue, morality, ethics, courage, courtesy, citizenship are old-fashioned words. Our children and youth are surrounded by cheap cynicism that tends to negate the good and the beautiful. . . . Behind the skills we can teach, beyond the programs we can provide, must come a deliberate, strong emphasis on the basic values of life. Let no one say that this is not the business of recreation, or that it should not be its major objective. If we place more emphasis on strength, fleetness of feet, quickness of eye and of wit, than we place on respect of human dignity, appreciation of goodness and beauty, and responsibility for the rights and privileges of all, then we are slated for oblivion, and we do not deserve the title of youth-serving, or character-building, agency.[3]

An acceptable public image of profession or program will evolve only when weaknesses are eliminated, challenges are accepted, and when satisfied program participants spread the word to others in the community.

[3] Virginia Musselman, "The White House Conference on Children and Youth—The Challenge to Program" in *Proceedings, 42nd National Recreation Congress* (New York: National Recreation Association, 1960), pp. 21–24. Reprinted by permission.

Good public relations must be founded on quality program. Honest reporting and interpretation of that sound program will eliminate misconceptions.

Changing Concepts

The recreation agency that continues to operate within the program scope deemed sufficient for the last twenty years is giving way to the agency with a more visionary outlook. Certain heartening evidences have been observed in the following areas:

1. There is an increasing awareness that agencies cannot operate as isolated units. More concepts of cooperative planning are being explored, with better programing resulting.
2. The cliché idea "What was good enough for us is good enough for our children" is being replaced by a new interest in creative ideas in facilities and program for both adults and children.
3. More emphasis is being placed on activities that allow individual expression and less on those that accent regimentation.
4. Increasing interest is being taken in the effect of a master plan upon programing. Such master plans do not discourage the initiative of the individual leaders but insure core programs of varied scope. More attention is being given to long-range planning.
5. Increased time and energy are being given to studies of program interests, effects of program on individuals and groups, unit costs of types of programing, and effect of leadership on program.
6. There is a new recognition of the need for interpretation of the recreation program and profession in twentieth-century living to give an honest and positive picture of the value of recreation to the individual and to the community.

Program planning will achieve its objectives only if the vision of its leadership expands with the fluctuating needs and interests of those who move in a constantly changing world. As amounts of leisure increase for greater numbers of people, program opportunities must keep pace by means of more and better leadership, wider varieties of challenging program ideas, and extended budgets for facilities and staff. Long-range and short-term planning are essential, if the creative, physical, cultural, and social recreation needs of individuals and groups are to be met in the modern community. We cannot be content with the status quo. Alert leaders, professionally trained, must, through quality research, continuously evaluate present offerings, explore new horizons, and plan creatively from factual data, if the recreation profession is to meet its mounting responsibilities in twentieth-century life.

SUGGESTED REFERENCES

Danford, Howard G., *Recreation in the American Community*. New York: Harper & Row, Inc., 1953.

Kraus, Richard, *Recreation Leaders' Handbook*. New York: McGraw-Hill Book Company, 1955.

Recreation for Community Living, Guiding Principles. Chicago: The Athletic Institute, 1952.

The Recreation Program. Chicago: The Athletic Institute, 1954.

"Variety is the mother of enjoyment."
BENJAMIN DISRAELI

17

Recreation Program Areas

The horizons of recreation are limitless, ranging from the simple to the complex, from the organized to the laissez-faire, from individual enjoyment to group fun, and from the mental and aesthetic to the physical. Many authors have attempted classification of recreation activities, with a variety of results. Any approach to program categorization is arbitrary and will meet with conflicting reactions. The activities in this book have been classified in eleven categories: arts and crafts; dance; drama; mental, linguistic, and literary activities; music; outdoor recreation; social recreation; sports and games; hobbies; service activities; and special events.

The many agencies that have responsibility for provision of recreation in the community have been described in the preceding chapters. The following pages introduce the recreation activities through which the organizations function. The scope, purposes, content, values, and methods of organization of the several program areas are explored.

Activities in themselves are meaningless unless they satisfy the creative, cultural, social, and physical needs and desires of people. Recreation leaders must place primary emphasis not on the activity but on what happens to individuals through the activity. Since recreation is voluntary, participants will not return to programs, and sponsoring agencies will not fulfill their objectives, unless basic recreation needs are served.

Arts and Crafts

Man's desire to express himself creatively with his hands in molding an object from clay, in weaving designs into a rug, or in sketching his imaginative creation on canvas is particularly revealing when scholars trace the development of arts and crafts through the centuries. In early times, craft objects were made primarily for utilitarian purposes. With the changing of time, cultures, and societies, the approach to arts and crafts has gradually changed.

In times of handicraft guilds, pottery, rugs, clothes, and baskets were made by skilled craftsmen, who earned their living by selling their products. Much of this work was done in the home. With the coming of the industrial age, machines gradually took over the craftsmen's jobs and left the people with a need for other creative outlets and satisfactions for personal accomplishments.

Today, arts and crafts can be found as an integral part of a community's leisure pursuits. Crafts in schools, especially in elementary education, enrich learning situations and are a source of creative experience. In the community recreation program, many outlets for arts and crafts are available in the community-center craft shop, as a part of a hobby group, on the playground, in the camp, or integrated with other cultural activities as a part of a community arts council. The vacation Bible school utilizes arts and crafts in its core program, whereas the various youth agencies, especially the Boy Scouts and Girl Scouts, consider crafts as an important part of creative development of youth. The great increase of craft hobbies, home workshops, and the sales of craft supplies provide proof of the growing interest in this area of recreation.

Scope

It is generally recognized that arts and crafts is a field that is as broad as the material available and as varied as people's imagination, curiosity, and knowledge of the various processes and characteristics of the materials with which they are working. However, the cost of materials is one factor that might limit the scope and type of activities that an agency can introduce. In recent years, the use of scrap or inexpensive materials has received increasing emphasis by agencies with limited budgets. Alert leaders and participants can find materials in the woods, on the seashore, and in the basement. Scrap materials can be procured from the carpenter's mill, linoleum store, shoe factory, or industrial plant; they provide unlimited resources of materials for a children's craft program.

Because arts and crafts appeal to people of all ages, backgrounds, interests, and abilities, there must be a wide variation of opportunities within each of the craft areas. Projects may vary from the simple uninhibited easel splashing of the two-year-old to the creative oil painting of the more mature participant. Within each area, it is possible to vary the processes in working with the material involved. Metalcraft, for example, might involve one or more of the following processes: cutting, etching, modeling, pounding, painting, or enameling. Projects can be made from inexpensive materials, such as "leftovers" from the shoe factory, or from more expensive materials, such as a quarter hide of high-grade leather, the processing of which would involve costly equipment.

A well-developed arts and crafts program should fit any pocketbook, motivate the novice as well as challenge the skilled, and involve the inept or mildly interested as well as the whole-hearted enthusiast. Opportunities for crafts in the community will vary according to the sponsoring agency and the program setting.

Values

If arts and crafts are to be considered purposeful leisure activities, more than beautiful objects must result. Crafts are more than just making things or keeping children busy. Individuals involved in these activities should be rewarded with positive values, if craft projects are to meet the real needs of all ages in our ever changing society. Some of the values that often result are:

1. *Serving as outlets for creative expression.* An arts and crafts program should be more than product-centered; it should be looked upon as being a creative experience. All people have certain creative urges. A child enjoys creating a new puppet and is thrilled by working with yarn, papier mâché, and other new materials. A creative program will encourage new activities and will stress imagination, ingenuity, and experimentation. A child molding clay or swirling water paint on paper with his fingers is stimulated to create his own object or design. Opportunities to experiment with new approaches, new materials, and new ideas are basic to creative endeavor.

2. *Offering opportunity to work with the hands.* Modern industrial society has been responsible for replacing man's individual efforts in making many of the necessities of everyday life. The urge to make something with one's own hands just for the joy of creating is strong. Howard Braucher presents the problems and the challenge as follows:

Starved, thwarted, twisted, are many of the men who have no chance to make things with their hands. A single repetitive motion day after day, year after year, does not satisfy the hand that aches to be making something that is a complete whole, that shall stand as a visible evidence of one-self as man the creator.

Call no man dull until you have seen his hands at work. Some gifted men are morons as far as their hands are concerned. Let hands be unused generation after generation and the fingers may atrophy and almost disappear.

Great as has been our waste of our natural resources in land and coal and oil, such waste is small compared to our waste of creative craft capacity in men and women for adding beauty of the world.

. . .

No recreation worker, seeking to give men and women everywhere the makings of an abundant life, can ignore what man hath wrought with his hands, what men do now in the crafts, what cravings lie deep inside men that will find satisfaction only in activity of the hands.[1]

3. *Stimulating creative hobbies.* Arts and crafts programs can develop interest, skills, and knowledges in children and adults that may provide enjoyment and satisfaction for the rest of the participants' lives. Often people become interested in some art or craft in which they have very little skill and knowledge and later develop a high degree of proficiency. As interest, knowledges, and skills in a craft become more pronounced, increased time and money are spent in pursuing the hobby.

4. *Producing therapeutic values.* Arts and crafts have certain therapeutic values for the normal as well as for the abnormal individual. Jay Broussard, Director of the Louisiana Art Commission, was very successful in his experimentation with art therapy among a group of exceptional children in Baton Rouge. Successful experiences resulted in getting spastic children to do finger painting.[2]

Crafts provide a change of pace and give satisfying, creative experiences to participants. It is agreed that such experiences usually result in the reduction of tensions of individuals and bring various desirable psychological reactions. Pounding a piece of clay into a grey elephant is often as therapeutic an outlet for aggressions as hitting a punching bag.

5. *Developing appreciation and recognition of beauty.* Although the primary emphasis of crafts should be placed on fun and the satisfaction of creating an object, leaders should constantly strive to have participants develop good taste and appreciation of beauty, form, and design. Appreciation of beauty is itself one of the highest forms of recreation. With each creative experience, a participant should further his appreciation of blending colors and shapes and should make an effort to develop better quality of work.

6. *Giving personal satisfaction—pride in accomplishment.* A boy who works hard in building a soapbox derby racer revels in joy and pride of

[1] Howard Braucher, A *Treasury of Living* (New York: National Recreation Association, 1950), pp. 137–139. Reprinted by permission.

[2] Edward Kerr, "Recreation Through Art," *Recreation*, XLVI, No. 2 (May 1952), 78.

accomplishment when others comment favorably on his finished product. A leader will get real satisfaction when he watches a group of small children proudly display their "animules" to their parents. Primary emphasis in arts and crafts, as in all other recreation activities, should be placed upon the personal satisfaction that the participating individuals derive from them.

Arts and crafts on the playground

Crafts are generally considered an integral part of a well-organized, varied playground program. In this setting, crafts are generally conducted in an informal atmosphere and employ inexpensive, easily produced projects geared to the needs and interests of children from 5 to 15 years of age. The craft program is usually conducted on tables located in a shady area adjacent to the shelter house. If space is available, crafts may be held in the shelter house, or, if the playground is conducted on a school site, in the school building. Projects offered generally require few special tools. In some cities, well-equipped arts and crafts mobile units travel from playground to playground in order to provide more adequate equipment and stimulate a higher quality of crafts. Examples of some of the types of playground crafts are: rhythm band instruments, nature leaf prints, lanyards, reed baskets, copper modeling, papier mâché masks and puppets, leather coin purses, clay modeling, and simple loom weaving. Playground crafts should be closely related to, or correlated with, other phases of the playground program. For example, making puppets and properties for puppet shows gives motivation to a craft program. Musical instruments can be made and then utilized in the music program.

Arts and crafts in camps

Arts and crafts in the camp setting should stress the use of indigenous materials to enhance the program of living in the out-of-doors. The collecting of native materials in a particular camp not only provides materials for an arts and crafts program but also increases camper awareness of nature and its resources. In the gathering of native materials, stress upon good conservation practices provides a most worthwhile by-product.

Many camps have a craft shelter or building, which serves as a storage place for materials and equipment. Craft activity can take place here or wherever the counselors and campers may choose to work in the natural setting.

Some of the arts and crafts projects that utilize native materials are: honeysuckle baskets and mats; nature prints; nature pixies; natural clay molding; carving and whittling projects, such as whistles, pins, brooms, forks, and knives. An Adirondack pack basket, a leather ax sheath, and metal tools or cooking utensils are but a few illustrations of some campcraft projects that have a utilitarian value in aiding the camper to live more effectively in the out-of-doors.

Arts and crafts in community centers

An indoor, building-centered program can offer varied arts and crafts opportunities for all age groups. The scope of the program in centers varies according to the needs and interests of the people and the facilities and leadership provided. Some centers have well-equipped craft shops, whereas others adapt rooms for craft purposes. Because of a long season, as compared to camps and playgrounds, and generally better facilities and equipment, more advanced types of arts and crafts can be offered. Crafts are often organized and conducted in classes, special-interest clubs, and workshops, under the direction of specialists.

The Fall Schedule of Activities of the Washington Community Recreation Center, Waterloo Recreation Commission, Waterloo, Iowa, indicates the wide variety of arts and crafts activities, for adults and children, which are offered as one part of this community center's total program. The day-by-day schedule of classes for adults is:

Monday
- Glass craft
- Lapidary
- Basketry and chair caneing
- Leather tooling
- Photo tinting

Tuesday
- Ceramics
- Hat making
- Woodworking

Wednesday
- Hat-making workshop
- Lapidary
- Jewelry
- Oil painting
- Upholstery

Thursday
- Water color
- Hat making
- Knitting
- Weaving
- Drawing and sketching
- Lapidary
- Pottery and ceramic sculpture
- Woodworking

Friday
- All-day painting workshop

The following activities for boys and girls, ages 6 through high school, are scheduled on Saturdays:

- Clay modeling
- Drawing and painting
- Junior lapidary
- Woodworking

Arts and crafts associations

Community-wide arts and crafts programs have received impetus and direction from the formation of arts and crafts associations in many communities. These associations or councils sometimes operate well-equipped art centers in which instructional classes are conducted, galleries are provided for exhibiting finished products, and art festivals are promoted. One of the early leaders in the arts and crafts association movement is found in Winston-Salem, North Carolina.

The Winston-Salem Arts and Crafts Association is one of the member groups of the Arts Council, Inc., of that city. The Arts Council is housed in the new million-dollar James Gordon Hanes Community Center. The Arts and Crafts Association sponsors a comprehensive program of workshops and classes for varied types of arts and crafts activities. A recent annual report published by the Association indicated that over 1,200 youths and adults took part in the instructional program offered at the Arts and Crafts Center during the year. Four terms of classes (spring, fall, winter, and summer) are scheduled each year with approximately 30 classes each term. The class offerings include: basic drawing, landscape, oil painting, portrait painting, water color, ceramics, decoupage, enameling, jewelry, lapidary, millinery, mosaics, needlework, rug hooking, and weaving. In the Art Council wing of the community center, the Craft House is operated. This store provides a sales outlet for some of the unusual handcrafted articles made at the Arts and Crafts Center.

Exhibits and festivals

The staging of an arts and crafts exhibit or festival is generally considered one of the highlights of the year for playgrounds, community centers, schools, art associations, or other organizations that present rich offerings in arts and crafts as a part of their program. Special events of this nature give opportunities for youth and adults to exhibit their work and an extra incentive for many of the community's creative hobbyists. They are also an excellent means of interpreting the arts and crafts program to the community.

Exhibits may vary from the children's playground show to a more elaborate and highly organized affair in the city's library, museum, community center, or art gallery. The successful public-relations technique of taking an exhibit "to the people" is receiving wide endorsement. Some recreation departments promote city-wide craft exhibits in downtown store windows, where thousands of shoppers pass. The Boston Arts Festival, held annually at the Public Garden in downtown Boston, is an extensive promotional affair combining all phases of the fine arts. In Red Bank, New Jersey, an Outdoor Festival of Art was staged on the main street. All kinds of arts and crafts projects were displayed. Active demonstrations, showing how a potter's wheel works or how an artist sculptures clay, added to the success of the affair. The Red Bank *Register,* in an editorial, viewed the events as follows: "The prestige of the Red Bank area as a cultural center zoomed and is still floating around in the heavens—the event was exciting, bold, and imaginative." [3]

Relationships of crafts to other program areas

Recreation leaders are in general agreement that a recreation program, whether in a camp, playground, or community center, should be an integrated, purposeful experience rather than a series of single, unrelated activities. If a handmade puppet can be utilized in a puppet show by the youngster who made it, certainly the making of the projects will be more meaningful to him. Similarly, when a group of children on a playground plan a minstrel show or stunt night, the arts and crafts groups may assist in making posters, costumes, and properties for the production.

A craft leader's role

An arts and crafts specialist or teacher is just as important to the success of a craft program as a coach is to the success of a basketball team. A teacher who is enthusiastic about his subject and sensitive to the people with whom he is working will do much to stimulate a creative craft program. His supreme role is to stimulate careful workmanship, stress originality, encourage free expression, and provide constructive guidance and inspiration.

Because of the wide range of craft activities, it is almost impossible for any one leader to be skilled in all areas. Through study, experimentation, and other aspects of in-service or formal education, a craft leader will be able to develop sufficient skills to do effective teaching. Community organizations should be ever alert to using creative hobbyists, artists, or other adults as volunteer leaders who might like to share their talents.

Dance

The word "dance" has a wide variety of meanings and conjures up diverse connotations, depending upon an individual's past associations with the term. Some kind of rhythmic expression has always been a part of man's activity. He has always danced. Early primitive dances had practical as well as aesthetic values. Man danced to worship his gods, to stimulate an emotional pitch that would catapult him into battle, to celebrate a victory, to ward off evil spirits, to communicate his feelings and ideas, or simply to release his energies. Dance has always been closely related to the folk patterns of the people, so that knowledge of the kinds of dance for a given period is often quite revealing in characterizing the life and spirit of the era.

[3] Quoted in Betty Bunn, "Art Comes to Main Street," *Recreation*, LII, No. 9 (November 1959), 382.

Through the years, dance has gained both favor and disfavor as wholesome recreation. From the primitive ritualistic dances to the occupational dances of the Middle Ages, the courtly gavottes or strict ballet of the Renaissance, the frenzied Charleston of the 1920's, the Big Apple of the 1930's, the Bunny Hop and jitterbug of World War II, to the Twist, which took society by storm in the 1960's, dance has been alternately praised or condemned; yet no social or religious organization has been powerful enough to eliminate dancing. The need to blend physical, mental, and emotional expression in rhythmic patterns is, indeed, universal.

Scope of dance in recreation

If dance is to gain its fullest potential as a program area in recreation, then a variety of offerings must be provided. The kinds of rhythmic movement must be varied in such a way that:

1. the novice as well as the more accomplished dancer may enjoy opportunities that will challenge without discouraging him;
2. there will be chances to explore simple creative rhythms or highly stylized dances;
3. chances to perform, to communicate through dance to an audience, will motivate participation and enhance enjoyment;
4. the handicapped may experience this exhilaration of dance as a recreative outlet; and
5. all age groups will have an opportunity to perform without embarrassment.

Kinds of dance activity

Many classifications of rhythmics and dance have been proposed. The types that are most frequently found within recreation programs include:

Creative rhythms. In recent years, the emphasis in all education and, indeed, in recreation has been on those experiences that allow freedom of expression for the participant. Rhythmic movement, under guidance that stimulates a child to create patterns from his own familiar experiences, helps a youngster to develop socially, mentally, and emotionally, as well as physically. Game activities or story-telling hours that whet the imagination often lead to creative dance experiments.

Alert leaders on playgrounds or in centers can do much to spark interest in creative activity by recognizing those moments when the group or an individual is ready to explore the fun of interpretation and communication through movement. Any child or adult has the basic urge and the physical equipment for this kind of activity. The leader must provide the environment in which the participant will feel free to express his ideas.

Play-party games. The play party is a distinct kind of game-dance combination that flourished in the early days of American history and lives in the pseudo-singing games of today. With frequent religious taboos on dance conflicting with the inherent desire of the early pioneers' carefree movement to music, the play party, in which words of a song gave directions for the action of the participating group, became a popular recreation activity that met the approval of the community. Young and old participated in games that took their origins from the German "Ach Ja" to the Irish "Galway Piper." The play party is extremely usable in recreation situations today because of its flexibility. Even though many of the tunes for play party activities have been recorded, the simple tunes and short verses are readily mastered by groups who enjoy singing their own musical accompaniment when the playground or camp makes electricity or public address system unavailable. The involvement of all the participants and infrequent coupling off or physical contact have made this kind of rhythmic activity popular with even the strictest of religious organizations.

Mixers. Dance activities in which couples change partners frequently have a dual purpose: the joy of moving in patterns to music and the opportunity to socialize with those who are similarly engaged. The dance mixer provides an excellent social recreation tool for large groups. Almost any kind of dance can be adjusted to provide change of partners and an opportunity to meet people. The creative leader learns to organize the program so that a few such experiences will be mingled with other kinds of dance.

One caution must be mentioned. The overzealous leader, in his goal to allow socialization for his group, must avoid two common mistakes: the inclusion of so many mixers that a couple who came to the dance together may never get a chance to be together again during the evening, and a program so jammed with activity that people who have met in a "mixer" will not be allowed time to get better acquainted. These two errors have given the "mixer" a poor reputation, which all too frequently decreases participation.

Folk dance. Folk and square dances, for a long time the outlet for the country environment and the less sophisticated American, have gained considerable popularity in the last twenty years. Festivals, television exhibitions, state dance competitions, and church approval all have helped to stimulate a revival of interest in dance patterns that have been handed down from the American pioneer or borrowed from the nations across the seas.

Tireless teachers like Lloyd Shaw, Ed Durlacher, and the Michael Hermans popularized square and round dancing during the 1930's and 1940's. The commercial opportunities in record making, square-dance calling, and spectator exhibitions also boosted the numbers involved in this kind of dance.

Unlike many of the other forms of art, such as drama and literature, folk dance was for a long time neglected. It was easy to hand down from one generation to another the beauty of a painting or the pleasure of the written word, but until the motion picture made visual recording of movement possible the folk dance lived in the hearts of the humble folk and had to be passed on through actually doing the dance. The folk dances of a different country are as diverse as the language—and just as distinctive. Part of the fun in executing the dance patterns of peoples in other lands and in other times is the knowledge of how those patterns depict the environment in which they lived, the occupations they performed, the important events of their lives, the restrictions of their faith, and their relationship with other forms of the performing arts.

The folk dances, national dances, or character dances differ from creative dance in that they are composed of specific basic patterns that must be learned. They run the gamut from the simple chain dances of the Greek Kritikos, which is reminiscent of the pastoral features of the rolling terrain, to the Irish lilts with their vertical movement and swift footwork, to the Lithuanian occupational Kalvelis dance, which depicts the smithy, to the more intricate Swedish Hambo. The beauty of the typical folk music stimulates participation, if intelligent leadership emphasizes the spirit of the dance as much as excellence of execution of the steps, particularly for beginners.

Square dance. Though it has its origins in the quadrille from across the sea, square dance is the only truly American folk dance, if one discounts the fads that have come and gone since the pioneer days. It evolved from the restrictions placed upon dance by the church in the early days of the nation and grew from the singing games and play-party patterns sanctioned by the church.

The popularity of square dancing has been increased by its inclusion in the school physical-education programs. Square-dance clubs for all ages have been promoted in agency, private, and municipal recreation programs. The format for the square dance remains fairly constant: introduction, basic dance sequence, break, and ending. Although the dance patterns are similar, there is opportunity for creative changes in the introductions, endings, and breaks. The music is lively, and the dance moves at a rapid pace. An earlier tendency to dress in Western attire to perform the dance has moved toward simplicity and variety of costume with the only criterion that of freedom of movement. Styles of dance patterns, calls, music, and costuming vary in different sections of the nation. Dance calls are sometimes as distinctively revealing as provincial dialects.

Square-dance calling. The art of square-dance calling has assumed such importance in today's dance world that state and national associations have arisen. Many persons have made a full-time career of teaching and calling square dances. Periodicals, trade magazines, instructional manuals, films, and promotional materials have flooded the market. Institutes, camps, conferences, workshops, and nation-wide tours have been arranged by popular leaders in the calling profession. Record suppliers have been quick to capitalize on the new demands for recorded music, and clothing manufacturers and jewelry designers have catered to the square-dance trade by supplying colorful costumes and insignia.

The longways set, or contra. The longways dance or New England contra is patterned after the old English reels. It is usually performed with about eight couples in straight lines but may be done with as few as six or as many as twenty-four. The caller stands at the head of the line, with ladies at his left and gentlemen at his right. In some dances, every other couple from the head of the line exchange places. Ralph Paige did much to popularize these dances in New England. They are less well known in other sections of the country. Contras vary from the extremely simple to the complicated. Excellent instruction is needed; all too frequently "Hull's Victory," a popular contra, becomes Hull's defeat because of inadequate or overcomplicated directions.

Kentucky running sets. Popular in the hills of Kentucky and spreading to the Midwest is the running set, a circle dance in which the caller is usually a part of the dance group. The dances are fast moving and energetic. Berea, Kentucky, features many such sets each year at its annual folk dance festival.

Couple dances or round dances. Lloyd Shaw and his Colorado enthusiasts renewed the popularity of the old time couple dances—the waltz, schottische, polka, or mazurka steps inspired by music of yesterday. Some of the basic steps have been and are still popular in the so-called social dance area, but the term "couple dance" here relates to the progression of specific patterns such as the Varsouvianna, the Rye Waltz, the Boston Two-Step, or the Texas Schottische. For years, the International Folk Festival at Chicago was not complete without an exhibition couple dance by Lloyd "Pappy" Shaw and one of his charming partners.

Social dance. The social dance has had a long period of struggle for approval and recognition. Although dances that allowed physical contact between the sexes were frowned upon by some religious groups, who felt that such proximity might prove a vestibule for further intimacy, such stigma have been slowly removed by all but a very few church groups.

The social dance, perhaps more than any of the other types, reveals the spirit of the times. Colonial restrictions and severity were evident in the stately minuet for the aristocracy; the barn dance offered an expression of the exuberance of the frontier. The eighteenth century saw the polka, the lancers, the military march, the quadrille, and finally the two-step in a revealing fluctuation between formalism and freedom of expression. The uncertainties of the wars and the depression brought such fads as the Charleston, the Conga, the Black Bottom, the Susie Q, the Mambo, the Stroll, the Hokey Pokey, and—as the Russians proceeded with a series of tests on 10- to 50-megaton bombs—in 1961, the Twist, executed, according to one graphic description, "by simulating the action of rubbing your lower back with a towel while trying to put out a cigarette with your right foot."

Those who have seen the rise and fall of popularity of the social dance find some reasons for such fluctuations. In the 1930's, when name dance bands could be hired at reasonable prices for college campuses, recreation halls, and special money-making projects, attendance at social dances was at an all-time high. Thirty years later, when popular stars were available on television, on the motion-picture screen, and on excellent recordings, high-school and college dances had difficulties in attracting enough participants to meet expenses.

Other problems arise in the changing customs at social dances. The absence of mixers, exchange dances, and opportunities for socialization has made the present social dance the least social of all of the types. John escorts Mary to the dance, dances each dance with her, and takes her home. Another obvious deterrent to the popularity of social dance is the seeming lack of skill on the part of the male population. School programs that fail to include dance in the boys' education, while including it in the girls', encourage the status quo. Too frequently, the emphasis in both school and community opportunities for boys is away from dance and toward sport activities. *Both are important*; such an attitude must be promoted by example as well as by word.

Modern dance. Ashton, noted dance instructor, states:

The spotlight on theater dance in this century is focused on "modern dance." Using the body freely as a medium of expression, modern dance is concerned with contemporary subject matter. It dares to be realistic instead of merely pretty, it dares to explore movement and space, and it dares to communicate by the use of emotional, psychological, sociological, and political problem themes. Contrary to some popular belief, modern dance has developed excellent techniques, basic principles, and sound philosophies of movement. These developments did not arise overnight. They were rooted deep in our cultural heritage to be drawn upon when the time and the place demanded their use.[4]

In the early years of the century, Ruth St. Denis and Ted Shawn emerged as leading exponents of a new American contribution to dance. Other creative artists like Charles Weidman, Martha Graham, Doris Humphrey,

[4] Dudley Ashton, "Dance History," *Journal of Health, Physical Education, and Recreation*, XXVII, No. 9 (December 1956), 21. Reprinted by permission.

and Martha Hill continued to popularize the new dance form, which allowed freer expression, fewer restrictions in technique, and a real challenge to explore and make use of the capabilities of the body. Many community agencies include modern dance classes for children and teenagers. Others promote attendance at dance presentations as spectator recreation. Modern dance, like modern art, must be understood to be appreciated. Education in the art of communication through freely expressed body movements will increase the numbers who can enjoy active or spectator participation in modern dance.

Ballet. The rigid technique of ballet requires many long hours of practice. Many dance teachers who are exponents of freer modes of expression in movement criticize the ballet as too formal, too restricted, and too disciplined. As a recreation offering, ballet is still popular among the 8- to 12-year-old girls, who endure hours of exacting practice for the thrill of a performance behind the footlights. The San Diego Park and Recreation Department reports increasing success with its ballet program, initiated in 1947. Participants advance to the Junior Civic Ballet, which closely allies its program with other cultural offerings of the department.

Acrobatic, tap, clog dancing. Although the popularity of these types of dances has waned in the last twenty years, they are often combined with other activities, such as baton twirling. The 1930's and the 1940's spurred the desire for tap dancing, in particular, as Gene Kelly, Fred Astaire, and Ginger Rogers tapped their way into the hearts of the people through the motion picture screen. Small communities that indulge in frequent home-town talent shows often provide a stimulus for classes and clubs in such activities.

Values in dance

Dependent upon the type of dance, the values and rewards move from opportunity for free expression to the satisfaction of submitting to the rigid discipline of exacting patterns. Inherent in most dancing done or seen for recreation are the following values:

1. Improved understanding of and control over body movement.
2. Exhilarating physical, mental, and emotional exercise, as thoughts and feelings are translated into movement.
3. Development of poise.
4. Relief of tension and a sense of accomplishment and personal enrichment.
5. Increased interest in music as an art form.
6. Improved understanding of dance forms.
7. Fulfillment of basic need for rhythmic outlets.

8. Cultural development as appreciations of other ethnic groups are realized.

In addition, modern dance develops freedom of expression, ability to use the imagination, creative skills, and understandings of people and how they express themselves. Folk dance also challenges better understanding of other cultures. Square dance, running sets, and contras lay emphasis on the social rewards, as does the social dance. Ballet, acrobatic, tap, and clog dancing develop rhythmic accuracy and disciplined control.

Organizational patterns for dance in the community program

The method of organization and extent of the dance offerings in the recreation program vary with the felt need, the leadership available, and the facilities at hand. The following are those types most commonly experienced:

1. *Classes.* Instructional classes in tap, modern, social, square, folk, and creative dance are found in many communities. Classes are usually arranged by age groupings. Square dance for the aged has become extremely popular as have the instructional classes in social dance for the middle-aged who are being sidelined by their teenage offspring.

2. *Drop-in centers with dancing offered for noon hour, after school, or evening informal activity.* A juke box or record player and enough floor space of smooth surface provide all that is needed for the pre-teen and teen-age sets in some communities.

3. *Clubs.* Folk, square and modern dance clubs, square-dance calling clubs, and family dance clubs offer consistent progression for those who would like to learn more challenging dances. They also offer opportunities for sustained interest in dance in industrial or hospital settings.

4. *Camps.* Camps in which dance is the main program offering in the outdoor setting have been popular as private ventures. The Michael Herman Folk Dance Camp exemplifies this type of organization, where in a natural environment the participants are steeped with the food, customs, and cultural tastes of other lands as well as their representative folk dances.

5. *Special events.* Community-center holiday dances, street dances on the playground areas, barn dances, social dance specials in the hospitals, disc-jockey nights in the teen centers, and cake walks all offer "specials" for dancing enthusiasts.

6. *Dance theater.* Some larger communities have been successful with dance theater for both adults and children. The Salt Lake City Dance Theater, a Mormon group, has gained national acclaim. Dance theater demands a high degree of achievement for a few performers and provides

fringe-area involvement for many more. It offers the chance to delight hundreds of spectators or to whet their appetites for active participation.

7. *Festivals.* Local, state, national, and international festivals have given large numbers of dancers of all ages an additional purpose for perfecting their talents. The annual state folk and square dance festival in Vermont, stimulated by Theresa Brungardt, the State Director of Recreation, increases in numbers of participants each year. Since 1936, the University of Pennsylvania has sponsored its Cultural Olympics, in which dance plays a major role. Indiana's State Fair provides impetus for square dancers throughout the state to come together for a festival.

8. *Dance for special groups.* The handicapped are no less desirous of experiencing the exhilaration of dance than are the normal. Much progress has been made in the last few years in wheel-chair dancing and other modifications.

Integration of dance with other program areas

The possibility of combining dance with drama, arts and crafts, and music is obvious. Productions such as any of the Broadway musicals, when transferred to the local stage, involve craftsmanship for stage settings and involvement of dance specialties with the music and the drama. Talent shows on playgrounds or in community centers give opportunity for solo, dual, or group performances. Even certain sports have resorted to dance to develop and discipline the movement and control of the human body.

Problems and pitfalls

The dance, like so many of the other performing arts, has found somewhat less than overwhelming support for its many program possibilities. Some areas of concern include:

Misconceptions about modern and creative dance. The picture of modern dance as uninhibited, undirected, undisciplined, and unfathomable has caused many to turn to other art forms for their creative expression. Social conditioning to the effect that this kind of dance is something "not for the boys" keeps the interested male from daring to participate. The use of ballet and modern dance as conditioning exercises for football players in two southern universities may eventually change this attitude. The truth of the matter is that dance of any sort is anything but "sissy" fare; it is rigorous, demanding, energetic use of the whole body. The generous use of dance on television programing may stimulate participation of both sexes as will the increasing tendency to hire male dance specialists.

Too much emphasis on expertism. Dance leaders sometimes kill the spirit of the participant by prolonged attention to the details of movement. Knowledge of the dance is necessary to find success and satisfaction, but too much concentration on "this is the authentic way," particularly in the folk dance field, has driven many to seek their fun elsewhere. By the same token, cliques of expert and polished square dancers may discourage the casual participant if they are allowed to "take over" in open dances. Special clubs will permit expert dancers to pursue their excellence without embarrassment or discouragement to others.

Monotonous music for square dance. For many years, potential square dancers refrained from the activity because they could not tolerate the monotonous beat of the "hoedown" music. Today's recordings for square dance are much more melodic and are attracting dancers from urban and rural sections, although some traditionals stick to the repetitious beat of the banjo and the fiddle.

Unfavorable social connotation of square dance. Square dance was, for a period of time, synonymous with "hillbilly" and "hick" for some groups. The costume of dungarees and boots furthered such an image and kept the urban group from the fun of square dance because of social prestige.

Anti-social social dances. Absence of informal coupling devices, mixers, and exchange dances plus lack of instructional classes make the high school or club dance a frightening and unfriendly affair for many. The overemphasis on formal clothes at early ages also keeps some away for economic reasons.

Lack of interested and skilled leaders. Too few men and women are being trained for teaching in the several dance areas. Too often the promotion and teaching of this special field are thrust upon an employee whose main talents, interests, and sympathies are elsewhere. The literature, too, has done dance an injustice. Some recreation program books give dance scanty treatment or completely omit it as a special program division.

Ray of hope for the future

The television and film bombardment of all kinds of dance gives the average child a heavier exposure to this program area than was previously possible. The increased numbers of schools that include dance in both the boys' and girls' physical-education classes, beginning in the elementary schools, cultivate a taste for further experiences in rhythmic expression. The initiation of more dance curriculums at the college level will provide more and better leaders as specialists. Camps such as the University of Kansas Fine Arts Camp, which started in 1925 as a music camp and now draws young enthusiasts of the performing arts from 40 states, help to spread the interest in dance. National emphasis on all the performing arts will stimulate more and better opportunities at the local level. The language of dance is a universal one that knows no boundaries. Intelligent and inspired leadership is needed to promote its use as a truly recreative outlet.

Drama

The world of make-believe holds an eternal magic for young and old. From the primitive caveman's early story-telling efforts through the ancient Greek dramatic classics to the ceremonial religious rites of the American Indian, drama has brought pleasure to people. From the cobbled innyards of Elizabethan England through the Mississippi showboats to the modern-day Broadway stage, television, and movie houses, the world of the theater has remained an enchanted realm in which humanity at large has found peculiar fascination.

Man's need to communicate with his fellow man, to share his thoughts, his emotions, and his problems, has been a constant motivation for expression. The art of dramatic communication, whether evidenced in the child's "let's pretend" or in Judith Anderson's emotional portrayal of Lady Macbeth, provides a vast, fertile area for recreation programing. Drama for recreative outlets should offer broad horizons for the talented or for the uninspired, since all who dare to explore the area find it one of the most challenging and rewarding of the performing arts.

Horizons

Community recreation programs should give attention to adequate areas, facilities, and leadership for the gamut of dramatic opportunities for young and old. They should extend from improvisation of imaginative story telling to polished performances of the written word in full-scale theatrical productions, which benefit the audience as well as the performers; from the "imagination stirrers" in the playgrounds, centers, camps, and parks to the simplest or the most elaborate community theater; from play reading to play going. Each participation, each setting, or each attendance at a performance should provide a step in a progression of opportunities in dramatic activity ranging from the simplest to the most sophisticated tastes, for all ages. The recreation program should include any and all activities in which there is opportunity for the individual to project himself in vocal and motor self-expression.

Why drama?

Drama, in its broadest sense, embodies one of the most universal of human interests. The love of the theater and the spark in the eyes of creative artists are the same, the world over. A sense of the dramatic is as necessary for enriched living as a sense of humor. Child and adult alike enjoy the release of being someone else, if only for a few moments; and the vicarious thrill, the empathy, of identifying with others who are performing can bring as great a pleasure.

Perspective

The emphasis in recreation drama is on the individual, not the vehicle. The important thing is not what the child or adult does to drama, but what drama does to the performer. Such a philosophy does not necessarily deny the value of performances that present a challenge and require polish. Community recreation is broadening opportunities for better quality as well as for more varied programs in drama. The expansion of leadership, facilities, and emphasis at the national level in such ventures as the National Cultural Center in Washington, D.C., is doing much to create an enthusiastic two-way avenue of inspiration and ideas from the local effort to the national organizations.

Kinds of dramatic programs

The scope, organization, and types of dramatic programs will depend on the sponsoring agency's philosophy and objectives and on its available leadership, areas and facilities, and budget. It is reasonable to suppose that camps, playgrounds, community centers, youth-serving agencies, churches, hospitals, and industries might offer some, if not all, of the following activities.

Informal dramatics. This term is applied most frequently to all those experiences in which ideas, events, or stories are improvised with action and/or dialogue without formal scripts, without rehearsal, and with or without the guidance of an adult leader. The following are examples of some program possibilities.

1. CREATIVE DRAMATICS. Scenes and stories that are developed through uninhibited expression of individual ideas and feelings form the realm of creative dramatics. Scenery and costumes are rarely used, and audiences are either nonexistent or incidental. The inherent sense of make-believe and the freedom of expression of children provide a fertile field for educational and recreation growth through creative dramatics as they "try on life" with the uninhibited abandon that only a child knows. Stimulation for creative dramatic situations might come from the leader who offers a small group of youngsters three objects with the casual question, "Now who do you think would use these things? What would they do?" The children react, become the characters who use such objects, and "the play is on." Other impetus might come from simply playing a record and then asking what kinds of things the music makes the youngsters feel. Adults, too, find enjoyment in creative drama. Recreationists in hospital settings are strong in their praise of this outlet for mental patients.

2. STORY TELLING. Vivid unfolding of a story is a dramatic activity at any age. *Reading or telling stories* of fact or fiction to elicit an emotional response from the audience is effective. *Songs* in which the group uses music and lyrics to express dramatic dialogue are popular. *Story plays,* in

which the listeners in groups or as a whole react with an action or dialogue on cue from the story teller, intrigue both young and old. *Imitative audience participation*, in which the group imitates words and actions of the leader, makes stunts like the "Lion Hunt" perennial favorites.

3. DRAMATIC GAMES. Many dramatic games have evolved from folk customs, ceremonial rituals, or political satires of former years. *Active and quiet games* based on the acting or speaking ability of individuals or groups are illustrated by such activities as "New Orleans" or "Charades." *Singing games* such as "Farmer in the Dell" combine song and drama through action directed by lyrics sung by the participants.

4. SKITS AND STUNTS. Skits and stunts can vary from the simple to the complex. All involve an informal portrayal of some situation. *Pantomimes*, the comic or serious expression of ideas through movement without words, form the basis of games, stunts, skits, or full-scale artistic productions. *Shadow plays*, playing out scenes behind a backlighted sheet in dark areas, are popular for parties and campfires. Creating a skit in a group, using a bag of objects as props, makes for exciting and often hilarious *nosebag drama*. The *record pantomime*, in which individuals perform by mouthing words soundlessly with appropriate gestures as a record plays, has gained recent popularity for informal fun or for talent shows.

5. FACILITY- OR EQUIPMENT-CENTERED ACTIVITIES. Mere availability of proper tools and environment will often inspire dramatic creativity. *Imagination stirrers* such as a trunk of old clothes and shoes or an old fire truck may instigate much impromptu dramatic play. The *sandbox* offers scenes for a battleground or a cave dwelling. *Finger puppets* can inspire unexpected hours of social and dramatic activity. *Campfires* offer opportunities for ceremonials or simply an imaginatively dramatic lighting of the fire.

Formal activities. More highly organized vehicles for displaying histrionic ability or for pleasing an audience are also within the responsibility of the recreation program. Such offerings present opportunities for development of talent, continuity of productions, rigor of rehearsal schedules, and a diverse choice of means for making an impact on the audiences available. Community programs throughout the country often offer one or more of the following types of production.

1. CHORAL SPEAKING GROUPS. All ages enjoy the opportunity to speak together in unison for dramatic depiction of story or mood.

2. TALENT SHOWS. One of the most enchanting of audience attractors is the show in which each child or adult displays his talent in music, dance, or drama with forceful showmanship.

3. PUPPET AND MARIONETTE SHOWS. Often the person who is reluctant to perform on stage will lose himself in the character of the puppet or marionette which he manipulates and into whose personality he projects without the necessity of facing an audience.

Fig. 23   *Puppet Theater—Austin, Texas*

4. MUSICALS, OPERETTAS, AND MINSTRELS. The combination of dance, music, or blackface joke-telling is popular and versatile in its offering for performer or audience.

5. CARNIVALS, CIRCUSES, AND PAGEANTS. The color and fanfare of the barker at the carnival booth, the portrayal of animal or trainer, and the special zest of the spirited pageant are dramatic special events.

6. RADIO AND TELEVISION SHOWS. Radio and television give challenges for creating and performing dramatic and informative productions for the listening and viewing public.

7. ONE-ACT OR THREE-ACT DRAMAS. The formal production on a stage of carefully prepared plots gives excellent experience in dramatic communication to those who have large or small parts.

8. PLAY TOURNAMENTS. Although drama is most frequently considered noncompetitive, some communities have stimulated interest in dramatic activity on regional or state levels by sponsoring play contests to determine excellence in acting, staging, and directing.

9. PLAY-READING AND PLAY-GOING CLUBS. Popular response has been given many programs in which individuals gather to read plays or to attend plays and discuss them afterwards.

10. INSTRUCTIONAL CLASSES. Cities that have offered classes in acting, make-up, or stage design have found an increasing interest from people of all ages.

Values in recreation drama

The values derived from dramatic experiences vary with the type of offering and the people involved. Here are benefits that could come from informal or formal productions.

1. *Socializing influence.* Dramatic effort is rarely solitary. The improvisation or the play interrelates and integrates a group of performers, whether they are five-year-olds dramatizing a nursery rhyme or forty-year-olds preparing *The Taming of the Shrew* for public performance. Drama is as much a team effort as any team sport. It is an experience in being an integral part of a successful undertaking, a practice in strongly motivated social cooperation.

2. *Understanding others.* Creation of a character makes mandatory a careful observation of people: how they act, how they feel, and how they show their emotions. In an impromptu skit or in a formal show, the individual must be subordinated for the good of the group. He obtains a better understanding of people and a deeper human sympathy through analyzing characters and situations.

3. *Therapy.* Losing oneself in another's character and problems is healthful and constructive. Drama gives the supreme opportunity for self-expression and for controlled emotional response. Many aggressions and tensions are released as the actor loses himself in the art of dramatic communication. The youngsters in the sandbox fighting wars with tin soldiers, the teenagers actively involved in charades, or the adults manipulating marionettes allow themselves the luxury of full expression often impossible in their other choices of activity. Role playing has long been an effective

technique for investigation and problem-solving in the fields of sociology and psychology. Whole-hearted surrender to a characterization can be just as therapeutic an outlet for the normal as for the disturbed individual.

4. *Personality development.* Cooperation, responsibility and loyalty to a common enterprise gain new importance as the performers learn that even the star of the show cannot shine successfully if the "bit" player forgets his cue. Drama gives a maximum of opportunity for conditioning attitudes and group reaction, and for developing imagination.

5. *Fun.* Drama is creative and recreative. The sheer joy of pretending, the abandon of assuming a new identity, the challenge of creating a new stage design, the pride in achievement of a measure of success, and the lift that comes from an audience reaction are just a few of the satisfactions that make drama a potent part of pleasure-packed recreation programing.

6. *Demand for a variety of talents.* Productions, formal or informal, require more than the vocal or motor talents of the actors. The individual who identifies with the theater, who is lured by the smell of greasepaint, but is reluctant or untalented in the communication of ideas, finds a niche in staging, costuming, ticket selling, lighting, promotions, or any of the other phases so necessary to the total program.

7. *Widening of appreciations and capacity for recognition of beauty in dramatic art.* With each brush with creative expression, with each opportunity to see or to participate in dramatic efforts of quality, comes a keener sense of appreciation of fine art, the discriminating taste for doing or seeing the best. In these days of constant exposure to the mediocre in television, on the stage, and on the screen, community recreation programs have a solemn challenge to offer opportunities for developing standards by which individuals may judge and choose their dramatic menu.

8. *Tools for integration of other program areas.* Drama becomes the melting pot for utilizing many of the other program offerings. The playground pageant or the Little Theater offers a culminating outlet for talents in the interest areas of crafts, music, dance, or service. A touch of drama adds to the sports play day or the camp hike, as awards are made or pioneers are challenged.

Settings and emphases

Drama in one form or another has proved popular in communities both large and small.

Drama on the playground. Storytelling by the playground leader or by a specialist who travels from playground to playground is the most common dramatic activity in this setting. *Weekly themes* around which activities are centered promote playground dramatics. In an effort to stimulate growth through self-initiated activity, the Bristol, New Hampshire, playground staff experimented with a "theme-of-the-week" plan. An "Early Settlers' Week" included outlets for costuming, building, and staging a Town Meeting, whereas a Pirate Week produced puppet shows and a pageant.

The *sandbox* provides inspiration for much creative and imaginative play. The tree-stump throne or the horizontal telephone pole in which a succession of seats has been gouged may inspire characterizations from fairy princesses to the posse after the latest television badman. Other more elaborate equipment to stimulate dramatic play is found in the new *creative playground equipment*. The Oakland, California, seahorse swing or the Jamison moon-rocket climbing apparatus proved enchanting bases for imaginative activity. Even the playground slide of yesteryear takes on new dramatic dimension when the child emerges through the wide-open mouth of a friendly whale.

Scrappy, the playground finger *puppet*, may give directions for cleanup or become a part of a puppet theater made from shoebox staging. Children have an effervescent desire to join the land of make-believe. It takes only mild stimulation to produce results in daily dramatic games or to finish the season with a culminating pageant. *Special events* in costume days, carnivals, and the like often provide a concentration of interest and effort in the dramatic aspects of programing.

Drama in the community center. The indoor center can stimulate winter activity through play-reading clubs, play-going clubs, creative dramatic classes, radio and television productions, talent shows, classes in stage design, instruction in dramatic technique, experience in make-up application, or one-act play tournaments with professional critiques. Often, the indoor centers provide extension of the school dramatic program.

Drama at camp. The camp provides an excellent setting for drama. A flickering campfire or a grove of trees at the foot of a hill sets the mood for inspirational performances never dreamed of on a wooden stage. Shadow stunts, ceremonials, and simple pageants are all popular. From the spectacular lighting of the campfire with a ball of fire seemingly dropped from the sky, through the humorous skits from the camp units, to the quiet notes of "Day Is Done" as the fire dies, the campfire program is drama-packed.

Show wagons. The traveling theater on wheels, gaining in popularity in many communities, is reminiscent of the old English guild carts from which the fifteenth-century mystery and morality plays were shown to audiences on street corners. Inexpensive, versatile show wagons can be formed on the flatbeds of trucks. Permanent wagons with dressing rooms and more ornate lighting and stage sets have also found favor in community programs. The stagemobiles move with ease to all parts of the city for "one-night stands."

The show wagon at Evansville, Indiana, has played to capacity audiences for years. The Boston Children's Theater stagemobile is available for individuals or groups during the summer months.

Children's theater. In 1953, the Children's Theater Conference, a division of the American Educational Theater Association, appointed a seven-man committee to interpret terms applied to drama done with and for children. The resulting interpretation describes children's theater as:

plays, written by living actors for child audiences. The players may be adults, children, or a combination of the two. Lines are memorized, action is directed, scenery and costumes are used.[5]

Many communities sponsor children's theater with a threefold purpose: giving the opportunity for children to learn through performance, offering the educational and emotional experience of watching a story come to life on stage, and fostering children's interest in artistic entertainment of all kinds.

The Children's Theater in Oak Park, Illinois, is co-sponsored by the playground and recreation board and the board of education of the public elementary schools. A council of 25 adults assists in selection and evaluation of programs. The director of recreation acts as chairman of the council. The program, considered one of the most successful, attracts over a thousand children each year.

Little theater. Many community programs sponsor or help sponsor separate theater operations for the increasingly popular formal production.

The little theater movement correctly designates the amateur production growth, for it was born and has grown because of people's love for drama as a community expression. Its origin may be traced to the classic drama of Greece, which was more closely allied to community drama than to the professional theater as we know it today. The little theater movement in America began in 1906 and 1907 with three groups of Chicago players. In the next fifteen years, scores of theaters mushroomed in rebuilt barns or bowling alleys from coast to coast.

Growth of community drama continues to spiral. Present statistics show numerous companies operating in rural and urban settings, from the art theater of the Cleveland Playhouse (now given professional status) to the Spartansburg Little Theater in Spartansburg, North Carolina. Some community theaters are sponsored by the municipal recreation departments;

[5] American Educational Theater Association, Committee on Interpretation, unpublished mimeographed material.

others are operated independently by private boards; still others are jointly operated by the recreation department and other agencies. The methods of organization, operation, and financing vary, as do the kinds of facilities used.

State tournaments. State tournaments and festivals often provide impetus for accelerated interest in dramatic efforts. The office of the state recreation director in Vermont sponsors an annual one-act play festival "to encourage little theater groups to do better work." Critique sessions follow each night's performance, and competition runs high for the citations awarded to best actor, best actress, best staging, and best direction. Outstanding judges are secured, and the festival attracts large groups of all ages. The Mormon church holds national and international drama festivals.

Instructional classes. Classes in acting technique, make-up, set design, and direction prove popular with teenagers, post-teens, and adults. Community centers find such classes a good "feeding system" for the little theater groups.

Puppet theater. The Oakland, California, hand puppet and marionette shows are transported to playgrounds and centers via a colorfully painted circus trailer with the puppet stage at one end and the marionette stage at the other.

Facilities, equipment, and supplies

The necessary tools for drama in its simplest form involve a place, some potential participants, and an inspired leader. The surroundings in which recreation drama takes place may vary from the community center lounge to the community-owned theater. For productions, formal or informal, the major concern is obtaining an area, free from distraction, in which atmosphere can be created. On the playground, some shady area backed by trees or bushes may suffice, or a piece of imaginative equipment may set the mood. In the natural setting of a camp, one needs only to find an open space before the proscenium of nature's backdrop. In the park, the foot of a sloping hill may produce a natural amphitheater, or a more permanent facility, such as Philadelphia's Robin Hood Dell, may be erected for the performing arts. The community playhouse may be as unpretentious as the community-built Birmingham, Michigan, theater or as complex as the Pasadena Playhouse. Recent experiments with "theater in the round" have proved that even a dining hall may provide an effective stage setting.

Equipment and supplies may vary from the meager to the elegant. The minimum requirements for productions demand some kind of lighting, intelligently used; some interchangeable flats for set design; a curtain; and a make-up kit.

Leadership

Until recent years, there has been a distinct void in leadership for recreation drama. The trend in most community programs is now to upgrade the dramatic program and broaden its scope. Municipal departments are looking for the leader who is trained in the philosophy of recreation and knowledgeable about the scope of recreation programs. He must be a master of the special techniques of acting, directing, and staging, but must also be capable of motivating simple and creative dramatic activities.

Needs in leadership. Every face-to-face leader on playgrounds, in camps, community centers, or hospitals should have some basic awareness of the informal dramatic activities possible in his profession. No program can effectively grow through specialists without the firm roots of the enthusiasm of the leader who sees his group from day to day and is willing to experiment even in areas in which he lacks confidence. The poor example of his leaders often causes the child who played Robin Hood with zest in the fifth-grade production to avoid the senior play or the community drama festival. Social conditioning and enthusiastic personnel, on the other hand, may alert the youngster to the pleasures in dramatic productions that he can enjoy all of his life.

Drama supervisor. If the drama program is to progress, it needs the stimulation of a special supervisor who can motivate, guide, and direct a progression of activities. Recreation drama should not deny opportunities to those who delight in pursuing and developing their dramatic activity to its most complex forms. The supervisor instigates and guides the informal programs but also develops the talents of those who desire a more challenging outlet for their dramatic interests.

Special problems in leadership. Possibly the greatest deterrent to effective promotion of dramatics in the recreation menu is the persistent feeling of the average recreation leader that he has no histrionic ability and is, therefore, unable to instigate or lead dramatic activities. Such reluctance can be successfully reduced by the drama supervisor or the recreation administrator through leadership institutes in dramatics. Institutes of this type should confine themselves to simple, informal dramatic activities. The leaders, having experienced success and fun, will carry away from the institute not only ideas of what activities to do and how to accomplish them, but a sudden realization that, after all, there's a little "ham" in almost everyone. Coupled with this realization comes the philosophy that every leader has a responsibility for the dramatic program area.

Community departments are becoming increasingly aware of the need for budget, special stimulation, facilities, and expert leadership in drama. With the increase in the demand for recreation dramatists, colleges and universities must produce leaders who can function as experts in formal dramatic production but who are sufficiently steeped in the philosophy and programing principles of recreation that they do not become too perfectionist-minded or too "long-haired" about all phases of recreation drama.

Another major concern of leaders who wish to produce amateur stage shows is the lack of good vehicles whose royalties are within reach of the meager budget. Most amateurs enjoy the thrill of audience reaction to their performance. Long hours of rehearsal are worthwhile because of the excitement of opening night. A play, after all, is a tool of communication. To perform without an audience is to diminish greatly the satisfaction and the pleasure of the performer. In most instances, however, royalties must be paid, even if no admission fee is charged, if the drama is presented before an audience. Frequently, because royalty charges for excellent plays have been prohibitive, directors have had to use dramas that are less expensive, yet less meaningful, less challenging, and less pleasurable for both actors and audience.

Integration of drama with other program areas

Almost every phase of programing can carry a dramatic overtone, if the leader capitalizes on the emotional possibilities of the moment. There are also many ways in which drama can be integrated with other areas in planned programs. Some examples of integration are included in the following chart (Fig. 24).

Fig. 24   *The Many Facets of Drama*

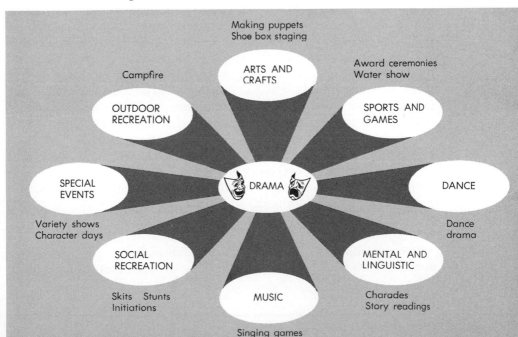

Progress report

A recent study that proposed to determine what dramatic activities are being carried on by public recreation departments throughout the United States presented a heartening picture of increased emphasis on a variety of programs in recreation drama. Thirty-six different kinds of dramatic activities, ranging from creative story telling to casting bureaus and costume services, revealed new interest and imagination in community drama in all age groups and in a variety of situations. Heartening, too, was the information that, in the majority of cases studied, the recreation budget was the most frequent source of funds. Drama, it seems, is assuming its rightful place as a wholesome recreation outlet that is worthy of a just share of leadership, facilities, and budget.

Literary, Mental, and Linguistic Activities

Few recreation activities could be described that would in no way make demands upon mental perception or linguistic ability. Just as there is rhythm in almost every recreation outlet, so there is also a thought process or a language emphasis. In the categories of music, drama, social recreation, and hobbies, for example, there may be many opportunities for mental activities. Puzzles are tried at a picnic; skits are written for dramatic production; mathematical hobbies are pursued; or musical memory quizzes are attempted. There are recreation activities that cannot be categorized elsewhere, however, which emphasize mental, linguistic, or literary efforts. These activities comprise this special category.

A child who has learned to love reading may travel to the ends of the earth without leaving his fireside. The teenager who spends his leisure in composing short stories enjoys the thrill and achievement of creative experience. The adult who masters a foreign language through individual study finds stimulating mental exercise. Many of these activities demand no audience and no cohort. Study, research, creative writing, reflective contemplation, and the like, can best be enjoyed in solitude. The home, the school, the church, and the recreation agencies can only hope to stimulate in their participants a desire for such individual enjoyment. Other mental and literary activities may involve several persons as the need arises to communicate, to display new skills or knowledge, or to compete against other minds. Recreation agencies have found success in offering the following opportunities that tax mental, literary, or linguistic abilities for individual or group enjoyment.

Reading

One who likes to read is never alone. Libraries are ever more keenly aware of their challenge and obligation to the leisure of all age groups.

From the children's story-telling hours in the library or on the playground to the reading clubs and contests for vacation months to the adult book-review clubs, reading takes its place as an inspiring and rewarding program for recreation agencies to encourage. Bookmobiles are now a popular program item for rural and municipal recreation offerings. Viscount Grey aptly describes the joys of reading in the following:

Books are the greatest and most satisfactory of recreations. I mean the use of books for pleasure. Without books, without having acquired the power of reading for pleasure, none of us can be independent, but if we can read we have a sure defence against boredom in solitude. If we have not that defence, we are dependent upon the charity of family, friends, or even strangers to save us from boredom; but if we can find delight in reading, even a long railway journey alone ceases to be tedious, and long winter evenings to ourselves are an inexhaustible opportunity for pleasure.[6]

Group discussions

Gathering in small groups to discuss music, philosophy, current events, religion, or innumerable other topics has always been a popular leisure pastime and a rewarding recreation. In modern society, the art of conversation has too often been overshadowed by radio, television, or other spectator activities. Clubs that meet regularly for discussion purposes may be organized, or special meetings to explore special-interest subjects may be scheduled. Although the thin line between adult education and recreation is ever present in such program undertakings, those who participate in stimulating discussions do so with as much thought of the joy of exhilarating mental exercise as of the incidental learning that will take place.

Language groups

Learning foreign languages by records and practicing in small groups affords opportunity for fun, challenge, and achievement. Plans for foreign tours sometimes stimulate the desire for mastery of a language for later use in the country to be toured.

Word puzzles

Crossword puzzles, acrostics, and other word games may be used as social recreation tools and also to fill the travel hours of many a wanderer. The lonely aged often resort to the challenge of crossword puzzles or magazine quick quizzes to fill otherwise empty hours.

Gameboard activities

Chess, checkers, Go, Parchesi, Scrabble, or their many variations provide mental exercise as well as competitive outlets. The national and interna-

[6] Viscount Grey of Fallodon, *Recreation* (New York: National Recreation Association, 1920), pp. 10–11. Reprinted by permission.

tional chess games that are played by correspondence often continue for long periods before a winner finally emerges.

Card games

Bridge, pinochle, canasta, and other card games are popular recreation choices for individual or group activity. The many kinds of solitaire provide fun for those who are alone from choice or circumstance; other card games provide social as well as mental rewards.

Letter writing and letter-writing clubs

Groups or individuals use many leisure hours in writing to friends, known and unknown. For example, a New England recreation department sets up correspondence with teenagers in South African communities. The exchange of letters leads to many hours of study and discussion of a foreign land. Club groups likewise often have "pen pals."

Public-speaking clubs

The desire to communicate intelligently and effectively brings many participants to those groups who are studying and practicing the art of public speaking. Many Toastmasters' Clubs are formed from a few adults in the Civic Center, Women's Club, church, or service club who are searching for worthwhile, challenging, and rewarding uses for leisure hours. Debating clubs provide additional stimulation for those who enjoy competitive argument.

Personal study

The exploration of any given topic by an individual is rarely the concern of the recreation program director, yet such continued diligence toward a goal is one of the most rewarding recreative experiences. Stimulation for such individual adventures can be provided by the recreation leader to his participants of any age. Discovering and exploring through research cannot be minimized as wholesome recreation opportunity.

Creative writing

Creative writing, whether the end result is a poem, short story, dramatic episode, or simply a brief message to a friend, is a recreative area that has been too long ignored. The beam on the face of a child who has just rhymed two lines for the first time, the pride in the voice of the eighty-year-old reading his description of the late fall colors, the anticipation of the teenager searching for the intriguing denouement for his short story all serve to exemplify the real worth of opening opportunities for creative writing. Many a soul whose creative urge may have been stifled by the assigned autobiographies in the school English class may soar to creative heights without fear of grade retribution as he explores the joys of communicating during a creative expression session at the camp or community center.

To explore all the ways in which lives might be enhanced through stimulation of mental abilities would be an impossible task. Suffice it to say that the area of literary, mental, and linguistic activities cannot be ignored, if our programs are going to achieve the broad scope of satisfactions necessary in a challenging world.

Music in Recreation

Music is often termed the most universal of the arts. The broad appeal of music in its many forms has been recognized in every culture from the beginning of time. From the pagan rhythmic chants to the latest popular tune, music has dynamically demonstrated its ability to blend human beings in the participation at hand.

The Greeks, believing that music "harmonized the soul," made music a part of the formal training of their youth. Early cultures in many lands found more functional values in musical activities, as they used them to incite a tribe to warfare or to attract the attention of the gods in religious rituals.

In spite of the repeated contentions that the American colonists, because of their preoccupation with life's hardships, had neither time nor inclination to cultivate the arts of music, the facts speak for themselves; the first book to be printed in America was a hymnal (the *Bay Psalm Book,* 1641); singing schools were instituted in the early eighteenth century, and the Philharmonic Society of New York had been founded by 1842. Even the Puritan and the Quaker, who frowned upon music in religious environments, were not completely immune to the joys of whistling or the rhythms of the spinning top.

The popularity of music for group participation or individual expression has progressed considerably since the depression years, when the Federal Arts Project gave a real impetus to the concept that music was an integral part of the recreation program. Modern education and recreation have found both practical and aesthetic reasons for including music in their program offerings.

Scope of program in recreation

Because tastes and appreciations in music must be cultivated and because there is a wide spectrum in native talent, which might influence ability in music activities, there is an urgent need to offer wide and diverse programs to whet the musical appetite of the novice or challenge the intellect or the emotions of the more accomplished musician. Kaplan outlines the general scope of the ideal community music program:

The ideal music program in recreation utilizes the full resources available to it in the home, neighborhood, racial and religious groups, school, community, and region.

The ideal music program in recreation provides both terminal and continuing activities.

The ideal music program in recreation provides both organized and spontaneous opportunities.

The ideal music program in recreation is concerned with developing leaders arising from its own participants.

The ideal music program in recreation brings together persons of a variety of social backgrounds and origins.

The ideal music program in recreation provides both self-sufficient activities and others which are closely integrated with the general recreation program.

The ideal music program in recreation contributes to an open-minded attitude and respect for music of all types, interests, and levels.[7]

The scope of program varies from simple rhythms on the playground to opportunities for choral work or orchestration, from spontaneous singing around the campfire to carefully planned music festivals or operas, from talent shows to instructional instrument classes, and from the mere provision of a facility to stimulation of the individual or group in a progression of meaningful steps.

Kinds of music for recreation

Music has appeal for people of every age and every capability. "Music is without a peer as a medium for recreation. Its appeal is so wide and its possibilities so infinite that its recreational potentialities can never be exhausted." [8]

The types, organization, and extent of program opportunities will depend upon the availability of competent leadership, the interests of the participants, and the philosophy of the sponsoring agency. The following chart affords a quick glance at a variety of musical activities, classified in six categories.

The lists are by no means all-inclusive but they do give a picture of some of the opportunities that are now a part of community recreation programs throughout the country. Any or all of the activities can take place in a number of settings and can move from the very simple to the most complex.

A different approach to classification might serve to clarify the scope of musical offerings. Two distinct categories are immediately apparent: those that occur somewhat spontaneously or with little formal scheduling or

[7] Max Kaplan, *Music in Recreation* (Champaign, Ill.: Stipes Publishing Co., 1955), pp. 69–71. Reprinted by permission.

[8] Charles Leonhard, *Recreation Through Music* (New York: The Ronald Press Company, 1952), p. 4. Reprinted by permission.

Classification of Music Activities [9]

Singing	Playing	Listening	Rhythmic Movement	Creating	Combined Activities
Informal singing	Rhythm instruments	Incidental hearing	Purely rhythmic	Song making	Folk dancing
Community sings	Simple melody instruments	Home music	Simple interpretive singing games	Other music making	Musical charades
Choruses		Records			Shadow plays
Quartets & other ensembles	Simple harmony instruments	Radio and television	Play-party games		Festivals
Glee clubs	Fretted instruments	Live concerts	Folk dances		Seasonal and holiday programs
A cappella choirs	Bands				Pageants
Madrigal groups	Orchestras				Caroling
Solos	Ensembles and chamber music groups				Community programs
	Solos				Talent shows
					Variety shows
					Sports events
					Swimming & skating
					Park concerts
					Operettas
					Opera workshops

direct leadership and those that, because of the numbers of people involved or the challenge of the musical medium, need more highly organized scheduling or more formal leadership. Examples of programs in each category follow.

Informal activities with little organization. Because music in some form is a satisfying means of self expression, individuals or small groups often turn to music with little or no stimulation on the part of any leader.

INFORMAL SINGING. Experimenting with voice tones starts long before a child can walk. As a means of personal expression or group integration,

[9] *The Recreation Program* (Chicago: The Athletic Institute, 1953), p. 211. Reprinted by permission.

lifting the voice in song has few equals in recreative experience. The teenager whistling or singing his way home from school, the youngster humming a tune with intermittent words as he plays at castle building in the playground sandpile, the children joining in the campfire songs, or the adults gathered around the recreation room piano are all indulging in informal music making. Fun songs, action songs, folk songs, or art songs all may evolve as individuals or groups spontaneously express themselves through singing. Even the child or adult who cannot carry a tune may find satisfaction in the community of spirit as he joins the singing group.

MUSICAL GAMES. Many simple games with a musical background afford pleasure for the Sunday-school group, the picnickers, the Bluebirds, the Scout troop, or the playground participants. Singing games such as Looby Loo, in which the instructions for the game are sung by the small group of participants, are popular among the very young. Mental competition activities that include songs guessed from rhythmic clapping, rhythm games with tapping feet, vibrating rhythm sticks, and flashcard picture contests to which the group reacts with a song are popular for young or old.

MUSICAL INSTRUMENTS. The child fingering the piano keys in his first attempt to compose a melody is lost in a pleasureful world of his own. The teenager who fondly strokes his ukulele or guitar may enjoy his music alone or as the center of attention when he accompanies a singing group. The professional harpist may turn to her harp for recreation after practice hours are over. Musical instruments from the simplest wooden whistle to the most expensive of pieces afford creative and recreative activity to an increasing number of individuals.

LISTENING ACTIVITIES. The flip of the dial on the television set or the turning of the switch on the record player may bring informal music activity to many. The record industry increases each year, with thousands of dollars being expended, particularly by the teenage group. The gamut of preference runs from Dixieland beats to Debussy, but the satisfactions of actually listening to music in informal situations, in the home, in the YWCA, or in the church social room are becoming more popular.

RHYTHM BANDS. An assortment of home-made or commercial bells, castanets, sandblocks, drums, cymbals, or sticks may form hours of enjoyment in rhythm bands. The arts and crafts program often provides handmade inner-tube or tin-can drums, castanets of wooden spoons, decorated wooden rulers, metal lamp-top cymbals, corn-filled paper plates, sleigh-bell bracelets, or a variety of paper-plate or bottle-cap tambourines. The experience of keeping time to music with heavy bass or lighter, faster beats is fundamental to future explorations with fun in music.

Musical activities that require more organization. Singing or playing an instrument alone provides one kind of enchantment and meets certain needs for self-expression. Playing an instrument or singing in cooperation with others who have similar interests affords the additional pleasures of communication and coordination for achievement. The following kinds of activities need some measure of organization.

MUSICAL OPPORTUNITIES FOR SMALL GROUPS. The *barber shop quartet*, which flourished in the Gay Nineties, has gained popularity in modern times. The community center or YMCA is often the focal point for weekly sessions of male singers from all walks of life. The Society for the Preservation and Encouragement of Barber Shop Quartet Singing in America, Inc., a national fraternity of male vocalists, was formed to promote barber shop singing.

Small groups of instrumentalists find relaxation and achievement in their concerted efforts. Youngsters enjoy playing simple melody instruments such as the tonette; others form *ensembles* of stringed instruments for simple or difficult renditions. *Stringed ensembles and brass quartets* are becoming more numerous in community recreation programs. *Harmonica bands* provide musical outlets for the youngsters or the senior citizens.

Some municipal departments give instruction in instruments during the summer months. Free instruction on the playground or in the center is so popular that administrators find that the demand far outreaches the ability of most communities to afford the opportunities. Policy usually dictates that no individual instruction will be given, but the class sessions provide the incentive for many individuals to explore greater accomplishment in private lessons. Song-writing classes are well attended.

Informally organized *listening hours* have been initiated on playgrounds, in club activities, and on college campuses. Walter Damrosch, in the 1920's, captivated the nation's school children with music appreciation hours. The listening hour on playgrounds becomes an informal avenue to appreciations that lead to better listening habits. If listening to music is to have real value, the individual must learn how to listen. Just as a youngster who has never learned to handle a bat finds little enjoyment in baseball, so the individual who would find most pleasure in music must know something about the medium.

ACTIVITIES WITH LARGE GROUPS. Possibly the most popular of the musical offerings with large groups is the community sing. Community sings are organized for particular interest groups and may be scheduled as continuing programs throughout the year. Parks, camps, and playgrounds offer outdoor settings, whereas the church, the community center, the club, and the school afford opportunities for indoor activity. Piano, guitar, autoharp, or ukulele accompaniment helps the leader of the large groups. The community sing is planned in advance, but its program may be flexible in terms of audience choices as the session progresses.

For many years, the community sing was synonymous with the less sophisticated, but with the impact of television singing programs and the early inclusion of group singing in the elementary school programs, even

Fig. 25 *Music under the Stars—Robin Hood Dell, Philadelphia*

the most aloof of sophisticates have come to know the joys of raising voices together in the sheer exuberance of melody.

More highly organized singing groups, with restricted participation because of talent requirements, are found in the a cappella choirs, glee clubs, and choruses of settlement houses, church fellowship groups, senior citizen clubs, agriculture extension clubs, and municipal recreation groups. The powerful unifying force of music is exemplified in Philadelphia's Singing City, which started with a handful of people in the 1930's with the objective of making Philadelphia a friendlier city. One of the means toward that objective was singing together, and from a small group of enthusiastic souls of dubious musical talent has grown a program of breadth and achievement complete with excellent choirs, conductors, groups, and training courses.

Many an ardent high-school bandsman has welcomed the opportunity for use of his trumpet or saxophone in his post high-school days. Municipal recreation programs and other community groups are finding a real enthusiasm for municipal bands, community orchestras, state symphonies, American Legion bands, Scout fife-and-drum corps, and similar organizations. Recreation agencies are in an excellent position to aid in the organization and coordination of such units and to make available facilities needed for practicing.

Club activities on a small or large scale whet the musical appetite of all

ages with concert-going activities, opera exploration, record or hi-fi concentration of interest, composing activities, or discussion groups. Baton-
twirling classes attract thousands to playgrounds and community centers
each year. Marching in a parade is a significant achievement for the child
displaying his talent with the spinning stick.

Special events that involve consumer and performer enjoyment include
talent shows, festivals, song-writing contests, concert tours, concert attendance, or special pageants. The Pittsfield, Massachusetts, Senior Citizen's
Club combines travel and musical fun with a trip to Tanglewood, a famous
music area, each year. All kinds of professional concerts for children are
opening new recreation outlooks for future generations. Symphonic music
is more available than ever before. In 1961, the Boston Symphony ended a
50-week marathon of 221 concerts, while the New York Philharmonic, the
oldest orchestra in the United States, had a considerably accelerated 120th
season.[10] Many radio stations fight the competition of television by offering long hours of the best in music.

Values in music as recreation

The values in recreation music to the performer or to the listener are
many. Music is perhaps the most adaptable, the most persuasive, and the
most democratic of the arts. Benefits derived from simple or complex recreation music activities include:

1. *A potent force in the control of behavior.* Musical taste and reaction
to rhythmic beat are folkways, so that music has the power to move individuals deeply, to build moods that will influence action, to stimulate and
inspire individuals or groups to decision, or to persuade in the direction
of custom or tradition. Carefully chosen songs slow the riotous laughter of
the campfire games and prepare campers for the somber inspirational clos-
ing of the program as the embers die. The heroine in the stage death scene
gets dramatic help for her histrionic talent as the music builds empathy
in the audience. The martial band music and fight songs whip the school
ballteam supporters into a frenzy of cheering. The housewife urges herself
to perform dull cleaning details with a Strauss waltz. Industries, knowing
that rhythm is a time saver, pipe in refreshing, lively tunes to step up assembly lines in the factories. A hasty rendition of the Star-Spangled Banner
has broken up many a servicemen's brawl. A quiet lullaby has carried many
an overtired youngster to the land of dreams.

2. *Milieu for group dynamics.* Music is said to be the most democratic
of the arts. In many forms, it seems to have a unifying effect on people
whether they are performing or listening. Group relationships are subtly

[10] "Life Guide," *Life* magazine, LI, No. 14 (October 1961), 21.

built. It is somehow difficult to hate the persons with whom you join in song. The fellowship that comes from participating in a chorus or orchestra provides a social and emotional integration of those who are involved. Music often serves to draw people together to identify as a group, whether that group be the Brownies singing their song, the state symphony orchestra playing a concert, the Old-Timers' Harmonica Band having a session, or the kindergarteners marching to their rhythm band.

3. *Means of individual expression or emotional outlet.* The young man creating a love song for his girl friend, the middle-aged housewife getting away from the dishwashing to play the piano, the child listening to the enchantment of the *Peer Gynt Suites,* and the teenager releasing his frustration on his set of drums are all finding outlets to communicate their emotions of the moment. Music is capable of removing us from the demands of the moment to appreciations, diversions, or emotional release at every age and level of folk taste.

4. *A therapeutic tool.* Music of all kinds has long been cherished as a means of effecting therapeutic results in normal or handicapped individuals. From the ancient priest-doctors of Egypt, who chanted music to influence the child-bearing capacity of women, to the Greek Zenocrates, who used harp music to quiet violently disturbed mental patients, to the music therapist in the modern mental hospital, the power of music to soothe, to divert, or to incite has long been recognized. Said Dr. Podolsky, "Physicians whose sole task is caring for the mentally ill have long realized that music is one of the best medicines for the mind." [11] Research in the effect of music on various types of mental illness has proved the worth of music in relieving lonely periods of prolonged hospitalization of patients in general hospitals. Research to prove the values of music in psychiatric settings is still in its infancy, but systematic observations have demonstrated the ability of music to soothe the disturbed or move the passive sufficiently to warrant the inclusion of music in the therapy program of most mental hospitals. The recreation program offers opportunities for active and passive participation in music.

5. *As a background or setting for other events.* Music, because of its mood-molding qualities, is frequently of value merely to set the stage for other recreation activities. The pleasant banquet is made more pleasurable with background dinner music; the stirring anthem may be a prelude to the discussion group's political topic of the evening; music may stimulate or moderate movement on the skating rink or in the swimming pool.

[11] Edward P. Podolsky, "Music and Mental Health," in *Music Therapy,* ed. Edward P. Podolsky (New York: Philosophical Library, 1954), p. 11.

6. *Lasting and cosmopolitan character.* The music lover has a lifetime of music ahead of him. The individual who enjoys playing the violin or singing may continue his recreation until arthritis knots his hands or cancer destroys his throat muscles. The person whose listening appetite has been encouraged has an intellectual and emotional outlet even after deafness allows him to "hear" the rhythm only through pulsations.

7. *Aesthetic values.* A defense of music simply as "unashamed embellishment of life" is made by John Mueller in the following statements:

Music has been, and now constitutes a large segment of our traditions. If we teach Shakespeare, we need not feel impelled to defend Beethoven and Mozart or Wagner. It is an unashamed embellishment of life. We do not strip life of embellishments; we do not speak naked, basic English; we do not restrict ourselves to K rations and merely nourishing food; we do not seek mere shelter and a minimum decent covering of the body. We simply do not live that way. Lowell Mason, under the influence of Pestalozzi, himself, when he defended the introduction of singing into the schools of Boston, asserted that it promoted worship of God, it served as entertainment, humanized the young. Not much more than that is needed today.[12]

Leadership in recreation music

As in any other of the performing arts, the leader in recreation music must know enough about the medium to use its unique potentialities to best advantage as satisfying recreation. The recreation leader, though he may not be a musical genius, must like music, know something about its characteristics and effects on people, and transfer his enthusiasm to the individual or the group with whom he is working. Early attempts to use specialists highly skilled in music areas were unsuccessful in many recreation programs. Although the highly talented and educated musician was extremely well qualified to work with those who had had an extensive musical background, he lacked the recreation philosophy that would allow participation for those who were less talented, less zealous, or less informed. Large municipal programs can afford to hire specialists for conducting large choruses, symphonies, or bands, but the recreation leader who works with the playground, the teen center, the church, the Scout troops, the 4-H clubs, and the hospital must have some concept and appreciation of music as a recreation tool.

Kaplan stresses that the recreation professional must acquire:

A wholesome respect for the standards of "good" music, as well as a respect for all types and styles of music which mean something to people.

[12] John H. Mueller, "The Social Nature of Musical Taste," *Journal of Research in Music Education,* IV, No. 2 (Fall 1956), 118.

A vision of the tremendous scope and variety of musical activities.

A clear understanding of the recreation philosophy and of pertinent social factors as they pertain to music.

A mastery of some essentials of music itself, together with an awareness of their own limitations and the location of other resources.[13]

The lack of confidence in the music area often deters leaders from program efforts that would be most rewarding for their participants. Institutes for in-service training can do much to stimulate more varied musical activities within the many recreation interests of the community.

Other problems in music programing

Too many music programs for recreation never progress past the very elementary stages of rhythm or jug-and-bottle bands, community singing, listening hours, and singing games. The adequate program must extend its offerings to provide challenges for those who would enjoy more demanding musical opportunities.

Budgets for programing in small communities are still not adequate for a broad cafeteria of opportunities for playing, listening, singing, or creating. Through better cooperation between the educational institutions and the recreation agencies, progression of outlets must be offered in leisure for those who have explored musical education in the school programs. Emphasis on and recognition for participation in instrumental or singing groups would help to stimulate interest of many who could profit by musical recreation long after they had ceased to kick footballs. Social conditioning should create a somewhat different public image of the musician and his abilities, so that joining the chorus will be just as attractive as going out for basketball.

Basic to the expansion of musical activity in community programs is the acceptance of the idea that tastes for musical activities differ radically but that those tastes may be cultivated. *Good* music may connote classical masterpieces to one individual and the latest popular tunes to another. Many a husband has suffered through an opera he could not understand or a symphony concert he could not interpret and has bravely called it his recreation. Musical tastes have too often become a mark of class or social distinction. In a recreation situation, the leader must find those musical activities that will prove enjoyable, give pleasure, and provide satisfaction for those participating. Too much emphasis on form and technique may make a tedious chore out of what could have been an emotional communication through music; on the other hand, complete lack of information may deny enjoyment for those who cannot interpret or participate successfully without such education. As in any of the arts, the leader must be

[13] Kaplan, *Music in Recreation*, p. i.

sensitive to the needs of his group in order to select intelligently, introduce enthusiastically, and lead in his musical medium sensitively.

Integration with other program areas

The possibilities for interweaving music with other program areas are so obvious and so numerous that little time will be spent on their enumeration. Music enhances or complements game activities, swimming, skating, dancing; it combines with drama in the opera, pageant, and festival; it joins with the nature program in the hiking songs or the concert under the stars; it shares in social gatherings, in hobbies, in special events of all kinds. Music knows no boundaries in setting; it takes place at the family table, in the camp ring, on the playground, in the YMCA, in the church basement, or at the Scout meeting place. It adapts readily to its setting or to its participants with a universal appeal upon which the recreation leader should capitalize.

Trends in recreation music

We have come a long way from the pre-Industrial Revolution days when it was necessary to travel to New York to hear Beethoven's Fifth Symphony. The New York Philharmonic performed in a half-dozen concerts in the year 1875. Their present schedule includes more than one hundred and fifty performances a year. For those who cannot coordinate their schedules with that of the New York Philharmonic, other local or state symphonies offer programs closer at hand. Literally millions are enrolled in the "society of music appreciators" through recordings. Thousands more are experiencing the pleasure of listening to talented stars on television, on radio, or in person in community concert series.

Recreation agencies of all types are broadening and enlivening their opportunities for musical enjoyment. The 1961 report published by the Music Section of the National Recreation Association Committee on the Performing Arts listed over 100 different activities offered by recreation agencies throughout the land. The American Music Conference in Chicago estimates that over eight million youngsters are now playing musical instruments. The authorization of the National Cultural Center in Washington, D.C., will serve to put music and the other performing arts in a rightful place of prominence in a new emphasis on cultural advancement in America.

Hospitals, industries, and penal institutions are increasing their opportunities for musical outlets in leisure. Schools are placing more emphasis on music in the elementary grades. There has been an increasing number of bandshells, auditoriums, and listening rooms in the plans of new recreation facilities. Music from simple rhythms to the complexities of the opera will continue to entice the American public in their leisure hours. In the words of V. K. Brown, former Director of Recreation for the Chicago Park District, "When music dies, recreation dies with it."

Outdoor Recreation

Under the heading of "outdoor recreation" we place those manifold pursuits related to the use, enjoyment, and understanding of the out-of-doors. Outdoor recreation encompasses fishing in a mountain stream, skiing down a snowy slope, contemplating a brilliant sunset, camping in a national park, planting a backyard garden, identifying an unusual bird, or gathering shells on a beach. The desires for outdoor experiences, adventure, knowledge, and beauty are well-nigh universal. It is these desires that outdoor recreation seeks to satisfy.

According to the findings of the Outdoor Recreation Resources Review Commission, driving and walking for pleasure, swimming, and picnicking lead the list of the outdoor activities in which Americans participate, and driving for pleasure is most popular of all. The ORRRC also found that about 90 percent of all Americans participated in some form of outdoor recreation in the summer of 1960. In total, they participated in one activity or another on 4.4 billion separate occasions.[14]

As American society takes on an urban character, as personal incomes

[14] Outdoor Recreation Resources Review Commission, *Outdoor Recreation for America* (Washington, D.C.: Government Printing Office, 1962), pp. 3–5.

Fig. 26   *Estimated Changes in Population, Income, Leisure, and Travel for the Years 1976 and 2000—Compared to 1960. Source:* Outdoor Recreation for America *(Washington, D.C.: Outdoor Recreation Resources Review Commission, 1962)*

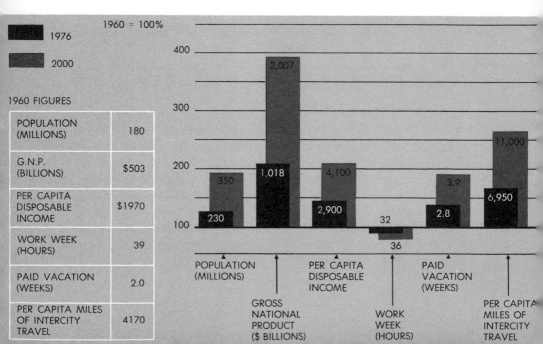

1960 FIGURES	
POPULATION (MILLIONS)	180
G.N.P. (BILLIONS)	$503
PER CAPITA DISPOSABLE INCOME	$1970
WORK WEEK (HOURS)	39
PAID VACATION (WEEKS)	2.0
PER CAPITA MILES OF INTERCITY TRAVEL	4170

Fig. 27   *Percent Distribution of U. S. Population 25 Years of Age and Over by Years of Formal Schooling— 1959 and Projected, 1980. Source:* Outdoor Recreation for America (*Washington, D.C.: Outdoor Recreation Resources Review Commission,* 1962)

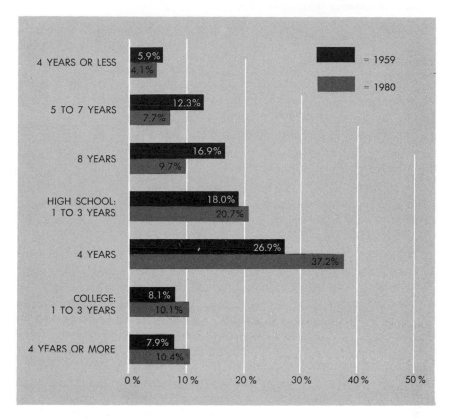

and amounts of leisure increase, and as transportation improves, the surge to the out-of-doors mounts. Figure 26 provides a comparison of some of the factors that determine people's ability to engage in recreation activities. The crowds in our parks and forests have created serious problems, particularly since the close of World War II, often destroying the beauty and isolation that the visitors themselves seek. A new generation is growing up that has had for the most part only a superficial contact with the out-of-doors. Many, lacking in the knowledge, skills, and appreciations necessary for the wise use of our outdoor resources, contribute to the problems of litter and vandalism that have become a national disgrace. General levels of education influence both tastes and popularity of outdoor recreation. A comparison of various factors related to education is the subject of Fig. 27.

Outdoor recreation programs developed by communities can not only provide opportunities for enjoyment but can also lessen the abuse of outdoor areas by helping to develop skills and attitudes that lead to considerate usage. Community provisions for outdoor recreation include land, facilities, programs, and leadership.

Values of outdoor recreation

Although the joy of participation and the satisfactions that come from outdoor experiences are worthy ends in themselves, outdoor recreation offers concomitant values:

1. The contact with nature meets deeply felt needs, counterbalancing the artificialities of modern life. Outdoor recreation thereby contributes to physical, mental, and emotional well-being.

2. Many outdoor interests are of such a nature that the participant may engage in them throughout his life. They contrast sharply in this respect with such recreation pursuits as active team sports, which can be engaged in for only a few years when physical vigor is at its height.

3. Outdoor living provides situations for the development of resourcefulness and self-reliance, qualities that may have survival value in the nuclear age ahead.

4. Many outdoor interests afford understandings of basic concepts, such as the cycle of life, the interrelatedness of living things, and man's dependence on his natural environment. Such insights should lead to appreciations and to assumption of responsibility for the wise use of natural resources.

Classification of recreation resources

The Outdoor Recreation Resources Review Commission recommended the following system of classifying recreation resources "to aid in the management of recreation resources, to enhance the quality of recreation opportunities, and to facilitate the orderly development of recreation areas":

Class I—High-Density Recreation Areas: Areas intensively developed and managed for mass use.

Class II—General Outdoor Recreation Areas: Areas subject to substantial development for a wide variety of specific recreation uses.

Class III—Natural Environment Areas: Various types of areas that are suitable for recreation in a natural environment and usually in combination with other uses.

Class IV—Unique Natural Areas: Areas of outstanding scenic splendor, natural wonder, or scientific importance.

Class V—Primitive Areas: Undisturbed roadless areas, characterized by natural, wild conditions, including "wilderness areas."

Class VI—Historic and Cultural Sites: Sites of major historic or cultural significance, either local, regional, or national.[15]

[15] *Outdoor Recreation for America*, pp. 96–97.

Community-held land

The basic requirement for outdoor recreation is land. Great numbers of people would be denied access to land were it not for public parks, forests, and reservations. As indicated elsewhere in this book, federal and state authorities control tremendous acreages, the federal government having authority over about 21.3 percent of the total land and the states, 4.2 percent. By comparison, the 18 million acres (1 percent) [16] owned by counties and municipalities are small, yet their proximity to population centers gives them value out of proportion to their size.

Unfortunately, this large acreage is not evenly distributed throughout the country. The West, with one seventh of the population, has about four fifths of the publicly owned open land. The Northeast, with one fourth of our population, has only one seventy-fifth. The North Central states and the South each have about two sevenths of the population, but only from one tenth to one twelfth of the federal lands.[17]

Our constantly growing country requires more land near its expanding centers of population. Since land is rapidly being turned to other uses, land available for recreation is dwindling fast. Recreation agencies must act without delay to save what they can before it is too late. Private lands have to a certain extent helped to satisfy the needs. Private power companies sometimes permit their lands to be used by the public. Timber companies have opened large tracts to public use, usually free of charge. About 1.5 million people, including hunters, fishermen, campers, picnickers, and skiers, used industrial forest lands in 1956.

Programs and facilities

Community provision for outdoor recreation varies greatly. Nature centers in the Cook County Forest Preserve (Illinois), Cleveland Metropolitan Parks (Ohio), and Columbus Parks (Ohio) emphasize the local natural environment. Outdoor recreation centers in Milwaukee and Pasadena stress camping, outdoor living skills, and outdoor sports as well as some of the nature interests. The programs of state and federal agencies have been considered in Chapters 11 and 12. Camps, parks, forests, game preserves, refuges, zoos, botanic gardens, museums, arboretums, gardens, streams, and lakes all contain possibilities for programs in outdoor recreation, on either an organized or individual basis.

Playgrounds and community centers, even though their major programs

[16] *Statistical Abstract of the United States, 1961* (Washington, D.C.: Department of Commerce, 1961), p. 184. The figures exclude Alaska and Hawaii. It is not to be assumed that all this acreage is available for recreation.

[17] *The Crisis in Open Land* (Wheeling, W. Va.: American Institute of Park Executives, 1959), p. 5.

lie in other directions, can provide some activities in outdoor recreation. These may be incidental or scheduled regularly under specialized leadership. What is done depends on the natural resources, man-made facilities, the interests of the clientele, and particularly the interests and abilities of the leaders. Some agencies are specifically oriented toward outdoor programs. Among them are the Boy Scouts, Girl Scouts, Camp Fire Girls, and hundreds of conservation clubs, garden clubs, mountain clubs, hiking clubs, and sportsmen's clubs—national, state, and local. Every community has some resources upon which outdoor recreation programs can be based so that it can provide a program that will afford satisfaction for the great numbers of human beings who enjoy the out-of-doors.

Leadership requirements

In recent years there has been an increasing demand for naturalists, camping specialists, leaders in outdoor-related sports, and other outdoor recreation specialists. In addition, general recreation leaders have been called upon to conduct outdoor recreation activities as part of their community recreation programs.

Special skills and knowledge are needed by leaders in each of the outdoor programs. Many activities require special knowledge of safety procedures or a field acquaintance with natural science. Opportunities for training leaders are offered in camp counselor training courses, nature and conservation camps, and various institutes and workshops. College and university programs for the education of professional recreation leaders include courses in science, gardening, camp counseling, and other outdoor recreation fields.

Volunteers render particularly valuable service in outdoor recreation. Adults with specialized outdoor interests are often happy to assist children and other adults. Courses are available to help volunteers attain proficiency in leadership capacities.

Forms of outdoor recreation

Many outdoor recreation activities could logically be classified as sports or games, social recreation, or arts and crafts. Their relationship to the natural environment is, however, the basis for their inclusion in this book as forms of outdoor recreation. Each of the following categories of outdoor recreation is discussed in the pages that follow: activities in natural science, outdoor-related arts and crafts, trips and outings, outdoor living, and outdoor-related sports.

Activities in natural science. Most people have at least a mild interest in the natural environment. Some have a passionate desire to learn all they can about the out-of-doors and find in the pursuit of the natural sciences a major source of satisfaction. The wide variance in interest demands programs with a diversity of approach. For some, merely viewing a beautiful scene may suffice; others want to know and understand all they can about that scene. To satisfy the numerous interests, the following activities have received acceptance in recreation programs.

DISCOVERY AND EXPLORATION. Trips for discovery and exploration are organized by recreation departments, schools, museums, nature centers, and youth agencies. The trips may be general in nature or may concentrate on one particular interest, such as tree identification, cave exploration, star observation, geology, birds, or flowers. Forests, parks, zoos, sanctuaries, and botanic gardens offer many possibilities for trips to pursue natural science interests.

COLLECTIONS. Most children and adults are natural collectors, and nature provides many possibilities for fascinating collections. Along with collecting goes the arrangement, display, study, and identification of things collected. However, caution must be exercised if individuals collect. In view of the diminishing of natural lands, collectors must observe strict conservation practices. Many things are best observed in their natural settings, and removing them leaves less to be enjoyed by those who follow the collector. Every would-be collector should ask himself, "What will be the effect of my taking this material? Will my action detract from the enjoyment of others?" Some natural objects should never be collected; others may be taken sparingly; and still others, freely. Most wildflowers should not be picked. If discretion is used, leaves of common trees may be picked. Except in populous areas or restricted areas, such as national parks, rocks and minerals, driftwood, nuts, berries, weeds, and insects may usually be collected. Nothing should be removed from private property without the owner's consent. The person whose collection consists of photographs he takes, sketches he makes, or notes he keeps may collect to his heart's content without injuring his environment.

TALKS AND DEMONSTRATIONS. Talks, illustrated lectures, and demonstrations by naturalists, travelers, and hobbyists provide another type of activity. Lecture series, such as the Audubon Screen Tours, bring professional speakers on outdoor-related subjects. Story hours and movies for young children can include nature and outdoor life. Many fine stories and movies are available.

CARE OF ANIMALS. Keeping of pets is for the most part a home-centered activity. For children who cannot have pets at home, pets at the recreation center offer joyous experiences and opportunities for learning. A bird feeding station, turtle pond, aquarium, or vivarium may be maintained almost anywhere. Keeping wild animals in captivity is inadvisable and cruel unless proper continued care is assured. Zoos occasionally lend traveling exhibits of living animals to park and playgrounds; some nature centers keep wild

Fig. 28   *Winter Bird Watching—Cleveland Metropolitan Park District*

animals and allow children to share in responsibility for their care. Traveling barnyards, set up in neighborhoods for several days at a time, are valuable and popular with city children.

OBSERVATIONS AND EXPERIMENTATION. Maintaining a weather station and making daily observations, records, and predictions, is an activity suitable for the nature center, camp, or playground. Other enjoyable projects include: operating a small observatory or a nature trail; maintaining bird feeding stations and bird baths; experimenting with seeds and soil; or keeping a calendar on which are recorded dates of the appearances of seasonal bird visitors, flowering of plants, or activities of animals.

NATURE GAMES. The natural science program can be enlivened by the introduction of games of various sorts. Outdoor scavenger hunts, treasure hunts, competitive games, and hiking games may all have natural science themes. Indoor games such as twenty questions, quizzes, quiz boards, and flash cards can also revolve around natural science. Observation games to provide fun on car trips are numerous.

GARDENING. For countless people there is no form of recreation as satisfying as gardening. The joy of sharing in the miracle of growth, the healthful outdoor exercise, and the gratifications of harvesting combine to make gardening an exhilarating pleasure for young and old alike.

As a community undertaking, gardening was given impetus by the federal government during the world wars, when raising one's own food was a patriotic gesture. Children and adults planted vegetable gardens in backyards and community plots. The interest in gardening continued in peace time. Garden clubs for adults today are numerous and are promoted by national organizations such as the Garden Club of America. For the most part, adults carry on their gardening on individual bases or through self-sufficient clubs; but in a few places tract gardens are provided by public agencies, industries, or apartment house owners for their tenants. The tract garden in the United States has not approached the popularity of the "allotment gardens" of Europe.

There are numerous children's gardens sponsored by schools, youth organizations, park and recreation agencies, adult garden clubs, or combinations of these. There are three major means of organizing these programs in a community.

1. Home gardens. The sponsoring group organizes the children into clubs or classes, gives instruction, and supervises the home gardens.

2. Group gardens. A class or club as a group cares for a garden in the school, playground, or other chosen area.

3. Tract gardens. Land is secured by the sponsoring group. It is divided into small plots, which range from 4 by 8 feet to 16 by 20 feet or larger, for which the children care individually or in groups of two or three. In a typical tract garden, children follow prepared plans in laying out and planting their plots. They care for the gardens under supervision and keep careful records of their harvests. This type of children's garden program has met with considerable success.

FARMS AND FORESTS. Some communities have developed forest and farm projects to which children may come for a day or longer to work at various chores or just to observe and enjoy the outdoor experience. Especially important in Minnesota, Wisconsin, and New England are community forests, some of which date from colonial times. There were in 1956 about 3,100 community forests, including 4.4 million acres of land.[18]

EXHIBITS AND DISPLAYS. Nature centers and museums usually have extensive natural science displays. Community centers, camps, and playgrounds may also set up exhibits. A "What Is It?" table, on which objects are placed until they can be identified, is a stimulus to learning. Collections and other interesting objects owned by individuals may be borrowed for temporary displays. Materials gathered on exploration trips, pictures, charts, electric boards, and diagrams that interpret the out-of-doors may all be utilized in exhibit areas or on bulletin boards.

CLUBS AND CLASSES. Fostering a serious study of natural science, clubs and classes are organized as parts of many community recreation programs. Astronomy, ornithology, mineralogy, meteorology, geology, conservation, and paleontology are only a few of the subjects of interest. These groups, if composed of adults, may be entirely self-sufficient and self-led. Children's

18 *Land, the Yearbook of Agriculture, 1958* (Washington, D.C.: Department of Agriculture, 1959), p. 52.

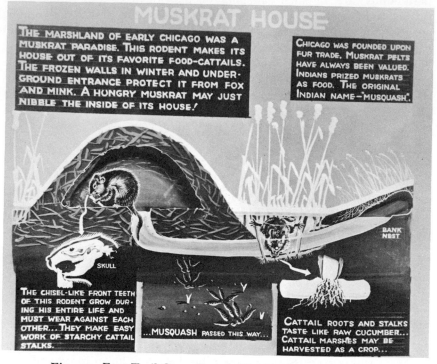

Fig. 29   *Foot-Trail Story Board—Cook County Forest Preserve, Illinois*

groups need the leadership and guidance of adults, often provided through recreation agencies.

SPECIAL EVENTS. Special events related to natural science include science fairs, pet shows, camping shows, camporees, zoo days, garden shows, hobby shows, and tours.

Outdoor-related arts and crafts. Arts and crafts related to the out-of-doors can contribute to the development of knowledge of nature, an awareness of natural beauty, and an appreciation of how man is linked to his environment.

ARTS AND CRAFTS USING NATIVE MATERIALS. Enjoyment of arts and crafts with native materials is enhanced immeasurably if the participant gathers the material himself. It is necessary, however, always to keep in mind the principles of conservation and to collect only what is permitted and what can be used. Through the process of locating, selecting, and preparing, the participant gains an understanding and respect for his medium that purchased material cannot inspire. Finding a bank of particularly fine-textured clay or a piece of wood with outstanding grain and color can spur creative efforts.

Common materials used are clay, wood, natural fibres, grasses, bark, seeds, nuts, cones, pine needles, cattails, rushes, honeysuckle, shells, driftwood, stones, and galls. Techniques used in transforming these objects into useful objects or works of art include ceramics, carving, jewelry making, weaving, and dyeing.

Crafts with materials from the natural environment can help one understand the life of the Indian and the pioneer. Many recreation programs include Indian crafts, such as the making of headdresses, tom-toms, and bows and arrows, and pioneer crafts, such as weaving and furniture making.

CONSTRUCTING TOOLS AND EQUIPMENT FOR USE IN OTHER ASPECTS OF THE OUTDOOR PROGRAM. Campers and hikers can enjoy making their own pack baskets, carrying cases, tin-can utensils, or even tents. Outdoor sports enthusiasts can make bows and arrows, fishing tackle, trout flies, and skiing equipment. Almost endless possibilities lie in making equipment used in the science programs: terraria and aquaria; bird feeding stations and bird baths; weather stations; insect nets, killing jars, and mounting boards; telescopes; quiz boards and other self-testing devices; and trailside exhibits and nature-trail labels.

PRINTS AND CASTS OF NATURAL OBJECTS. Perishable materials may be reproduced in various ways, the most common being the plaster of paris cast. The shapes of leaves may be preserved as attractive prints through such techniques as blue printing, ozalid printing, ink printing, and smoke printing.

Trips and outings. Trips and outings may be participated in by individuals, families, small organized groups, or scheduled touring groups. Scheduled tours are sometimes sponsored and conducted by youth organizations, churches, public recreation departments, or other agencies. Means of travel may be by foot, car, bicycle, horseback, plane, or boat, depending upon the interests and the physical and financial resources of the participants. Those who are too young or too old to undertake these ventures themselves are the ones most responsive to organized community offerings in this area of recreation.

Short trips, for a few hours or a day, made to nearby sanctuaries, arboretums, parks, zoos, farms, dairies, and other places of interest, are popular with camp, club, school, center, and playground groups. The chief purpose may be to see an area or to enjoy a cookout or a picnic.

More lengthy trips may take the form of travel camping and youth hosteling. For the physically fit, there are few experiences that can equal in pleasure a trip into a wild and roadless land, where there are no stores, no hotels, no television, no electricity, no agriculture, and no industries. All the food and equipment needed for the entire stay, be it two days or two months, must be taken in by the visitor. Such a trip, by canoe in the Quetico-Superior, by foot in the High Sierra, with perhaps a burro to carry the load, or by horseback in the wilderness of the Selway-Bitterroots, is an exhilarating, never-to-be-forgotten experience. For those who hesitate to organize a trip themselves, there are many camps, conservation organizations, and private guides who are experienced in conducting back-country trips. In children's camps, a wilderness trip is often the culminating experience of the summer.

Outdoor living. Outdoor living is simple "housekeeping" in the out-of-doors, such as is engaged in on the family camping trip, the day camp, the overnight camp, the picnic, and the cookout. Community agencies may not only sponsor such activities but may offer instruction in the skills required of participants, such as outdoor cooking, fire building, construction and erection of shelters and simple camp furnishings, use of tools, selection and care of gear, and the use of a map and compass. Camping is discussed in more detail in Chapter 8.

Outdoor-related sports. The term "outdoor-related sports" is here applied to outdoor physical activities that do not require a high degree of organization or special playing fields, courts, or stadiums. Outdoor-related sports depend for their full enjoyment on natural land or water areas and, for the most part, may be engaged in on an individual basis. The popularity of outdoor-related sports has burgeoned in recent years. Community recreation agencies have contributed to this growth by teaching the skills required and by offering these sports as part of their recreation programs. Public park and forest agencies have been put under great pressure to provide lands and waters to meet the demand.

WATER SPORTS AND WINTER SPORTS. Both water sports and winter sports depend heavily upon the adequacy of outdoor areas. These sports are discussed in this chapter in the section entitled "Sports and Games."

HUNTING AND FISHING. The providing of land and water areas for these popular sports is for the most part a public responsibility. In certain places community agencies offer instruction in casting and gun safety and organize fishing contests of various kinds.

WALKING, CLIMBING, AND CYCLING. There are those who say that the use of legs for transportation is fast becoming a "lost art." Mechanized travel has reduced the amount of walking in the United States, and dangerous highways have discouraged cycling. Nonetheless, walking and cycling remain among the best forms of exercise and among the most pleasurable for the participant. Special hiking and cycling trails would do much to revive these activities. Clubs catering to hikers, mountain climbers, and cyclists are found in many schools and community recreation agencies. Significant contributions to these activities have been made by the Youth Hostels and regional mountain clubs, such as the Sierra Club.

WIDE-AREA GAMES. Wide-area games are those that require a great deal of land. They may extend over several miles and require hours to complete. One of the newer games is orienteering, which combines cross-country running with the use of map and compass. Orienteering was introduced into this country from northern Europe and is now being promoted in many communities and camps. Treasure hunts and trailing games are other wide-area games.

Organizations concerned with outdoor recreation

In addition to recreation agencies—governmental and voluntary—that offer outdoor recreation, there are hundreds of organizations that promote participation in outdoor-related sports, agitate for the acquisition of land and water areas, urge the conservation of natural resources, or in other ways encourage outdoor recreation. The conservation organizations put their efforts toward saving the wildlife, wilderness, trees, water, wildflowers, fish, or resources in general. The yacht clubs, mountain-climbing clubs, skiing clubs, speleological clubs, hunting and fishing clubs, and many others promote the use of these resources in recreation; and the more conscientious of them join in the conservation effort. The limitations of space permit mention of only a few of the larger organizations that have made particularly significant contributions to outdoor recreation and that have not received attention elsewhere in the book.

Hiking, cycling, and mountaineering clubs. The American Youth Hostels, Inc., is concerned with providing travel and outdoor experiences at a low cost primarily for young people. It maintains low-cost hostels, where travelers by foot or bicycle may stay. The youth hostel movement has been more extensive in Europe than in the United States, but increasing interest in its expansion is being demonstrated in the United States.

There are numerous mountaineering and hiking groups in the country. The Sierra Club of California and the Colorado Mountain Club are illustrative of organizations that not only provide a variety of outdoor experiences to their members but are also important conservation forces in their respective areas. The various hiking and mountain clubs along the Appalachian mountains have banded together in the Appalachian Trail Conference. The various clubs maintain extensive outing programs and have been related to the development of the Appalachian Trail, which extends the length of the Appalachian mountain chain.

A large number of local hiking and outing clubs exist; some organized by museums, park and recreation departments, YMCAs, YWCAs, colleges, and other organizations. Some are self-sufficient, with no relationship to any sponsor. Examples of hiking clubs are the Prairie Hikers of the Chicago area, the Minni Hikers of Minneapolis, and the Dartmouth Outing Club.

Conservation and outdoor education groups. An organization that has contributed greatly to recreation is the National Audubon Society, which carries on a wide variety of club activities for adults, conducts four leadership training camps, maintains sanctuaries and nature centers, organizes Audubon Wildlife Films, carries on research, conducts tours, and sponsors a very extensive Audubon Junior program for school-age children.

The Izaak Walton League is primarily concerned with the problems of water conservation but has given support to conservation education enterprises and to the protection of all of the outdoor recreation resources of the country.

Keep America Beautiful devotes its energies to the reduction of litter and vandalism through a constant flow of publicity. The National Parks Association serves as the lay arm of the national parks and is dedicated to the preservation of park ideals. The Wilderness Society aggressively defends the dwindling wilderness of the country and promotes legislation to protect it. The National Wildlife Federation carries on a varied educational program, sponsors National Wildlife Week and the sale of wildlife stamps, and keeps its eye on legislation. The American Forestry Association is concerned with the protection of forests. Of all of these groups it may be said that the recreation function, though important, is incidental.

These are but a handful of many organizations that devote themselves to various aspects of conservation and conservation education. Their tireless determination has retarded the diminution of our natural resources and has stimulated appreciation of those resources.

Special-interest organizations. Organizations such as the Garden Club of America and the National Council of State Garden Clubs have supported the expansion of gardening for outdoor enjoyment, both for their own members and for youth groups.

There exists a wide variety of outdoor science organizations, spanning the alphabet from archeology to zoology. The American Association of Museums has promoted special programs for both adults and children. Nature Centers for Young America, now affiliated with the National Audubon Society, and the Natural Science for Youth Foundation were organized to encourage the development of children's museums and nature centers. Camping groups such as the Family Camping Association and the American Camping Association are interested in the promotion of outdoor living. Science Clubs of America, an affiliation of about 25,000 high-school science clubs, includes many groups with outdoor interests.

National youth organizations. We have discussed the youth agencies in Chapter 6. We wish here merely to call attention to the importance of outdoor recreation in their programs. Camping, hiking, playing, and learning out-of-doors constitute part of the program of each of these agencies and the heart of the program of several of them. It should be recognized that the above-mentioned organizations are merely illustrative of the types of groups concerned with outdoor recreation. Their existence and vitality are proof of the significance of outdoor recreation to the American people.

A paradox

There is a seeming contradiction in the effort of recreation agencies to encourage use of outdoor resources for recreation while at the same time these agencies deplore the destruction of the resources through overuse. One might ask if we are "trying to eat our cake and have it too." The intelligent solution lies in two directions: (1) long-term planning and acquisition of needed lands and (2) managing these resources according to conservation principles and educating the public to use its land with respect. These steps cannot be taken too soon if we are to assure the continued benefits of leisure spent in places of natural attractiveness.

Social Recreation

There is nothing new about social recreation. It is as old as people. Whenever two or more individuals come together, there is a potential social recreation situation. On the streets of ancient Greece, social recreation was found in the leisurely, pleasant or the bombastic, persuasive discussions of those who met for social conversation. In early London, the coffeehouses, like the grand ballrooms, afforded a chance for fun and fellowship with others. The earliest social recreation in America was found perhaps in the clandestine taverns of the seventeenth century or in the kissing games and card parties of the eighteenth century. The early American quilting bee was, undoubtedly, the forerunner of today's "Stitch and Chat Club," in which the emphasis is placed more on interrelationships of people than on the materials evolved when people gather. The hardy pioneers combined their work and play to engage in wrestling contests or country dancing after a day of husking or barn-raising had brought neighbors together. In essence, social recreation can, and does, involve almost any activity, any age group, and any setting. One has only to look at the objectives of those involved in participation to determine what activities lie within the confines of this area.

Why social recreation?

Man, by his basic nature, is gregarious; he yearns to belong. Whether he lives in an urban or rural setting, he wants to know other people. Offerings in social recreation will allow him to become a part of his community, whether that community is a hospital, a school, a prison, a small town, or a large city. Regardless of the setting or the program medium, doing or seeing an activity with others usually enhances the enjoyment produced. Hearing a joke or seeing a film multiplies in pleasurable reward if there is someone with whom to share the laugh. Being able to show the reed basket to an interested person at your side is part of the fun involved in its creation. Being with a friend or a potential friend is a security measure for participation in many activities.

Definition and scope

Social recreation may best be defined as any recreation activity in which the stimulating or motivating force for participation is the basic social drive, the need to interrelate with people. Within such a definition, the scope of social recreation is limited only by the imagination and the ingenuity of the leadership available. The media through which social recreation can take place may run from mere conversation to parlor games, or from dance to arts and crafts. If the young mother joins the "Slimnastics Club" to get acquainted in a new town, or if the young man goes to the dance to meet his own or the opposite sex, then physical activity and dance have become social recreation. Regardless of the medium, the underlying objective is the same. The participants are seeking *fun through fellowship,* the camaraderie that takes place when persons come together to know each other better in a relaxed atmosphere conducive to the building of cooperation rather than competition.

Although many activities may be simultaneously within the categories of social recreation and other types of recreation, depending upon the objectives involved, the following traits usually characterize the purely social event.

1. The emphasis in social recreation is on the interrelationships of people. The participants attend or are involved primarily because they want to meet others, whether the meeting takes place while knitting, playing ball, or dancing.

2. Social recreation demands no advance preparation on the part of the participant. He uses whatever talents he possesses without feeling the need to upgrade his skills before the involvement.

3. The emphasis on degree of skill for performers is minimized. The dramatic social recreation experience allows the talented thespian or the novice to have equal opportunity for dramatic group fun.

4. The emphasis is on cooperation, not competition.

5. The approach to the activity is usually informal.

6. The event can take place anytime, anywhere, and with any number.

7. No special equipment is needed by the participant. Many items may be needed by the leader, however; the tools of social recreation are varied.

8. The event should be an *integrating* activity, if it is truly in the social recreation realm. It should give repeated opportunities for the participants to meet or mingle.

Kinds of social recreation

Although music, drama, art, or any other kind of recreation that involves more than one person may be used as a tool for social recreation, certain activities are noted for their primary emphasis on social objectives. They may involve one or more activity media. The following list is selective rather than inclusive.

1. Conversation, sometimes known as "the lost art," allows for better understanding of feelings and ideas of others, whether the social interchange takes place in restaurant, home, car, or park.
2. Teas and coffee hours may range from the informal college coffee-break to the very formal tea.
3. Parties centered around anything from a television sport event to a holiday get together are basic socializers.
4. Banquets, dinners, and picnics involve a meal, before, during, and after which groups find fellowship.
5. Game rooms and drop-in centers provide facilities in which people get acquainted or renew friendship over a game of checkers, cards, box hockey, or ping pong.
6. Co-recreation sports nights allow "boy-meets-girl" opportunities through swimming, badminton, volleyball, and similar activities.
7. Outings that allow groups to travel together by foot, car, bus, horseback, train, or plane afford social recreation experiences.
8. Special events such as festivals, fairs, carnivals, and campfires provide the atmosphere and media for social participation.

Into these social events, characterized by a particular method of organization or by a special environment, the leader may weave arts and crafts, sports and games of both active and quiet nature, dance, dramatic outlets, music, nature lore, or mental and linguistic activities.

Values in social recreation

The broad scope of social recreation possibilities provides a host of rewards for the participant or the sponsoring organization. Values might include:

1. Opportunities for meeting people of the same or opposite sex in accepted social situations.
2. Bolstering democratic community spirit and group security.
3. Fulfillment of basic psychological needs such as the need to belong, the need for response, and the need for recognition.
4. Variety of outlets for creative self-expression.

5. Chance to serve others.
6. Opportunity to explore new leisure interests as they are introduced in group situations.
7. Opportunity to develop skills in an informal atmosphere.
8. More ready understanding of human nature without prejudice of competitive pressures.
9. Public-relations opportunities for the sponsoring organization to introduce or get support for other program areas.

Man's need to socialize is a pressing one. Programs must offer wholesome opportunities for young and old to get acquainted, to meet their future mates, or just to establish communication with their fellow man. In large cities, neighbors may never know each other's names until they meet at a recreation program possibly five miles from home. This situation holds true particularly for the aged, who are most in need of social contacts. After the mandatory relationships in school and work have stopped in retirement, all too often the aged withdraw into isolation. Social recreation becomes a most needed program area, if the aged are to continue to be happy, contributing citizens.

Leadership in social recreation

The social recreation specialist is a social engineer, and, as such, must be personable, dynamic enough to move the larger groups, and sensitive enough to involve the smaller gatherings. At times, his leadership must assume proportions of showmanship adequate to call a dance for 100 square dancers; at times, his best leadership technique is the inconspicuous prodding he does as a functioning member of a group in a songfest around a campfire. The wise leader learns to study the situation, feel the pulse of those involved, and recognize when to assert direct and forceful stimulation or control and when to allow the sequence of events seemingly to evolve from the participants. He must have enough social poise to disguise any insecurity he may feel before a group and enough humility and good sense to share the spotlight with others when the opportunity arises.

The demand for leaders qualified to organize a picnic for 100 adult couples or a party for a Brownie troop has increased tremendously in the last ten years. More job opportunities that have a social recreation emphasis are being offered with private clubs, commercial resorts, transoceanic steamships, and industries. The hospitals for the mentally disturbed are directing more of their recreation time and energies to those events that allow the patient a chance to interrelate with one, two, ten, or 100 others through social recreation. Church recreation institutes place a heavy emphasis on the need for wholesome social recreation opportunities for their parishioners.

The leader must be an expert in human relations and group processes. He must be aware of the limitations, both physical and mental, of others.

His success depends upon his ability to discern quickly reactions of the group and be guided by them. He must be well versed in motivational techniques. Though he may not be an excellent vocalist, or a fine actor, he must master techniques that will allow him to involve participants in music or drama for group fun. His repertoire should include firstcomers, icebreakers, socializers, grouping devices, theme ideas, refreshment and decoration inspirations, rhythms, and audience-participation activities, as well as active and quiet games with a variety of demands on mental or physical abilities. He must be able to organize and plan, and, having carefully planned, he must learn to adjust those plans as they meet with success or failure with his group.

Planning for social recreation

Good social recreation experiences don't just happen. They are skillfully planned. Factors that a leader must consider before planning a picnic, dance, party, or other event include:

1. *The participants.* The more a leader knows about the people with whom he will be working, the more intelligently he can plan. *Age* is an important conditioning factor. Youngsters come to a party on a higher emotional plane and have less need than adults for contrived gimmicks to stimulate participation. They sometimes need a carefully planned sequence of events to tone down the ascending emotional pitch of the group. Both teens and adults need to be made a part of the planning process, but committee action is particularly important with teenage groups. Other advance information needed by the leader and concerned with the participants includes: *numbers* involved, whether or not they will be a mixed group or all of one *sex*, their *interests*, past *experiences*, *prejudices*, *mores*, *socioeconomic status*, and mental and physical *abilities*. It is often impossible to obtain all such data, and the leader must plan for intelligent alternatives with the information available.

2. *The facility.* The location in which an event is to take place will affect planning. The leader, in planning activities, must consider the area's *size*, *safety hazards*, *ventilation* available, and its *accessibility* to those for whom the event is scheduled.

3. *The time.* How long the social event will last, at what time of day, week, and year it will take place, and how often this kind of activity is offered all affect what the leader will use as program material. An event that will occur every week may need much more careful progression in planning than a "one-shot" special in which all the leader's "sure-fire" favorites may be used in one evening.

4. *Finance.* Who will pay for the activity, how it will be paid for, and why the charge is necessary all condition the planning.

5. *Resources available.* Personnel, facilities, equipment, and finances available will enlarge or confine the planning.

6. *Integration.* Integration of this particular social event with whatever has gone before or what will follow is too often neglected in the planning process. No program can operate in a vacuum. Social recreation programing is no exception.

The plan itself should be carefully thought out ·after investigating the factors discussed above. Experience has proved that most successful social recreation events hang their activities upon a skeleton provided by a theme that lends unity and continuity; adds interest and atmosphere; inspires publicity, decoration, and refreshment ideas; and facilitates use of program activities made more exciting by adaptation to the theme. The program itself should provide for welcoming and involving individuals upon arrival; give opportunities for frequent changes of pace, position,·and group; utilize a wide variety of media for integrating the group; and lead to a climax that signals, with interesting but firm precision, that the party is over. Important, too, in the committee plans is an evaluation when the event is over, so that future similar activities may profit by experiences that went well or may avoid repeating former errors.

Services to the community in social recreation

In the realms of social recreation the municipal recreation department's responsibility does not and must not stop with the provision of a staff member reasonably versed in the arts of planning and executing social recreation gatherings, though provision of a social recreation specialist might be expected to help motivate the following types of services.

Face-to-face leadership with large or small community groups. The social recreationist might plan and conduct picnics, banquets, or parties with clubs, churches, schools, or industry.

Consultant services for individuals or organizations. The specialist should be available for ideas or guidance in planning with committees from organizations who will sponsor and conduct their own programs but need help in planning.

Organization. The municipal agency is in an excellent position to stimulate coordination of social recreation events that involve large segments of the population. Publishing a calendar of events or acting as a clearing house when dates for socials are being considered greatly increases the chances for successful programs in the community. Some cities have found that the organization of a council to handle coordination and other social recreation needs has been a worthwhile innovation.

Resources. Some recreation departments lend backyard and picnic kits on a sign-out basis and have found that the demand far exceeds the supply. Other recreation departments offer the use of books, films, and public-address systems for social recreation events. Providing a card file of social recreation ideas at the department office and publishing monthly idea bulletins for parties have proved popular services. Establishing a name file of volunteers able to help with social recreation gatherings gives a double service. It gives service opportunities to persons with special capabilities who like to work with group singing, square-dance calling, or children's parties and, at the same time, enlarges the amount of social recreation leadership, otherwise financially impossible.

Training. The demand for persons to help in the planning and execution of social recreation activities always exceeds the available personnel. The recreation department is often in the best position to organize social recreation institutes, which may involve the training of volunteers, sub-professionals or professionals from churches, schools, youth-serving agencies, 4-H clubs, and industry.

Special problems in social recreation

As is the case in most program areas, social recreation finds itself with special problems, which include:

False impressions. Probably the greatest problem that arises in the social recreation area is the tardiness of the profession as a whole to recognize the social recreationist as a specialist, instead of a personable "Jack-of-all-trades," who is expected to pull something exciting out of a hat if a lull is experienced in any group setting.

Lack of careful planning. Too often, the inexperienced group relies on the false philosophy that if you get people together, they will naturally have great fun. A careful, if inconspicuous, plan from making the first arrivals feel welcome to sending off the group before enthusiasm wanes is social insurance. Inflexible leaders who stick to a plan that is not working create just as much havoc.

Failure to involve people in the planning. Plans must be made *with*, not *for*, the people who are going to be involved. The social recreation leader who superimposes his plan without consultation or guidance from representative committees may expect difficulties. Social recreation is a "we" proposition.

The overenthusiastic leader. In social recreation, the novice leader all too frequently keeps the party going at such a fast pace of activity that participants have no time in which to explore further the interesting new friends whom they met in the last mixer. Some overambitious leaders make possible a situation in which a wife who comes with her husband to a dance or party gets to talk with him again only on their way home. Overplanning of activities without breaks and overemphasis on constant participation defeat the very purpose of the event and lend a somewhat odious reputation to the social recreation specialty. Intelligent planning and controlled zeal remedy such situations.

Absence of petty cash funds. The amount of money spent by most social recreation specialists during any given year would add up to cash totals that could not be called "petty." In spite of the reluctance of most departments to establish petty cash funds, the area of social recreation frequently necessitates unexpected expenditures of small amounts. Items such as balloons, string, and crepe paper can be estimated and provided for in yearly budget plans, but the need for candies, potatoes, oranges, or a variety of other perishables that enhance an otherwise ordinary relay or provide prizes for a party may not be so easily predictable. Petty cash funds are a necessity for the social recreation leader.

Lack of evaluation. All too frequently, the important evaluation of what happened and why it happened at the social event is minimized with the statement, "Well, I guess they all had fun together." Until the social recreation leader looks objectively at each experience and explores with the committees the reasons for the successful or the unsuccessful moments, the quality of the experiences cannot hope to improve. The need for careful evaluation cannot be too strongly emphasized.

Formula for success

Here are guideposts for those who seek to meet the community needs in social recreation more effectively.

1. Keep the program balanced by offerings that are varied in nature, attract all age groups, and occur at different times of the day.
2. Plan *with*, not *for*, the groups involved.
3. Keep the public informed about events in their neighborhood. A street dance or a cakewalk in the vicinity may annoy people if they have not been invited or if it has come without advance warning.
4. Be aware of the mores and customs of the community in which you operate before planning events. Prevailing local social customs cannot be ignored, if your program is to prosper.
5. Evaluate after every experience. In sports activities, it is more obvious that the team won or lost, was successful or unsuccessful. Losses in social recreation may be just as significant, if less obvious. Learn how to observe and analyze results.

6. Minimize the importance of winning by de-emphasizing prizes of tangible value.

7. Have courage to try new ideas with groups.

New ideas and techniques are around every corner. The leader must move rapidly in order not to lose ground. Intelligent trial and error with groups bring rewarding results. As George Bernard Shaw said in his preface to *Dark Lady of the Sonnets*, "It is by exhausting all the hypotheses that we reach the verifiable one; and, after all, the wrong road always leads somewhere." So it is with social recreation.

Sports and Games

Sports and games are both universal and old. Certainly, many of our sport activities can be traced to early civilizations. From generation to generation, the national character and customs of the people have influenced both the type of sport practiced and the basic reasons for participation. Primitive man, for example, engaged in running, fishing, hunting, and throwing primarily as a means of obtaining food and clothing. The sports of the early Greeks and Romans served as a means of conditioning and preparing for combat. The Roman gladiatorial combats were evidence of the more bloody tastes in spectator sports of that era. During the Middle Ages and the Puritan times, religion greatly influenced the prevalence of sport activities, which were considered wicked and a waste of time.

Gradually, throughout the ages, the recreation emphasis in sports became more and more evident. Each people and each period has had a significant role in the fostering of sports and games. Although the popularity of sports throughout the years has been unquestioned, today public interest centers on the simple recreational value of sports. The growth of sports and games in the United States has been phenomenal. Sports and games, either in the form of actual participation or spectator interest, appeal to all ages. Including both participants and spectators, this form of recreation attracts more people than any other.

A casual drive through the average community reveals the drawing power that sports and games have in our leisure hours. A pick-up softball game on the vacant lot, children playing hop-scotch on the sidewalk, the basketball goals above the garage doors, and the increasing number of boats on trailers standing in the driveways are but a few indications of the widespread participation in sports.

Cities, through their park and recreation departments, are confronted with increased demands for tennis courts, swimming pools, ballfields, skating rinks, marinas, golf courses, driving ranges, and other facilities normally found in our playgrounds, playfields, and parks. Our present facilities are jammed to capacity.

The tremendous numbers of commercial recreation activities, such as bowling, roller skating, playing miniature golf, or practicing at driving ranges, indicate that the American public is willing to pay for its recreation. Some of the new "bowling palaces" are actually extensive recreation centers and a far cry from the smoke-filled bowling alleys of the past. It is encouraging to find the new respectability that bowling and billiards have attained.

Each year new highs are reached in the attendance at amateur and professional sports events. Additional teams and leagues in professional baseball and football have been necessitated by the increased demands for more baseball and football in cities throughout the country.

Sports are not strictly a city phenomenon, nor are they participated in exclusively by youth. These activities appeal to all ages, both sexes, the physically strong as well as the handicapped, and people in all environs. Children are introduced to sports at an early age in our schools, community centers, playgrounds, camps, youth-serving agencies, churches, and homes. Because of these backgrounds, sports are perhaps the easiest of all recreation activities to promote. Both children and adults seek activities of this nature, and the mere mention of "Let's play ball" usually brings forth favorable responses.

Types of activities

Sports and games, as a part of a community's total recreation program, should be organized to meet the needs and interests of the many, not the few, of the novice as well as the highly skilled, of the young and the old, of the physically strong and the handicapped, and of the women and girls along with the boys and men. Activities that will meet the needs of the above are many. They can be classified under the following major groupings.

Low organized games and contests. Activities of this type have real value and interest especially to younger children. They are informal in nature and do not require a high degree of organization. Few rules are needed, and usually a variable number of players can participate. Skills needed are simple but are most important in that they provide lead-up experience for the more complex and highly organized games. Games of this type can be participated in by individuals of various age levels and therefore must be adapted to the physical skills, mental abilities, and interests of each age group. The many variations of low organized games make it possible for these activities to be easily adapted to needs of all age levels. Low organized games are of fundamental importance to camp, playground, and such programs. Several examples of such games and contests are: tag, hide-and-seek, drop-the-handkerchief, dodge ball, relays, club snatch, and three deep.

Individual sports. Although man actually is a sociable creature, many people also enjoy solitary activities. Some actually prefer these. In other cases, where friends are not available, lone participation in an activity may be a necessity. Regardless of the reason, there are activities that can be engaged in on an individual basis. They include such sports as: hunting, fishing, skiing, riding, hiking, golf, skating, archery, swimming, bicycling, and boating.

Dual sports. All of the previously mentioned examples of individual sports can be engaged in by two or more people. In fact, most people prefer the sociability of other persons while playing golf, hiking, or bowling. Also, friendly competition offers added incentive and enjoyment to many sports. Some activities require a minimum of at least two persons for successful participation in the game. Boxing, tennis, badminton, table tennis, horseshoes, fencing, wrestling, and handball are examples of dual activities.

Team sports. "Making the team" is an important goal of almost every boy. Team play has gained in popularity as a spectator as well as a participant sport. It is in team play that the development of cooperative efforts toward common goals is achieved. Competitive play among teams requires a higher degree of organization than most other kinds of sport activities. More rules and regulations are necessary in conducting team sports. Today, team sports have gained tremendous support in our school, college, and recreation agency programs, with millions of participants in such team activities as basketball, baseball, softball, volleyball, football, and soccer.

Values

There are many values that ought to accrue from a well-organized sports program. Four main values are:

1. *Fun.* People who engage in sports and games for recreation do so primarily for fun. These activities, therefore, should be conducted in an atmosphere of fun and adventure. The actual enjoyment, satisfaction, and sense of accomplishment received by the participants are perhaps the richest rewards that can be achieved.

2. *Competition.* The desire to compete with another individual or team or against a standard motivates many to participate in sports activities. This urge starts at an early age when small children "choose sides" to play capture the flag or alley basketball. Competition continues throughout life, as is evidenced by the popularity of Little League baseball, high-school sports, city-wide golf tournaments, tennis meets, swimming contests, or sailing regattas. It is in the area of sports and games that competition in leisure activities is most dominant. Competition is present in other forms of recreation but to a far lesser degree and with less emphasis.

3. *Catharsis.* Sports, especially through competition, offer, to both participants and spectators, wholesome outlets for hostile tendencies. Oppor-

tunities are provided for the release of tensions and nervous strain concomitant with our modern way of living.

4. *Physical fitness.* A concern for physical fitness or personal well-being is responsible for many individuals' voluntarily choosing sports as a leisure activity. New emphasis has been placed upon "keeping in good shape" as a health and social measure. Physical exercise, most often found in sports, is basic to the fitness needed by individuals to perform satisfactorily their daily tasks efficiently and without undue fatigue. President Eisenhower's conferences on youth fitness were instrumental in alerting the nation to the problem of fitness of the American public. Through their athletic and physical education programs, schools and other recreation agencies are charged with the responsibility of raising the fitness level of American youth and adults. Recreation's role is presented by Sapora and Mitchell as follows:

It is the task of the recreation leader to utilize scientific information to promote activities that are beneficial and conducive to the development of total fitness for living. These activities must motivate people to participate regularly —of their own volition— in physical activities of sufficient intensity to maintain a minimum level of fitness. At the same time these exercises must also involve some play and recreation to allow for self-expression and emotional release to help meet the needs, interests, and desires of people.[19]

Competition

Competition is a way of life. Just as sports are wholesome and essential, competition is wholesome and right. However, success of any competitive sports program is based upon "a sound philosophy, good leaders, and continuous education of the players and spectators."[20] Competition must be geared to the player's skill, age level, and physical and emotional health.

Many professionals in education, health, medicine, and recreation view with growing alarm the emphasis placed on highly competitive sports at the junior high school level and below. Much has been said and written concerning such nationally sponsored sport programs as Biddy Basketball, Little League, and Pop Warner football. These programs have been charged with "overemphasis on winning," "exploitation of youth for commercial advertising," "parental vanity," and approaches to competition that affect the child's physical and emotional health. Programs of this nature also tend to favor the few highly skilled players instead of the majority. Many communities are taking a critical look at these and other athletic programs provided for boys of this age level and are attempting to modify many of the

---

[19] Allen V. Sapora and Elmer D. Mitchell, *The Theory of Play and Recreation*, 3rd ed. (New York: The Ronald Press Company, 1961), pp. 251–252. Reprinted by permission.

[20] *The Recreation Program*, p. 127.

undesirable features. Further study is needed to evaluate objectively programs that provide highly organized competition for the 8- to 12-year-old boy.

Classification. Some method of classification of players is essential, if fair and keen competition is to result. A team or individual that is out-matched in skill or physical ability offers weak competition, with player dissatisfaction and mild spectator interest resulting. The two most commonly used methods of classification for competition in community sports and games are age and skill.

Age classification is commonly used for boys and girls in intra- and inter-playground, city-wide, and inter-city competition. A two-year differential is generally recommended. The following system is used by the Division of Recreation, Board of Education, Madison, Wisconsin, to classify the competitive activities in that city.

> Midgets—under 12 years of age
> Juniors —12 to 15 years of age
> Seniors —15 to 18 years of age
> Adults —18 years of age or older

Skill is considered the best method of classification for adult activities. In bowling and golf, for instance, averages are determined and handicaps established so that even mediocre players may compete with the best with some hope of success.

Methods of competition. The following are some of the methods of conducting sport activities in communities.

Method	Definition	Specific Examples
Leagues	Teams or individuals engaged in round-robin competition in a sport	Interplayground leagues in softball, soccer, and volleyball Little League baseball Babe Ruth baseball City-wide leagues— baseball, basketball, softball, and soccer
Tournaments	Special event whereby an individual or team champion is determined	Weekly playground tournament City-wide softball tournament
Meets—Contests	Special event in which a number of separate events are conducted during the short period provided	Hole-in-one contest Swimming meet Silver skates ice skating derby Track meet Golf meet

Method	*Definition*	*Specific Examples*
Play Days or Field Days	Special event composed of a wide variety of activities, with emphasis on fun rather than extreme competition	G.A.A. Play Days Interplayground field day

Sports for girls and women

Sports for girls and women have been neglected in far too many cities. A wide variety of sport activities is just as necessary for girls and women as for boys and men. If communities are to uphold the philosophy that recreation should be for all ages and for both sexes, then an accelerated program of sports for girls and women must be instituted. Social customs that at one time placed a taboo on women's participation in sport events have gradually changed, and girls are no longer considered "tomboys" if they actively engage in golf, swimming, tennis, and other sport events. Because of this background, the lag in programing for women and girls is still great. On the positive side, it is encouraging to find a definite trend toward the employment of women sport supervisors by municipal recreation departments. Gradually, recreation administrators are recognizing that girls and women are entitled to a fair share of the leadership, facilities, and programing.

Various professional organizations have formulated approved programs and suitable standards for women and girls in this area. It is generally accepted that a wide variety of sport activities should be provided for each age level. The hiring of competent female leaders and officials is a necessity. Girls' rules, adopted by the National Division for Girls' and Women's Sports, should be utilized, and precautions should be taken to protect the participants' health and safety.

Water sports

The desire to be on, in, or near the water entices millions of people yearly to our seashores, beaches, lakes, rivers, pools, and other water areas. Water sports are one of our most rapidly growing programs. This increased interest has placed new demands upon municipal, state, regional, and federal agencies to develop adequate marinas, pools, beaches, docks, and other basic facilities essential to meet the increased demands of water enthusiasts. With facilities jammed with fishermen, water skiers, sailors, swimmers, skin divers, and speedboat enthusiasts, authorities are faced with the tremendous problems of assuring safe and satisfying experiences to the varied interest groups. Administrators of water recreation areas have three primary functions to perform: the development and maintenance of adequate areas and facilities, the supervision and control of the use of such facilities, and the

Fig. 30   *Waterfront Activities—Chicago Park District*

provision of an extensive program of activities and instruction in the necessary skills basic to the many water sports.

The first function, that of developing and maintaining adequate areas and facilities, was discussed in detail in Chapter 4. The planning, financing, and maintaining of the facilities that are provided to meet the needs and interests of water enthusiasts are huge tasks in most cities. For example, the Chicago Park District provides mooring and docking facilities for 2,195 boats, operates 19 indoor natatoriums and 39 outdoor pools. Also, seven launching ramps are in operation. Attendance at the beaches depends somewhat on the weather but varies from 11 million to 13 million each summer.

The increased number of drownings and accidents taking place each year in our rivers, lakes, and ponds emphasizes the need for better supervision and control of water activities. Control is essential to reduce problems concerning proper use of water areas, particularly when one considers the wide variety of user groups. For instance, the fishermen in many places have become disturbed at the speed boaters because they are disrupting the fishing. Sailboaters become equally disgruntled when water skiers cross their bows in a crucial regatta. Administrators must establish the necessary controls and coordinate the use of these many different activities so that safe operation is assured and maximum and most enjoyable use of the water results. Controls may take the form of restricting activities on certain lakes, of zoning the water area for different types of activities, of setting and properly enforcing speed limitations for motorboats, and, most important of all, of educating all groups as to the nature, extent, regulations, and problems inherent in each water sport.

Millions of youth and adults have learned to swim in programs sponsored by the American Red Cross, YMCA, schools, and recreation agencies. In recent years, skin and scuba diving have attained tremendous popularity. Many cities, especially on the west coast, have met this challenge by providing instruction in these fascinating new water sports. Sailing clubs, both private and public, have stimulated instruction to the novices of this sport, which draws well over two and one half million Americans each year.

Winter sports

A wooded park, a shallow lagoon, or a hill on a playfield, covered with snow and ice, offers an inviting setting for winter sports. Under conditions that are largely dependent upon weather, hockey, sliding, skiing, skating, tobogganing, and other winter sports take the spotlight. The success of the winter sports program is certainly influenced by the weather but is guided by good facilities and competent leaders.

A neighborhood park or playfield equipped with sled slides, skating rinks, toboggan runs, and hockey rinks can serve as a winter playground for the entire family. With creative leadership, a comprehensive program can be initiated. Music can be added to make open skating sessions more enjoy-

Fig. 31   *Winter Sports—Lincoln Center, Columbus, Indiana*
(Courtesy Public Service Company of Indiana, Inc.)

able. Leagues in hockey offer rugged competition. The sculpturing of ice castles or figures adds a creative touch. Speed skating races among rinks on a city-wide basis provide competition for those interested in this particular phase of winter sports. Instruction in figure skating, speed skating, and hockey can take place. Children and adults love to play in the snow and on the ice in such a setting. The winter playground adds much to a well-rounded community recreation program.

One of the outstanding special events staged in winter sports is the annual St. Paul Winter Carnival. This event rivals the Indianapolis 500-mile auto race or New Orleans' Mardi Gras as a civic promotional event. Winter sports such as ice sculpturing, curling bonspiels, silver skating championships, ice fishing contests, ice boat racing, ski meets, dogsled races, and parades are all coordinated in this sensational event.

In warmer climates, artificial hockey, curling, and skating rinks have made possible the enjoyment of these activities during the winter. The Lincoln Center Rink in Columbus, Indiana, exemplifies the new modern design in recreation buildings and the development of ice rinks in places that have warmer climates.

Leadership

The coach, umpire, referee, instructor, and sports supervisor all have important roles to play in determining the success of sports and games as a part of the total community recreation program. Qualified, inspired leadership is essential to the success of any recreation venture. Sports and games are no exception.

Most community recreation agencies employ sport supervisors to plan, promote, and direct comprehensive sports programs. YMCAs hire physical directors for the physical program of the Y. The responsibility of these supervisors is to hire and train the coaches, umpires, instructors, and other personnel deemed essential to carry out the sports program.

Skills in various sports are essential, if fun and satisfaction are to result. Personnel employed in the sports and games program are charged with the responsibility of teaching these skills. Leaders may discharge this responsibility by informal instruction on the playground or in the camp, by sports clinics in the community, or by "kids' baseball schools," which utilize the most talented sports instructors in the community. Classes may also be offered in many other sports.

Whether the job is that of teaching skills, supervising a sports area or facility, or conducting a sports program, qualified leaders play a significant role in the success of the activity.

Formula for success

If sports and games are to play an important role in the community's recreation program, it is essential that recreation agencies should:

1. Provide for a wide variety of sports and games activities for each age level and for both sexes.
2. Create opportunities for co-recreation sports at each age level.
3. Provide sports and games for the unskilled as well as the skilled.
4. Provide good leadership and well-qualified officials to organize and conduct competitive sports.
5. Carefully consider the physical and emotional characteristics of various age groups in the planning of sports.
6. Insure the health and safety of the participants and spectators.
7. Provide adequate areas and facilities, properly maintained and accessible to children and adults of the community.
8. Consider the importance of teaching skills in sports and promote classes, clinics, and other activities to meet this function.
9. Keep the sports and games phase of the community recreation program in proper balance with other aspects of the program.

Service to the Community

Voluntary services and citizenship participation represent a traditional American ideal of value in community living. To be of service to one's fellow man is a most satisfying choice of leisure activity at any age. Many recreation agencies augment their own program offerings as they create opportunities for individuals to give service to others. The desire to be needed and wanted is basic; service activities help to satisfy this elemental urge. The entire organization of volunteer leadership is grounded in the satisfactions that people feel as they contribute to the happiness of others.

Most agencies that offer recreation programs have ample opportunity for stimulating service activities. Not all agencies have been wise enough to make use of this challenge. The youth-serving organizations that depend largely on volunteers for their face-to-face leaders capitalize on this approach. The result provides not only needed services for those under whose auspices the program is sponsored but rewarding leisure outlets for those who choose to be of service.

We often forget the strong service urge of the teenager as he gropes in that half-suspension of being not still a child and not yet an adult. Services to others give him a feeling of worth and dignity as well as recognition. The retired person also finds in services to his community an opportunity to keep in contact and a substitute for the busy demands, social role, or sense of contribution, often lost in withdrawal from the labor force, loss of immediate family, or decreased participation in political, religious, or school affairs.

The horizons of service possibilities through which one may aid the community or any individual within its confines would make an endless list. They depend upon the needs of the community and the talents of those who would serve. The following ideas are representative of some that give benefit both to the giver and to the receiver of the service.

Cleanup projects

Active teenagers and adults find that the repainting or cleaning of a center, clubroom, home for the aged, or the like provides a pleasure and a challenge with the hard work. Yard cleanups for the sick and elderly, help weeks, and "spruceups" for the park or playground are favorite community projects.

Fund raising

Car washes by the teenagers; soliciting for special projects such as the mental-health fund; aid in promotion of community bond drives through articles, mass media interviews, or personal contacts; ticket selling for special attractions; duty at the concession stand; or candy sales by the youngsters are just a few of the money-raising services by all ages.

Professional services

Representatives of most professions give of their talents and their energies to concerns of the community. Guidance in planning and layout of facilities, physical examinations for youngsters who are to participate in sport or camp activities, direction of discussions or lectures, writing or drawing of promotional materials, and instruction of special classes are examples of free services by professionals whose talents augment the programs serviced.

Transportation and communication

Many would not be able to participate in activities such as concerts, tournament play, and camping trips if it were not for those who give service by chauffeuring the young, the elderly, the handicapped, or others who are without transportation. Organized transportation corps in large cities offer those who enjoy driving a chance to meet a variety of individuals as they trek pre-schoolers to the church party, the aged to the center ceramics class, or the ball club to the neighboring school. The homebound, who are unable to participate in other activities, find a real opportunity to help community organizations by providing telephone contacting service for special events. Such contact makes the handicapped feel less isolated from the world around him.

Visiting the ill and handicapped

Individuals and groups find visiting the homebound or institutionalized, in person or by letter, a rewarding service. The "forgotten patient" programs in the mental hospitals give patient and visitor satisfactions and rewards that are lasting.

Officiating at athletic events

Whether the sport activity is a seasonal special or a weekly affair, good officiating is necessary. Extra manpower is always needed for official timing, scoring, refereeing, and umpiring, if the event is to be beneficial for the participants. Many adults find pleasure in coaching athletic teams in the community leagues.

One-time specials

Special events give wide opportunity for service activities. The garden club holds a "planting day" to give the playground or park a much-needed landscape facelifting; the aged widow who no longer has a family for whom to cook prepares the pre-performance meal for the high-school drama club; many prominent citizens judge costume parades or pet shows in the recreation programs; the former music teacher consents to accompany the performances for the first grade's Christmas party program. Such specials lend variety to the service and do not commit the volunteer to extended obligations.

Continuing leadership roles

Accepting responsibility for a Scout troop, instruction of a class, Grey Lady duty at the hospital, sponsorship of a church young people's group, or coaching of a team all provide opportunities for continuing service. Frequently, the rewards for service in such jobs are greater, though more time consuming, because the individual can watch progress, growth, and development of his project.

Service clubs

The programs of service clubs are dealt with in Chapter 9. Suffice it to say that the organizations are initiated and developed with a service motive. Each has one or more special projects that involve the members in effecting services to individuals or to groups in their own communities and, in turn, helping to finance programs throughout the world.

Rewards for service

And so it goes; the opportunities for service are great. So are the rewards. No talent is too small when a helping hand is needed. The entire area of service to others is perhaps the most rewarding use of leisure. The warm friendliness in the face of the crippled child who has enjoyed the puppet show that you made possible; the firm handshake of the aged gentleman as you return him to his home after the tour of autumn scenery; the sincere, "You really know how to call them," of the Little Leaguer whose game you've just umpired; the contented faces on those who have just eaten the meal you prepared for the needy; the squeal of delight from the child who has just received his glasses made possible by your fund-raising project; the heartening development of the camp for underprivileged that your service club sponsored are but a few satisfactory returns from time and energies expended.

Hobbies

A hobby may be defined as a leisure interest that absorbs an individual's attention over a long period of time and with considerable intensity. Most hobbies can be pursued on an individual and independent basis. The hobbyist does not "select" a hobby; he adopts it. There is nothing half-hearted about the pursuit of a hobby.

How a hobby is adopted is sometimes a mystery even to the hobbyist. The mere mention of raising orchids, exploring a cave, breeding parakeets, or collecting oak galls may cause one person's eyes to light up while another shrugs his shoulders in indifference. Perhaps the greatest influence in the spread of hobbies from person to person is the contagious enthusiasm of the hobbyist. The hobbyist—be he a scuba diver in a rubber suit, a stamp collector hurrying to the post office for the latest commemorative, a would-be Grandma Moses setting up an easel, or a child collecting pictures of horses—has one distinguishing charactcristic: he has singled out a pursuit so engrossing to him that it makes other things dwindle in importance.

Today, with more time and money available for hobbies, the hobbyists are legion. Individually and in groups they follow their chosen interests with a dedication that at times makes a hobby resemble a cult, complete with its own literature and esoteric language.

Most hobbies fall into one of the program categories previously discussed: arts and crafts; dance; music; drama; sports and games; outdoor recreation; and literary, mental, and linguistic activities. Hobbies are considered separately here because of three considerations:

1. The intensity and continuity of participation distinguish hobbies from other forms of recreation.
2. Some hobbies, such as certain types of collections, are difficult to classify under any other category. For instance, where would you classify stamp collecting or raising pets?
3. The way in which recreation agencies conduct hobby programs is often different from that of the other program categories.

Adding zest to life

Almost everyone can find personal enrichment in hobbies, but they give particular purpose and pleasure to the lives of the retired, the ill, the lonely, and the bored. A hobby enjoyed by an entire family brings the family into fuller enjoyment of their relationships. A hobbyist in a strange place is sure to ferret out those who share his zeal; wherever he goes, the common bond soon cements new friendships and wins esteem for the newcomer.

To most adult hobbyists, a hobby is a rewarding pursuit that is an end in itself. For the young, hobbies can be far more; they can provide an entree into vocations. They offer exploratory experiences in fields from which lifetime careers may later emerge. A young fossil collector may become a paleontologist; the little chaser of butterflies, an entomologist. Many adults who achieve outstanding success, particularly in the arts and sciences, attribute their careers to childhood hobbies. Most hobbies might be classified as collecting, creative, learning, performing, and service hobbies.

Community provision for hobbies

Hobby clubs. A pleasure shared is often a pleasure multiplied. Although most hobbies can be carried on independently, many a hobbyist prefers to share his hobby with others by joining a hobby club. Clubs have been organized in practically all of the hobby fields, and many of them have national affiliations and their own periodicals. Recreation agencies often contribute to their success by helping in getting clubs organized, publicizing meetings, and in some cases providing leadership and meeting rooms.

The clubs make possible pursuit of a hobby to an extent often impossible on an individual basis. For example, a photography club may obtain and equip a darkroom that an individual member might not be able to afford by himself; or the club may jointly own books, lights, and cameras. Club members encourage and stimulate each other through demonstrations and discussions on the art and history of photography, instruction in new techniques, and thoughtful assessment of fellow members' work. The club may secure outstanding authorities as speakers; plan photographic field trips; organize photography shows and contests of community-wide interest, which reward the hobbyists with recognition of their merit; and in other ways create and spread enthusiasm for photography. Mutually shared hobby interests are great socializers. Conversation flows easily and ice is broken quickly among those with common interests. The member of a hobby club quickly surrounds himself with a circle of warm friends.

Hobby shows. Recreation agencies can initiate and organize one of the most enjoyable of community-wide events—the hobby show. The worth of the show is tested not so much by the number in attendance—though this is important—as by the number of active participants. Hobby clubs, women's groups, civic clubs, schools, youth-serving organizations, municipal authorities for recreation, and individual hobbyists, working together in the show, can give stimulus to wholesome recreation through hobbies. The displays may be supplemented by demonstrations of how to carry on specific hobbies and by performances that include dancing, musical numbers, and dramatic skits.

If commercial exhibitors share in the hobby show, it may take on tremendous proportions. An example is the Indianapolis Star Hobby and Gift Show, which, in 1961, was a week-long event. The show was preceded by a parade, with children in costume and a high-school band. During the show there were special demonstrations in bowling, billiards, and trampoline gymnastics as well as a variety show and animal act. Active demonstrations included ceramics, use of power tools, Christmas decoration making, painting, weaving, wall paneling, glassblowing, leather tooling, gem polishing, and others. More than 200 hobbies were represented. Proceeds of the show benefited the Police Athletic League (PAL) Clubs.

By way of contrast is the simple playground hobby show to which neighborhood children bring their dolls, pets, and collections of shells, rocks, stamps, matchbooks, and buttons. Since the chief value of the hobby show is received by displayers rather than viewers, and since most playground hobby show participants are displayers, the value is great for the energy expended. Shows limited to particular hobbies are also successful. There may be garden shows, pet shows, camping demonstrations, showings of paintings by local artists, and the like.

Displays. Community recreation agencies can promote hobbies in additional ways. Printed information, pictures, and sometimes hobby materials themselves may find a place on bulletin boards in community centers, on playgrounds, in schools, in camps, or elsewhere where they may be seen by interested persons. Tables and cases for display of unusual collections, crafts, and works of art may also be provided.

Talks and demonstrations. In order to spread knowledge of hobbies from one group to another, recreation agencies may sponsor talks and demonstrations given by individuals with interesting hobbies. Such occasions provide not only inspiration to others but satisfying experiences to the hobbyists. If enough interest is evinced, clubs or classes may be organized around the hobby.

Hobby centers. Some communities maintain specialized centers catering to particular hobby interests. Art centers, children's museums, nature centers, and garden centers are illustrations of such specialized developments.

Leadership

Since many hobbies are individual pursuits, leadership assumes a somewhat different function from that in other recreation activities. Emphasis is on developing the ability of individuals to carry on under their own initiative. Leaders can provide the climate and the incentives for the development of hobby interests but cannot superimpose their own dedication to a hobby upon participants. Perhaps the most important qualities of the leader of a hobby are a zest for the hobby itself and a desire to interest others. The leader can show beginning hobbyists how to explore the dimensions of their hobbies. He may help the sea shell enthusiast want not only to collect shells and admire their beauty but to learn something about the magnificent world of marine life. He may encourage the stamp collector to know something about the history of the countries whose stamps he possesses. A leader can make a hobby a broadening, not a limiting, experience.

Should everyone have a hobby?

There are those who insist that everyone should have a hobby. In an age in which leisure hours exceed work hours for many people, hobbies are more important than ever before. For a few people, particularly those in the higher professions, work itself is so engrossing that it becomes a hobby; and no other hobby is wanted. For the great majority of people, however, hobbies are means of enriching life and reaching heights of achievement and recognition denied them in their work. Community recreation agencies can do much to encourage hobbies that grant these rewards.

Special Events

The public spotlight in community recreation programs is frequently trained on special events. They add color, light, and excitement to the routine fare. Leaders must be cautioned, however, that successful recreation programing must be grounded firmly in a well-balanced, day-to-day schedule of interesting opportunities in all program areas. Just as a well-balanced meal of staple foods is enhanced by an inviting dessert, so the recreation menu may be enlarged and embellished by special activities that depart from the regular recreation diet. A meal composed only of desserts, delectable though each may be, would be unbalanced and unhealthful; by the same token, a recreation program with a preponderance of special events is unwholesome and undesirable.

Definition and scope

The term "special event" is, as the name implies, an event which, because of its uniqueness, its departure from normal routine, its extraordinary demands in organizational pattern or coordination of personnel, or its infrequency of production, becomes something special for those whom it attracts. Camps, playgrounds, parks, community centers, clubs, or hospitals find that special events add stimulation to their program offerings. Ideas for such events may range from the informal weekly dance at the hospital to the grandiose Mardi Gras on a community-wide basis. Over the years, some special events become a part of the yearly routine but still remain within the category of special events because of the uniqueness of their appeal or their infrequent occurrence.

The horizons of ideas for special events stretch as far as the imagination, budget, and facilities of the sponsoring agencies. Ordinarily, special events fall into three major categories:

1. *Special days that involve the participants and parents in any one organization or area.* Examples of such programs would be the special campfire for campers and their parents, the style show for patients at the hospital, or the pet show on one of the playgrounds.

2. *Intra-agency or inter-area attractions.* When the Girl Scout troops in the city combine efforts to join in a mother-daughter banquet, we have another kind of special event with different organizational needs. A comparable affair would evolve in the interplayground craft show.

3. *City-wide community affairs.* When organizations join forces in a special event that attracts the interest of the general public, then still a different type of pattern evolves. Jointly sponsored historical pageants, city-wide dance festivals, or community hobby shows might exemplify this category.

Some recreation programs include also "program peps" or "semi-specials" to spark their weekly offerings, particularly in day-to-day offerings such as those found in community centers, playgrounds, or hospitals. The ladder tournament day for checkers or Zell ball on the playground or the spur-of-the-moment alphabet nature hike at camp offer few prolonged efforts in organization but they lend semi-climactic moments to the pleasures of the daily offerings. Many program experts also include such activities in the special-event category.

Values in special events

There is much to be gained from the break in routine in a special setting or in the community-wide approach. Some values in special events, for sponsoring organizations or for participants, are:

1. To provide added incentive for those already involved in the program and forcefully motivate those who have not yet attended the basic offerings.
2. To offer chances to show with pride work well done in a crafts exhibit, hobby show, or nature display.
3. To serve as excellent public-relations tools to sell the program to those who would not otherwise be aware of the activities. If the

talent show were not publicized or the costume parade did not flow down Main Street, many citizens would be oblivious to recreation offerings.

4. To give excellent opportunities for involving adult volunteers who help in organization or execution of the specialty and then become interested in the basic program.

5. To integrate and make more meaningful separate program offerings as agencies, clubs, or even special supervisors within a recreation staff start working together toward a common goal.

6. To add glamor and spice, and give participants added incentive to practice their creative or physical skills.

7. To provide opportunities for education, as the child learns to groom his pet for the pet show or explore historical lore for the pageant costume or set design.

8. To provide a "shot in the arm," which lifts the morale for both staff and participants.

9. To bring the recreation program to the people and the people to the program. Many a mother is unaware of the facilities and areas within walking distance, until the child next door asks for her baby for the playground baby show and stimulates a visit to the playground.

10. To alert community leaders to the values of the recreation program, as recreation offerings involve them in the judging of some special event.

11. To provide a spirit of competition as participants meet in a community-wide or interplayground special event. Such competitive spirit, sparked by a loyalty to the "home" organization, creates additional zeal and incentives for better and more closely coordinated preparations.

12. To make changes of pace, which constantly afford the adventure and excitement of the surprise appeal.

Special events on the playground

Experience has proved that a weekly special event will provide exciting and climactic activity for the day-to-day participants and will attract additional devotees, who are lured by the special event and enticed into a more regular attendance. Special events for playground may involve "on the grounds" or "off-playground" opportunities. Choices of events and frequency of occurrence will depend on available staff, needs and interests of participants, local color, and budget. Following are a few examples of feasible specialties for weekly fun that do not require excessive organization or promotion.

On the playground:

Doll shows. Each child brings a doll; awards are made for the prettiest, ugliest, most unique, et cetera.

Pet shows. Anything classifies as a pet from the beribboned worm in a matchbox to the purebred collie. Such a show requires organization to avoid hazards of fighting dogs, fish eaten by cats, or thirsty animals.

Rodeo days. Ranch activities and real pony rides can make this day a keen attraction.

Diaper Derby. The nine- to twelve-month-old crawlers are coaxed across a tarpaulin racetrack to the finish line. Rear-view camera shots are always popular.

Off the playground:

Bus or train trips. In the American state of opulence in which cars are owned by most families, the children may enjoy their first taste of the bus

Fig. 32 *Rodeo Day—Detroit Zoological Park*

or train ride in a playground special event. Destination may add excitement, with a ballgame or concert in store at the end of the trip.

Hikes. Excursions to fish hatcheries, museums, or firehouses are educational, as well as pleasurable.

Nature outings. Some playgrounds offer a series of one-day camp experiences in an off-the-playground special.

Other less-frequent special events involve playgrounds on a city-wide basis in hobby shows, interplayground field days, fishing derbies, or talent show playoffs. Such events require careful, long-range planning and are usually scheduled, organized, planned, and coordinated by the top administrator, with the help of the personnel from each participating playground.

Playgrounds frequently finish the summer season with an extravaganza, which may take the form of a carnival, playday, circus, pageant, field day, or holiday party for the playground participants and their friends. This end-of-the-season "send-off" integrates and culminates all phases of the playground program. One caution needs to be observed as plans are formulated for the grand event. Concentration of efforts toward the finale should not deny or detract from the daily routine, which is still the heart of the continuing success or failure of the playground program.

Special events for the community centers

The community center, whether it is established for the needs of children, youth, or adults, needs some special program "peps" to break the certainty of the daily routine. Special tournaments in ping pong or cards (with final playoffs), holiday parties, dances, progressive game nights, charm school nights, or disc jockey specials have all proved popular.

Several community centers have combined forces with parents to stage all-night "after-prom" parties in an attempt to eliminate unwholesome activities or accidents in driving sprees after the junior or senior prom. Special committees involving recreation-center personnel, parents, school faculties, and interested citizens have paved the way for saner and more satisfying expenditure of the early hours of the morning after the prom band has played for the last dance.

Hospital special events

Parties and game nights on the ward and weekly hospital dances, style shows, or musical concerts for those who are allowed to go off the ward add new zest for patients. Hours or days of anticipation go into the simulated radio show displayed for patients and staff. Less highly organized events such as daily ladder tournaments for ping pong or musical listening hours give a lift to the daily routine. Picnics in nearby parks offer new vistas and special rewards.

City-wide special events

All segments of the city or town can be attracted to mass participation in any of the program areas. The highly popular Halloween celebration in Pittsfield, Massachusetts, combines the efforts of industry, police, recreation department, and interested citizens from the huge parade to after-parade parties for all ages. Such civic cooperation has not only contributed to the enjoyment of participants and spectators but has cut down significantly on delinquent behavior on the night when youth feels the urge to howl with the witches.

Water shows that involve participants from many organizations integrate music, dramatics, swimming, diving, and skills in costume and set designing.

The Christmas season or patriotic holidays offer stimulation for community-wide celebrations in religious observances, parades, or field days.

Scout jamborees occur on city-wide and nation-wide bases and prove to be incentives for better participation in the other aspects of program offerings. Community sings, band concerts, and music festivals have proved popular as have square-dance festivals and hobby shows. Joint sponsorship by agencies and organizations results in best promotion of and involvement in city-wide events.

Organization of special events

It would be impossible to write general principles of planning for special events as a program feature, since the type and extent of such events are so varied. Generally speaking, the larger the spectacular, the more people must be involved in the plan, the more budget allowance is needed, and the more detailed the plans must be. Every special event, large or small, should have a general planning committee, at the head of which is one person who has over-all responsibility, who is "in charge." A steering committee not only divides and absorbs the details of responsibilities but also proves a liaison between the planning committee and those whom they wish to attract with the special event. Planning is done in light of objectives, interests, needs, budget, and personnel available. Responsibilities for promotion, facilities, program, personnel, finance, awards, judging, evaluation, and cleanup must be assigned.

Formula for success

Types of special events are so diverse that no attempt will be made to specify guideposts for any of the separate kinds. A few generalizations that might heighten success in some situations are:

1. *Keep special events in balance.* They lose their appeal if there are too many, and they tend to overshadow the other phases of the program.

2. *Do not sacrifice the daily program by concentrating the energies of staff and participants on weekly or monthly specials.* If the Brownie troop must work each weekly meeting on nothing but the scheduled carnival, then perhaps the carnival is too complicated a special event for this group.

3. *Avoid big prizes.* Think up all the superlatives possible for the vehicle parade or the comic-strip character day. It's the *activity* the participants should remember, not the prize. A large number of small prizes or ribbons will be more effective than a small number of expensive awards.

4. *Obtain advance registrations for pet shows, talent shows, kite contests, and similar activities.* They help in the planning and execution of the events.

5. *Secure a police escort for parades of any sort.* Escorts are needed for any special event that will gather more than the ordinary number in any particular area.

6. *For best public relations, notify the residents when a special event will be planned in their immediate area.* The street dance noise is less bothersome for the neighbor who has been notified and consulted concerning time and objectives for the gathering.

7. *Secure written permission from parents for all "off-the-grounds" activities.*

8. *Allow the general public to become more appreciative of program efforts through publicity in promotional materials or post-event pictures and stories.*

9. *Prepare a master plan of city-wide special events.* Supplement it by individual daily or weekly specials on each area to provide coordination and integration of basic program offerings.

10. *Keep a first-aid kit on the playground or a first-aid mobile unit at the parade or carnival site.* Special events gather crowds. As too many recreation directors have already learned, there is not always "safety in numbers."

Special events highlight, integrate, and culminate all other program areas. Those events that deal with other specific areas, such as sports, arts and crafts, or drama, are dealt with in other sections of this book. Again, emphasis must be placed on the fact that recreation programs must be anchored in enriched, day-to-day scheduling of interesting activities. Special events provide the icing for the cake for those loyal stalwarts who would have eaten the plain cake anyway and entice those who want desserts before they will sample the bread and butter.

SUGGESTED REFERENCES

Benson, Kenneth R., *Creative Crafts for Children*. Englewood Cliffs, N.J.: Prentice-Hall, Inc., 1958.

Borst, Evelyne and Elmer D. Mitchell, *Social Games for Recreation*. New York: The Ronald Press Company, 1959.

Brockman, C. Frank, *Recreational Use of Wild Lands*. New York: McGraw-Hill Book Company, 1959.

Butler, George D., ed., *Community Sports and Athletics: Organization, Administration, Program*. New York: The Ronald Press Company, 1949.

Corbin, H. Dan, *Recreation Leadership*. Englewood Cliffs, N.J.: Prentice-Hall, Inc., 1953.

Hammett, Catherine T. and Carol M. Horrocks, *Creative Crafts for Campers*. New York: Association Press, 1957.

Hillcourt, William, *Field Book of Nature Activities*. New York: G. P. Putnam's Sons, 1950.

Jenny, John H., *Introduction to Recreation Education*. Philadelphia: W. B. Saunders Company, 1955.

Kaplan, Max, *Music in Recreation*. Champaign, Ill.: Stipes Publishing Co., 1955.

Kraus, Richard, *Recreation Leader's Handbook*. New York: McGraw-Hill Book Company, 1955.

Leonhard, Charles, *Recreation Through Music*. New York: The Ronald Press Company, 1952.

Mattil, Edward L., *Meaning in Crafts*. Englewood Cliffs, N.J.: Prentice-Hall, Inc., 1959.

Parson, Ruben L., *Conserving American Resources*. Englewood Cliffs, N.J.: Prentice-Hall, Inc., 1956.

Shaw, Lloyd, *The Round Dance Book*. Caldwell, Idaho: Caxton Printers, Ltd., 1950.

Staples, Frank, *Arts and Crafts Program Manual*. New York: National Recreation Association, 1954.

The Recreation Program. Chicago: The Athletic Institute, Revised 1963.

Vannier, Maryhelen, *Methods and Materials in Recreation Leadership*. Philadelphia: W. B. Saunders Company, 1956.

"To know how to grow old is the master work of wisdom, and one of the most difficult chapters of living."

CHARLES REED

18

Recreation
Serves Special Needs

Social, cultural, economic, and technological transitions often create new problems. In today's society, there have emerged many groups of individuals who are atypical either because of infirmity, disease, mental deficiencies, extended age, or lack of freedom to choose their living and working environment. Since changes in society are, in part, responsible for creating these problem individuals, a democratic society must be responsible for offering compensatory opportunities for them. Inasmuch as recreation is deemed a basic human need for all, the recreation profession must accept the challenge to provide recreation outlets for the aged, the institutionalized, and others who require special attention. This chapter is concerned with the problems inherent in meeting the recreation needs of these segments of society.

Recreation in the Later Years

For many years, the plight of the aged population in the countries of the world was principally a family affair or an individual responsibility. In a three-generation household and a rural environment, the senior citizen who succeeded in accumulating an unbelievable 70 chronological years in his life-span could expect preferential social or family status, a community deference to his superior wisdom and strength, a dependence upon his experience, or a lessening of his economic burdens. Such community reciprocation for services rendered has become today a complex, if not at times impossible, responsibility, which has focused dramatic attention on the acute problems of the aged in our country.

In the last sixty years, the composition of our society has undergone a revolution, which was at first gradual, then accelerated. Since 1900, the numbers of aged in the United States more than quadrupled, while the rest of the population only doubled. Social, economic, technological, and scientific developments have created changes that demand drastic adjustments in the lives of those who are over 65 years of age. As millions of people live to become aged, the concerns of this age group must become the interest and problem of the community; solutions to problems are rarely found solely through individual effort to adjust to circumstances beyond individual control.

A look at the problem

Reasons for the increased concern for the welfare of the aged include several factors that must alert the recreation profession to the needs of this segment of the population.

Increase in the numbers of persons over 65 years of age. In 1960, there were about 17 million persons in the United States who had reached or passed their sixty-fifth birthday. Population predictions made by the Department of Health, Education, and Welfare indicate that in the forty years between 1960 and 2000 the aged population will more than double in number.[1]

These figures become more meaningful when described as percentages of the total population. The aged have increased their proportion from approximately one out of twenty, in 1900, to one out of eleven in 1960. Better diet, advances in preventive medicine and medical care, better sanitation and health practices, and technological advances that have raised the standard of living and decreased the mortality rate have combined to add years to normal life expectancy. Average life expectancy at birth has increased by more than twenty years for women and seventeen for men in a period of the last fifty years. Thus, there are more persons who can expect to live more years; there remains a challenge to make those additional years meaningful and satisfying.

Decrease in job opportunities and increase in compulsory retirement. The increasing tempo of the so-called Machine Age, initiated by the In-

[1] Senate Special Committee on Aging, *New Population Facts on Older Americans*, 1960, 87th Congress, 1st session (Washington, D.C.: Government Printing Office, 1961), p. 9.

dustrial Revolution, tends to give employment advantages to younger individuals. Emphasis on speed and physical strength tends to put the older person in the unenviable position of being stereotyped as a poor job-risk, despite research that has arrived at favorable conclusions as to his efficiency, his low rate of absenteeism, and the worthiness of his contribution. In the labor force discrimination against hiring those over 60 years of age is prevalent. Our present system of compulsory retirement, without careful regard to economic need, physical ability, mental acumen, or education for use of leisure, carries with it a psychological impact for which few retirees are prepared.

Attitudes of and toward the aged. Not the least of the problems blocking fruitful use of leisure in the later years are the attitude of younger generations toward the aged and the feelings of emptiness that the aged themselves experience. Americans live in a youth-oriented society, which tends to glorify accomplishments that demand the speed and power of youth. They need to be taught that numbers of calendar years are not always an indication of mental aptitude or of physical productivity.

The Social Security Act, though initiated to alleviate the problems of the aged, has done much to condition the thinking of the nation to the point of view that the attainment of age 65 must automatically throw the worker on the economic and social scrapheap. We need to outgrow the assumption that youth is the best of life and that old age is the denouement after the real climax has been reached. The aged person himself must not succumb to the stereotypes of age as a period of dependency, ill health, immobility, eccentricity, isolation, and uselessness, all of which deter him from courageously exploring new roles. Too often, the oldster "gives up" physically and mentally long before his capabilities have dictated such action. As one author puts it, hardening of the arteries is less prevalent than hardening of the attitudes. Education toward a new concept of his place in society is needed both for the aged and for the community at large. If the aged are to have sympathetic understanding and a feeling of self-worth, there must be a more positive attitude toward what the later years can entail.

Changing role and status of the aged. As the numbers of aged have increased, their prestige has decreased. The use of age as a reference point for establishing status is almost universal. Most societies recognize three groupings: the child, the adult, and the aged. Unfortunately, the third stage has lost status in our society. The adult roles command the highest prestige in present communities. It is very difficult realistically to equate prestige, respect, material wealth, or prominence with the average older person in the United States.

The lack of a precise role to play, sudden retirement from the satisfying functions of an occupation, relaxing of family ties with the death of a spouse or the mobility of children, and indecision concerning the use of increased leisure all bring psychological effects that may be devastating. The sense of being needed and useful is often lost in the transition from the labor force into retirement. Attitudes of society as a whole toward retirement must be changed before the retiree can look forward optimistically to the later years as meaningful, significant, and satisfying. The attitude of the older person is greatly dependent upon how useful he feels in his surroundings.

Financial difficulties. Many of the aged are living on reduced or fixed incomes. With ever-increasing costs of living, discretionary income for this age bracket does not correspond with the increase in discretionary time. In spite of extended Social Security benefits, many aged persons have incomes inadequate to meet anything but the bare necessities of life. The 1960 census listed the majority of those over 65 as having less than $1,000 annual income. Under such conditions, even the transportation fee to and from leisure activity could deny participation to many.

Changing environment. A three-generation household in a rural environment kept the aged of a past generation busily useful in the daily demands of a rugged existence. The reduction in numbers and proportions of farmers or owners of small businesses has made us a nation of wage earners from whose market the sixty-five year old has been banished.

The new trend in homes differs from the rambling farm house in which each of three generations held a useful, interdependent position. The present, smaller, two-generation unit gives the aged person little room, little privacy, and little sense of personal contribution. Rather than face the crises of such an environment, 77 percent of the aged live alone, creating further problems for those who wish to reach them for group activities.

Job opportunities in a new business and industrial world, coupled with easier, less expensive transportation, have scattered families, often leaving the aged isolated from those on whom they most depend for emotional security. Reluctance on the part of the aged person to move from his hometown leaves him all too often without family, without friends, and with little heart to continue his lonely existence.

Providing the aged with housing that is within their financial means and that offers a stimulating, satisfying environment as well as mere shelter is a challenge to the architects of our time. Many attempts are being made to accept this challenge, both by the federal government and by private agencies.

The living environment for the aged is an individual choice, just as it is for any other age group. Some want group housing; some need institutional life; some prefer housing units integrated with the total community; others seek independent units within a colony of retirees. There is no rubber stamp that can magically afford the answer to housing needs.

Among those needs, however, is access to areas and facilities that provide recreation outlets for expanded leisure.

Health of the aged. Maintaining health and vigor in later maturity becomes a problem in situations in which diet may be faulty and opportunity or stimulation of desire for healthful exercise may be at a minimum. Physical difficulties occur at a more rapid rate than in youth. Susceptibility to mental illness may increase because of organic difficulties or psychological maladjustment resulting from loss of sight or hearing or the decline of meaningful social roles.

Increase in leisure hours. For the majority of the aged population, leisure is a new experience. Vacations with pay, the eight-hour day, and the 40-hour week are comparatively recent innovations. The 12- to 16-hour day in a rural setting left no time for a problem of leisure use. Before our machine culture decreased man-hours needed for work, the elderly could continue their crafts, their farming, or their small businesses, without too much change in their standard of living or too much risk of being swallowed by competition from larger concerns.

Urbanization, change in living area, influx of machinery, improved transportation and communication, new technological and scientific inventions have all created more leisure for more persons. Volumes have been written about the use or misuse of this leisure by teenagers. Just as important is the impact of this leisure on the aged. It is, perhaps, more important, because the aged had no gradual introduction to leisure and because they were educated for the most part to a philosophy that proclaimed the godliness of work and the sinfulness of idleness. As a nation, we still have much to learn at any age with respect to adequate, creative, and recreative outlets for leisure. A general change in attitude toward the potential of leisure might leave the retired senior citizen with a sense of freedom rather than loss and uselessness in his new-found hours.

The challenge to recreation

The first half of the twentieth century in the United States saw a concerted effort toward better opportunities for youth. The last half of the century may well be spent in showing like concern for the aged. The human life-span seems to be evolving into three phases of emphasis: a first devoted to basic education, a second involved with family and vocational responsibilities, and a third given to retirement. With the current predictions on drastic elongation of life expectancy in the future (some say we may be living to the age of 125), this third phase may well prove to be the largest. How we prepare for it may determine whether or not it can become "the last of life, for which the first was made."

Compulsory retirement, elongation of the expected life-span, reduction of work opportunities, loss of social status and contacts because of withdrawal from the work force, difficult housing conditions, little outlet for creative self-expression, and decreasing chances for maintaining physical and mental health have produced a large population of potentially lonely persons with a large number of leisure hours. Projections indicate that the future will increase both the numbers of the aged and their amounts of leisure. What the aged do in that leisure may help them in their social and psychological adjustments or may condemn them to an elongated period of "graveyard watching."

Needs of the aging

Basic psychological needs for the aged do not differ radically from those of any other age group. The needs for new experience, recognition, response, participation, security, self-expression, and the aesthetic or creative are constant. Many writers have developed lists of special needs for those in later maturity.

The pamphlet *Enriching the Added Years* lists the basic needs of the aging as: economic security, preservation of health, maintaining personal contacts, useful activity, good living arrangements, and meaningful use of free time.[2] Regardless of the terminology used, the lists of needs include wholesome leisure activities to provide fullness, growth, and enrichment in the later years—the opportunity to *grow* old, not merely to *get* old.

The section of the 1961 White House Conference on Aging that dealt with population trends and the social and economic implications thereof evolved a Senior Citizen's Charter, which detailed both the rights that the aged should expect as citizens and their obligations to their communities. Included in the compilation of rights was "the right to a fair share of the community's recreational, educational, and medical resources." Pertinent obligations of the aging included "the obligation of each citizen to prepare himself to become and resolve to remain active, alert, capable, self-supporting, and useful so long as health and circumstances permit and plan for ultimate retirement," "the obligation to seek and develop potential avenues of service in the years of retirement," and "the obligation to make available the benefits of his experience and knowledge."[3] The section affirmed strongly that society must adopt a new philosophy, one that denies the concept that gainful employment is the sole symbol of human worth and dignity and that fosters the concept that constructive leisure activity is a meaningful source of human values.

[2] Department of Health, Education, and Welfare, *Enriching the Added Years* (Washington, D.C.: Government Printing Office, 1959).

[3] Department of Health, Education, and Welfare, *The Nation and Its Older People* (Washington, D.C.: Government Printing Office, 1961), p. 118.

A look at history

Although historically old age has always been with us, the concentration of attention on this segment of the population in the United States did not reach a climax until after World War II. The sharp rise in numbers of those over 65 years of age activated an increased concern for all aspects of aging and its accompanying adjustments.

At that time the federal and the state governments gave attention to medical care, housing, income maintenance, and research. Committees and commissions were appointed in most states to explore the special needs of the aged. State and regional conferences were held. Two national conferences were called. Medicine and the social sciences formed special societies to deal with physical diseases or other problems of this age group (American Geriatric Society, 1942, and the Gerontological Society, 1944). Legislation concerning improvement of institutional living for the aged has been enacted in some states. The federal government has established the Special Staff on Aging in the Department of Health, Education, and Welfare.

Educational efforts. Educators have focused attention on the aged with the formation of permanent Institutes of Gerontology in state universities such as those in Florida, Michigan, Iowa, and Connecticut. During the late 1950's, four major interdisciplinary research centers (Duke University, Albert Einstein Medical School, Western Reserve, and University of Miami) were established with support from the National Institutes of Health. Courses in gerontology and courses for the aged are being included in the offerings of colleges and universities. Thirty-two national organizations have educational programs about the aging. Churches are becoming increasingly more aware of their obligations to their aged members. Social services for the elderly are reported in a majority of states.

Private and public agencies are becoming concerned with housing for those over sixty-five. A profusion of literature dealing with every aspect of the aging process has been offered to the public since 1950. All kinds of national organizations that distribute monthly periodicals catering to the interests of the aged are ever more popular. Private philanthropic foundations are spending millions of dollars on projects for the aged.

Much of the present attention is the result of two national conferences. The First National Conference on Aging, in 1950, brought together 816 participants from all parts of the country with the underlying purposes of focusing attention on the needs and problems of the aged and exploring means of solving those problems. The years following the conference saw some improvements in several areas, but the decision to implement a White House Conference on the Aging, in 1961, arose from a feeling that there had been more words than action in the campaign for better living for the elderly.

White House Conference on the Aging. Congressman John E. Fogarty introduced a bill to provide funds for the national conference. Each state was offered an amount up to $15,000 to enable it to convene leaders, to explore its own needs and resources, and to send its conclusions and recommendations through its representative delegates to the national meeting. The meeting of 3,000 delegates was followed by state and regional conferences to make reports and to outline plans of action. Stimulation of community concern both before and after the White House Conference was perhaps the most dramatic consequence of the national gathering.

All fifty states assigned delegates to the section of the White House Conference that dealt with Free-Time Activities: Recreation, Voluntary Services, Citizenship Participation. Most of those convened agreed that the term recreation might encompass the second and third terms also. Recommendations of the section on free time emphasized the need for extended programs, better facilities, cooperative planning, more adequate leadership, more research, and more adequate preparation for retirement.

Recreation programs for the aged

Although the Church of Latter Day Saints is said to have organized leisure activities for its older members as early as 1875, greatest attention to recreation for elder citizens was initiated in the years following World War II. Stimulating activities are necessary at any age, but in the years of retirement—when social contacts, demands of work, and family obligations decrease while leisure hours increase—worthwhile, creative, meaningful participation is mandatory for healthful living. Figure 33 shows how a community organizes to serve the recreational needs of older people.

Leisure programs for the aged are currently sponsored by public recreation departments, voluntary agencies, organizations, private foundations, welfare councils, labor unions, religions, industries, national associations such as Volunteers of America, philanthropic clubs such as Altrusa Club, service organizations, lodges, and associations of the aged themselves. A survey by the National Committee on Aging, in 1960, reported 218 centers and 803 clubs, though there is no complete information available as to numbers of clubs or aged served on a national scale. The 1961 Recreation and Park Yearbook of the National Recreation Association listed 645 cities and 36 counties that reported special recreation programs for the aged of their communities.

Types of programs. The programs suitable for the aged duplicate somewhat those suitable at any adult age. Programs that have proved successful in communities include:

SPORTS. Bowling, horseshoes, shuffleboard, hunting, tennis, fishing, golf, sailing, and watching team sports are popular with those over sixty-five. Participation depends somewhat on finance, past experience with sports, and involvement by other household members such as grandchildren.

Fig. 33   *How a Community Organizes To Serve the Recreational Needs of Older People. Source:* Recreation for Older People in California (*Sacramento, Calif.: California Recreation Commission, October 1951*)

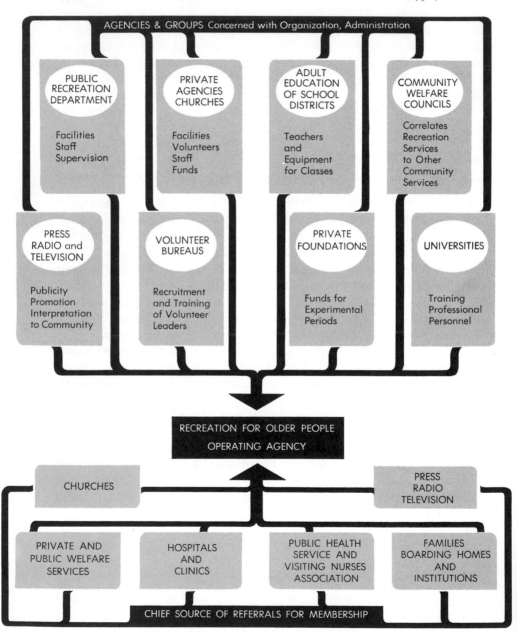

CLASSES AND DEMONSTRATIONS. Cooking, home nursing, flower arrangements, hat design, painting, sewing, wood carving, and machine tool operation are some of the possibilities for educational and recreational classes. Especially useful is instruction in activities that the aged can carry on in their own homes outside of class hours.

OUTDOOR RECREATION. Camping for senior citizens is gaining enthusiastic support. Gardening and hiking are replacing the solitary park-sitting days of some elder citizens.

SOCIAL CLUBS AND INTEREST CLUBS. Formation of a club of those over sixty-five has been the starting point for other program efforts in most communities. Some of the more common names used to designate clubs composed of elderly members are: Sunset, Senior Citizen, Borrowed Timer, Golden Age, Happy Seventies, Evergreen, and Gay Nineties. The social clubs meet to celebrate birthdays, play cards, sing together, and engage in a variety of service activities. After initial organization, they usually elect officers, run their own programs, and in general operate with little support or leadership from the sponsoring agency. Many states have organized state associations of Golden Age Clubs, and the National Association of Senior Citizens' Clubs meets annually. Special-interest clubs include choral groups, dance enthusiasts, discussion groups, play reading, poetry writing, and many others.

MUSIC, DANCE, AND DRAMA. Many interest clubs are formed in these program areas, but centers also offer playgoing excursions, band concerts, record listening hours, lectures on opera, free movies, harmonica bands, and informal singing around the piano.

TRAVEL. Interest in travel is expressed in attendance at travelog programs and in the popular trips to scenic or historic places. The elderly are more mobile than one might expect, and the planned tour that adds social companionship to the pleasure of seeing things makes an exciting program.

SERVICE ACTIVITIES. Opportunities to serve others in the community make life worthwhile for many aged. Participating in political activities, visiting the sick, teaching crafts or music, umpiring ballgames, babysitting, and serving the church are all socially valuable experiences from which the elderly gain satisfaction.

INFORMAL ACTIVITIES. Card playing, reading, and letter writing are forms of recreation left to individual choice at home or at a center.

A *typical program.* Programs vary with the needs of the individuals. A typical monthly program in one center included: free movies with titles that ranged from "Van Gogh—Darkness to Light" to "Famous Fish I Have Met"; a tour to see autumn foliage; two birthday parties; a speech on "United States Politics in World Affairs"; lessons in bridge, knitting, oil painting, cooking, and stage design; a craft session to make Christmas decorations; a high school performance of an excerpt from "The King and I"; a stag party for men; a "This Is Your Life" review of a member; a costume party; a hobby show; and the regular drop-in reading, visiting, and card-playing activities of the center.

Facilities

Recreation facilities for the aged are getting a share of the attention of present planning committees. Whether it is feasible or desirable to have a center for the exclusive use of the aged is a point for discussion and can be determined only by local situations. Wings of civic or community centers that are designated for use of senior citizens are sometimes

Fig. 34   *Quiet Fun—Golden Age Camp, Atlanta, Georgia*

preferable. Churches and other agencies sometimes provide one large social room.

Whether the facility is a part of a center or a complete building, two considerations are of paramount importance—the location and the design. The senior citizen in most instances has decreased energy for walking and a limited budget for transportation. It is important to establish neighborhood facilities that are readily accessible. The facility should be designed with consideration for the increasing infirmities of this age group. First-floor accommodations with rampways or stairs with handrails are desirable. Good lighting and heating are mandatory. Hallways that allow a wheelchair to pass must also be considered.

Who pays?

Can the older adult pay for his own recreation needs? In the average case, the answer to this question is definitely "No." Much has been done for the elderly through religious organizations, voluntary agencies, and associations for retired employees. The elderly person must be allotted a fairer share of the recreation tax dollar, if increasing needs are to be serviced.

Leadership needs

More attention must be given in recreation curriculums of colleges and universities to the nature of the aging process, the special needs of the aged in the population, and the interests of these people. Practical field experience, which involves working in a variety of situations with persons over sixty-five years of age, should be included. Research efforts to discover better ways of meeting the recreation needs of the aged must be accelerated.

Coordination

There are now so many organizations that are trying to minister to the needs of the aged that particular attention must be given at the local level to avoid duplication of effort and to coordinate existing programs and facilities. "Doing for the aged" has become a popular philanthropic bandwagon. Conscientious efforts to coordinate such energies must be forthcoming.

Guides to successful planning for the future

Stieglitz informs us that "success or failure in the second forty years, measured in terms of happiness, is determined more by how we use or abuse our leisure than by any other factor." [4] Such a statement proves challenging for the recreation profession. If the recreation needs of the aged of the future are to be met, we must:

[4] Edward J. Stieglitz, *The Second Forty Years* (Philadelphia: J. B. Lippincott Company, 1946), p. 260.

1. Help to change public attitudes toward retirement so that this period of leisure may be so meaningful and rewarding that it will no longer be dreaded.

2. Help to create social values that will lend social status and prestige to the leisure roles of the aged.

3. Realize that the aged of the future may not duplicate the attributes of the aged of today, since they will have lived through different leisure experiences unknown in the earlier years of our present aged.

4. Recognize that people spanning the years from 65 to 100 cannot be dealt with as one age group. Knowledge of the aging process and its physical and psychological toll is important to the program planning.

5. Plan programs that will integrate the aged with other age groups as well as those that will allow them to associate with their peers.

6. Create a greater variety of program opportunities with increasing emphasis on social, mental, and cultural activities, including classes that will teach new skills.

7. Use every available means of contact to encourage the isolated aged to participate in recreation.

8. Encourage provision for recreation facilities and leadership in retirement communities and homes for the aged.

9. Plan *with*, not *for* this age group. Involvement in planning is especially significant for the elder citizens.

10. Keep fees and charges low. Although some senior citizen clubs are self-supporting, it is usually desirable to keep fees and charges at a minimum.

11. Legislate to upgrade current standards for institutional care of the aged to provide better recreation facilities and leadership.

12. Educate now for the recreation literacy of the future, so that coming generations of aged will not know loneliness and boredom in their leisure hours.

Dr. T. Glynne Williams states:

There are three main barriers to the development of good programs for older people. Perhaps number one is the pessimistic attitude toward the aged among professionals, families, and the aged themselves. The others are the shortages of trained and professional personnel and failure to budget adequately. When we start taking significant strides toward overcoming these obstacles, emancipation of our aging citizens will not be far off.[5]

[5] T. Glynne Williams, "Adjustment Problems of the Aged," *Journal of Rehabilitation*, XXVII, No. 1 (January–February 1961), 24.

Joseph Lee, father of the playground movement, said, "We do not cease playing because we are old; we grow old because we cease playing." The recreation profession must look to the needs of the aged so that they may retire *to*, not *from* life.

Therapeutic Recreation

The basic democratic principle of the right to "life, liberty, and the pursuit of happiness" demands an increasing awareness of obligations to minority groups. As one of these minorities, the ill and handicapped today present new challenges for society as their numbers continue to grow at an alarming rate. Predictions for 1970 estimate that one out of every six persons in the United States will be chronically impaired. Over half of the beds in the hospitals today are occupied by mentally disturbed individuals. Estimates predict that one out of every three people may need psychiatric attention within the next 15 years. Reasons for increased concern for these segments of the population include:

1. Medical science now succeeds in keeping alive many who would have died from their difficulties, even twenty-five years ago. They continue to exist with permanent handicaps.

2. Increases in the tempo of twentieth-century living result in increased accidents or in emotional disturbances. Man has changed little in the last several thousand years; his environment has altered considerably. In primitive days, man could either fight or flee the causes of his tensions; today, in a more civilized world, he must withstand the tensions or provide substitute emotional outlets. Often, the strain is too great.

3. The wars of this century have added to the numbers of known physically and mentally handicapped, either directly as a result of war casualties, or indirectly, as a result of the discovery of impairments when servicemen were examined for active duty.

4. A modern philosophy fosters the concept that even the handicapped person should be allowed to develop to his fullest potential.

5. Those who work with the mentally and physically handicapped are increasingly aware that recreation plays a vital part in the lives of those patients being rehabilitated for return to their community life, those who must spend the rest of their lives in institutions, and those who, in the newer methods of therapy, are brought to a clinic where they can relate to companions and surroundings, though they are not institutionalized.

If the recreation profession is to maintain the ideal of "recreation for all," then the needs of the handicapped are a matter of immediate concern. To service those needs, therapeutic recreation has emerged as a professional specialty in the general field of recreation. By definition, the term *therapeutic recreation*

describes the recreation services given to people who are ill, disabled, or handicapped, and consequently unable to participate in the recreation program for able-bodied provided by the community unless special provisions are made in community settings for their inclusion.[6]

Who are the handicapped?

Emphasis has been placed on the numbers of handicapped. Who are they? What are their impairments? Hunt identifies them thus:

There are subgroups of people within our culture who frequently behave differently from the "normal." They have degrees of difference as well as kinds of difference in their biological makeup; and these differences affect their social environment and its meaning to them. Personality strains may result. Disabled people constitute one of these subgroups, one that has become a deep concern for educators, physicians, and social workers. People have called them "handicapped"—a word that is steeped with the meaning of their role in society. . . . The word "handicapped" is used to describe persons with degrees of difference physically, psychologically, and socially. It no longer refers to the extent of the physical crippling except as the crippling or actual defect limits the person competitively. An inability to compete successfully in all areas of life labels a person as handicapped.[7]

The ill and the handicapped, then, are those in our society who cannot maintain normal living experiences. The degree of an individual's handicap is conditioned not so much by the degree of disability as by his power to compensate for his deficiency.

Types of handicap

There are many types of handicap with which the recreation professional may come in contact within the community or within special institutions. They include:

The blind and the deaf. Those who have lost their sight and those who have lost their hearing frequently have feelings of rejection that multiply the difficulties of their handicaps. They are not usually hospitalized.

The cardiac, the diabetic, and the tubercular. These chronic ailments do not necessarily incapacitate the individual but may limit the type or degree of his activity.

[6] Howard Rusk, M. D., "Therapeutic Recreation," *Hospital Management,* LXXXIV, No. 4 (April 1960), 34.

[7] Valerie V. Hunt, *Recreation for the Handicapped* (Englewood Cliffs, N.J.: Prentice-Hall, Inc., 1955), pp. 44–45. Reprinted by permission.

The orthopedically handicapped. The adjustment of those with obvious crippling of limbs is often made more difficult because of their treatment by others. Visible physical defects often cause in others a reaction that complicates the emotional adjustment of the handicapped individual. Because of this, these individuals need special care.

The neurologically handicapped. Handicaps caused by cerebral palsy, brain injury, muscular dystrophy, spinal nerve injury, and similar disorders are perhaps most complex because they may involve impairment of sensory, motor, intellectual, or emotional capacities. The social rejection caused by such impairment makes necessary special and usually separate recreation programs.

The mentally retarded. Those who differ from the normal in intellectual capacity need special attention because of their inability to cope with the tempo of the normal environment. Depending upon their degree of retardation, they may or may not be institutionalized.

The mentally ill. The term "mentally ill" encompasses a wide variety of mental disorders, which range from slight emotional disturbances to severe psychoses. Most of those individuals who have been diagnosed as psychotic are under psychiatric care either within a mental hospital or as out-patients in a clinic or hospital. Better understanding of the problems and increased concern for treating the whole person, not just his ailment, have helped improve the lot of those who were once locked up and forgotten.

The physically ill. Those with physical illnesses of short- or long-term duration may be homebound or may be hospitalized. The emotional impact of being incapacitated for any length of time brings need for special attention to this group.

Where are the handicapped?

The physically and mentally handicapped are found in many places in the community. Some are confined to their homes, unable to compete physically or mentally with the environment outside their immediate surroundings. Some are in nursing homes; others are in homes for the aged. The private and state psychiatric hospitals house a great number of handicapped; the crippled children's homes service others. The general hospitals accommodate those with short-term difficulties; the Veterans' Administration hospitals service those whose handicaps were of military origin. The homes for the feeble-minded carry their burden. In short, the handicapped are all around us, some making perfect adjustment to their difficulties, some hopelessly withdrawn from a world with which they are not equipped to cope.

What are the needs of the handicapped?

Basic universal needs of man do not change simply because a person loses a portion of either mental or physical efficiency. The ill and the handicapped still have the same need to belong, to create, to feel secure, to love and be loved, to feel significant, and to experience new adventure. The needs are the same, but they are accentuated through privation. The cerebral-palsied youngster with convulsive motor patterns needs acceptance as much as his pretty, well-coordinated sister. Though the afflicted child may not get recognition for beauty or for motor ability, he must have substitute experiences in which he can feel successful and accepted. The prejudices and fears of society often deny to the handicapped the opportunity for finding their optimum usefulness and happiness.

What is the challenge to recreation?

The increasing numbers of the ill and handicapped provide a threefold challenge for the recreation profession. In a fast-moving world in which stresses and strains increase the incidence of emotional difficulties, the first challenge comes in offering wholesome, satisfying recreation activities that will relieve tensions, create substitute experiences for meeting basic needs, and act as an aid to mental health, thus helping to decrease the numbers of mentally incompetent. Recreation, then, can play a part in the *prevention* of disorder.

Second, when a person is incapacitated either because of physical or mental difficulties, wholesome recreation opportunities can provide meaningful activity during his increased leisure hours, thus helping make the patient more receptive to treatment through a happier environment.

The third challenge is the one most frequently ignored. There should be better coordination between community recreation agencies and institutions so that the recreation agency will be aware of the patient who has been released from the hospital and will know his limitations and needs. Those patients who are returning to the community are not usually ready to operate at optimum capacity. Recreation may help bridge the gap and help in the reorientation of the patient to community life.

The values of recreation, then, with regard to handicaps, are involved with prevention of illness through contributing to better mental and physical health, therapy while the patient is disabled, and rehabilitation to community life.

Recreation as an aid to mental and physical health. Doctors state that with increased emotional conflict come anxiety, fear, and tension. The normal individual under control is like an inactive geyser. When the pressure of his problems becomes too great, the result is ... Old Faithful. Recreation activities can act as ventilation for emotional tensions.

Recreation can satisfy basic needs not met in work situations. The pioneer had no need to find outlets for aggressive or creative urges in his leisure. Each day brought new adventure, the excitement of the fight against man or nature, and the need to improvise to stay alive. Opportunities for such experiences may come now to some people only through competitive sports, creative hobbies, or travel.

Physical fitness, in a world in which many jobs are becoming ever more sedentary, is dependent upon the physical exercise available in leisure. America is a "nation on wheels." Frequently, the man who will not walk half a block to work needs the stimulation of the golf or tennis game or the lure of sailing or hunting to make him use his physical energies.

Recreation as therapy. The controversy still exists among recreation and medical professionals as to whether recreation can be termed therapy. Following are some opinions, which may serve as a basis for discussion. Hunt states:

Most recreational philosophers have expressed the value of recreation as therapy or have stressed that recreation must not be geared to therapy. These diverse opinions express a semantic interpretation of the words recreation and therapy. It is this writer's feeling that play and recreation are not synonymous with therapy, but that they may act as therapy. Narrowly conceived, therapy is a thing, a medication, a surgery, or a treatment of a behavior difficulty, but such a narrow conception is as fallacious as to say that recreation is golf. Golf may be recreation as play may be therapeutic. If we look not at the act but at what it does, we must alter our concept of therapy as we have changed our interpretation of recreation—and therapy becomes the purposeful change rather than the agent that produces it. And as not all medication and treatment has the same effect upon everyone, not all activities have recreation value for all people.[8]

Menninger wrote:

It has been the privilege of many of us practicing medicine in psychiatry to have some very rewarding experiences in the use of recreation as an adjunctive method of treatment. Along with direct psychological help, hydrotherapy, shock and insulin therapy, many of us have, for years, used various forms of education, recreation, and occupation in the treatment of our patients. . . . Recreation has not only played an important part in the treatment program of many mental illnesses, but it has been a considerable factor in enabling former patients to remain well.[9]

Haun indicates another viewpoint:

Today the recreation worker is the only member of the hospital's staff who can make the patient's healthy psychologic needs his sole and exclusive con-

[8] *Recreation for the Handicapped*, p. 54.
[9] William C. Menninger, M. D., "Recreation and Mental Health," reprinted from *Recreation* (November 1948), p. 2.

cern. This is far more than providing a place for the patient to go during the hours he is not "needed" in therapy. And, to be both honest as well as effective, it must not in my view serve as subterfuge for some disguised and unspoken purpose. All patients, and particularly psychiatric patients, are in desperate need of getting away on occasion, from the stare of clinical appraisal, of being able to do something with another person, of talking to a friend, of silently sharing the warmth of companionship, without fear of being booby trapped into a clinically significant admission. . . .

The hospital recreation worker performs many services essential, in my opinion, to the welfare of the patient. I can not, however, regard any of them as therapeutic, first because I have never been convinced that recreation in any of its forms is a specific instrument for the modification of a disease process comparable say to penicillin in the treatment of syphilis; second, because I am so fully persuaded of the psychiatric patient's need for recreation *as recreation* that I grudge any dilution of its potency through adulteration with alternative purposes. I endorse the pure food and drug act. When I prescribe aspirin for my patient, the pharmacist is going to have to do a lot of fast explaining if he substitutes quinine for it. When I "prescribe" recreation for my patient, I would be saddened to think he had fallen into the hands of an earnest, highly motivated junior clinician who was attempting to treat the illness with a baseball. . . .

It is because I believe that recreation is an essential human need that I want it for my patients.[10]

Wolffe has commented on the subject thus:

It is quite apparent that it will take time until everybody concerned comes to realize that recreation activities are an effective form of therapeutics and prophylaxis. Many patients do not yet understand the medical value of properly supervised recreation activities.[11]

Recreation as the road back to community life. The road back to reality or to adjustment to a physical handicap may start at the hospital but should continue in the community. For the physically ill or disabled, recreation activities may provide the needed stimulus for exercising to improve physical health. For the mentally disturbed, recreation outlets help him to relate to others in dance, drama, social recreation, or the many other community offerings. Without the pressures of work-related demands, he may gain confidence and build his self-respect and ability to interrelate with people again.

Other values. Recreation within or outside the institution may enlarge the range of physical and mental activity, may help in the education

[10] Paul Haun, M. D., "Hospital Recreation—A Medical Viewpoint" in *Recreation for the Mentally Ill* (Washington, D.C.: American Association for Health, Physical Education, and Recreation, 1958), pp. 57–8. Reprinted by permission.

[11] Joseph B. Wolffe, M. D., *Recreation, Medicine, and the Humanities* (Chapel Hill, N.C.: University of North Carolina, 1957), p. 13. Reprinted by permission.

of the retarded, may create new interests, may develop new skills, may provide a happier environment in which a patient may be more receptive to treatment, may provide recognition, may give creative outlets, may return the neuropsychic to the group, or may simply provide meaningful activity for enforced leisure.

A look at history

Recreation for the ill is not new. Florence Nightingale made efforts to ease the life of the injured soldiers during the Crimean War with reading rooms, lectures, games, social hours, and concerts. World War I found the American Red Cross giving valuable recreation services to the wounded, while many took a new attitude toward the contribution of recreation to mental and physical well-being because numbers of draftees were refused because of physical or mental deficiencies.

The WPA staffed hospitals with recreation specialists during the depression years of the 1930's, and World War II proved again the worth of recreation as a morale booster before or after war casualties. The year 1945 brought two major events: the establishment of the Recreation Service as part of the Office of Special Services of the Veterans' Administration and the national conference sponsored by the American Red Cross to investigate training resources for hospital recreation workers.

The American Psychiatric Association formed its Leisure Time Committee in 1948; the American Recreation Society established a Hospital Recreation Section in 1949, and the University of Minnesota initiated its curriculum in hospital recreation a year later. The early 1950's found other special sections and associations being formed on national levels: The Recreation Therapy Section of the American Association for Health, Physical Education, and Recreation; the Consulting Service on Recreation for the Ill and Handicapped of the National Recreation Association, and the National Association of Recreation Therapists. These joined forces for coordination and cooperation in the Council for the Advancement of Hospital Recreation, formed in 1953.

The AAHPER held its conference on recreation for the mentally ill in November of 1957, gathering educators, practitioners, and psychiatrists to explore the needs of the fast growing specialty. The Consulting Service on Recreation for the Ill and Handicapped of the NRA, under the able leadership of Mrs. Beatrice Hill, sponsored institutes and ·workshops; gathered and published pertinent materials; conducted surveys of leadership needs and existing programs; set up a graduate fellowship program to recruit leaders for this specialty; and developed interpretive films dealing with recreation and its contribution to the ill and handicapped. The Service was responsible for a curriculum conference in 1961 to explore ways and means for getting some common agreement and standards for content of curriculums in therapeutic recreation.

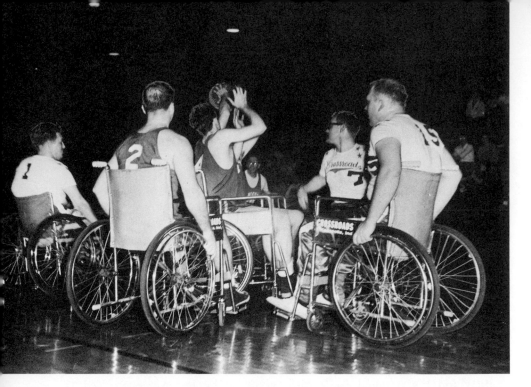

Fig. 35 *Wheelchair Basketball—Crossroads Rehabilitation Center, Indianapolis*

Comeback, Inc., "the only national organization which is concerned solely with therapeutic recreation," was born in 1961. Though much has been accomplished, the picture today with respect to therapeutic recreation still leaves much to be desired. There are few institutions of higher learning that are offering curriculums in this specialization. Leadership needs are not being met. Voluntary registration of professionals has been encouraged since 1957, yet there are still many subprofessionals being employed because of lack of qualified leadership available.

Programs for the handicapped

It would be impossible to make an inclusive list of programs that are popular with different types of handicaps. Some programs that have brought special enjoyment, however, can be mentioned. The mentally retarded learn through circle and singing games, puzzles, record listening, marionettes, and parties. The cerebral-palsied enjoy swimming, adapted crafts, trips, and quiet games. The crippled participate in wheelchair basketball or square dance. Music and drama are outlets for most of the handicapped. Radio and television shows, glee clubs, and parties help relate the mentally ill to reality. Camping is beneficial and pleasureable for most.

The city recreation department in Boston, in 1952, initiated Pleasure

Island, a playground exclusively for the retarded. Mrs. Janet Pomeroy successfully adapted a full program of recreation activities for the Recreation Center for the Cerebral Palsied in San Francisco. Even the potter's wheel can be conquered with the toes, if flailing arms make the usual methods impossible. Visitations to the ill make an enjoyable service activity for normal people and give pleasure also to the handicapped who are visited.

Camp Kno-Koma in South Charleston, West Virginia, provides full camp experiences for diabetics. Bradford Woods at Martinsville, Indiana, accommodates all kinds of handicapped children at its Camp Riley. Programs for the handicapped are limited only by the imagination of the leader and his ability to adapt activities to the limitations of his group.

Facilities

Hospitals, sheltered workshops, clinics, and recreation centers are becoming more aware of their obligation to serve the special needs of those who are atypical. State mental hospitals are building extensive activity therapy buildings and outdoor areas. Communities are adapting center facilities and camps for the use of the handicapped. General hospitals are including recreation rooms. Day centers and sheltered workshops are being constructed for exclusive use of handicapped groups. The supply of special facilities has not kept up with the demands, but those whose responsibility it is to offer recreation in the community are giving the handicapped a fairer share of the program than heretofore.

Leadership

The demands for professional recreators who understand medical and psychiatric concepts of health and disease, who are aware of the social, cultural, and psychological effects of illness and disability, and who are acquainted with the settings in which patients are cared for, far exceed the present ability of the recreation profession to meet the need. Therapeutic recreation cannot make its fullest contribution until there are available professionals who are educated, not only in the broad field of recreation, but in this specialty.

Demands for increased leadership have been met in some instances by sharing professionals among several agencies. The Forest Park Foundation of Peoria, Illinois, set up an activity therapy program with six cooperating agencies. The National Recreation Association ran a pilot project that proved the expediency of sharing recreation personnel among several nursing homes.

Types of positions. Leadership positions within an institution are frequently classified as: recreation leader, recreation supervisor, recreation director, and coordinator of activity therapy. The suggestion has been made within the profession that sub-professional aides be used to meet the gross needs of face-to-face leadership. It is the hope of the authors that improved recruitment practices and working situations may prevent the profession from resorting to such a measure. The face-to-face leader is as important to the recreation profession as is the first-grade teacher to the education world.

Several conferences have designated qualities, skills, and knowledges to be desired in the person who works in therapeutic recreation. There is some agreement within the profession that such specialization should come preferably at the graduate level, though many individuals presently engaged in such work hold only a bachelor's degree.

Curriculum conference. Participants at the 1961 Therapeutic Recreation Curriculum Development Conference evolved a list of needs pertinent to the development of curriculums for preparation of specialists for therapeutic recreation. Suggested needs included:

Recreation specialists who are prepared to conduct research in recreation for the ill, disabled and/or handicapped.

Recreation specialists with a broad body of knowledge concerning medical-care problems, administration and organization of hospitals and other health agencies, designs of specific treatment plans, and the role of recreation in comprehensive rehabilitation programs.

Recreation specialists with a variety of communication skills to interpret philosophy, basic concepts, and objectives of therapeutic recreation to workers in their own and related fields.

Measures to curtail the growing isolation of the specialist in recreation for ill, aged, disabled, and/or handicapped from the field of recreation as a whole. . . .

Improved salaries, increased status, and improved programs in education for leadership in recreation for the ill and handicapped to attract more students and ultimately reduce the shortage of persons prepared to provide all the types of therapeutic recreation.

A stronger and more dynamic total professional effort through existing associations and societies.[12]

In-service training. Because so few persons have been trained in the specialty of therapeutic recreation, in-service training before and during work experiences is mandatory to orient the individual to the setting and the special problems with which he will be working.

Use of volunteers. Volunteers may assume many important roles in this specialization. They may relieve the professional worker of clerical duties, help him in the program, and supervise activities. This type of service is a popular choice for those who wish to ease the plight of those less fortunate than themselves. The handicapped themselves are sometimes the first to offer help to others in service opportunities.

[12] *Therapeutic Recreation Curriculum Conference* (New York: Comeback, Inc., 1961), pp. 11–14.

Future prospects and needs

Predictions for the future indicate increased numbers of physically and mentally handicapped. Although personal observations of both doctors and recreation leaders seem to credit recreation activity with both preventive and curative powers, additional scientific research is needed to prove the extent of the value of recreation to this special group. Future recreation leaders must measure such contribution, must recruit for this specialization, must maintain standards of excellence, must initiate more opportunities to study this specialty in recognized curriculums, must unite within the profession and coordinate efforts with other phases of recreation, must instigate better coordination between community and institution, and most importantly, must educate for recreation choices that will help prevent illness.

Dr. Wolffe predicts that:

Recreation, properly employed as an auxiliary therapeutic measure, will yet prove to be equally as important as any of the so-called "miracle" drugs.

More importantly, re-created patients helped by a skilled team of therapists who respect and care for each of them as a complete person, will symbolize the interrelated values of recreation, medicine, and the humanities.[13]

Penal and Correctional Institutions

Despite the many social forces that have, over the years, attempted to stamp out the causes of delinquency, there are still individuals of varied ages who find themselves barred from society because they committed some antisocial act. The old-fashioned penal and correctional institution, the reform school, or the federal penitentiary fostered the concept that the inmate had given up his rights as a citizen and had lost all his privileges except those that would keep him physically alive. The best treatment that the first-time offender or the hardened criminal could expect was a marching drill in the yard or hours of sitting because he was neither required nor permitted to do otherwise.

Fortunately, modern philosophy of treatment of those who have for various reasons been deprived of their freedom in society shows a more enlightened thinking. In spite of insufficient funds, lack of trained leadership, and—sometimes—adverse public opinion, prison administrators are consistently making efforts to provide meaningful activities for the leisure of prisoners.

Need for recreation program

Recreation programs are far from being a luxury in the environment of the prison. Conversely, they are mandatory, not only for the rehabilita-

[13] Wolffe, *Recreation, Medicine, and the Humanities*, p. 3.

tion of the offender himself but for the society to which he will return. Recreation is being offered, in most instances, not so much to relieve the boredom of the inmates, but to help them in the process of again becoming potential contributing, law-abiding citizens.

Values of recreation

The values of recreation to the prisoner or to the confined juvenile delinquent duplicate those values inherent for any individual. Physical recreation affords stimulating exercise, a release of energies, a safety-valve or sublimation of aggressive urges. Team activities may teach a prisoner new lessons in self-control, cooperation, the assumption of responsibility, or an awareness of his own and others' limitations. He may learn skills in art, music, or other areas, which will broaden his horizons for future recreation choices. He may gain recognition in socially acceptable outlets with his pantomime in the talent show or his solo on music night. New interests are awakened; new insights are gained; new skills are learned to assist him in his rehabilitation. These are some of the rewards for the individual who is confined.

For the prison administration, recreation activities seem to cut down on needs for disciplinary measures. Maintaining order is easier; control through taking away recreation privileges is often more successful than more drastic forms of punishment.

For society as a whole, rewards come in two ways. The inmate who has been successfully rehabilitated is less apt to return to prison as a continued tax burden. Lessons learned may not only divert him from further misdemeanors but will help him make his adjustment as a contributing member of society.

Programs for prisoners

The recreation needs of individuals behind bars are as varied as those of their counterparts outside the prison walls. Unfortunately, their choice is much more confined. Usual offerings consist of team sports, cards, checkers, chess, reading, some music activities such as choral and instrumental groups, hobby pursuits, and films. Programs are dependent upon available facilities and leadership. Opportunities to do service jobs for organizations in neighboring communities are often popular.

Facilities

Existing facilities in penal institutions are varied in scope and extent. All have some provision for recreation programing. Most prisons have limited outdoor areas for sports activities. There is a need for more space allocated to indoor activities. Libraries range from mobile carts to well-equipped, professionally staffed units. Hobby rooms and craft shops are sometimes available.

Leadership

Few correctional or penal institutions have adequate recreation leadership. Such deficiencies seriously curtail program opportunities. The outdoor sports are often run by an athletically-inclined inmate; the indoor program is all too often of a laissez-faire variety. The meagerness of the offerings is explained by the fact that money from the canteen provides the principal source of recreation funds in many instances. Until such time as the general public, who support these institutions through their taxes, can be made more vitally aware of the need for expanded recreation leadership, facilities, and program, much that could help rehabilitate the delinquent will be impossible.

Future needs

Perhaps the greatest need in the area of recreation for correctional institutions is that of better public understanding of the problem. Garrett Heyns reminds us of our responsibility in the following statement:

> The public should remember that the reason many men are behind bars is due in no small measure to lack of adequate recreation facilities in the free world. Institution heads who are trying to succeed with individuals in whose cases society has thus far failed should not be handicapped because of lack of facilities. The public is often remiss in its efforts at prevention; it should not now be niggardly in the program of rehabilitation.
>
> One of the primary functions of penal and correctional institutions is to protect the public from those who violate the law. However, society is protected from any individual criminal only as long as he is kept safely within an institution. As soon as he is released to go his predatory way, this protection ceases. It is only when a change has been brought about within the offender so that he goes back to the free world with his thinking and his aspirations in accord with those which are socially acceptable that society is free from danger in his case. It is the duty of the institution to help bring about this change.[14]

Hopefully, extended recreation programs under professional leadership in improved facilities might help in such rehabilitation.

[14] Garrett Heyns, "Penal Institutions" in *Recreation In The Age of Automation* (Philadelphia: the American Academy of Political and Social Sciences, 1957), The Annals of the Academy, Vol. 313, pp. 73, 75. Reprinted by permission.

SUGGESTED REFERENCES

Chapman, Frederick M., *Recreation Activities for the Handicapped*. New York: The Ronald Press Company, 1960.

Hunt, Valerie V., *Recreation for the Handicapped*. Englewood Cliffs, N.J.: Prentice-Hall, Inc., 1955.

Kleemeier, Robert W., *Aging and Leisure*. New York: Oxford University Press, 1961.

Rathbone, Josephine L. and Carol Lucas, *Recreation in Total Rehabilitation*. Springfield, Ill.: Charles C. Thomas, Publisher, 1959.

United States Department of Health, Education, and Welfare, *The Nation and Its Older People*. Washington, D.C.: Government Printing Office, 1961.

Williams, Arthur, *Recreation for the Aging*. New York: Association Press, 1953.

6

LOOKING AHEAD

19

The Fabulous Future

One hundred years ago no one could possibly have foreseen all of the developments of the 1960's. There was no knowledge then that could have predicted atomic energy, nor the vacuum tube that made television possible. Rapid change has been one of the most significant characteristics of our day. The last fifty years have seen greater scientific changes than the past 2,000 years, and there is every reason to believe that, barring some great catastrophe, the changes of the next fifty years will be even greater. Any effort to look into the future can be predicated only upon seeing what is happening in the world about us today, looking backward at the recent changes, and endeavouring to determine trends that might continue.

In the following pages, in which we look into the future, we assume that we will escape the catastrophe of atomic war; although we must also assume that for many years a large part of the income and energy of our nation will be devoted to keeping America strong, both militarily and economically. On the other hand, if the tremendous burden of armaments could be lifted from the nations of the world, the release of monies earmarked for defense would make possible a great leap forward. Putting these funds to other use could provide untold benefits to humanity. Let us take a look at those factors in modern society that will have a bearing upon the future use of leisure.

Factors Influencing Leisure Use

Automation and new sources of power

Automation and atomic power may well presage the second great industrial revolution, the consequences of which may be even more far reaching than the first. The science of electronics, coupled with the development of atomic power, may do away with many of the routine jobs in industry. Production per man-hour should continue to increase as it has during the past fifty years, but the rise will be more spectacular. The numbers of workers needed in industry will be greatly reduced.

Today over $6 billion per year is spent in all types of research, and this expenditure is increasing each year. New materials, new and more efficient methods of manufacture, and new ways of using power all give promise of continuing rapid changes in the world of production. They mean new wealth, higher production, and more leisure.

Increased leisure

Although there has been no sharp decrease in the weekly hours of work during the past few years, there still remains the possibility of further decrease in future years. There is every reason to believe that, if it were not for the tremendous expenditures on defense, the increased ability to produce would lead to a reduction in the work week. The 40-hour work week may drop to 32, and some even predict an eventual decrease to 24 hours in the manufacturing industries. This condition may mean that the working man may have from 72 to 80 hours per week available as discretionary time.

Will the same increase in leisure be available for all segments of the population? Probably, the answer is "No." Management responsibilities, many service occupations, and the professions do not now share in the great decrease in working time; they have little expectation of sharing equally with labor in the future. In many fields, work itself provides the major satisfaction of life. We are, however, going through a radical change of attitude towards work. It is recognized that, for many, work still provides the great satisfactions of life; however, where work does not provide opportunities for creativity, we must increasingly turn to leisure for some of the deep satisfactions of life.

Increased income

If present trends continue, we may expect the average real income per family to continue to rise. How high and how fast this growth will be is difficult to say, but there are some predictions that by the year 2000 we will attain a family average of $15,000 per year. It is predicted that there will be a smaller percentage of our people in the lower income brackets and that the opportunity to earn adequately for a decent standard of living will be open to all. As labor requirements decrease with the increase of automation, a larger and larger number of people will be absorbed into the service occupations. With more income and more free time, industries, businesses, and services supplying leisure needs of people will assume an ever-increasing importance.

Greater health and longevity

Modern science has conquered many of the great killers of the past, and there is every reason to believe that in coming years great progress will be made in combating heart disease, cancer, and mental illness. Life expectancy in the United States has gradually increased until it now stands at 68 years for men and 73 for women. The new knowledge of geriatrics may well increase these figures to 80 or 85. More important, it may make the aging years more pleasant and vigorous. Our aged may have 25 or more years of life after their years of labor. One of the greatest challenges of this post-retirement period will be to find worthy and creative activities for this large leisure class.

It is not only the aged that will benefit from the new discoveries of medicine. At all ages, people may well live with greater vigor and health than in the past. Fitness through participation in physical recreation pursuits may assume proportions undreamed of today.

Higher standard of living

As income rises, medical knowledge increases, and more leisure is available, the standard of living of the American people should continue to improve. It may, however, move in new directions. Homes will be more comfortable and practical; home automation will effect further reductions in the labor involved in maintaining the home. It may well be that there will, however, be a renewed interest in cooking and home-making, not as labor, but as art. Home workshops, recreation rooms, musical instruments, high-fidelity recordings, and television will become almost universal. A larger and larger percentage of income will be available for education, travel, music, entertainment, and reading.

David Sarnoff expressed his feelings about the future thus:

Not labor but leisure will be the great problem in the decades ahead. That prospect should be accepted as a God-given opportunity to add dimensions of enjoyment and grace to life. We have reason to foresee a fantastic rise in demand for and appreciation of the better, and perhaps the best, in art, music and letters.[1]

[1] David Sarnoff, "The Fabulous Future," *Fortune* magazine (January 1955), p. 115. Courtesy of *Fortune* magazine.

Greater mobility

Although Americans are on the move as are no other people of the world, it is probable that they will be even more mobile in future years. Whereas the average American travels 5,000 miles per year today, this figure will probably increase to at least 9,000 miles by the year 2000. New highways and ease of motor travel will be responsible for part of the increase, but more rapid and possibly more economical transportation by jet aircraft, which will place all parts of the world within easy reach, should attract most of the increase. So-called "out-of-the-way," unspoiled, picturesque places may cease to exist. Unless great care is exercised, extreme pressures will be put on parks, forests, and wilderness areas, and wildlife will suffer under the impact. Natural areas of solitude and silence may be lost forever.

Population changes

Our population will continue to grow, although possibly at a decreasing rate. It is estimated that by the year 2000 we may be a nation of more than 300 million people. The population of the world, if present rates continue, will double in less than 50 years. This population will have greater numbers in the younger and the older segments. Probably only 50 percent of our population will be in the active working force. This growth in population will create problems of overcrowding, food scarcity, transportation difficulties, and lack of adequate land and water.

In a crowded nation and in a crowded world, great care will be needed to provide for the amenities of life, for housing with privacy, and for access to open spaces. Much greater consideration will need to be given to the recreation needs of society in the planning of cities and suburbs.

Needs and Problems

The recreation movement faces many problems, due in part to the rapidity of its growth and in part to the recency of its development. The social changes mentioned earlier in this chapter have been largely responsible for the development of the recreation movement as well as for the complexities of modern life that have resulted in many of the problems that the movement faces. If the recreation profession is to meet its future obligations, it must recognize its difficulties and problems and endeavor to find solutions.

Need for better understanding of recreation

The lay public, other professional groups, and the members of the recreation profession need to develop a better understanding of the nature, significance, and place of recreation in modern life. There is a need for a concept of recreation that will include the large sphere of recreation interests and their relation to the development of personality. There is also a need for a better understanding of the role of the various agencies engaged in providing recreation services in order that their efforts may be made more effective.

Roy Sorensen, speaking at the National Recreation Congress in 1960, expressed this need in the following words:

The concept must be big enough to comprehend within it the changed and major role of leisure in our society and an understanding of the forces and pressures which mold leisure values and pursuits of the young. A more comprehensive view of leisure in our time is needed by interested citizens, by parents, by educators, by legislators and public officials, by young people themselves and by those who work in public and voluntary recreational agencies.[2]

Need for broadening the program base

Every effort should be made to make more varied and imaginative the programs provided by community agencies. There needs to be a much increased emphasis on the cultural activities—music, art, and dramatics. Quality, rather than quantity, should be emphasized. The need for programs emphasizing physical fitness will be even greater than in the past; and efforts should be made to provide opportunities for people of all ages to find appropriate and satisfying opportunities for physical activities. The movement to the out-of-doors can be expected to continue to expand as boating, hunting, fishing, camping, and touring attract more adherents. Increased provision to care for these interests must be made, but there will be a particular need to teach people to use resources wisely. The opportunity for all to belong to and actively participate in social and cultural activities should be made available, with special efforts to provide for those most in need of social experiences.

More and more people will seek opportunities for creative experiences through community arts and crafts programs and through home workshops. The old concept of community recreation as concerned only with playgrounds needs drastic revision. All ages and all segments of society should be able to find satisfying and creative outlets in the community recreation program.

Need for leadership

As the recreation movement expands, there will be an ever-increasing demand for dynamic leadership. There will be need for planners, managers, and advisers, as well as leaders directly concerned in the conducting and organizing of activities. There will need to be more emphasis on a broad liberal background followed by professional technical training. Salaries

[2] Roy Sorensen, *Selected Papers Presented at the 42nd National Recreation Congress* (New York: National Recreation Association, 1960), p. 8.

will need to continue to rise and community recognition for imaginative leadership should be given to make this a rewarding and satisfying field of endeavour.

Universities and colleges should greatly expand their professional programs and emphasis should be placed on education for community services rather than on promoting activities for their own sake. As it expands and its opportunities for professional leadership become better known, the recreation movement should attract more young people of intelligence and ability. The opportunities for service in a new and growing professional field need to be brought to the attention of young men and women.

Need for education in the world of tomorrow

Because of increased leisure and the technical changes of tomorrow, the need for education, broadly conceived, will be greater than ever. More highly trained technicians will be needed. The field of knowledge will continue to grow, and the educated man will need to be acquainted with the vast areas of science as well as humanities. The demands of medicine, education, and the other professions will be greater; those of highest ability and dedication to their callings will be needed. Even more important, however, will be the development of those attitudes and values that will make possible an effective society in the years ahead. The problems will not be solved merely by increased knowledge but will require imagination, curiosity, resourcefulness, and skill in analysis. Each citizen will be concerned not only with making a living but also with community responsibility to help solve the problems of living together in a complex society. Education will need to place increased attention on education for leisure. Those interested in recreation will join with those in the humanities in endeavoring to provide the climate and skills for enriched living.

Need for cooperation and coordination of services

Each of the agencies and organizations providing recreation services has a distinctive contribution to make. There is need, however, for a clearer definition of what these contributions are and how these services may best be rendered. There is particularly a need for the various groups to work more cooperatively in order that the total services provided may be greater and more effective. A first consideration in such cooperation is the development of mutual respect and understanding of the special functions and purposes of each agency. This respect and understanding can come only through more opportunities for exchange of information and the cross-fertilization that comes through group discussion and efforts to solve common problems.

There is need on a community, state, and national level for better machinery for cooperative action. When the various agencies work jointly on projects of great urgency that affect them all, greater understanding and mutual respect result. The White House Conferences on Children and Youth and the similar conference on the aging illustrate the types of joint cooperative action that should be encouraged in the future.

Need for upgrading recreation through research

From the behavioral sciences comes new knowledge applicable to the field of recreation. Learning more about the individual and the interaction of people in groups should make possible new services in the recreation movement. Research in the problems of leisure should become more widespread and more significant in the coming years. The direction of study should turn more and more toward the effects of the experiences on the participant within the group.

Competition for time

Along with our increase in leisure has come an increase in the competition for time. A child's leisure is demanded by radio, television, motion pictures, Little League, Scouts, music and dancing lessons, little theater, school clubs, sports, summer camps, playground activities, reading, and parties. Parents more often complain that there are too many things for children to do rather than too few. With all the present offerings, one may ask why we need more and why schools, youth agencies, and park and recreation departments should continually endeavour to expand their programs.

Time is a precious commodity, the very stuff of life, and how it is used determines the happiness of the individual and the health of society. Every individual must select from a wide variety of choices, those activities that seem to be worthwhile. Parents and educators have the obligation of helping children develop standards for the use of leisure. Some forms of amusements may have all the elements of a drug, in which ever-increasing doses are demanded. Some guideposts in deciding how leisure time should be allotted are:

Seek a balanced leisure diet. The Greek ideal involved physical, intellectual, and aesthetic development. A variety of leisure activities, selected from a number of different fields, is desirable.

Develop recreation interests with a lifetime value. Some recreation activities are most pertinent at a particular age level; others may be enjoyed throughout the life span.

Use recreation activities to help overcome weaknesses. Physical and social development may be furthered through participation in activities that develop these capacities.

Find time for solitude and contemplation. We belong to an activity-centered culture, but all people need time for reading, solitude, and contemplation.

As community agencies develop recreation programs, they need to be mindful of the children and adults that do not belong to many organizations and that are not generally attracted to traditional programs. We have mentioned the many demands on a child's leisure, but studies indicate that in every school, while some children are already involved in more activities than are good for them, another 25 to 50 percent of the pupils need additional participation.

Competition for funds

In any community there is competition for private contributions and tax funds for recreation and other public services. It is estimated that only 2 or 3 percent of the expenditures for recreation are those of public or private nonprofit organizations. With the rising tax rate, there has been increasing competition for school, park, and recreation funds.

Considering the vast expenditures for commercial recreation, one might well ask whether this area might not provide more and more recreation. There are of course many desirable services that have come to be regarded as the exclusive prerogative of private enterprise. There are others that both commercial and social agencies provide. For example, swimming pools are sometimes a profitable field for private enterprise. The cost of providing swimming commercially, however, often prohibits participation of children from low-income families. Many other services should be deemed primarily the responsibility of nonprofit agencies because of their importance in the physical, mental, and moral development of youth. Many youth clubs, playground, and community center programs, and school co-curricular activities fall into this category.

There are still many communities that have not yet recognized recreation as a function of government. In coming years, public agencies not only will need to continue to prove their importance but also will need to do a better job of interpreting their functions to the community at large and particularly to those responsible for allotting funds. Park and recreation funds will probably always be a very small percentage of the total cost of government, but programs can function effectively only when reasonable amounts of money are available. It is easy to explain to city fathers the need for more policemen, better roads, and new public buildings. It is more difficult to interpret the values of recreation in the lives of children, in making communities better places to live, and in the possible reduction in social problems.

The same problem, that of adequate financing, faces the voluntary agencies. Here occurs the competition between welfare agencies, health agencies, and group work and recreation agencies. Here many of the same arguments for adequate support hold as they do in the case of the tax-supported agencies. Financing through united funds has given stability to the voluntary agencies, but it has also in many cases made it difficult for the more aggressive of them to expand their programs.

Every effort will be needed in the future to secure the kind of financing that will make possible programs of high quality to meet the needs of those not provided for adequately by other means. The needs of recreation are as urgent as those of education and should be interpreted to the public in the same light.

Crisis in land

The rapid growth of population, urbanization, urban sprawl, the automobile, and new highways have created a crisis in the amount of land available for recreation. Marion Clawson, economist for Resources for the Future, estimates that, if present trends continue, by the year 2000 land needs on a local level will be four times as great and land needs in rural and distant areas may be 16 times as great as they are at present.[3] Although many communities and states are endeavoring to anticipate land needs, the time is already past when land can be acquired at a reasonable cost. Each year that passes makes it more difficult to secure needed areas for playgrounds, playfields, parks, forests, wildlife areas, camps, and nature preserves.

Private lands for recreation will need to be made available in ever-increasing amounts. Commercial fishing and hunting areas, private camps, picnic spots, and scenic areas can provide income to owners and services to the public.

Planning for future land needs is essential. Such planning must be done cooperatively by the various levels of government and the voluntary agencies concerned. Many states have developed long-range recreation plans, and other states are now in the process. Large metropolitan centers of population need to plan on a regional basis, as the land problems transcend political boundaries. Only through careful planning for the future will it be possible to meet the needs of future Americans for adequate land resources.

Water resources of America are particularly in need of a long-range program of rehabilitation and expansion. No other recreation pursuit has had during recent years a rate of growth comparable to that of the water-related activities. Pollution, sedimentation, and, in some cases, drainage have greatly reduced the value of many of our present resources.

[3] Marion Clawson, "The Crisis in Outdoor Recreation," reprinted from *American Forests* (March–April 1959), p. 15. Used by permission.

The need for quality in leisure pursuits

Recreation includes many things of a passing or ephemeral nature, and no one would gainsay their value. We could become too serious and too concerned that all the activities of life be purposeful. There is need for play, relaxation, light conversation, and fun. Nevertheless, as leisure increases in quantity, the social institutions concerned with leisure will need to give more attention to making recreation more creative and to providing those things that in the long run provide the greatest satisfaction to people and the greatest good to society.

The problem that confronts us is twofold: first, what constitutes the good, better, or best; and second, how we achieve the good, better, or best in the lives of possible participants. Too often it is assumed that what the majority regards as valuable is the standard by which to abide. We cannot ignore what the majority desires, but any leadership worthy of the name should be concerned with raising the quality of the experience of participants. The participant is attracted to recreation programs only as he attains satisfaction from the experience. Leadership, therefore, must serve an educational function to develop interest in those things that have value in the long run.

How may we determine what higher values are? Certainly some credence should be given to the experience of those who are authorities in given fields, such as music, art, science, and who are acquainted with needs of people at various age levels and the ways these needs may be met. By his very nature, man is a maker of value judgments, and the seeking of other than material values is important to him. If increased leisure is to be satisfying rather than deadening or demoralizing, there must be a continuous pursuit of excellence and a striving for quality, for intellectual and spiritual satisfactions, for higher levels of skills, and for participation in those pursuits that lead to personality integration rather than disintegration. The quality of our civilization will be determined more by its leisure than by its work.

Trends

This book has been concerned largely with social institutions and their efforts to provide for people's leisure. Trends have been indicated in many chapters, although seldom have they been labeled as such. We are here listing briefly some of the trends, assuming that they will continue and that they point the way to the recreation movement of tomorrow.

The recreation movement provided by public and private agencies has been growing at a rapid rate, as evidenced in the increasing number of participants, increased financial support, and increased appreciation of the purposes and values of good recreation services.

Family recreation has shown a marked increase, with home provisions for family rooms, recreation rooms, workrooms, hobby equipment, back-yard play equipment, musical instruments, and family vacations.

There has been a rapid rise in the expenditures for commercial recreation and a growth in forms of commercial recreation that attract the whole family.

There is a growing trend toward the development of private neighborhood recreation centers. Such centers may include recreation buildings, swimming pools, athletic facilities, and children's playgrounds.

Organized camping has expanded. In recent years there has been a particularly rapid growth in day camping, camping by religious organizations, school camping, and camping for handicapped and emotionally disturbed children.

Cultural aspects of recreation are increasing in importance, and special leadership is being provided in these fields.

Concern for physical fitness has brought a renewed interest in physical activities adapted for various age levels and organized to reach those who may not have great proficiency in particular sports.

Aquatic activities have expanded at an explosive rate. Marinas, boating areas, and swimming facilities are being developed in ever-increasing numbers.

There has been a general upgrading of leadership. This has come about as a result of better salaries, improved status, and the expanded curriculums of colleges and universities.

There is a trend toward more attractive and well-equipped neighborhood centers. More originality in the development and design of outdoor areas is evident, and play equipment for children is becoming more creative.

The federal government has expanded its recreation services on public lands. The Outdoor Recreation Resources Review Committee has suggested guidelines for meeting future needs.

There is an emphasis on community planning to meet future recreation needs. Such planning is increasingly including the schools and the voluntary and private organizations along with the various public agencies.

There is increased concern, at all levels of government, regarding the problems related to the use of water resources. Extensive programs are under way to reduce pollution and sedimentation as well as to develop artificial lakes for multi-purpose use, including recreation.

Special efforts are being made to provide recreation services to the aged. Programs for senior citizens are expected to expand rapidly as more funds become available and as the percentage of aged in the population increases. Early retirement will continue to be an important factor.

Recreation services in hospitals are becoming more widespread. Mental hospitals, in particular, are expanding their recreation programs.

Parents are turning more and more to the voluntary youth-serving agencies to provide informal, small-group character-building experiences for their children.

There is recognition at the local level that the tax-supported park and recreation departments must serve the basic community recreation needs.

There is a trend towards the combining of parks and recreation departments.

There is a striking increase in the number of new recreation systems established and in the financial support for public recreation programs of all types.

There is a trend toward the establishment of park and recreation programs on a county or regional basis.

State agencies are improving their services to local political subdivisions.

In many states, extensive programs are under way to develop long-range plans for developing and financing outdoor recreation resources.

It is recognized that these are only a few of the trends evident in the recreation movement, but they indicate the desire to meet the needs of the coming generation. A projection of the total recreation picture by the summer of 2000 is presented in Fig. 36.

Recreation and the Good Life

Philosophers and religious leaders have through the ages debated the purposes of life. If the peoples of the future have more leisure with less concern for earning the bread of life, whole new vistas of spiritual, social, and cultural development lie ahead. If this opportunity is lost in the pursuit of hedonistic pleasure, the pessimists' predictions that our civilization will crumble through internal decay may well come true.

In the Christian ethic, work has been considered the great good in life. If, by *work*, we mean drudgery and the unpleasant labor of routine tasks, then we must change our thinking; for in the future these tasks can be done better by machinery. If, on the other hand, *work* involves the creative aspects of life and the essential purpose of contributing to a better society, then work will continue to be a central purpose for people engaged in those occupations or professions where such rewards are possible. For large segments of the population, however, leisure pursuits rather than work will provide the major satisfactions of life.

Here we must ask ourselves, "What is time for? How shall it be used

Fig. 36   *Number of Occasions of Participation in Outdoor Summer Recreation—1960 Compared with 1976 and 2000 (by Millions). Source:* Outdoor Recreation for America (Washington, D.C.: Outdoor Recreation Resources Review Commission, 1962)

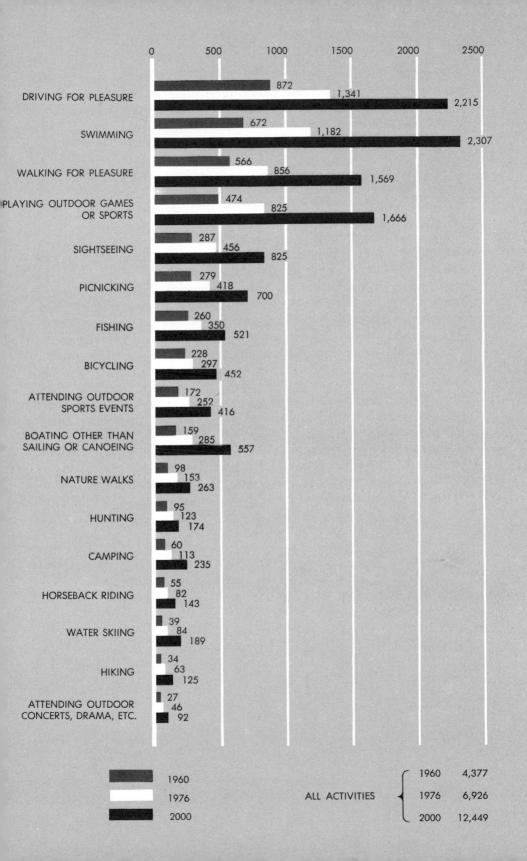

for the good of man and society?" In leisure the use of time becomes largely an individual matter, and each person must make his own choices. How choices are made will depend on many factors, but particularly on those values, standards, attitudes, and skills that have been inculcated in children and youth—and also on the opportunities provided by the culture in which we live.

Man will always want to feel useful and needed. Through community service, through the social and religious organizations, and through voluntary leadership of youth, leisure, as well as work, provides opportunities to achieve a sense of purpose.

Man is an active, participating being. Mental alertness and physical fitness can be achieved through those pursuits that challenge and that provide opportunities for healthful physical activity.

Man is a creative being and desires opportunities for self-expression, whether these come through the home do-it-yourself experiences or through music, art, or dramatics. Aesthetic appreciation, whether through the performing arts, literature, or the world of nature, meets deep-seated needs.

Man is a social being and needs the companionship of others and the feeling of belonging. Recreation can help fill these needs.

Man is a spiritual being, and it is part of his nature to search for meaning in the world in which he lives. His sense of wonder, his curiosity about his world, and his response to beauty in all of its manifestations have spiritual connotations.

The recreation movement should strive to make its influence felt, to help Americans find for themselves the most satisfying uses of leisure, not only as an avenue to personal happiness but also as a channel to social well-being. This is the challenge of recreation in American life.

Index

A

Abramovitz, Moses, 198
Addams, Jane, 36
Aesthetic values, 19
Aged
  needs of, 483
  problems of, 478-491
  recreation programs for, 485-489
American Camping Association, 177
American Forestry Association, 33
American Library Association, 47
American Physical Education Association, 47
American Recreation Society, 48
American Red Cross, 48, 49, 295
Amusement, 78-79
Anderson, Jackson M., 219
Armed forces, recreation for, 294-298
Ashton, Dudley, 404
Astor, Charlotte, 223
Astor, William, 223
Automation, 16, 508

B

Balch, Ernest, 33
Bobbitt, Franklin, 114
Botanic gardens, 231-232
Boy Scouts of America, 133-136
  divisions of, 134
Boys' Clubs of America, 136-137
Braucher, Howard, 6, 42, 48, 195, 395
Brightbill, Charles K., 6, 200-201,
  219, 322
Brockman, C. Frank, 224
Bunn, Betty, 399
Bureau of Fisheries, 33
Bureau of Indian Affairs, 285
Bureau of Land Management,
  284-285
Bureau of Outdoor Recreation, 52,
  293-294
Bureau of Public Roads, 292
Bureau of Reclamation, 287
Bureau of the Census, 291
Butler, George D., 6, 36, 41, 103,
  120, 240

523